Beginning PHP 5 and MySQL: From Novice to Professional

W. JASON GILMORE

Beginning PHP 5 and MySQL: From Novice to Professional

Copyright © 2004 by W. Jason Gilmore

ISBN (pbk): 1-893115-51-8

Printed and bound in the United States of America 9 8 7 6 5 4 3 2

Trademarked names may appear in this book. Rather than use a trademark symbol with every occurrence of a trademarked name, we use the names only in an editorial fashion and to the benefit of the trademark owner, with no intention of infringement of the trademark.

Lead Editor: Chris Mills

Technical Reviewer: Matt Wade

Editorial Board: Steve Anglin, Dan Appleman, Ewan Buckingham, Gary Cornell, Tony Davis, John Franklin, Jason Gilmore, Chris Mills, Steve Rycroft, Dominic Shakeshaft, Jim Sumser, Karen Watterson, Gavin Wray, John Zukowski

Project Managers: Nate McFadden, Laura Cheu

Copy Edit Manager: Nicole LeClerc

Copy Editor: Brian MacDonald

Production Manager: Kari Brooks

Production Editor: Kelly Winquist

Compositor: Diana Van Winkle, Van Winkle Design Group

Proofreader: Linda Seifert, Christy Wagner

Indexer: Kevin Broccoli

Artist: Kinetic Publishing Services, LLC

Cover Designer: Kurt Krames

Manufacturing Manager: Tom Debolski

Distributed to the book trade in the United States by Springer-Verlag New York, Inc., 175 Fifth Avenue, New York, NY 10010 and outside the United States by Springer-Verlag GmbH & Co. KG, Tiergartenstr. 17, 69112 Heidelberg, Germany.

In the United States: phone 1-800-SPRINGER, e-mail orders@springer-ny.com, or visit http://www.springer-ny.com. Outside the United States: fax +49 6221 345229, e-mail orders@springer.de, or visit http://www.springer.de.

For information on translations, please contact Apress directly at 2560 Ninth Street, Suite 219, Berkeley, CA 94710. Phone 510-549-5930, fax 510-549-5939, e-mail info@apress.com, or visit http://www.apress.com.

The source code for this book is available to readers at http://www.apress.com in the Downloads section.

Per Alessia. Anche se questo lavoro enorme dimostra che sono un uomo di molte parole, mi è impossibile dirti quanto ti amo.

Contents at a Glance

Contents

Chapter 10 Working with the File and Operating System...........227

Chapter 11 Forms and Navigational Cues 259

Chapter 15 PHP and LDAP 353

Chapter 16 Session Handlers 381

About the Author

W. Jason Gilmore is the Open Source Editorial Director for Apress. He has developed hundreds of PHP and MySQL applications over the past six years, and has almost 50 articles to his credit on this and other topics pertinent to Internet application development. Among others, his work has been featured within the pages of *Linux Magazine*, the O'Reilly Network, Developer.com, and Dev Shed. In addition to PHP, he regularly obsesses over the Perl, Python, and C# languages. When not slouched in front of his laptop, Jason can be found reading, praising the virtues of professional boxing, or on the phone with his father getting the latest in home repair advice. This is his second book.

About the Technical Reviewer

Matt Wade is a database analyst by day and a freelance PHP developer by night. He has extensive experience with database technologies ranging from Microsoft SQL Server to MySQL. Matt is also an accomplished systems administrator, and has experience with all flavors of Windows and FreeBSD.

Matt resides in Florida with his wife Michelle and two children, Matthew and Amanda. When he isn't busy working, he can be found at church or fiddling with one of his many aquariums. Matt can be found at his home on the Web, Codewalkers.com, which is a resource for PHP developers.

Acknowledgments

I'D LIKE TO THANK Apress's co-founder and publisher Gary Cornell for the opportunity to both write and work for the greatest publishing company on the planet. It's an honor to call you a colleague and friend.

Working with the Apress publication team is akin to hitting the jackpot, with the diligence, enthusiasm, and knowledge of each member worth its weight in gold. Special thanks is in order for several individuals. Project Manager Nate McFadden deserves a medal for his efficiency, patience, and unbounded optimism throughout this long, hard slog. My excellent Technical Reviewer Matt Wade deserves thanks for his profound technical acumen and candid advice throughout the project. Copy editor Brian MacDonald did a tremendous job reining in my rampant abuse of the English language. Lead Editor Chris Mills offered excellent advice and regular encouragement. Production editor Kelly Winquist constantly impressed me with her attention to detail regarding the final drafts. I'm grateful to project manager Laura Cheu for the late-stage encouragement, direction, and advice. I remain beholden to all of you, not to mention those unnamed members of the Apress staff who have done so much to bring this book to fruition.

This book, not to mention much of my professional programming and writing career, would not exist without the tireless efforts of Open Source developers and enthusiasts around the world. Never before has the metaphor "standing on the shoulders of giants" seemed more fitting.

Ed Copony, Jon Shoberg, Rob Kinney, and Brian Wilson all deserve special mention for withstanding my barrage of book-related e-mails throughout this process. Thanks for the input, guys.

To Alessia and my family, my campaigns against words and code have kept me away for the past several months. To your great chagrin, you'll be seeing much more of me soon enough.

Any errors in this book are mine and mine alone.

Introduction

MOST GREAT PROGRAMMING books sway far more towards the realm of the practical than of the academic. Although I have no illusions regarding my place among the great technical authors of our time, I always strive to write with this point in mind, shying away from details that most would consider superfluous, and drawing upon both my own real-world experience and that of others in an attempt produce material that readers will be able to immediately grasp as well as apply to their own situation. Given the size of this book, it's also apparent that I try to squeeze out every last drop of such practicality from the subject matter. That said, if you're interested in gaining practical and comprehensive insight into the PHP programming language and MySQL database server, with special emphasis on how the two work together to create dynamic, powerful Web applications, this book is for you.

If you've already perused this book's table of contents, it's apparent that the majority of the material is focused on topics specific to the PHP language. There are simply so many amazingly practical language features that I would not have felt this book complete if I had omitted even one. In fact, the first twenty chapters are devoted to PHP features and extensions. I devote the first five chapters to a thorough introduction of the language's core features, such as installation and configuration issues, variables, data types, arrays, and functions. Chapters 6 and 7 offer insight into PHP's object-oriented programming features, with special emphasis on the vast assortment of upgrades made available in version 5. Chapter 8 shows you how to take advantage of PHP's error-detection and reporting abilities, and includes a dedicated section on the exception handling feature new to PHP 5. Finally, Chapter 9 offers a lengthy discourse on PHP's powerful string-handling libraries, including a detailed overview of its two POSIX- and Perl-based regular expression libraries.

The next 10 chapters take you on a tour of many of the language's fascinating features and extensions, starting with its file and operating system functions. The following chapters cover Web form integration and navigational cues, HTTP authentication, file upload management, and networking capabilities. Enterprise developers will likely find the LDAP, session management, and templating chapters to be highly useful. Chapter 18, one of my personal favorites of the book, is devoted to Web Services, and covers a gamut of topics. I introduce PHP 5's new SOAP and SimpleXML extensions, and demonstrate two third-party extensions, namely NuSOAP and MagpieRSS. I even demonstrate cross-platform interoperability by showing you how to connect a C#-based Web Services client to a PHP-based server. Chapter 19 is dedicated to a topic that should be close to the heart of all Internet application developers: security. Finally, Chapter 20 rounds out the PHP-specific discussion with an introduction to PHP 5's new SQLite database extension, a feature that I predict will skyrocket in popularity in the coming months.

Chapters 21 through 25 lead you through a whirlwind introduction of MySQL-specific features. Although MySQL requires considerably less overhead and knowledge than its competitors, it nonetheless has a learning curve that can be daunting for some. In an effort to eliminate much of the initial research required by beginners, I've strived to offer a highly practical introduction that focuses solely on those topics that most effectively contribute to your ability to begin effectively using and maintaining the server and data. Topics covered include installation and configuration, a thorough overview of key MySQL clients such as mysql, mysqladmin, and mysqldump, a brief introduction to GUI-based administration clients, table structures and data types, security, and user management. This material sets the stage for Chapters 26 through 30, where I turn attention to PHP and MySQL integration issues. In Chapter 26, I introduce PHP's MySQL library, and demonstrate how to select, insert, delete, and update MySQL data using PHP-driven Web interfaces. In Chapter 27, I present an object-oriented MySQL data class used to abstract the data mining operations from your PHP application logic. After several precursory examples demonstrating class usage, I proceed to offer numerous real-world examples, showing you how to output results in an user-friendly tabular format, accompany output with actionable options, sort tabular output, and created paged results. Chapter 28 introduces the concept of database indexing. After an introduction to primary, unique, normal, and full-text indexes, I show you how to create PHP-based search interfaces for quickly sifting through even enormous data stores. Chapter 29 shows you how to implement database transactions in MySQL, and demonstrates the process first on the command line and then within a Web application. Finally, Chapter 30 covers the topic of data import and export, offering introductions to several useful MySQL clients and commands such as mysqlimport and load data infile, and then demonstrates how easy it is to use PHP as a means for loading delimited data to a MySQL table.

If you're new to PHP, I heartily recommend starting with Chapter 1, because it's likely that first gaining foundational knowledge will be of considerable benefit in later chapters. More advanced readers are invited to jump around as necessary; after all, this isn't a romance novel. Regardless of your reading strategy, I've attempted to compartamentalize each chapter into a neat little package, enabling you to get the most from each chapter without having to necessarily master other chapters beyond those that concentrate on the basics of each technology.

Newcomers and seasoned PHP and MySQL developers alike have something to gain from this book, as I've intentionally organized it in a format of both tutorial and reference. I appreciate the fact that you or your employer has traded hard-earned cash for this book, and therefore have strived to present the material in a fashion that will prove useful not only the first few times you peruse it, but far into the future.

Contact Me!

I love answering reader questions, and welcome feedback, even the abusive sort. Feel free to e-mail me at jason@wjgilmore.com, or peruse my personal Web site, http://www.wjgilmore.com/.

CHAPTER 1

An Introduction
to PHP

THIS CHAPTER SERVES to better acquaint you with the basics of PHP, offering insight into its roots, popularity, and users. This information sets the stage for a discussion of PHP's feature set, including the new features in PHP 5. By the conclusion of this chapter, you'll learn:

- How a Canadian developer's Web page hit counter spawned one of the world's most popular scripting languages

- What PHP's developers have done to once again reinvent the language, making version 5 the best yet released

- Which features of PHP continue to attract new programmers

History

The origins of PHP date back to 1995, when an independent software development contractor named Rasmus Lerdorf developed a Perl/CGI script that enabled him to know how many visitors were reading his online résumé. His script performed two tasks: logging visitor information, and displaying the count of visitors to the Web page. Because the Web as we know it today was still young at that time, tools such as these were nonexistent, and they prompted e-mails inquiring about Lerdorf's scripts. Lerdorf thus began giving away his toolset, dubbed *Personal Home Page* (PHP).

The clamor for the PHP toolset prompted Lerdorf to begin developing additions to PHP, one of which converted data entered in an HTML form into symbolic variables that allowed users to export them to other systems. To accomplish this, he opted to continue development in C code rather than Perl. Ongoing additions to the PHP toolset culminated in November 1997 with the release of PHP 2.0, or Personal Home Page — Form Interpreter (PHP-FI). As a result of PHP's rising popularity, the 2.0 release was accompanied by a number of enhancements and improvements from programmers worldwide.

The new PHP release was extremely popular, and a core team of developers soon joined Lerdorf. They kept the original concept of incorporating code directly alongside HTML and rewrote the parsing engine, giving birth to PHP 3.0. By the June 1998 release of version 3.0, over 50,000 users were using PHP to enhance their Web pages.

> **NOTE** *1997 also saw the change of the words underlying the PHP abbreviation from Personal Home Page to Hypertext Preprocessor.*

Development continued at a hectic pace over the next two years, with hundreds of functions being added and the user count growing in leaps and bounds. At the beginning of 1999, Netcraft (`http://www.netcraft.com/`) reported a conservative estimate of a user base surpassing 1,000,000, making PHP one of the most popular scripting languages in the world. Its popularity surpassed even the greatest expectations of the developers, as it soon became apparent that users intended to use PHP to power far larger applications than was originally anticipated. Two core developers, Zeev Suraski and Andi Gutmans, took the initiative to spearhead a complete rethinking of the way PHP operated, culminating in a rewriting of the PHP parser, dubbed the Zend scripting engine. The result of this work was seen in the release of PHP 4.

> **NOTE** *In addition to leading development of the Zend engine, and playing a major role in steering the overall development of the PHP language, Zend Technologies Ltd. (`http://www.zend.com/`), based in Israel, offers a host of tools for developing and deploying PHP. These include the Zend Development Studio, Zend Encoder, and the Zend Optimizer, among others. Check out the Zend Web site for more information.*

PHP 4

On May 22, 2000, roughly 18 months after the first official announcement of the new development effort, PHP 4.0 was released. Many considered the release of PHP 4 to be the language's official debut within the enterprise development scene, an opinion backed by the language's meteoric rise in popularity. Just a few months after the major release, Netcraft (`http://www.netcraft.net/`) estimated that PHP had been installed on over 3.6 million domains, making it one of the most popular scripting languages in the world.

Features

PHP 4 included several enterprise-level improvements, including the following:

- **Improved resource handling:** One of version 3.*x*'s primary drawbacks was scalability. This was largely because the designers underestimated how much the language would be used for large-scale applications. The language wasn't originally intended to run enterprise-class Web sites, and subsequent attempts to do so caused the developers to rethink much of the language's mechanics. The result was vastly improved resource-handling functionality in version 4.

- **Object-oriented support:** Version 4 incorporated a degree of object-oriented functionality, although it was largely considered an unexceptional implementation. Nonetheless, the new features played an important role in attracting users used to working with traditional object-oriented programming (OOP) languages. Standard class and object development methodologies were made available, in addition to object overloading, and run-time class information. A much more comprehensive OOP implementation has been made available in version 5, and is introduced in Chapter 5.

- **Native session-handling support:** HTTP session-handling, available to version 3.*x* users through the third-party package PHPLIB (http://phplib.sourceforge.net), was natively incorporated into version 4. This feature offers developers a means for tracking user/site interactions with unparalleled efficiency and ease. Chapter 13 covers PHP's session-handling capabilities.

- **Encryption:** The MCrypt (http://mcrypt.sourceforge.net) library was incorporated into the default distribution, offering users both full and hash encryption using encryption algorithms including Blowfish, MD5, SHA1, and TripleDES, among others. Chapter 16 delves into PHP's encryption capabilities.

- **ISAPI support:** ISAPI support offered users the ability to use PHP in conjunction with Microsoft's IIS Web server as an ISAPI module, greatly increasing its performance and security.

- **Native COM/DCOM support:** Another bonus for Windows users is PHP 4's ability to access and instantiate COM objects. This functionality opens up a wide range of interoperability with Windows applications.

- **Native Java support:** In another boost to PHP's interoperability, support for binding to Java objects from a PHP application was made available in version 4.0.

- **Perl Compatible Regular Expressions (PCRE) library:** The Perl language has long been heralded as the reigning royalty of the string parsing kingdom. The developers knew that powerful regular expression functionality would play a major role in the widespread acceptance of PHP, and opted to simply incorporate Perl's functionality rather than reproduce it, rolling the PCRE library package into PHP's default distribution (as of version 4.2.0). Chapter 9 introduces this important feature in great detail, and offers a general introduction to the often confusing regular expression syntax.

In addition to these features, literally hundreds of functions were added to version 4, greatly enhancing the language's capabilities. Throughout the course of this book, I'll discuss much of this functionality, as it remains equally important in the version 5 release.

Drawbacks

PHP 4 represented a gigantic leap forward in the language's maturity. The new functionality, power, and scalability offered by the new version swayed an enormous number of burgeoning and expert developers alike, resulting in its firm establishment among the Web scripting behemoths. Yet maintaining user adoration in the language business is a difficult task; programmers often hold a "what have you done for me lately" mindset. The PHP development team kept this notion close at hand, because it wasn't too long before they began yet another monumental task, one that could establish PHP as the 800-pound gorilla of Web scripting languages: Version 5.

PHP 5

Version 5, in beta at the time of this writing, is sizing up to be yet another watershed in the evolution of the PHP language. Although previous major releases had enormous numbers of new library additions, version 5 contains improvements over existing functionality and adds several features commonly associated with mature programming language architectures.

- **Vastly improved object-oriented capabilities:** Improvements to PHP's object-oriented architecture is version 5's most visible feature. Version 5 includes numerous functional additions such as explicit constructors and destructors, object cloning, class abstraction, variable scoping, interfaces, and a major improvement regarding how PHP handles object management. Chapters 6 and 7 delve into the subject of object-oriented PHP.

- **Try/catch exception handling:** Devising custom error-handling strategies within structural programming languages is, ironically, error-prone and inconsistent. To remedy this problem, version 5 now supports exception handling. Long a mainstay of error management in many languages, C++, C#, Python, and Java included, exception handling offers an excellent means for standardizing your error reporting logic. This new and convenient methodology is introduced in Chapter 8.

- **Improved string handling:** Prior versions of PHP have treated strings as arrays by default, a practice indicative of the language's traditional loose-knit attitude towards datatypes. This strategy has been tweaked in version 5, in which a specialized string offset syntax has been introduced, and the previous methodology has been deprecated. The new features, changes, and effects offered by this new syntax are discussed in Chapter 9.

- **Improved XML and Web Services support:** XML support is now based on the libxml2 library, and a new and rather promising extension for parsing and manipulating XML, known as SimpleXML, has been introduced. In addition, a SOAP extension is now available. In Chapter 18 I'll introduce SimpleXML and the new SOAP extension, and also demonstrate a number of slick third-party Web Services extensions.

- **Native support for SQLite:** Always keen on choice, the developers have added support for the powerful yet compact SQLite database server. SQLite offers a convenient solution for developers looking for many of the features found in some of the heavyweight database products without incurring the accompanying administrative overhead. I introduce SQLite and PHP's support for this powerful database engine in Chapter 20.

A host of other improvements and additions are offered in version 5, many of which I'll introduce as relevant throughout the book. When practical, I'll be sure to introduce these improvements as the book proceeds.

As the release of PHP 5 draws near, PHP's prevalence is at a historical high. At press time, PHP has been installed on more than 15 million domains (Netcraft, http://www.netcraft.com/). According to E-Soft, Inc. (http://www.securityspace.com/), PHP is by far the most popular Apache module, present on over 50 percent of all Apache installations.

So far, I've only discussed version-specific features of the language. Each version shares a common set of characteristics that play a very important role in attracting and retaining a large user base. In the next section, you'll learn about these foundational features.

General Language Features

Every user has his or her own specific reason for using PHP to implement a mission-critical application, although I find that such motives tend to fall into what I like to call the four pillars of PHP: Practicality, Power, Possibility, and Price.

Practicality

From the very start, the PHP language was created with practicality in mind. After all, Lerdorf's original intention was not to design an entirely new language, but to resolve a problem that had no immediately applicable solution. Furthermore, much of PHP's early evolution was not the result of the explicit intention to improve the language itself, but rather to increase its utility to the user. The result is what I like to call a *minimalist* language, in terms of what is required of the user, and in terms of the language's syntactical requirements. For starters, a useful PHP script can consist of as little as one line; there is no need for the mandatory inclusion of libraries like in C. For example, the following represents a complete PHP script, the purpose of which is to output the current date, such as March 16, 2004:

```
<?php echo date("F j, Y");?>
```

Another example of the language's penchant for compactness is its ability to nest functions. For example, I can effect numerous changes to a value on the same line by stacking functions in a particular order, in this case producing a pseudorandom string of five alphanumeric characters, such as "a3jh8":

```
$randomString = substr(md5(microtime()), 0, 5);
```

PHP is a loosely-typed language, which also increases its practicality. For example, there is no need to explicitly create, typecast, or destroy a variable, although you are not prevented from doing so. PHP handles all of this for you, creating variables on the fly as they are called in a script, employing a best guess formula for automatically typecasting variables, and finally, automatically destroying variables and returning resources back to the system when the script completes. In these and many other respects, the language allows the developer to concentrate almost exclusively on the final goal (a working application), attempting to handle many of the administrative aspects of programming internally.

Power

In the earlier introduction to PHP 5, I alluded to the fact that the new version is more qualitative than quantitative in comparison to previous versions. Previous major versions were accompanied by enormous additions to PHP's default libraries, to the tune of several hundred new functions per release. Presently, 113 libraries are available, collectively containing well over 1,000 functions. Although you're likely aware of PHP's ability to interface with databases, manipulate form information, and create pages dynamically, did you know that PHP can:

- Create and manipulate Macromedia Flash, image, and Portable Document Format (PDF) files

- Evaluate a password for guessability by comparing it to language dictionaries, and easily broken patterns

- Communicate with the Lightweight Directory Access Protocol (LDAP)

- Parse even the most complex of strings using both the POSIX and Perl-based regular expression libraries

- Authenticate users against login credentials stored in flat files, databases, and even Microsoft's Active Directory

- Communicate with a wide variety of protocols, including IMAP, POP3, NNTP, and DNS, among others

- Communicate with a wide array of credit-card processing solutions

Of course, I'll strive to cover as many of PHP's interesting and useful features as possible in the coming chapters.

Possibility

PHP developers are rarely bound to any single implementation solution. On the contrary, a user can easily be overwhelmed by the number of choices offered by the language. For example, consider PHP's array of database support options. Native support is offered for over twenty-five database products, including Adabas D, dBase, Empress, FilePro, FrontBase, Hyperwave, IBM DB2, Informix, Ingres, Interbase, mSQL, direct MS-SQL, MySQL, Oracle, Ovrimos, PostgreSQL, Solid, Sybase, Unix dbm, and Velocis. In addition, abstraction layer functions are available for accessing Berkeley DB-style databases. Finally, two database abstraction layers are available, one called the dbx module, and another via PEAR, titled the PEAR DB.

PHP's powerful string-parsing capabilities is another feature indicative of the possibility offered to users. In addition to more than eighty-five string manipulation functions, two distinct regular expression formats are supported POSIX and Perl-compatible. This flexibility not only offers users of differing skill sets the opportunity to immediately begin performing complex string operations, but also to quickly port programs of similar functionality (such as Perl and Python) over to PHP.

Do you prefer a language that embraces functional programming? How about one that embraces the object-oriented paradigm? PHP offers comprehensive support for both. Although PHP was originally a solely functional language, the developers soon came to realize the importance of offering the popular OOP paradigm, and took the steps to implement an extensive solution.

The recurring theme here is that PHP allows you to quickly capitalize on your current skill set with very little time investment. The examples set forth here are but a small sampling of this idea, which can be found repeatedly throughout the language.

Price

Since its inception, PHP has been without usage, modification, and redistribution restrictions. In recent years, software meeting such open licensing qualifications been referred to as *open-source* software. Open-source software and the Internet go together like bread and butter. Open-source projects like Sendmail, Bind, Linux, and Apache all play enormous roles in the ongoing operations of the Internet at large. Although the fact that open-source software is available free has been the characteristic most promoted by the media, several other characteristics are equally important if not more so:

- **Free of licensing restrictions imposed by most commercial products.** Open Source software users are freed of the vast majority of licensing restrictions one would expect of commercial counterparts. Although some discrepancies do exist among license variants, users are largely free to modify, redistribute, and integrate the software into other products.

- **Open development and auditing process.** Although there have been some incidents, open-source software has long enjoyed a stellar security record. Such high standards are a result of the open development and auditing process. Because the source code is freely available for examination by anyone who wants to, security holes and potential problems are rapidly found and fixed. This advantage was perhaps best summarized by open-source advocate Eric S. Raymond, who wrote, "Given enough eyeballs, all bugs are shallow."

- **Everyone is free to participate.** Development teams are not limited to a particular organization. Anyone who has the interest and the ability is free to join the project. The absence of member restrictions greatly enhances the talent pool for a given project, ultimately contributing to a higher quality product.

Summary

This chapter has provided a bit of foreshadowing about this wonderful language to which much of this book is devoted. We looked first at PHP's history, before outlining version 4 and 5's core features, setting the stage for later chapters.

In Chapter 2, prepare to get your hands dirty, as you'll delve into the PHP installation and configuration process. Although readers often liken most such chapters to scratching nails on a chalkboard, you can gain much from learning more about this process. Much like a professional cyclist or race car driver, the programmer with hands-on knowledge of the tweaking and maintenance process often holds an advantage over those without, by virtue of a better understanding of the software's configurable behaviors and quirks. So grab a snack and snuggle up to your workstation; it's time to build.

## CHAPTER 2

Installing and Configuring PHP

IN THIS CHAPTER, you'll learn how to install and configure PHP, and in the process learn how to install the Apache Web server. If you don't already have a working Apache/PHP server at your disposal, the material covered here will prove invaluable for working with the examples in later chapters, not to mention for carrying out your own experiments. Specifically, in this chapter, you will learn about:

- How to install Apache and PHP as an Apache server module on both the Unix and Windows platforms

- How to test your installation to ensure that all of the components are properly working

- Common installation pitfalls and their resolutions

- The purpose, scope, and default values of many of PHP's most commonly used configuration directives. You'll also learn the various ways in which you can modify PHP's configuration directives.

Installation

In this section, you'll carry out all of the steps required to install an operational Apache/PHP server. By its conclusion, you'll be able to execute PHP scripts on the server, and view their results in a browser.

Obtaining the Source Code

Before you being the installation, you'll need to download the source code. In this section, I'll provide instructions regarding how to do so.

Downloading Apache

Apache's popularity and open source license has prompted practically all Unix developers to package the software with their respective distribution. Because of Apache's rapid release schedule, however, you should consult the Apache Web site and download the latest version. At the time of this writing, the following page offered a listing of 162 mirrors located in 46 different countries:

```
http://www.apache.org/mirrors/
```

Alternatively, if you'd like the Apache Web site to suggest a mirror, navigate to:

```
http://httpd.apache.org/download.cgi
```

Once you've chosen a suitable mirror, it's time to download the software. The distribution is available in two formats: source and binary.

- **Source:** If your target server platform is a Unix variant, I suggest downloading the source code. Although there is certainly nothing wrong with using one of the superbly built binary versions, the extra time invested in learning how to compile from source will provide you with greater flexibility in the long run. If your target platform is Windows, and you'd like to compile from source, note that a separate source package intended for the Win32 platform is available for download.

- **Binary:** At the time of this writing, binaries are available for 29 operating systems. If your target server platform is Windows, I suggest downloading the relevant binary version. Alternatively, consider compiling from source, because of the greater flexibility it provides in the long-run.

> **NOTE** *At the time of this writing, a binary version of Apache 2 with SSL support was not yet available, although it's possible that by the time you read this, the situation has changed. However, if it hasn't and you require SSL support on Windows, you'll need to build from source.*

Downloading PHP

Although PHP comes bundled with most Linux distributions nowadays, I recommend that you download the latest stable version from the PHP Web site. To decrease download time, choose from almost 100 official mirrors residing in over 50 countries, a list of which is available here: `http://www.php.net/mirrors.php`.

Once you've chosen the closest mirror, navigate to the downloads page and choose the appropriate format, from these three:

- **Source:** If Unix is your target server platform, or if you're planning on compiling from source for the Windows platform, choose the source format. Building from source on Windows isn't recommended, and isn't discussed in this book. Unless your situation warrants very special circumstances, chances are that the pre-built Windows binary will suit your needs just fine.

- **Windows zip package:** This binary includes both the CGI binary and various server module versions. If you're planning on using PHP in conjunction with Apache, you should to download this version.

- **Windows installer:** This CGI-only binary offers a convenient Windows installer interface for installing and configuring PHP, and support for automatically configuring the IIS, PWS, and Xitami servers. Although you could use this version in conjunction with Apache, it is not recommended. Instead, use the Windows zip package version.

If you are interested in playing with the very latest PHP development snapshots, you can download both source and binary versions here: `http://snaps.php.net/`.

Keep in mind that some of the versions made available via this Web site are not intended for production use.

Downloading the Manuals

Regardless of your experience level, you'll likely refer to the Apache and PHP documentation regularly. Both manuals are wonderfully comprehensive, not to mention well-organized. In addition, several formats are available for download, allowing you to browse each manual locally, saving you the hassle of having to repeatedly return to the product Web site simply to peruse the documentation. Therefore, although not a prerequisite, I recommend that you take a few moments to download each manual in your preferred format, because I guarantee you'll save yourself time, not to mention bandwidth, for the foreseeable future. Check out `http://www.php.net/` and `http://httpd.apache.org/` for links to the latest documentation versions.

> **NOTE** *The Apache distribution comes with an HTML-formatted manual by default. If you'd like some other format, check out the Apache Web site.*

The Installation Process

Because the primary focus of this chapter is on PHP, and not on the Apache server, a comprehensive (or even preliminary) discussion of the many features made available to you during the Apache build process is beyond the scope of this chapter. For additional information regarding these features, I suggest taking some time to peruse the Apache documentation.

The remainder of this section is devoted to the PHP installation procedure.

> **NOTE** *Licensing conflicts between PHP and MySQL have resulted in the removal of the MySQL libraries from PHP 5. Therefore, if you want to use PHP 5 and MySQL together (as is quite likely, given that you're reading this book), you'll need to take the necessary steps to make the MySQL libraries available to PHP 5. I'll discuss this matter in further detail in Chapter 22. As to licensing arrangements, the general rule of thumb is that if you're using PHP 5 and MySQL to create a commercial application, you should purchase the MySQL commercial license. Otherwise, use MySQL's GPL-licensed version.*

Compiling Apache and PHP From Source for Unix

This section guides you through the process of building Apache and PHP from source, targeting the Unix platform. You'll need a respectable ANSI-C compiler and build system, two items that are commonplace on the vast majority of distributions available today. In addition, PHP requires the Flex and Bison packages, while Apache requires at least Perl version 5.003. Again, all three items are prevalent on most, if not all, modern Unix platforms. Finally, you'll require root access to the target server.

Before beginning the installation process, consider moving both packages to a common location, /usr/src/ for example. The installation process follows:

1. Unzip and untar Apache and PHP:

   ```
   %>gunzip httpd-2_X_XX.tar.gz
   %>tar xvf httpd-2_X_XX.tar
   %>gunzip php-XX.tar.gz
   %>tar xvf php-XX.tar
   ```

2. Configure and build Apache:

   ```
   %>cd httpd-2_X_XX
   %>./configure --enable-so [other options]
   %>make
   ```

3. Install Apache:

   ```
   %>make install
   ```

4. Configure, build, and install PHP (see the section "Customizing the Build" for information regarding modifying installation defaults and incorporating third-party extensions into PHP).

   ```
   %>cd ../php-X_XX
   %>./configure --with-apxs2=/usr/local/apache2/bin/apxs [other options]
   %>make
   %>make install
   ```

5. Copy the php.ini file to its default location. The php.ini file is PHP's main configuration channel. In the next section, "Configuration," php.ini's purpose and contents are examined in detail.

    ```
    %>cp php.ini-dist /usr/local/lib/php.ini
    ```

6. Open up the httpd.conf file and ensure that the following lines have been added:

    ```
    LoadModule php5_module modules/libphp5.so
    AddType application/x-httpd-php .php
    ```

Believe it or not, that's it! Restart the Apache server with the following command:

```
%>/usr/local/apache/bin/apachectl restart
```

Now proceed to the section, "Testing Your Installation."

> **TIP** *The* AddType *directive binds a MIME-type to a particular extension or extensions. The* .php *extension is only a suggestion; you can use any extension you'd like, including* .html, .php4, *or even* .jason. *In addition, you can designate multiple extensions simply by including them all on the line, each separated by a space.*

Installing Apache and PHP on Windows

Before the release of Apache 2, the Apache Web site officially warned users against deploying the software on the Windows platform for purposes other than testing. The code base was optimized for the Unix platform, and differences between Unix and the Win32 platform are plenty, resulting in both performance and scalability degradation on Windows. However, because of the complete rewrite of the software for the Windows platform, you can finally feel at ease deploying Apache 2 and PHP in an environment that was once maligned for its instability and poor performance. Even if you don't plan on deploying your application on the Windows platform, it nonetheless makes for a great localized testing environment for those users (myself included) who find it easier to code, test, and document on a Windows workstation. The installation process follows:

1. Start the Apache installer by double-clicking the apache_X.X.XX-win32-x86 icon.

2. The installation process will begin with a welcome screen. Take a moment to read the screen and click Next.

3. The License agreement is displayed next. Carefully read through the license. Assuming that you agree with the license stipulations, click Next.

4. A screen containing various items pertinent to the Apache server is displayed next. Take a moment to read through this information and click Next.

5. You will be prompted for various items pertinent to the server's operation, including the Network Domain, Server Name, and Administrator's Email Address. If you know this information, fill it in now; otherwise, just use "localhost" for the first two items, and put in any e-mail address for the last. You can always change this information later in the `httpd.conf` file. When you're finished, click Next.

6. You'll next be prompted for a Setup Type: Typical or Custom. Unless there is a specific reason you don't want the Apache documentation installed, choose Typical and click Next. Otherwise, choose Custom, click Next, and on the next screen uncheck the "Apache Documentation" option.

7. You're next prompted for the Destination folder. By default, this is `C:\Program Files\Apache Group`. I suggest changing this to `C:\Apache2`. Regardless of what you choose, keep in mind that I'll be using the latter for sake of convention. Click Next.

8. Finally, click Install to complete the installation. That's it for Apache. Next you'll install PHP.

9. Unzip the PHP package, placing the contents into `C:\php5\`. You can chose another installation directory if you'd like; I advise against choosing a path containing spaces. Regardless, I'll continue to use the installation directory `C:\php5\` for consistency.

10. Navigate to `C:\php5\sapi\` directory.

11. Copy the `php5ts.dll` and `php5apache2.dll` into the appropriate system directory. On Windows 95, 98, or ME, this is typically `C:\Windows\system`, and on Windows NT or 2000 this is typically `C:\winnt\system32\` or `C:\winnt40\system32\`. Finally, on Windows XP this is typically `C:\windows\system32\`. Alternatively, you could copy these files into any directory in your Windows PATH environment variable.

12. Navigate to `C:\php5\`.

13. Copy php.ini-recommended to the appropriate Windows directory, renaming it as php.ini. On Windows 98, ME, or XP, this is typically C:\Windows\, while on Windows NT or 2000, this is typically C:\winnt\ or C:\winnt40\.

14. Navigate to C:\apache2\conf and open httpd.conf for editing.

15. Add the following two lines to the httpd.conf file. I suggest adding them directly below the block of LoadModule entries located in the bottom of the Global Environment section.

```
LoadModule php5_module c:/php5/sapi/php5apache2.dll
AddType application/x-httpd-php .php .html
```

16. If you're using Windows NT, 2000, or XP, navigate to Settings ➤ Control Panel ➤ Administrative Tools, and open up Services.

17. Locate Apache in the list, and make sure that it is started. If not, highlight the label and click Start the service, located to the left of the label. Right-click Apache and choose Properties. Ensure that the startup type is set to Automatic. If you're still using Windows 95/98, you'll need to start Apache manually via the shortcut provided on the Start menu.

Testing Your Installation

The best way to verify your PHP installation is by attempting to execute a PHP script. Open up your favorite text editor and add the following lines to a new file. Then save that file within a web-accessible directory as phpinfo.php:

```php
<?php
    phpinfo();
?>
```

Now open a browser and access this file just like you would any other Web document. For example:

```
http://www.example.com/pmnp/1/phpinfo.php
```

If all goes well, you should see output similar to that shown in Figure 2-1.

> **TIP** *The* phpinfo() *function offers a plethora of useful information pertinent to your PHP installation.*

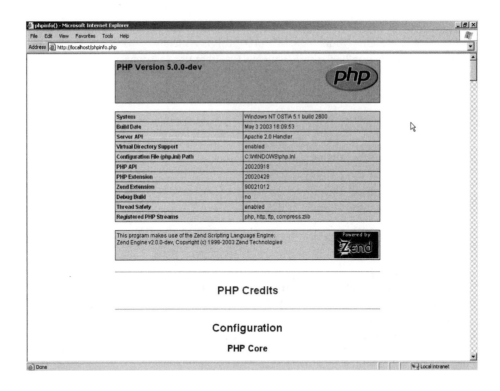

Figure 2-1. Output from PHP's phpinfo() function

Help! I'm Getting an Error!

Assuming that you encountered no noticeable errors during the build process, you may not be seeing the cool `phpinfo()` output due to one or more of the following reasons:

- Apache was not started or restarted after the build process was complete.

- A typing error was introduced into the code in the `phpinfo.php` file. If a parse error message is resulting in the browser input, then this is almost certainly the case.

- Something went awry during the build process. Consider rebuilding, watching closely for errors. Don't forget to execute a make clean from within each of the respective distribution directories before reconfiguring and rebuilding.

Customizing the Unix Build

Although the base PHP installation is sufficient for most beginning users, the chances are that you'll soon want to make adjustments to the default configuration settings and possibly experiment with some of the third-party extensions not built into the distribution by default. You can view a complete list of configuration flags (there are over 150) by executing:

```
%>./configure --help
```

To make adjustments to the build process, you just need to add one or more of these arguments to PHP's `configure` command, including a value assignment if necessary. For example, suppose you wanted to enable PHP's FTP functionality, a feature not enabled by default. Just modify the configuration step of the PHP build process like so:

```
%>./configure --with-apxs2=/usr/local/apache2/bin/apxs --enable-ftp
```

As another example, suppose you want to enable PHP's Java extension. Just change step four to read:

```
%>./configure --with-apxs2=/usr/local/apache2/bin/apxs --enable-java=[JDK-INSTALL-DIR]
```

One common point of confusion among beginners is to assume that simply including additional flags will automatically make this functionality available via PHP. This is not necessarily the case. Keep in mind that you also need to install the software ultimately responsible for enabling the extension support. In the case of the Java example, you need the Java JDK.

Customizing the Windows Build

A total of 33 extensions come with PHP's Windows distribution, all of which are located in the `INSTALL_DIR\extensions\` directory. However, to actually use any of these extensions, you'll need to uncomment the appropriate line within the `php.ini` file. For example, if you'd like to enable PHP's IMAP extension, you need to make two minor adjustments to your php.ini file.

1. Open up the `php.ini` file, located in the Windows directory. To determine which directory that is, see installation Step 13 of the "Installing Apache and PHP on Windows" section. Locate the `extension_dir` directive, and assign it `C:\php5\extensions\`. If you installed PHP in another directory, modify this path accordingly.

2. Locate the line `;extension=php_imap.dll`. Uncomment this line by removing the preceding semicolon. Save and close the file.

3. Restart Apache, and the extension is ready for use from within PHP. Keep in mind that some extensions require further modifications to the PHP file before they can be used properly. See the "Configuration" section for a discussion of the `php.ini` file.

Common Pitfalls

It's common to experience some initial problems bringing your first PHP-enabled page online. I'll touch upon some of the more commonplace symptoms in this section.

- Changes made to Apache's configuration do not take effect until it has been restarted. Therefore, be sure to restart Apache after adding the necessary PHP-specific lines to the file.

- When you modify the Apache configuration file, you may accidentally introduce an invalid character, causing Apache to fail upon an attempt to restart. If Apache will not start, go back and review your changes.

- Verify that the file indeed ends in the PHP-specific extension as specified in the httpd.conf file. For example, if you've defined .php as the extension, don't try to embed PHP code in an .html file.

- Make sure that you've delimited the PHP code within the file. Neglecting to do this will cause the code to simply output to the browser.

- You've created a file named index.php and are trying unsuccessfully to call it as you would a default directory index. Remember that, by default, Apache only recognizes index.html in this fashion. Therefore you'll need to add index.php to Apache's DirectoryIndex directive.

Configuration

If you've made it this far, congratulations! You have an operating Apache and PHP server at your disposal. However, you'll probably want to make at least a few other run-time changes before the software is working to your satisfaction. The vast majority of these changes are handled through Apache's httpd.conf file and PHP's php.ini file. Each file contains a myriad of configuration directives that collectively control the behavior of each product. For the remainder of this chapter, we'll focus on PHP's most commonly used configuration directives, introducing the purpose, scope, and default value of each.

Managing PHP's Configuration Directives

Before delving into the specifics of each directive, I'll demonstrate the various ways in which these directives can be manipulated, including through the php.ini file, the httpd.conf and .htaccess files, and directly through a PHP script.

The php.ini File

The PHP distribution comes with two configuration templates, php.ini-dist and php.ini-recommended. In the installation section, I suggested using the latter, because many of the parameters found within it have already been set to their suggested settings. Taking this advice will likely save you a good deal of initial time and effort securing and tweaking your installation, because there are more than 230 distinct configuration parameters in this file. Although the default values go a long way towards helping you to quickly deploy PHP, you'll probably want to make additional adjustments to PHP's behavior, and you'll need to learn a bit more about this file and its many configuration parameters. The section "PHP Configuration Directives" presents a comprehensive introduction to many of these parameters, explaining the purpose, scope, and range of each.

The php.ini file is PHP's global configuration file, much like httpd.conf is to Apache, or my.cnf (my.ini on Windows) is to MySQL. This file addresses eleven different aspects of PHP's behavior. These sections include:

- Language Options

- Safe Mode

- Resource Limits

- Miscellaneous

- Error Handling and Logging

- Data Handling

- Paths and Directories

- File Uploads

- fopen Wrappers

- Dynamic Extensions

- Module Settings

Each section is introduced along with its respective parameters in the "PHP Configuration Directives" section. Before introducing them however, take a moment to review the php.ini file's general syntactical characteristics. The php.ini file is a simple text file, consisting solely of comments and parameter=key assignment pairs. Here's a sample snippet from the file:

```
;
; Safe Mode
;
safe_mode = Off
```

Lines beginning with a semicolon are comments; The parameter safe_mode is assigned the value Off.

> **TIP** *Once you're comfortable with a configuration parameter's purpose, consider deleting the corresponding comments to streamline the file's contents, thereby decreasing later editing time.*

Exactly when changes take effect depends on how you installed PHP. If PHP is installed as a CGI, the php.ini file is re-read every time PHP is invoked, thus making changes instantaneous. If PHP is installed as an Apache module, then php.ini is only read in once, when the Apache daemon is first started. Therefore, if PHP is installed in the latter fashion, you must restart Apache before any new behaviors take effect.

The Apache httpd.conf and .htaccess Files

When PHP is running as an Apache module, you can modify many of the directives through either the httpd.conf file, or through .htaccess. This is accomplished by prefixing the name = value pair with one of the following keywords:

- php_value: Sets the value of the specified directive.

- php_flag: Sets the value of the specified Boolean directive.

- php_admin_value: Sets the value of the specified directive. This differs from php_value in that it cannot be used within an .htaccess file, and cannot be overridden within virtual hosts or .htaccess.

- php_admin_flag: Sets the value of the specified directive. This differs from php_value in that it cannot be used within an .htaccess file, and cannot be overridden within virtual hosts or .htaccess.

Within the Executing Script

The third, and most localized, means for manipulating PHP's configuration variables is via the ini_set() function. For example, suppose you wanted to modify PHP's maximum execution time for a given script. Just embed the following command into the top of the script:

```
ini_set("max_execution_time","60");
```

Configuration Directive Scope

Can configuration directives be modified anywhere? Good question. The answer is no, for a variety of reasons, mostly security related. Each directive is assigned a scope, and the directive can only be modified within that scope. In total, there are four scopes:

- PHP_INI_PERDIR: Directive can be modified within the php.ini, httpd.conf, or .htaccess files

- PHP_INI_SYSTEM: Directive can be modified within the php.ini and httpd.conf files

- PHP_INI_USER: Directive can be modified within user scripts

- PHP_INI_ALL: Directive can be modified anywhere

Throughout the book, I'll accompany the introduction of each configuration directive with a reference to its scope.

PHP's Configuration Directives

The following sections introduce many of PHP's core configuration directives. In addition to a general definition, I'll include its scope and default value. Because you'll probably spend the majority of your time working with these variables from within php.ini, I'll introduce the directives as they appear in this file.

Note that the directives introduced in this section are largely relevant solely to PHP's general behavior; directives pertinent to extensions, or to topics in which considerable attention is given later in the book, are not introduced in this section, but are rather introduced in the appropriate chapter. For example, MySQL's configuration directives are introduced in Chapter 26.

Language Options

The directives located in this initial section determine some of the language's most basic behavior. You'll definitely want to take a few moments to become acquainted with these configuration possibilities.

engine (On, Off)
Scope: PHP_INI_ALL, Default value: On
This parameter is simply responsible for determining whether the PHP engine is available. Turning it off will prevent you from using PHP at all. Obviously, you should leave this enabled if you're planning on using PHP.

short_open_tag (On, Off)
Scope: `PHP_INI_ALL`, Default value: On
PHP script components are enclosed within escape syntax. There are four different escape formats, the shortest of which is known as *short open tags*, and looks like this:

```
<?
   echo "Some PHP statement";
?>
```

You may recognize this syntax is shared with XML, which could cause issues in certain environments. Thus, a means for disabling this particular format has been provided. When `short_open_tag` is enabled (On), short tags are allowed; when disabled (Off), they are not.

asp_tags (On, Off)
Scope: `PHP_INI_ALL`, Default value: Off
PHP supports ASP-style script delimiters, which look like this:

```
<%
   echo "Some PHP statement";
%>
```

If you're coming from an ASP background, and you prefer to continue using this delimiter syntax, you can do so by enabling this tag.

precision (integer)
Scope: `PHP_INI_ALL`, Default value: 14
PHP supports a wide variety of data types, including floating-point. The `precision` parameter specifies the number of significant digits displayed in a floating-point number representation.

y2k_compliance (On, Off)
Scope: `PHP_INI_ALL`, Default value: Off
Who can forget the Y2K scare of just a few years ago? Although superhuman efforts were undertaken to eliminate the problems posed by non-Y2K compliant software, some users continue to use non-compliant browsers. If for some bizarre reason you're sure that a great number of your site's users fall into this group, then disable the `y2k_compliance` parameter; if not, it should be enabled.

output_buffering ((On, Off) or (integer))
Scope: `PHP_INI_SYSTEM`, Default value: Off
Anybody with even minimal PHP experience is likely quite familiar with the following two messages:

```
"Cannot add header information - headers already sent"
"Oops, php_set_cookie called after header has been sent"
```

These messages occur when a script attempts to modify a header after it has already been sent back to the requesting user. Most commonly, they are the result of the programmer attempting to send a cookie to the user after some output has already been sent back to the browser, an impossibility because the header (not seen by the user, but used by the browser) will always precede that output. PHP version 4.0 offered a solution to this annoying problem, introducing the concept of output buffering. When enabled, output buffering tells PHP to send all output at once, after the script has been completed. This way, any subsequent changes to the header can be made throughout the script, because it hasn't yet been sent. Enabling the output_buffering directive turns output buffering on. Alternatively, you can limit the size of the output buffer (thereby implicitly enabling output buffering) by setting it to the maximum number of bytes you'd like this buffer to contain.

If you do not plan to use output buffering, you should disable this directive, as it will hinder performance slightly.

output_handler (string)
Scope: PHP_INI_ALL, Default value: Null
This interesting and useful directive tells PHP to pass all output through a function before returning it to the requesting user. For example, suppose you want to compress all output before returning it to the browser, a feature supported by all mainstream HTTP/1.1-compliant browsers. You can assign output_handler like so:

```
output_handler = "ob_gzhandler"
```

ob_gzhandler() is PHP's compression-handler function, located in PHP's output control library. Keep in mind that you cannot simultaneously set output_handler to ob_gzhandler() and enable zlib.output_compression (discussed next).

zlib.output_compression ((On, Off) or (integer))
Scope: PHP_INI_SYSTEM, Default value: Off
Compressing output before it is returned to the browser can save bandwidth and time. This HTTP/1.1 feature is supported by most modern browsers, and can be safely used in most applications. You enable automatic output compression by setting zlib.output_compression to On. In addition, you can simultaneously enable output compression and set a compression buffer size (in bytes) by assigning zlib.output_compression an integer value.

zlib.output_handler (string)
Scope: PHP_INI_SYSTEM, Default value: Null
The zlib.output_handler specifies a particular compression library if the zlib library is not available.

implicit_flush (On, Off)
Scope: PHP_INI_SYSTEM, Default value: Off
Enabling implicit_flush results in automatically clearing, or *flushing*, the output buffer of its contents after each call to print(), echo(), and completion of each embedded HTML block.

unserialize_callback_func (string)
Scope: `PHP_INI_ALL`, Default value: Null
This directive allows you to control the response of the unserializer when a request is made to instantiate an undefined class. For most users, this directive is irrelevant, because PHP already outputs a warning in such instances, if PHP's error reporting is tuned to the appropriate level.

allow_call_time_pass_reference (On, Off)
Scope: `PHP_INI_SYSTEM`, Default value: On
Function arguments can be passed in two ways: by value and by reference. Exactly how each argument is passed to a function at function call time can be specified in the function definition, which is the recommended means for doing so. However, you can force all arguments to be passed by reference at function call time by enabling `allow_call_time_pass_reference`.

The discussion of PHP functions in Chapter 4 discusses how functional arguments can be passed both by value and reference, and the implications of doing so.

Syntax Highlighting

PHP can display and highlight source code. You can enable this feature either by assigning the PHP script the extension `.phps` (this is the default extension, and can be modified), or via the `show_source()` or `highlight_file()` function. You can control the color of strings, comments, keywords, the background, default text, and HTML components of the highlighted source through the following six directives. Each can be assigned an rgb, hexadecimal, or keyword representation of each color. For example, the color we commonly refer to as "black" can be represented as `rgb(0,0,0)`, #000000, or `black`, respectively.

> **TIP** *To make use of the* `.phps` *extension, you need to add the following line to httpd.conf:*
>
> `AddType application/x-httpd-php-source .phps`

highlight.string (string)
Scope: `PHP_INI_ALL`, Default value: #DD0000

highlight.comment (string)
Scope: `PHP_INI_ALL`, Default value: #FF9900

highlight.keyword (string)
Scope: `PHP_INI_ALL`, Default value: #007700

highlight.bg (string)
Scope: `PHP_INI_ALL`, Default value: #FFFFFF

highlight.default (string)
Scope: PHP_INI_ALL, Default value: #0000BB

highlight.html (string)
Scope: PHP_INI_ALL, Default value: #000000

Safe Mode

When you deploy PHP in a multi-user environment, such as that found on an ISP's shared server, you might want to limit its functionality. As you might imagine, offering all users full reign over all PHP's functions could open up the possibility for exploiting or damaging server resources and files. As a safeguard for using PHP on shared servers, PHP can be run in a restricted, or *safe mode*.

Enabling safe mode has a great many implications, including the automatic disabling of quite a few functions and various features deemed to be potentially insecure and thus possibly damaging if they are misused within a local script. A small sampling of these disabled functions and features include: parse_ini_file(), chmod(), chown(), chgrp(), exec(), system() and backtick operators. In addition, enabling safe mode opens up the possibility for activating a number of other restrictions via other PHP configuration directives, each of which is introduced in this section.

safe_mode (On, Off)
Scope: PHP_INI_SYSTEM, Default value: Off
Enabling the safe_mode directive results in PHP being run in the restricted safe mode.

safe_mode_gid (On, Off)
Scope: PHP_INI_SYSTEM, Default value: Off
When safe_mode is enabled, an enabled safe_mode_gid will enforce a GID (group ID) check when opening files. When safe_mode_gid is disabled, a more restrictive UID (user ID) check is enforced.

safe_mode_include_dir (string)
Scope: PHP_INI_SYSTEM, Default value: Null
The safe_mode_include_dir provides a safe haven from the UID/GID checks enforced when safe_mode and potentially safe_mode_gid are enabled. UID/GID checks are ignored when files are opened from its assigned directory.

safe_mode_exec_dir (string)
Scope: PHP_INI_SYSTEM, Default value: Null
When safe_mode is enabled, the safe_mode_exec_dir parameter will restrict execution of executables via the exec() function to the assigned directory. For examples, if you wanted to restrict execution to functions found in /usr/local/bin, you would use this directive:

```
safe_mode_exec_dir = "/usr/local/bin"
```

safe_mode_allowed_env_vars (string)
Scope: `PHP_INI_SYSTEM`, Default value: `PHP_`
When safe mode is enabled, you can restrict which operating system-level environment variables users can modify through PHP scripts with the `safe_mode_allowed_env_vars` directive. For example, setting this directive like the following will limit modification to only those variables with an `PHP_` or `MYSQL_` prefix:

```
safe_mode_allowed_env_vars = "PHP_,MYSQL_"
```

Keep in mind that leaving this directive blank means that the user can modify any environment variable.

safe_mode_protected_env_vars (string)
Scope: `PHP_INI_SYSTEM`, Default value: LD_LIBRARY_PATH
The `safe_mode_protected_env_vars` directive offers a means for explicitly preventing certain environment variables from being modified. For example, if you wanted to prevent the user from modifying the `PATH` and `LD_LIBRARY_PATH` variables, you would use this directive:

```
safe_mode_protected_env_vars = "PATH, LD_LIBRARY_PATH"
```

open_basedir (string)
Scope: `PHP_INI_SYSTEM`, Default value: Null
Much like Apache's `DocumentRoot`, PHP's `open_basedir` directive can establish a base directory to which all file operations will be restricted. This prevents users from entering otherwise restricted areas of the server. For example, suppose all Web material is located within the directory /home/www. To prevent users from viewing and potentially manipulating files like /etc/passwd via a few simple PHP commands, consider setting `open_basedir` like this:

```
open_basedir = "/home/www/"
```

Note that the influence exercised by this directive is not dependent upon the `safe_mode` directive.

disable_functions (string)
Scope: `PHP_INI_SYSTEM`, Default value: Null
In certain environments you may want to completely disallow the use of certain default functions, such as `exec()` and `system()`. Such functions can be disabled by assigning them to the `disable_functions` parameter, like this:

```
disable_functions = "exec, system";
```

Note that the influence exercised by this directive is not dependent upon the `safe_mode` directive.

disable_classes (string)
Scope: PHP_INI_SYSTEM, Default value: Null
Given the new functionality offered by PHP's embrace of the object-oriented paradigm, it likely won't be too long before you're using large sets of class libraries. There may be certain classes found within these libraries that you'd rather not make available, however. You can prevent the use of these classes via the disable_classes directive. For example, suppose that you wanted to disable two particular classes, named administrator and janitor:

```
disable_classes = "administrator, janitor"
```

Note that the influence exercised by this directive is not dependent upon the safe_mode directive.

Resource Limits

Although version 5 features numerous advances in PHP's resource-handling capabilities, you must still be careful to ensure that scripts do not monopolize server resources as a result of either programmer- or user-initiated actions. Three particular areas where such overconsumption is prevalent are script execution time, script input processing time, and memory. Each can be controlled via the following three directives.

max_execution_time (integer)
Scope: PHP_INI_ALL, Default value: 30
The max_execution_time parameter places an upper-limit on the amount of time, in seconds, that a PHP script can execute. Setting this parameter to zero will disable any maximum limit. Note that any time consumed by an external program executed by PHP commands, such as exec() and system(), does not count towards this limit.

max_input_time (integer)
Scope: PHP_INI_ALL, Default value: 60
The max_input_time parameter places a limit on the amount of time, in seconds, that a PHP script will devote to parsing request data. This parameter is particularly important when you upload large files using PHP's file upload feature, which is discussed in Chapter 13.

memory_limit (integer)M
Scope: PHP_INI_ALL, Default value: 8M
The memory_limit parameter determines the maximum amount of memory, in MB, that can be allocated to a PHP script.

Miscellaneous

The Miscellaneous category consists of a single directive, expose_php.

expose_php (On, Off)
Scope: PHP_INI_SYSTEM, Default value: On
Each scrap of information a potential attacker can gather about a Web server increases the chances that he will successfully compromise it. One simple way to obtain key information about server characteristics is via the server signature. For example, Apache will broadcast the following information within each response-header by default:

```
Apache/2.0.44 (Unix) DAV/2 PHP/5.0.0-dev Server at www.example.com Port 80
```

Disabling expose_php will prevent the Web server signature (if enabled) from broadcasting the fact that PHP is installed. Although you need to take other steps to ensure sufficient server protection, obscuring server properties such as this one is nonetheless heartily recommended.

> **NOTE** *You can completely disable Apache's broadcast of its server signature by setting* ServerSignature *to off in the* httpd.conf *file.*

Error Handling and Logging

PHP offers a convenient and flexible means for reporting and logging errors, warnings, and notices generated by PHP at compile-time, run-time, and as a result of some user action. The developer has control over the reporting sensitivity, whether and how this information is displayed to the browser, and whether the information is logged to either a file or the system log (syslog on Unix, event log on Windows). The next fifteen directives control this behavior.

error_reporting (string)
Scope: PHP_INI_ALL, Default value: Null
The error_reporting directive determines PHP's level of error-reporting sensitivity. There are twelve assigned error levels, each unique in terms of its pertinence to the functioning of the application or server. These levels are defined in Table 2-1.

You can set error_reporting to any single level, or a combination of these levels, using Boolean operators. For example, suppose you wanted to report just errors. You'd use this setting:

```
error_reporting = E_ERROR|E_CORE_ERROR|E_COMPILE_ERROR|E_USER_ERROR
```

If you wanted to track all errors, except for user-generated warnings and notices, you'd use this setting:

```
error_reporting = E_ALL & ~E_USER_WARNING & ~E_USER_NOTICE
```

During the application development and initial deployment stages, you should turn sensitivity to the highest level, or E_ALL. However, once all major bugs have been dealt with, consider turning the sensitivity down a bit.

Table 2-1: PHP's error reporting Levels

NAME	DESCRIPTION
E_ALL	Report all errors and warnings
E_ERROR	Report fatal run-time errors
E_WARNING	Report non-fatal run-time errors
E_PARSE	Report compile-time parse errors
E_NOTICE	Report run-time notices, like uninitialized variables
E_STRICT	PHP version portability suggestions
E_CORE_ERROR	Report fatal errors occurring during PHP's startup
E_CORE_WARNING	Report non-fatal errors occurring during PHP's startup
E_COMPILE_ERROR	Report fatal compile-time errors
E_COMPILE_WARNING	Report non-fatal compile-time errors
E_USER_ERROR	Report user-generated fatal error messages
E_USER_WARNING	Report user-generated non-fatal error messages
E_USER_NOTICE	Report user-generated notices

display_errors (On, Off)
Scope: PHP_INI_ALL, Default value: On
When display_errors is enabled, all errors of at least the level specified by error_reporting will be output. Consider enabling this parameter during the development stage. When your application is deployed, all errors should be logged instead, accomplished by enabling log_errors and specifying the destination of the log, using error_log.

display_startup_errors (On, Off)
Scope: PHP_INI_ALL, Default value: Off
Disabling display_startup_errors will prevent errors specific to PHP's startup procedure from being displayed to the user.

log_errors (On, Off)
Scope: PHP_INI_ALL, Default value: Off
Error messages can prove invaluable in determining potential issues that arise during the execution of your PHP application. Enabling log_errors tells PHP that these errors should be logged, either to a particular file or the syslog. The exact destination is determined by another parameter, error_log.

log_errors_max_len (integer)
Scope: PHP_INI_ALL, Default value: 1024
This parameter determines the maximum length of a single log message, in bytes. Setting this parameter to zero results in no maximum imposed limit.

ignore_repeated_errors (On, Off)
Scope: PHP_INI_ALL, Default value: Off
If you're reviewing the log regularly, there really is no need to note errors that repeatedly occur on the same line of the same file. Disabling this parameter will prevent such repeated errors from being logged.

ignore_repeated_source (On, Off)
Scope: PHP_INI_ALL, Default value: Off
Disabling this variant on the ignore_repeated_errors parameter will disregard the source of the errors when ignoring repeated errors. This means that only a maximum of one instance of each error message can be logged.

report_memleaks (On, Off)
Scope: PHP_INI_ALL, Default value: Off
This parameter, only relevant when PHP is compiled in debug mode, determines whether memory leaks are displayed or logged. In addition to the debug mode constraint, an error level of at least E_WARNING must be in effect.

track_errors (On, Off)
Scope: PHP_INI_ALL, Default value: Off
Enabling track_errors causes PHP to store the most recent error message in the variable $php_error_msg. The scope of this variable is limited to the particular script in which the error occurs.

html_errors (On, Off)
Scope: PHP_INI_SYSTEM, Default value: On
PHP encloses error messages within HTML tags by default. Sometimes, because you might not always to do so, a means for disabling this behavior is offered via the html_errors parameter.

docref_root (string)
Scope: PHP_INI_ALL, Default value: Null
If html_errors is enabled, PHP will include a link to a detailed description of any error, found in the official manual. However, rather than linking to the official Web site, you should point the user to a local copy of the manual. The location of the local manual is determined by the path specified by docref_root.

docref_ext (string)
Scope: PHP_INI_ALL, Default value: Null
The docref_ext informs PHP of the local manual's page extensions when used to provide additional information about errors (see docref_root).

error_prepend_string (string)
Scope: PHP_INI_ALL, Default value: Null
If you want to pass additional information to the user before outputting an error, you can prepend a string (including formatting tags) to the automatically generated error-output using the error_prepend_string parameter.

error_append_string (string)
Scope: PHP_INI_ALL, Default value: Null
If you want to pass additional information to the user after outputting an error, you can append a string (including formatting tags) to the automatically generated error-output using the error_append_string parameter.

error_log (string)
Scope: PHP_INI_ALL, Default value: Null
If log_errors is enabled, the error_log directive specifies the message destination. PHP supports logging to both a specific file, or the operating system syslog. On Windows, setting error_log to syslog will result in messages being logged to the event log.

Data Handling

The parameters introduced in this section affect the way that PHP handles external variables; that is, variables passed into the script via some outside source. GET, POST, cookies, the operating system, and the server are all possible candidates for providing external data. Other parameters located in this section determine PHP's default character set, MIME-type, and whether external files will be automatically prepended or appended to PHP's returned output.

arg_separator.output (string)
Scope: PHP_INI_ALL, Default value: &
PHP is capable of automatically generating URLs, and will use the standard ampersand (&) for separating input variables. However, if you need to override this convention, you can do so using the arg_separator.output directive.

arg_separator.input (string)
Scope: PHP_INI_ALL, Default value: &
The ampersand (&) is the standard character used to separate input variables passed in via the POST or GET method. If you need to override this convention within your PHP applications, you can do so using the arg_separator.input directive.

variables_order (string)
Scope: PHP_INI_ALL, Default value: Null
The variables_order directive determines which and in which order the EGPCS (Environment, Get, Post, Cookie, Server) variables are parsed.

register_globals (On, Off)
Scope: PHP_INI_SYSTEM, Default value: Off
If you have used PHP before version 4, the mere mention of this directive is enough to evoke gnashing of the teeth and pulling of the hair. In version 4.2.0 this directive was disabled by default, forcing many long-time PHP users to entirely rethink (and in some cases rewrite) their Web application development methodology. This change, although done at a cost of considerable confusion, ultimately serves the best interests of developers in terms of greater application security. If you're new to all of this, what's the big deal?

Historically, all external variables were automatically registered in the global scope. That is, any incoming variable of the types COOKIE, ENVIRONMENT, GET, POST and SERVER were made available globally. Because they were available globally, they were also globally modifiable. Although this might seem convenient to some, it also introduced a security deficiency, because variables intended to solely be managed using a cookie could also potentially be modified via the URL. For example, suppose that a session identifier uniquely identifying the user is communicated across pages via a cookie. Nobody but that user should see the data which is ultimately mapped to the user identified by that session identifier. A user could open the cookie, copy the session identifier, and paste it onto the end of the URL, like this:

```
http://www.example.com/secretdata.php?sessionid=4x5bh5H793adK
```

The user then e-mails this link to some other user, who subsequently opens it. If there are no other security restrictions in place (IP identification, for example), this user will be able to see the otherwise confidential data. Disabling the register_globals directive prevents such behavior from occurring. While these external variables remain in the global scope, each must be referred to in conjunction with its type. For example, the sessionid variable used in the previous example would instead be referred to solely as:

```
$_COOKIE['sessionid']
```

Any attempts to modify this parameter using any other means (GET or POST for example) cause a new variable in the global scope of that means ($_GET['sessionid'] or $_POST['sessionid']). The section "PHP's Superglobal Variables," in Chapter 3, offers a thorough introduction to external variables of the COOKIE, ENVIRONMENT, GET, POST, and SERVER types.

Although disabling register_globals is unequivocally a good idea, keep in mind that it isn't the only thing you need to do to secure your application. Chapter 19 has more information about securing your applications.

register_long_arrays (On, Off)
Scope: PHP_INI_SYSTEM, Default value: Off
This directive determines whether to continue registering the various input arrays (environment, get, post, cookie, system) using the deprecated syntax, such as HTTP_*_VARS. Disabling this directive is recommended for performance reasons.

register_argc_argv (On, Off)
Scope: PHP_INI_SYSTEM, Default value: On
Passing in variable information via the GET method is analogous to passing arguments to an executable. Many languages process such arguments in terms of argc and argv. argc is the argument count, and argv is an indexed array containing the arguments. If you would like to declare variables $argc and $argv and mimic this functionality, enable register_argc_argv.

post_max_size (integer)M
Scope: `PHP_INI_SYSTEM`, Default value: 8M
Of the two methods for passing data between requests, POST is better equipped to transport large amounts such as what might be sent via a Web form. However, for both security and performance reasons, you might wish to place an upper ceiling on exactly how much data can be sent via this method to a PHP script; this can be accomplished using `post_max_size`.

gpc_order (string)
Scope: `PHP_INI_ALL`, Default value: GPC
This parameter determines the order in which variables passed in via GET, POST and cookies are parsed. For example, maintaining the default setting of `GPC` results in any GET variable values being overwritten by any POST variable values of the same name. Setting this parameter to `GC` causes POST variables to be ignored entirely.

> **NOTE** *Quotes, both of the single and double variety, have long played a special role in programming. Because they are commonly used both as string delimiters and in written language, you need a way to differentiate between the two in programming to eliminate confusion. The solution is simple: escape any quote mark not intended to delimit the string. If you don't do this, unexpected errors could occur. Consider the following:*
>
> ```
> $sentence = "John said, "I love racing cars!"";
> ```
>
> *Which quote is intended to delimit the string, and which are used to delimit John's utterance? PHP doesn't know, unless certain quote marks are escaped, like this:*
>
> ```
> $sentence = "John said, \"I love racing cars!\"";
> ```
>
> *Escaping non-delimiting quote marks is known as enabling* magic quotes. *This process could be automatic, done by enabling the directive* magic_quotes_gpc *introduced in this section, or it could be handled manually using the functions* addslashes() *and* stripslashes(). *The latter strategy is recommended, because it enables the developer to wield total control over the application, although in those cases where you're trying to use an application in which the automatic escaping of quotations is expected, you'll need to enable this behavior accordingly. Three parameters determine how PHP behaves in this regards:* magic_quotes_gpc, magic_quotes_runtime, *and* magic_quotes_sybase.

magic_quotes_gpc (On, Off)
Scope: `PHP_INI_SYSTEM`, Default value: On
This parameter determines whether magic quotes are enabled for data transmitted via the GET, POST and Cookie methodologies. When enabled, all single and double quotes, backslashes, and null characters are automatically escaped with a backslash.

magic_quotes_runtime (On, Off)
Scope: PHP_INI_ALL, Default value: Off
Enabling this parameter results in the automatic escaping (using a backslash) of any quote marks located within data returned from an external resource, such as a database or text file.

magic_quotes_sybase (On, Off)
Scope: PHP_INI_ALL, Default value: Off
This parameter is only of interest in the case that magic_quotes_runtime is enabled. If magic_quotes_sybase is enabled, all data returned from an external resource will be escaped using a single quote, rather than a backslash. This is useful when the data is being returned from a Sybase database, which employs a rather unorthodox requirement of escaping special characters with a single quote rather than a backslash.

auto_prepend_file (string)
Scope: PHP_INI_SYSTEM, Default value: Null
Creating page header templates or including code libraries before a PHP script is executed is most commonly done using the include() or require() function. You can automate this process and forego the inclusion of these functions within your scripts by assigning the file name and corresponding path to the auto_prepend_file directive.

auto_append_file (string)
Scope: PHP_INI_SYSTEM, Default value: Null
Automatically inserting footer templates after a PHP script is executed is most commonly done using the include() or require() functions. You can automate this process and forego the inclusion of these functions within your scripts by assigning the template file name and corresponding path to the auto_append_file directive.

default_mimetype (string)
Scope: PHP_INI_ALL, Default value: SAPI_DEFAULT_MIMETYPE
MIME types offer a standard means for classifying file types on the Internet. You can serve any of these file types via PHP applications, the most common of which is text/html. If you're using PHP in other fashions, however, such as a content generator for WML (Wireless Markup Languages) applications for example, you need to adjust the MIME type accordingly. You can do so by modifying the default_mimetype directive.

default_charset (string)
Scope: PHP_INI_ALL, Default value: SAPI_DEFAULT_CHARSET
As of version 4.0b4, PHP will output a character encoding in the Content-type header. By default this is set to iso-8859-1, which supports languages such as English, Spanish, German, Italian, and Portuguese, among others. If your application is geared towards languages such as Japanese, Chinese, or Hebrew, however, the default_charset directive allows you to update this character set setting accordingly.

Paths and Directories

This section introduces directives that determine PHP's default path settings. These paths are used for including libraries and extensions, as well as for determining user Web directories and Web document roots.

include_path (string)
Scope: `PHP_INI_ALL`, Default value: `PHP_INCLUDE_PATH`
The path to which this parameter is set serves as the base path used by functions such as `include()`, `require()`, and `fopen_with_path()`. You can specify multiple directories by separating each with a semicolon, for example:

```
include_path="/usr/local/include/php;/home/php"
```

By default, this parameter is set to the path defined by the environment variable `PHP_INCLUDE_PATH`.

doc_root (string)
Scope: `PHP_INI_SYSTEM`, Default value: Null
This parameter determines the default from which all PHP scripts will be served. It's only used if non-empty.

user_dir (string)
Scope: `PHP_INI_SYSTEM`, Default value: Null
The `user_dir` directive specifies the absolute directory PHP uses when opening files using the `/~username` convention. For example, when `user_dir` is set to `/home/users` and a user attempts to open the file `~/gilmore/collections/books.txt`, PHP will know that the absolute path is `/home/users/gilmore/collections/books.txt`.

extension_dir (string)
Scope: `PHP_INI_SYSTEM`, Default value: `PHP_EXTENSION_DIR`
The `extension_dir` directive tells PHP where its loadable extensions (modules) are located. By default, this is set to `./`, which means the same directory as the executing script. In the Windows environment, if `extension_dir` is not set, it will default to `C:\INSTALLATION-DIRECTORY\extensions\`. In the Unix environment, the exact location of this directory depends on several factors, although its quite likely that the location will be `INSTALLATION-DIRECTORY/lib/php/extensions/no-debug-zts-RELEASE-BUILD-DATE/`.

enable_dl (On, Off)
Scope: `PHP_INI_SYSTEM`, Default value: On
The `dl()` function allows a user to load a PHP extension at runtime, that is, during a script's execution.

File Uploads

PHP supports the uploading and subsequent administrative processing of both text and binary files via the POST method. Three directives are available for maintaining this functionality, each of which is introduced in this section.

> **TIP** *PHP's file upload functionality is introduced in Chapter 13.*

file_uploads (On, Off)
Scope: PHP_INI_SYSTEM, Default value: On
The file_uploads directive determines whether PHP file uploading is enabled.

upload_tmp_dir (string)
Scope: PHP_INI_SYSTEM, Default value: Null
When files are first uploaded to the server, most operating systems place them in a staging, or temporary directory. You can specify this directory for files uploaded via PHP using the upload_tmp_dir directive.

upload_max_filesize (integer)M
Scope: PHP_INI_SYSTEM, Default value: 2M
The upload_max_filesize directive sets an upper limit, in megabytes, on the size of a file processed using PHP's upload mechanism.

fopen Wrappers

This section contains five directives pertinent to the access and manipulation of remote files.

allow_url_fopen (On, Off)
Scope: PHP_INI_ALL, Default value: On
Enabling allow_url_fopen allows PHP to treat remote files almost as if they were local. When enabled, a PHP script can access and modify files residing on remote servers, if the file has the correct permissions.

from (string)
Scope: PHP_INI_ALL, Default value: Null
The from directive is perhaps misleading in its title in that it actually determines the password, rather than the identity, of the anonymous user used to perform FTP connections. Therefore, if from is set like this:

```
from = "jason@example.com"
```

The username anonymous and password jason@example.com will be passed to the server when authentication is requested.

user_agent (string)
Scope: PHP_INI_ALL, Default value: Null
PHP always sends a content header along with its processed output, including a user
agent attribute. This directive determines the value of that attribute.

default_socket_timeout (integer)
Scope: PHP_INI_ALL, Default value: 60
This directive determines the timeout value of a socket-based stream, in seconds.

auto_detect_line_endings (On, Off)
Scope: PHP_INI_ALL, Default value: Off
One never-ending source of developer frustration is derived from the end-of-line
(EOL) character, because of the varying syntax employed by different operating systems.
Enabling auto_detect_line_endings determines whether the data read by fgets() and
file() uses Macintosh, MS-DOS, or Unix file conventions.

Dynamic Extensions

The Dynamic Extensions section contains a single directive, extension.

extension (string)
Scope: PHP_INI_ALL, Default value: Null
The extension directive is used to dynamically load a particular module. On the Win32
operating system, a module might be loaded like this:

```
extension = php_java.dll
```

On Unix, it would be loaded like this:

```
extension = php_java.so
```

Module Settings

The directives found in this section affect the behavior of PHP's interaction with various operating system functions and non-default extensions, such as Java and various
database servers. I'll touch upon a few in this section, and elaborate upon numerous
others in later chapters.

Syslog

define_syslog_variables (On, Off)
Scope: PHP_INI_ALL, Default value: Off
This directive specifies whether or not syslog variables such as $LOG_PID and $LOG_CRON
should be automatically defined. For performance reasons, disabling this directive is
recommended.

Mail

PHP's mail() function offers a convenient means for sending e-mail messages via PHP scripts. Four directives are available for determining PHP's behavior in this respect.

SMTP (string)
Scope: PHP_INI_ALL, Default value: localhost
The SMTP directive, applicable only for Win32 operating systems, determines the DNS name or IP address of the SMTP server PHP should use when sending mail.

smtp_port (int)
Scope: PHP_INI_ALL, Default value: 25
The smtp_port directive, applicable only for Win32 operating systems, specifies the port PHP should use when sending mail via the server designated by the SMTP directive.

sendmail_from (string)
Scope: PHP_INI_ALL, Default value: Null
The sendmail_from directive, applicable only for Win32 operating systems, designates the sender identity when PHP is used to initiate the delivery of e-mail.

sendmail_path (string)
Scope: PHP_INI_SYSTEM, Default value: DEFAULT_SENDMAIL_PATH
The sendmail_path directive, applicable only for Unix operating systems, is primarily used to pass additional options to the sendmail daemon, although it could also be used to determine the location of sendmail when installed in a nonstandard directory.

Java

PHP can instantiate Java classes via its Java extension. The following four directives determine PHP's behavior in this respect.

java.class.path (string)
Scope: PHP_INI_ALL, Default value: Null
The java.class.path directory specifies the location where your Java classes are stored.

java.home (string)
Scope: PHP_INI_ALL, Default value: Null
The java.home directive specifies the location of the Java Development Kit (JDK) binary directory.

java.library (string)
Scope: PHP_INI_ALL, Default value: JAVALIB
The java.library directive specifies the location of the Java Virtual Machine (JVM).

java.library.path (string)
Scope: PHP_INI_ALL, Default value: Null
The java.library.path directive specifies the location of PHP's Java extension.

Summary

This chapter provided you with the information you need to establish an operational Apache/PHP server, and valuable insight regarding PHP's run-time configuration options and capabilities. This was a major step, because you'll now be able to use this platform to test examples throughout the remainder of the book.

In the next chapter, you'll learn all about the basic syntactical properties of the PHP language. By its conclusion, you'll be able to create simplistic, yet nonetheless quite useful scripts. This material sets the stage for subsequent chapters, where you'll gain the knowledge required to start building some really cool applications.

CHAPTER 3

PHP Basics

THUS FAR, we've covered quite a bit of ground regarding the PHP language. You're familiar with the language's background and history, and have delved deep into the installation and configuration concepts and procedures. This material set the stage for what will form the crux of the remainder of this book: Creating powerful PHP applications. This chapter initiates this discussion, introducing a great number of the language's foundational features. Specifically, chapter topics include:

- How to delimit PHP code, which provides the parsing engine with a means for determining which areas of the script should be parsed and executed, and which should be ignored.

- An introduction to commenting code using the various methodologies borrowed from the Unix shell scripting, C, and C++ languages.

- How to output data using the `echo()`, `print()`, `printf()`, and `sprintf()` statements.

- A discussion of PHP's data types, variables, operators, and statements.

- A thorough dissertation of PHP's key control structures and statements including `if-else-elseif`, `while`, `foreach`, `include`/`require`, `break`, `continue`, and `declare`.

By the conclusion, you'll possess not only the knowledge necessary to create basic but useful PHP applications, but also an understanding of what's required to make the most of the material covered in later chapters.

Escaping to PHP

One of PHP's advantages is that you can embed PHP code directly into static HTML pages. For the code to do anything, the page must be passed to the PHP engine for interpretation. It would be highly inefficient for the interpreter to consider every line as a potential PHP command, however. Therefore, the parser needs some means to immediately determine which areas of the page are PHP-enabled. This is logically accomplished by delimiting the PHP code. There are four delimitation variants, all of which are introduced in this section.

Default Syntax

The default delimiter syntax opens with <?php and concludes with ?>, like this:

```
<h3>Welcome!</h3>
<?php
    print "<p>This is a PHP example.</p>";
?>
<p>Some static information found here...</p>
```

If you save this above code as test.php and call it from a PHP-enabled Web server, output such as that shown in Figure 3-1 follows:

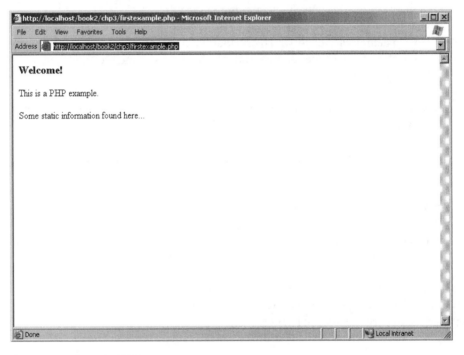

Figure 3-1. Sample PHP output

Short-Tags

For the lazy, an even shorter delimiter syntax is available. This syntax, known as *short-tags*, foregoes the php reference required in the default syntax. However, to use this feature you'll need to enable PHP's short_open_tag directive. An example follows:

```
<?
    print "This is another PHP example.";
?>
```

> **CAUTION** *Although short-tag delimiters are convenient, keep in mind that they clash with XML, and thus XHTML syntax. Therefore, for conformance reasons, you should use the default syntax.*

Typically, information is displayed using `print` or `echo` statements. When short-tags are enabled, you can omit these statements using an output variation known as *short-circuit syntax*:

```
<?="This is another PHP example.";?>
```

Which is functionally equivalent to both of the following:

```
<? print "This is another PHP example."; ?>
<?php print "This is another PHP example.";?>
```

Script

Historically, certain editors, Microsoft's FrontPage editor in particular, have had problems dealing with escape syntax such as that employed by PHP. Therefore, support for another mainstream delimiter variant, `<script>`, was incorporated into PHP:

```
<script language="php">
    print "This is another PHP example.";
</script>
```

> **TIP** *Microsoft's FrontPage editor also recognizes ASP-style delimiter syntax, introduced next.*

ASP-Style

Microsoft ASP pages employ a similar strategy, delimiting static from dynamic syntax using a predefined character pattern, opening dynamic syntax with `<%` and concluding with `%>`. If you're coming from an ASP background, and prefer to continue using this syntax, PHP supports it. Here's an example:

```
<%
    print "This is another PHP example.";
%>
```

Embedding Multiple Code Blocks

You can escape to and from PHP as many times as you require throughout a given page. For example, the following is completely acceptable:

```
<html>
    <head>
        <title><?php echo "Welcome to my site!";?></title>
    </head>
    <body>
        <?php
            $date = "May 18, 2003";
        ?>
        <h3>Today's date is <?=$date;?></h3>
    </body>
</html>
```

Note that any variables declared in a prior code block is "remembered" for later blocks, as was the case with the $date variable in this example.

Comments

I can't overstate the importance of providing thorough comments in code. PHP offers several syntactical variations, each of which is introduced in this section.

Single-line C++ Syntax

Comments often require no more than a single line. Because of its brevity, there is no need to delimit the comment's conclusion, because the newline (\n) character fills this need quite nicely. PHP supports C++ single-line comment syntax, which is prefaced with a double-slash (//), like this:

```
<?php
    // Title: My PHP program
    // Author: Jason
    print "This is a PHP program";
?>
```

Shell Syntax

PHP also supports an alternative to the C++-style single-line syntax, known as *shell syntax*, which is prefaced with a hash mark (#). Revising the previous example:

```
<?php
    # Title: My PHP program
    # Author: Jason
    print "This is a PHP program";
?>
```

Multiple-line C Syntax

It's often convenient to include somewhat more verbose functional descriptions or other explanatory notes within code, which logically warrant numerous lines. Although you could preface each line with C++ or Shell-style delimiters, PHP also offers a multiple-line variant that both opens and closes the comment. Consider the following multi-line comment:

```php
<?php
/*
Title: My PHP Program
Author: Jason
Date: May 10, 2003
*/
?>
```

Multi-line commentary syntax is particularly useful when generating documentation from code, because it offers a definitive means for distinguishing between disparate comments, a convenience not easily possible using single-line syntax.

Output

Most Web applications involve a high degree of interactivity. Well-written scripts are constantly communicating with users, both via tool interfaces and request responses. PHP offers a number of means for displaying information, each of which is discussed in this section.

print()

```
boolean print(argument)
```

The print statement is responsible for providing user feedback, and it is capable of displaying both raw strings and variables. All of the following statements are plausible print statements:

```php
<?php
print("<p>I love the summertime.</p>");
?>

<?php
$season = "summertime";
print "<p>I love the $season.</p>";
?>

<?php
print "<p>I love the
summertime.</p>";
?>
```

```php
<?php
$season = "summertime";
print "<p>I love the ".$season."</p>";
?>
```

All these statements result in the following:

```
I love the summertime.
```

While the first three variations are likely quite easy to understand, the last one might not be so straightforward. In this last variation, I concatenated three string items together using a period, which when used in this context is known as the *concatenation* operator. This practice is commonly employed when concatenating variables, constants and static strings together. You'll see this strategy used repeatedly throughout the entire book.

> **NOTE** *Although the official syntax calls for the use of parentheses to enclose the argument, you have the option of omitting them. I tend towards omission, simply because the target argument is equally apparent without them.*

echo()

```
void echo(string argument1 [, ...string argumentN])
```

The echo statement operates similarly to print, except for two differences. First, it cannot be used as part of a complex expression because it returns void whereas print returns a boolean. Second, echo is capable of outputting multiple strings. The utility of this particular trait is questionable; I can't recall a single occasion in which I've ever used it, although this seems to be a matter of preference more than anything else. Nonetheless, it's available should you feel the need. Here's an example:

```php
<?php
    $heavyweight = "Lennox Lewis";
    $lightweight = "Floyd Mayweather";
    echo $heavyweight, " and ", $lightweight, " are great fighters.";
?>
```

This code produces the following:

```
Lennox Lewis and Floyd Mayweather are great fighters.
```

> **TIP** *Which is faster,* echo() *or* print()*? The fact that they are functionally inter-changeable leaves many pondering this question. The answer is that the* echo() *function is a tad faster, because it returns nothing, whereas* print() *returns a Boolean value informing the caller whether or not the statement was successfully output. It's quite unlikely that you'll notice any speed difference, however, so you can consider the usage decision to be one of stylistic concern.*

printf()

```
boolean printf (string format [, mixed args])
```

The printf() function is functionally identical to print(), outputting the arguments specified in args, except that the output is formatted according to format. This lets you wield considerable control over the output data, be it in terms of alignment, precision, type, or position. The argument consists of up to five components, which should appear in format in the following order:

- **Padding specifier:** This optional component determines which character will be used to pad the outcome to the correct string size. The default is a space character. An alternative character is specified by preceding it with a single quotation.

- **Alignment specifier:** This optional component determines whether the outcome should be left- or right-justified. The default is right-justified; You can set the alignment to left with a negative sign.

- **Width specifier:** This optional component determines the minimum number of characters that should be output by the function.

- **Precision specifier:** This optional component determines the number of decimal digits that should be displayed. This component affects only data of type float.

- **Type specifier:** This component determines how the argument will be cast. The supported type specifiers are listed in Table 3-1.

Table 3-1. Supported Type Specifiers

TYPE	DESCRIPTION
%b	Argument considered an integer; presented as a binary number.
%c	Argument considered an integer; presented as a character corresponding to that ASCII value.
%d	Argument considered an integer; presented as a signed decimal number.
%f	Argument considered a floating point number; presented as a floating-point number.
%o	Argument considered an integer; presented as an octal number.
%s	Argument considered a string; presented as a string.
%u	Argument considered an integer; presented as an unsigned decimal number.
%x	Argument considered an integer; presented as a lowercase hexadecimal number.
%X	Argument considered an integer; presented as an uppercase hexadecimal number.

Consider a few examples:

```
printf("$%01.2f", 43.2); // $43.20
printf("%d bottles of beer on %s", 100, "the wall");
       // 100 bottles of beer on the wall
printf("%15s", "Some text");  // Some text
```

Sometimes it's convenient to change the output order of the arguments, or repeat the output of a particular argument, without explicitly repeating it in the argument list. This is done by making reference to the argument in accordance with its position. For example, %2$ indicates the argument located in the second position of the argument list, while %3$ indicates the third. However, when placed within the format string, the dollar-sign must be escaped, like this: %2\$. Two examples follow:

```
printf("The %2\$s likes to %1\$s", "bark", "dog"); // The dog likes to bark
printf("The %1\$s says: %2\$s, %2\$s.", "dog", "bark");
       // The dog says: bark, bar.
```

sprintf()

```
string sprintf (string format [, mixed arguments])
```

The sprintf() function is functionally identical to printf(), except that the output is assigned to a string rather than output directly to standard output. An example follows:

```
$cost = sprintf("$%01.2f", 43.2); // $cost = $43.20
```

Data Types

A *data type* is the generic name assigned to any set of data sharing a common set of characteristics. Common data types include *strings, integers, floats,* and *Booleans.* PHP has long offered a rich set of data types, and has further increased this yield in version 5. In this section, I'll review these data types, all of which can be broken into three categories: *scalar, compound,* and *special.*

Scalar Data Types

Scalar data types are capable of containing a single item of information. Several data types fall under this category, including *boolean, integer, float,* and *string.*

Boolean

The boolean data type is named after George Boole (1815–1864), a mathematician who is considered to be one of the founding fathers of information theory. A Boolean variable represents truth, supporting only two values: TRUE or FALSE (case-insensitive). Alternatively, you can use zero to represent FALSE, and any nonzero value to represent TRUE. A few examples follow:

```
$alive = false;      # $alive is false.
$alive = 1;          # $alive is true.
$alive = -1;         # $alive is true.
$alive = 5;          # $alive is true.
$alive = 0;          # $alive is false.
```

Integer

An integer is quite simply a whole number, or one that does not contain fractional parts. Decimal (base 10), octal (base 8), and hexadecimal (base 16) numbers all fall under this category. Several examples follow:

```
42          # decimal
-678900     # decimal
0755        # octal
0xC4E       # hexadecimal
```

The maximum supported integer size is platform-dependent, although this is typically positive or negative 2^{31}. If you attempt to surpass this limit within a PHP script, the number will be automatically converted to a float. An example follows:

```
<?php
    $val = 45678945939390393678976;
    echo $val + 5;
?>
```

This is the result:

```
4.567894593939E+022
```

Float

Floating point numbers, also referred to as floats, doubles, or real numbers, allow you to specify numbers that contain fractional parts. Floats are used to represent monetary values, weights, distances, and a whole host of other representations in which a simple integer value won't suffice. PHP's floats can be specified in a variety of ways, each of which is exemplified here:

```
4.5678
4.0
8.7e4
1.23E+11
```

String

Simply put, a string is a sequence of characters treated as a contiguous group. Such groups are typically delimited by single or double quotes, although PHP also supports another delimitation methodology introduced in the later section "String Interpolation." The ramifications of all three delimitation methods are also discussed in this section.

The following are all examples of valid strings:

```
"whoop-de-do"
'subway\n'
"123$%^789"
```

Historically, PHP treated strings in the same fashion as arrays (see the next section, "Compound Data Types," for more information about arrays), allowing for specific characters to be accessed via array offset notation. For example, consider the following string:

```
$color = "maroon";
```

You could retrieve and display a particular character of the string by treating the string as an array, like this:

```
echo $color[2]; // outputs 'r'
```

Although this is convenient, it can lead to some confusion, and thus PHP 5 introduces specialized string offset functionality, which Chapter 9 covers in some detail. Additionally, Chapter 9 is devoted to a thorough presentation of many of PHP's valuable string and regular expression functions.

Compound Data Types

Compound data types allow for multiple items of the same type to be aggregated under a single representative entity. The *array* and the *object* fall into this category.

Array

It's often useful to aggregate a series of similar items together, arranging and referencing them in some specific way. These data structures, known as *arrays*, are formally defined as an indexed collection of data values. Each member of the array index (also known as the key) references a corresponding value, and can be a simple numerical reference to the value's position in the series, or it could have some direct correlation to the value. For example, if I were interested in aggregating a list of U.S. states, I could use a numerically indexed array, like so:

```
$state[0] = "Alabama";
$state[1] = "Alaska";
$state[2] = "Arizona";
...
$state[49] = "Wyoming";
```

What if I wanted to correlate U.S. states to their capitals, however? Rather than base my keys on a numerical index, I might instead use an associative index, like this:

```
$state["Alabama"] = "Montgomery";
$state["Alaska"] = "Juneau";
$state["Arizona"] = "Phoenix";
...
$state["Wyoming"] = "Cheyenne";
```

I offer a formal introduction to the concept of arrays in Chapter 5, so don't worry too much about the matter if you don't completely understand these concepts right now. Just keep in mind that the array data type is indeed supported by the PHP language.

> **NOTE** *PHP also supports arrays consisting of several dimensions, better known as* multidimensional arrays. *This concept is introduced in Chapter 5.*

Object

The other compound data type supported by PHP is the *object*. The object is a central concept of the object-oriented programming paradigm. If you're new to object-oriented programming, don't worry, because I devote Chapters 6 and 7 to a complete introduction to the matter as applied to PHP.

Unlike the other data types contained in the PHP language, an object must be explicitly declared. This declaration of an object's characteristics and behavior takes place within something called a *class*. Here's a general example of class declaration and subsequent object instantiation:

```
class appliance {
            private $power;
            function set_power($status) {
                            $this->power = $status;
            }
}
. . .
$blender = new appliance;
```

A class definition creates several attributes and functions pertinent to a data structure, in this case a data structure named *appliance*. So far, the appliance isn't very functional. There is only one attribute: power. This attribute can be modified by using the method set_power().

Remember, however, that a class definition is a template and cannot itself be manipulated. Instead, objects are created based on this template. This is accomplished via the new keyword. Therefore, in the last line of the previous listing, an object of class appliance named *blender* is created.

The blender's power attribute can then be set by making use of the method set_power():

```
$blender->set_power("on");
```

Improvements to PHP's object-oriented development model are a highlight of PHP 5. Chapters 6 and 7 are devoted to thorough coverage of this important feature.

Special Data Types

Special data types encompass those types serving some sort of niche purpose, which makes it impossible to group them in any other type category. The *resource* and *null* data types fall under this category.

Resource

PHP is often used to interact with some external data source: databases, files, and network streams all come to mind here. Typically this interaction takes place through *handles*, which are named at the time a connection to that resource is successfully initiated. These handles remain the main point of reference for that resource until communication is completed, at which time the handle is destroyed. These handles are of the resource data type.

Not all functions return resources; only those that are responsible for binding a resource to a variable found within the PHP script do. Examples of such functions include fopen(), mysql_connect(), and pdf_new(). For example, $link is of type resource in the following example:

```
$link = mysql_connect("localhost","testuser","secret");
```

Variables of type resource don't actually hold a value; rather, they hold a pointer to the opened resource connection. In fact, if you try to output the contents, you'll see a reference to a resource id number.

Null

Null, a term meaning "nothing," has long been a concept that has perplexed beginning programmers. Null does not mean blank space, nor does it mean zero; it means no value, or nothing. In PHP, a value is considered to be Null if:

- It has not been set to any predefined value.

- It has been specifically assigned the value Null.

- It has been erased using the function unset().

The Null data type recognizes only one value: Null:

```
<?php
    $default = Null;
?>
```

Type Casting

Forcing a variable to behave as a type other than the one originally intended for it is known as *type casting*. A variable can be evaluated once as a different type by casting it to another. This is accomplished by placing the intended type in front of the variable to be cast. A type can be cast by inserting one of the casts shown in Table 3-2 in front of the variable:

Table 3-2. Type Casting Operators

CAST OPERATORS	CONVERSION
(array)	Array
(bool) or (boolean)	Boolean
(int) or (integer)	Integer
(object)	Object
(real) or (double) or (float)	Float
(string)	String

Let's consider several examples. Suppose you'd like to cast an integer as a double:

```
$variable1 = 13;
$variable2 = (double) $variable1;  // $variable2 is assigned the value 13.0
```

Although $variable1 originally held the integer value 13, the double cast temporarily converted the type to double (and in turn, 13 became 13.0). This value was then assigned to $variable2.

Now consider the opposite scenario. Type casting a value of type double to type integer has an effect that you might not expect:

```
$variable1 = 4.7;
$variable2 = 5;
$variable3 = (int) $variable1 + $variable2;        // $variable3 =  9
```

The decimal was truncated from the double. Note that the double will be rounded down every time, regardless of the decimal value.

You can also cast a data type to be a member of an array. The value being cast simply becomes the first element of the array:

```
$variable1 = 1114;
$array1 = (array) $variable1;
print $array1[0];                  // The value 1114 is output.
```

Note that this shouldn't be considered standard practice for adding items to an array, because this only seems to work for the very first member of a newly created array. If it is cast against an existing array, that array will be wiped out, leaving only the newly cast value in the first position.

What happens if you cast a string data type to that of an integer? Let's find out:

```
$sentence = "This is a sentence";
echo (int) $sentence; // returns 0
```

That doesn't do too much good. How about the opposite procedure, casting an integer to a string? In light of PHP's loosely typed design, it will simply return the integer value unmodified. However, as you'll see in the next section, PHP will sometimes take the initiative and cast a type to best fit the requirements of a given situation.

One final example: any data type can be cast as an object. The result is that the variable becomes an attribute of the object, the attribute having the name `scalar`:

```
$model = "Toyota";
$new_obj = (object) $model;
```

The value can then be referenced as:

```
print $new_obj->scalar; // returns "Toyota"
```

Type Juggling

Because of PHP's lax attitude toward type definitions, variables are sometimes automatically cast to best fit the circumstances in which they are referenced. Consider the following snippet:

```
<?php
    $total = 5;
    $count = "15";
    $total += $count; // $total = 20;
?>
```

The outcome is the expected one; $total is assigned "20", converting the $count variable from a string to an integer in order to do so. Here's another example:

```
<?php
    $total = "45 fire engines";
    $incoming = 10;
    $total = $incoming + $total; // $total = 55
?>
```

Because the original $total string begins with an integer value, this value is used in the calculation. However, if it begins with anything other than a numerical representation, the value is zero. Consider another example:

```
<?php
    $total = "1.0";
    if ($total) echo "The total count is positive";
?>
```

In this example, a string is converted to Boolean type in order to evaluate the `if` statement. This is indeed common practice in PHP programming, something you'll see on a regular basis, and useful if you prefer streamlined code.

Consider one last, particularly interesting, example. If a string used in a mathematical calculation includes a ".", "e", or "E", it will be evaluated as a float:

```php
<?php
    $val1 = "1.2e3";
    $val2 = 2;
    echo $val1 * $val2; // outputs 2400
?>
```

Type-Related Functions

A few functions are available for both verifying and converting data types, and those are covered in this section.

settype()

```
boolean settype (mixed var, string type)
```

The settype() function converts a variable, specified by var, to the type specified by type. Seven possible type values are available: array, boolean, float, integer, null, object, and string. If the conversion is successful, TRUE is returned; otherwise, FALSE is returned.

gettype()

```
string gettype (mixed var)
```

The gettype() function returns the type of the variable specified by var. In total, eight possible return values are available: array, boolean, double, integer, object, resource, string, and unknown type.

Type Identifier Functions

A number of functions are available for determining a variable's type, including is_array(), is_bool(), is_float(), is_integer(), is_null(), is_numeric(), is_object(), is_resource(), is_scalar(), and is_string(). Because all these functions follow the same naming convention, arguments, and return values, I'll consolidate their introduction down to a single general form, presented here.

is_name()

```
boolean is_name (mixed var)
```

All of these functions are grouped under a single-heading, because each ultimately accomplishes the same task. Each determines whether a variable, specified by var, satisfies a particular condition specified by the function name. If var is indeed of that type, TRUE is returned; otherwise, FALSE is returned. An example follows:

```php
<?php
    $item = 43;
    echo "The variable \$item is of type array: ".is_array($item)."<br />";
    echo "The variable \$item is of type integer: ".is_integer($item)."<br />";
    echo "The variable \$item is numeric: ".is_numeric($item)."<br />";
?>
```

This code returns the following:

```
The variable $item is of type array:
The variable $item is of type integer: 1
The variable $item is numeric: 1
```

Note that in the case of a falsehood, nothing is returned.

Identifiers

An *identifier* is a general term applied to variables, functions, and various other user-defined objects. There are several properties that PHP identifiers must abide by:

- An identifier can consist of one or more characters and must begin with a letter or an underscore. Furthermore, identifiers can only consist of letters, numbers, underscore characters, and other ASCII characters from 127 through 255. Consider a few examples:

VALID	INVALID
my_function	This&that
Size	!counter
_someword	4ward

- Identifiers are case sensitive. Therefore, a variable named $recipe is different from variables named $Recipe, $rEciPe, or $recipE.

- Identifiers can be any length. This is advantageous, because it enables a programmer to accurately describe the identifier's purpose via the identifier name.

- Finally, an identifier name can't be identical to any of PHP's predefined keywords. You can find a complete list of these keywords in the PHP manual appendix.

Variables

Although variables have been used within numerous examples found in this chapter, I've yet to formally introduce the concept. In this section I'll do so, starting with a definition. Simply put, a *variable* is a symbol that can store different values at different times. For example, suppose you create a Web-based calculator capable of performing mathematical tasks. Of course, the user will want to plug in values of his choosing; therefore, the program must be able to dynamically store those values and perform calculations accordingly. At the same time, the programmer requires a user-friendly means for referring to these value-holders within the application. The variable accomplishes both tasks.

Given the importance of this programming concept, it would be wise to explicitly lay the groundwork as to how variables are declared and manipulated. I'll now examine these rules in detail.

> **NOTE** *A variable is a named memory location that contains data and may be manipulated throughout the execution of the program.*

Variable Declaration

A variable always begins with a dollar sign, $, which is then followed by the variable name. Variable names follow the same naming rules as identifiers. That is, a variable name can begin with either a letter or an underscore, and can consist of letters, underscores, numbers, or other ASCII characters ranging from 127 through 255. The following are all valid variables:

```
$color
$operating_system
$_some_variable
$model
```

Note that variables are case-sensitive. The following variables bear absolutely no relation to one another:

```
$color
$Color
$COLOR
```

Interestingly, variables do not have to be explicitly declared in PHP. Rather, variables can be declared and assigned values simultaneously. Nonetheless, just because you can do something doesn't mean you should. Good programming practice dictates that all variables should be declared prior to use, preferably with an accompanying comment.

Once you've declared your variables, you can begin assigning values to them. Two methodologies are available for variable assignment: by value and by reference. Both are introduced next.

Value Assignment

Assignment by value simply involves copying the value of the assigned expression to the variable assignee. This is the most common type of assignment. A few examples follow:

```
$color = "red";
$number = 12;
$age = 12;
$sum = 12 + "15"; /* $sum = 27 */
```

You need to understand that each of these variables possess copies of the expression assigned to them. For example, $number and $age each possess their own unique copy of the value 12. If you'd rather that two variables point to the same copy of a value, you'll need to assign by reference, introduced next.

Reference Assignment

PHP 4 introduced the ability to assign variables by reference, which essentially means that you can create a variable that refers to the same content as another variable does. Therefore, a change to any variable referencing a particular item of variable content will be reflected among all other variables referencing that same content. You can assign variables by reference by appending an ampersand (&) to the equals sign. Let's consider an example:

```
<?php
    $value1 = "Hello";
    $value2 =& $value1;    /* $value1 and $value2 both equal "Hello". */
    $value2 = "Goodbye";   /* $value1 and $value2 both equal "Goodbye". */
?>
```

An alternative reference assignment syntax is also supported which involves appending the ampersand to the front of the variable being referenced. to the following example adheres to this new syntax:

```
<?php
    $value1 = "Hello";
    $value2 = &$value1;    /* $value1 and $value2 both equal "Hello". */
    $value2 = "Goodbye";   /* $value1 and $value2 both equal "Goodbye". */
?>
```

References also play an important role in both function arguments and return values, as well as in object-oriented programming. Chapters 4 and 6 cover these features.

Variable Scope

However you declare your variables (by value or by reference), you can declare variables anywhere in a PHP script. The location of the declaration greatly influences the realm in which a variable can be accessed, however. This accessibility domain is known as its *scope*.

PHP variables can be one of four scope types:

- Local variables

- Function parameters

- Global variables

- Static variables

Local Variables

A variable declared in a function is considered *local*. That is, it can be referenced only in that function. Any assignment outside of that function will be considered to be an entirely different variable from the one contained in the function. Note that when you exit the function in which a local variable has been declared, that variable and its corresponding value will be destroyed.

Local variables are helpful because they eliminate the possibility of unexpected side effects, which can result from globally accessible variables that are modified, intentionally or not. Consider this listing:

```
$x  = 4;
function assignx () {
    $x = 0;
    print "\ $x inside function is $x. <br>";
}
assignx();
print "\ $x outside of function is $x. <br>";
```

Executing this listing results in:

```
$x inside function is 0.
$x outside of function is 4.
```

As you can see, two different values for $x are output. This is because the $x located inside the assignx() function is local. Modifying the value of the local $x has no bearing on any values located outside of the function. On the same note, modifying the $x located outside of the function has no bearing on any variables contained in assignx().

Function Parameters

As in many other programming languages, in PHP, any function that accepts arguments must declare these arguments in the function header. Although these arguments accept values that come from outside of the function, they are no longer accessible once the function has exited.

> **NOTE** *This section only applies to parameters passed by value, and not by reference. Parameters passed by reference will indeed be affected by any changes made to the parameter from within the function. See Chapter 4 for additional details.*

Function parameters are declared after the function name and inside parentheses. They are declared much like a typical variable would be:

```
// multiply a value by 10 and return it to the caller
function x10 ($value) {
        $value = $value * 10;
        return $value;
}
```

You should realize that, although you can access and manipulate any function parameter in the function in which it is declared, it is destroyed when the function execution ends.

Global Variables

In contrast to local variables, a *global variable* can be accessed in any part of the program. To modify a global variable, however, it must be explicitly declared to be global in the function in which it is to be modified. This is accomplished, conveniently enough, by placing the keyword GLOBAL in front of the variable that should be recognized as global. Placing this keyword in front of an already existing variable tells PHP to use the variable having that name. Consider an example:

```
$somevar = 15;

function addit() {
        GLOBAL $somevar;
        $somevar++;
        print "Somevar is $somevar";
}
addit();
```

The displayed value of $somevar would be 16. However, if you were to omit this line:

```
GLOBAL $somevar;
```

The variable $somevar would be assigned the value 1, because $somevar would then be considered local within the addit() function. This local declaration would be implicitly set to 0, and then incremented by 1 to display the value 1.

An alternative method for declaring a variable to be global is to use PHP's $GLOBALS array, formally introduced in the next section. Reconsidering the above example, you can use this array to declare the variable $somevar to be global:

```
$somevar = 15;

function addit() {
            $GLOBALS["somevar"]++;
}

addit();
print "Somevar is ".$GLOBALS["somevar"];
```

Returning:

```
Somevar is 16
```

Regardless of the method you choose to convert a variable to global scope, be aware that the global scope has long been a cause of grief among programmers due to unexpected results that may arise from their careless use. Therefore, although global variables can be extremely useful, be prudent when using them.

Static Variables

The final type of variable scoping to discuss is known as *static*. In contrast to the variables declared as function parameters, which are destroyed on the function's exit, a static variable does not lose its value when the function exits, and will still hold that value if function is called again. You can declare a variable to be static simply by placing the keyword STATIC in front of the variable name:

```
STATIC $somevar;
```

Consider an example:

```
function keep_track() {
   STATIC $count  = 0;
   $count++;
   print $count;
```

```
    print "<br>";
}

keep_track();
keep_track();
keep_track();
```

What would you expect the outcome of this script to be? If the variable $count were not designated to be static (thus making $count a local variable), the outcome would be:

```
1
1
1
```

However, because $count is static, it retains its previous value each time the function is executed. Therefore, the outcome is:

```
1
2
3
```

Static scoping is particularly useful for recursive functions. *Recursive functions* are a powerful programming concept in which a function repeatedly calls itself until a particular condition is met. Recursive functions are covered in detail in Chapter 4.

PHP's Superglobal Variables

PHP offers a number of useful predefined variables, which are accessible from anywhere within the executing script, and serve to provide the developer with a substantial amount of environment-specific information. You can sift through these variables to retrieve details about the current user session, the user's operating environment, the local operating environment, and more. PHP creates some of the variables, while the availability and value of many of the other variables are specific to the operating system and Web server. Therefore, rather than exhaustively attempt to assemble a comprehensive list of all possible predefined variables and their possible values, I'll instead show you how to easily output your system-specific variables and their respective values. For instance, the following code outputs all predefined variables pertinent to the Web server and the script's execution environment:

```
while (list($var,$value) = each ($_SERVER)) {
    echo "$var => $value <br />";
}
```

This returns a list of variables similar to the following. Take a moment to peruse the listing produced by the this code as executed on a Windows server. You'll see some of these variables again in the examples that follow.

```
HTTP_ACCEPT => */*
HTTP_ACCEPT_LANGUAGE => en-us
HTTP_ACCEPT_ENCODING => gzip, deflate
HTTP_USER_AGENT => Mozilla/4.0 (compatible; MSIE 6.0; Windows NT 5.1;)
HTTP_HOST => localhost
HTTP_CONNECTION => Keep-Alive
PATH => C:\Perl\bin\;C:\WINDOWS\system32;C:\WINDOWS;
SystemRoot => C:\WINDOWS
COMSPEC => C:\WINDOWS\system32\cmd.exe
PATHEXT => .COM;.EXE;.BAT;.CMD;.VBS;.VBE;.JS;.JSE;.WSF;.WSH
WINDIR => C:\WINDOWS
SERVER_SIGNATURE => Apache/2.0.45 (Win32) PHP/5.0.0 Server at localhost Port 80
SERVER_SOFTWARE => Apache/2.0.45 (Win32) PHP/5.0.0-dev
SERVER_NAME => localhost
SERVER_ADDR => 127.0.0.1
SERVER_PORT => 80
REMOTE_ADDR => 127.0.0.1
DOCUMENT_ROOT => C:/Apache2/htdocs
SERVER_ADMIN => wj@wjgilmore.com
SCRIPT_FILENAME => C:/Apache2/htdocs/book2/chp3/globals.php
REMOTE_PORT => 1393
GATEWAY_INTERFACE => CGI/1.1
SERVER_PROTOCOL => HTTP/1.1
REQUEST_METHOD => GET
QUERY_STRING =>
REQUEST_URI => /pmnp/3/globals.php
SCRIPT_NAME => /pmnp/3/globals.php
PHP_SELF => /pmnp/3/globals.php
```

As you can see, quite a bit of information is available, some useful, some not so useful. You can display just one of these variables simply by treating it as a regular variable. For example, use this to display the user's IP address:

```
print "Hi! Your IP address is: $_SERVER['REMOTE_ADDR']";
```

This returns a numerical IP address, such as 123.456.789.000.

You can also gain information regarding the user's browser and operating system. Consider the following one-liner:

```
print "Your browser is: $_SERVER['HTTP_USER_AGENT']";
```

This returns information similar to the following:

```
Your browser is: Mozilla/4.0 (compatible; MSIE 6.0; Windows NT 5.1; .NET CLR 1.0.3705)
```

This example illustrates only one of PHP's nine predefined variable arrays. The rest of this section is devoted to introducing the purpose and contents of each.

> **NOTE** *To use the predefined variable arrays, the configuration parameter* track_vars *must be enabled in the php.ini file. As of PHP 4.03,* track_vars *is always enabled.*

$_SERVER

The $_SERVER superglobal contains information created by the Web server, and offers a bevy of information regarding the server and client configuration and the current request environment. Although the value and number of variables found in $_SERVER varies by server, you can typically expect to find those defined in the CGI 1.1 specification (available at the National Center for Supercomputing Applications, at http://hoohoo.ncsa.uiuc.edu/cgi/env.html). You'll likely find all of these variables to be immensely useful in your applications, some of which include:

- $_SERVER['HTTP_REFERER']: The URL of the page that referred the user to the current location.

- $_SERVER['REMOTE_ADDR']: The client's IP address.

- $_SERVER['REQUEST_URI']: The path component of the URL. For example, if the URL is http://www.example.com/blog/apache/index.html, then the URI is /blog/apache/index.html.

- $_SERVER['HTTP_USER_AGENT']: The client's user agent, which typically offers information about both the operating system and browser.

$_GET

The $_GET superglobal contains information pertinent to any parameters passed using the GET method. If the URL
http://www.example.com/index.html?category=apache&articleid=157 was requested, you could access the following variables using the GET superglobal:

```
$_GET['category'] = "apache"
$_GET['articleid'] = "157"
```

The $_GET superglobal, by default, is the only way that you can access variables passed via the GET method. You cannot reference GET variables like this: $category, $articleid. See Chapter 19 for an explanation of why this is the recommended means for accessing GET information.

$_POST

Like GET, the $_POST superglobal contains information pertinent to any parameters passed using the POST method. Consider the following form, used to solicit subscriber information:

```
<form action="subscribe.php" method="post">
    <p>
        Email address:<br />
        <input type="text" name="email" size="20" maxlength="50" value="" />
    </p>
    <p>
        Password:<br />
        <input type="password" name="pswd" size="20" maxlength="15" value="" />
    </p>
    <p>
    <input type="submit" name="subscribe" value="subscribe!" />
    </p>
</form>
```

The following POST variables will be made available via the target subscribe.php script:

```
$_POST['email'] = "jason@example.com";
$_POST['pswd'] = "rainyday";
$_POST['subscribe'] = "subscribe!";
```

Like $_GET, the $_POST superglobal is by default the only way to access POST variables. You cannot reference POST variables like this: $email, $pswd, $subscribe.

$_COOKIE

The $_COOKIE superglobal stores information passed into the script through HTTP cookies. Such cookies are typically set by a previously executed PHP script through the PHP function setcookie(). For example, suppose that you use setcookie() to store a cookie named example.com with the value ab2213. You could later retrieve that value by calling $_COOKIE["example.com"]. Chapter 16 introduces PHP's cookie-handling functionality in detail.

$_FILES

The $_FILES superglobal contains information regarding data uploaded to the server via the POST method. This superglobal is a tad different from the others in that it is a two-dimensional array containing five elements. The first subscript refers to the name of the form's file upload form element; the second is one of five predefined subscripts which describe a particular attribute of the uploaded file:

- $_FILES['upload-name']['name']: The name of the file as uploaded from the client to the server.

- $_FILES['upload-name']['type']: The MIME type of the uploaded file. Whether this variable is assigned depends on the browser capabilities.

- $_FILES['upload-name']['size']: The byte-size of the uploaded file.

- $_FILES['upload-name']['tmp_name']: Once uploaded, the file will be assigned a temporary name before it is moved to its final location.

- $_FILES['upload-name']['error']: An upload status code. Despite the name, this variable will be populated even in the case of success. There are five possible values:

  - UPLOAD_ERR_OK: The file was successfully uploaded.

  - UPLOAD_ERR_INI_SIZE: The file size exceeds the maximum size imposed by the upload_max_filesize directive.

  - UPLOAD_ERR_FORM_SIZE: The file size exceeds the maximum imposed by an optional MAX_FILE_SIZE hidden form-field parameter.

  - UPLOAD_ERR_PARTIAL: The file was only partially uploaded.

  - UPLOAD_ERR_NO_FILE: A file was not specified in the upload form prompt.

Chapter 13 is devoted to a complete introduction of PHP's file-upload functionality.

$_ENV

The $_ENV superglobal offers information regarding the PHP parser's underlying server environment. Some of the variables found in this array include:

- $_ENV['HOSTNAME']: The server host name.

- $_ENV['SHELL']: The system shell.

$_REQUEST

The $_REQUEST superglobal is a catch-all of sorts, recording variables passed to a script via any input method, specifically GET, POST, and Cookie. The order of these variables doesn't depend on the order in which they appear in the sending script, but by the order specified by the variables_order configuration directive. Although it may be tempting, do not use this superglobal to handle variables, because it is insecure. See Chapter 19 for an explanation.

$_SESSION

The $_SESSION superglobal contains information regarding all session variables. Registering session information allows you the convenience of referring to it throughout your entire Web site, without the hassle of explicitly passing the data via GET or POST. Chapter 16 is devoted to PHP's formidable session-handling feature.

$GLOBALS

The $GLOBALS superglobal array can be thought of as the superglobal superset, and contains a comprehensive listing of all variables found in the global scope. You can view a dump of all variables found in $GLOBALS by executing the following:

```
print '<pre>';
print_r($GLOBALS);
PRINT '</pre>';
```

Variable Variables

On occasion you may want to make use of variables whose contents can be treated dynamically as a variable in itself. Consider this typical variable assignment:

```
$recipe = "spaghetti";
```

Interestingly, you can then treat the value "spaghetti" as a variable by placing a second dollar sign ($) in front of the original variable name and again assigning another value:

```
$$recipe = "& meatballs";
```

This in effect assigns "& meatballs" to a variable named "spaghetti".
Therefore, the following two snippets of code produce the same result:

```
print $recipe $spaghetti;
print $recipe ${$recipe};
```

The result of both is the string "spaghetti & meatballs"

Constants

A *constant* is a value that cannot be modified throughout the execution of a program. Constants are particularly useful when working with values that definitely will not require modification, such as pi (3.141592), or a specific distance such as the number of feet in a mile (5,280). Once a constant has been defined, it cannot be changed (or redefined) at any other point of the program. Constants are defined using the define() function.

define()

```
bool define(string name, mixed value [, bool case_insensitive])
```

The define() function defines a constant, specified by name, assigning it the value value. If the optional parameter case-insensitive is included and assigned TRUE, subsequent references to the constant will be case insensitive. Consider the following example, in which the mathematical constant PI is defined:

```
define("PI", 3.141592);
```

The constant is subsequently used in the following listing:

```
print "The value of pi is ".PI.".<br />";
$pi2 = 2 * PI;
print "Pi doubled equals $pi2.";
```

This code produces the following results:

```
The value of pi is 3.141592.
Pi doubled equals 6.283184.
```

There are two points to note regarding the previous listing: The first is that constant references are not prefaced with a dollar sign. The second is that you can't redefine or undefine the constant once it has been defined (for example, 2*PI); if you need to produce a value based on the constant, the value must be stored in another variable. Finally, constants are global; they can be referenced anywhere in your script.

Expressions

An *expression* is a phrase representing a particular action in a program. All expressions consist of at least one operand and one or more operators. A few examples follow:

```
$a = 5;                     // assign integer value 5 to the variable $a
$a = "5";                   // assign string value "5" to the variable $a
$sum = 50 + $some_int;      // assign sum of 50 + $some_int to $sum
$wine = "Zinfandel";        // assign "Zinfandel" to the variable $wine
$inventory++;               // increment the variable $inventory by 1
```

Operands

Operands are the inputs of an expression. You might already be familiar with the manipulation and use of operands not only through everyday mathematical calculations, but also through prior programming experience. Some examples of operands follow:

```
$a++; // $a is the operand
$sum = $val1 + val2; // $sum, $val1 and $val2 are operands
```

Operators

An *operator* is a symbol that specifies a particular action in an expression. Many operators may be familiar to you. Regardless, you should remember that PHP's automatic type conversion will convert types based on the type of operator placed between the two operands, which is not always the case in other programming languages.

The precedence and associativity of operators are significant characteristics of a programming language. Both concepts are introduced below. Table 3-3 contains a complete listing of all operators, ordered from highest to lowest precedence. The sections following the table discuss each of these topics in further detail.

Table 3-3. Operator Precedence, Associativity, and Purpose

OPERATOR	ASSOCIATIVITY	PURPOSE
new	NA	Object instantiation
( )	NA	Expression sub-grouping
[ ]	R	Index enclosure
! ~ ++ --	R	Boolean NOT, bitwise NOT, increment, decrement
@	R	Error suppression
/ * %	Left	Division, multiplication, modulus
+ - .	Left	Addition, subtraction, concatenation
<< >>	Left	Shift left, shift right (bitwise)

(continued)

Table 3-3. Operator Precedence, Associativity, and Purpose (continued)

OPERATOR	ASSOCIATIVITY	PURPOSE
`< <= > >=`	NA	Less than, less than or equal to, greater than, greater than or equal to
`== != === <>`	NA	Is equal to, is not equal to, is identical to, is not equal to
`& ^ |`	Left	Bitwise AND, bitwise XOR, bitwise OR
`&& ||`	Left	Boolean AND, Boolean OR
`?:`	Right	Ternary operator
`= += *= /= .= %=&= |= ^= <<= >>=`	Right	Assignment operators
`AND XOR OR`	Left	Boolean AND, boolean XOR, boolean OR
`,`	Left	Expression separation. Example: `$days = array(1=>"Monday", 2=>"Tuesday")`

Operator Precedence

Operator precedence is a characteristic of operators that determines the order in which they evaluate the operands surrounding them. PHP follows the standard precedence rules used in elementary school math class. Consider a few examples:

```
$total_cost = $cost + $cost * 0.06;
```

This is the same as writing:

```
$total_cost = $cost + ($cost * 0.06);
```

This is because the multiplication operator has higher precedence than the addition operator.

Operator Associativity

The *associativity* characteristic of an operator specifies how operations of the same precedence (having the same precedence value as displayed in Table 3-3) are evaluated as they are executed. Associativity can be performed in two directions, left-to-right or right-to-left. Left-to-right associativity means that the various operations making up the expression are evaluated from left to right. Consider the following example:

```
$value = 3 * 4 * 5 * 7 * 2;
```

This is the same as:

```
$value = ((((3 * 4) * 5) * 7) * 2);
```

This expression results in the value 840. This is because the multiplication (*) operator is left-to-right associative. In contrast, right-to-left associativity evaluates operators of the same precedence from right to left:

```
$c = 5;
print $value = $a = $b = $c;
```

This is the same as:

```
$c = 5;
$value = ($a = ($b = $c));
```

When this expression is evaluated, variables $value, $a, $b, and $c will all contain the value 5. This is because the assignment operator (=) has right-to-left associativity.

Arithmetic Operators

The arithmetic operators, listed in Table 3-4, perform various mathematical operations and will probably be used frequently in most PHP programs. Fortunately, they are easy to use.

Table 3-4. Arithmetic Operators

EXAMPLE	LABEL	OUTCOME
$a + $b	Addition	Sum of $a and $b
$a - $b	Subtraction	Difference of $a and $b
$a * $b	Multiplication	Product of $a and $b
$a / $b	Division	Quotient of $a and $b
$a % $b	Modulus	Remainder of $a divided by $b

Incidentally, PHP provides a vast assortment of predefined mathematical functions, capable of performing base conversions and calculating logarithms, square roots, geometric values, and more. Check the manual for an updated list of these functions.

Assignment Operators

The *assignment operators* assign a data value to a variable. The simplest form of assignment operator just assigns some value, while others (known as *shortcut assignment operators*) perform some other operation before making the assignment. Table 3-5 lists examples using this type of operator.

Table 3-5. Assignment Operators

EXAMPLE	LABEL	OUTCOME
$a = 5	Assignment	$a equals 5
$a += 5	Addition-assignment	$a equals $a plus 5
$a *= 5	Multiplication-assignment	$a equals $a multiplied by 5
$a /= 5	Division-assignment	$a equals $a divided by 5
$a .= 5	Concatenation-assignment	$a equals $a concatenated with 5

String Operators

PHP's *string operators* (see Table 3-6) provide a convenient way in which to concatenate strings together. There are two such operators, including the concatenation operator (.) and the concatenation assignment operator (.=), discussed in the previous section.

> **NOTE** Concatenate *means to combine two or more objects together to form one single entity.*

Table 3-6. String Operators

EXAMPLE	LABEL	OUTCOME
$a = "abc"."def";	Concatenation	$a is assigned the string "abcdef"
$a .= "ghijkl";	Concatenation-assignment	$a equals its current value concatenated with "ghijkl"

Here is an example of usage of the string operators:

```
// $a contains the string value "Spaghetti & Meatballs";
$a = "Spaghetti" . "& Meatballs";

$a .= " are delicious";
// $a contains the value "Spaghetti & Meatballs are delicious."
```

The two concatenation operators are hardly the extent of PHP's string-handling capabilities. Read Chapter 9 for a complete accounting of this functionality.

Increment and Decrement Operators

The *increment* (++) and *decrement* (--) operators listed in Table 3-7 present a minor convenience in terms of code clarity, providing shortened means by which you can add 1 to or subtract 1 from the current value of a variable.

Table 3-7. Increment and Decrement Operators

EXAMPLE	LABEL	OUTCOME
++$a, $a++	Increment	Increment $a by 1
--$a, $a--	Decrement	Decrement $a by 1

These operators can be placed on either side of a variable, and the side on which they are placed provides a slightly different effect. Consider the outcomes of the following examples:

```
$inv = 15;        /* Assign integer value 15 to $inv. */
$oldInv = $inv--;  /* Assign $oldInv the value of $inv, then decrement $inv.*/
$origInv = ++$inv; /*Increment $inv, then assign the new $inv value to $origInv.*/
```

As you can see, the order in which the increment and decrement operators are used has an important effect on the value of a variable. Prefixing the operand with one of these operators is known as a preincrement and predecrement operation, while postfixing the operand is known as a postincrement and postdecrement operation.

Logical Operators

Much like the arithmetic operators, *logical operators* (see Table 3-8) will probably play a major role in many of your PHP applications, providing a way to make decisions based on the values of multiple variables. Logical operators make it possible to direct the flow of a program, and are used frequently with control structures, such as the if conditional and the while and for loops.

Table 3-8. Logical Operators

EXAMPLE	LABEL	OUTCOME
$a && $b	And	True if both $a and $b are true
$a AND $b	And	True if both $a and $b are true
$a || $b	Or	True if either $a or $b is true
$a OR $b	Or	True if either $a or $b are true
! $a	Not	True if $a is not true
NOT $a	Not	True if $a is not true
$a XOR $b	Exclusive Or	True if only $a or only $b is true

Logical operators are also commonly used to provide details about the outcome of other operations, particularly those that return a value:

```
file_exists("filename.txt") OR print "File does not exist!";
```

One of two outcomes will occur:

- The file `filename.txt` exists

- The sentence "File does not exist!" will be output.

Equality Operators

Equality operators (see Table 3-9) are used to compare two values, testing for equivalence.

Table 3-9. Equality Operators

EXAMPLE	LABEL	OUTCOME
$a == $b	Is equal to	True if $a and $b are equivalent.
$a != $b	Is not equal to	True if $a is not equal to $b
$a === $b	Is identical to	True if $a and $b are equivalent *and* $a and $b have the same type

It is a common mistake for even experienced programmers to attempt to test for equality using just one equal sign (for example, $a = $b). Keep in mind that this will result in the assignment of the contents of $b to $a, and will not produce the expected results.

Comparison Operators

Comparison operators (see Table 3-10), like logical operators, provide a method by which to direct program flow through examination of the comparative values of two or more variables.

Table 3-10. Comparison Operators

EXAMPLE	LABEL	OUTCOME
$a < $b	Less than	True if $a is less than $b
$a > $b	Greater than	True if $a is greater than $b
$a <= $b	Less than or equal to	True if $a is less than or equal to $b
$a >= $b	Greater than or equal to	True if $a is greater than or equal to $b
($a == 12) ? 5 : -1	Ternary	If $a equals 12, the return value is 5; otherwise the return value is –1

Note that the comparison operators should be used only for comparing numerical values. Although you may be tempted to compare strings with these operators, you will most likely not arrive at the expected outcome if you do so. There is a substantial set of predefined functions that compare string values, which are discussed in detail in Chapter 9.

Bitwise Operators

Bitwise operators examine and manipulate integer values on the level of individual bits that make up the integer value (thus the name). To fully understand this concept, you need at least an introductory knowledge of the binary representation of decimal integers. Table 3-11 presents a few decimal integers and their corresponding binary representations.

Table 3-11. Binary Representations

DECIMAL INTEGER	BINARY REPRESENTATION
2	10
5	101
10	1010
12	1100
145	10010001
1,452,012	101100010011111101100

The bitwise operators listed in Table 3-12 are variations on some of the logical operators, but can result in drastically different outcomes.

Table 3-12. Bitwise Operators

EXAMPLE	LABEL	OUTCOME
$a & $b	And	And together each bit contained in $a and $b
$a | $b	Or	Or together each bit contained in $a and $b
$a ^ $b	Xor	Exclusive-or together each bit contained in $a and $b
~ $b	Not	Negate each bit in $b
$a << $b	Shift left	$a will receive the value of $b shifted left two bits
$a >> $b	Shift right	$a will receive the value of $b shifted right two bits

If you are interested in learning more about binary encoding, bitwise operators, and why they are important, I suggest Randall Hyde's massive online reference, "The Art of Assembly Language Programming," available at http://webster.cs.ucr.edu/ Page_asm/0_Page_asm.html. It's by far the best resource I've found thus far on the Web.

String Interpolation

To offer developers the maximum flexibility when working with string values, PHP offers a means for both literal and figurative interpretation. For example, consider the following string:

```
The $animal jumped over the wall.\n
```

You might assume that $animal is a variable, and \n is a newline character, and therefore both should be interpreted accordingly. However, what if you wanted to output the string exactly as it is written, or perhaps you wanted the newline to be rendered, but wanted the variable to display in its literal form ($animal), or vice versa? All these variations are possible in PHP, depending on how the strings are enclosed and whether certain key characters are escaped through a predefined sequence. These topics are the focus of this section.

Double Quotes

Strings enclosed in double quotes are the most commonly used in most PHP scripts, because they offer the most flexibility. This is because both variables and escape sequences will be parsed accordingly. Consider the following example:

```php
<?php
    $sport = "boxing";
    echo "Jason's favorite sport is $sport.";
?>
```

This example returns:

```
Jason's favorite sport is boxing.
```

Escape sequences are also parsed. Consider this example:

```php
<?php
    $output = "This is one line.\nAnd this is another line.";
    echo $output;
?>
```

Returning within the browser source:

```
This is one line.
And this is another line.
```

Note that I stated "browser source" and not "browser". This is because newline characters of this fashion are ignored by the browser window. However, if you view the source, you'll see that the output in fact appears on two separate lines. The same idea holds true if the data were output to a textfile.

In addition to the newline (\n) character, PHP recognizes a number of special escape sequences, all of which are listed in Table 3-13.

Table 3-13. Recognized Escape Sequences

SEQUENCE	DESCRIPTION
\n	Newline character
\r	Carriage return
\t	Horizontal tab
\\	Backslash
\$	Dollar sign
\"	Double quote
\[0-7]{1,3}	Octal notation
\x[0-9A-Fa-f]{1,2}	Hexadecimal notation

Single Quotes

Enclosing a string within single quotes is useful when the string should be interpreted exactly as stated. This means that both variables and escape sequences will not be interpreted when the string is parsed. For example, consider the following single-quoted string:

```
echo 'This string will $print exactly as it\'s \n declared.';
```

This results in:

```
This string will $print exactly as it's \n declared.
```

Note that the single quote located in "it's" was escaped. Omitting the backslash escape character will result in a syntax error, unless the magic_quotes_gpc configuration directive is enabled.. Consider another example:

```
echo 'This is another string.\\';
```

This results in:

```
This is another string.\
```

In this example, the backslash appearing at the conclusion of the string had to be escaped itself, otherwise the PHP parser would have understood that the trailing single quote was to be escaped. However, if the backslash were to appear anywhere else within the string, there would be no need to escape it.

heredoc

heredoc syntax offers a convenient means for outputting large amounts of text. Rather than delimiting strings with double or single quotes, two identical identifiers are employed. An example follows:

```php
<?php
$website = "http://www.romatermini.it";
echo <<<EXCERPT
<p>Rome's central train station, known as <a href = "$website">Roma Termini</a>,
was built in 1867. Because it had fallen into severe disrepair in the late 20th
century, the government knew that considerable resources were required to
rehabilitate the station prior to the 50-year <i>Giubileo</i>.</p>
EXCERPT;
?>
```

Several points are worth noting regarding this example:

- The opening and closing identifiers, in the case of this example, `EXCERPT`, must be identical. You can choose any identifier you please, but they must exactly match. The only constraint is that the identifier must consist of solely alphanumeric characters and underscores, and must not begin with a digit or underscore.

- The opening identifier must be preceded with three left-angle brackets, `<<<`.

- heredoc syntax follows the same parsing rules as strings enclosed in double quotes. That is, both variables and escape sequences are parsed. The only difference is that double quotes do not need to be escaped.

- The closing identifier must begin at the very beginning of a line. It cannot be preceded with spaces, or any other extraneous character.

heredoc syntax is particularly useful when you need to manipulate a substantial amount of material, but you do not want to put up with the hassle of escaping quotes.

Control Structures

Control structures determine the flow of code within an application, defining execution characteristics like whether and how many times a particular code statement will execute, as well as when a code block will relinquish execution control. These structures also offer a simple means to introduce entirely new sections of code (via file-inclusion statements) into a currently executing script. In this section, you'll learn about all such control structures available to the PHP language.

Execution Control Statements

The return and declare statements offer fine-tuned means for controlling when a particular code block begins and ends, respectively.

declare()

```
declare(directive) statement
```

The declare statement is used to determine the execution frequency of a specified block of code. Only one directive is currently supported: the *tick*. PHP defines a tick as a event occurring upon the execution of a certain number of low-level statements by the PHP parser. You might use a tick for benchmarking code, debugging, simple multitasking, or any other task in which control over the execution of low-level statements is required.

This event is defined within a function, and registered as a tick event via the register_tick_function(). These events can subsequently be unregistered via the unregister_tick_function(). Both functions are introduced next. The event frequency is specified by setting the declare function's directive accordingly, like the: ticks=N, where N is the number of low-level statements occurring between invocations of the event.

register_tick_function()

```
void register_tick_function (callback function [, mixed arg])
```

The register_tick_function() function registers the function specified by function as a tick event.

unregister_tick_function()

```
void unregister_tick_function (string function)
```

The unregister_tick_function() function unregisters the previously registered function specified by function.

return()

The return() statement is typically used within a function body, returning outcome to the function caller. If return() is called from the global scope, script execution ends immediately. If it is called from within a script that has been included using include() or require(), then control is returned to the file caller. Enclosing its argument in parentheses is optional. An example follows:

```
function cubed($value) {
    return $value * $value * value;
}
```

Calling this function will return the result to the caller:

```
$answer = cubed(3); // $answer = 27
```

Conditional Statements

Conditional statements make it possible for your computer program to respond accordingly to a wide variety of inputs, using logic to discern between various conditions based on input value. This functionality is so basic to the creation of computer software that it shouldn't come as a surprise that a variety of conditional statements are a staple of all mainstream programming languages, PHP included.

if

The if conditional is one of the most commonplace constructs of any mainstream programming language, offering a convenient means for conditional code execution. The syntax is:

```
if (expression) {
    statement
}
```

Considering an example, suppose you wanted a congratulatory message displayed if the user guesses a predetermined secret number:

```
<?php
    $secretNumber = 453;
    if ($_POST['guess'] == $secretNumber) {
        echo "<p>Congratulations! You guessed it!</p>";
    }
?>
```

The hopelessly lazy can forego the use of brackets when the conditional body consists of only a single statement. Here's a revision of the previous example:

```
<?php
    $secretNumber = 453;
    if ($_POST['guess'] == $secretNumber)
        echo"<p>Congratulations! You guessed it!</p>";
?>
```

> **NOTE** *Alternative enclosure syntax is available for the* if, while, for, foreach, *and* switch *control structures. This involves replacing the opening bracket with a colon (:) and replacing the closing bracket with* endif;, endwhile;, endfor;, endforeach;, *and* endswitch;, *respectively. I've been told that this syntax will be deprecated in the upcoming version, although it is likely to remain valid for the foreseeable future.*

else

The problem with the previous example is that output is only offered for the user who correctly guesses the secret number. All other users are left destitute, completely snubbed for reasons presumably linked to their lack of psychic power. What if you wanted to provide a tailored response no matter the outcome? To do so, you'll need a way to handle those not meeting the if conditional requirements, a function handily offered by way of the else statement. Here's a revision of the previous example, this time offering a response in both cases:

```php
<?php
    $secretNumber = 453;
    if ($_POST['guess'] == $secretNumber) {
        echo "<p>Congratulations! You guessed it!</p>";
    } else {
        echo "<p>Sorry. Apparently you lack psychic powers!</p>";
    }
?>
```

Like if, the else statement brackets can be skipped if only a single code statement is enclosed.

elseif

The if-else combination works nicely in an "either-or" situation; that is, a situation in which only two possible outcomes are available. What if there are several outcome possibilities? You would need a means for considering each possible outcome, which is accomplished with the elseif statement. I'll revise the secret number example again, this time offering a message if the user's guess is relatively close (within 10) of the secret number:

```php
<?php
    $secretNumber = 453;
    $_POST['guess'] = 442;
    if ($_POST['guess'] == $secretNumber) {
        echo "<p>Congratulations! You guessed it!</p>";
    } else if abs ($_POST['guess'] - $secretNumber) < 10) {
        echo "<p>You're getting close!</p>";
    } else {
```

```php
        echo "<p>Sorry. Apparently you lack psychic powers!</p>";
    }
?>
```

Like all conditionals, `elseif` supports the elimination of bracketing when only a single statement is enclosed.

switch

You can think of the `switch` statement as a variant of the `if-else` statement, often used when you need to compare a variable against a large number of values.

```php
<?php
switch($category) {
    case "news":
        print "<p>What's happening around the World</p>";
        break;
    case "weather":
        print "<p>Your weekly forecast</p>";
        break;
    case "sports":
        print "<p>Latest sports highlights</p>";
        break;
    default:
        print "<p>Welcome to my Web site</p>";
}
?>
```

Note the presence of the `break` statement at the conclusion of each `case` block. If a `break` statement isn't present, all subsequent `case` blocks will execute until a `break` statement is located. As an illustration of this quirk, let's assume that the `break` statements were removed from the above example, and that $category was set to "weather." You'd get the following results:

```
Your weekly forecast
Latest sports highlights
Welcome to my Web site
```

Looping Statements

Although varied approaches exist, looping statements are a fixture in every widespread programming language. This isn't a surprise, because looping mechanisms offer a simple means for accomplishing a commonplace task in programming: repeating a sequence of instructions until a specific condition is satisfied. PHP offers several such mechanisms, none of which should come as a surprise if you're familiar with other programming languages.

while

The while statement specifies a condition that must be met before execution of its embedded code is terminated. Its syntax is:

```
while (expression) {
     statements
}
```

In the following example, $count is initialized to the value 1. The value of $count is then squared, and output. The $count variable is then incremented by 1, and the loop is repeated until the value of $count reaches 5.

```php
<?php
$count = 1;
while ($count < 5) {
     echo "$count squared = ".pow($count,2). "<br />";
     $count++;
}
?>
```

The output looks like this:

```
1 squared = 1
2 squared = 4
3 squared = 9
4 squared = 16
```

Like all other control structures, multiple conditional expressions may also be embedded into the while statement. For instance, the following while block evaluates either until it reaches the end-of-file or until five lines have been read and output:

```php
<?php
$linecount = 1;
$fh = fopen("sports.txt","r");
while (!feof($fh) && $linecount<=5) {
     $line = fgets($fh, 4096);
     echo $line. "<br />";
     $linecount++;
}
?>
```

Given these conditionals, a maximum of five lines will be output from the sports.txt file, regardless of its size.

do...while

The do...while looping conditional is a variant of while, but it verifies the loop conditional at the conclusion of the block rather than at the beginning. Its syntax is:

```
do {
    statements
} while (expression);
```

Both while and do...while are similar in function; the only real difference is that although it's possible that the code embedded within a while statement could never be executed, the code embedded within a do...while statement will always execute at least once. Consider the following example:

```
<?php
    $count = 11;
    do {
        echo "$count squared = ".pow($count,2). "<br />";
    } while ($count < 10);
?>
```

The outcome is:

```
11 squared = 121
```

Despite the fact that 11 is out-of-bounds of the while conditional, the embedded code will execute once, because the conditional is not evaluated until the conclusion!

for

The for statement offers a somewhat more complex looping mechanism than its sibling, while. Its syntax is:

```
for (expression1; expression2; expression3) {
    statements
}
```

There are a few rules to keep in mind when using PHP's for loops:

- The first expression, expression1, is evaluated by default at the first iteration of the loop.

- The second expression, expression2, is evaluated at the beginning of each iteration. This expression determines whether looping will continue.

- The third expression, expression3, is evaluated at the conclusion of each loop.

- Any of the expressions can be empty, their purpose substituted by logic embedded within the for block.

With these rules in mind, consider the following examples. All display a partial kilometer/mile equivalency chart:

```
// Example One
for ($kilometers = 1; $kilometers <= 5; $kilometers++) {
    echo "$kilometers kilometers = ".$kilometers*0.62140. " miles. <br />";
}

// Example Two
for ($kilometers = 1; ; $kilometers++) {
    if ($kilometers > 5) break;
    echo "$kilometers kilometers = ".$kilometers*0.62140. " miles. <br />";
}

// Example Three
$kilometers = 1;
for (;;) {
    if ($kilometers > 5) break;
    echo "$kilometers kilometers = ".$kilometers*0.62140. " miles. <br />";
    $kilometers++;
}
```

The results for all three examples are:

```
1 kilometers = 0.6214 miles
2 kilometers = 1.2428 miles
3 kilometers = 1.8642 miles
4 kilometers = 2.4856 miles
5 kilometers = 3.107 miles
```

foreach

The foreach looping construct syntax is adept at looping through arrays, pulling each key/value pair from the array until all items have been retrieved, or some other internal conditional has been met. Two syntax variations are available, each of which is presented with an example.

The first syntax variant strips each value from the array, moving the pointer closer to the end with each iteration. Its syntax is:

```
foreach(array_expr as $value) {
    statement
}
```

Consider an example. Suppose you wanted to output an array of links:

```php
<?php
    $links = array("www.mysql.com","www.php.net","www.apache.org");
    echo "<b>Online Resources</b>:<br />";
    foreach($links as $link) {
        echo "<a href=\"http://$link\">$link</a><br />";
    }
?>
```

This would result in:

```
Online Resources:
www.mysql.com
www.php.net
www.apache.org
```

The second variation is well-suited for working with both the key and value of an array. The syntax follows:

```php
foreach(array_expr as $key => $value) {
    statement
}
```

Revising the previous example, suppose that the $links array contained both a link and corresponding link title:

```php
$links = array("The Official Apache Web site" => "www.apache.org",
               "The Official MySQL Web site" => "www.mysql.com",
               "The Official PHP Web site" => "www.php.net");
```

Each array item consists of both a key and a corresponding value. The foreach statement can easily peel each key/value pair from the array, like this:

```php
echo "<b>Online Resources</b>:<br />";
foreach($links as $title => $link) {
        echo "<a href=\"http://$link\">$title</a><br />";
}
```

The resulting would be that each link is embedded under its respective title, like this:

```
Online Resources:
The Official Apache Web site
The Official MySQL Web site
The Official PHP Web site
```

There are many other variations on this method of key/value retrieval, all of which are introduced in Chapter 5.

break

Encountering a break statement will immediately end execution of a do...while, for, foreach, switch, or while block. For example, the following while loop will terminate if a prime number is pseudo-randomly happened upon:

```php
<?php
$primes = array(2,3,5,7,11,13,17,19,23,29,31,37,41,43,47);
for($count = 1; $count++; $count < 1000) {
    $randomNumber = rand(1,50);
    if (in_array($randomNumber,$primes)) {
        break;
    } else {
        echo "<p>Non-prime number encountered: $randomNumber</p>";
    }
}
?>
```

Sample output follows:

```
Non-prime number encountered: 48
Non-prime number encountered: 42
Prime number encountered: 17
```

continue

The continue statement causes execution of the current loop iteration to end and commence at the beginning of the next iteration. For example, execution of the following while body will recommence if $usernames[$x] is found to have the value "missing":

```php
<?php
    $usernames = array("grace","doris","gary","nate","missing","tom");
    for ($x=0; $x < count($usernames); $x++) {
        if ($usernames[$x] == "missing") continue;
        echo "Staff member: $usernames[$x] <br />";
    }
?>
```

This results in the following output:

```
Staff member: grace
Staff member: doris
Staff member: gary
Staff member: nate
Staff member: tom
```

File Inclusion Statements

Efficient programmers are always thinking in terms of ensuring reusability and modularity. The most prevalent means for doing this is by isolating functional components into separate files, and then reassembling these files as needed. PHP offers four statements for including such files into applications, each of which is introduced in this section.

include()

The include() statement does exactly what its name implies; it includes a file. Including a file is the same as if you copied the data from the file argument into the location in which the statement appears. Its syntax follows:

```
include (/path/to/filename)
```

Like the print and echo statements, you have the option of omitting the parentheses. For example, if you wanted to include a series of preliminary MySQL server and database connection functions, you could place them into a separate file (called mysql-connect.php, for example), and then include that file within the top of each PHP script, like this:

```php
<?php
    include "/usr/local/lib/php/wjgilmore/mysql.connect.php";
    /* the script continues here */
?>
```

> **TIP** *You can optionally surround the* include() *argument with parentheses.*

You can also execute include() statements conditionally. For example, if an include() statement is placed in an if statement, the file will be included only if the if statement in which it is enclosed evaluates to true. One quirk regarding the use of include() in a conditional is that it must be enclosed in statement block curly brackets or in the alternative statement enclosure. Consider the difference in syntax between Listings 3-1 and 3-2.

Listing 3-1. Incorrect Use of include()

```php
<?php
if (expression)
    include ('filename');
else
    include ('another_filename');
?>
```

Listing 3-2. Correct Use of include()

```php
<?php
if (expression) {
    include ('filename');
} else {
    include ('another_filename');
}
?>
```

One misleading aspect of the include() statement is that any PHP code in the included file *must* be escaped with valid PHP enclosure tags, even though it is already embedded in a PHP execution block. Therefore, you could not just place a PHP command in a file and expect it to parse correctly, such as the one found here:

```php
print "this is an invalid include file";
```

Instead, any PHP statements must be enclosed with the correct escape tags, as shown here:

```php
<?php
    print "this is an invalid include file";
?>
```

> **TIP** *Any code found within an included file will inherit the variable scope of the location of its caller.*

Interestingly, all include statements support the inclusion of files residing on remote servers by prefacing include()'s argument with a supported URL. If the resident server is PHP-enabled, any variables found within the included file can be parsed by passing the necessary key/value pairs as would be done in a GET request, like this:

```php
include "http://www.wjgilmore.com/index.html?background=blue";
```

Two requirements must be satisfied before the inclusion of remote files is possible. First, the allow_url_fopen configuration directive must be enabled, and second, the URL wrapper must be supported. I discuss the latter requirement in further detail in Chapter 14.

include_once()

The include_once() function has the same purpose as include(), except that it first verifies whether or not the file has already been included. If it has been, include_once() will not execute. Otherwise, it will include the file as necessary. Other than this difference, include_once() operates in exactly the same way as include(). Its syntax follows:

include_once (*filename*)

The same quirk pertinent to enclosing include() within conditional statements also applies to include_once().

require()

For the most part, require() operates like include(), including a template into the file in which the require() call is located. It has this syntax:

require(*filename*)

However, there are two important differences between require() and include(). First, the file will be included in the script in which the require() construct appears regardless of where require() is located. For instance, if require() were placed within an if statement that evaluated to false, the file would be included anyway!

> **TIP** *A URL can be used with* require() *only if "URL fopen wrappers" is enabled, which by default it is.*

Second, script execution will stop if a require() fails, whereas it may continue in the case of an include(). One possible explanation for the failure of a require() statement is an incorrectly referenced target path.

require_once()

As your site grows, you may find yourself redundantly including certain files. Although this might not always be a problem, sometimes you will not want modified variables in the included file to be overwritten by a later inclusion of the same file. Another problem that arises is the clashing of function names should they exist in the inclusion file. You can solve these problems with the `require_once()` function.

The `require_once()` function ensures that the insertion file is included only once in your script. After `require_once()` is encountered, any subsequent attempts to include the same file will be ignored. Its syntax follows:

```
require_once(insertion_file)
```

Other than the verification procedure of `require_once()`, all other aspects of the function are the same as for `require()`.

Summary

Although the material presented here is not as glamorous as later chapters, it is invaluable to your success as a PHP programmer, because all subsequent functionality is based on these building blocks. This will soon become apparent.

The next chapter is entirely devoted to the construction and invocation of functions, reusable chunks of code intended to perform a specific task. This material starts you down the path necessary to begin building modular, reusable PHP applications.

CHAPTER 4

Functions

EVEN IN TRIVIAL APPLICATIONS, repetitive processes are likely to exist. For non-trivial applications, such repetition is a given. For example, in an e-commerce application, you might need to query a customer's profile information numerous times: at login, checkout, and when verifying a shipping address. However, repeating the profile querying process throughout the application would not only be error-prone, but also a nightmare to maintain. What happens if a new field has been added to the customer's profile? You might need to sift through each page of the application, modifying the query as necessary, likely introducing errors in the process.

Thankfully, the concept of embodying these repetitive processes within a named section of code, and then invoking this name as necessary, has long been a key component of any respectable computer language. These sections of code are known as *functions*, and they grant you the convenience of a singular point of modification if the embodied process requires changes in the future, which greatly reduces both the possibility of programming errors and maintenance overhead. In this chapter, you'll learn all about PHP functions, including how to create and invoke them, pass input, return both single and multiple values to the caller, and create and include function libraries. In additionally, I'll touch upon some functional "black magic," and discuss both *recursive* and *variable* functions.

Invoking a Function

Over 1,000 standard functions are built into the standard PHP distribution, many of which you'll see throughout this book. You can invoke the function you want simply by specifying the function name, assuming that the function has been made available either through the library's compilation into the installed distribution, or via the include()/require() statements. For example, suppose you wanted to raise 5 to the third power. You could invoke PHP's pow() function like this:

```php
<?php
    $value = pow(5,3); // returns 125
    echo $value;
?>
```

If you simply want to output the function outcome, you can forego assigning the value to a variable, like this:

```php
<?php
    echo pow(5,3);
?>
```

If you want to output function outcome within a larger string, you'll need to concatenate it like this:

```
echo "Five raised to the third power equals ".pow(5,3).".";
```

Creating a Function

Although PHP's vast assortment of function libraries are a tremendous benefit to the programmer seeking to avoid reinventing the programmatic wheel, sooner or later you'll need to go beyond what is offered in the standard distribution, which means you'll need to create custom functions or even entire function libraries. To do so, you'll need to define a function using a predefined syntactical pattern, like so:

```
function function_name (parameters) {
    function-body
}
```

For example, consider the following function, generate_footer(), which outputs a page footer:

```
function generate_footer() {
    echo "<p>Copyright &copy; 2003-2004 W. Jason Gilmore</p>";
}
```

Once it is defined, you can then call this function as you would any other. For example:

```
<?php
    generate_footer();
?>
```

This yields the following result:

```
<p>Copyright &copy; 2003-2004 W. Jason Gilmore</p>
```

Passing Arguments By Value

You'll often find it useful to pass data into a function. As an example, I'll create a function that calculates an item's total cost by determining its sales tax and then adding that amount to the price:

```
function salestax($price,$tax) {
    $total = $price + ($price * $tax);
    echo "Total cost: $total";
}
```

This function accepts two parameters, aptly named $price and $tax, which are used in the calculation. Although these parameters are intended to be floats, because of PHP's loose typing, nothing prevents you from passing in variables of any data type, but the outcome might not be as one would expect. In addition, you're allowed to define as few or as many parameters as you deem necessary; there are no language-imposed constraints in this regard.

Once the function is defined, you can then invoke it, as was demonstrated in the previous section. For example, the salestax() function would be called like so:

```
salestax(15.00,.075);
```

Of course, you're not bound to passing static values into the function. You can pass variables like this:

```php
<?php
    $pricetag = 15.00;
    $salestax = .075;
    salestax($pricetag, $salestax);
?>
```

When you pass an argument in this manner, it's called *passing by value*. This means that any changes made to those values within the scope of the function are ignored outside of the function. If you want these changes to be reflected outside of the function's scope, you can pass the argument *by reference*, introduced next.

> **NOTE** *Note that you don't necessarily need to define the function before it's invoked, because PHP reads the entire script into the engine before execution. Therefore, you could actually call* salestax() *before it is defined, although such haphazard practice is not recommended.*

Passing Arguments by Reference

On occasion, you may want any changes made to an argument within a function to be reflected outside of the function's scope. Passing the argument by reference accomplishes this need. Passing an argument by reference is done by appending an ampersand to the front of the argument. An example follows:

```php
<?php
    $cost = 20.00;
    $tax = 0.05;
    function calculate_cost(&$cost, $tax)
    {
        // Modify the $cost variable
        $cost = $cost + ($cost * $tax);
```

```
        // Perform some random change to the $tax variable.
        $tax += 4;
    }
    calculate_cost($cost,$tax);
    echo "Tax is: ". $tax*100."<br />";
    echo "Cost is: $". $cost."<br />";
?>
```

Here's the result:

```
Tax is 5%
Cost is $21
```

Note that the value of $tax remains the same, although $cost has changed.

Default Argument Values

Default values can be assigned to input arguments, which will be automatically assigned to the argument if no other value is provided. To revise the sales tax example, suppose that the majority of your sales are to take place in Franklin county, located in the great state of Ohio. You could then assign $tax the default value of 5.75%, like this:

```
function salestax($price,$tax=.0575) {
    $total = $price + ($price * $tax);
    echo "Total cost: $total";
}
```

Keep in mind that you can still pass $tax another taxation rate. 5.75% will only be used if salestax() is invoked like this:

```
$price = 15.47;
salestax($price);
```

Note that default argument values must be constant expressions; you cannot assign non-constant values such as functions calls or variables.

Optional Arguments

You can designate certain arguments as *optional* by placing them at the end of the list, and assigning them a default value of nothing, like so:

```
function salestax($price,$tax="") {
    $total = $price + ($price * $tax);
    echo "Total cost: $total";
}
```

This allows you to call `salestax()` without the second parameter if there is no sales tax:

```
salestax(42.00);
```

This returns the following:

```
Total cost: $42.00
```

If multiple optional arguments are specified, you can selectively choose which ones are passed along. Consider this example:

```
function calculate($price,$price2="",$price3="") {
    echo $price + $price2 + $price3;
}
```

You can then call `calculate()`, passing along just $price and $price3, like so:

```
calculate(10,"",3);
```

This returns the value:

```
13
```

Returning Values From a Function

Often, it isn't enough to blindly rely on a function to do something; a script's outcome might depend on a function's outcome, or on changes in data resulting from its execution. Yet variable scoping prevents information from easily being passed from a function body back to its caller, so how can such data from being passed? You can pass data back to the caller by way of the `return` keyword.

return()

The `return` statement returns any ensuing value back to the function caller, returning program control back to the caller's scope in the process. If `return` is called from within the global scope, the script execution is terminated. Revising the sales tax function again, suppose you didn't want to immediately echo the sales total back to the user upon calculation, but rather wanted to return the value to the calling block:

```
function salestax($price,$tax=.0575) {
    $total = $price + ($price * $tax);
    return $total;
}
```

Alternatively, you could have returned the calculation directly without even assigning it to $total, like this:

```
function salestax($price,$tax=.0575) {
    return $price + ($price * $tax);
}
```

Here's an example of how you would call this function:

```
<?php
    $price = 6.50;
    $total = salestax($price);
?>
```

Returning Multiple Values

It's often quite convenient to return multiple values from a function. For example, suppose that you'd like to create a function that retrieves user data from a MySQL database, say the user's name, e-mail address, and phone number, and returns it to the caller. This is accomplished much easier than you might think, done with the help of a very useful language construct, list(). The list() construct offers a convenient means for retrieving values from an array, like so:

```
<?php
    $colors = array("red","blue","green");
    list($red,$blue,$green) = $colors; // $red="red", $blue="blue", $green="green"
?>
```

Building on this example, you can imagine how the three prerequisite values might be returned from a function using list():

```
<?php
    function retrieve_user_profile() {
        $user[] = "Jason";
        $user[] = "jason@example.com";
        $user[] = "English";
        return $user;
    }
    list($name,$email,$language) = retrieve_user_profile();
    echo "Name: $name, email: $email, preferred language: $language";
?>
```

Executing this script returns:

```
Name: Jason, email: jason@example.com, preferred language: $language
```

This concept is useful and will be used repeatedly throughout this book.

Nesting Functions

PHP supports *nesting functions,* or defining and invoking functions within functions. For example, a dollar-to-pound conversion function, convert_pound(), could be both defined and invoked entirely within the salestax() function, like this:

```
function salestax($price,$tax) {
   function convert_pound($dollars, $conversion=1.6) {
      return $dollars * $conversion;
   }
   $total = $price + ($price * $tax);
   echo "Total cost in dollars: $total. Cost in British pounds: "
      .convert_pound($total);
}
```

Note that PHP does not restrict the scope of a nested function. For example, I could still call convert_pound() outside of salestax(), like this:

```
salestax(15.00,.075);
echo convert_pound(15);
```

Recursive Functions

Recursive functions, or functions that call themselves, offer immense practical value to the programmer. This strategy is used to divide an otherwise complex problem into a simple case, reiterating that case until the problem is resolved.

Practically every introductory recursion example I have ever encountered involves factorial computation. Yawn. Let's do something a tad more practical. I'll demonstrate how to create a loan payment calculator. Specifically, the following example uses recursion to create a payment schedule, telling you the principal and interest amounts required of each payment installment to repay the loan. The recursive function, amortizationTable(), is introduced in Listing 4-1. It takes as input four arguments: $paymentNum, which identifies the payment number, $periodicPayment, which carries the total monthly payment, $balance, which indicates the remaining loan balance, and $monthlyInterest, which determines the monthly interest percentage rate. These items are designated or determined in the script listed in Listing 4-2, titled mortgage.php.

Listing 4-1. The Payment Calculator Function, amortizationTable()

```
function amortizationTable($paymentNum, $periodicPayment, $balance,
                                       $monthlyInterest) {
    $paymentInterest = round($balance * $monthlyInterest,2);
    $paymentPrincipal = round($periodicPayment - $paymentInterest,2);
    $newBalance = round($balance - $paymentPrincipal,2);
    print "<tr>
            <td>$paymentNum</td>
            <td>\$".number_format($balance,2)."</td>
            <td>\$".number_format($periodicPayment,2)."</td>
```

```
            <td>\$".number_format($paymentInterest,2)."</td>
            <td>\$".number_format($paymentPrincipal,2)."</td>
            </tr>";
     # If balance not yet zero, recursively call amortizationTable()
     if ($newBalance > 0) {
        $paymentNum++;
        amortizationTable($paymentNum, $periodicPayment, $newBalance,
                        $monthlyInterest);
     } else {
        exit;
     }
  } #end amortizationTable()
```

After setting pertinent variables and performing a few preliminary calculations, Listing 4-2 invokes the amortizationTable() function. Because this function calls itself recursively, all amortization table calculations will be performed internal to this function; once complete, control is returned to the caller.

Listing 4-2. A Payment Schedule Calculator Using Recursion (mortgage.php)

```
<?php
   # Set some initial variables
   # Loan balance
   $balance = 200000.00;
   # Loan interest rate
   $interestRate = .0575;
   # Monthly interest rate
   $monthlyInterest = .0575 / 12;
   # Term length of the loan, in years.
      $termLength = 30;
   # Number of payments per year.
      $paymentsPerYear = 12;
    # Payment iteration
   $paymentNumber = 1;
   # Perform preliminary calculations
   $totalPayments = $termLength * $paymentsPerYear;
   $intCalc = 1 + $interestRate / $paymentsPerYear;
   $periodicPayment = $balance * pow($intCalc,$totalPayments) * ($intCalc - 1) /
                            (pow($intCalc,$totalPayments) - 1);
   $periodicPayment = round($periodicPayment,2);
   # Create table
   echo "<table width='50%' align='center' border='1'>";
   print "<tr>
            <th>Payment Number</th><th>Balance</th>
            <th>Payment</th><th>Interest</th><th>Principal</th>
            </tr>";
   # Call recursive function
   amortizationTable($paymentNumber, $periodicPayment, $balance, $monthlyInterest);
   # Close table
   print "</table>";
?>
```

Figure 4-1 shows sample output, based on monthly payments made on a 30 year fixed loan of $200,000.00 at 6.25% interest. For reasons of space conservation, just the first ten payment iterations are listed.

Payment Number	Balance	Payment	Interest	Principal
1	$200,000.00	$1,660.82	$958.33	$702.48
2	$199,297.52	$1,660.82	$954.96	$705.85
3	$198,591.67	$1,660.82	$951.58	$709.23
4	$197,882.44	$1,660.82	$948.18	$712.64
5	$197,169.80	$1,660.82	$944.77	$716.05
6	$196,453.75	$1,660.82	$941.34	$719.47
7	$195,734.28	$1,660.82	$937.89	$722.93
8	$195,011.35	$1,660.82	$934.42	$726.40
9	$194,284.95	$1,660.82	$930.94	$729.87
10	$193,555.08	$1,660.82	$927.45	$733.36

Figure 4-1. Sample output from mortgage.php

Employing a recursive strategy often results in significant code savings and promotes reusability. Although recursive functions are not always the optimal solution, they are often a welcome addition to any language's repertoire.

Variable Functions

One of PHP's most attractive traits is its syntactical clarity. On occasion, however, taking a somewhat more abstract programmatic route can eliminate a great deal of coding overhead. For example, consider a scenario in which several data retrieval functions have been created: retrieveUser(), retrieveNews(), and retrieveWeather(), where the name of each function implies its purpose. In order to trigger a given function, you could use a URL parameter and an if conditional statement, like this:

```php
<?php
    if ($trigger == "retrieveUser") {
        retrieveUser($rowid);
    } else if ($trigger == "retrieveNews") {
        retrieveNews($rowid);
    } else if ($trigger == "retrieveWeather") {
        retrieveWeather($rowid);
    }
?>
```

This code allows you to pass along URLs like this:

```
http://www.example.com/content/index.php?trigger=retrieveUser&rowid=5
```

The `index.php` file will then use `$trigger` to determine which function should be executed. Although this works just fine, it is tedious, particularly if a large number of retrieval functions are required. An alternative, much shorter means for accomplishing the same goal is through *variable functions*. A variable function is a function whose name is also evaluated before execution, meaning that its exact name is not known until execution time. Variable functions are prefaced with a dollar sign, just like regular variables, like this:

```php
$function();
```

Using variable functions, let's revisit the previous example:

```php
<?php
$trigger($rowid);
?>
```

Although variable functions are at times convenient, you should keep in mind that they do present certain security risks. Most notably, an attacker could execute any function in PHP's repertoire simply by modifying the variable used to declare the function name. For example, consider the ramifications of modifying the `$trigger` variable in the previous example to hold the value "exec", and the `$rowid` to hold "rm -rf /". PHP's `exec()` command will happily attempt to execute its argument on the system level. The command `rm -rf /` will attempt to recursively delete all files starting at the root level directory. The results could be catastrophic. Therefore, as always, be sure to sanitize all user information; you never know what will be attempted next.

Function Libraries

Great programmers are lazy, and lazy programmers think in terms of reusability. Functions form the crux of such efforts, and are often collectively assembled into *libraries*, and subsequently repeatedly reused within similar applications. PHP libraries are created via the simple aggregation of function definitions in a single file, like this:

```php
<?php
    function local_tax($grossIncome, $taxRate) {
        // function body here
    }
    function state_tax($grossIncome, $taxRate) {
        // function body here
    }
    function medicare($grossIncome, $medicareRate) {
        // function body here
    }
?>
```

Save this library, preferably using a naming convention that will clearly denote its purpose, like taxes.library.php. You can then insert this function into scripts using include(), include_once(), require(), or require_once(), each of which was introduced in Chapter 3. (Alternatively, you could use PHP's auto_prepend configuration directive to automate the task of script/template insertion for you.) For example, assuming that you titled this library taxation.library.php, you could include it into a script like this:

```php
<?php
    require_once("taxation.library.php");
    ...
?>
```

Once included, any of the three functions found in this library can be invoked as needed.

Summary

This chapter concentrated on one of the basic building blocks of modern day programming languages: reusability through functional programming. You learned how to create and invoke functions, pass information to and from the function block, nest functions, and create both recursive and variable functions. Finally, you learned how to aggregate functions together as libraries and include them into the script as needed.

In the next chapter, I'll switch gears, turning our attention to PHP's array functionality. I'll run the entire gamut of array manipulation, and introduce PHP 5's new character array-handling features.

CHAPTER 5

Arrays

PROGRAMMERS SPEND A considerable amount of time working with sets of related data. The names of all employees at the XYZ corporation, U.S. Presidents and their corresponding birth dates, and years between 1900 and 1975 are all examples of related data sets. Because working with such groups of data is so prevalent, it might not come as a surprise that a means for managing these groups within code is a common feature across all mainstream programming languages. This means typically centers around the compound data type *array*, which offers an ideal means for storing, manipulating, sorting, and retrieving data sets. PHP's solution is no different, supporting the *array* data type, in addition to an accompanying host of behaviors and functions directed towards array manipulation. In this chapter, you'll learn all about those array-based features and functions supported by PHP. Although it is beyond the scope of this book to provide a comprehensive list of all predefined functions, you'll nonetheless find information regarding the majority of array functions in this chapter, because PHP's array-handling capabilities are just so darned useful.

Because I introduce so many functions in this chapter, I thought it wise to divide them into the following categories:

- Outputting arrays

- Creating arrays

- Testing for an array

- Adding and removing array elements

- Locating array elements

- Traversing arrays

- Determining array size and element uniqueness

- Sorting arrays

- Merging, slicing, splicing, and dissecting arrays

Rather than simply list them alphabetically, the categorical division should aid in later reference when searching for a viable solution to some future problem. Before beginning this review, I'll start the chapter with a brief recap of the array definition and structure.

What Is an Array?

An *array* is traditionally defined as a group of items that share the same characteristics and are distinguished by their lookup key (more about this key in a bit). I use the word *traditionally* because you can flaunt this definition and group entirely unrelated entities together in an array structure. PHP takes this a step further, foregoing the requirement that they even share the same datatype. For example, an array might contain items like state names, zip codes, exam scores, or playing card suits. Each entity consists of two items: a *key* and a *value*. The key serves as the lookup facility for retrieving its counterpart, the value. These keys can be numerical, and bear no real relation to the value other than the value's position in the array. As an example, the array could consist of an alphabetically sorted list of state names, with key 0 representing "Alabama", and key 49 representing "Wyoming". Using PHP syntax, this might look like this:

```
$states = array (0 => "Alabama", "1" => "Alaska"..."49" => "Wyoming");
```

Using numerical indexing, you could reference the first state like so:

```
$states[0]
```

> **NOTE** *PHP's numerically indexed arrays begin with position 0, not 1.*

Alternatively, key mappings can be associative, where the key bears some relation to the value other than its array position. Mapping arrays associatively is particularly convenient when using numerical index values just doesn't make sense. For example, I might want to create an array that maps state abbreviations to their names, like this: OH/Ohio, PA/Pennsylvania, and NY/New York. Using PHP syntax, this might look like:

```
$states = array ("OH" => "Ohio", "PA" => "Pennsylvania", "NY" => "New York")
```

You could then reference "Ohio" like so:

```
$states["OH"]
```

Arrays consisting solely of atomic entities are referred to as being single-dimensional. Multidimensional arrays consist of other arrays. For example, you could use a multidimensional array to store U.S. state information. Using PHP syntax, it might look like this:

```
$states = array (
    "Ohio" => array ("population" => "11,353,140", "capital" => "Columbus"),
    "Nebraska" => array("population" => "1,711,263", "capital" => "Omaha")
)
```

You could then reference Ohio's population like so:

```
$states["Ohio"]["population"]
```

This would return the following value:

```
11,353,140
```

In addition to offering a means for creating and populating an array, the language must also offer a means for traversing it. As you'll learn throughout this chapter, PHP offers many ways for doing so. Regardless of which way you use, keep in mind that all rely on the use of a central feature known as an *array pointer*. The array pointer acts like a bookmark, telling you the position of the array that you're presently examining. You won't work with the array pointer directly, but instead will traverse the array either using built-in language features or functions. Still, it's useful to understand this basic concept.

Outputting Arrays

Although it might not necessarily make sense to learn how to output an array before even knowing how to create one in PHP, this function is so heavily used throughout this chapter, and indeed, throughout you daily programming life, that it merits first mention in this chapter.

print_r()

```
boolean print_r(mixed variable [, boolean return])
```

The print_r() function takes as input any *variable* and sends its contents to standard output, returning TRUE on success and FALSE otherwise. This in itself isn't particularly exciting, until you take into account that it will organize array contents (as well as an object's) into a very readable format before displaying them. For example, suppose you wanted to view the contents of an associative array consisting of states and their corresponding state capitals. You could call print_r() like this:

```
print_r($states);
```

This returns the following:

```
Array ( [Ohio] => Columbus [Iowa] => Des Moines [Arizona] => Phoenix )
```

The optional parameter *return* modifies the function's behavior, causing it to return the output to the caller, rather than sending it to standard output. Therefore, if you want to return the contents of the above $states array, you just set *return* to TRUE:

```
$stateCapitals = print_r($states, TRUE);
```

This function is used repeatedly throughout this chapter as a simple means for displaying the results of the example at hand.

> **TIP** *The* print_r() *function isn't the only way to output an array, but rather offers a convenient means for doing so. You're free to output arrays using a looping conditional (such as* while *or* for*), and in fact these sorts of loops are required to implement many application features. I'll come back to this method repeatedly throughout not only this chapter, but also throughout the entire book.*

Creating an Array

Unlike other, much more annoying array implementations of other languages, PHP doesn't require that you assign a size to an array at creation time. In fact, because it's a loosely-typed language, PHP doesn't even require that you declare the array before you use it. Despite the lack of restriction, PHP offers both a formalized and informal array declaration methodology. Each has its advantages, and both are worth learning. We'll examine both in this section, starting with the informal variety.

You reference the individual elements of a PHP array by denoting the element between a pair of square brackets. Because there is no size limitation on the array, you can create the array simply by making reference to it, like this:

```
$state[0] = "Delaware";
```

You could then display the first element of the array $state like this:

```
echo $state[0];
```

You can then add additional values by referencing the intended value in conjunction with the array index, like this:

```
$state[1] = "Pennsylvania";
$state[2] = "New Jersey";
...
$state[49] = "Hawaii";
```

Interestingly, if you assume the index value is numerical and ascending, you can choose to omit the index value at creation time:

```
$state[] = "Pennsylvania";
$state[] = "New Jersey";
...
$state[] = "Hawaii";
```

Creating associative arrays in this fashion is equally trivial, except that the associative index reference is always required. The following example creates an array that matches U.S. state names with their date of entry into the Union:

```
$state["Delaware"] = "December 7, 1787";
$state["Pennsylvania"] = "December 12, 1787";
$state["New Jersey"] = "December 18, 1787";
...
$state["Hawaii"] = "August 21, 1959";
```

Next I'll discuss a functionally identical, yet somewhat more formal means for creating arrays: via the array() function.

array()

```
array array([item1 [,item2 ... [,itemN]]])
```

The array() function takes as its input zero or more *items* and returns an array consisting of these input elements. Here is an example of using array() to create an indexed array:

```
$languages = array ("English", "Gaelic", "Spanish");
// $languages[0] = "English", $languages[1] = "Gaelic", $languages[2] = "Spanish"
```

You can also use array() to create an associative array, like this:

```
$languages = array ("Spain" => "Spanish",
                    "Ireland" => "Gaelic",
                    "United States" => "English");
// $languages["Spain"] = "Spanish"
// $languages["Ireland"] = "Gaelic"
// $languages["United States"] = "English"
```

list()

```
void list(mixed...)
```

The list() function is similar to array(), though it's used to make simultaneous variable assignments from values extracted from an array in just one operation. This construct can be particularly useful when you're extracting information from a database or file. For example, suppose you wanted to format and output information read from a text file. Each line of the file contains user information, including name, occupation, and favorite color, with each piece of information delimited by a vertical bar (|). A typical line would look similar to the following:

```
Nino Sanzi|Professional Golfer|green
```

Using list(), a simple loop could read each line, assign each piece of data to a variable, and format and display the data as needed. Here's how you could use list() to make multiple variable assignments simultaneously:

```
// While the EOF hasn't been reached, get next line
while ($line = fgets ($user_file, 4096)) {
    // use explode() to separate each piece of data.
    list ($name, $occupation, $color) = explode ("|", $line);
    // format and output the data
    print "Name: $name <br />";
    print "Occupation: $occupation <br />";
    print "Favorite color: $color <br />";
}
```

Each line would in turn be read and formatted similar to this:

```
Name: Nino Sanzi
Occupation: Professional Golfer
Favorite Color: green
```

Reviewing the example, list() depends on the function explode()to split each line into three elements, which in turn uses the vertical bar as the element delimiter. The explode() function is formally introduced in Chapter 9. These elements are then assigned to $name, $occupation, and $color. At that point, it's just a matter of formatting for display to the browser.

range()

```
array range(int low, int high [,int step])
```

The range() function provides an easy way to quickly create and fill an array consisting of a range of *low* and *high* integer values. An array containing all integer values in this range is returned. As an example, suppose you need an array consisting of all possible face values of a die:

```
$die = range(0,6);
// Same as specifying $die = array(0,1,2,3,4,5,6)
```

The optional *step* parameter offers a convenient means for determining the increment between members of the range. For example, if you want an array consisting of all even values between 0 and 20, you could use an step value of 2:

```
$even = range(0,20,2);
// $even = array(0,2,4,6,8,10,12,14,16,18,20);
```

The range() function can also be used for character sequences. For example, suppose you wanted to create an array consisting of the letters A through F:

```
$letters = range("A","F");
// $letters = array("A,","B","C","D","E","F");
```

Testing for an Array

When you incorporate arrays into your application, you'll sometimes need to know whether a particular variable is an array. A built-in function, is_array(), is available for accomplishing this task.

is_array()

```
boolean is_array(mixed variable)
```

The is_array() function determines whether *variable* is an array, returning TRUE if it is, and FALSE otherwise. Note that even an array consisting of a single value will still be considered an array. An example follows:

```
$states = array("Florida");
$state = "Ohio";
echo "\$states is an array: ".is_array($states)."<br />";
echo "\$state is an array: ".is_array($state)."<br />";
```

The results are:

```
$states is an array: 1
$state is an array:
```

Adding and Removing Array Elements

PHP provides a number of functions for both growing and shrinking an array. Some of these functions are provided as a convenience to programmers who wish to mimic various queue implementations (FIFO, LIFO, and so on), as reflected by their names (push, pop, shift, and unshift). Even if you don't know what queue implementations are, don't worry; these functions are easy to use, and examples are provided for each.

> **NOTE** *A traditional queue is a data structure in which the elements are removed in the same order that they were entered, known as first-in-first-out, or FIFO. In contrast, a stack is a data structure in which the elements are removed in the order opposite to that in which they were entered, known as last-in-first-out, or LIFO.*

$arrayname[]

This isn't a function, but a language feature. You can add array elements simply by executing the assignment, like so:

```
$states["Ohio"] = "March 1, 1803";
```

In the case of a numerical index, you can append a new element like this:

```
$state[] = "Ohio";
```

Sometimes, however, you'll require a somewhat more sophisticated means for adding array elements (and subtracting array elements, a feature not readily available in the fashion described for adding elements). These functions are introduced throughout the remainder of this section.

array_push()

```
int array_push(array target_array, mixed variable [, mixed variable...])
```

The array_push() function adds *variable* onto the end of the *target_array*, returning TRUE on success and FALSE otherwise. You can push multiple variables onto the array simultaneously, by passing these variables into the function as input parameters. An example follows:

```
$states = array("Ohio","New York");
array_push($states,"California","Texas");
// $states = array("Ohio","New York","California","Texas");
```

array_pop()

```
mixed array_pop(array target_array)
```

The array_pop() function returns the last element from *target_array*, resetting the array pointer upon completion. An example follows:

```
$states = array("Ohio","New York","California","Texas");
$state = array_pop($states); // $state = "Texas"
```

array_shift()

mixed array_shift(array *target_array*)

The array_shift() function is similar to array_pop(), except that it returns the first array item found on the *target_array*, rather than the last. As a result, if numerical keys are used, all corresponding values will be shifted down, whereas arrays using associative keys will not be affected. An example follows:

```
$states = array("Ohio","New York","California","Texas");
$state = array_shift($states);
// $states = array("New York","California","Texas")
// $state = "Ohio"
```

Like array_pop(), array_shift() also resets the pointer after completion.

array_unshift()

int array_unshift(array *target_array*, mixed *variable* [, mixed *variable*...])

The array_unshift() function is similar to array_push(), except that it adds elements onto the front of the array, rather than add them to the end. All pre-existing numerical keys are modified to reflect their new position in the array, but associative keys aren't affected. An example follows:

```
$states = array("Ohio","New York");
array_unshift($states,"California","Texas");
// $states = array("California","Texas","Ohio","New York");
```

array_pad()

array array_pad(array *target*, integer *length*, mixed *pad_value*)

The array_pad() function modifies the *target* array, increasing its size to the length specified by *length*. This is done by padding the array with the value specified by *pad_value*. If *pad_value* is positive, the array will be padded on the right-side (the end); if it is negative, the array will be padded to the left (the beginning). If *length* is equal to or less than the current *target* size, no action will be taken. An example follows:

```
$states = array("Alaska","Hawaii");
$states = array_pad($states,4,"New colony?");
$states = array("Alaska","Hawaii","New colony?","New colony?");
```

Locating Array Elements

Often, the value of data can be determined by the ability to easily identify items of value, rather than the amount accumulated. If you aren't able to quickly navigate the information, little good is done accumulating it. In this section, I'll introduce several functions that enable you to sift through arrays, in an effort to locate items of interest efficiently.

in_array()

```
boolean in_array(mixed needle, array haystack [,boolean strict])
```

The in_array() function searches the haystack array for *needle*, returning TRUE if found, and FALSE otherwise. The optional third parameter, *strict*, forces in_array() to also consider type. An example follows:

```
$grades = array(100,94.7,67,89,100);
if (in_array("100",$grades)) echo "Somebody studied for the test!";
if (in_array("100",$grades,1)) echo "Somebody studied for the test!";
```

Returning:

```
Somebody studied for the test!
```

This string was output only once, because the second test required that the datatypes match. Because the second test compared an integer with a string, the test failed.

array_keys()

```
array array_keys(array target_array [, mixed search_value])
```

The array_keys() function returns an array consisting of all keys located in the array *target_array*. If the optional *search_value* parameter is included, only keys matching that value will be returned. An example follows:

```
$state["Delaware"] = "December 7, 1787";
$state["Pennsylvania"] = "December 12, 1787";
$state["New Jersey"] = "December 18, 1787";
$keys = array_keys($state);
print_r($keys);
// Array ( [0] => Delaware [1] => Pennsylvania [2] => New Jersey )
```

array_key_exists()

```
boolean array_key_exists(mixed key, array target_array)
```

The function array_key_exists() returns TRUE if the supplied *key* is found in the array *target_array*, and FALSE otherwise. An example follows:

```
$state["Delaware"] = "December 7, 1787";
$state["Pennsylvania"] = "December 12, 1787";
$state["Ohio"] = "March 1, 1803";
if (array_key_exists("Ohio", $state)) echo "Ohio joined the Union on $state[Ohio]";
```

The result is:

```
Ohio joined the Union on March 1, 1803
```

array_values()

array array_values(array *target_array*)

The array_values() function returns all values located in the array *target_array*, automatically providing numeric indexes for the returned array. For example:

```
$population = array("Ohio" => "11,421,267", "Iowa" => "2,936,760");
$popvalues = array_values($population);
print_r($popvalues);
// Array ( [0] => 11,421,267 [1] => 2,936,760 )
```

array_search()

mixed array_search(mixed *needle*, array *haystack* [, boolean *strict*])

The array_search() function searches the array *haystack* for the value *needle*, returning its key if located, and FALSE otherwise. For example:

```
$state["Ohio"] = "March 1";
$state["Delaware"] = "December 7";
$state["Pennsylvania"] = "December 12";
$founded = array_search("December 7", $state);
if ($founded) echo "The state $founded was founded on $state[$founded]";
```

Traversing Arrays

The need to travel across an array and retrieve various keys, values, or both is a commonplace affair, so it's not a surprise that PHP offers numerous functions for navigating throughout. Many of these functions do double-duty, both retrieving the key or value residing at the current pointer location, and also moving the pointer to the next appropriate location. We'll review these functions in this section.

key()

```
mixed key(array input_array)
```

The key() function returns the key element located at the current pointer position of *input_array*. Consider the following example:

```
$capitals = array("Ohio" => "Columbus", "Iowa" => "Des Moines","Arizona" => "Phoenix");
echo "<p>Can you name the capitals of these states?</p>";
while($key = key($capitals)) {
    echo $key."<br />";
    next($capitals);
}
```

This returns:

```
Ohio
Iowa
Arizona
```

Note that key() does not advance the pointer with each call. Rather, you use the next() function, whose sole purpose is to accomplish this task. This function is formally introduced later in this section.

reset()

```
mixed reset(array input_array)
```

The reset() function serves to set the *input_array* pointer back to the beginning of the array. This function is commonly used when you need to review or manipulate an array multiple times within a script, or when sorting has completed.

each()

```
array each(array input_array)
```

The each() function returns the current key/value pair from the *input_array*, and advances the pointer one position. The returned array consists of four keys, with keys *0* and *key* containing the key name, and keys *1* and *value* containing the corresponding data. If the pointer is residing at the end of the array before executing each(), FALSE will be returned.

current()

```
mixed current(array target_array)
```

The current() function returns the array value residing at the current pointer position of the *target_array*. Note that unlike the next(), prev(), and end() functions, it does not move the pointer. An example follows:

```
$fruits = array("apple", "orange", "banana");
$fruit = current($fruits); // returns "apple"
$fruit = next($fruits); // returns "orange"
$fruit = prev($fruits); // returns "apple"
```

end()

```
mixed end(array target_array)
```

The end() function moves the pointer to the last position of the *target_array*, returning the last element. An example follows:

```
$fruits = array("apple", "orange", "banana");
$fruit = current($fruits); // returns "apple"
$fruit = end($fruits); // returns "banana"
```

next()

```
mixed next(array target_array)
```

The next() function returns the array value residing at the position immediately following that of the current array pointer. An example follows:

```
$fruits = array("apple", "orange", "banana");
$fruit = next($fruits); // returns "orange"
$fruit = next($fruits); // returns "banana"
```

prev()

```
mixed prev(array target_array)
```

The prev() function returns the array value residing at the location preceding the current pointer location, or FALSE if the pointer resides at the first position in the array.

array_walk()

```
boolean array_walk(array input_array, callback function [, mixed userdata])
```

The array_walk() function will pass each element of *input_array* to the user-defined *function*. This is useful when you need to perform a particular action based on each array element. Note that if you intend to actually modify the array key/value pairs, you'll need to pass each key/value to the function as a reference.

The user-defined function must take two parameters as input: the first represents the array's current value and the second the current key. If the optional *userdata* parameter is present in the call to array_walk(), then its value will be passed as a third parameter to the user-defined function.

You are probably scratching your head, wondering why this function could possibly be of any use (c'mon, you can admit it). Admittedly, I initially thought the same, until I did a bit of brainstorming. Perhaps one of the most effective examples involves the sanity-checking of user-supplied form data. Suppose the user was asked to provide six keywords that he thought best-described his state. That form source code might look like that shown in Listing 5-1.

Listing 5-1. Using an Array in a Form

```
<form action="submitdata.php" method="post">
    <p>
    Provide up to six keywords that you believe best describe the state in
    which you live:
    </p>
    <p>Keyword 1:<br />
    <input type="text" name="keyword[]" size="20" maxlength="20" value="" /></p>
    <p>Keyword 2:<br />
    <input type="text" name="keyword[]" size="20" maxlength="20" value="" /></p>
    <p>Keyword 3:<br />
    <input type="text" name="keyword[]" size="20" maxlength="20" value="" /></p>
    <p>Keyword 4:<br />
    <input type="text" name="keyword[]" size="20" maxlength="20" value="" /></p>
    <p>Keyword 5:<br />
    <input type="text" name="keyword[]" size="20" maxlength="20" value="" /></p>
    <p>Keyword 6:<br />
    <input type="text" name="keyword[]" size="20" maxlength="20" value="" /></p>
    <p><input type="submit" value="Submit!"></p>
</form>
```

This form information is then sent to some script, referred to as submitdata.php in the form. This script should sanitize user data, then insert it into a database for later review. Using array_walk(), you can easily sanitize the keywords using a function stored in a form validation class:

```
<?php
    function sanitize_data(&$value, $key) {
        $value = strip_tags($value);
    }

    array_walk($_POST['keyword'],"sanitize_data");
?>
```

The result is that each value in the array is run through the strip_tags() function, which results in any HTML and PHP tags being deleted from the value. Of course, additional input checking would be necessary, but this should suffice to illustrate the utility of array_walk().

array_reverse()

array array_reverse(array *target* [, boolean *preserve_keys*])

The array_reverse() function reverses the element order of the *target* array. If the optional *preserve_keys* parameter is set to TRUE, the key mappings are maintained. Otherwise, each newly rearranged value will assume the key of the value previously presiding at that position.

```
$states = array("Delaware","Pennsylvania","New Jersey");
print_r(array_reverse($states));
// Array ( [0] => New Jersey [1] => Pennsylvania [2] => Delaware )
```

Contrast this behavior with that resulting from enabling *preserve_keys*:

```
$states = array("Delaware","Pennsylvania","New Jersey");
print_r(array_reverse($states,1));
// Array ( [2] => New Jersey [1] => Pennsylvania [0] => Delaware )
```

Arrays with associative keys are not affected by *preserve_keys*; key mappings are always preserved in this case.

array_flip()

array array_flip(array *target_array*)

The array_flip() function reverses the roles of the keys and their corresponding values in the array *target_array*. An example follows:

```
$state = array("Delaware","Pennsylvania","New Jersey");
$state = array_flip($state);
print_r($state);
// Array ( [Delaware] => 0 [Pennsylvania] => 1 [New Jersey] => 2 )
```

Determining Array Size and Uniqueness

A few functions are available for determining the number of total and unique array values. I'll introduce these functions in this section.

count()

```
integer count(array input_array [, int mode])
```

The count() function, quite simply, returns the total number of values found in the *input_array*. If the optional *mode* parameter is enabled (set to 1), the array will be counted recursively, a feature useful when counting all elements of a multidimensional array. An example follows:

```
$locations = array("Italy","Amsterdam",array("Boston","Des Moines"),"Miami");
echo count($locations,1);
```

This returns:

```
6
```

You may be scratching your head at this outcome, because there appears to be only five elements in the array. The array entity holding "Boston" and "Des Moines" is counted as an item, just as its contents are.

> **NOTE** *The* sizeof() *function is an alias of* count(). *It is functionally identical.*

array_count_values()

```
array array_count_values(array input_array)
```

The array_count_values() function returns an array consisting of associative key/value pairs. Each key represents a value found in the *input_array*, and its corresponding value denoting the frequency of that key's appearance (as a value) in the *input_array*. An example follows:

```
$states = array("Ohio","Iowa","Arizona","Iowa","Ohio");
$stateFrequency = array_count_values($states);
print_r($stateFrequency);
```

This returns:

```
Array ( [Ohio] => 2 [Iowa] => 2 [Arizona] => 1 )
```

array_unique()

```
array array_unique(array input_array)
```

The array_unique() function removes all duplicate values found in *input_array*, returning an array consisting of solely unique values. An example follows:

```
$states = array("Ohio","Iowa","Arizona","Iowa","Ohio");
$uniqueStates = array_unique($states);
print_r($uniqueStates);
```

This returns:

```
Array ( [0] => Ohio [1] => Iowa [2] => Arizona )
```

Sorting Arrays

To be sure, data sorting is one of computer science's core topics. Anybody who's had the pleasure of taking an entry-level programming class is well aware of sorting algorithms such as *bubble, heap, shell,* and *quick.* This subject rears its head so often during the application development process that the process is as common as creating an if conditional or a while loop, if the language offers a sorting library. This is the case with the PHP language, which offers a multitude of useful functions in this category. We'll review those functions in this section.

> **TIP** *By default PHP's sorting functions sort in accordance with the rules as specified by the English language. If you need to sort in another language, say French or German, you'll need to modify this default behavior by setting your locale using the setlocale() function.*

sort()

```
void sort(array target_array [, int sort_flags])
```

The sort() function sorts the *target_array*, ordering elements from lowest to highest value. Note that it doesn't return the sorted array. Instead, it sorts the array "in place," returning nothing regardless of outcome. The optional *sort_flags* parameter modifies the function's default behavior in accordance with its assigned value:

- SORT_NUMERIC: Sort items numerically. This is useful when sorting integers or floats.

- SORT_REGULAR: Sort items by their ASCII value. This means that B will come before a, for instance. Search the Internet for ASCII table to view a comprehensive character ordering.

- SORT_STRING: Sort items in a fashion that might better correspond with how a human might perceive the correct order. See natsort() for further information about this matter, introduced later in this section.

Consider an example. Suppose you wanted to sort exam grades from lowest to highest:

```
$grades = array(42,57,98,100,100,43,78,12);
sort($grades);
print_r($grades);
```

The outcome looks like this:

```
Array ( [0] => 12 [1] => 42 [2] => 43 [3] => 57 [4] => 78 [5] => 98
[6] => 100 [7] => 100 )
```

It's important to note that key/value associations are not maintained. Consider the following example:

```
$states = array("OH" => "Ohio", "CA" => "California", "MD" => "Maryland");
sort($states);
print_r($states);
```

Here's the output:

```
Array ( [0] => California [1] => Maryland [2] => Ohio )
```

To maintain these associations, use asort(), introduced later in this section.

natsort()

```
void natsort(array target_array)
```

The natsort() function is intended to offer a sorting mechanism comparable to those people normally use. The PHP manual offers an excellent example of what is meant by this; Consider the following items: picture1.jpg, picture2.jpg, picture10.jpg, picture20.jpg. Sorting these items using typical algorithms results in the following ordering:

```
picture1.jpg, picture10.jpg, picture2.jpg, picture20.jpg
```

Certainly not what you might have expected, right? The natsort() function resolves this dilemma, sorting the *target_array* in the order you would expect, like so:

```
picture1.jpg, picture2.jpg, picture10.jpg, picture20.jpg
```

natcasesort()

```
void natcasesort(array target_array)
```

The function natcasesort() is functionally identical to natsort(), except that it is case-insensitive. Returning to the file sorting dilemma raised in the natsort() section, suppose that the pictures were named like this: Picture1.JPG, picture2.jpg, PICTURE10.jpg, picture20.jpg. The natsort() function would do its best, sorting these items like so:

```
PICTURE10.jpg, Picture1.JPG, picture2.jpg, picture20.jpg
```

The natcasesort() function resolves this idiosyncrasy, sorting as you might expect:

```
Picture1.jpg, PICTURE10.jpg, picture2.jpg, picture20.jpg
```

rsort()

```
void rsort(array target_array [, int sort_flags])
```

The rsort() function is identical to sort(), except that it sorts array items in reverse (descending) order. An example follows:

```
$states = array("Ohio","Florida","Massachusetts","Montana");
sort($states);
print_r($states)
// Array ( [0] => Ohio [1] => Montana [2] => Massachusetts [3] => Florida )
```

If the optional *sort_flags* parameter is included, then the exact sorting behavior is determined by its value, as explained in the sort() section.

asort()

```
void asort(array target_array [,integer sort_flags])
```

The asort() function is identical to sort(), sorting the *target_array* in ascending order, except that the key/value correspondence is maintained. Consider an array that contains the states in the order in which they joined the Union:

```
$state[0] = "Delaware";
$state[1] = "Pennsylvania";
$state[2] = "New Jersey"
```

Sorting this array using sort() causes the associative correlation to be lost, which is probably a bad idea. Sorting using sort() and then outputting the results using print_r() results in the following:

```
Array ( [0] => Delaware [1] => New Jersey [2] => Pennsylvania )
```

However, sorting with rsort() results in:

```
Array ( [0] => Delaware [2] => New Jersey [1] => Pennsylvania )
```

If you use the optional *sort_flags* parameter, the exact sorting behavior is determined by its value, as described in the sort() section.

array_multisort()

```
boolean array_multisort(array array [, mixed arg [, mixed arg2...]])
```

The array_multisort() function can sort several arrays at once, and can sort multidimensional arrays in a number of fashions, returning TRUE on success and FALSE otherwise. It takes as input one or more arrays, each of which can be followed by flags that determine sorting behavior. There are two categories of sorting flags: order and type. Each flag is described in Table 5-1.

Table 5-1. array_multisort() Flags

FLAG	TYPE	PURPOSE
SORT_ASC	Order	Sort in ascending order
SORT_DESC	Order	Sort in descending order
SORT_REGULAR	Type	Compare items normally
SORT_NUMERIC	Type	Compare items numerically
SORT_STRING	Type	Compare items as strings

Consider an example. Suppose that you want to sort the surname column of a multidimensional array consisting of staff information. To ensure that the entire name (given-name surname) is sorted properly, you would then sort by the given name:

```php
<?php
    $staff["givenname"][0] = "Jason";
    $staff["givenname"][1] = "Manny";
    $staff["givenname"][2] = "Gary";
    $staff["givenname"][3] = "James";
    $staff["surname"][0] = "Gilmore";
    $staff["surname"][1] = "Champy";
    $staff["surname"][2] = "Grisold";
    $staff["surname"][3] = "Gilmore";

$res = array_multisort($staff["surname"],SORT_STRING,SORT_ASC,
                       $staff["givenname"],SORT_STRING,SORT_ASC);

print_r($staff);
?>
```

This returns the following:

```
Array ( [givenname] => Array ( [0] => Manny [1] => James [2] => Jason [3] => Gary )
         [surname] => Array ( [0] => Champy [1] => Gilmore [2] =>
                              Gilmore [3] => Grisold ) )
```

arsort()

```
void arsort(array array [, int sort_flags])
```

Like asort(), arsort() maintains key/value correlation. However, it sorts the array in reverse order. An example follows:

```php
$states = array("Delaware","Pennsylvania","New Jersey");
arsort($states);
print_r($states);
// Array ( [1] => Pennsylvania [2] => New Jersey [0] => Delaware )
```

If the optional *sort_flags* parameter is included, the exact sorting behavior is determined by its value, as described in the sort() section.

ksort()

```
integer ksort(array array [,int sort_flags])
```

The ksort() function sorts the input array *array* by its keys, returning TRUE on success and FALSE otherwise. If the optional *sort_flags* parameter is included, then the exact sorting behavior is determined by its value, as described in the sort() section. Keep in mind that the behavior will be applied to key sorting, rather than value sorting.

krsort()

```
integer krsort(array array [,int sort_flags])
```

The krsort() function operates identically to ksort(), sorting by key, except that it sorts in reverse (descending) order.

usort()

```
void usort(array array, callback function_name)
```

The usort() function offers a means for sorting an array using a user-defined comparison algorithm, embodied within a function. This is useful when you need to sort data in a fashion not offered by one of PHP's built-in sorting functions.

The user-defined function must take as input two arguments, and must return a negative integer, zero, or a positive integer based on whether the first argument is less than, equal to, or greater than the second argument. Not surprisingly, this function must be made available to the same scope in which usort() is being called.

A particularly applicable example of usort() involves the ordering of American-format dates. Suppose that you want to sort an array of dates in ascending order:

```php
<?php
$dates = array('10-10-2003', '2-17-2002', '2-16-2003', '1-01-2005', '10-10-2004');
sort($dates);
// Array ( [0] => 10-01-2002 [1] => 10-10-2003 [2] => 2-16-2003 [3] => 8-18-2002 )

natsort($dates);
// Array ( [2] => 2-16-2003 [3] => 8-18-2002 [1] => 10-01-2002 [0] => 10-10-2003 )

function DateSort($a, $b) {

    // If the dates are equal, do nothing.
    if($a == $b) return 0;

    // Dissassemble dates
    list($amonth, $aday, $ayear) = explode('-',$a);
    list($bmonth, $bday, $byear) = explode('-',$b);

    // Pad the month with a leading zero if leading number not present
    $amonth = str_pad($amonth, 2, "0", STR_PAD_LEFT);
    $bmonth = str_pad($bmonth, 2, "0", STR_PAD_LEFT);

    // Pad the day with a leading zero if leading number not present
    $aday = str_pad($aday, 2, "0", STR_PAD_LEFT);
    $bday = str_pad($bday, 2, "0", STR_PAD_LEFT);

    // Reassemble dates
    $a = $ayear . $amonth . $aday;
    $b = $byear . $bmonth . $bday;
```

```
    // Determine whether date $a > $date b
    return ($a > $b) ? 1 : -1;
}

usort($dates, 'DateSort');

print_r($dates);
?>
```

This returns the desired result:

```
Array ( [0] => 8-18-2002 [1] => 10-01-2002 [2] => 2-16-2003 [3] => 10-10-2003 )
```

Merging, Slicing, Splicing, and Dissecting Arrays

In this section, I introduce a number of functions that are capable of performing somewhat more complex array manipulation tasks, such as combining and merging multiple arrays, extracting a cross-section of array elements, and comparing arrays.

array_combine()

```
array array_combine(array keys, array values)
```

The array_combine() function produces a new array consisting of keys residing in the input parameter array *keys*, and corresponding values found in the input parameter array *values*. Note that both input arrays must be of equal size, and that neither can be empty. An example follows:

```
$abbreviations = array("AL","AK","AZ","AR");
$states = array("Alabama","Alaska","Arizona","Arkansas");
$stateMap = array_combine($abbreviations,$states);
print_r($stateMap);
```

This returns:

```
Array ( [AL] => Alabama [AK] => Alaska [AZ] => Arizona [AR] => Arkansas )
```

array_merge()

```
array array_merge(array input_array1, array input_array2 [..., array input_arrayN])
```

The array_merge() function appends arrays together, returning a single, unified array. The resulting array will begin with the first input array parameter, appending each subsequent array parameter in the order of appearance. If an input array contains a string key that already exists in the resulting array, that key/value pair will overwrite the pre-viously existing entry. This behavior does not hold true for numerical keys, in which case the key/value pair will be appended to the array. An example follows:

```
$face = array("J","Q","K","A");
$numbered = array("2","3","4","5","6","7","8","9");
$cards = array_merge($face, $numbered);
shuffle($cards);
print_r($cards);
```

This returns something along the lines of the following (your results will vary because of the shuffle):

```
Array ( [0] => 8 [1] => 6 [2] => K [3] => Q [4] => 9 [5] => 5
                  [6] => 3 [7] => 2 [8] => 7 [9] => 4 [10] => A [11] => J )
```

array_merge_recursive()

```
array array_merge_recursive(array input_array1, array input_array2 [, array...])
```

The array_merge_recursive() function operates identically to array_merge(), joining two or more arrays together to form a single, unified array. The difference between the two functions lies in the way that this function behaves when a string key located in one of the input arrays already exists within the resulting array. array_merge() will sim-ply overwrite the preexisting key/value pair, replacing it with the one found in the cur-rent input array. array_merge_recursive() will instead merge the values together, forming a new array with the preexisting key as its name. An example follows:

```
$class1 = array("John" => 100, "James" => 85);
$class2 = array("Micky" => 78, "John" => 45);
$classScores = array_merge_recursive($class1, $class2);
print_r($classScores);
```

This returns the following:

```
Array ( [John] => Array ( [0] => 100 [1] => 45 ) [James] => 85 [Micky] => 78 )
```

Note that the key "John" now points to a numerically indexed array consisting of two scores.

array_slice()

```
array array_slice(array input_array, int offset [, int length])
```

The array_slice() function returns the section of *input_array* starting at the key *offset*, and ending at position *offset* + *length*. A positive offset value will cause the slice to begin that many positions from the beginning of the array, while a negative offset will start the slice that many positions from the end of the array. If the optional *length* parameter is omitted, the slice will start at *offset* and end at the last element of the array. If *length* is provided and is positive, it will end at *offset + length* positions from the beginning of the array. Conversely, if *length* is provided and is negative, it will end at count(*input_array*) − *length* positions from the end of the array. Consider an example:

```
$states = array("Alabama", "Alaska", "Arizona", "Arkansas",
                "California", "Colorado", "Connecticut");
$subset = array_slice($states, 4);
print_r($subset);
```

This returns:

```
Array ( [0] => California [1] => Colorado [2] => Connecticut )
```

Consider a second example, this one involving a negative length:

```
$states = array("Alabama", "Alaska", "Arizona", "Arkansas",
                "California", "Colorado", "Connecticut");
$subset = array_slice($states, 2, -2);
print_r($subset);
```

This returns:

```
Array ( [0] => Arizona [1] => Arkansas [2] => California )
```

array_splice()

```
array array_splice(array input, int offset [, int length [, array replacement]])
```

The array_splice() function removes all elements of an array starting at offset, and ending at position *offset + length*, and will return those removed elements in the form of an array. A positive offset value will cause the splice to begin that many positions from the beginning of the array, while a negative offset will start the splice that many positions from the end of the array. If the optional *length* parameter is omitted, all elements from the offset position to the conclusion of the array will be removed. If *length* is provided and is positive, the splice will end at *offset + length* positions from the beginning of the array. Conversely, if *length* is provided and is negative, the splice will end at count(*input_array*) − *length* positions from the end of the array. An example follows:

```
$states = array("Alabama", "Alaska", "Arizona", "Arkansas", "California",
"Connecticut");
$subset = array_splice($states, 4);
```

```
print_r($states);
print_r($subset);
```

This returns:

```
Array ( [0] => Alabama [1] => Alaska [2] => Arizona [3] => Arkansas )
Array ( [0] => California [1] => Connecticut )
```

You can use the optional parameter *replacement* to specify an array that will replace the target segment. An illustration follows:

```
$states = array("Alabama", "Alaska", "Arizona", "Arkansas", "California",
"Connecticut");
$subset = array_splice($states, 2, -1, array("New York", "Florida"));
print_r($states);
```

This returns the following:

```
Array ( [0] => Alabama [1] => Alaska [2] => New York [3] => Florida [4] => Connecticut )
```

array_intersect()

```
array array_intersect(array input_array1, array input_array2 [, array...])
```

The array_intersect() function returns a key-preserved array consisting only of those values present in *input_array1* that are also present in each of other the input arrays. An example follows:

```
$array1 = array("OH","CA","NY","HI","CT");
$array2 = array("OH","CA","HI","NY","IA");
$array3 = array("TX","MD","NE","OH","HI");
$intersection = array_intersect($array1, $array2, $array3);
print_r($intersection);
```

This returns:

```
Array ( [0] => OH [3] => HI )
```

Note that array_intersect() only considers two items to be equal if they also share the same datatype.

array_intersect_assoc()

array array_intersect(array *input_array1*, array *input_array2* [, array...])

The function array_intersect_assoc() operates identically to array_intersect(), except that it also considers array keys in the comparison. Therefore, only key/value pairs located in *input_array1* that are also found in all other input arrays will be returned in the resulting array. An example follows:

```
$array1 = array("OH" => "Ohio", "CA" => "California", "HI" => "Hawaii");
$array2 = array("50" => "Hawaii", "CA" => "California", "OH" => "Ohio");
$array3 = array("TX" => "Texas", "MD" => "Maryland", "OH" => "Ohio");
$intersection = array_intersect_assoc($array1, $array2, $array3);
print_r($intersection);
```

This returns:

```
Array ( [OH] => Ohio )
```

Note that Hawaii was not returned because the corresponding key in $array2 is "50", rather than "HI" (as is the case in the other two arrays.)

array_diff()

array array_diff(array *input_array1*, array *input_array2* [, array...])

The function array_diff() returns those values located in *input_array1* that are not located in any of the other input arrays. This function is essentially to the opposite of array_intersect(). An example follows:

```
$array1 = array("OH","CA","NY","HI","CT");
$array2 = array("OH","CA","HI","NY","IA");
$array3 = array("TX","MD","NE","OH","HI");
$diff = array_diff($array1, $array2, $array3);
print_r($intersection);
```

This returns:

```
Array ( [0] => CT )
```

array_diff_assoc()

```
array array_diff_assoc(array input_array1, array input_array2 [, array...])
```

The function array_diff_assoc() operates identically to array_diff(),except that it also considers array keys in the comparison. Therefore only key/value pairs located in *input_array1*, and not appearing in any of the other input arrays, will be returned in the result array. An example follows:

```
$array1 = array("OH" => "Ohio", "CA" => "California", "HI" => "Hawaii");
$array2 = array("50" => "Hawaii", "CA" => "California", "OH" => "Ohio");
$array3 = array("TX" => "Texas", "MD" => "Maryland", "KS" => "Kansas");
$diff = array_diff_assoc($array1, $array2, $array3);
print_r($diff);
```

This returns:

```
Array ( [HI] => Hawaii )
```

Other Useful Array Functions

In this section I introduce a number of array functions that perhaps don't easily fall into one of the prior sections, but are nonetheless quite useful.

array_rand()

```
mixed array_rand(array input_array [, int num_entries])
```

The array_rand() function will return one or more keys found in *input_array*. If you omit the optional *num_entries* parameter, only one random value will be returned. If *num_entries* is set to greater than one, that many keys will be returned. An example follows:

```
$states = array("Ohio" => "Columbus", "Iowa" => "Des Moines","Arizona" => "Phoenix");
$randomStates = array_rand($states, 2);
print_r($randomStates);
```

This returns:

```
Array ( [0] => Arizona [1] => Ohio )
```

shuffle()

```
void shuffle(array input_array)
```

The shuffle() function randomly reorders the elements of *input_array*. Consider an array containing values representing playing cards:

```
$cards = array("jh","js","jd","jc","qh","qs","qd","qc",
               "kh","ks","kd","kc","ah","as","ad","ac");
// shuffle the cards
shuffle($cards);
print_r($positions);
```

This returns something along the lines of the following (your results will vary because of the shuffle):

```
Array ( [0] => js [1] => ks [2] => kh [3] => jd
          [4] => ad [5] => qd [6] => qc [7] => ah
          [8] => kc [9] => qh [10] => kd [11] => as
          [12] => ac [13] => jc [14] => jh [15] => qs )
```

array_sum()

```
mixed array_sum(array input_array)
```

The array_sum() function adds all the values of *input_array* together, returning the final sum. Of course, the values should be either integers or floats. If other datatypes (a string, for example) are found in the array, they will be ignored. An example follows:

```
<?php
    $grades = array(42,"hello",42);
    $total = array_sum($grades);
    print $total;
?>
```

This returns:

array_chunk()

```
array array_chunk(array input_array, int size [, boolean preserve_keys])
```

The array_chunk() function breaks *input_array* into a multidimensional array consisting of several smaller arrays consisting of *size* elements. If the input array can't be evenly divided by *size*, the last array will consist of fewer than *size* elements. Enabling the optional parameter *preserve_keys* will preserve each value's corresponding key. Omitting or disabling this parameter results in numerical indexing starting from zero for each array. An example follows:

```
$cards = array("jh","js","jd","jc","qh","qs","qd","qc",
               "kh","ks","kd","kc","ah","as","ad","ac");
// shuffle the cards
shuffle($cards);
// Use array_chunk() to divide the cards into four equal "hands"
$hands = array_chunk($cards, 4);
print_r($hands);
```

This returns the following (your results will vary because of the shuffle):

```
Array ( [0] => Array ( [0] => jc [1] => ks [2] => js [3] => qd )
        [1] => Array ( [0] => kh [1] => qh [2] => jd [3] => kd )
        [2] => Array ( [0] => jh [1] => kc [2] => ac [3] => as )
        [3] => Array ( [0] => ad [1] => ah [2] => qc [3] => qs ) )
```

Summary

Arrays play an indispensable role in programming, and are ubiquitous in every imaginable type of application, Web-based or not. The purpose of this chapter was to bring you up to speed regarding many of the PHP functions that will make your programming life much easier as you deal with these arrays.

The next chapter focuses on yet another very important topic: object-oriented programming. This topic has a particularly special role in PHP 5, because the process has been entirely redesigned for this major release.

CHAPTER 6

Object-Oriented PHP

THIS CHAPTER AND the next introduce what is surely PHP 5's shining star: the vast improvements and enhancements to PHP's object-oriented functionality. If you're familiar with PHP, you may be wondering what the buzz is all about. After all, PHP 4 offered object-oriented capabilities, right? Although the answer to this question is technically yes, version 4's object-oriented functionality was less than optimal. Although the very basic premises of object-oriented programming (OOP) were offered in version 4, several deficiencies existed, including:

- An unorthodox object referencing methodology

- No means for setting the scope (public, private, protected, abstract) of fields or methods

- Lack of a sensible convention for naming constructors

- Absence of object destructors

- Lack of an object cloning feature

- Lack of support for interfaces

In fact, PHP 4's adherence to the traditional OOP model is so bad that in my first book, *A Programmer's Introduction to PHP 4.0*, I devoted more time to demonstrating hacks than actually introducing useful OOP features. I'm happy to announce that version 5 eliminates all of the aforementioned hindrances. PHP 5 brings substantial improvements to the original implementation, as well as a bevy of new OO features. This chapter and the following aim to introduce these new features and enhanced functionality. Before doing so, however, I'll take a moment to discuss the advantages of the OOP development model.

The Benefits of OOP

The birth of object-oriented programming represented a major paradigm shift in development strategy, refocusing attention on an application's data rather than its logic. To put it another way, OOP shifts the focus from a program's procedural events towards the real-life entities it ultimately models. The result is an application closely resembling the world around us.

In this section, I'll examine three of OOP's foundational concepts: *encapsulation*, *inheritance*, and *polymorphism*. Together, these three ideals form the basis for the most powerful programming model yet devised.

Encapsulation

Programmers are typically rabidly curious individuals. We enjoy taking things apart, and learning how all of the little pieces work together. Although mentally gratifying, attaining such in-depth knowledge of an item's inner-workings isn't a requirement. For example, millions of people use a computer every day, yet few know how it actually works. The same idea applies to automobiles, microwaves, televisions, and any number of commonplace items we use on a regular basis. We can get away with such ignorance through the use of interfaces. For example, you know that turning the radio dial allows you to change radio stations (610 AM, for example); never mind the fact that what you're actually doing is telling the radio to listen to the signal transmitted at 610,000 hertz, a feat accomplished using a demodulator, and so on and so forth. Failing to understand this process does not prevent you from using the radio, because the interface hides such details from you. The practice of separating the user from the true inner workings of an application through well-known interfaces is known as *encapsulation*.

Object-oriented programming promotes the same notion of hiding the inner workings of the application from the user. You're expected to manipulate data through a series of well-known interfaces, known as *objects*. In fact, you are typically required to do so. Objects are created from a template known as a *class*, used to embody both the data and the behavior you would expect of a particular entity. This class exposes certain behaviors through functions known as *methods*, which are in turn used to manipulate class characteristics, known as *fields*. This strategy offers several advantages:

- The developer can change the application implementation without affecting the user, because the user's only interaction with the application is via the interface.

- The potential for user error is reduced, because of the control exercised over the user's interaction with the application.

Inheritance

Despite the chaos that typically engulfs our lives, much of what surrounds us can be modeled using a fairly well-defined set of rules. Take, for example, the concept of an employee. An employee can be loosely defined as somebody who works for an organization. All employees share a common set of characteristics: a name, employee ID, and wage, for instance. However, there are many different classes of employees: clerks, supervisors, cashiers, and chief executive offers, among others, each of which likely possesses some superset of those characteristics defined by the generic employee definition. In object-oriented terms, these various employee classes *inherit* the general employee definition, and all of the characteristics and behaviors that contribute to this definition. In turn, each of these specific employee classes could be in turn inherited by yet another, more specific class. For example, the "clerk" type might be inherited by a day clerk and a night clerk, each of which inherits all traits specified by both the employee definition and the clerk definition. Building on this idea, you could then later create a "human" class, and then make the "employee" class a subclass of human. The effect would be that the employee class and all of its derived classes (clerk, cashier, CEO, and so on) would immediately inherit all characteristics and behaviors defined by human.

The object-oriented development methodology places great stock in the concept of inheritance. This strategy promotes code reusability, because it assumes that one will be able to use well-designed classes within numerous applications, because the code in these classes will be of a degree of abstraction allowing for such reuse.

Polymorphism

Polymorphism, a term originating from the Greek language meaning "having multiple forms," is perhaps the coolest feature of object-oriented programming. Simply defined, polymorphism defines OOP's ability to redefine, or morph, a class's characteristic or behavior depending upon the context in which it is used. This is perhaps best explained with an example.

Returning to the employee example from the previous section, suppose that a behavior titled clock_in was included within the employee definition. For employees of class "clerk," this behavior might involve actually using a time clock to timestamp a card. For other types of employees, "programmers" for instance, clocking in might involve signing on to the corporate network. Although both classes derive this behavior from the employee class, the actual implementation of each is dependent upon the context in which "clocking in" is implemented. This is the power of polymorphism.

These three key OOP concepts, encapsulation, inheritance, and polymorphism, are touched upon as they apply to PHP's OOP implementation through this chapter and the next.

Key OOP Concepts

This section introduces key object-oriented implementation concepts, including PHP-specific examples.

Classes

Our everyday environment consists of innumerable entities: plants, people, vehicles, food...we could go on for hours just listing them. Each entity is defined by a particular set of characteristics and behaviors that ultimately serve to define the entity for what it is. For example, a vehicle might be defined as having characteristics such as color, number of tires, make, model, and capacity, and behaviors such as stop, go, turn, and honk horn. In object-oriented programming, such an embodiment of an entity's defining attributes and behaviors is known as a *class*.

Classes are intended to represent those real-life items that you'd like to manipulate within an application. For example, if you wanted to create an application for managing a public library, you'd probably want to include classes representing books, magazines, staff, special events, patrons, and anything else that would require oversight. Each of these entities embodies a certain set of characteristics and behaviors, better known in OOP as *fields* and *methods* respectively, that defines the entity as what it is. PHP's generalized class creation syntax follows:

```
class classname
{
    // Field declarations defined here
    // Method declarations defined here
}
```

Listing 6-1 depicts a class representing organizational staff members.

Listing 6-1. Class Creation

```
class Staff
{
    private $name;
    private $title;
    protected $wage;
    protected function clockIn() {
        echo "Member $this->name clocked in at ".date("h:i:s");
    }
    protected function clockOut() {
        echo "Member $this->name clocked out at ".date("h:i:s");
    }
}
```

This class, titled Staff, defines three fields: name, title, and wage, in addition to two methods: clock in and clock out. Don't worry if you're not familiar with some of the grammar and syntax (private/protected and $this, particularly); I'll cover each of these topics in detail soon enough.

Objects

A class is quite similar to a recipe, or template, that defines both the characteristics and behavior of a particular concept or tangible item. This template provides a basis from which you can create specific instances of the entity the class models, better known as *objects*. For example, an employee management application may include a Staff class, which serves as the template for managing employee information. Based on these set specifications, you can create and maintain specific instances of the staff class, Sally and Jim, for example.

NOTE *The practice of creating objects based on predefined classes is often referred to as* class instantiation.

Objects are created using the new keyword, like this:

```
$employee = new Staff();
```

Once the object is created, all of the characteristics and behaviors defined within the class are made available to the newly instantiated object. Exactly how this is accomplished is revealed in the following sections.

Fields

Fields are attributes intended to describe some aspect of a class. They are quite similar to normal PHP variables, except for a few minor differences, which I'll touch upon in this section. You'll also learn how to declare and invoke fields, and all about field scopes.

Declaring Fields

The rules regarding field declaration are quite similar to those in place for variable declaration: essentially, there are none. Because PHP is a loosely-typed language, fields don't even necessarily need to be declared at all; they can simply be created and assigned simultaneously by a class object, although you'll rarely want to do that. Instead, it is common practice for fields to be declared at the beginning of the class. Optionally, you can assign them initial values at this time. An example follows:

```
class Staff
{
    public $name = "Lackey";
    private $wage;
}
```

In this example, the two fields, name and wage, are prefaced with a scope descriptor (public or private), a common practice when declaring fields. Once declared, each field can be used under the terms accorded to it by the scope descriptor. If you don't know what role scope plays in class fields, don't worry; that topic is covered later in this chapter.

Invoking Fields

Fields are referred to using the -> operator, and are not prefaced with a dollar sign as is the case with variables. Furthermore, because a field's value typically is specific to a given object, it is correlated to said object like this:

```
$object->field
```

For example, the Staff class described at the beginning of this chapter included the fields name, title, and wage. If you created an object named $employee of type Staff, you would refer to these fields like this:

```
$employee->name
$employee->title
$employee->wage
```

When you refer to a field from within the class in which it is defined, it is still prefaced with the -> operator, although instead of correlating it to the class name, you use the $this keyword. $this implies that you're referring to the field residing in the same class in which the field is being accessed or manipulated. Therefore, if you were to create a method for setting the name field in the aforementioned Staff class, it might look like this:

```
function setName($name)
{
    $this->name = $name;
}
```

Field Scopes

PHP supports five class field scopes: *public, private, protected, final,* and *static.* The first four are introduced in this section, and the static scope is introduced in the later section, "Static Class Members."

Public

You can declare fields in the public scope simply by prefacing the field with the keyword public. An example follows:

```
class Staff
{
    public $name;
    /* Other field and method declarations follow... */
}
```

Public fields can then be manipulated and accessed directly by a corresponding object, like so:

```
$employee = new Staff();
$employee->name = "Mary Swanson";
$name = $employee->name;
echo "New staff member: $name";
```

Not surprisingly, executing this code results in:

```
New staff member: Mary Swanson
```

Although this might seem like a logical means for maintaining class fields, public fields are actually generally considered taboo to OOP, and for good reason. The reason for shunning such an implementation is that such direct access robs the class of a convenient means for enforcing any sort of data validation. For example, what is to prevent the user from assigning "name" like so:

```
$employee->name = "12345";
```

This is certainly not the kind of input you were expecting. To prevent such mishaps from occurring, two solutions are available. One solution involves encapsulating the data within the object, making it available only via a series of interfaces, known as *public methods*. Data encapsulated in this way is said to be *private* in scope. The second recommended solution involves the use of *properties*, and is actually quite similar to the first, although it is a tad more convenient in most cases. Private scoping is introduced next, whereas properties are discussed in the later section, "Properties."

Private

Private fields are only accessible from within the class in which they are defined.

```
class Staff
{
    private $name;
    private $telephone;
}
```

Fields designated as private are not directly accessible by an instantiated object, nor are they available to subclasses. If you want to make these fields available to subclasses, consider using the protected scope instead, introduced next. Instead, private fields must be accessed via publicly exposed interfaces, which satisfies one of OOP's main tenets introduced at the beginning of this chapter: data encapsulation. Consider the following example, in which a private field is manipulated by a public method:

```
<?php
  class Staff
  {
     private $name;
     public function setName($name) {
        $this->name = $name;
     }
  }
  $staff = new Staff;
  $staff->setName("Mary");
?>
```

Encapsulating the management of such fields within a method enables the developer to maintain tight control over how that field is set. For example, you could add to the setName() method's capabilities, validating that the name is set to solely alphabetical characters, and ensuring that it isn't blank. This strategy is much more reliable than leaving it to the end user to provide valid information.

protected

Just like functions often require variables intended for use only within the function, classes can include fields used for solely internal purposes. Such fields are deemed *protected*, and are prefaced accordingly:

```
class Staff
{
     protected $wage;
}
```

Protected fields are also made available to inherited classes for access and manipulation, a trait not shared by private fields. Any attempt by an object to access a protected field will result in a fatal error. Therefore, if you plan on extending the class, you should use protected fields in lieu of private fields.

final

Marking a field as final prevents it from being overridden by a subclass, a matter I'll discuss in further detail in the next chapter. A finalized field is declared like so:

```
class Staff
{
     final $ssn;
     ...
}
```

You can also declare methods as final; the procedure for doing so is described in the later section, "Methods."

Properties

Properties are a particularly convincing example of the powerful features OOP has to offer, ensuring protection of fields by forcing access and manipulation to take place through methods, yet allowing the data to be accessed as if it were a public field. These methods, known as *accessors* and *mutators*, or more lovingly as *getters* and *setters*, are automatically triggered whenever the field is accessed or manipulated, respectively.

Unfortunately, as applied to properties, PHP 5 does not offer the functionality that you might be used to if you're familiar with other OO-languages like C++ and Java. Therefore, you'll need to make do with using public methods for imitating such functionality. For example, you might create getter and setter methods for the property name, by declaring two functions, getName() and setName(), respectively, and embedding the appropriate syntax within each. I offer an example of this strategy at the conclusion of this section.

PHP 5 does offer some semblance of support for properties, which does offer a few interesting features. This support is made available by overloading the __set and __get methods. These methods are invoked if you attempt to reference a member variable that does not exist within the class definition. You could use them for a variety of purposes, for example invoking an error message, or even extending the class by actually creating new variables on the fly. Each is introduced in the following sections.

__set()

```
boolean __set([string property_name],[mixed value_to_assign])
```

The *mutator*, or *setter* method, is responsible for both hiding implementation and validating class data before assigning it to a class field. It takes as input a property name and a corresponding value, returning TRUE if the method is successfully executed, and FALSE otherwise. An example follows:

```
class Staff
{
    var $name;
    function __set($propName, $propValue)
    {
        echo "Nonexistent variable: \$$propName!";
    }
}

$employee = new Staff();
$employee->name = "Mario";
$employee->title = "Executive Chef";
```

This results in the following output:

```
Nonexistent variable: $title!
```

Of course, you could use this method to actually extend the class with new properties, like this:

```
class Staff
{
    var $name;
    function __set($propName, $propValue)
    {
        $this->$propName = $propValue;
    }
}

$employee = new Staff();
$employee->name = "Mario";
$employee->title = "Executive Chef";
echo "Name: ".$employee->name;
echo "<br />";
echo "Title: ".$employee->title;
```

This results in:

```
Name: Mario
Title: Executive Chef
```

__get()

```
boolean __get([string property_name])
```

The *accessor*, or *getter* method, is responsible for encapsulating the code required for retrieving a class variable. It takes as input one parameter, the name of the property whose value you'd like to retrieve. It should return the value TRUE on successful execution, and FALSE otherwise. An example follows:

```
class Staff
{
    var $name;
    var $city;
    protected $wage;

    function __get($propName)
    {
        echo "__get called!<br />";
        $vars = array("name","city");
        if (in_array($propName, $vars))
        {
            return $this->$propName;
        } else {
            return "No such variable!";
```

```
            }
        }

    }

    $employee = new Staff();
    $employee->name = "Mario";

    echo $employee->name."<br />";
    echo $employee->age;
```

This returns the following:

```
Mario
__get called!
No such variable!
```

Creating Custom Getters and Setters

Frankly, although I see some benefits to the aforementioned __set() and __get() methods, they really aren't sufficient for managing properties in a complex object-oriented application. Because PHP doesn't offer support for the creation of properties in the fashion that Java or C# does, you'll need to implement your own methodology. I prefer to create two methods for each private field, like so:

```php
<?php
class Staff {
    private $name;
    // Getter
    public function getName() {
        return $this->name;
    }
    // Setter
    public function setName($name) {
        $this->name = $name;
    }
}
?>
```

Although such a strategy doesn't offer the same convenience as properties do, it does encapsulate management and retrieval tasks using a standardized naming convention. Of course, you should add additional validation functionality to the setter, however this simple example should suffice to drive the point home.

Constants

You can define *constants*, or values that are not intended to change, within a class. These values will remain unchanged throughout the lifetime of any object instantiated from that class. Class constants are created like so:

```
const NAME = 'VALUE';
```

For example, suppose you created a math class that contained a number of methods defining mathematical functions, in addition to numerous constants:

```
class math_functions
{
    const PI = '3.14159265';
    const E = '2.7182818284';
    const EULER = '0.5772156649';
    /* define other constants and methods here... */
}
```

Class constants can then be called like this:

```
echo math_functions::PI;
```

Methods

A *method* is quite similar to a function, except that it is intended to define the behavior of a particular class. Like a function, a method can accept arguments as input and can return a value to the caller. Methods are also invoked like functions, except that the method is prefaced with the name of the object invoking the method, like this:

```
$object->method_name();
```

In this section you'll learn all about methods, including method declaration, method invocation, and scope.

Declaring Methods

Methods are created in exactly the same fashion as functions, using identical syntax. The only difference between methods and normal functions is that the method declaration is typically prefaced with a scope descriptor. The generalized syntax follows:

```
scope function functionName()
{
    /* Function body goes here */
}
```

For example, if you wanted to declare a public method titled `calculateSalary()`, it might look like this:

```php
public function calculateSalary()
{
    return $this->wage * $this->hours;
}
```

In this example, the method is directly invoking two class fields, `wage` and `hours`, using the $this keyword. It calculates a salary by multiplying the two field values together, and returning the result just like a function might. Note, however, that a method isn't confined to working solely with class fields; it's perfectly valid to pass in arguments in the same way you can with a function.

> **TIP** *In the case of public methods, you can forego explicitly declaring the scope, and just declare the method like you would a function (without any scope).*

Invoking Methods

Methods are invoked almost exactly in the same fashion as functions. Continuing with the previous example, you could invoke the `calculateSalary()` method like so:

```php
$employee = new staff("Janie");
$salary = $employee->calculateSalary();
```

Method Scopes

PHP supports six method scopes: *public, private, protected, abstract, final,* and *static*. The first five scopes are introduced in this section. The sixth, static, is introduced in the later section, "Static Members."

Public

Public methods can be accessed from anywhere, at any time. You declare a public method by prefacing it with the keyword `public`, or by foregoing any prefacing whatsoever. The following example demonstrates both declaration practices, in addition to demonstrating how public methods can be called from outside the class:

```php
<?php
    class Visitors
    {
        public function greetVisitor()
        {
```

```
        echo "Hello<br />";
    }
    function sayGoodbye()
    {
        echo "Goodbye<br />";
    }
}
Visitors::greetVisitor();
$visitor = new Visitors();
$visitor->sayGoodbye();
?>
```

The result:

```
Hello
Goodbye
```

Private

Methods marked as *private* are only available for use within the originating class, and cannot be called by the instantiated object, nor by any of the originating class's subclasses. Methods solely intended to be helpers for other methods located within the class should be marked as private. For example, consider a method, called validateCardNumber(), used to determine the syntactical validity of a patron's library card number. Although this method would certainly prove useful for satisfying a number of tasks, such as creating patrons and self-checkout, the function has no use when executed alone. Therefore validateCardNumber() should be marked as private, like this:

```
private function validateCardNumber($number)
{
    if (! ereg('^([0-9]{4})-([0-9]{3})-([0-9]{2})') ) return FALSE;
      else return TRUE;
}
```

Attempts to call this method from an instantiated object result in a fatal error.

Protected

Class methods marked as *protected* are available only to the originating class and its subclasses. Such methods might be used for helping the class or subclass perform internal computations. For example, before retrieving information about a particular staff member, you might want to verify the employee identification number (EIN), passed in as an argument to the class instantiator. You would then verify this EIN for syntactical correctness using the verify_ein() method. Because this method is intended for use only by other methods within the class, and could potentially be useful to classes derived from Staff, it should be declared protected:

```php
<?php
    class Staff
    {
        private $ein;
        function __construct($ein)
        {
            if ($this->verify_ein($ein)) {

                echo "EIN verified. Finish";
            }

        }
        protected function verify_ein($ein)
        {
            return TRUE;
        }
    }
    $employee = new Staff("123-45-6789");
?>
```

Attempts to call verify_ein() from outside of the class will result in a fatal error, because of its protected scope status.

Abstract

Abstract methods are special in that they are only declared within a parent class, but implemented in child classes. Only classes declared as abstract can contain abstract methods. You might declare an abstract method if you'd like to define an API that can later be used as a model for implementation. A developer would know that his particular implementation of that method should work as long as he meets all requirements as defined by the abstract method. Abstract methods are declared like this:

```php
abstract function methodName();
```

Suppose that you wanted to create an abstract Staff class, which would then serve as the base class for a variety of staff types (manager, clerk, cashier, and so on):

```php
abstract class Staff
{
    abstract function hire();
    abstract function fire();
    abstract function promote();
    abstract demote();
}
```

This class could then be extended by the respective staffing classes, like manager, clerk, and cashier. In the next chapter, I'll expand upon this concept, and look much more deeply at abstract classes.

Final

Marking a method as *final* prevents it from being overridden by a subclass. A finalized method is declared like this:

```
class staff
{
    ...
    final function getName() {
    ...
    }
}
```

Attempts to later override a finalized method results in a fatal error.

> **NOTE** *The topics of class inheritance and the overriding of methods and fields are discussed in the next chapter.*

Type Hinting

Type hinting is a feature new to PHP 5. Type hinting ensures that the object being passed to the method is indeed a member of the expected class. For example, it makes sense that only objects of class staff should be passed to the take_lunchbreak() method. Therefore you can preface the method definition's sole input parameter $employee with staff, enforcing this rule. An example follows:

```
private function take_lunchbreak (staff $employee)
{
    ...
}
```

Keep in mind that type hinting only works for objects. You can't offer hints for types such as integers, floats, or strings.

Constructors and Destructors

Often, you'll want to execute a number of tasks when creating and destroying objects. For example, you might want to immediately assign several fields of a newly instantiated object. However, if you have to do so manually, you'll almost certainly forget to execute all of the required tasks. Object-oriented programming goes a long way towards removing the possibility for such errors by offering special methods called *constructors* and *destructors*, which automate the object creation and destruction process.

Constructors

You often want to initialize certain fields and even trigger the execution of methods found when an object is newly instantiated. There's nothing wrong with doing so immediately after instantiation, but it would be easier if this were done for you automatically. Such a mechanism exists in OOP, known as a *constructor*. Quite simply, a constructor is defined as a block of code that automatically executes at the time of object instantiation. OOP constructors offer a number of advantages:

- Constructors can accept parameters, which are assigned to specific object fields at creation time.

- Constructors can call class methods or other functions.

- Class constructors can call on other constructors, including those from the class parent.

In this section, I'll review how all these advantages work with PHP 5's improved constructor functionality.

> **NOTE** *PHP 4 also offered class constructors, except using a different, more cumbersome syntax than that offered in version 5. Version 4 constructors were simply class methods of the same name as the class it represented. Such a convention made it tedious to move or rename a class. The new constructor naming convention resolves these issues. For reasons of compatibility, however, if a class is found to not contain a constructor satisfying the new naming convention, that class will then be searched for a method bearing the same name as the class; if located, this method is considered the constructor.*

PHP recognizes constructors by the name __construct. The general syntax for constructor declaration follows:

```
function __construct([argument1, argument2, ..., argumentN])
{
    /* Class initialization code */
}
```

As an example, suppose you wanted to immediately populate certain book fields with information specific to a supplied ISBN. For example, you might want to know the title and author of the book, in addition to how many copies the library owns, and how many are presently available for loan.

```php
<?php
    class book
    {
        private $title;
```

```
    private $isbn;
    private $copies;

    public function __construct($isbn)
    {
        $this->setIsbn($isbn);
        $this->getTitle();
        $this->getNumberCopies();
    }

    public function setIsbn($isbn)
    {
        $this->isbn = $isbn;
    }

    public function getTitle() {
        $this->title = "Practical Python";
        print "Title: ".$this->title."<br />";
    }

    public function getNumberCopies() {
        $this->copies = "5";
        print "Number copies available: ".$this->copies."<br />";
    }
}

$book = new book("1590590066");
?>
```

This results in:

```
Title: Practical Python
Number copies available: 5
```

Although of course a real-life implementation would likely involve somewhat more intelligent *get* methods (methods that query a database, for example), the point is made. Instantiating the book object results in the automatic invocation of the constructor, which in turn calls the setIsbn(), getTitle(), and getNumberCopies() methods. If you know that such method should be called whenever a new object is instantiated, you're far better off automating the calls via the constructor than attempting to manually call them yourself.

Additionally, if you would like to make sure that these methods are called only via the constructor, you should set their scope to private, ensuring that they cannot be directly called by the object nor by a subclass.

Invoking Parent Constructors

PHP does not automatically call the parent constructor; you must call it explicitly using the parent keyword.

An example follows:

```php
<?php
class Staff
{
    protected $name;
    protected $title;

    function __construct()
    {
        echo "<p>Staff constructor called!</p>";
    }
}

class Manager extends Staff
{
    function __construct()
    {
        parent::__construct();
        echo "<p>Manager constructor called!</p>";
    }
}

$employee = new Manager();
?>
```

This results in:

```
Staff constructor called!
Manager constructor called!
```

Neglecting to include the call to parent::__construct() results in the invocation of only the manager constructor, like this:

```
Manager constructor called!
```

Invoking Unrelated Constructors

You can invoke class constructors that don't have any relation to the instantiated object, simply by prefacing __constructor with the class name, like so:

```
classname::__construct()
```

As an example, assume that the `Manager` and `Staff` classes used in the previous example bear no hierarchical relationship; instead, they are simply two classes located within the same library. The `Staff` constructor could still be invoked within `Manager`'s constructor, like this:

```
Staff::__construct()
```

Calling the `Staff` constructor like this results in the same outcome as that shown in the previous example.

> **NOTE** *You may be wondering why I've neglected to discuss the extremely useful constructor overloading feature, available in many OOP languages. I haven't forgotten; PHP does not support this feature.*

Destructors

Although objects were automatically destroyed upon script completion in PHP 4, it wasn't possible to customize this cleanup process. With the introduction of destructors in PHP 5, this constraint is no more. Destructors are created like any other method, but must be titled __destruct(). An example follows:

```php
<?php
    class Book
    {
        private $title;
        private $isbn;
        private $copies;

        function __construct($isbn)
        {
            echo "<p>Book class instance created.</p>";
        }

        function __destruct()
        {
            echo "<p>Book class instance destroyed.</p>";
        }
    }

    $book = new Book("1893115852");
?>
```

Here's the result:

```
Book class instance created.
Book class instance destroyed.
```

Of course, when the script is complete, PHP will destroy any objects that reside in memory. Therefore, if the instantiated class and any information created as a result of the instantiation reside in RAM, you're not required to explicitly declare a destructor. However, if less volatile data were created (say, stored in a database) as a result of the instantiation, and should be destroyed at the time of object destruction, you'll need to create a custom destructor.

Static Class Members

Sometimes it's useful to create fields and methods that are not invoked by any particular object, but rather are pertinent to, and are shared by, all class instances. For example, suppose that you wrote a class that tracks the number of Web page visitors. You wouldn't want the visitor count resetting back to zero every time the class was instantiated, and therefore should set the field to be of the static scope.

```php
<?php
    class visitors
    {
        private static $visitors = 0;

        function __construct()
        {
            self::$visitors++;
        }
        static function getVisitors()
        {
            return self::$visitors;
        }

    }
    /* Instantiate the visitors class. */
    $visits = new visitors();

    echo visitors::getVisitors()."<br />";
    /* Instantiate another visitors class. */
    $visits2 = new visitors();

    echo visitors::getVisitors()."<br />";

?>
```

The results are:

```
1
2
```

Because the $visitors field was declared as static, any changes made to its value (in this case via the class constructor) are reflected across all instantiated objects. Also note that static fields and methods are referred to using the self keyword and class name, rather than via the this and arrow operators. This is because referring to static fields using the means allowed for their "regular" siblings is not possible, and will result in a syntax error if attempted.

> **NOTE** *You can't use $this within a class to refer to a field declared as* static.

The instanceof Keyword

Another newcomer to PHP5 is the addition of the instanceof keyword. With it, you can determine whether an object is an instance of a class, is a subclass of a class, or implements a particular interface, and do something accordingly. For example, suppose you wanted to learn whether an object called manager is derived from the class Staff:

```
$manager = new Staff();
...
if ($manager instanceof staff) echo "Yes";
```

There are two points worth noting here. First, note that the class name is not surrounded by any sort of delimiters (quotes). Doing so will result in a syntax error. Second, if this comparison fails, then the script will abort execution! This keyword is particularly useful when you're working with a number of objects simultaneously. For example, you might be repeatedly calling a particular function, but want to tweak that function's behavior in accordance with a given type of object. You might use a case statement and the instanceof keyword to manage behavior in this fashion.

Helper Functions

A number of functions are available for helping the developer manage and use class libraries. These functions are introduced in this section.

class_exists()

```
boolean class_exists(string class_name)
```

The class_exists() function returns TRUE if the class specified by *class_name* exists within the currently executing script context, and FALSE otherwise.

get_class()

```
string get_class(object object)
```

The get_class() function returns the name of the class to which *object* belongs, and FALSE if *object* is not an object.

get_class_methods()

```
array get_class_methods (mixed class_name)
```

The get_class_methods() function returns an array containing all method names defined by the class *class_name*.

get_class_vars()

```
array get_class_vars (string class_name)
```

The get_class_vars() function returns an associative array containing the names of all fields and their corresponding values defined within the class specified by *class_name*.

get_declared_classes()

```
array get_declared_classes(void)
```

The function get_declared_classes() returns an array containing the names of all classes defined within the currently executing script.

> **NOTE** *Three predefined classes are also included at the beginning of this array,* stdClass, OverloadedTestClass, *and* Directory. *Therefore, you'll need to disregard these classes if you're using this function to do any script-specific class analysis.*

get_object_vars()

`array get_object_vars(object object)`

The function get_object_vars() returns an associative array containing the defined fields available to *object*, and their corresponding values. Those fields that don't possess a value will be assigned NULL within the associative array.

get_parent_class()

`string get_parent_class(mixed object)`

The get_parent_class() function returns the name of the parent of the class to which *object* belongs. If *object*'s class is a base class, then that class name will be returned.

is_a()

`boolean is_a(object object, string class_name)`

The is_a() function returns TRUE if *object* belongs to a class of type *class_name*, or if it belongs to a class that is a child of *class_name*. If *object* bears no relation to the *class_name* type, FALSE is returned.

is_subclass_of()

`boolean is_subclass_of (object object, string class_name)`

The is_subclass_of() function returns TRUE if *object* belongs to a class inherited from *class_name*, and FALSE otherwise.

method_exists()

`boolean method_exists(object object, string method_name)`

The method_exists() function returns TRUE if a method named *method_name* is available to the object *object*, and FALSE otherwise.

Summary

This chapter introduced PHP's object-oriented features, devoting special attention to those enhancements and additions new to PHP 5. In the next chapter, we'll build upon this introductory information, turning attention to PHP's advanced OOP functionality.

CHAPTER 7

Advanced
OOP Features

IN THE LAST CHAPTER, I introduced the fundamentals of object-oriented PHP programming. In this chapter, I'll build on that foundation, introducing several of the more advanced OOP features that you should take into consideration once you've got the basics down pat. Specifically I'll talk about four features:

- **Object Cloning:** One of the major improvements to PHP's OOP model in version 5 is the treatment of all objects as references rather than values. However, how do you go about creating a copy of an object if they're all treated as references? By *cloning* the object, a feature new to PHP 5. I'll show you how cloning is accomplished using the clone keyword.

- **Inheritance:** As I mentioned in Chapter 6, the ability to build class hierarchies through *inheritance* is a key concept of object-oriented programming. I'll introduce inheritance, PHP 5's inheritance syntax, and offer several examples demonstrating this key OOP feature.

- **Interfaces:** An *interface* is a collection of unimplemented method definitions and constants that serve as a class blueprint of sorts. Interfaces define exactly what can be done with the class, without getting bogged down into implementation-specific details. I'll further introduce interfaces, present PHP 5's interface support (new to this version), and offer several examples demonstrating this powerful OOP feature.

- **Abstract Classes:** An *abstract class* is essentially a class that cannot be instantiated. Abstract classes are intended to be inherited by a class that can be instantiated, better known as a *concrete* class. Abstract classes can be fully implemented, partially implemented, or not implemented at all. I'll introduce general concepts surrounding abstract classes, and show you how to abstract classes are implemented in PHP 5.

You Didn't Cover...How Come?

If you have experience in other object-oriented languages, by the end of this chapter, you might be scratching your head over why I didn't cover a particular feature. It might well be because PHP doesn't support it. Therefore, I'll save you the suspense and enumerate those advanced OOP topics that aren't covered in this chapter. It isn't because of oversight, but rather because they aren't supported by the language.

- **Namespaces:** Although originally planned as a PHP 5 feature, development has since stopped. It isn't clear whether namespace support will be integrated into a future version.

- **Method overloading:** The ability to effect polymorphism through functional overloading did not make the cut this time around. According to a discussion on the Zend Technologies Web site, it probably never will. See the article "Ask the Experts About the Future of PHP" at http://www.zend.com/php/ask_experts.php.

- **Operator overloading:** The ability to assign additional meanings to operators based upon the type of data you're attempting to modify did not make the cut this time around. According to the aforementioned Zend Technologies Web site discussion, it is unlikely that this feature will ever be implemented.

- **Multiple inheritance:** PHP does not support multiple inheritance. Implementation of multiple interfaces is supported, however.

Only time will tell whether any or all of these features will be supported in the future.

Object Cloning

One of the biggest drawbacks to PHP 4's object-oriented capabilities was the fact that it treated objects like any other data type. This practice impeded the use of many common OOP methodologies, such as the use of design patterns, because such methodologies depend on the ability to pass objects to other class methods as references, rather than as values, which was PHP's default practice. Thankfully, this matter has been resolved with PHP 5, and now all objects are treated by default as references. Because all objects are treated as references rather than values, however, it is now more difficult to copy an object. If you try to copy a referenced object, it would simply point back to the addressing location of the original object. To remedy this, PHP offers an explicit means for *cloning* an object.

CAUTION *Changes to PHP 5's cloning syntax were still being made as late as beta 4.*

Cloning Example

You clone an object by prefacing it with the clone keyword, like so:

destinationobject = clone *targetobject*;

Listing 7-1 offers a comprehensive object cloning example. In this example, I've created a sample class, named corporatedrone, which contains two members (employeeid and tiecolor), and corresponding getters and setters for these members. I'll instantiate a corporatedrone object and use it as the basis for demonstrating the effects of a clone operation.

Listing 7-1. Cloning an Object with clone

```php
<?php
    class corporatedrone {
        private $employeeid;
        private $tiecolor;
        // Define a setter and getter for $employeeid
        function setEmployeeID($employeeid) {
            $this->employeeid = $employeeid;
        }
        function getEmployeeID() {
            return $this->employeeid;
        }
        // Define a setter and getter for $tiecolor
        function setTiecolor($tiecolor) {
            $this->tiecolor = $tiecolor;
        }
        function getTiecolor() {
            return $this->tiecolor;
        }
    }
    // Create new corporatedrone object
    $drone1 = new corporatedrone();
    // Set the $drone1 employeeid member
    $drone1->setEmployeeID("12345");
    // Set the $drone1 tiecolor member
    $drone1->setTiecolor("red");
    // Clone the $drone1 object
    $drone2 = clone $drone1;
    // Set the $drone2 employeeid member
    $drone2->setEmployeeID("67890");
    // Output the $drone1 and $drone2 employeeid members
    echo "drone1 employeeID: ".$drone1->getEmployeeID()."<br />";
    echo "drone1 tie color: ".$drone1->getTiecolor()."<br />";
    echo "drone2 employeeID: ".$drone2->getEmployeeID()."<br />";
    echo "drone2 tie color: ".$drone2->getTiecolor()."<br />";
?>
```

Executing this code returns the following:

```
drone1 employeeID: 12345
drone1 tie color: red
drone2 employeeID: 67890
drone2 tie color: red
```

As you can see, $drone2 became an object of type corporatedrone and inherited the member values of $drone1. To further demonstrate that $drone2 is indeed of type corporatedrone, I also reassigned its employeeid member.

The __clone() Method

You can tweak an object's cloning behavior by defining a __clone() method within the object class. Anything that takes place in this method will execute in addition to the copying of all existing object members to the target object. As an example, I'll revise the corporatedrone class, adding the following method:

```
function __clone() {
    $this->tiecolor = "blue";
}
```

With this in place, I'll create a new corporatedrone object, add the employeeid member value, clone it, and then output some data to show that the cloned object's tiecolor was indeed set through the __clone() method. Listing 7-2 offers the example.

Listing 7-2. Extending clone's Capabilities with the __clone() Method

```
// Create new corporatedrone object
$drone1 = new corporatedrone();
// Set the $drone1 employeeid member
$drone1->setEmployeeID("12345");
// Clone the $drone1 object
$drone2 = clone $drone1;
// Set the $drone2 employeeid member
$drone2->setEmployeeID("67890");
// Output the $drone1 and $drone2 employeeid members
echo "drone1 employeeID: ".$drone1->getEmployeeID()."<br />";
echo "drone2 employeeID: ".$drone2->getEmployeeID()."<br />";
echo "drone2 tiecolor: ".$drone2->getTiecolor()."<br />";
```

Executing this code returns:

```
drone1 employeeID: 12345
drone2 employeeID: 67890
drone2 tiecolor: blue
```

Inheritance

People are quite adept at thinking in such terms of organizational hierarchies; thus it doesn't come as a surprise that we make widespread use of this conceptual view for managing many aspects of our everyday lives. Corporate management structures, the United States tax system, and our view of the plant and animal kingdoms are just a few examples of systems that rely heavily on hierarchical concepts. Because object-oriented programming is based on the premise of allowing us humans to closely model the properties and behaviors of the real-world environment we're trying to implement in code, it makes sense to be able to represent these hierarchical relationships as well.

For example, suppose that your application called for a class titled employee, which is intended to represent the characteristics and behaviors that one might come to expect from an employee. Some class members might include:

- name: The employee's name

- age: The employee's age

- salary: The employee's salary

- years_employed: The number of years for which the employee has been with the company

Some employee class methods might include:

- doWork: Perform some work-related task.

- eatLunch: Take a lunch break.

- takeVacation: Make the most of those valuable two weeks.

These characteristics and behaviors would be relevant to all types of employees, regardless of the employee's purpose or stature within the organization. Obviously, though, there are also differences among employees; for example, the executive might hold stock options and be able to pillage the company, while other employees are not afforded such luxuries. A assistant must be able to take a memo, and an office manager needs to take supply inventories. Yet despite these differences, it would be quite inefficient if you had to create and maintain redundant class structures for those attributes that all classes share. The OOP development paradigm takes this into account, allowing you to inherit from and build upon existing classes.

Class Inheritance

As applied to PHP, class inheritance is accomplished using the extends keyword. Listing 7-3 demonstrates this ability, first creating an Employee class, and then creating an Executive class which inherits from Employee.

> **NOTE** *A class that inherits another class is known as a child class, or a subclass. The child class inherits from the* parent *class, or a base class.*

Listing 7-3. Inheriting from a Base Class

```php
<?php
    # Define a base Employee class
    class Employee {

        private $name;
        # Define a setter for the private $name member.
        function setName($name) {
            if ($name == "") echo "Name cannot be blank!";
            else $this->name = $name;
        }
        # Define a getter for the private $name member
        function getName() {
            return "My name is ".$this->name."<br />";
        }
    } #end Employee class
    # Define an Executive class that inherits Employee
    class Executive extends Employee {
        # Define a method unique to Employee
        function pillageCompany() {
            echo "I'm selling company assets to finance my yacht!";
        }
    } #end Executive class
    # Create a new Executive object
    $exec = new Executive();
    # Call the setName() method, defined in the Employee class
    $exec->setName("Richard");
    # Call the getName() method
    echo $exec->getName();
    # Call the pillageCompany() method
    $exec->pillageCompany();
?>
```

This returns the following:

```
My name is Richard.
I'm selling company assets to finance my yacht!
```

Because all employees have a name, the Executive class inherits from the Employee class, saving you the hassle of having to recreate the name member and the corresponding getter and setter. You can then focus solely on those characteristics that are specific to an executive, in this case a method named pillageCompany(). This method is available solely to objects of type Executive, and not to the Employee class or any other class, unless of course we create a class that inherits from Executive. Next, I'll demonstrate that concept. The following example offers a class titled CEO, which inherits from Executive.

```php
<?php
class Employee {

   ...

}
class Executive extends Employee {

   ...

}
class CEO extends Executive {
   function getFacelift() {
      echo "nip nip tuck tuck";
   }
}
$ceo = new CEO();
$ceo->setName("Bernie");
$ceo->pillageCompany();
$ceo->getFacelift();
?>
```

Because Executive has inherited from Employee, objects of type CEO also have all of the members and methods as made available to Executive.

Inheritance and Constructors

A common question pertinent to class inheritance has to do with the use of constructors. Does a parent class constructor execute when a child is instantiated? If this is so, what happens if the child class also has its own constructor? Does it execute in addition to the parent constructor, or does it override the parent? I'll answer such questions in this section.

If a parent class offers a constructor, it does execute when the child class is instantiated, provided that the child class does not also have a constructor. For example, suppose that the Employee class offers this constructor:

```php
function __construct($name) {
   $this->setName($name);
}
```

Then you instantiate the CEO class and retrieve the name member:

```php
$ceo = new CEO("Dennis");
echo $ceo->getName();
```

It will yield:

```
My name is Dennis
```

However, if the child class also has a constructor, it will execute when the child class is instantiated, regardless of whether the parent class also has a constructor. For example, suppose that in addition to the Employee class containing the above constructor, the CEO class contains this:

```
function __construct() {
    echo "<p>CEO object created!</p>";
}
```

Then you instantiate the CEO class:

```
$ceo = new CEO("Dennis");
echo $ceo->getName();
```

This time it will yield:

```
CEO object created!
My name is
```

This is because the CEO constructor overrides the Employee constructor. When it comes time to retrieve the name member, you find that it's blank because the setName() method, which executes in the Employee constructor, never fires. Of course, it's quite likely that you're going to want those parent constructors to also fire. Not to fear, there is a simple solution. Modify the CEO constructor like so:

```
function __construct($name) {
    parent::__construct($name);
    echo "<p>CEO object created!</p>";
}
```

Again instantiating the CEO class and executing getName() in the same fashion as above, this time you'll see a different outcome:

```
CEO object created!
My name is Dennis
```

You should understand that when parent::__construct() was encountered, PHP began a search upwards through the parent classes for an appropriate constructor. Because one was not found in Executive, it continued the search up to the Employee class, at which point one was located. If a constructor was located in the Employee class, then it would have fired. If you wanted both the Employee and Executive constructors to fire, then you need to place a call to parent::__construct() in the Executive constructor.

You also have the option to reference parent constructors in another fashion. For example, suppose that I'd like both the Employee and the Executive constructors to execute when a new CEO object is created. As I mentioned in the last chapter, I could reference these constructors explicitly within my CEO constructor like so:

```
function __construct($name) {
    Employee::__construct($name);
    Executive::__construct();
    echo "<p>CEO object created!</p>";
}
```

Interfaces

An *interface* defines a general specification for implementing a particular service, declaring the required functions and constants, without specifying exactly how it must be implemented. Implementation details aren't provided because different entities might need to implement the published method definitions in different ways. The point is to establish a general set of guidelines that must be implemented in order for the interface to be considered *implemented*.

> **CAUTION** *Class members are not defined within interfaces! This is a matter left entirely to the implementing class.*

Take for example the concept of pillaging a company. This task might be accomplished in a variety of ways, depending upon who is doing the dirty work. For example, a typical employee might do his part by using the office credit card to purchase shoes and movie tickets, writing the purchases off as "office expenses," while an executive might force his assistant to reallocate funds to his Swiss bank account through the online accounting system. Both employees are intent on accomplishing the task, but each goes about it in a different way. In this case, the goal of the interface is to define a set of guidelines for pillaging the company, and then ask the respective classes to implement that interface accordingly. For example, the interface might consist of just two methods:

```
emptyBankAccount()
burnDocuments()
```

You can then ask the Employee and Executive classes to implement these features. In this section, I'll show you how this is accomplished. First however, I'd like to take a moment to introduce how PHP 5 implements interfaces. In PHP, an interface is created like so:

```
interface IinterfaceName
{
    CONST 1;
    ...
    CONST N;

    function methodName1();
    ...
    function methodNameN();
}
```

> **TIP** *It's common practice to preface the name of an interface with the letter* I *to make them easier to recognize.*

The contract is completed when a class *implements* the interface, via the imple-ments keyword. All methods must be implemented, or the implementing class must be declared *abstract* (a concept I'll introduce in the next section), or else a fatal error simi-lar to the following will occur:

```
Fatal error: Class Executive contains 1 abstract methods and must
therefore be declared abstract (pillageCompany::emptyBankAccount) in
/www/htdocs/pmnp/7/executive.php on line 30
```

The general syntax for implementing the above interface follows:

```
class className implements interfaceName
{
    function methodName1()
    {
        /* methodName1() implementation */
    }
    ....
    function methodNameN()
    {
        /* methodName1() implementation */
    }
}
```

Implementing a Single Interface

Next I'll create a working example of PHP's interface implementation by creating and implementing an interface used for pillaging our company, named IPillage:

```
interface IPillage
{
    function emptyBankAccount();
    function burnDocuments();
}
```

This interface is then implemented for use by the Executive class:

```
class Executive extends Employee implements IPillage
{
    private $totalStockOptions;

    function emptyBankAccount()
    {
        echo "Call CFO and ask to transfer funds to Swiss bank account.";
    }

    function burnDocuments()
    {
        echo "Torch the office suite.";
    }
}
```

Because pillaging should be carried out at all levels of the company, we can implement the same interface by the Assistant class:

```
class Assistant extends Employee implements IPillage
{
    function takeMemo() {
        echo "Taking memo...";
    }

    function emptyBankAccount()
    {
        echo "Go on shopping spree with office credit card.";
    }

    function burnDocuments()
    {
        echo "Start small fire in the trash can.";
    }
}
```

As you can see, interfaces are particularly useful because although they define the number and name of the methods required for some behavior to occur, they acknowledge the fact that different classes might require different ways of carrying those methods out. In this example, the Assistant class burns documents by setting them on fire in a trash can, while the Executive class does so through somewhat more aggressive means (setting his office on fire).

Implementing Multiple Interfaces

Of course, it wouldn't be fair if we allowed outside contractors to pillage the company; after all, it was upon the backs of our full-time employees that the organization was built. That said, how can we provide our employees with the ability to both do their job and pillage the company, while limiting contractors solely to the tasks required of them? By breaking these tasks down into several tasks and then implementing multiple interfaces as necessary. Such a feature is available to PHP 5. Consider this example:

```php
<?php
    interface IEmployee {...}
    interface IDeveloper {...}
    interface IPillage {...}

    class Employee implements IEmployee, IDeveloper, iPillage {

    ...
    }

    class Contractor implements IEmployee, IDeveloper {

    ...
    }
?>
```

As you can see, all three interfaces (IEmployee, IDeveloper, and IPillage) have been made available to the employee, while only IEmployee and IDeveloper have been made available to the contractor.

Abstract Classes

An *abstract class* is a class that really isn't supposed to ever be instantiated, but instead serves as a base class to be inherited by other classes. For example, consider a class titled Media, intended to embody the common characteristics of various types of published materials, such as newspapers, books, and CDs. Because the Media class doesn't represent a real-life entity, but is instead a generalized representation of a range of similar entities, you'd never want to instantiate it directly. To ensure that this doesn't happen, the class is deemed *abstract*. The various derived Media classes then inherit this abstract class, ensuring conformity among the child classes, because all methods defined in that abstract class must be implemented within the subclass.

A class is declared abstract simply by prefacing the definition with the word abstract, like so:

```
abstract class classname
{
        // insert attribute definitions here
        // insert method definitions here
}
```

Attempting to instantiate an abstract class results in the following error message:

Fatal error: Cannot instantiate abstract class staff in
/www/book/chapter06/class.inc.php.

Abstract classes ensure conformity because any classes derived from them must implement all abstract methods derived within the class. Attempting to forego implementation of any abstract method defined in the class results in a fatal error.

....

Abstract Class or Interface?

When should you use an interface instead of an abstract class, and vice versa? This can be quite confusing and is often a matter of considerable debate. However, there are a few factors that can help you formulate a decision in this regards:

- If you intend to create a model that will be assumed by a number of closely related objects, use an abstract class. If you intend to create functionality that will subsequently be embraced by a number of unrelated objects, use an interface.

- If your object must inherit behavior from a number of sources, use an interface. PHP classes can inherit multiple interfaces but cannot extend multiple abstract classes.

- If you know that all classes will share a common behavior implementation, use an abstract class and implement the behavior there. You cannot implement behavior in an interface.

....

Summary

Over this chapter and the previous one, I introduced you to the entire gamut of PHP's OOP features, both old and new. Although the PHP development team was careful to ensure that users aren't constrained to use these features, there is little doubt that the improvements and additions made regarding PHP's ability to operate in conjunction with this important development paradigm represents a quantum leap forward for the language. If you're an old hand at object-oriented programming, hopefully these last two chapters have left you smiling ear-to-ear over the long-awaited capabilities introduced within these pages. If you're new to the concept, I'll be satisfied if I was able to effectively introduce you to some of the key OOP concepts and leave you wanting to perform additional experimentation and research into the matter.

In the next chapter, I'll introduce yet another new, and certainly long-awaited feature of PHP 5: exception handling.

CHAPTER 8

Error and Exception Handling

EVEN IF YOU WEAR an S on your chest when it comes to programming, you can be sure that errors will be introduced into all but the most trivial of applications throughout the development cycle. Accordingly, you and your team will require an efficient means for detecting, logging, and reporting issues that may arise during program execution. Some of these errors are programmer-induced; that is, they're the result of blunders during the development process. Others are user-induced, caused by the end user's unwillingness or inability to conform to application constraints. For example, the user might enter "12341234" when asked for an e-mail address, obviously ignoring what would otherwise be expected as valid input. Regardless of the source, your application must be able to encounter and react to such unexpected errors in a graceful fashion, hopefully doing so without a loss of data or program or system crash. In addition, your application should be able to log recurring errors, as well as provide the user with the feedback necessary to understand the reason for the error and potentially adjust its behavior accordingly.

In this chapter, I'll demonstrate the tremendous number of features PHP has to offer for error handling. Specifically, I'll delve into the following topics, in this order:

- **Configuration Directives:** PHP's error-related configuration directives determine the bulk of the language's error-handling behavior. I'll introduce many of the most pertinent directives in this section.

- **Error Logging:** Keeping a running log of application errors is the best way to record progress regarding the correction of repeated errors, as well as quickly take note of newly introduced problems. I'll show you how to log messages to both your operating system syslog and a custom log file in this section.

- **Exception Handling:** This long-awaited feature, prevalent among many popular languages (Java, C#, and Python, to name a few), and new to PHP 5, offers a standardized process for detecting, reacting to, and reporting errors.

Historically, the development community has been notoriously lax in implementing proper application error handling. This doesn't really come as a surprise, given that the feature offers little in terms of sex appeal; it's just not as cool as the other features we provide via our applications. However, as applications continue to grow increasingly complex and unwieldy, the importance of incorporating proper error-handling strategies into your daily development routine cannot be understated. Therefore, you should invest some time becoming familiar with the many features PHP has to offer in this regard.

Configuration Directives

Numerous configuration directives determine PHP's error reporting behavior. Many of these directives are introduced in this section.

error_reporting (string)
Scope: PHP_INI_ALL, Default value: E_ALL & ~E_NOTICE & ~E_STRICT
The error_reporting directive determines the reporting sensitivity level. Thirteen separate levels are available, and any combination of these levels is valid. See Table 8-1 for a complete list of these levels.

Table 8-1. PHP's Error Reporting Levels

LEVEL	DESCRIPTION
E_ALL	All errors and warnings
E_ERROR	Fatal run-time errors
E_WARNING	Run-time warnings
E_PARSE	Compile-time parse errors
E_NOTICE	Run-time notices
E_STRICT	PHP version portability suggestions
E_CORE_ERROR	Fatal errors that occur during PHP's initial start
E_CORE_WARNING	Warnings that occur during PHP's initial start
E_COMPILE_ERROR	Fatal compile-time errors
E_COMPILE_WARNING	Compile-time warnings
E_USER_ERROR	User-generated error
E_USER_WARNING	User-generated warning
E_USER_NOTICE	User-generated notice

I'd like to make special note of E_STRICT, because it's new to PHP 5. E_STRICT makes suggestions pertaining to the core developers' determinations as to proper coding methodologies, and is intended to ensure portability across PHP versions. E_STRICT comes into play in situations such as when deprecated functions or syntax is used, references are used incorrectly, var is used for class fields rather than a scope level, and other stylistic discrepancies.

> **NOTE** *The logical operator NOT is represented by the tilde character (~). This meaning is specific to this directive, as the exclamation mark (!) bears this significance throughout all other parts of the language.*

During the development stage of any project, you'll likely want all errors to be reported. Therefore, consider setting the directive like this:

```
error_reporting E_ALL
```

However, suppose that you were only concerned with fatal run-time, parse, and core errors. You could use logical operators to set the directive as follows:

```
error_reporting E_ERROR | E_PARSE | E_CORE_ERROR
```

As a final example, suppose you wanted all errors reported except for user-generated ones:

```
error_reporting E_ALL & ~(E_USER_ERROR | E_USER_WARNING | E_USER_NOTICE)
```

As is often the case, the name of the game is to remain well informed about the ongoing issues of your application without becoming so inundated with information that you quit looking at the logs. I suggest spending some time experimenting with the various levels during the development process, at least until you're well aware of the various types of reporting data that each configuration provides.

display_errors (On | Off)
Scope: PHP_INI_ALL, Default value: On
Enabling the display_errors directive results in the display of any errors meeting the criteria defined by error_reporting. You should only have this directive enabled during testing, and keep it disabled when the site is live. Not only will the display of such messages likely serve to only further confuse the end user, but they could also provide more information about your application/server than you might like to make available. For example, suppose you were using a flat file to store newsletter subscriber e-mail addresses. Due to a permissions misconfiguration, the application could not write to the file. Yet rather than catch the error and offer a user-friendly response, you instead opt to allow PHP to report the matter to the end user. The displayed error would look something like:

```
Warning: fopen(subscribers.txt): failed to open stream: Permission denied in
/home/www/htdocs/pmnp/8/displayerrors.php on line 3
```

Granted, you've already broken a cardinal rule by placing a sensitive file within the document root tree, but now you've greatly exacerbated the problem by informing the user of the exact location and name of the file. The user can then simply enter a URL similar to http://www.example.com/subscribers.txt, and proceed to do what he will with your soon-to-be furious subscriber base.

display_startup_errors (On | Off)

Scope: PHP_INI_ALL, Default value: Off

Enabling the display_startup_errors directive will display any errors encountered during the initialization of the PHP engine. Like display_errors, you should have this directive enabled during testing, and disabled when the site is live.

log_errors (On | Off)

Scope: PHP_INI_ALL, Default value: Off

Errors should be logged in every instance, because such records provide the most valuable means for determining problems specific to your application and the PHP engine. Therefore, you should keep log_errors enabled at all times. Exactly to where these log statements are recorded depends on the error_log directive.

error_log (string)

Scope: PHP_INI_ALL, Default value: Null

Errors can be sent to the system syslog, or can be sent to a file specified by the administrator via the error_log directive. If this directive is set to syslog, error statements will be sent to the syslog on Linux, or to the event log on Windows.

   If you're unfamiliar with the syslog, it's a Unix-based logging facility that offers an API for logging messages pertinent to system and application execution. The Windows event log is essentially the equivalent to the Unix syslog. These logs are commonly viewed using the Event Viewer.

log_errors_max_len (integer)

Scope: PHP_INI_ALL, Default value: 1024

This directive sets the maximum length, in bytes, of each logged item. The default is 1,024 bytes. Setting this directive to 0 means that no maximum length is imposed.

ignore_repeated_errors (On | Off)

Scope: PHP_INI_ALL, Default value: Off

Enabling this directive causes PHP to disregard repeated error messages that occur within the same file and on the same line.

ignore_repeated_source (On | Off)

Scope: PHP_INI_ALL, Default value: Off

Enabling this directive causes PHP to disregard repeated error messages emanating from different files or lines within the same file.

track_errors (On | Off)

Scope: PHP_INI_ALL, Default value: Off

Enabling this directive stores the most recent error message in the variable $php_errormsg. Once registered, you can do as you please with the variable data, including outputting it, saving it to a database, or any other task suiting a variable.

Error Logging

If you've decided to log your error to a separate text file, you'll need to ensure that the user running the Web server process has adequate permission to write to this file. In addition, be sure to place this file outside of the document root. When you write to the syslog, the error messages look like this:

```
Dec  5 10:56:37 example.com httpd: PHP Warning:
fopen(/home/www/htdocs/subscribers.txt): failed to open stream: Permission
denied in /home/www/htdocs/book/8/displayerrors.php on line 3
```

When you write to a separate text file, the error messages look like this:

```
[05-Dec-2003 10:53:47] PHP Warning:
fopen(/home/www/htdocs/subscribers.txt): failed to open stream: Permission
denied in /home/www/htdocs/book/8/displayerrors.php on line 3
```

As to which one to use, that is a decision that can be made on a per-environment basis. Personally, I prefer to use a separate file, although the decision is largely based on my preference. The syslog does offer several nice features however. My advice is to examine both routes and choose the strategy that best fits with your overall server environment configuration.

Sending Custom Messages to the syslog

PHP enables you to send custom messages as well as general error output to the system syslog. Four functions facilitate this feature. I'll examine these functions in this section, and offer an example at the conclusion.

define_syslog_variables()

```
void define_syslog_variables(void)
```

The define_syslog_variables() function initializes the constants necessary for using the openlog(), closelog(), and syslog() functions. You need to execute this function before using any of the following logging functions.

openlog()

```
int openlog(string ident, int option, int facility)
```

The openlog() function opens a connection to the platform's system logger, and sets the stage for the insertion of one or more messages into the system log by designating several parameters which will be used within the log context:

- *ident*: A message identifier added to the beginning of each entry. Typically this value is set to the name of the program. Therefore, you might want to identify PHP-related messages as "PHP" or "PHP5".

- *option*: Determines which logging options are used when generating the message. A list of available options is offered in Table 8-2. If more than one option is required, separate each option with a vertical bar. For example, you could specify three of the options like so: LOG_ODELAY | LOG_PERROR | LOG_PID.

- *facility*: Helps determine what category of program is logging the message. There are several categories, including: LOG_KERN, LOG_USER, LOG_MAIL, LOG_DAEMON, LOG_AUTH, LOG_LPR, and LOG_LOCAL*N*, where *N* is a value ranging between 0 and 7. Note that the designated facility determines the message destination. For example, designating LOG_CRON will result in the submission of subsequent messages to the cron log, whereas designating LOG_USER will result in the transmission of messages to the messages file. Unless PHP is being used as a command-line interpreter, you'll likely want to set this to LOG_USER. I also regularly use LOG_CRON when executing PHP scripts from a crontab. See the syslog documentation for more information about this matter.

Table 8-2. Logging Options

OPTION	DESCRIPTION
LOG_CONS	If error occurs when writing to the syslog, send output to the system console.
LOG_NDELAY	Immediately open the connection to the syslog.
LOG_ODELAY	Do not open the connection until the first message has been submitted for logging. This is the default.
LOG_PERROR	Output the logged message to both the syslog and standard error.
LOG_PID	Accompany each message with the process id (PID).

closelog()

```
int closelog(void)
```

The closelog() function closes the connection opened by openlog().

syslog()

```
int syslog(int priority, string message)
```

The syslog() function is responsible for sending a custom message to the syslog. The first parameter, *priority*, specifies the syslog priority level, presented in order of severity here:

- LOG_EMERG: A serious system problem, likely signaling a crash.

- LOG_ALERT: A condition that must be immediately resolved to avert jeopardizing system integrity.

- LOG_CRIT: Critical errors, which although they could render a service unusable, do not necessarily place the system in danger.

- LOG_ERR: General errors

- LOG_WARNING: General warnings

- LOG_NOTICE: Normal, but notable conditions

- LOG_INFO: General informational messages

- LOG_DEBUG: Information that is typically only relevant when debugging an application.

The second parameter, *message*, specifies the text of the message that you'd like to log. If you'd like to log the error message as provided by the PHP engine, you can include the string %m in the message. This string will be replaced by the error message string (strerror) as offered by the engine at execution time.

Now that you've been acquainted with the relevant functions, here's an example:

```php
<?php
    define_syslog_variables();
    openlog("CHP8", LOG_PID, LOG_USER);
    syslog(LOG_WARNING,"Chapter 8 example warning.");
    closelog();
?>
```

This snippet would produce a log entry in the messages file similar to the following:

```
Dec  5 20:09:29 www.example.com CHP8[30326]: Chapter 8 example warning.
```

Exception Handling

Languages such as Java, C#, and Python have long been heralded for their efficient error management abilities, done through the use of exception handling. If you have prior experience working with exception handlers, you likely scratch your head when working with any language, PHP included, that doesn't offer similar capabilities. This sentiment is apparently a common one across the PHP community, because as of version 5, exception handler capabilities have been incorporated into the language. In this section I'll teach you all about this new feature, introducing the basic concepts, syntax, and best practices, always accompanied by usage examples. Because exception handling is an entirely new feature to the PHP language, you may not have any prior experience incorporating this feature into your applications. Therefore I'll devote some time to a general overview regarding the matter. If you're already familiar with the basic concepts, feel free to skip ahead to the PHP-specific material later in this section.

Why Exception Handling Is Handy

In a perfect world, your program would run like a well-oiled machine, devoid of both internal and user-initiated errors that disrupt the flow of execution. However, programming, like the real-world, remains anything but an idyllic dream, and unforeseen events that disrupt the ordinary chain of events happen all the time. In programmer's lingo, these unexpected events are known as *exceptions*. Some programming languages are capable of attempting to react gracefully to an exception, attempting to locate a code block capable of handling the error. This is referred to as *throwing the exception*. In turn, the error handling code takes ownership of the exception, or *catches* it. The advantages to such a strategy are many.

For starters, exception handling essentially brings order to the error-management process through the use of a generalized strategy for both identifying and reporting application errors, as well as specifying what the program should do once an error is encountered. Furthermore, its syntax promotes the separation of error handlers from the general application logic, resulting in considerably more organized, readable code. Most languages that implement exception handling abstract the process into four components:

1. Attempt something.

2. If the attempt fails, throw an exception.

3. The assigned handler catches the exception, and performs any necessary tasks.

4. Clean up any resources consumed during the attempt.

Almost all languages have borrowed from the C++ language's handler syntax, known as try/catch. Here's a simple pseudocode example:

```
try {
    perform some task
    if something goes wrong
        throw exception("Something bad happened")
// Catch the thrown exception
} catch(exception) {
    output the exception message
}
```

You can also set up multiple handler blocks, which enable you to account for a variety of errors. This is accomplished by either making use of various predefined handlers, or by extending one of the predefined handlers, essentially creating your own custom handler. PHP currently only offers a single handler, exception. However, you can extend that handler if you need to. I suspect that additional default handlers will be made available in future releases. For the purposes of illustration, I'll build on the previous pseudocode example, using contrived handler classes to manage I/O and division-related errors:

```
try {
    perform some task
    if something goes wrong
        throw IOexception("Something bad happened")
    if something else goes wrong
        throw Numberexception("Something really bad happened")
// Catch IOexception
} catch(IOexception) {
    output the IOexception message
}
// Catch Numberexception
} catch(Numberexception) {
    output the Numberexception message
}
```

If you're new to exceptions, I'm sure that such a syntactical error-handling standard seems like a breath of fresh air. In the next section, I'll apply these concepts to PHP, introducing and demonstrating the variety of new exception-handling procedures made available in version 5.

PHP's Exception-Handling Implementation

In this section I'll demonstrate PHP's new exception-handling feature. Specifically I'll touch upon the base exception class internals, and demonstrate how to extend this base class, define multiple catch blocks, in addition to various other advanced handling tasks. Let's begin with the basics: the base exception class.

PHP's Base Exception Class

PHP's base exception class is actually quite simple in nature, offering a default constructor consisting of no parameters, an overloaded constructor consisting of two optional parameters, and six methods. Each is introduced in this section.

The Default Constructor

The default exception constructor is called with no parameters. For example, you can invoke the exception class like so:

```
throw new Exception();
```

Once the exception has been instantiated, you can use any of the six methods introduced later in this section. However, only four will be of any use; the other two are useful only if you instantiate the class with the overloaded constructor, introduced next.

The Overloaded Constructor

The overloaded constructor offers additional functionality not available to the default constructor through the acceptance of two optional parameters:

- message: The message parameter is intended to be a user-friendly explanation that will presumably be passed to the user via the getMessage() method, introduced in the following section.

- error code: The error code parameter is intended to hold an error identifier which would presumably be mapped to some identifier-to-message table. Error codes are often used for reasons of internationalization and localization. This error code is made available via the getCode() method, introduced in the next section. Later, I'll demonstrate how the base exception class can be extended to compute id/message table lookups.

You can call this constructor in a variety of ways. I'll demonstrate each here:

```
throw new Exception("Something bad just happened", 4)
throw new Exception("Something bad just happened");
throw new Exception("",4);
```

Of course, nothing actually happens to the exception until it's caught, as demonstrated later in this section.

Methods

Six methods are available to the exception class:

- getMessage(): Returns the message, if it was passed to the constructor.

- getCode(): Returns the error code, if it was passed to the constructor.

- getLine(): Returns the line number for which the exception is thrown.

- getFile(): Returns the name of the file throwing the exception.

- getTrace(): Returns an array consisting of information pertinent to the context in which the error occurred. Specifically, this array includes the file name, line, function, and function parameters.

- getTraceAsString(): Returns all of the same information as is made available by getTrace(), except that this information is returned as a string rather than as an array.

> **CAUTION** *Although you can extend the exception base class, you cannot override any of the above methods, because they are final.*

Listing 8-1 offers a simple example that embodies the use of the overloaded base class constructor, as well as several of the methods.

Listing 8-1. Raising an Exception

```
try {
    $conn = mysql_connect("localhost","webuser","secret");
    if (! $conn) {
        throw new Exception("Could not connect!");
    }
}
catch (Exception $e) {
    echo "Error (File: ".getFile().", line ".$e->getLine()."): ".$e->getMessage();
}
```

If the exception is raised, something like the following would be output:

```
Error (File: \www\htdocs\pmnp\8\mysqlconnect.php, line 6): Could not connect!
```

Extending the Exception Class

PHP's base exception class offers some nifty features, however, in some situations you'll likely want to extend the class to allow for additional capabilities. For example, suppose you want to internationalize your application to allow for the translation of error messages. These messages reside in an array located in a separate text file. The extended exception class will read from this flat file, mapping the error code passed into the constructor to the appropriate message (which has been presumably localized to the appropriate language). A sample flat file follows:

```
1,Could not connect to the database!
2,Incorrect password. Please try again.
3,Username not found.
4,You do not possess adequate privileges to execute this command.
```

When MyException is instantiated with a language and error code, it will read in the appropriate language file, parsing each line into an associative array consisting of the error code and its corresponding message. The MyException class and a usage example are found in Listing 8-2.

Listing 8-2. The MyException Class in Action

```php
class MyException extends Exception {
    function __construct($language,$errorcode) {
        $this->language = $language;
        $this->errorcode = $errorcode;
    }

    function getMessageMap() {
        $errors = file("errors/".$this->language.".txt");
        foreach($errors as $error) {
            list($key,$value) = explode(",",$error,2);
            $errorArray[$key] = $value;
        }
        return $errorArray[$this->errorcode];
    }
} # end MyException

try {
    throw new MyException("english",4);
}
catch (MyException $e) {
    echo $e->getMessageMap();
}
```

Catching Multiple Exceptions

Good programmers must always ensure that all possible scenarios are taken into account. Consider a scenario in which your site offers an HTML form from which the user could subscribe to a newsletter by submitting his or her e-mail address. Several outcomes are possible. For example, the user could:

- Provide a valid e-mail address

- Provide an invalid e-mail address

- Neglect to enter any address at all

- Attempt to mount a server attack such as an SQL injection

Proper exception handling will account for all such scenarios. However, in order to do so, you need a means for catching each exception. Thankfully, this is easily possible with PHP. Listing 8-3 shows the code that satisfies this scenario.

Listing 8-3. Catching Multiple Exceptions

```php
<?php
/* The InvalidEmailException class is responsible for notifying the site
    administrator in the case that the e-mail is deemed invalid. */
class InvalidEmailException extends Exception {

    function __construct($message, $email) {
        $this->message = $message;
        $this->notifyAdmin($email);
    }

    private function notifyAdmin($email) {
        mail("admin@wjgilmore.com","INVALID EMAIL",$email,"From:web@example.com");
    }

}

/* The subscribe class is responsible for validating an e-mail address
    and adding the user e-mail address to the database. */
class subscribe {

    function validateEmail($email) {
        try {
            if ($email == "") {
                throw new Exception("You must enter an e-mail address!");
            } else {
                list($user,$domain) = explode("@", $email);
                if (! checkdnsrr($domain, "MX"))
                {
```

```
                    throw new InvalidEmailException("Invalid e-mail address!", $email);
                } else {
                    return 1;
                }
            }
        } catch (Exception $e) {
            echo $e->getMessage();
        } catch (InvalidEmailException $e) {
            echo $e->getMessage();
        }

    }
    /* This method would presumably add the user's e-mail address to
        a database. */
    function subscribeUser() {
        echo $this->email." added to the database!";
    }

} #end subscribe class

/* Assume that the e-mail address came from a subscription form. */

$_POST['email'] = "someuser@example.com";

/* Attempt to validate and add address to database. */
if (isset($_POST['email'])) {
    $subscribe = new subscribe();
    if($subscribe->validateEmail($_POST['email']))
        $subscribe->subscribeUser($_POST['email']);
}

?>
```

You can see that its possible for two different exceptions to fire, one derived from the base class, and one extended from the base class, InvalidEmailException.

Summary

The topics covered in this chapter touch upon many of the core error-handling practices used in today's programming industry. While the implementation of such non-sexy features remain more preference than policy, the introduction of capabilities such as logging and error handling have contributed substantially to the ability to detect and respond to otherwise unforeseen problems to our code.

In the next chapter, I offer an in-depth introduction to PHP's string parsing capabilities, covering the language's powerful regular expression features, and offering insight into many of the powerful string manipulation functions.

CHAPTER 9

Strings and Regular Expressions

FORGET THE DISSERTATIONS about application servers, programming languages, and Backus-Naur forms, a good programmer defines his profession as ten letters comprising three vowels and seven consonants, uttered in three syllables, and consuming ten bytes of memory. The dissection of data is the lifeblood of our vocation. It doesn't matter if it's a gourmet recipe, store sales receipts, or poetry; we build applications that are based on establishing rules surrounding the parsing, classification, storage, and display of information. In this chapter, we'll examine many of the PHP functions that you'll undoubtedly use on a regular basis when performing such tasks.

This chapter is divided into three sections:

- **PHP 5's New String Offset Syntax:** In an effort to remove ambiguity and pave the way for potential optimizing of run-time string processing, a change to the string offset syntax has been made official in PHP 5. In the opening section, I'll discuss this change.

- **Regular Expressions:** In the opening section, I'll offer a brief introduction to regular expressions, touching upon the features and syntax of PHP's two supported regular expression implementations: POSIX and Perl. In addition, I'll offer a complete introduction to PHP's respective function libraries.

- **String Manipulation:** It's conceivable that throughout your programming career, you'll somehow be required to modify every conceivable aspect of a string. In this section, I'll introduce many of the powerful PHP functions which can help you do so.

Complex (Curly) Offset Syntax

Because PHP is a loosely-typed language, it makes sense that a string could also easily be treated as an array. Therefore any string, "php" for example, could be treated as both a contiguous entity and as a collection of three characters. Therefore, you could output such a string in two fashions:

```php
<?php
    $thing = "php";
    echo $thing;
    echo "<br />";
    echo $thing[0];
    echo $thing[1];
    echo $thing[2];
?>
```

This returns the following:

```
php
php
```

Although this behavior is quite convenient, it isn't without problems. For starters, it invites ambiguity. Looking at the code, was it the developer's intention to treat this data as a string or an array? Also, this lax syntax prevents you from creating any sort of run-time code optimization intended solely for strings, because the scripting engine can't differentiate between the two. To resolve this problem, the square bracket offset syntax has been deprecated in preference to curly bracket syntax when working with strings. Here's another look at the previous example, this time using the preferred syntax:

```php
<?php
    $thing = "php";
    echo $thing;
    echo "<br />";
    echo $thing{0};
    echo $thing{1};
    echo $thing{2};
?>
```

This example yields the same results as the original version.

The square bracket syntax has been around so long that it's unlikely to go away any time soon, if ever. Nonetheless, in the spirit of clean programming practice, it's suggested that you migrate to the curly bracketing syntax style.

Regular Expressions

Regular expressions provide the foundation for pattern-matching functionality. A regular expression is nothing more than a pattern of characters itself, matched against the text in which a search has been requested. This sequence may be a pattern with which you are already familiar, such as the word "dog," or it may be a pattern with specific meaning in the context of the world of pattern-matching, <(?)>.*<\ /.?> for example.

PHP offers functions specific to two sets of regular expression functions, each corresponding to a certain type of regular expression: POSIX and Perl-style. Each has its own unique style of syntax and is discussed accordingly in later sections. Keep in mind that innumerable tutorials have been written regarding this matter; you can find them both on the Web and in various books. Therefore, I will provide you with a basic introduction to both and leave it to you to search out further information should you be so inclined.

If you are not already familiar with the mechanics of general expressions, please take some time to read through the short tutorial comprising the remainder of this section. If you are already a regular expression pro, feel free to skip past the tutorial to subsequent sections.

Regular Expression Syntax (POSIX)

The structure of a POSIX regular expression is similar to that of a typical arithmetic expression: various elements (operators) are combined to form more complex expressions. The meaning of the combined regular expression elements is what makes them so powerful. You can not only locate literal expressions, such as a specific word or number, but also locate a multitude of semantically different but syntactically similar strings, for instance, all HTML tags in a file.

The simplest regular expression is one that matches a single character, such as g, which would match strings such as g, *haggle*, and *bag*. You could combine several letters together to form larger expressions, such as gan, which logically would match any string containing *gan*; *gang, organize,* or *Reagan,* for example.

You can also simultaneously test for several different expressions by using the pipe (|) operator. For example, you could test for *php or zend* via the regular expression php|zend.

Brackets

Brackets ([ ]) have a special meaning when used in the context of regular expressions, used to find a *range* of characters. Contrary to the regular expression php, which will find strings containing the explicit string *php*, the regular expression [php] will find any string containing the character *p* or *h*. Bracketing plays a significant role in regular expressions, because many times you may be interested in finding strings containing any of a range of characters. Several commonly used character ranges follow:

- [0-9] matches any decimal digit from 0 through 9.

- [a-z] matches any character from lowercase *a* through lowercase *z*.

- [A-Z] matches any character from uppercase *A* through uppercase *Z*.

- [A-Za-z] matches any character from uppercase *A* through lowercase *z*.

Of course, the ranges shown here are general; you could also use the range [0-3] to match any decimal digit ranging from 0 through 3, or the range [b-v] to match any lowercase character ranging from *b* through *v*. In short, you are free to specify whatever range you wish.

Quantifiers

The frequency or position of bracketed character sequences and single characters can be denoted by a special character, with each special character having a specific connotation. The +, *, ?, {int. range}, and $ flags all follow a character sequence:

- p+ matches any string containing at least one *p*.

- p* matches any string containing zero or more *p*'s.

- p? matches any string containing zero or one *p*'s.

- p{2} matches any string containing a sequence of two *p*'s.

- p{2,3} matches any string containing a sequence of two or three *p*'s.

- p{2,} matches any string containing a sequence of at least two *p*'s.

- p$ matches any string with *p* at the end of it.

Still other flags can precede and be inserted before and within a character sequence:

- ^p matches any string with *p* at the beginning of it.

- [^a-zA-Z] matches any string *not* containing any of the characters ranging from *a* through *z* and *A* through *Z*.

- p.p matches any string containing *p*, followed by any character, in turn followed by another *p*.

You can also combine special characters to form more complex expressions. Consider the following examples:

- ^.{2}$ matches any string containing *exactly* two characters.

- <b>(.*)</b> matches any string enclosed within <b> and </b> (presumably HTML bold tags).

- p(hp)* matches any string containing a *p* followed by zero or more instances of the sequence *hp*.

You may wish to search for these special characters in strings instead of using them in the special context just described. If you want to do so, the characters must be escaped with a backslash (\). For example, if you wanted to search for a dollar amount, a plausible regular expression would be as follows: ([\$])([0-9]+), that is, a dollar sign followed by one or more integers. Notice the backslash preceding the dollar sign. Potential matches of this regular expression include $42, $560, and $3.

Predefined Character Ranges (Character Classes)

For your programming convenience, several predefined character ranges, also known as *character classes*, are available. Character classes specify an entire range of characters, for example, the alphabet or an integer set. Standard classes include:

- [:alpha:]: Lowercase and uppercase alphabetical characters. This can also be specified as [A-Za-z].

- [:alnum:]: Lowercase and uppercase alphabetical characters and numerical digits. This can also be specified as [A-Za-z0-9].

- [:cntrl:]: Control characters such as a tab, escape, or backspace.

- [:digit:]: Numerical digits 0 through 9. This can also be specified as [0-9].

- [:graph:]: Printable characters found in the range of ASCII 33 to 126.

- [:lower:]: Lowercase alphabetical characters. This can also be specified as [a-z].

- [:punct:]: Punctuation characters, including ~ ` ! @ # $ % ^ & * ( ) - _ + = { } [ ] : ; ' < > , . ? and /.

- [:upper:]: Uppercase alphabetical characters. This can also be specified as [A-Z].

- [:space:]: White space characters including the space, horizontal tab, vertical tab, new line, form feed, or carriage return.

- [:xdigit:]: Hexadecimal characters. This can also be specified as [a-fA-F0-9].

PHP's Regular Expression Functions (POSIX Extended)

PHP currently offers seven functions for searching strings using POSIX-style regular expressions: ereg(), ereg_replace(), eregi(), eregi_replace(), split(), spliti(), and sql_regcase(). These functions are discussed in this section.

ereg()

```
boolean ereg(string pattern, string string [, array regs])
```

The ereg() function executes a case-sensitive search of *string* for *pattern*, returning TRUE if the pattern is found, and FALSE otherwise. Here's how you could use ereg() to ensure that a username consists solely of lowercase letters:

```php
<?php
    $username = "jasoN";
    if (ereg("([^a-z])",$username)) echo "Username must be all lowercase!";
?>
```

In this case, ereg() will return TRUE, causing the error message to output.

The optional input parameter *regs* contains an array of all matched expressions that were grouped by parentheses in the regular expression. Making use of this array, you could segment a URL into several pieces, as shown here:

```php
<?php
    $url = "http://www.apress.com";

    // break $url down into three distinct pieces:
    // "http://www", "apress", and "com"
    $parts = ereg("^(http://www)\.([[:alnum:]]+)\.([[:alnum:]]+)", $url, $regs);

    echo $regs[0];      // outputs the entire string "http://www.apress.com"
    echo "<br>";
```

```php
echo $regs[1];      // outputs "http://www"
echo "<br>";
echo $regs[2];      // outputs "apress"
echo "<br>";
echo $regs[3];      // outputs "com"
?>
```

This returns:

```
http://www.apress.com
http://www
apress
com
```

eregi()

```
int eregi(string pattern, string string, [array regs])
```

The eregi() function searches *string* for *pattern*. Unlike ereg(), the search is case insensitive. This function can be useful when checking the validity of strings, such as passwords. This concept is illustrated in the following example:

```php
<?php
    $pswd = "jasongild";
    if (!eregi("^[a-zA-Z0-9]{8,10}$", $pswd))
    echo "The password must consist solely of letters,
        and must be 8-10 characters in length!";

?>
```

Any password consisting of non-alphanumeric characters, or of length less than eight characters, or greater than ten characters will return the error message.

ereg_replace()

```
string ereg_replace (string pattern, string replacement, string string)
```

The ereg_replace() function operates much like ereg(), except that the functionality is extended to finding and replacing *pattern* with *replacement* instead of simply locating it. If no matches are found, the string will remain unchanged. Like ereg(), ereg_replace() is case sensitive. Consider an example:

```php
<?php
    $text = "This is a link to http://www.wjgilmore.com/.";
    echo ereg_replace("http://([a-zA-Z0-9./-]+)$", "<a href=\"\\0\">\\0</a>",
                    $text);
?>
```

This returns:

```
This is a link to
<a href="http://www.wjgilmore.com/">http://www.wjgilmore.com</a>.
```

A rather interesting feature of PHP's string-replacement capability is the ability to back-reference parenthesized substrings. This works much like the optional input parameter *regs* in the function ereg(), except that the substrings are referenced using backslashes, such as \0, \1, \2, and so on, where \0 refers to the entire string, \1 the first successful match, and so on. Up to nine back references can be used. This example shows how to replace all references to a URL with a working hyperlink:

```
$url = "Apress (http://www.apress.com)";
$url = ereg_replace("http://([a-zA-Z0-9./-]+)([a-zA-Z/]+)",
                    "<a href=\"\\0\">\\0</a>", $url);
print $url;
// Displays Apress (<a href="http://www.apress.com">http://www.apress.com</a>)
```

> **NOTE** *Although* ereg_replace() *works just fine, another predefined function named* str_replace() *is actually much faster when complex regular expressions are not required.* str_replace() *is discussed later in this chapter.*

eregi_replace()

string eregi_replace (string *pattern*, string *replacement*, string *string*)

The eregi_replace() function operates exactly like ereg_replace(), except that the search for a pattern in string is not case sensitive.

split()

array split (string *pattern*, string *string* [, int *limit*])

The split() function divides *string* into various elements, with the boundaries of each element based on the occurrence of *pattern* in string.

The optional input parameter *limit* is used to specify the number of elements into which the string should be divided, starting from the left end of the string and working rightward. In cases where the pattern is an alphabetical character, split() is case-sensitive. Here's how you would use split() to break a string into pieces based on occurrences of horizontal tabs and newline characters:

```php
<?php
    $text = "this is\tsome text that\nwe might like to parse.";
    print_r(split("[\n\t]",$text));
?>
```

This returns:

```
Array ( [0] => this is [1] => some text that [2] => we might like to parse. )
```

spliti()

```
array split (string pattern, string string [, int limit])
```

The spliti() function operates exactly in the same manner as its sibling split(), except that it is case insensitive.

sql_regcase()

```
string sql_regcase (string string)
```

The sql_regcase() function converts each character in string into a bracketed expression containing two characters. If the character is alphabetic, the bracket will contain both forms; otherwise, the original character will be left unchanged. This function is particularly useful when PHP is used in conjunction with products that support only case-sensitive regular expressions. Here's how you would use sql_regcase() to convert a string:

```php
<?php
    $version = "php 4.0";
    print sql_regcase($version);
    // outputs [Pp] [Hh] [Pp] 4.0
?>
```

Regular Expression Syntax (Perl Style)

Perl has long been considered one of the greatest parsing languages ever written, and it provides a comprehensive regular expression language that can be used to search and replace even the most complicated of string patterns. The developers of PHP felt that instead of reinventing the regular expression wheel, so to speak, they should make the famed Perl regular expression syntax available to PHP users, thus the Perl-style functions.

Perl-style regular expressions are similar to their POSIX counterparts. In fact, Perl's regular expression syntax is a derivation of the POSIX implementation, resulting in considerable similarities between the two. In fact, you can use any of the quantifiers introduced in the previous POSIX section. I devote the remainder of this section to a brief introduction of Perl regular expression syntax. Let's start with a simple example of a Perl-based regular expression:

`/food/`

Notice that the string *food* is enclosed between two forward slashes. Just like with POSIX regular expressions, you can build a more complex string through the use of quantifiers:

`/fo+/`

This will match *fo* followed by one or more characters. Some potential matches include *food*, *fool*, and *fo4*. Here is another example of using a quantifier:

`/fo{2,4}/`

This matches *f* followed by two to four occurrences of *o*. Some potential matches include *fool*, *fooool*, and *foosball*.

Modifiers

Often you'll want to tweak the interpretation of a regular expression, for example telling it to execute a case-insensitive search, or ignore comments embedded within its syntax. These tweaks are known as *modifiers*, and they go a long way towards helping you to write short and concise expressions. I offer a few of the more interesting ones in Table 9-1.

Table 9-1. Six Sample Modifiers

MODIFIER	DESCRIPTION
i	Perform a case-insensitive search.
g	Find all occurrences (perform a global search).
m	Treats a string as several (*m* for multiple) lines. By default, the ^ and $ characters match at the very start and very end of the string in question. Using the m modifier will allow for ^ and $ to match at the beginning of any line in a string.
s	Accomplishes just the opposite of the m modifier, treating a string as a single line, ignoring any newline characters found within.
x	Ignore white space and comments within the regular expression.
U	Many quantifiers are "greedy"; they match the pattern as many times as possible, rather than just stopping at the first match. You can cause them to be "ungreedy" with this modifier.

These modifiers are placed directly after the regular expression, for example, /string/i. Let's consider a few examples:

- /wmd/i: Matches *WMD, wMD, WMd, wmd*, and any other case-variation of the string *wmd*.

- /taxation/gi: Case insensitively locates all occurrences of the word *taxation*. You might use the global modifier to tally up the total number of occurrences, or in conjunction with a replacement feature for replacing all occurrences with some other string.

Metacharacters

Another cool thing you can do with Perl regular expressions is use various metacharacters to search for matches. A metacharacter is simply an alphabetical character preceded by a backslash that symbolizes special meaning. A list of useful metacharacters follows:

- \A: Matches only at the beginning of the string.

- \b: Matches a word boundary.

- \B: Matches anything but a word boundary.

- \d: Matches a digit character. This is the same as [0-9].

- \D: Matches a non-digit character.

- \s: Matches a white space character.

- \S: Matches a non-white space character.

- []: Encloses a character class. A list of useful character classes was provided in the previous section.

- (): Encloses a character grouping or defines a back reference.

- $: Matches the end of a line.

- ^: Matches the beginning of a line.

- .: Matches any character except for the newline.

- \: Quote the next metacharacter.

- \w: Matches any string containing solely underscore and alphanumeric characters. This is the same as [a-zA-Z0-9_].

- \W: Matches a string, omitting the underscore and alphanumeric characters.

Consider a few examples:

```
/sa\b/
```

Because the word boundary is defined to be on the right side of the strings, this will match strings like *pisa* and *lisa* but not *sand*.

```
/\blinux\b/i
```

This returns the first case-insensitive occurrence of the word *linux*.

```
/sa\B/
```

The opposite of the word boundary metacharacter is \B. This matches on anything but a word boundary. This will match strings like *sand* and *Sally*, but not *Melissa*.

```
/\$\d+\g
```

This returns all instances of strings matching a dollar sign followed by one or more digits.

PHP's Regular Expression Functions (Perl Compatible)

PHP offers seven functions for searching strings using Perl-compatible regular expressions: preg_grep(), preg_match(), preg_match_all(), preg_quote(), preg_replace(), preg_replace_callback(), and preg_split().These functions are introduced in the following sections.

preg_grep()

```
array preg_grep (string pattern, array input [, flags])
```

The preg_grep() function searches all elements of the array *input*, returning an array consisting of all elements matching *pattern*. Consider an example that uses this function to search an array for foods beginning with *p*:

```php
<?php
    $foods = array("pasta", "steak", "fish", "potatoes");
    $food = preg_grep("/^p/", $foods);
    print_r($food);
?>
```

This returns:

```
Array ( [0] => pasta [3] => potatoes )
```

Note that the array corresponds to the indexed order of the input array. If the value at that index position matches, it's included in the corresponding position of the output array. Otherwise, that position is empty. If you want to remove those instances of the array which are blank, filter the output array through the function array_values(), introduced in Chapter 5.

The optional input parameter *flags* was added in PHP version 4.3. It accepts one value, PREG_GREP_INVERT. Passing this flag will result in retrieval of those array elements that do *not* match the pattern.

preg_match()

```
int preg_match (string pattern, string string [, array matches]
[, int flags [, int offset]]])
```

The preg_match() function searches *string* for *pattern*, returning TRUE if it exists, and FALSE otherwise. The optional input parameter *pattern_array* can contain various sections of the subpatterns contained in the search pattern, if applicable. Here's an example that uses preg_match() to perform a case-sensitive search:

```php
<?php
    $line = "Vim is the greatest word processor ever created!";
    if (preg_match("/\bVim\b/i", $line, $match)) print "Match found!";
?>
```

For instance, this script will confirm a match if the word *Vim* or *vim* is located, but not *simplevim*, *vims*, or *evim*.

preg_match_all()

```
int preg_match_all (string pattern, string string, array pattern_array
[, int order])
```

The preg_match_all() function matches all occurrences of pattern in string, assigning each occurrence to array *pattern_array* in the order you specify via the optional input parameter *order*. The *order* parameter accepts two values:

- PREG_PATTERN_ORDER is the default if the optional *order* parameter is not included. PREG_PATTERN_ORDER specifies the order in the way that you might think most logical: $pattern_array[0] is an array of all complete pattern matches, $pattern_array[1] is an array of all strings matching the first parenthesized regular expression, and so on.

- PREG_SET_ORDER orders the array a bit differently than the default setting. $pattern_array[0] contains elements matched by the first parenthesized regular expression, $pattern_array[1] will contain elements matched by the second parenthesized regular expression, and so on.

Here's how you would use preg_match_all() to find all strings enclosed in bold HTML tags:

```php
<?php
    $userinfo = "Name: <b>Zeev Suraski</b> <br> Title: <b>PHP Guru</b>";
    preg_match_all ("/<b>(.*)<\/b>/U", $userinfo, $pat_array);
    print $pat_array[0][0]." <br> ".$pat_array[0][1]."\n";
?>
```

This returns:

```
Zeev Suraski
PHP Guru
```

preg_quote()

```
string preg_quote(string str [, string delimiter])
```

The function preg_quote()inserts a backslash delimiter before every character of special significance to regular expression syntax. These special characters include: $ ^ * ( ) + = { } [ ] | \\ : < >. The optional parameter *delimiter* is used to specify what delimiter is used for the regular expression, causing it to also be escaped by a backslash. Consider an example:

```php
<?php
    $text = "Tickets for the bout are going for $500.";
echo preg_quote($text);
?>
```

This returns:

```
Tickets for the bout are going for \$500\.
```

preg_replace()

```
mixed preg_replace (mixed pattern, mixed replacement, mixed str [, int limit])
```

The preg_replace() function operates identically to ereg_replace(), except that it employs use of a Perl-based regular expression syntax, replacing all occurrences of *pattern* with *replacement*, and returning the modified result. The optional input parameter *limit* specifies how many matches should take place. Failing to set *limit* or setting it to –1 will result in the replacement of all occurrences. Consider an example:

```php
<?php
    $text = "This is a link to http://www.wjgilmore.com/.";
    echo preg_replace("/http:\/\/(.*)\//", "<a href=\"\${0}\">\${0}</a>", $text);
?>
```

This returns:

```
This is a link to
<a href="http://www.wjgilmore.com/">http://www.wjgilmore.com/</a>.
```

Interestingly, the *pattern* and *replacement* input parameters can also be arrays. This function will cycle through each element of each array, making replacements as they are found. Consider this example, which I'll market as the CEO corporate report generator:

```php
<?php
    $draft = "In 2004 the company faced plummeting revenues and scandal.";
    $keywords = array("/faced/", "/plummeting/", "/scandal/");
    $replacements = array("celebrated", "skyrocketing", "expansion");
    echo preg_replace($keywords, $replacements, $draft);
?>
```

This returns:

```
In 2004 the company celebrated skyrocketing revenues and expansion.
```

preg_replace_callback()

```
mixed preg_replace_callback(mixed pattern, callback callback, mixed str
[, int limit])
```

Rather than handling the replacement procedure itself, the preg_replace_callback() function delegates the string replacement procedure to some other user-defined function. The *pattern* parameter determines what you're looking for, while the *str* parameter defines the string you're searching. The *callback* parameter defines the name of the function to be used for the replacement task. The optional parameter *limit* specifies how many matches should take place. Failing to set *limit* or setting it to –1 will result in the replacement of all occurrences. In the following example, a function named acronym() is passed into preg_replace_callback() and is used to insert the long form of various acronyms into the target string:

```php
<?php
    // This function will add the acronym long form
    // directly after any acronyms found in $matches
    function acronym($matches) {
        $acronyms = array(
            'WWW' => 'World Wide Web',
            'IRS' => 'Internal Revenue Service',
            'PDF' => 'Portable Document Format');
        if (isset($acronyms[$matches[1]]))
            return $matches[1] . " (" . $acronyms[$matches[1]] . ")";
        else
            return $matches[1];
    }


        // The target text
    $text = "The <acronym>IRS</acronym> offers tax forms in
                 <acronym>PDF</acronym> format on the <acronym>WWW</acronym>.";
    // Add the acronyms' long forms to the target text
    $newtext = preg_replace_callback("/<acronym>(.*)<\/acronym>/U", 'acronym',
                                     $text);

    print_r($newtext);
?>
```

This returns:

```
The IRS (Internal Revenue Service) offers tax forms
in PDF (Portable Document Format) on the WWW (World Wide Web).
```

preg_split()

array preg_split (string pattern, string *string* [, int *limit* [, int *flags*]])

The preg_split() function operates exactly like split(), except that *pattern* can also be defined in terms of a regular expression. If the optional input parameter *limit* is specified, only *limit* number of substrings are returned. Consider an example:

```php
<?php
    $delimitedText = "+Jason+++Gilmore+++++++++++Columbus+++OH";
    $fields = preg_split("/\+{1,}/", $delimitedText);
    foreach($fields as $field) echo $field."<br />";
?>
```

This returns the following:

```
Jason
Gilmore
Columbus
OH
```

Other String-Specific Functions

In addition to the regular expression-based functions discussed in the first half of this chapter, PHP offers over 100 functions collectively capable of manipulating practically every imaginable aspect of a string. To introduce each function would be out of the scope of this book and would only repeat much of the information in the PHP documentation. Instead, I've opted to devote the remainder of this chapter to a categorical FAQ of sorts, focusing upon the string-related issues that seem to most frequently appear within community forums. The remainder of this chapter is divided into the following topics:

- Determining string length

- Comparing string length

- Manipulating string case

- Converting to and from HTML

- Alternatives for regular expression functions

- Padding and compacting a string

Determining the Length of a String

Determining string length is a repeated action within countless applications. The PHP function strlen() accomplishes this task quite nicely.

strlen()

```
int strlen (string str)
```

You can determine the length of a string with the strlen() function. This function returns the length of a string, where each character in the string is equivalent to one unit. The following example verifies whether a user password is of acceptable length:

```php
<?php
    $pswd = "secretpswd";
    if (strlen($string) < 10) echo "Password is too short!";
?>
```

In this case, the error message will not appear, because the chosen password consists of 10 characters, whereas the conditional expression validates if the target string consists of less than 10 characters.

Comparing Two Strings

String comparison is arguably one of the most important features of the string-handling capabilities of any language. Although there are many ways in which two strings can be compared for equality, PHP provides four functions for performing this task: strcmp(), strcasecmp(), strspn(), and strcspn(). These functions are discussed in the following sections.

strcmp()

```
int strcmp (string str1, string str2)
```

The strcmp() function performs a binary-safe case-sensitive comparison of the strings *str1* and *str2*, returning one of three possible values:

- 0 if *str1* and *str2* are equal

- −1 if *str1* is less than *str2*

- 1 if *str2* is less than *str1*

Web sites often require that a registering user enter and confirm his chosen password, lessening the possibility of an incorrectly entered password as a result of a typing error. Because passwords are often case-sensitive, strcmp() is a great function for comparing the two:

```php
<?php
    $pswd = "supersecret";
    $pswd2 = "supersecret";
    if (strcmp($pswd,$pswd2) != 0) echo "Your passwords do not match!";
?>
```

Note that the strings must match exactly for strcmp() to consider them equal. For example, *Supersecret* is different from *supersecret*. If you're looking to compare two strings case-insensitively, consider strcasecmp(), introduced next.

Another common point of confusion regarding this function surrounds its behavior of returning 0 if the two strings are equal. This is different from executing a string comparison using the == operator, like so:

```
if ($str1 == $str2)
```

While both accomplish the same goal, which is to compare two strings, keep in mind that the values they return in doing so are different.

strcasecmp()

```
int strcasecmp (string str1, string str2)
```

The strcasecmp() function operates exactly like strcmp(), except that its comparison is case-insensitive. The following example compares two e-mail addresses, an ideal use for strcasecmp() because casing does not determine an e-mail address' uniqueness:

```php
<?php
    $email1 = "admin@example.com";
    $email2 = "ADMIN@example.com";

    if (! strcasecmp($email1, $email2))
        print "The email addresses are identical!";
?>
```

In this case the message is output, because strcasecmp() performs a case-insensitive comparison of $email1 and $email2, and determines that they are indeed identical.

strspn()

```
int strspn (string str1, string str2)
```

The strspn() function returns the length of the first segment in *str1* containing characters also in *str2*. Here's how you might use strspn() to ensure that a password does not consist solely of numbers:

```php
<?php
    $password = "3312345";
    if (strspn($password, "1234567890") == strlen($password))
        echo "The password cannot consist solely of numbers!";
?>
```

In this case, the error message is returned, because $password does indeed consist solely of digits.

strcspn()

```
int strcspn (string str1, string str2)
```

The strcspn() function returns the length of the first segment in *str1* containing characters not in *str2*. Here's an example of password validation using strcspn():

```php
<?php
    $password = "a12345";
    if (strcspn($password, "1234567890") == 0) {
        print "Password cannot consist solely of numbers! ";
    }
?>
```

In this case, the error message will not be displayed, because $password does not consist solely of numbers.

Manipulating String Case

Four functions are available to aid you in manipulating the case of characters in a string: strtolower(), strtoupper(), ucfirst(), and ucwords(). These functions are discussed in this section.

strtolower()

```
string strtolower (string str)
```

The strtolower() function converts str to all lowercase letters, returning the modified string. Nonalphabetical characters are not affected. The following example uses strtolower() to convert a URL to all lowercase letters:

```php
<?php
    $url = "http://WWW.EXAMPLE.COM/";
    echo strtolower($url);
?>
```

This returns:

```
http://www.example.com/
```

strtoupper()

```
string strtoupper (string str)
```

Just as you can convert a string to lowercase, you can convert it to uppercase. This is accomplished with the function strtoupper(). Nonalphabetical characters are not affected. This example uses strtoupper() to convert a string to all uppercase letters:

```php
<?php
    $msg = "i annoy people by capitalizing e-mail text.";
    echo strtoupper($msg);
?>
```

This returns:

```
I ANNOY PEOPLE BY CAPITALIZING E-MAIL TEXT.
```

ucfirst()

```
string ucfirst (string str)
```

The ucfirst() function capitalizes the first letter of the string *str*, if it is alphabetical. Nonalphabetical characters will not be affected. Additionally, any capitalized characters found in the string will be left untouched. Consider this example:

```php
<?php
    $sentence = "the newest version of PHP was released today!";
    echo ucfirst($sentence);
?>
```

This returns:

```
The newest version of PHP was released today!
```

Note that while the first letter is indeed capitalized, the capitalized word "PHP" was also left untouched.

ucwords()

```
string ucwords (string str)
```

The ucwords() function capitalizes the first letter of each word in a string. Nonalphabetical characters are not affected. This example uses ucwords() to capitalize each word in a string:

```php
<?php
    $title = "O'Malley wins the heavyweight championship!";
    echo ucwords($title);
?>
```

This returns:

```
O'Malley Wins The Heavyweight Championship!
```

Note that if "O'Malley" was accidentally written as "O'malley," ucwords() would not catch the error, as it considers a word to be defined as a string of characters separated from other entities in the string by a blank space on each side.

Converting Strings to and from HTML

Converting a string or an entire file into one suitable for viewing on the Web (and vice versa) is easier than you would think. Several functions are suited for such tasks, all of which are introduced in this section. For convenience, I'll divide this section into two parts: "Converting Plain Text to HTML" and "Converting HTML to Plain Text."

Converting Plain Text to HTML

It is often useful to be able to quickly convert plain text into HTML for readability within a Web browser. Several functions can aid you in doing so. These functions are the subject of this section.

nl2br()

```
string nl2br (string str)
```

The nl2br() function converts all newline (\n) characters in a string to their XHTML-compliant equivalent, <br />. The newline characters could be created via a carriage return, or explicitly written into the string. The following example translates a text string to HTML format:

```php
<?php
    $recipe = "3 tablespoons Dijon mustard
    1/3 cup Caesar salad dressing
    8 ounces grilled chicken breast
    3 cups romaine lettuce";
    // convert the newlines to <br />'s.
    echo nl2br($recipe);
?>
```

Executing this example results in the following output:

```
3 tablespoons Dijon mustard<br />
1/3 cup Caesar salad dressing<br />
8 ounces grilled chicken breast<br />
3 cups romaine lettuce
```

htmlentities()

```
string htmlentities (string str [, int quote_style [, int charset]])
```

During the general course of communication you may come across many characters that are not included in a document's text encoding, or are not readily available on the keyboard. Examples of such characters include the copyright symbol (©), cent sign (¢), and the French accent grave (è). To facilitate such shortcomings, a set of universal key codes was devised, known as *character entity references*. When these entities are parsed by the browser, they will be converted into their recognizable counterparts. For example, the three aforementioned characters would be presented as ©, ¢, and È, respectively.

The htmlentities() function converts all such characters found in *str* into their HTML-equivalents. Because of the special nature of quote marks within markup, the optional *quote_style* parameter offers the opportunity to choose how they will be handled. Three values are accepted:

- ENT_COMPAT: Convert double-quotes and ignore single quotes. This is the default.

- ENT_NOQUOTES: Ignore both double and single quotes.

- ENT_QUOTES: Convert both double and single quotes.

A second optional parameter, *charset*, determines the character set used for the conversion. Table 9-2 offers the list of supported character sets. If *charset* is omitted, it will default to ISO-8859-1.

Table 9-2. htmlentities()'s Supported Character Sets.

CHARACTER SET	DESCRIPTION
BIG5	Traditional Chinese.
BIG5-HKSCS	BIG5 with additional Hong Kong extensions, traditional Chinese.
cp866	DOS-specific Cyrillic character set.
cp1251	Windows-specific Cyrillic character set
cp1252	Windows-specific character set for Western Europe
EUC-JP	Japanese
GB2312	Simplified Chinese
ISO-8859-1	Western European, Latin-1
ISO-8859-15	Western European, Latin-9
KOI8-R	Russian
Shift-JIS	Japanese
UTF-8	ASCII compatible multi-byte 8 encode

The following example converts the necessary characters for Web display:

```php
<?php
    $advertisement = "Coffee at 'Cafè Française' costs $2.25.";
    echo htmlentities($advertisement);
?>
```

This returns:

```
Coffee at 'Caf&egrave; Fran&ccedil;aise' costs $2.25.
```

Two characters were converted, the accent grave (è) and the cedilla (ç). The single-quotes were ignored due to the default *quote_style* setting ENT_COMPAT.

htmlspecialchars()

string htmlspecialchars (string *str* [, int *quote_style* [, string *charset*]])

Several characters play a dual role in both markup languages and the human language. When used in the latter fashion, these characters must be converted into their displayable equivalents. For example, an ampersand must be converted to &, whereas a greater-than character must be converted to >. The htmlspecialchars() function can do this for you, converting the following characters into their compatible equivalents:

- & becomes &

- "(double quote) becomes "

- ' (single quote) becomes '

- < becomes <

- > becomes >

This function is particularly useful in preventing users from entering HTML markup into an interactive Web application, for example a message board.

The following example converts potentially harmful characters using htmlspecialchars():

```php
<?php
    $input = "I just can't get <<enough>> of PHP!";
    echo htmlspecialchars($input);
?>
```

Viewing the source, you'll see:

```
I just can't get &lt;&lt;enough&gt;&gt; of PHP &amp!
```

If the translation isn't necessary, perhaps a more efficient way to do this is to use strip_tags(), which deletes the tags from the string altogether.

> **TIP** *If you are using* gethtmlspecialchars() *in conjunction with a function like* nl2br(), *you should execute* nl2br() *after* gethtmlspecialchars(), *otherwise the*
's generated with nl2br() *will be converted to visible characters.*

get_html_translation_table()

array get_html_translation_table (int *table* [, int *quote_style*])

Using get_html_translation_table() is a convenient way to translate text to its HTML equivalent, returning one of the two translation tables (HTML_SPECIALCHARS or HTML_ENTITIES) specified by *table*. This returned value can then be used in conjunction with another predefined function, strtr() (formally introduced later in this section), to essentially translate the text into its corresponding HTML code.

The following sample uses get_html_translation_table() to convert text to HTML:

```
<?php
    $string = "La pasta é il piatto piú amato in Italia";
    $translate = get_html_translation_table(HTML_ENTITIES);
    echo strtr($string, $translate);
?>
```

This returns the string formatted as necessary for browser rendering:

```
La pasta &eacute; il piatto pi&uacute; amato in Italia
```

Interestingly, array_flip() is capable of reversing the text-to-HTML translation and vice versa. Assume that instead of printing the result of strtr() in the preceding code sample, you assigned it to the variable $translated_string.

The next example uses array_flip() to return a string back to its original value:

```
<?php
    $entities = get_html_translation_table(HTML_ENTITIES);
    $translate = array_flip($entities);
    $string = "La pasta &eacute; il piatto pi&uacute; amato in Italia";
    echo strtr($string, $translate);
?>
```

This returns the following:

```
La pasta é il piatto piú amato in italia
```

strtr()

```
string strtr (string str, array replacements)
```

The strtr() function converts all characters in *str* to their corresponding match found in *replacements*. This example converts the deprecated bold (<b>) character to its XHTML equivalent:

```php
<?php
    $table = array("<b>" => "<strong>", "</b>" => "</strong>");
    $html = "<b>Today In PHP-Powered News</b>";
    echo strtr($html, $table);
?>
```

This returns the following:

```
<strong>Today In PHP-Powered News</strong>
```

Converting HTML to Plain Text

You may sometimes need to convert an HTML file to plain text. The following function can help you accomplish this.

strip_tags()

```
string strip_tags (string str [, string allowable_tags])
```

The strip_tags() function removes all HTML and PHP tags from *str*, leaving only the text entities. The optional *allowable_tags* parameter allows you to specify which tags you would like to be skipped during this process. This example uses strip_tags() to delete all HTML tags from a string:

```php
<?php
    $input = "Email <a href='spammer@example.com'>spammer@example.com</a>";
    echo strip_tags($input);
?>
```

This returns the following:

```
Email spammer@example.com
```

The following sample strips all tags except the `<a>` tag:

```php
<?php
    $input = "This <a href='http://www.example.com/'>example</a>
                is <b>awesome</b>!";
    echo strip_tags($input, "<a>");
?>
```

This returns the following:

```
This <a href='http://www.example.com/'>example</a> is awesome!
```

> **NOTE** *Another function that behaves like* strip_tags() *is* fgetss(). *This function is described in Chapter 10.*

Alternatives for Regular Expression Functions

When you're processing large amounts of information, the regular expression functions can slow matters dramatically. You should use these functions only when you are interested in parsing relatively complicated strings that require the use of regular expressions. If you are instead interested in parsing for simple expressions, there are a variety of predefined functions that speed up the process considerably. Each of these functions is described in this section.

strtok()

```
string strtok (string str, string tokens)
```

The strtok() function parses the string *str* based on the characters found in *tokens*. One oddity about strtok() is that it must be continually called in order to completely tokenize a string; each call only tokenizes the next piece of the string. However, the *str* parameter only needs to be specified once, because the function keeps track of its position in string until it either completely tokenizes string or a new string parameter is specified. Its behavior is best explained via an example:

```php
<?php
    $info = "J. Gilmore:jason@example.com|Columbus, Ohio";

    // delimiters include colon (:), vertical bar (|), and comma (,)
    $tokens = ":|,";
```

```php
    $tokenized = strtok($info, $tokens);
    // print out each element in the $tokenized array
    while ($tokenized) {
        echo "Element = $tokenized<br>";
        // Don't include the first argument in subsequent calls.
        $tokenized = strtok($tokens);
    }
?>
```

This returns the following:

```
Element =J. Gilmore
Element = jason@example.com
Element = Columbus
Element = Ohio
```

parse_str()

```
void parse_str (string str [, array arr]))
```

The parse_str() function parses string into various variables, setting the variables
in the current scope. If the optional parameter *arr* is included, the variables will be
placed in that array instead. This function is particularly useful when handling URLs
that contain HTML form or otherwise extended information. The following example
parses information passed via a URL. This string is the common form for a grouping
of data that is passed from one page to another, compiled either directly in a hyperlink
or in an HTML form:

```php
<?php
    // suppose that the URL is http://www.example.com?ln=gilmore&zip=43210
    parse_str($_SERVER['QUERY_STRING']);
    // after execution of parse_str(), the following variables are available:
    // $ln = "gilmore"
    // $zip = "43210"
?>
```

Note that parse_str() is unable to correctly parse the first variable of the query
string if the string leads off with a question mark. Therefore, if you use a means other
than $_SERVER['QUERY_STRING'] for retrieving this parameter string, make sure you
delete that preceding question mark before passing the string to parse_str(). The
ltrim() function, introduced later in the chapter, is ideal for such tasks.

explode()

array explode (string *separator*, string *str* [, int *limit*])

The explode() function divides the string *str* into an array of substrings. The original string is divided into distinct elements by separating it based on the character *separator*. The number of elements can be limited with the optional inclusion of *limit*. Let's use explode() in conjunction with sizeof() and strip_tags() to determine the total number of words in a given block of text:

```php
<?php
$summary = <<< summary
In the latest installment of the ongoing Developer.com PHP series,
I discuss the many improvements and additions to
<a href="http://www.php.net">PHP 5's</a> object-oriented architecture.
summary;
$words = sizeof(explode(' ',strip_tags($summary)));
echo "Total words in summary: $words";
?>
```

This returns:

Total words in summary: 22

The explode() function will always be considerably faster than preg_split(), split(), and spliti(). Therefore, always use it instead of the others when a regular expression isn't necessary.

implode()

string implode (string *delimiter*, array *pieces*)

Just as you can use the explode() function to divide a delimited string into various array elements, so can you concatenate array elements to form a single, delimited string. This is accomplished with the implode() function. This example forms a string out of the elements of an array:

```php
<?php
    $cities = array("Columbus", "Akron", "Cleveland", "Cincinnati");
    echo implode("|", $cities);
?>
```

This returns:

```
Columbus|Akron|Cleveland|Cincinnati
```

> **NOTE** join() *is an alias for* implode().

strpos()

```
int strpos (string str, string substr [, int offset])
```

The strpos() function finds the position of the first case-sensitive occurrence of *substr* in *str*. The optional input parameter *offset* specifies the position at which to begin the search. If *substr* is not in string, strpos() will return FALSE. The optional parameter *offset* determines the position from which strpos() will begin searching. The following example determines the timestamp of the first time *index.html* is accessed:

```php
<?php
    $substr = "index.html";
$log = <<< logfile
192.168.1.11:/www/htdocs/index.html:[2004/02/10:20:36:50]
192.168.1.13:/www/htdocs/about.html:[2004/02/11:04:15:23]
192.168.1.15:/www/htdocs/index.html:[2004/02/15:17:25]
logfile;

    // what is first occurrence of the time $substr in log?
    $pos = strpos($log, $substr);

    // Find the numerical position of the end of the line
    $pos2 = strpos($log,"\n",$pos);

    // Calculate the beginning of the timestamp
    $pos = $pos + strlen($substr) + 1;

    // Retrieve the timestamp
    $timestamp = substr($log,$pos,$pos2-$pos);

    echo "The file $substr was first accessed on: $timestamp";
?>
```

This returns the position in which the file index.html was first accessed:

```
The file index.html was first accessed on: [2004/02/10:20:36:50]
```

stripos()

```
int stripos(string str, string substr [, int offset])
```

The function stripos() operates identically to strpos(), except that that it executes its search case-insensitively.

strrpos()

```
int strrpos (string str, char substr [, offset])
```

The strrpos() function finds the last occurrence of *substr* in *str*, returning its numerical position. The optional parameter *offset* determines the position from which strrpos() will begin searching. Suppose you wanted to pare down lengthy news summaries, truncating the summary and replacing the truncated component with an ellipsis. However, rather than simply cut off the summary explicitly at the desired length, you want it to operate in a user-friendly fashion, truncating at the end of the word closest to the truncation length. This function is ideal for such a task. Consider this example:

```php
<?php
    // Limit $summary to how many characters?
    $limit = 100;

    $summary = <<< summary
    In the latest installment of the ongoing Developer.com PHP series,
    I discuss the many improvements and additions to
    <a href="http://www.php.net">PHP 5's</a> object-oriented
    architecture.
summary;

    if (strlen($summary) > $limit)
        $summary = substr($summary, 0, strrpos(substr($summary, 0, $limit),
                          ' ')) . '...';
    echo $summary;
?>
```

This returns:

```
In the latest installment of the ongoing Developer.com PHP series,
I discuss the many...
```

---

str_replace()

```
mixed str_replace (string occurrence, mixed replacement, mixed str [, int count])
```

The str_replace() function executes a case-sensitive search for *occurrence* in *str*, replacing all instances with *replacement*. If *occurrence* is not found in *str*, then *str* is returned unmodified. If the optional parameter *count* is defined, then only *count occurrences* found in *str* will be replaced.

This function is ideal for hiding e-mail addresses from automated e-mail address retrieval programs:

```php
<?php
    $author = "jason@example.com";
    $author = str_replace("@","(at)",$author);
    echo "Contact the author of this article at $author.";
?>
```

This returns:

```
Contact the author of this article at jason(at)example.com.
```

str_ireplace()

```
mixed str_ireplace(mixed occurrence, mixed replacement, mixed str [, int count])
```

The function str_ireplace() operates identically to str_replace(), except that it is capable of executing a case-insensitive search.

strstr()

```
string strstr (string str, string occurrence)
```

The strstr() function returns the remainder of *str* beginning at the first *occurrence*. This example uses the function in conjunction with the ltrim() function to retrieve the domain name of an e-mail address:

```php
<?php
    $url = "sales@example.com";
    echo ltrim(strstr($url, "@"),"@");
?>
```

This returns the following:

```
example.com
```

substr()

```
string substr(string str, int start [, int length])
```

The substr() function returns the part of the *str* located between the *start* and *start+length* positions. If the optional *length* parameter is not specified, the substring is considered to be the string starting at *start* and ending at the end of string. There are four points to keep in mind when using this function:

- If *start* is positive, the returned string will begin at the *start* position of the string.

- If *start* is negative, the returned string will begin at the string length – *start* position of the string.

- If *length* is provided and is positive, the returned string will consist of the characters between *start* and (*start* + *length*). If this distance surpasses the total string length, then only the string between *start* and the string's end will be returned.

- If *length* is provided and is negative, the returned string will end *length* characters from the end of string.

Keep in mind that *start* is the offset from the first character of the string; therefore the returned string will actually start at character position (*start* + 1).

Consider a basic example:

```php
<?php
    $car = "1944 Ford";
    echo substr($car, 5);
?>
```

This returns the following:

```
Ford
```

The following example uses the *length* parameter:

```php
<?php
    $car = "1944 Ford";
    echo substr($car, 0, 4);
?>
```

This returns the following:

```
1944
```

The final example uses a negative length parameter:

```php
<?php
    $car = "1944 Ford";
    $yr = echo substr($car, 2, -5);
?>
```

This returns:

```
44
```

substr_count()

```
int substr_count (string str, string substring)
```

The substr_count() function returns the number of times *substring* occurs in *str*. The following example determines the number of times an IT consultant uses various buzzwords in his presentation:

```php
<?php
    $buzzwords = array("mindshare", "synergy", "space");
$talk = <<< talk
I'm certain that we could dominate mindshare in this space with our new product,
establishing a true synergy between the marketing and product development teams.
We'll own this space in three months.
talk;
    foreach($buzzwords as $bw) {
        echo "The word $bw appears ".substr_count($talk,$bw)." time(s).<br />";
    }
?>
```

This returns the following:

```
The word mindshare appears 1 time(s).
The word synergy appears 1 time(s).
The word space appears 2 time(s).
```

substr_replace()

```
string substr_replace (string str, string replacement, int start [, int length])
```

The substr_replace() function replaces a portion of *str* with *replacement*, beginning the *replacement* at *start* position of the string, and ending at *start* + *length* (assuming that the optional input parameter *length* is included). Alternatively, the *replacement* will stop on the complete placement of *replacement* in string. There are several behaviors you should keep in mind regarding the values of *start* and *length*:

- If *start* is positive, *replacement* will begin at character *start*.

- If *start* is negative, *replacement* will begin at (string length – *start*).

- If *length* is provided and is positive, *replacement* will be *length* characters long.

- If *length* is provided and is negative, *replacement* will end at (*str* length − *length*) characters.

Suppose you built an e-commerce site, and within the user profile interface, you want to show just the last four digits of the provided credit card number. This function is ideal for such a task:

```php
<?php
    $ccnumber = "1234567899991111";
    echo substr_replace($ccnumber,"************",0,12);
?>
```

This returns:

************1111

Padding and Stripping a String

For formatting reasons, you sometimes need to modify the string length via either padding or stripping characters. PHP provides a number of functions for doing so. I'll examine many of the commonly used functions in this section.

ltrim()

string ltrim (string *str* [, string *charlist*])

The ltrim() function removes various characters from the beginning of *str*, including white space, the horizontal tab (\t), newline (\n), carriage return (\r), NULL (\0), and vertical tab (\x0b).You can designate other characters for removal by defining them in the optional parameter *charlist*.

rtrim()

string rtrim(string *str* [, string *charlist*])

The rtrim() function operates identically to ltrim(), except that it removes the desig-nated characters from the right side of *str*.

trim()

string trim (string *str* [, string *charlist*])

You can think of the trim() function as a combination of ltrim() and rtrim(), except that it removes the designated characters from both sides of *str*.

str_pad()

```
string str_pad (string str, int length [, string pad_string [, int pad_type]])
```

The str_pad() function pads *str* to *length* characters. If the optional parameter *pad_string* is not defined, *str* will be padded with blank spaces; otherwise it will be padded with the character pattern specified by *pad_string*. By default, the string will be padded to the right; however, the optional parameter *pad_type* may be assigned the values STR_PAD_RIGHT, STR_PAD_LEFT, or STR_PAD_BOTH, padding the string accordingly. This example shows how to pad a string using str_pad():

```php
<?php
    echo str_pad("Salad", 10)." is good.";
?>
```

This returns the following:

```
Salad     is good.
```

This example makes use of str_pad()'s optional parameters:

```php
<?php
    $header = "Log Report";
    echo str_pad ($header, 20, "=+", STR_PAD_BOTH);
?>
```

This returns:

```
=+=+=Log Report=+=+=
```

Note that str_pad() truncates the pattern defined by *pad_string* if *length* is reached before completing an entire repetition of the pattern.

Counting Characters and Words

It's often useful to determine the total number of characters or words in a given string. Although PHP's considerable capabilities in string parsing has long made this task trivial, two functions were recently added that formalize the process. Both functions are introduced in this section.

count_chars()

```
mixed count_chars(string str [, mode])
```

The function count_chars() offers information regarding the characters found in *str*. It's behavior depends upon how the optional parameter *mode* is defined:

- 0: Returns an array consisting of each found byte-value as the key and the corresponding frequency as the value, even if the frequency is zero. This is the default.

- 1: Same as 0, but returns only those byte-values with a frequency greater than zero.

- 2: Same as 0, but returns only those byte-values with a frequency of zero.

- 3: Returns a string containing all located byte-values.

- 4: Returns a string containing all unused byte-values.

The following example counts the frequency of each character in $sentence:

```php
<?php
    $sentence = "The rain in Spain falls mainly on the plain";
    // Retrieve located characters and their corresponding frequency.
    $chart = count_chars($sentence, 1);

    foreach($chart as $letter=>$frequency)
        echo "Character ".chr($letter)." appears $frequency times<br />";
?>
```

This returns the following:

```
Character   appears 8 times
Character S appears 1 times
Character T appears 1 times
Character a appears 5 times
Character e appears 2 times
Character f appears 1 times
Character h appears 2 times
Character i appears 5 times
Character l appears 4 times
Character m appears 1 times
Character n appears 6 times
Character o appears 1 times
Character p appears 2 times
Character r appears 1 times
Character s appears 1 times
Character t appears 1 times
Character y appears 1 times
```

str_word_count()

```
mixed str_word_count (string str [, int format])
```

The function str_word_count() offers information regarding the total number of words found in *str*. If the optional parameter *format* is not defined, it will simply return the total number of words. If *format* is defined, it modifies the function's behavior based on its value:

- 1: Returns an array consisting of all words located in *str*.

- 2: Returns an associative array, where the key is the numerical position of the word in *str*, and the value is the word itself.

Consider an example:

```
<?php
$summary = <<< summary
In the latest installment of the ongoing Developer.com PHP series,
I discuss the many improvements and additions to PHP 5's
object-oriented architecture.
summary;
    $words = str_word_count($summary);
    echo "Total words in summary: $words";
?>
```

This returns the following:

```
Total words in summary: 23
```

You can use this function in conjunction with array_count_values() to determine the frequency in which each word appears within the string:

```
<?php
$summary = <<< summary
In the latest installment of the ongoing Developer.com PHP series,
I discuss the many improvements and additions to PHP 5's
object-oriented architecture.
summary;
    $words = str_word_count($summary,2);
    $frequency = array_count_values($words);
    print_r($frequency);
?>
```

This returns the following:

```
Array ( [In] => 1 [the] => 3 [latest] => 1 [installment] => 1 [of] => 1
[ongoing] => 1 [Developer] => 1 [com] => 1 [PHP] => 2 [series] => 1
[I] => 1 [discuss] => 1 [many] => 1 [improvements] => 1 [and] => 1
[additions] => 1 [to] => 1 [s] => 1 [object-oriented] => 1
[architecture] => 1 )
```

Summary

Many of the functions introduced in this chapter will be among the most commonly used within your PHP applications, as they form the crux of the language's string manipulation capabilities.

In the next chapter, we'll turn our attention towards another set of well-worn functions: those devoted to working with the file and operating system.

CHAPTER 10

Working with the File and Operating System

IT'S QUITE RARE to write an application that is entirely self-sufficient; that is, a program that does not rely on at least some level of interaction with external resources, such as the underlying file and operating system, and even other programming languages. The reason for this is quite simple: As languages, file systems, and operating systems have matured, the opportunities for creating much more efficient, scalable and timely applications have increased greatly as a result of the developer's ability to integrate the tried-and-true features of each component into a singular product. Of course, the trick is to choose a language that offers a convenient and efficient means for doing so. Luckily, PHP satisfies both conditions quite nicely, offering the programmer a wonderful array of tools for not only handling file system input and output, but also executing programs at the shell level. This chapter serves as an introduction to all such functionality, covering the following topics:

- **Learning About Files and Directories:** In this section, you'll learn how to perform file system forensics, revealing details including file and directory size and location, modification and access times, file pointers (both the hard and symbolic types), and more.

- **File Ownership and Permissions:** All mainstream operating systems offer a means for securing system data through a permission system based on user and group ownership and rights. In this section, you'll learn how to both determine and manipulate these controls.

- **File I/O:** In this section you'll learn how to interact with data files, which will let you perform a variety of practical tasks, including creating, deleting, reading, and writing files.

- **Reading Directory Contents:** In this section you'll learn how to easily retrieve directory contents.

- **Executing Shell Commands:** You can take advantage of operating system and other language-level functionality from within a PHP application through a number of built-in functions and mechanisms. You'll learn all about them in this section. I also demonstrate PHP's input sanitization capabilities, showing you how to prevent users from passing data that could potentially cause harm to your data and operating system.

> **NOTE** *PHP is particularly adept at working with the underlying file system, so much so that it is gaining popularity as a command-line interpreter. Although this topic is out of the scope of this book, you can find additional information in the PHP manual.*

Learning About Files and Directories

Organizing related data into entities commonly referred to as *files* and *directories* has long been a core concept in the computing environment. For this reason, programmers need to have a means for obtaining important details about files and directories, such as the location, size, last modification time, last access time, and other defining information. This section introduces many of PHP's built-in functions for doing just this.

Parsing Directory Paths

It's often useful to parse directory paths for various attributes such as the tailing extension name, directory component, and base name. A host of functions are available for performing such tasks, all of which are introduced in this section.

basename()

```
string basename (string path [, string suffix])
```

The basename() function returns the filename component of *path*. If the optional *suffix* parameter is supplied, that suffix will be omitted if the returned filename contains that extension. An example follows:

```php
<?php
    $path = "/home/www/data/users.txt";
    $filename = basename($path); // $filename contains "users.txt"
    $filename2 = basename($path, ".txt"); // $filename2 contains "users"
?>
```

dirname()

```
string dirname (string path)
```

The dirname() function is essentially the counterpart to basename(), instead providing the directory component of *path*. Reconsidering the previous example:

```php
<?php
    $path = "/home/www/data/users.txt";
    $dirname = dirname($path); // $dirname contains "/home/www/data"
?>
```

pathinfo()

```
array pathinfo (string path)
```

The pathinfo() function creates an associative array containing three components of the path specified by *path*: directory name, base name, and extension, referred to by the array keys dirname, basename, and extension, respectively. Consider the following path:

```
/home/www/htdocs/book/chapter10/index.html
```

As is relevant to pathinfo(), this path contains three components:

- dirname: /home/www/htdocs/book/chapter10

- basename: index.html

- extension: html

Therefore, you can use pathinfo() like this to retrieve this information:

```php
<?php
    $pathinfo = pathinfo("/home/www/htdocs/book/chapter10/index.html");
    echo "Dir name: $pathinfo[dirname]<br />\n";
    echo "Base name: $pathinfo[basename] <br />\n";
    echo "Extension: $pathinfo[extension] <br />\n";
?>
```

This returns:

```
Dir name: /home/www/htdocs/book/chapter10
Base name: index.html
Extension: html
```

realpath()

```
string realpath (string path)
```

The superbly useful realpath() function converts all symbolic links, and relative path references located in *path* to their absolute counterparts. For example, suppose your directory structure assumed the following path:

```
/home/www/htdocs/book/images/
```

You can then use `realpath()` to resolve any local path references:

```php
<?php
    $imgPath = "../../images/cover.gif";
    $absolutePath = realpath($imgPath);
    // Returns /www/htdocs/book/images/cover.gif


?>
```

File Types and Links

Numerous functions are available for learning various details about files and links (or file pointers) found on a file system. I'll introduce those functions in this section.

filetype()

```
string filetype (string filename)
```

The `filetype()` function determines and returns the file type of *filename*. Seven values are possible, including:

- `block`: The file is a block device.

- `char`: The file is a character device. A character device is responsible for a non-buffered exchange of data between the operating system and a device such as a terminal or printer.

- `dir`: The file is a directory.

- `fifo`: The file is a named pipe. Named pipes are commonly used to facilitate the passage of information from one process to another.

- `file`: The file is, well, a file (technically, a hard link).

- `link`: The file is a symbolic link. A symbolic link is a pointer to the pointer of a file.

- `unknown`: The file type is not known.

Consider three examples. In the first example, you determine the type of a CD-ROM drive:

```
echo filetype("/mnt/cdrom"); // char
```

Next, you determine the type of a Linux partition:

```
echo filetype("/dev/sda6"); // block
```

Finally, you can determine the type of a regular old HTML file:

```
echo filetype("/home/www/htdocs/index.html"); // file
```

link()

```
int link (string target, string link)
```

The link() function creates a hard link, *link*, to *target*, returning TRUE on success and FALSE otherwise. Note that because PHP scripts typically execute under the guise of the server daemon process owner, this function will fail unless that user has write permissions within the directory in which *link* is to reside.

linkinfo()

```
int linkinfo (string path)
```

The Unix lstat() function is used to return useful information about a symbolic link, including items such as the size, time of last modification, and the owner's user ID. The linkinfo() function returns one particular item offered by the lstat() function, used to determine whether the symbolic link specified by *path* really exists.

lstat()

```
array lstat (string symlink)
```

The lstat() function returns numerous items of useful information regarding the symbolic link referenced by *symlink*. See fstat() for a complete accounting of the returned array.

fstat()

```
array fstat (resource filepointer)
```

The fstat() function retrieves an array of useful information pertinent to a file referenced by a file pointer, *filepointer*. This array can be accessed either numerically, or via associative indices, each of which is listed in their numerically indexed position:

- **dev (0):** The device number upon which the file resides.

- **ino (1):** The file's inode number. The *inode* number is the unique numerical identifier associated with each filename, and is used to reference the associated entry in the inode table that contains information about the file's size, type, location, and other key characteristics.

- **mode (2):** The file's inode protection mode. This value determines the access and modification privileges assigned to the file.

- **nlink (3):** The number of hard links associated with the file.

- **uid (4):** The file owner's user ID (UID).

- **gid (5):** The file group's group ID (GID)

- **rdev (6):** The device type, if the inode device is available. Note that this element is not available on Win32 operating systems.

- **size (7):** The file size, in bytes.

- **atime (8):** The time of the file's last access, in Unix timestamp format.

- **mtime (9):** The time of the file's last modification, in Unix timestamp format.

- **ctime (10):** The time of the file's last change, in Unix timestamp format.

- **blksize (11):** The filesystem's block size. Note that this element is not available on Win32 operating systems.

- **blocks (12):** The number of blocks allocated to the file.

Consider the example shown in Listing 10-1.

Listing 10-1. Retrieving Core File Information

```php
<?php

/* Convert timestamp to desired format. */
function tstamp_to_date($tstamp) {
    return date("m-d-y  g:i:sa", $tstamp);
}

$file = "/usr/local/apache2/htdocs/book/chapter10/stat.php";
/* Open the file */
$fh = fopen($file, "r");

/* Retrieve file information */
$fileinfo = fstat($fh);

/* Output some juicy information about the file. */
echo "Filename: ".basename($file)."<br />";
echo "Filesize: ".round(($fileinfo["size"]/1024), 2)." kb <br />";
echo "Last accessed: ".tstamp_to_date($fileinfo["atime"])."<br />";
echo "Last modified: ".tstamp_to_date($fileinfo["mtime"])."<br />";
?>
```

This code returns:

```
Filename: stat.php
Filesize: 2.16 kb
Last accessed: 06-09-03 12:03:00pm
Last modified: 06-09-03 12:02:59pm
```

stat()

```
array stat (string filename)
```

The stat() function returns an array of useful information about the file specified by
filename, or FALSE if it fails. This function operates exactly like fstat(), returning all of
the same array elements; the only difference is that it requires an actual file name and
path rather than a resource handle..

If *filename* is a symbolic link, then the information will be pertinent to the file the
symbolic link points to, and not the symbolic link itself. To retrieve information about a
symbolic link, use lstat(). The lstat() function was introduced earlier in this chapter.

readlink()

```
string readlink (string path)
```

The readlink() function returns the target of the symbolic link specified by *path*, or FALSE if an error occurs. Therefore, if link test-link.txt is a symbolic link pointing to test.txt, the following will return the absolute pathname to the file:

```
echo readlink("/home/jason/test-link.txt");
// returns /home/jason/myfiles/test.txt
```

symlink()

```
int symlink (string target, string link)
```

The symlink() function creates a symbolic link named *link* to the existing *target*, returning TRUE on success and FALSE otherwise. Note that because PHP scripts typically execute under the guise of the server daemon process owner, this function will fail unless that daemon owner has write permissions within the directory in which *link* is to reside. Consider this example, in which a symbolic link "03" is pointed to the directory "2003":

```
<?php
    $link = symlink("/www/htdocs/stats/2003", "/www/htdocs/stats/03");
?>
```

Calculating File, Directory, and Disk Sizes

Calculating file, directory, and disk sizes is a common task in all sorts of applications. In this section, I'll introduce a number of standard PHP functions suited to this task.

filesize()

```
int filesize (string filename)
```

The filesize() function returns the size, in bytes, of *filename*. An example follows:

```
<?php
    $file = "/www/htdocs/book/chapter1.pdf";
    $bytes = filesize("$file"); // Returns 91815
    echo "File ".basename($file)." is $bytes bytes, or
        ".round($bytes / 1024, 2)." kilobytes.";
?>
```

This returns the following:

```
File 852Chapter16R.rtf is 91815 bytes, or 89.66 kilobytes
```

---

disk_free_space()

```
float disk_free_space (string directory)
```

The disk_free_space() function returns the available space, in bytes, allocated to the disk partition housing the directory specified by *directory*. An example follows:

```php
<?php
    $drive = "/usr";
    echo round((disk_free_space($drive) / 1048576), 2);
?>
```

This returns:

```
2141.29
```

Note that the returned number is in megabytes (MB), because the value returned from disk_free_space() was divided by 1,048,576, which is equivalent to one MB.

disk_total_space()

```
float disk_total_space (string directory)
```

The disk_total_space() function returns the total size, in bytes, consumed by the disk partition housing the directory specified by *directory*. If you use this function in conjunction with disk_free_space(), it's easy to offer useful space allocation statistics:

```php
<?php
    $systempartitions = array("/", "/home","/usr", "/www");
    foreach ($systempartitions as $partition) {
        $totalSpace = disk_total_space($partition) / 1048576;
        $usedSpace = $totalSpace - disk_free_space($partition) / 1048576;
        echo "Partition: $partition (Allocated: $totalSpace MB. Used: $usedSpace MB.)";
    }
?>
```

This returns:

```
Partition: / (Allocated: 3099.292 MB. Used: 343.652 MB.)
Partition: /home (Allocated: 5510.664 MB. Used: 344.448 MB.)
Partition: /usr (Allocated: 4127.108 MB. Used: 1985.716 MB.)
Partition: /usr/local/apache2/htdocs (Allocated: 4127.108 MB. Used: 1985.716 MB.)
```

Retrieving a Directory Size

PHP doesn't currently offer a standard function for retrieving the total size of a directory; a task often more applicable than retrieving total disk space (see disk_total_space()). And although you could make a system level call to du using exec() or system() (both of which are introduced later in this chapter), such functions are often disabled for security reasons. The alternative solution is to write a custom PHP function capable of carrying out this task. A recursive function seems particularly well-suited for this task. One possible variation is offered in Listing 10-2.

> **NOTE** *The* du *command will summarize disk usage of a file or directory. See the* man *page for usage information.*

Listing 10-2. Determining the Size of a Directory's Contents

```php
<?php
function directory_size($directory) {
    $directorySize=0;
    /* Open the directory and read its contents. */
    if ($dh = @opendir($directory)) {
        /* Iterate through each directory entry. */
        while (($filename = readdir ($dh))) {
            /* Filter out some of the unwanted directory entries. */
            if ($filename != "." && $filename != "..")
            {
                // File, so determine size and add to total.
                if (is_file($directory."/".$filename))
                    $directorySize += filesize($directory."/".$filename);
                // New directory, so initiate recursion. */
                if (is_dir($directory."/".$filename))
                    $directorySize += directory_size($directory."/".$filename);
            }
        } #endWHILE
    } #endIF
    @closedir($dh);
    return $directorySize;
} #end directory_size()
```

```
$directory = "/usr/local/apache2/htdocs/book/chapter10/";
$totalSize = round((directory_size($directory) / 1024), 2);
echo "Directory $directory: ".$totalSize. "kb.";
?>
```

Access and Modification Times

The ability to determine a file's last access and modification time plays an important role in many administrative tasks, especially in Web applications that involve network or CPU-intensive update operations. PHP offers three functions for determining a file's access, creation, and last modification time, all of which are introduced in this section.

fileatime()

```
int fileatime (string filename)
```

The fileatime() function returns *filename*'s last access time in Unix timestamp format, or FALSE on error. An example follows:

```
<?php
    $file = "/usr/local/apache2/htdocs/book/chapter10/stat.php";
    echo "File last accessed: ".date("m-d-y  g:i:sa", fileatime($file));
?>
```

This returns:

```
File last accessed: 06-09-03 1:26:14pm
```

filectime()

```
int filectime (string filename)
```

The filectime() function returns *filename*'s last changed time in Unix timestamp format, or FALSE on error. An example follows:

```
<?php
    $file = "/usr/local/apache2/htdocs/book/chapter10/stat.php";
    echo "File inode last changed: ".date("m-d-y  g:i:sa", fileatime($file));
?>
```

This returns:

```
File inode last changed: 06-09-03 1:26:14pm
```

237

> **NOTE** *The "last changed time" differs from the "last modified time" in that the last changed time refers to any change in the file's inode data, including changes to permissions, owner, group, or other inode-specific information, whereas the last modified time refers to changes to the file's content (specifically, bytesize).*

filemtime()

```
int filemtime (string filename)
```

The filemtime() function returns *filename*'s last modification time in Unix timestamp format, or FALSE otherwise. The following code demonstrates how to place a "last modified" timestamp on a Web page:

```php
<?php
    $file = "/usr/local/apache2/htdocs/book/chapter10/stat.php";
    echo "File last updated: ".date("m-d-y  g:i:sa", filemtime($file));
?>
```

This returns:

```
File last updated: 06-09-03 1:26:14pm
```

File Ownership and Permissions

These days, security is paramount to any server installation, large or small. Most modern operating systems have embraced the concept of the separation of file rights via a user/group ownership paradigm, which, when properly configured, offers a wonderfully convenient and powerful means for securing data. In this section, you'll learn how to use PHP's built-in functionality to review and manage these permissions.

Note that because PHP scripts typically execute under the guise of the server daemon process owner, some of these functions will fail unless highly insecure actions are taken to run the server as a privileged user. Thus, keep in mind that some of the functionality introduced in this chapter is much better suited for use when running PHP as a command-line interpreter.

chown()

```
int chown (string filename, mixed user)
```

The chown() function attempts to change the owner of *filename* to *user* (specified either by the user's username or UID), returning TRUE on success and FALSE otherwise.

chgrp()

```
int chgrp (string filename, mixed group)
```

The chgrp() function will attempt to change the group membership of *filename* to *group*, returning TRUE on success and FALSE otherwise.

fileperms()

```
int fileperms (string filename)
```

The fileperms() function returns *filename*'s permissions in decimal format, or FALSE in case of error. Because the decimal permissions representation is almost certainly not the desired format, you'll need to convert fileperms() return value. This is easily accomplished using the base_convert() function in conjunction with substr(). The base_convert() function converts a value from one number base to another; therefore you can use it to convert fileperms() returned decimal value from base 10 to the desired base 8. The substr() function is then used to retrieve only the final three digits of base_convert()'s returned value, which are the only ones referred to when discussing Unix file permissions. Consider the following example:

```php
<?php
    echo substr(base_convert(fileperms("/etc/passwd"), 10, 8), 3);
?>
```

This returns:

```
644
```

---

filegroup()

```
int filegroup (string filename)
```

The filegroup() function returns the group ID (GID) of the *filename* owner, and FALSE if the GID cannot be determined.

```php
<?php
    $gid = filegroup("/etc/passwd");
    // Returns "0" on Unix, because root usually has GID of 0.
?>
```

Note that filegroup() returns the GID, and not the group name.

fileowner()

```
int fileowner (string filename)
```

The fileowner() function returns the user ID (UID) of the *filename* owner, or FALSE if the UID cannot be determined. Consider this example:

```php
<?php
    $uid = fileowner("/etc/passwd");
    // Returns "0" on Linux, as root typically has UID of 0.
?>
```

Note that fileowner() returns the UID, and not the username.

isexecutable()

```
boolean isexecutable (string filename)
```

The isexecutable() function returns TRUE if *filename* exists and is executable, and FALSE otherwise. Note that this function is not available on Win32 installations.

isreadable()

```
boolean isreadable (string filename)
```

The isreadable() function returns TRUE if *filename* exists and is readable, and FALSE otherwise. If a directory name is passed in as *filename*, isreadable() will determine whether that directory is readable.

iswriteable()

```
boolean iswriteable (string filename)
```

The iswriteable() function returns TRUE if *filename* exists and is writable, and FALSE otherwise. If a directory name is passed in as *filename*, iswriteable() will determine whether that directory is writable.

umask

```
int umask ([int mask])
```

The umask determines the level of permissions assigned to a newly created file. The umask() function calculates PHP's umask to be the result of *mask* bitwise ANDed with 0777, and returns the old mask. Keep in mind that *mask* is a three or four digit code representing the permission level. PHP will then use this umask when creating files and directories throughout the script. Omitting the optional parameter *mask* will result in the retrieval of PHP's currently configured umask value.

File I/O

Writing exciting, useful programs almost always requires that the program work with some sort of external data source. Two prime examples of such data sources are files and databases. In this section, we'll delve deep into working with files. Prior to beginning an introduction of PHP's numerous standard file-related functions, I'd like to introduce a few basic concepts pertinent to this topic.

The Concept of a Resource

The term *resource* is commonly attached to any entity from which an input or output stream can be initiated. Standard input or output, files, and network sockets are all examples of resources.

Newline

The newline character, which has the syntax \n, represents the end of a line within a file. Keep this in mind when you need to input or output information one line at a time. Several functions introduced throughout the remainder of this chapter offer functionality tailored to working with the newline for exactly this reason. Some of these functions include file(), fgetcsv(), and fgets().

End-of-file

Programs require a standardized means for discerning when the end of a file has been reached. This standard is commonly referred to as the end-of-file, or EOF character. This is such an important concept that almost every language I can think of offers a built-in function for verifying whether or not the parser has arrived at the EOF. In the case of PHP, this function is feof(), described next.

feof()

```
int feof(string resource)
```

The feof() function determines whether *resource*'s EOF has been reached. It is used quite commonly in file I/O operations. An example follows:

```php
<?php
    $fh = fopen("/home/www/data/users.txt", "rt");
    while (!feof($fh)) echo fgets($fh);
    fclose($fh);
?>
```

Opening and Closing a File

You'll often need to establish a connection to a file resource before you can do anything with its contents. Likewise, once you've finished working with that resource, you should close the connection. Two standard functions are available for such tasks, both of which are introduced in this section.

fopen()

```
resource fopen (string resource, string mode [, int use_include_path
[, resource zcontext]])
```

The fopen() function binds a *resource* to a stream, or handler. Once bound, the script can interact with this resource via the handle. Most commonly, it's used to open files for reading and manipulation. However fopen() is also capable of opening resources via a number of protocols, including HTTP, HTTPS, and FTP, a concept discussed in Chapter 14.

The *mode*, assigned at the time a *resource* is opened, determines the level of access available to that resource. The various modes are defined in Table 10-1.

Table 10-1. File Modes

MODE	DESCRIPTION
r	Read-only. The file pointer is placed at the beginning of the file.
r+	Read and write. The file pointer is placed at the beginning of the file.
w	Write only. Before writing, delete the file contents and return file pointer to the beginning of the file. If the file does not exist, attempt to create it.
w+	Read and write. Before reading or writing, delete the file contents and return file pointer to the beginning of the file. If the file does not exist, attempt to create it.
a	Write only. The file pointer is placed at the end of the file. If the file does not exist, attempt to create it. This mode is better known as Append.
a+	Read and write. The file pointer is placed at the end of the file. If the file does not exist, attempt to create it. This mode is better known as Append.
b	Open the file in binary mode.
t	Open the file in text mode.

If the resource is found on the local file system, PHP expects the resource to be available either by the local or relative path prefacing it. Alternatively, you can assign fopen()'s *use_include_path* parameter the value of 1, which will cause PHP to consider the paths specified in the include_path configuration directive.

The final parameter, *zcontext*, is used for setting configuration parameters specific to the file or stream, and for sharing file- or stream-specific information across multiple fopen() requests. I'll talk more about this topic in Chapter 14.

So now consider a few examples. The first opens a read-only stream to a text file residing on the local server:

```
$fh = fopen("/usr/local/apache/data/users.txt","rt");
```

The next example demonstrates opening a write stream to a Microsoft Word document. Because Word documents are binary, you should specify the binary b mode variation.

```
$fh = fopen("/usr/local/apache/data/docs/summary.doc","wb");
```

The next example refers to the same Word document, except this time PHP will search for the file in the paths specified by the include_path directive:

```
$fh = fopen("summary.doc","wb", 1);
```

In the final example, you'll open a read-only stream to a remote index.html file:

```
$fh = fopen("http://www.example.com/", "rt");
```

You'll see this function in numerous examples throughout this and the next chapter.

fclose()

```
boolean fclose (resource filehandle)
```

Good programming practice dictates that you should destroy pointers to any resources once you're finished with them. The fclose() function handles this for you, closing the previously opened file pointer specified by *filehandle*, returning TRUE on success and FALSE otherwise. The *filehandle* must be an existing file pointer opened using fopen() or fsockopen().

Reading from a File

PHP offers numerous methods for reading data from a file, ranging from reading in just one character at a time, to reading in the entire file with a single operation. I'll examine the entire gamut here.

file()

```
array file (string filename [int use_ include_path [, resource context]])
```

The immensely useful file() function is capable of reading a file into an array, separating each element by the newline character, with the newline still attached to the end of each element. Although simplistic, the importance of this function can't be understated, and therefore it warrants a simple demonstration. Consider the following sample text file, named users.txt:

```
Ale ale@example.com
Nicole nicole@example.com
Laura laura@example.com
```

The following script reads in `users.txt`, and parses and converts the data into a convenient Web-based format:

```php
<?php
    $users = file("users.txt");
    foreach ($users as $user) {
        list($name, $email) = explode(" ", $user);
        // Remove newline from $email
        $email = trim($email);
        echo "<a href=\"mailto:$email\">$name</a> <br />\n";
    }
?>
```

This script results in the following HTML output:

```
<a href="ale@example.com">Ale</a><br />
<a href="nicole@example.com">Nicole</a><br />
<a href="laura@example.com">Laura</a><br />
```

Like `fopen()`, you can tell `file()` to search through the paths specified in the include_path configuration parameter by setting *use_include_path* to 1. The *context* parameter refers to a stream context. You'll learn more about this topic in Chapter 14.

file_get_contents()

```
string file_get_contents (string filename [, int use_include_path
[resource context]])
```

The `file_get_contents()` function reads the contents of *filename* into a string. Revising the above script to use this function instead of `file()`, you get the following code:

```php
<?php
    $userfile= file_get_contents("users.txt");
    // Place each line of $userfile into array
    $users = explode("\n",$userfile);
    foreach ($users as $user) {
        list($name, $email) = explode(" ", $user);
        echo "<a href=\"mailto:$email\">$name/a> <br />";
    }
?>
```

The *context* parameter refers to a stream context. You'll learn more about this topic in Chapter 14.

fgetc()

```
string fgetc (resource handle)
```

The fgetc() function reads a single character from the open resource stream specified by *handle*. If the EOF is encountered, a value of FALSE is returned.

fgetcsv()

```
array fgetcsv (resource handle, int length [, string delimiter
[, string enclosure]])
```

The convenient fgetcsv() function parses each line of a file delimited file specified by *handle*, and delimited by *delimiter* placing each field into an array. Reading does not stop on a newline; rather, it stops either when *length* characters have been read or the closing *enclosure* character is located. Therefore, it is always a good idea to choose a number that will certainly surpass the longest line in the file.

Consider a scenario in which weekly newsletter subscriber data is cached to a file for perusal by the corporate marketing staff. Always eager to barrage the IT department with dubious requests, they ask that the information be also made available for viewing on the Web. Thankfully, this is easily accomplished with fgetcsv(). The following example parses the already cached file:

```php
<?php
    $fh = fopen("/home/www/data/subscribers.csv", "r");
    while (list($name, $email, $phone) = fgetcsv($fh, 1024, ",")) {
        echo "<p>$name ($email) Tel. $phone</p>";
    }
?>
```

Note that you don't have to use fgetcsv() to parse such files; the file() and list() functions accomplish the job quite nicely. Reconsidering the above example:

```php
<?php
    $users = file("users.txt");
    foreach ($users as $user) {
        list($name, $email, $phone) = explode(",", $user);
        echo "<p>$name ($email) Tel. $phone</p>";
    }
?>
```

> **NOTE** *Comma-separated Value (CSV) files are commonly used when importing files between applications. Microsoft Excel and Access, MySQL, Oracle, and PostgreSQL are just a few of the applications and databases capable of both importing and exporting CSV data. Additionally, languages such as Perl, Python, and PHP are particularly efficient at parsing delimited data.*

fgets()

```
fgets (resource handle [, int length])
```

The fgets() function returns either length – 1 bytes from the opened resource referred to by *handle*, or everything it has read up to the point that a newline or the EOF is encountered. If the optional *length* parameter is omitted, 1024 characters is assumed. In most situations, this means that fgets() will encounter a newline character before reading 1024 characters, thereby returning the next line with each successive call. An example follows:

```php
<?php
    $fh = fopen("/home/www/data/users.txt", "rt");
    while (!feof($fh)) echo fgets($fh);
    fclose($fh);
?>
```

fgetss()

```
string fgetss (resource handle, int length [, string allowable_tags])
```

The fgetss() function operates similarly to fgets(), save for that it strips any HTML and PHP tags from *handle*. If you'd like certain tags to be ignored, include them in the *allowable_tags* parameter. As an example, consider a scenario in which authors are expected to submit their work in HTML format using a specified subset of HTML tags. Of course, the authors (this one included) don't always follow instructions, so the file must be scanned for tag misuse before it can be published. With fgetss(), this is trivial:

```php
<?php
    /* Build list of acceptable tags */
    $tags = "<h2><h3><p><b><a><img>";
    /* Open the article, and read its contents. */
    $fh = fopen("gilmore.html", "rt");
    while (!feof($fh)) {
        $article .= fgetss($fh, 1024, $tags);
    }
    fclose($fh);
    /* Open the file up in write mode
        and write $article contents. */
    $fh = fopen("gilmore.html", "wt");
    fwrite($fh, $article);
    fclose($fh);
?>
```

> **TIP** *If you want to remove HTML tags from user input submitted via a form, check out the* strip_tags() *function, introduced in Chapter 9.*

fread()

```
string fread (resource handle, int length)
```

The fread() function reads *length* characters from the resource specified by *handle*. Reading will stop when the EOF is reached or when *length* characters have been read. Note that unlike other read functions, newline characters are irrelevant when using fread(), therefore it's often convenient to read the entire file in at once using filesize() to determine the number of characters that should be read in:

```php
<?php
    $file = "/home/www/data/users.txt";
    $fh = fopen($file, "rt");
    $userdata = fread($fh, filesize($file));
    fclose($fh);
?>
```

The variable $userdata now contains the contents of the users.txt file.

readfile()

```
int readfile (string filename [, int use_include_path])
```

The readfile() function reads an entire file specified by *filename* and immediately outputs it to the output buffer, returning the number of bytes read. Enabling the optional *use_include_path* parameter tells PHP to search the paths specified by the include_path configuration parameter. After sanitizing the article discussed in the fgetss() section, it can be output to the browser quite easily using readfile(). This revised example is shown here:

```php
<?php
    $file = "/home/www/articles/gilmore.html";
    /* Build list of acceptable tags */
    $tags = "<h2><h3><p><b><a><img>";
    /* Open the article, and read its contents. */
    $fh = fopen($file, "rt");
    while (!feof($fh))
        $article .= fgetss($fh, 1024, $tags);
    fclose($fh);
    /* Open the article, overwriting it with the sanitized material */
    $fh = fopen($file, "wt");
    fwrite($fh, $article);
    fclose($fh);
    /* Output the article to the browser. */
    $bytes = readfile($file);
?>
```

Like many other of PHP's file I/O functions, remote files can be opened via their URL if the configuration parameter fopen_wrappers is enabled.

fscanf()

```
mixed fscanf (resource handle, string format [, string var1])
```

The fscanf() function offers a convenient means for parsing the resource specified by *handle* in accordance with the format specified by *format*. Suppose you wanted to parse the following file consisting of social security numbers (socsecurity.txt):

```
123-45-6789
234-56-7890
345-67-8901
```

The following example parses the socsecurity.txt file:

```php
<?php
    $fh = fopen("socsecurity.txt", "r");
    /* Parse each SSN in accordance with
       integer-integer-integer format. */
    while ($user = fscanf($fh, "%d-%d-%d")) {
        list ($part1,$part2,$part3) = $user;

        ...
    }
    fclose($fh);
?>
```

With each iteration, the variables $part1, $part2, and $part3 will be assigned the three components of each SSN, respectively.

Moving the File Pointer

It's often useful to jump around within a file, reading from and writing to various locations. Several PHP functions are available for doing just this.

fseek()

```
int fseek (resource handle, int offset [, int whence])
```

The fseek() function moves the *handle*'s pointer to the location specified by *offset*. If the optional parameter *whence* is omitted, the position is set *offset* bytes from the beginning of the file. Otherwise, *whence* can be set to one of three possible values, which affect the pointer's position:

- SEEK_CUR: Sets the pointer position to the current position plus *offset* bytes.

- SEEK_END: Sets the pointer position to the EOF plus *offset* bytes. In this case, *offset* must be set to a negative value.

- SEEK_SET: Sets the pointer position to *offset* bytes. This has the same effect as omitting *whence*.

ftell()

```
int ftell (resource handle)
```

The ftell() function retrieves the current position of the file pointer's offset within the resource specified by *handle*.

rewind()

```
int rewind (resource handle)
```

The rewind() function moves the file pointer back to the beginning of the resource specified by *handle*.

Writing to a File

This section highlights several of the functions used to output data to a file.

fwrite()

```
int fwrite (resource handle, string string, [, int length])
```

The fwrite() function outputs the contents of *string* to the resource pointed to by *handle*. If the optional *length* parameter is provided, fwrite() will stop writing when *length* characters have been written. Otherwise, writing will stop when the end of the *string* is found. Consider this example:

```php
<?php
    $subscriberInfo = "Jason Gilmore|wj@example.com";
    $fh = fopen("/home/www/data/subscribers.txt", "at");
    fwrite($fh, $subscriberInfo);
    fclose($fh);
?>
```

> **TIP** *If the length parameter is not supplied, the* magic_quotes_runtime *configuration parameter will be disregarded. See Chapters 2 and 9 for more information about this parameter.*

fputs()

```
int fputs (resource handle, string string [, int length])
```

The fputs() function operates identically to fwrite(). Presumably it was incorporated into the language to satisfy the terminology preferences of C/C++ programmers.

Reading Directory Contents

The process required for reading a directory's contents is quite similar to that involved in reading a file. In this section, I'll introduce the functions available for this task, and also introduce a function new to PHP 5 that reads a directory's contents into an array.

opendir()

```
resource opendir (string path)
```

Just as fopen() opens a file pointer to a given file, opendir() opens a directory stream specified by *path*.

closedir()

```
void closedir (resource directory_handle)
```

The closedir() function closes the directory stream pointed to by *directory_handle*.

readdir()

```
string readdir (int directory_handle)
```

The readdir() function returns each element in the directory specified by *directory_handle*. You can use this function to list all files and child directories in a given directory:

```php
<?php
    $dh = opendir('/usr/local/apache2/htdocs/');
    while ($file = readdir($dh))
        echo "$file <br>";
    closedir($dh);
?>
```

Sample output follows:

```
.
..
articles
images
news
test.php
```

Note that readdir() also returns the . and .. entries common to a typical Unix directory listing. You can easily filter these out with an if statement:

```
if($file != "." AND $file != "..")…
```

scandir()

```
array scandir(string directory [,int sorting_order [, resource context]])
```

The scandir() function, which is new to PHP 5, returns an array consisting of files and directories found in *directory*, or returns FALSE on error. Setting the optional *sorting_order* parameter to 1 sorts the contents in descending order, overriding the default of ascending order. Revisiting the previous example:

```php
<?php
    print_r(scandir("/usr/local/apache2/htdocs"));
?>
```

This returns:

```
Array ( [0] => . [1] => .. [2] => articles [3] => images
[4] => news [5] => test.php )
```

The *context* parameter refers to a stream context. You'll learn more about this topic in Chapter 14.

Executing Shell Commands

The ability to interact with the underlying operating system is a crucial feature of any programming language. In this section, I'll introduce PHP's capabilities in this regard.

PHP's Built-in System Commands

Although you could conceivably execute any system-level command using a function like exec() or system(), some of these functions are so commonplace that the developers thought it a good idea to incorporate them directly into the language. Several of those functions are introduced in this section.

rmdir()

```
int rmdir (string dirname)
```

The rmdir() function removes the directory specified by *dirname*, returning TRUE on success and FALSE otherwise. As with many of PHP's file system functions, permissions must be properly set in order for rmdir() to successfully remove the directory. Because PHP scripts typically execute under the guise of the server daemon process owner, rmdir() will fail unless that user has write permissions to the directory. Also, the directory must be empty.

To remove a non-empty directory, you can either use a function capable of executing a system level command, like system() or exec(), or you can write a recursive function that will remove all file contents before attempting to remove the directory. Note that in either case the executing user (server daemon process daemon owner) requires write access to the *parent* of the target directory.

```php
<?php
    function delete_directory($dir)
    {
        if ($dh = @opendir($dir))
        {
            /* Iterate through directory contents. */
            while (($file = readdir ($dh)) != false)
            {
                if (($file == ".") || ($file == "..")) continue;
                if (is_dir($dir . '/' . $file))
                    delete_directory($dir . '/' . $file);
                else
                    unlink($dir . '/' . $file);
            } #endWHILE
            @closedir($dh);
            rmdir($dir);
        } #endIF
    } #end delete_directory()
    $dir = "/usr/local/apache2/htdocs/book/chapter10/test/";
    delete_directory($dir);
?>
```

rename()

```
boolean rename (string oldname, string newname)
```

The rename() function renames a file specified by *oldname* to the new name *newname*, returning TRUE on success and FALSE otherwise. Because PHP scripts typically execute under the guise of the server daemon process owner, rename() will fail unless that user has write permissions to that file.

touch()

```
int touch (string filename [, int time [, int atime]])
```

The touch() function will set the file *filename*'s last-modified and last-accessed times, returning TRUE on success or FALSE on error. If *time* is not provided, the present time (as specified by the server) is used. If the optional *atime* parameter is provided, the access time will be set to this value; otherwise, like the modification time, it will be set to either *time* or the present server time.

Note that if *filename* does not exist, it will be created, assuming that the script's owner possesses adequate permissions.

System-Level Program Execution

Truly lazy programmers know how to make the most of their entire server environment when developing applications, exploiting the functionality of the operating system, file system, installed program base, and programming languages whenever necessary. In this section, you'll learn how PHP can interact with the operating system to call both OS-level programs, and third-party installed applications. Done properly, it adds a whole new level of functionality to your PHP programming repertoire. Done poorly, it can be catastrophic to not only your application, but to your server's data integrity. That said, before delving into this powerful feature, I'd like to take a moment to discuss the topic of sanitizing user input before passing it to the shell level.

Sanitizing the Input

Before introducing any of PHP's program execution functions, I want to say a few words about the importance of sanitizing any user input which that may subsequently be passed to system level functions. Neglecting to do so could allow attackers to do massive internal damage to your information store and operating system, deface or delete Web files, and otherwise gain unrestricted access to your server. And that's only the beginning.

NOTE *See Chapter 19 for a discussion of secure PHP programming.*

As an example of why this is so important, consider a real-world scenario. Suppose that you offered an online service that generated PDFs from an input URL. A great tool for accomplishing just this is HTMLDOC, a program that converts HTML documents to indexed HTML, Adobe PostScript, and PDF files. HTMLDOC is a product of Easy Software Products (http://www.easysw.com/), and is released under the GNU General Public License. HTMLDOC can be invoked from the command line, like so:

```
%>htmldoc --webpage -f webpage.pdf http://www.wjgilmore.com/
```

This would result in the creation of a PDF named webpage.pdf, which would contain a snapshot of my Web site's index page. Of course, most users will not have command-line access to your server; therefore, you'll need to create a much more controlled interface to the service, perhaps the most obvious of which being via a Web page. Using PHP's passthru() function (introduced later in this chapter), you can call HTMLDOC and return the desired PDF, like so:

```
$document = $_POST['userurl'];
passthru("htmldoc --webpage -f webpage.pdf $document);
```

What if an enterprising attacker took the liberty of passing through additional input, unrelated to the desired HTML page, entering something like this:

```
http://www.wjgilmore.com/ ; cd /usr/local/apache/htdocs/; rm -rf *
```

Most Unix shells would interpret the passthru() request as three separate commands. The first is:

```
htmldoc --webpage -f webpage.pdf http://www.wjgilmore.com/
```

The second command is:

```
cd /usr/local/apache/htdocs/
```

And the final command is:

```
rm -rf *
```

Those last two commands were certainly unexpected, and could result in the deletion of your entire Web document tree. One way to safeguard against such attempts is to sanitize user input before it is passed to any of PHP's program execution functions. Two standard functions are conveniently available for doing so: escapeshellarg() and escapeshellcmd(). I'll examine each in this section.

escapeshellarg()

```
string escapeshellarg (string arguments)
```

The escapeshellarg() function delimits *arguments* with single quotes and prefixes (escapes) quotes found within *arguments*. The effect is that when *arguments* is passed to a shell command, it will be considered a single argument. This is significant because it lessens the possibility that an attacker could masquerade additional commands as shell command arguments. Therefore, in the nightmare scenario I just described, the entire user input would be enclosed in single quotes, like so:

```
'http://www.wjgilmore.com/ ; cd /usr/local/apache/htdoc/; rm -rf *'
```

The result would be that HTMLDOC would simply return an error because it could not resolve a URL possessing this syntax, rather than deleting an entire directory tree.

escapeshellcmd()

```
string escapeshellcmd (string command)
```

The escapeshellcmd() function operates under the same premise as escapeshellarg(), sanitizing potentially dangerous input by escaping shell metacharacters. These characters include: # & ; ` , | * ? , ~ < > ^ ( ) [ ] { } $ \\

PHP's Program Execution Functions

This section introduces several functions (in addition to the backticks execution operator) used to execute system-level programs via a PHP script. Although at first glance they all appear to be operationally identical, each offers its own syntactical nuances.

exec()

```
string exec (string command [, array output [, int return_var]])
```

The exec() function is best-suited for executing an operating system-level application (designated by *command*) intended to continue executing in the server background. Although the last line of output will be returned, chances are that you'd like to have all of the output returned for review; you can do this by including the optional parameter *output*, which will be populated with each line of output upon completion of the command specified by exec(). In addition, you can discover the executed command's return status by including the optional parameter *return_var*.

Although I could take the easy way out and demonstrate how exec() can be used to execute an ls command (dir for the Windows folks), returning the directory listing, I'd rather take this opportunity to offer a somewhat more practical example; how to call a Perl script from PHP. Consider the below Perl script (languages.pl):

```
#! /usr/bin/perl
my @languages = qw[perl php python java c];
foreach $language (@languages) {
    print $language."<br />";
}
```

The Perl script is quite simple; I purposely decided not to require any modules so that you could test this example with little time investment. If you're running Linux, chances are very good that you could run this example immediately, because Perl is installed on every respectable distribution. If you're running Windows, check out ActiveState's (http://www.activestate.com/) fantastic ActivePerl distribution.

Like *languages.pl*, the PHP script shown here isn't exactly rocket science; it simply calls the Perl script, specifying that the outcome be placed into an array named $results. The contents of $results are then output to the browser.

```php
<?php
    $outcome = exec("languages.pl", $results);
    foreach ($results as $result) echo $result;
?>
```

The results are as follows:

```
perl
php
python
java
c
```

system()

```
string system (string command [, int return_var])
```

The system() function is useful when you want to output the executed command's results. Rather than return output via an optional parameter, as is the case with exec(), the output is returned directly to the caller. However, if you would like to review the execution status of the called program, you need to designate a variable using the optional parameter *return_var*.

For example, suppose you'd like to list all files located within a specific directory:

```
$mymp3s = system("ls -1 /home/jason/mp3s/");
```

Or, revising the previous PHP script to again call the languages.pl using system():

```php
<?php
    $outcome = exec("languages.pl", $results);
    echo $outcome
?>
```

passthru()

```
void passthru (string command [, int return_var])
```

The passthru() function is similar in function to exec(), except that it should be used if you'd like to return binary output to the caller. For example, suppose you wanted to convert GIF images to PNG before displaying them to the browser. You could use the

Netpbm graphics package, available at `http://netpbm.sourceforge.net/` under the
GPL license:

```
<?php
   header("ContentType:image/png");
   passthru("giftopnm cover.gif | pnmtopng > cover.png");
?>
```

Backticks

Delimiting a string with backticks signals to PHP that the string should be executed as
a shell command, returning any output. Note that backticks are not single quotes, but
rather are a slanted cousin, commonly sharing a key with the tilde (~) on most Ameri-
can keyboards. An example follows:

```
<?php
   $result = `date`;
   echo "<p>The server timestamp is: $result</p>";
?>
```

This returns something similar to:

```
The server timestamp is: Sun Jun 15 15:32:14 EDT 2003
```

The backtick operator is operationally identical to the `shellexec()` function, introduced next.

shell_exec()

```
string shell_exec (string command)
```

The `shell_exec()` function offers an syntactical alternative to backticks, executing a
shell command and returning the output. Reconsidering the preceding example:

```
<?php
    $result = shell_exec("date");
    echo "<p>The server timestamp is: $result</p>";
?>
```

Summary

Although you can certainly go a very long way using solely PHP to build interesting and
powerful Web applications, such capabilities are greatly expanded when functionality
is integrated with the underlying platform and other technologies. As applied to this
chapter, these technologies include the underlying operating and file systems. You'll

see this theme repeatedly throughout the remainder of this book, as I demonstrate how PHP is used with a wide variety of technologies like LDAP, SOAP, and MySQL.

In the next chapter, you'll examine two key aspects of any Web application: Web forms and navigational cues.

CHAPTER 11

Forms and
Navigational Cues

YOU CAN THROW ABOUT technical terms such as *relational database*, *Web services*, *session-handling*, and *LDAP*, but when it comes down to it, you started learning PHP because you wanted to build cool, interactive Web sites. After all, one of the Web's most alluring aspects is that it's a two-way media; not only can you disseminate information, but it also offers a highly effective means for compiling it. In this chapter I'll formally introduce one of the most common ways in which you can use PHP to interact with the user: Web forms. In addition, I'll also discuss a few commonplace site design strategies that will help the user to better engage with your site and even recall key aspects of your site structure more easily. These strategies are typically referred to as *navigational cues*; I'll show you how to implement three such cues, namely user-friendly URLs, breadcrumb trails, and custom error pages.

In all, the majority of the material covered in this chapter should be a relatively simple to understand, yet nonetheless crucial for anybody interested in building even the most basic of Web sites. In total, we'll talk about the following topics:

- Basic PHP and Web form concepts

- Passing form data to PHP functions

- Working with multi-valued form components

- Automating form generation

- Forms auto-completion

- PHP and JavaScript integration

- Creating friendly URLs with PHP and Apache

- Creating breadcrumb navigation trails

- Creating custom 404 handlers

PHP and Web Forms

Although using hyperlinks as a means for interaction is indeed useful, often you'll require a means for allowing the user to actually input raw data into the application. For example, what if you wanted to enable a user to enter his name and e-mail address so he could subscribe to a newsletter? You'd use a form, of course. Because you're surely quite aware of what a Web form is, and have undoubtedly made use of Web forms, at least on the level of an end user, hundreds, if not thousands of times, I'm not going to devote any time to introducing form syntax. If you require a primer or a refresher course regarding how to create basic forms I'd like to suggest taking time to review any of the many tutorials made available on the Web. Two of my favorite sites that include forms-specific tutorials follow:

- W3 Schools: `http://www.w3schools.com/`

- HTML Goodies: `http://www.htmlgoodies.com/`

Instead, what I am going to discuss is how you can use Web forms in conjunction with PHP to gather and process valuable user data.

There are two common methods for passing data from one script to another: GET and POST. Although GET is the default, you'll typically want to use POST, because it's capable of handling considerably more data, an important behavior when you're using forms to insert and modify large blocks of text. If you use POST, any posted data sent to a PHP script must be referenced using the `$_POST` syntax, as was first introduced in Chapter 3. For example, suppose the form contains a text-field named `email` that looks like this:

```
<input type="text" name="email" size="20" maxlength="40" value="" />
```

Once this form is submitted, you can reference that text-field value like so:

```
$_POST['email']
```

Keep in mind that other than the odd naming convention, `$_POST` variables are just like any other variable. They're simply referenced in this fashion in an effort to definitively compartmentalize an external variable's origination. As you learned in Chapter 3, such a convention is available for variables originating from the GET method, cookies, sessions, the server, and uploaded files. Think of it as namespaces for variables.

In this section, I'll discuss numerous scenarios in which PHP can play a highly effective role in not only managing form data, but in actually creating the form itself. For starters though, I'll begin with a proof-of-concept example.

A Simple Example

The following script renders a form, which prompts the user for his name and e-mail address. Once completed and submitted, the script (named subscribe.php) will display this information back to the browser window:

```php
<?php
    // If the submit button has been pressed
    if (isset($_POST['submit']))
    {
        echo "Hi ".$_POST['name']."!<br />";
        echo "The address ".$_POST['email']." will soon be a spam-magnet!<br />";
    }
?>

<form action="subscribe.php" method="post">
    <p>
        Name:<br />
        <input type="text" name="name" size="20" maxlength="40" value="" />
    </p>
    <p>
        Email Address:<br />
        <input type="text" name="email" size="20" maxlength="40" value="" />
</p>
    <input type="submit" name = "submit" value="Go!" />
</form>
```

Note that in this example the form refers to the script in which it is found, rather than another script. Although both practices are regularly employed, it's quite commonplace to refer back to the originating document and use conditional logic to determine which actions should be performed. In this case, the conditional logic dictates that the echo statements will only occur if the user has submitted (posted) the form.

Passing Form Data to a Function

Passing form data to a function is like working with any other variable; you simply pass the posted form data as function parameters. Consider an example. Suppose you wanted to incorporate some server-side validation into the previous example, using a custom function to ensure that the e-mail address is valid. Listing 11-1 offers this revised script.

Listing 11-1. Passing Form Data to a Function

```php
<?php
    // Function used to check email syntax
    function validate_email($email)
    {
        // Create the syntactical validation regular expression
```

```
        $regexp = "^([_a-z0-9-]+)(\.[_a-z0-9-]+)*@([a-z0-9-]+)
                    (\.[a-z0-9-]+)*(\.[a-z]{2,4})$";

        // Validate the syntax
        if (eregi($regexp, $email)) return 1;
            else return 0;
    }

    // Has the form been submitted?
    if (isset($_POST['submit']))
    {
        echo "Hi ".$_POST['name']."!<br />";
        if (validate_email($_POST['email']))
            echo "The address ".$_POST['email']." is valid!";
        else
            echo "The address <strong>".$_POST['email']."</strong> is invalid!";
    }
?>

<form action="subscribe.php" method="post">
    <p>
        Name:<br />
        <input type="text" name="name" size="20" maxlength="40" value="" />
    </p>

    <p>
        Email Address:<br />
        <input type="text" name="email" size="20" maxlength="40" value="" />
    </p>

    <input type="submit" name = "submit" value="Go!" />
</form>
```

Working with Multi-valued Form Components

Multi-valued form components such as checkboxes and multiple-select boxes greatly enhance your Web-based data collection capabilities, because they afford the user the opportunity to simultaneously select multiple values for a given form item. For example, consider a form used to gauge a user's computer-related interests. You would like to ask the user to indicate those programming languages that interest him. Using checkboxes or a multiple-select box, this form item might look similar to that shown in Figure 11-1.

The basic HTML for rendering the checkboxes looks like this:

```
<input type="checkbox" name="languages" value="csharp" />C#<br />
<input type="checkbox" name="languages" value="jscript" />JavaScript<br />
<input type="checkbox" name="languages" value="perl" />Perl<br />
<input type="checkbox" name="languages" value="php" />PHP<br />
```

What's your favorite programming language?
(check all that apply)

☐ C#

☐ JavaScript

☐ Perl

☐ PHP

What's your favorite programming language?
(select all that apply)

```
C#
JavaScript
Perl
PHP
```

Figure 11-1. Representing the same data using two different form items.

The HTML for the multi-select box looks like this:

```
<select name="languages" multiple="multiple">
    <option value="csharp">C#</option>
    <option value="jscript">JavaScript</option>
    <option value="perl">Perl</option>
    <option value="php">PHP</option>
</select>
```

Because these components are multi-valued, the form processor must be able to recognize that there may be several values assigned to a single form variable. In the case of the above examples, note that both use the name "languages" to reference several language entries. How does PHP handle the matter? Perhaps not surprisingly, by considering it an array. To do so, however, you need to make a minor change to the form item name, appending a pair of square brackets to it. Therefore, instead of languages, the name would read languages[]. Once renamed, PHP will treat the posted variable just like any other array. Consider a complete example, found in the file multiplevaluesexample.php:

```php
<?php
    if (isset($_POST['submit']))
    {
        echo "You chose the following languages:<br />";
        foreach($_POST['languages'] AS $language) echo "$language<br />";
    }
?>

<form action="multiplevalueexample.php" method="post">
```

```
What's your favorite programming language?<br /> (check all that apply):<br />
<input type="checkbox" name="languages[]" value="csharp" />C#<br />
<input type="checkbox" name="languages[]" value="jscript" />JavaScript<br />
<input type="checkbox" name="languages[]" value="perl" />Perl<br />
<input type="checkbox" name="languages[]" value="php" />PHP<br />
<input type="submit" name="submit" value="Go!" />
</form>
```

If the user were to choose the languages "C#" and "PHP," he would be greeted with the following output:

```
You chose the following languages:
csharp
php
```

Generating Forms with PHP

Of course, many Web-based forms are a tad more involved than just a few text fields. Items such as checkboxes, radio buttons, and drop-down boxes are all quite useful, and can add considerably to the utility of a form. However, you'll often want to base the values assigned to such items on data retrieved from some dynamic source, such as a database. PHP renders such a task trivial, as I'll explain in this section.

Suppose your site offers a registration form that prompts for the user's preferred language, among other things. That language will serve as the default for future e-mail correspondence. However, the choice of languages depends upon the language capabilities of your support staff, the records of which are maintained by the human resources department. Therefore, rather than take the chance of offering an outdated list of available languages, you link the drop-down list used for this form item directly to there language table used by the HR department. Furthermore, because you know that each element of a drop-down list consists of three items: a name identifying the list itself, and a value and name for each list item, you can create a function that abstracts this task. This function, which I'll creatively call create_dropdown(), takes four parameters as input:

- $identifier: The name assigned to the drop-down list, determining how the posted variable will be referenced.

- $pairs: An associative array that contains the key-value pairs used to create the selection menu entries.

- $firstentry: Serves as a visual cue for the dropdown menu, and is placed in the very first position.

- $multiple: Should this drop-down list allow for multiple selection? If yes, pass in "multiple," if no, pass in nothing (the parameter is optional).

The function follows:

```
function create_dropdown($identifier,$pairs,$firstentry,$multiple="")
{
    // Start the dropdown list with the <select> element and title
    $dropdown = "<select name=\"$identifier\" multiple=\"$multiple\">";
    $dropdown .= "<option name=\"\">$firstentry</option>";

    // Create the dropdown elements
    foreach($pairs AS $value => $name)
    {
        $dropdown .= "<option name=\"$value\">$name</option>";
    }
    // Conclude the dropdown and return it
    echo "</select>";
    return $dropdown;
}
```

The following code snippet makes use of the function.

```
<?php
// Connect to the db server and select a database
mysql_connect("localhost","webuser","secret");
mysql_select_db("chapter11");

// Retrieve the language table data
$query = "SELECT id,name FROM language ORDER BY name";
$result = mysql_query($query);

// Create an associative array based on the table data
while($row = mysql_fetch_array($result))
{
    $value = $row["id"];
    $name = $row["name"];
    $pairs["$value"] = $name;
}

echo "Choose your preferred language: <br />";
echo create_dropdown("language",$pairs,"Choose One:");

?>
```

Figure 11-2 offers a rendering of the form once the values have been retrieved.

Choose your preferred language:

Figure 11-2. A PHP-generated form element

Form Auto-Selection

In the world of user-interface design, users simply do not like inconsistency. That said, it's always a good idea to strive for visual harmony across the entire site, particularly within those components that the user will come into direct contact with, forms, for example. I like to actually reuse forms wherever possible, re-enlisting the same template for both data insertion and modification. Of course, you might imagine that such a strategy could quickly result in a mish-mash of logic and presentation. However, with a bit of forethought, it's actually quite simple to encourage form reuse while maintaining some semblance of good coding conduct. In this section, I'll show you one way to do so.

In the last section, I showed you how to create a general function for creating dynamically generated drop-down lists. To illustrate the concepts introduced in this section, I'll continue that theme, except this time I'll revise the create_dropdown() function to both generate the dynamic list, as well as auto-select a predetermined value. I'll add this extra feature simply by defining another parameter, named:

- $selectedkey: This optional parameter holds the value of the element to be auto-selected. If it is not assigned, then no values will be auto-selected.

The function determines whether a particular element should be auto-selected by comparing each to the $selectedkey while building the dropdown list. For the purposes of slightly more compact code, I'll use the ternary operator to make this comparison. The revised function follows:

```
function create_dropdown($identifier,$pairs,$firstentry,$multiple="",$selectedkey="")
{
    $dropdown = "<select name=\"$identifier\" multiple=\"$multiple\">";
    $dropdown .= "<option name=\"\">$firstentry</option>";

    foreach($pairs AS $value => $name)
    {
        $dropdown .= ($value==$selectedkey) ?
                    "<option name=\"$value\" selected=\"selected\">$name</option>" :
                    "<option name=\"$value\">$name</option>";
    }
    echo "</select>";
    return $dropdown;
}
```

If you want to auto-select the element "Italian," you just pass in its corresponding identifier, for example "2," like this:

```
echo create_dropdown("language",$pairs,"Choose One:", "", 2);
```

This results in HTML being output like so (formatted for readability):

```
Choose your preferred language: <br />
<select name="language" >
   <option name="">Choose One:</option>
   <option name="4">Dutch</option>
   <option name="1">English</option>
   <option name="2" selected="selected">Italian</option>
   <option name="3">Spanish</option>
</select>
```

Note that the "Italian" element has been selected.

PHP, Web Forms, and JavaScript

Of course, just because you're using PHP as a primary scripting language for a given application doesn't mean that you should rely on it to do everything. In fact, using PHP in conjunction with a client-side language such as JavaScript often greatly extends the application's flexibility. However, a point of common confusion involves the ability to make one language talk to another, because JavaScript executes on the client-side, and PHP on the server-side. It's probably easier than you think, as I will illustrate in the following example.

Many Web sites offer the ability to e-mail an article or news story to a friend. Sometimes this is accomplished by using a "pop-up" window, which in turn prompts the user for the recipient's address and some other information. Upon submitting the form, the article is mailed to the recipient, and the user in turn closes the window. Often the pop-up action is accomplished using JavaScript, while the mail submission is done using PHP. However, because JavaScript is launching the new window, it must be able to pass some bit of information, such as an article ID, that uniquely identifies the article.

The following script demonstrates this task, showing how easy it is to pass a PHP variable into a JavaScript function. In the document header, a JavaScript function named mail() is defined. This function opens a new fixed-size window to a PHP script, which in turn prompts for and then processes the mail submission.

```
<!DOCTYPE html PUBLIC "-//W3C//DTD XHTML 1.0 Transitional//EN"
                    "http://www.w3.org/TR/xhtml1/DTD/xhtml1-transitional.dtd">
<html>
   <head>
   <title>An Example.com article</title>
   <script type="text/javascript">
      function mail(id) {
```

```
            window.open("mail.php?id=" + id, "info",
                            "width=250,height=250,scrollbars=0,resizable=0")
    }
</script>
</head>
<body bgcolor="#ffffff" text="#000000" link="#0000ff"
      vlink="#800080" alink="#ff0000">
  <a href="#" onClick="mail(<?php echo $id; ?>);">
  Mail this article to a friend</a>
  Article content goes here...
</body>
</html>
```

Once clicked, a form similar to that shown in Figure 11-3 is opened.

Figure 11-3. The article mailer form.

In particular, take note that you passed the PHP variable $id into the call to the JavaScript function mail() simply by escaping to PHP, outputting the variable, and then escaping back to the HTML. Clicking the link triggers the onClick() event, which opens the following script:

```
<?php
    // If the mail form has been submitted
    if (isset($_POST['submit']))
    {
        // Designate a mail header and body
```

```
    $headers = "FROM:editor@example.com\n";
    $body = "Your friend ".$_POST['name']." thought you'd be interested in this
            article:\nhttp://www.example.com/article.html?id=".$_POST['id'];
    // Mail the article URL
    mail($_POST['recipient'],"Example.com News Article",$body,$headers);
    // Notify the user
    echo "The article has been mailed to ".$_POST['recipient'];
  }
?>
<p>
   Email this article to a friend!
</p>
<form action="mail.html" method="post">
   <input type="hidden" name="id" value="<?php echo $_GET['id'];?>" />
   <p>
      Recipient email:<br />
      <input type="text" name="recipient" size="20" maxlength="40" value="" />
   </p>
   <p>
      Your name:<br />
      <input type="text" name="name" size="20" maxlength="40" value="" />
   </p>
   <input type="submit" name="submit" value="Send Article" />
</form>
```

Although a predefined URL was used to provide the recipient with a reference to the article, you could just as easily offer the option to retrieve the article from the database using the available unique identifier ($id), and embed the article information directly into the e-mail.

Navigational Cues

The word *usability* ranks up there with some of the most overused terms of the dot-com bust, and indeed to hear the mere mention of it in conversation still manages to turn me a pale shade of green. Nonetheless, once you get by the word's connotations as applied to recent memory, site usability is indeed a matter of utmost concern to the site developer. But what does the term mean? Strictly defined, the degree to which a Web application is "usable" is determined by the degree of effectiveness and satisfaction derived from its use. In other words, has the interface been designed in such a manner that users feel comfortable and perhaps even empowered using it? Can they easily locate the tools and data they require? Does it offer multiple means to the same ends, often accomplished through readily available visual cues? Taken together, characteristics such as these define an application's "usability."

In this section, I'm going to discuss three of my favorite navigational aids: user-friendly URLs, breadcrumb trails, and custom error files. All three can be implemented with a minimum of effort, and provide considerable value to the user.

User-Friendly URLs

Back in the boring old days of the Web, coming across a URL like this was pretty impressive:

```
http://www.example.com/sports/football/buckeyes.html
```

This user undoubtedly meant business! After all, he's taken the time to categorize his site material, and judging from the URL structure, his site might be so vast that he might talk about more than one football team, or even more than one sport. These days however, it's not uncommon to come across a URL that looks like this:

```
http://www.example.com/articles.php?category=php&id=145
```

Although greater URL complexity is the result of the greater complexity of the development tools and strategies available, what has been lost is the friendliness of URLs. You see, although the amount of material made available via that avant-garde Web site of the early 1990's is likely laughable when compared to many of today's sports-related Web sites, we've managed to lose the help of a key navigational aid, the URL, in the process. What if you could rewrite the above URL in a much more user-oriented fashion, all without sacrificing use of cutting-edge technologies such as PHP? For example, what if you could rewrite it like so:

```
http://www.example.com/articles/php/145/
```

Indeed, this is much more "friendly" than its uglier predecessor. However, how is it possible to do this and still pass the required variables to the necessary PHP script? Furthermore, how does Apache even know which script to serve? Because I've presented both versions of the URL, you know that php and 145 are parameters, and that this location does not actually exist within the server document structure. Believe it or not, Apache is capable of recognizing this as well, and employing a little-known feature known as *lookback* in an attempt to discern the intended destination. I'll now run through an example of how this feature operates.

Suppose Apache receives a request for this user-friendly URL, which you know doesn't exist. When lookback is enabled, Apache will actually begin to "look backwards" down the URL searching for a suitable destination. So given this URL, Apache will first examine:

```
http://www.example.com/articles/php/145/
```

Because an index file is not found at that location, Apache will then look for a file named 145. Because nothing is found, Apache then examines:

```
http://www.example.com/articles/php/
```

Repeating the same process as that used in the first step. Because no suitable match is presumably located, Apache will then examine:

```
http://www.example.com/articles/
```

Assuming that there is no index file in a directory at that location named `articles`, Apache will then look for a *file* named `articles`. Indeed, it finds `articles.php`, and serves that file.

Once the file `articles.php` is served, anything following `articles` within the URL is assigned to the Apache environment variable PATH_INFO, and accessible from a PHP script using the variable:

```
$_SERVER['PATH_INFO']
```

Therefore, in the case of this example, this variable would be assigned:

```
/php/145/
```

So, now you know the basic premise behind how this feature works. Next I'll actually implement the feature, starting with the required changes to Apache's configuration.

Configuring Apache's Lookback Feature

Apache's lookback feature is made possible through working with three configuration directives: `Files`, `ForceType`, and `AcceptPathInfo`. I'll introduce each as it applies to this feature in this section.

> **NOTE** *You can accomplish the same task via Apache's rewrite feature. Indeed, this might even be the preferred method, because it eliminates the need to embed additional code within your application with the sole purpose of parsing the URL. However, because many users run their Web sites through a third-party host, and thus do not possess adequate privileges to manipulate Apache's configuration, Apache's lookback feature can offer an ideal solution.*

Files

The `Files` directive is a container enabling you to modify the behavior of certain requests based on the filename destination. I'll provide a usage example in conjunction with `ForceType`, introduced next.

ForceType

The ForceType directive allows you to force the mapping of a particular MIME type in a given instance. For example, you could use this directive in conjunction with the Files container to force the mapping of the PHP MIME type to any file named articles:

```
<Files articles>
    ForceType application/x-httpd-php
</Files>
```

If the context of the above Files container were applied at the document root level, I could create a file named articles (with no extension), and place various PHP commands within it. I could then execute that script like so:

```
http://www.example.com/articles
```

This causes the file to be parsed and executed like any other PHP script. When used in conjunction with the next directive, AcceptPathInfo, you've completed the Apache configuration requirements.

> **NOTE** *Discussing the context in which Apache directives and containers are applied is out of the scope of this book. Please consult the excellent Apache documentation at* http://httpd.apache.org/ *for more information.*

AcceptPathInfo

The AcceptPathInfo directive is the key component of Apache's lookback feature. When enabled, Apache understands that a URL might not explicitly map to the intended destination. Turning this directive on causes Apache to begin searching the requested URL path for a viable destination, and placing any trailing URL components into the PATH_INFO variable.

This directive is typically used in conjunction with a Directory container. Therefore, if you enable lookback capabilities at the document root level of your Web server, you might enable AcceptPathInfo like so:

```
<Directory />
    # Other directives go here...
    AcceptPathInfo On
</Directory>
```

Putting it All Together

What follows is a sample snippet from Apache's httpd.conf file, used to configure
Apache's lookback feature:

```
<Directory content>
   AcceptPathInfo On
   <Files articles>
      ForceType application/x-httpd-php
   </Files>
   <Files news>
      ForceType application/x-httpd-php
   </Files>
</Directory>
```

The PHP Code

Once you've reconfigured Apache, all that's left to do is write a tiny bit of PHP code to
handle the data placed in the PATH_INFO environment variable. For starters, however,
you'll just output this data. Assuming that you configured your Apache as explained
previously, place the following in the articles file (again, no extension):

```
<?php
   echo $_SERVER['PATH_INFO'];
?>
```

Next, navigate to the example URL, replacing the domain with your own:

```
http://www.example.com/articles/php/145/
```

The following should appear within the browser:

```
/php/145/
```

However, you need to parse that information. According to our original "unfriendly"
URL, two parameters are required, category and id. You can use two predefined PHP
functions, list() and explode() to retrieve these parameter values from
$_SERVER['PATH_INFO']:

```
list($category, $id) = explode("/", $_SERVER['PATH_INFO']);
```

Pretty simple, huh? Indeed it is. Just place this at the top of your articles script,
and then use the resulting variables as necessary to retrieve the intended article. Note
that it's not necessary to modify any other aspect of the article retrieval script, because
the variable names used to retrieve the article information presumably do not change.

Breadcrumb Trails

Navigational trails, or as they are more affectionately titled, *breadcrumb trails*, are implemented quite frequently within Web applications, because of the readily visible and intuitive navigational aid they offer to users. By breaking down a user's present location into a path of hyperlinks that provide a summary view of the current document's location as it relates to the site at large, the user has a far more practical and efficient navigational tool at his disposal than is offered by the browser, and serves to complement or even replace a typical site's localized menu system. Figure 11-4 depicts a breadcrumb trail in action.

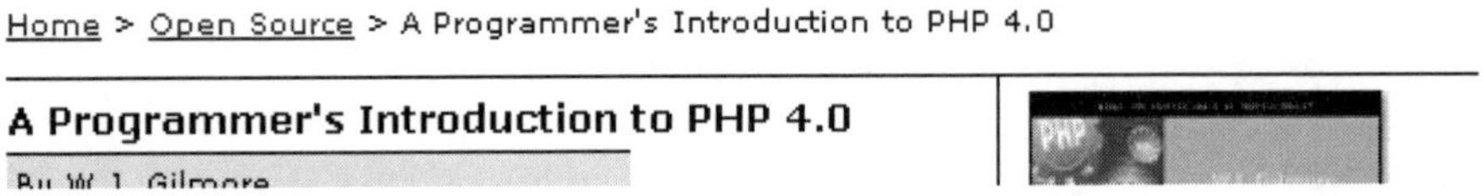

Figure 11-4. A typical navigational trail.

This section is devoted to a demonstration of two separate breadcrumb trail implementations. The first makes use of an array to transform an unwieldy URL tree into a much more user-friendly naming convention. This implementation is particularly useful for creating navigational trees that correspond to largely static pages. The second implementation expands upon the first, this time using a MySQL database to create user-friendly navigational mappings for a database-driven Website. Although each follows a different approach, both accomplish the same goal. In fact, it's often useful to implement a hybrid mapping strategy: that is, one that can handle both static and database driven pages as necessary.

Creating Breadcrumbs From Static Data

One rather simple means for implementing breadcrumb trails using PHP is to create an associative array that maps the entire directory structure to corresponding user-friendly titles. When each page is loaded, the URL is parsed, and converted to its corresponding linked list of those user-friendly titles as specified within the array. The generalized process for realizing this implementation follows:

1. Map the Web site directory structure.

2. Create an associative array, which is used to provide user-friendly names to the breadcrumbs. This array is typically stored in a global site header.

3. Create the URL parsing and mapping function, create_crumbs(). Store it in the global site header

4. Execute the create_crumbs() function where necessary within each page intended to contain the crumb trail.

Listing 11-2 shows the create_crumbs() function.

Listing 11-2. The create_crumbs() Function

```
function create_crumbs($crumb_site, $home_label, $crumb_labels) {
    // Start the crumb trail
    $crumb_trail = "<a href=\"$crumb_site\">$home_label</a>";

    // Parse the requested URL path
    $crumb_tree = explode('/', $_SERVER['PHP_SELF']);

    // Start the URL path used within the trail
    $crumb_path = $crumb_site.'/';

    // Assemble the crumb trail
    for($x=1; $x<sizeof($crumb_tree)-1; $x++) {
        $crumb_path .= $crumb_tree[$x].'/';
        $crumb_trail .= ' &gt; <a href="'.$crumb_path.'">'
            .$crumb_labels[$crumb_tree[$x]].'</a>';
    }

    return $crumb_trail;
}
```

Next you need to create the three input parameters. The purpose of each is explained here:

- $crumb_site: The base URL of the path. This is useful because it allows you to easily start new trails within subsections of your site.

- $home_label: The name given to the very first crumb in the path. This will point back to the URL specified by $crumb_site.

- $crumb_labels: The array containing the URL component to friendly name mappings.

Typically these variables would be placed in an application configuration file. However for the sake of space I'll just include them in the same script as the call to the create_crumbs() function:

```
<?php
    include "breadcrumbs.php";
    $crumb_site = "http://www.example.com/";
    $crumb_labels = array("articles" => "Recent Articles",
                        "php" => "Advanced PHP",
                        "mysql" => "MySQL",
                        "pmnp" => "PHP 5 and MySQL Pro");
    echo create_crumbs($crumb_site, $crumb_labels);
?>
```

Now place this script into a document tree at this location:

```
http://www.example.com/pmnp/articles/mysql/
```

The following breadcrumb trail will appear:

```
Home > PHP 5 and MySQL Pro > Recent Articles > MySQL
```

Creating Breadcrumbs From Database Table Data

In the previous section, you learned that URLs could be easily parsed and formatted for display as a navigational trail. This simply involved the translation of each URL directory component to its corresponding array value. But what about generating breadcrumbs based on data stored within a database? For example, consider the following URL (note the user-friendly URL):

```
http://www.example.com/books/1893115852/
```

How would you go about translating this URL into the following breadcrumb trail?

```
Home > Books > A Programmer's Introduction to PHP 4.0
```

At first glance, it would seem that you could use the first breadcrumb implementation. After all, it seems as if a simple translation is taking place, that is the replacement of a user-unfriendly ISBN (1893115852) with the user-friendly book title, "A Programmer's Introduction to PHP 4.0." Making use of an array isn't always the most convenient means for storing dynamic information, however. Given that most corporate Web sites retrieve content from a relational database system, it would be impractical to redundantly store some of this information in both a database and a separate file-based array. With that in mind, the remainder of this section will demonstrate a mechanism for creating navigational trails using a MySQL database.

> **NOTE** *If you're unfamiliar with the MySQL server and are confused by the syntax found in the following example, consider reviewing the material found in Chapters 21, 23, and 26.*

The following MySQL table, books, is used to store information about a publisher's book offerings.

```
create table books (
    bookID mediumint unsigned not null auto_increment,
    categoryID mediumint unsigned not null,
    isbn varchar(10) not null,
    authorID mediumint unsigned not null,
```

```
title varchar(45) not null,
description mediumtext not null,
primary key(bookID));
```

The following table, bookCategories, provides the 1-to-N mapping of a book category to books stored within the books table:

```
create table bookCategories (
   categoryID mediumint unsigned not null auto_increment,
   categoryName varchar(15) not null,
   primary key(categoryID));
```

Note that a similar author table mapping would exist in a real implementation, but I'm omitting it here for the sake of space.

In addition to the aforementioned user-friendly URL, you would like to provide a navigational trail at the top of the page to allow for quick recognition of current site location, and the potential for easily navigating back up the site directory tree. The intended goal is to create a navigation trail that resembles the following:

```
Home > Open Source > A Programmer's Introduction to PHP 4.0
```

Listing 11-3 demonstrates the modified create_crumbs() function, this one capable of parsing the URL and building a navigation trail consisting of retrieved table data.

Listing 11-3. The create_crumbs() *Function Revisited*

```
<?

   // The revised create_crumbs() function. Note that this version is
   // much simpler, as it's customized specifically for use with the book catalog.
   function create_crumbs($siteURL, $categoryID, $categoryName, $title) {

      $crumb = "<a href = \"$siteURL\">Home</a> &gt;
                     <a href = \"$siteURL/category/$categoryID/\">
                     $categoryName</a> &gt; $title";

      print $crumb;

   } # end create_crumbs definition

   $siteURL = "http://www.example.com";
   // connect to the db server and select the database
   mysql_pconnect("localhost","jason","secret");
   mysql_select_db("chapter11");

   // assume that this would be parsed from the user-friendly URL
   $isbn = "1893115852";

   // Execute the query. To improve performance, this same query could also
```

```
                // be used to retrieve the book data for the page.
                $result = mysql_query("SELECT b.categoryID, c.categoryName, b.isbn,
                                       b.authorID, b.title, b.description
                                       FROM books b, bookCategories c
                                       WHERE b.isbn = $isbn AND
                                       b.categoryID = c.categoryID");

            $row = mysql_fetch_assoc($result);
            // Retrieve the query values
            $categoryID = $row["categoryID"];
            $categoryName = $row["categoryName"];
            $isbn = $row["isbn"];
            $authorID = $row["authorID"];
            $title = $row["title"];

            // Execute the function
            create_crumbs($siteURL, $categoryID, $categoryName, $title);

        ?>
```

Creating Custom Error Handlers

It can be quite irritating for a user to happen upon a moved or removed Web page, only to see the dreaded "HTTP 404 - File not found" message. That said, site maintainers should take every step necessary to ensure that "link rot" does not occur. However, there are times when this cannot be easily avoided, particularly when major site migrations or updates are taking place. Fortunately, Apache offers a configuration directive that makes it possible to forward all requests ending in a particular server error (404, 403, and 500, for example) to a predetermined page. The directive, named ErrorDocument, can be placed with httpd.conf's main configuration container, as well as within virtual host, directory, and .htaccess containers (with the appropriate permissions, of course). For example, you could point all 404 errors to a document named error.html, which is located in the particular context's base directory, like so:

```
ErrorDocument 404 /error.html
```

Pointing 404s to such a page is useful because it could provide the user with further information regarding the reason for page removal, an update pertinent to Web site upgrade progress, or even a search interface. Using it in combination with PHP, such a page could also attempt to discern the page that the user is attempting to access, and forward accordingly, e-mail the site administrator, letting him know that an error has occurred, create custom error logs, or really anything else that you'd like it to do. In this section, I'll demonstrate how to use PHP to gather some statistics pertinent to the missing file and mail that information to a site administrator. Hopefully this example will provide you with a few ideas as to how you can begin creating custom 404 handlers suited for their own specific needs.

NOTE *I fully realize that some of the concepts described in this chapter are already handled quite efficiently by the URL rewriting capability of the Apache Web server.. However, before looking up my e-mail address and berating me on the matter, keep in mind that many readers make use of shared servers for Web hosting, and thus do not have the luxury of wielding total control over the behavior of their Web server. That said, the concepts described here serve to get the reader thinking about the alternatives made available to him in the case that those made available via administration of the Web server are not.*

In this example, you'll create a script that e-mails the site administrator with a detailed report of the error, and displays a message begging the user's forgiveness. To start, create an .htaccess file that redirects the 404 errors to the custom script:

```
ErrorDocument 404 /www/htdocs/errormessage.html
```

If you want this behavior to occur throughout the site, place it in the root directory of your Web site. If you're unfamiliar with .htaccess files, see the Apache documentation for more information.

Next, create the script that handles the error by e-mailing the site administrator and displaying an appropriate message. This script is provided in Listing 11-4.

Listing 11-4. E-mail Notification and Simple Message Display

```php
<?
    $servername = $_SERVER['SERVER_NAME'];
    $recipient = "webmaster@example.com";
    $subject = "404 error detected: ".$_SERVER['PHP_SELF'];
    $timestamp = date( "F d, Y G:i:s", time() );
    $referrer = $_SERVER['HTTP_REFERER'];
    $ip = $_SERVER['REMOTE_ADDR'];
    $redirect = $_SERVER['REQUEST_URI'];

    $body = <<< body
        A 404 error was detected at: $timestamp.

        Server: $servername
        Missing page: $redirect
        Referring document: $referrer
        User IP Address: $ip
    body;

    mail($recipient, $subject, $body, "From: administrator\r\n");
?>

<h3>File Not Found</h3>
<p>
```

```
Please forgive us, as our Web site is currently undergoing maintenance.
As a result, you may experience occasional difficulties accessing documents
and/or services.
The site administrator has been emailed with a detailed event log of this matter.
</p>
Thank you,<br />
The Web site Crew
```

Of course, if your site is particularly large, you might want to consider writing error information to a log file rather than sending it via e-mail.

Summary

One of the Web's great strengths is the ease it offers in not only disseminating, but also compiling and aggregating user information. As a result, as developers we spend an enormous amount of time building and maintaining a multitude of user interfaces, many of which are complex HTML forms. Hopefully you'll be able to use some of the concepts described in this chapter to decrease that time a tad.

In addition, I discussed a few commonplace strategies to improve general user experience working with your application. Although it is not an exhaustive list, perhaps the material presented in this chapter will act as a springboard for further experimentation, not to mention help you to decrease time investment in what is surely another of the more consuming aspects of Web development: improving user experience.

In the next chapter I'll switch gears a bit, showing you how to protect sensitive areas of your Web site by forcing users to supply a username and password prior to entry.

CHAPTER 12

Authentication

AUTHENTICATING USER IDENTITIES is common practice in today's Web applications. This is done not only for security-related reasons, but also to offer customization features based on user preferences and type. Typically, users are prompted for a username and password, which when taken together form a unique identifying value for that user. In this chapter, you'll learn how to prompt for and validate this information, using PHP's built-in authentication capabilities. Specifically, in this chapter you'll learn about:

- Basic HTTP-based authentication concepts

- PHP's authentication variables, namely $_SERVER['PHP_AUTH_USER'] and $_SERVER['PHP_AUTH_PW']

- Several PHP functions that are commonly used to implement authentication procedures

- Three commonplace authentication methodologies: hard-coding the login pair (username and password) directly into the script, file-based authentication, and database-based authentication

- Further restricting authentication credentials with a user's IP address

- Testing password guessability using the CrackLib extension

- Recovering lost passwords using one-time URLs

HTTP Authentication Concepts

The HTTP protocol offers a fairly simple, yet effective, means for user authentication, used by the server to challenge a resource request, and by the client (browser) to provide information pertinent to the authentication procedure. A typical authentication process goes like this:

1. The client requests a resource that has been restricted.

2. The server responds to this request with a 401 (Unauthorized access) response message.

3. The client (browser) recognizes the 401 response, and produces a pop-up authentication prompt similar to the one shown in Figure 12-1. Most modern

281

browsers are capable of understanding HTTP authentication and offering appropriate capabilities, including Internet Explorer, Netscape Navigator, Mozilla, and Opera.

4. The user either supplies proper credentials (username and password), which are sent back to the server for validation, and is subsequently allowed to access the resource, or offers incorrect or blank credentials, and is denied access.

5. If the user is validated, the browser will store the authentication information within its authentication cache. This cache information remains within the browser until the cache is cleared, or until another 401 server response is sent to the browser.

Figure 12-1. An authentication prompt

You should understand that although HTTP authentication effectively controls access to restricted resources, it does not secure the channel in which authentication information travels. That is, it is quite trivial for a well-positioned attacker to *sniff*, or monitor, all traffic taking place between a server and a client. Both the supplied username and password are included in this traffic, both unencrypted. Therefore, to eliminate the possibility of compromise through such a method, you'll need to implement a secure communications channel, typically accomplished using the Secure Sockets Layer (SSL). SSL support is available for all mainstream Web servers, Apache and IIS included.

PHP Authentication

Integrating user authentication directly into your Web application logic is convenient and flexible; convenient because it consolidates what would otherwise require some level of inter-process communication, and flexible because integrated authentication provides a much simpler means for integrating with other components of an application, such as content customization and user privilege designation. For the remainder of this chapter, we'll examine PHP's built-in authentication feature, and demonstrate several authentication methodologies that you can immediately begin incorporating into your applications.

Authentication Variables

PHP makes use of two predefined variables to authenticate a user: `$_SERVER['PHP_AUTH_USER']` and `$_SERVER['PHP_AUTH_PW']`. These variables hold the two components needed for authentication, specifically the username and the password, respectively. Their usage will become apparent in the following examples. For the moment, however, there are two important caveats to keep in mind when using these predefined variables:

- Both variables must be verified at the start of *every* restricted page. This is easily accomplished by wrapping each restricted page by including the authentication code in a separate file and including it using the `REQUIRE()` function.

- These variables do not function properly with the CGI version of PHP, nor do they function on the Microsoft IIS server. See the sidebar about PHP authentication and IIS.

....

PHP Authentication and IIS

If you're using IIS in conjunction with PHP's ISAPI module, and you want to use PHP's HTTP authentication capabilities, you'll need to make a minor modification to the examples offered throughout this chapter. The username and password variables are still available to PHP when using IIS, but not via `$_SERVER['PHP_AUTH_USER']` and `$_SERVER['PHP_AUTH_PW']`. Instead, these values must be parsed from another server global variable, `$_SERVER['HTTP_AUTHORIZATION']`. So for example, you'll need to parse out these variables like so:

```
list($user, $pswd) =
   explode(':', base64_decode(
   substr($_SERVER['HTTP_AUTHORIZATION'], 6)));
```

....

Useful Functions

Two standard functions are commonly used when using handling authentication via PHP, header() and isset(). I'll introduce both in this section.

header()

```
void header(string string [, boolean replace [, int http_response_code]])
```

The header() function sends a raw HTTP header to the browser. The *string* parameter specifies the header information sent to the browser. The optional *replace* parameter determines whether this information should replace or accompany a previously sent header. Finally, the optional *http_response_code* parameter defines a specific response code that will accompany the header information. Note that you can include this code in the string, as I'll demonstrate. Applied to user authentication, this function is useful for sending the WWW authentication header to the browser, causing the pop-up authentication prompt to be displayed. It is also useful for sending the 401 header message to the user, if incorrect authentication credentials are submitted. An example follows:

```php
<?php
header('WWW-Authenticate: Basic Realm="Book Projects"');
header("HTTP/1.1 401 Unauthorized");
...
?>
```

Note that unless output buffering is enabled, these commands must be executed before any output is returned. Neglecting this rule will result in a server error because of the violation of the HTTP specification.

isset()

```
boolean isset(mixed var [, mixed var [,...]])
```

The isset() function determines whether or not a variable has been assigned a value. It returns TRUE if the variable contains a value, and FALSE if it does not. Applied to user authentication, the isset() function is useful for determining whether or not the $_SERVER['PHP_AUTH_USER'] and the $_SERVER['PHP_AUTH_PW'] variables are properly set. Listing 12-1 offers a usage example.

Listing 12-1. Using isset() *to Verify Whether a Variable Contains a Value*

```php
<?php
if (isset($_SERVER['PHP_AUTH_USER']) and isset($_SERVER['PHP_AUTH_PW'])) {
    // execute additional authentication tasks
} else {
```

```
        echo "<p>Please enter both a username and a password!</p>";
}
?>
```

Authentication Methodologies

There are several ways you can implement authentication via a PHP script. You should consider the scope and complexity of each when the need to invoke such a feature arises. In particular, I'll discuss three implementation methodologies: hard-coding a login pair directly into the script, file-based authentication, and database-based authentication.

Hard-Coded Authentication

The simplest way to restrict resource access is through hard-coding the username and password directly into the script. Listing 12-2 offers an example of how to accomplish this.

Listing 12-2. Authenticating Against a Hard-Coded Login Pair

```
if (($_SERVER['PHP_AUTH_USER'] != 'specialuser') ||
    ($_SERVER['PHP_AUTH_PW'] != 'secretpassword')) {
        header('WWW-Authenticate: Basic Realm="Secret Stash"');
        header('HTTP/1.0 401 Unauthorized');
        print('You must provide the proper credentials!');
        exit;
}
```

The logic in this example is quite simple. If $_SERVER['PHP_AUTH_USER'] and $_SERVER['PHP_AUTH_PW'] are set to "specialuser" and "secretpassword," respectively, the code block will not execute, and anything ensuing that block will execute. Otherwise, the user is prompted for the username and password until either the proper information is provided, or a 401 Unauthorized message is displayed due to multiple authentication failures.

Although using a hard-coded authentication pair is very quick and easy to configure, it has several drawbacks. First, as this code currently stands, all users requiring access to that resource must use the same authentication pair. Usually, in real-world situations, each user must be uniquely identified so that user-specific preferences or resources can be made available. Although you could allow for multiple login pairs by adding additional logic, the ensuing code would be highly unwieldy. Second, changing the username or password can only be done by entering the code and making the manual adjustment. The next two methodologies satisfy this need.

File-based Authentication

Often you need to provide each user with a unique login pair, making it possible to log user-specific login times, movements, and actions. You can do this easily with a text file, much like the one commonly used to store information about Unix users (/etc/passwd). Listing 12-3 offers such a file. Each line contains a username and an encrypted password pair, with the two elements separated by a colon (:).

Listing 12-3. authenticationFile.txt

```
jason:60d99e58d66a5e0f4f89ec3ddd1d9a80
donald:d5fc4b0e45c8f9a333c0056492c191cf
mickey:bc180dbc583491c00f8a1cd134f7517b
```

A crucial security consideration regarding authenticationFile.txt is that this file should be stored outside the server document root. If not, an attacker could discover the file through brute-force guessing, revealing half of the login combination. In addition, although you could skip encrypting the password instead storing it in plain-text format, it is strongly discouraged, because users with access to the server might be able to view the login information if file permissions are not correctly configured.

The PHP script required to parse this file and authenticate a user against a given login pair is only a tad more complicated than the one used to authenticate against a hard-coded authentication pair. The difference lies in the fact that the script must also read the text file into an array, and then cycle through that array searching for a match. This involves the use of several functions, including the following:

- file(string *filename*): The file() function reads a file into an array, with each element of the array consisting of a line in the file.

- explode(string *separator*, string *string* [, int *limit*]): The explode() function splits a string into a series of substrings, with each string boundary determined by a specific separator.

- md5(string *str*): The md5() function calculates an MD5 hash of a string, using RSA Data Security Inc.'s MD5 Message-Digest algorithm (http://www.rsa.com).

> **NOTE** *Although they are similar in function, you should use* explode() *instead of* split(), *because* split() *is a tad slower due to its invocation of PHP's regular expression parsing engine.*

Listing 12-4 illustrates a PHP script capable of parsing authenticationFile.txt, potentially matching a user's input to a login pair.

Listing 12-4. Authenticating a User Against a Flat File Login Repository

```php
<?php
    // Preset authentication status to false.
    $authorized = FALSE;
    if (isset($_SERVER['PHP_AUTH_USER']) && isset($_SERVER['PHP_AUTH_PW'])) {
        // Read the authentication file into an array
        $authFile = file("/usr/local/lib/php/site/authenticate.txt");
        // Cycle through each line in file, searching for authentication match.
        foreach ($authFile as $login) {
            list($username, $password) = explode(":", $login);
            // Remove the newline from the password
            $password = trim($password);
            if (($username == $_SERVER['PHP_AUTH_USER']) &&
                ($password == md5($_SERVER['PHP_AUTH_PW']))) {
                $authorized = TRUE;
                break;
            }
        }
    }
    # If not authorized, display authentication prompt or 401 error
    if (! $authorized) {
        header('WWW-Authenticate: Basic Realm="Secret Stash"');
        header('HTTP/1.0 401 Unauthorized');
        print('You must provide the proper credentials!');
        exit;
    }
    // restricted material goes here...
?>
```

Although the file-based authentication system works great for relatively small, static authentication lists, this strategy can become somewhat inconvenient when you're handling a large number of users, when users are regularly being added, deleted, and modified, or when you need to incorporate an authentication scheme into a larger information infrastructure (into a pre-existing user table, for example). Such requirements are better satisfied by implementing a database-based solution. The following section demonstrates just such a solution, using a MySQL database to store authentication pairs.

Database Authentication

Of all the various authentication methodologies discussed in this chapter, implementing a database-based solution is the most powerful, due not only to reasons of administrative convenience and scalability, but also because such a solution can be integrated into a larger database infrastructure. For purposes of this example, we'll limit the datastore to four fields—a primary key, the user's name, a username, and a password. These columns are placed into a table that we'll call user, shown in Listing 12-5.

> **NOTE** *If you're unfamiliar with the MySQL server and are confused by the syntax found in the following example, consider reviewing the material found in Chapters 21, 23, and 26.*

Listing 12-5. A User Authentication Table.

```
create table user (
    rowID tinyint unsigned not null auto_increment,
    commonName varchar(35) not null,
    username varchar(8) not null,
    pswd char(32) not null,
    primary key(rowID) );
```

Listing 12-6 displays the code used to authenticate a user-supplied username and password against the information stored within the user table.

Listing 12-6. Authenticating a User Against a MySQL Table.

```php
<?php
/* Because the authentication prompt needs to be invoked twice,
   embed it within a function.
*/
function authenticate_user() {
    header('WWW-Authenticate: Basic realm="Secret Stash"');
    header("HTTP/1.0 401 Unauthorized");
    exit;
}

/* If $_SERVER['PHP_AUTH_USER'] is blank, the user has not yet been prompted for
the authentication information.
*/
if (! isset($_SERVER['PHP_AUTH_USER'])) {
    authenticate_user();
} else {
    // Connect to the MySQL database
    mysql_pconnect("localhost","authenticator","secret")
                or die("Can't connect to database server!");
    mysql_select_db("gilmorebook")
                or die("Can't select authentication database!");

    // Create and execute the selection query.
    $query = "SELECT username, pswd FROM user
            WHERE username='$_SERVER[PHP_AUTH_USER]' AND
            pswd=MD5('$_SERVER[PHP_AUTH_PW]')";
```

```
    $result = mysql_query($query);
    // If nothing was found, reprompt the user for the login information.
    if (mysql_num_rows($result) == 0) {
        authenticate_user();
    }
}
?>
```

Although MySQL authentication is more powerful than the previous two method-ologies, it is really quite trivial to implement. Simply execute a selection query against the user table, using the entered username and password as criteria for the query. Of course, such a solution is not dependent upon specific use of a MySQL database; any relational database could be used in its place.

IP-based Authentication

Sometimes you need an even greater level of access restriction to ensure the validity of the user. Of course, a username/password combination is not foolproof; this infor-mation can be given to someone else, or stolen from a user. It could also be guessed through deduction or brute force, particularly if the user chooses a poor login combi-nation, which is still quite common. To combat this, one effective way to further enforce authentication validity is to not only require a valid username/password login pair, but also a specific IP address. To do so, you only need to slightly modify the user table used in the previous section, and make a tiny modification to the query used in Listing 12-6. First the table, displayed in Listing 12-7.

Listing 12-7. The User Table Revisited

```
create table user (
    rowID mediumint unsigned not null auto_increment,
    commonName varchar(35) not null,
    username char(8) not null,
    pswd char(32) not null,
    ipAddress char(15) not null,
    primary key(rowID) );
```

The code for validating both the username/password and IP address is displayed in Listing 12-8.

Listing 12-8: Authenticating Using a Login Pair and an IP Address

```
<?php
function authenticate_user() {
    header('WWW-Authenticate: Basic realm="Secret Stash"');
    header("HTTP/1.0 401 Unauthorized");
    exit;
}
```

```
if(! isset($_SERVER['PHP_AUTH_USER'])) {
    authenticate_user();
} else {

    mysql_connect("localhost","authenticator","secret")
                    or die("Can't connect to database server!");

    mysql_select_db("gilmorebook")
                    or die("Can't select authentication database!");

    $query = "SELECT username, pswd FROM user
                WHERE username='$_SERVER[PHP_AUTH_USER]' AND
                pswd=MD5('$_SERVER[PHP_AUTH_PW]')
                AND ipAddress='$_SERVER[REMOTE_ADDR]'";

    $result = mysql_query($query);

    if (mysql_num_rows($result) == 0)
            authenticate_user();
    mysql_close();

} # end if
?>
```

Although this additional layer of security works quite well, you should understand that it is not foolproof. The practice of *IP spoofing*, or tricking a network into thinking that traffic is emanating from a particular IP address, has long been a tool in the savvy attacker's toolbox. Therefore, if such an attacker gains access to a user's username and password, they could conceivably circumvent your IP-based security obstacles.

User Login Administration

When you incorporate user logins into your application, providing a sound authentication mechanism is only part of the total picture. How do you ensure that the user chooses a sound password, of sufficient difficulty that attackers cannot use it as a possible attack route? Furthermore, how do you deal with the inevitable event when the user forgets his password? Both topics are covered in detail in this section.

Password Designation

Passwords are often assigned during some sort of user registration process, typically when the user signs up to become a site member. In addition to providing various items of information such as the user's given name and e-mail address, the user is often also prompted to designate a username and password, to be later used for logging in to the site. You'll create a working example of such a registration process, using the table displayed in Listing 12-9 to store the user data.

Listing 12-9. The user *Table*

```
CREATE TABLE user {
    rowID smallint unsigned not null auto_increment,
    name char(40) not null,
    email char(55) not null,
    username char(15) not null,
    pswd char(32) not null,
    primary key(rowID)
);
```

Listing 12-10 offers the registration code. For sake of space conservation, I'll forego presenting the registration form HTML, as it is assumed by now that you're quite familiar with such syntax. This form is stored in a file called registration.html, and is displayed using the file_get_contents() function. A screenshot of this registration form is available in Figure 12-2.

Name:

Email Address:

Username:

Password:

Verify Password:

Register!

Figure 12-2. The registration form

The user provides the necessary input, and submits the form data. The script will then confirm that the password and password verification strings match, displaying an error if they do not. If the password checks out, a connection to the MySQL server is made, and an appropriate insertion query executed.

Listing 12-10: User Registration (registration.php)

```php
<?php
/*
Has the user submitted data?
If not, display the registration form.
*/
if (! isset($_POST['submitbutton'])) {
    echo file_get_contents("/templates/registration.html");
/* Form data has been submitted. */
} else {
    /* Connect to the MySQL server and select database.  */
    mysql_connect("localhost","authenticator","secret");
    mysql_select_db("chapter12");
    /* Ensure that the password and password verifier match. */
    if ($_POST['pswd'] != $_POST['pswdagain']) {
        echo "<p>The passwords do not match. Please go back and try again.</p>";
    /* Passwords match, so attempt to insert information into user table.   */
    } else {
        try {
            $query = "INSERT INTO user SET rowID=NULL, name='$_POST[name]',
                            email='$_POST[email]', username='$_POST[username]',
                            pswd=MD5('$_POST[pswd]')";
            $result = mysql_query($query);
            if (! $result) {
                throw new Exception(
                    "Registration problems were encountered!"
                );
            } else {
                echo "<p>Registration was successful!</p>";
            }
        } catch(Exception $e) {
            echo "<p>".$e->getMessage()."</p>";
        } #endCatch
    } #endIF
} #endIF
?>
```

The registration script provided here is for demonstration purposes only; if you want to use such a script in a mission-critical application, you'll need to include additional error checking mechanisms. Here are just a few items to make sure of:

- All fields have been completed.

- The e-mail address is valid, because this is likely to be the main avenue of communication for matters such as password recovery (a topic discussed in the next section).

- The password and password verification strings match (done in the preceding example).

- The user does not already exist in the database.

- No potentially malicious code has been inserted into the fields. This matter is discussed in some detail in Chapter 19.

- Password length and syntax. Shorter passwords consisting of solely letters or numbers are much more likely to be broken, given a concerted attempt.

Testing Password Guessability with the CrackLib Library

In an ill-conceived effort to prevent forgetting passwords, users tend to choose something easy to remember; the name of their dog, their mother's maiden name, or worse, their own name or age. Ironically, this practice often doesn't help users to remember the password, and even worse, it offers attackers a rather simple route into an otherwise restricted system, either by researching the user's background and attempting various passwords until the correct one is found, or by using brute-force to discern the password through numerous repeated attempts. In either case, the password is typically broken because the user has chosen a password that is easily guessable, resulting in not only the possible compromise of the user's personal data, but also of the system itself.

Reducing the possibility that such easily guessable passwords could be introduced into the system is quite simple, by turning the procedure of unchallenged password creation into one of automated password approval. PHP offers a wonderful means for doing so via the CrackLib library, created by Alec Muffett (http://www.crypticide.org/users/alecm/). CrackLib is intended to test the strength of a password by setting certain benchmarks that determine its guessability, including:

- **Length:** Passwords must be longer than four characters.

- **Case:** Passwords cannot be all lowercase.

- **Distinction:** Passwords must contain adequate different characters. In addition, the password cannot be blank.

- **Familiarity:** Passwords cannot be based on a word found in a dictionary. In addition, the password cannot be based on a *reversed* word found in the dictionary. I'll talk more about dictionaries in a bit.

- **Standard Numbering:** Because CrackLib's author is British, he thought it a good idea to check against patterns similar to what is known as a National Insurance (NI) Number. The NI Number is used in Britain for taxation, much like the Social Security Number (SSN) is used in America. Coincidentally, both numbers are nine characters long, allowing this mechanism to efficiently prevent the use of either, if a user is stupid enough to use such a sensitive identifier for this purpose.

Installing PHP's CrackLib Extension

To use the CrackLib extension, you need to first download and install the CrackLib library, available at http://www.crypticide.org/users/alecm/. If you're running a Linux/Unix variant, it might already be installed, because CrackLib is often packaged with these operating systems. Complete installation instructions are available in the README found in the tar package (short instructions: configure, make, make install). Next, compile PHP with the --with-crack[=DIR] option. Remember, if you heeded my advice in Chapter 2, and compiled PHP as an Apache module, you do not need to recompile Apache. Once the PHP recompilation is complete, just start and stop Apache, and the CrackLib features are immediately made available to you.

Once CrackLib is installed, you'll need to make sure that the crack.default_ dictionary directive in php.ini is pointing to a password dictionary. Such dictionaries abound on the Internet, so executing a search will turn up numerous results. Later in this section I offer some information regarding various types of dictionaries.

Using the CrackLib Extension

Using PHP's CrackLib extension is quite easy. Listing 12-11 offers a complete usage example.

Listing 12-11. Using PHP's CrackLib Extension

```php
<?php
    $pswd = "567hejk39";

    /* Open the dictionary. Note that the dictionary
       filename does NOT include the extension.
    */
    $dictionary = crack_opendict('/usr/lib/cracklib_dict');
    // Check password for guessability
    $check = crack_check($dictionary, $pswd);
    // Retrieve outcome
    echo crack_getlastmessage();
    // Close dictionary
    crack_closedict($dictionary);
?>
```

In this particular example, crack_getlastmessage() returns the string "strong password", because the password denoted by $pswd is sufficiently difficult to guess.

However, if the password is weak, one of a number of different messages could be returned. Table 12-1 offers a few other passwords, and the resulting outcome from passing them through crack_check().

Table 12-1. Password Candidates and the crack_check() *Function's Response*

PASSWORD	RESPONSE
mary	it is too short
12	it's WAY too short
1234567	it is too simplistic/systematic
street	it does not contain enough DIFFERENT characters

By writing a short conditional statement, you can create user-friendly, detailed responses based on the information returned from CrackLib. Of course, if the response is "strong password," you can allow the user's password choice to take effect.

Dictionaries

In Listing 12-11, I used the cracklib_dict.pwd dictionary, which is generated by CrackLib during the installation process. Note that in the example I did not include the extension (.pwd) when referring to the file. This seems to be a quirk with the way that PHP wants to refer to this file, and could change sometime in the future, so that the extension is also required.

You are also free to use other dictionaries, of which there are many freely available on the Internet. Furthermore, you can find dictionaries for practically every spoken language. One particularly complete repository of such dictionaries is available on the University of Oxford's FTP site: ftp.ox.ac.uk. In addition to quite a few language dictionaries, the site offers a number of interesting specialized dictionaries, including one containing keywords from many *Star Trek* plot summaries. At any rate, regardless of the dictionary you decide to use, simply assign its location to the crack.default_dictionary directive, or open it using crack_opendict().

One-Time URLs and Password Recovery

As sure as the sun rises, your application users will forget their passwords. All of us are guilty of forgetting such information, and it's not entirely our fault. Take a moment to list all of the different login combinations you regularly use; my guess is that it's at least twelve. E-mail, workstations, servers, bank accounts, utilities, online commerce, securities and mortgage brokerages... We use passwords to manage nearly everything these days. Because your application will assumedly be adding yet another login pair to the user's list, a simple, automated mechanism should be in place for retrieving or resetting the user's password when he or she forgets it. Depending on the sensitivity of the material protected by the login, retrieving the password might require a phone call or sending the password via the postal service. As always, use discretion when you devise mechanisms that may be exploited by an intruder. I'll examine one such mechanism in this chapter, which is referred to as a one-time URL.

A one-time URL is commonly used given to a user to ensure uniqueness when no other authentication mechanisms are available, or when the user would find authentication perhaps too tedious for the task-at-hand. For example, suppose you maintain a list of newsletter subscribers, and you wanted to know which and how many subscribers were actually reading each monthly issue. Simply embedding the newsletter into an e-mail won't do, because you would never know how many subscribers were simply deleting the e-mail from their inboxes without even glancing at the contents (something I do regularly). Rather, you could offer them a one-time URL pointing to the newsletter, one of which might look like this:

```
http://www.example.com/newsletter/0503.php?id=9b758e7f08a2165d664c2684fddbcde2
```

In order to know exactly which users showed interest in the newsletter issue, a unique id parameter like the one shown in the above URL has been assigned to each user, and stored in some subscriber table. Such values are typically pseudorandom, derived using PHP's md5() and uniqid() functions, like so:

```
$id = md5(uniqid(rand(),1));
```

The subscriber table might look something like the following:

```
CREATE TABLE subscriber (
    rowID smallint unsigned not null auto_increment,
    email varchar(55) not null,
    uniqueid char(32) not null,
    readNewsletter ENUM('Y','N') not null default 'N',
    primary key(rowID)
    );
```

When the user clicks on this link, taking him to the newsletter, a function similar to the following could execute before displaying the newsletter:

```
function read_newsletter($id) {
    $query = "UPDATE subscriber SET readNewsletter='Y' WHERE uniqueid='$id'";
    return mysql_query($query);
}
```

The result is that you will know exactly how many subscribers showed interest in the newsletter, because they all actively clicked on the link.

This very same concept can be applied to password recovery. To illustrate how this is accomplished, consider the user table, shown in Listing 12-12.

Listing 12-12. A Revised user *Table*

```
create table user (
    rowID mediumint unsigned not null auto_increment,
    commonName varchar(35) not null,
```

```
username char(8) not null,
pswd char(32) not null,
uniqueIdentifier char(32) not null,
primary key(rowID)
);
```

Suppose one of the users found in this table forgets his password, and thus clicks on the "Forgot password?" link commonly found near a login prompt. The user will arrive at a page in which he is asked to enter his e-mail address. Upon entering the address and submitting the form, a script is executed similar to that shown in Listing 12-13:

Listing 12-13. A One-Time URL Generator

```php
<?php
// Create unique identifier
$id = md5(uniqid(rand(),1));
// Set user's uniqueIdentifier field to a unique id.
$query = "UPDATE user SET uniqueIdentifier='$id' WHERE email=$_POST[email]";
$result = mysql_query($query);

$email = <<< email
Dear user,
Click on the following link to reset your password:
http://www.example.com/users/lostpassword.php?id=$id
email;

// Email user password reset options
mail($_POST['email'],"Password recovery","$email","FROM:services@example.com");
echo "<p>Instructions regarding resetting your password have been sent to
        $_POST[email]</p>";
?>
```

When the user receives this e-mail, and clicks on the link, he is taken to the script lostpassword.php, shown in Listing 12-14.

Listing 12-14. Resetting a User's Password

```php
<?php
    // Create a pseudorandom password five characters in length
    $pswd = substr(md5(uniqid(rand(),1),5));
    // Update the user table with the new password.
    $query = "UPDATE user SET pswd='$pswd' WHERE uniqueIdentifier=$_GET[id]";
    $result = mysql_query($query);

    // Display the new password to the user
    echo "<p>Your password has been reset to $pswd. Please log in and change
            your password to one of your liking.</p>";
?>
```

Of course, this is only one of many recovery mechanisms. For example, you could use a similar script to provide the user with a form for resetting his own password.

Summary

This chapter introduced PHP's authentication capabilities, features that are practically guaranteed to be incorporated into many of your future applications. In addition to discussing the basic concepts surrounding this functionality, I investigated several common authentication methodologies, including authenticating against hard-coded values, file-based authentication, and database-based authentication. I took a look at decreasing password guessability using PHP's CrackLib extension, and finally offered a discussion of recovering passwords using one-time URLs.

In the next chapter, I'll discuss another set of commonly used PHP functionality—handling file uploads via the browser.

CHAPTER 13

Handling File Uploads

DESPITE THE HYPE, glory, and often rumors of magical powers bestowed upon it almost from birth, the Web is really nothing more than a global file server. More specifically, it's a global file server farm. And although HTML files of course make up the vast majority of all files transferred via the HTTP protocol, it has become quite common-place to make Word documents, PDFs, executables, MPEGs, and any number of other file types accessible via the Web. Although FTP has historically been the common means for uploading files to a server, such file transfers are becoming increasingly prevalent via a Web-based interface. In this chapter, you'll learn all about PHP's file-upload handling capabilities. In particular, chapter topics include:

- PHP's file upload configuration directives

- PHP's $_FILES superglobal array, used to handle file upload data

- PHP's built-in upload functions: is_uploaded_file() and move_uploaded_file()

- A review of possible values returned from an upload script

As always, numerous real-world examples are offered throughout this chapter, providing you with applicable insight into this topic.

Uploading Files via the HTTP Protocol

The way files are uploaded via a Web browser was officially formalized in around November 1995, when Ernesto Nebel and Larry Masinter of the Xerox Corporation proposed a standardized methodology for doing so within RFC 1867 (http://www.ietf.org/rfc/rfc1867.txt.). This memo, which formulated the groundwork for making the additions necessary to HTML to allow for file uploads (subsequently incorporated into HTML 3.0), also offered the specification for a new Internet Media Type, *multipart/form-data*. This new media type was desired, because the standard type used to encode "normal" form values, *application/x-www-form-urlencoded*, is considered too inefficient to handle large quantities of binary data such as that which might be uploaded via such a form interface. An example follows, and a screenshot of the corresponding output is shown in Figure 13-1:

```
<form action="uploadmanager.html" enctype="multipart/form-data" method="post">
    Name:<br /> <input type="text" name="name" value="" /><br />
    Email:<br /> <input type="text" name="email" value="" /><br />
    Homework:<br /> <input type="file" name="homework" value="" /><br />
    <p><input type="submit" name="submit" value="Submit Homework" /></p>
</form>
```

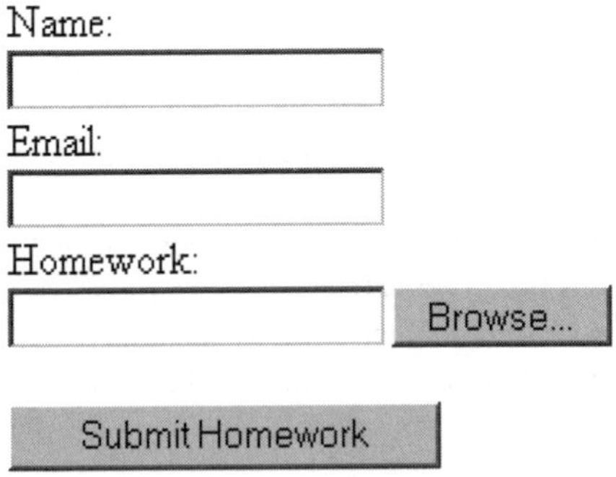

Name:

Email:

Homework:

Browse...

Submit Homework

Figure 13-1. HTML form incorporating the "file" input type tag

Understand that this offers only half of the desired result; whereas the file input type and other upload-related attributes standardize the way files are sent to the server via an HTML page, no capabilities are offered for determining what happens once that file gets there! The reception and subsequent handling of the uploaded files is a function of an upload handler, created using some server process, or capable server-side language, like Perl, Java, or PHP. We'll devote the remainder of this chapter to this aspect of the upload process.

Handling Uploads with PHP

Successfully managing file uploads via PHP is the result of cooperation between various configuration directives, the $_FILES superglobal, and a properly coded Web form. In the following sections, I'll introduce all three topics and conclude with a number of examples.

PHP's File Upload/Resource Directives

Several configuration directives are available for fine-tuning PHP's file upload capabilities. These directives determine whether PHP's file upload support is enabled, the maximum allowable uploadable file size, the maximum allowable script memory allocation, and various other important resource benchmarks. I'll introduce these directives in this section.

file_uploads (boolean)
Scope: `PHP_INI_SYSTEM`, Default value: 1
The `file_uploads` directive determines whether PHP scripts on the server can accept file uploads.

max_execution_time (integer)
Scope: `PHP_INI_ALL`, Default value: 30
The `max_execution_time` directive determines the maximum amount of time, in seconds, that a PHP script will execute before registering a fatal error.

memory_limit (integer)M
Scope: `PHP_INI_ALL`, Default value: 8M
The `memory_limit` directive sets a maximum allowable amount of memory, in megabytes, that a script can allocate. Note that the integer value must be followed by an "M" in order for this setting to work properly. This prevents runaway scripts from monopolizing server memory, and even crashing the server in certain situations. This directive only takes effect if the `--enable-memory-limit` flag was set at compile-time.

upload_max_filesize (integer)M
Scope: `PHP_INI_SYSTEM`, Default value: 2M
The `upload_max_filesize` directive determines the maximum size, in megabytes, of an uploaded file. This directive should be smaller than `post_max_size` (introduced in a later section), because it applies only to information passed via the `file` input type, and not to all information passed via the `POST` instance. Like `memory_limit`, note that an `M` must follow the integer value.

upload_tmp_dir (string)
Scope: `PHP_INI_SYSTEM`, Default value: NULL
Because an uploaded file must be successfully transferred to the server before subsequent processing on that file can begin, a staging area of sorts must be designated for such files as the location where they can be temporarily placed until moved to their final location. This location is specified using the `upload_tmp_dir` directive. For example, suppose you wanted to temporarily store uploaded files in the `/tmp/phpuploads/` directory:

```
upload_tmp_dir = "/tmp/phpuploads/"
```

Keep in mind that this directory must be writable by the user owning the server process. Therefore, if user "nobody" owns the Apache process, then user "nobody" should either be made owner of the temporary upload directory, or should be made a member of the group owning that directory. If this is not done, user "nobody" will be unable to write the file to the directory, unless world write permissions are assigned to the directory.

post_max_size (integer)M

Scope: PHP_INI_SYSTEM, Default value: 8M

The post_max_size directive determines the maximum allowable size, in megabytes, of information that can be accepted via the POST method. As a rule of thumb, this directive setting should be larger than upload_max_filesize, to account for any other form fields that may be passed in addition to the uploaded file. Like memory_limit and upload_max_filesize, note that an M must follow the integer value.

The $_FILES Array

The $_FILES superglobal is special in that it is the only one of the predefined EGCPFS (Environment, Get, Cookie, Put, Files, Server) superglobal arrays that is two-dimensional. Its purpose is to store a variety of information pertinent to a file (or files) uploaded to the server via a PHP script. In total, five items are available in this array, each of which is introduced in this section.

> **NOTE** *Each of the items introduced in this section makes reference to* userfile. *This is simply a placeholder for the name assigned to the file upload form element. Therefore, this value will likely change in accordance to your chosen name assignment.*

$_FILES['userfile']['error']

The $_FILES['userfile']['error'] array value offers important information pertinent to the outcome of the upload attempt. In total, five return values are possible, one signifying a successful outcome, and four others denoting specific errors which arise from the attempt. The names and meanings of each return value are introduced in the later section, "Upload Error Messages."

$_FILES['userfile']['name']

The $_FILES['userfile']['name'] variable specifies the original name of the file, including the extension, as declared on the client machine. Therefore, if you browse to a file named vacation.jpg, and upload it via the form, this variable will be assigned the value vacation.jpg.

$_FILES['userfile']['size']

The $_FILES['userfile']['size'] variable specifies the size, in bytes, of the file uploaded from the client machine. Therefore, in the case of the vacation.jpg file, this variable could plausibly be assigned a value like 5253, or roughly 5 kilobytes.

$_FILES['userfile']['tmp_name']

The $_FILES['userfile']['tmp_name'] variable specifies the temporary name assigned to the file once it has been uploaded to the server. This is the name of the file assigned to it while stored in the temporary directory (specified by the PHP directive upload_tmp_dir).

$_FILES['userfile']['type']

The $_FILES['userfile']['type'] variable specifies the mime-type of the file uploaded from the client machine. Therefore, in the case of the vacation.jpg file, this variable would be assigned the value image/jpeg. If a PDF were uploaded, then the value application/pdf would be assigned.

Because this variable sometimes produces unexpected results, you should explicitly verify it yourself from within the script.

PHP's Upload Functions

In addition to the host of file-handling functions made available via PHP's file system library (see Chapter 10 for more information), PHP offers two functions specifically intended to aid in the upload process, is_uploaded_file() and move_uploaded_file(). Each function is introduced in this section.

is_uploaded_file()

boolean is_uploaded_file(string *filename*)

The is_uploaded_file() function determines whether a file specified by the input parameter *filename* was uploaded using the POST method. This function is intended to prevent a potential attacker from manipulating files not intended for interaction via the script in question. For example, consider a scenario in which uploaded files were made immediately available for viewing via a public site repository. Say an attacker wanted to make a file somewhat juicier than boring old class notes available for his perusal, say /etc/passwd. So rather than navigate to a class notes file as would be expected, the attacker instead types /etc/passwd directly into the form's file upload field.

Now consider the following uploadmanager.php script:

```php
<?php
    copy($_FILES['classnotes']['tmp_name'],
            "/www/htdocs/classnotes/".basename($classnotes));
?>
```

The result in this poorly written example would be that the /etc/passwd file is copied to a publicly-accessible directory. (Go ahead, try it. Scary, isn't it?) To avoid such a problem, use the is_uploaded_file() function to ensure that the file denoted by the form field, in this case classnotes, is indeed a file that has been uploaded via the form. Revising the uploadmanager.php code:

```php
<?php
if (is_uploaded_file($_FILES['classnotes']['tmp_name'])) {
    copy($_FILES['classnotes']['tmp_name'],
            "/www/htdocs/classnotes/".$_FILES['classnotes']['name']);
} else {
    echo "<p>Potential script abuse attempt detected.</p>";
}
?>
```

In the revised script, is_uploaded_file() checks whether the file denoted by $_FILES['classnotes']['tmp_name'] has indeed been uploaded. If the answer is yes, the file is copied to the desired destination Otherwise, an appropriate error message is displayed.

move_uploaded_file()

boolean move_uploaded_file(string *filename*, string *destination*)

The move_uploaded_file() function was introduced in version 4.0.3 as a convenient means for moving an uploaded file from the temporary directory to a final location. Although copy() works equally well, move_uploaded_file() offers one additional feature that this function does not: It will check to ensure that the file denoted by the *filename* input parameter was in fact uploaded via PHP's HTTP POST upload mechanism. If the file has indeed not been uploaded, the move will fail and a FALSE value will be returned. Because of this, you can forego using is_uploaded_file() as a precursor condition to using move_uploaded_file().

Using move_uploaded_file() is quite simple. Consider a scenario in which you want to move the uploaded class notes file to the directory /www/htdocs/classnotes/, while also preserving the filename as specified on the client:

```
move_uploaded_file($_FILES['classnotes']['tmp_name'],
                   "/www/htdocs/classnotes/".$_FILES['classnotes']['name']);
```

Of course you could rename the file to anything you wish when it's moved. It's important, however, that you properly reference the file's temporary name within the first (source) parameter.

Upload Error Messages

Like any other application component involving user interaction, you need a means to assess the outcome, successful or otherwise. How do you definitively know that the file-upload procedure was successful? And if something goes awry during the upload process, how do you know what caused the error? Thankfully, sufficient information for determining the outcome, and in the case of an error, the reason for the error, is provided in $_FILES['userfile']['error'].

UPLOAD_ERR_OK (Value = 0)
A value of 0 is returned if the upload is successful.

UPLOAD_ERR_INI_SIZE (Value = 1)
A value of 1 is returned if there is an attempt to upload a file whose size exceeds the specified by the upload_max_filesize directive.

UPLOAD_ERR_FORM_SIZE (Value = 2)
A value of 2 is returned if there is an attempt to upload a file whose size exceeds the value of the MAX_FILE_SIZE directive, which can be embedded into the HTML form.

UPLOAD_ERR_PARTIAL (Value = 3)

A value of 3 is returned if a file was not completely uploaded. This might occur if a network error occurs that results in a disruption of the upload process.

UPLOAD_ERR_NO_FILE (Value = 4)

A value of 4 is returned if the user submits the form without specifying a file for upload.

File Upload Examples

Now that the groundwork has been set regarding the basic concepts, it's time to consider a few practical examples.

A Simple Upload Example

The first example actually implements the class notes example referred to throughout this chapter. To formalize the scenario, suppose that a professor invites students to post class notes to his Web site, the idea being that everyone might have something to gain from such a collaborative effort. Of course, credit should nonetheless be given where credit is due, so each file upload should be renamed to the last name of the student. In addition, only PDF files are accepted. Listing 13-1 offers an example:

Listing 13-1. A Simple File Upload Example

```
<form action="uploadmanager.php" enctype="multipart/form-data" method="post">
    Last Name:<br /> <input type="text" name="name" value="" /><br />
    Class Notes:<br /> <input type="file" name="classnotes" value="" /><br />
    <p><input type="submit" name="submit" value="Submit Notes" /></p>
</form>

<?php
/* Set a few constants */
define ("FILEREPOSITORY","/home/www/htdocs/class/classnotes/");

/* Make sure that the file was POSTed. */
if (is_uploaded_file($_FILES['classnotes']['tmp_name'])) {

    /* Was the file a PDF? */
    if ($_FILES['classnotes']['type'] != "application/pdf") {
        echo "<p>Class notes must be uploaded in PDF format.</p>";
    } else {
```

```
/* move uploaded file to final destination. */
        $name = $_POST['name'];

        $result = move_uploaded_file($_FILES['classnotes']['tmp_name'],
        FILEREPOSITORY."/$name.pdf");

        if ($result == 1) echo "<p>File successfully uploaded.</p>";
            else echo "<p>There was a problem uploading the file.</p>";

    } #endIF

} #endIF
?>
```

> **CAUTION** *Remember that files are both uploaded and moved under the guise of the Web server daemon owner. Failing to assign adequate permissions to both the temporary upload directory and the final directory destination for this user will result in failure to properly execute the file upload procedure.*

Categorizing Uploaded Files by Date

The professor, delighted by the students' participation in the class notes project, has decided to move all class correspondence online. His current project involves providing an interface that will allow students to submit their daily homework via the Web. Like the class notes, the homework is to be submitted in PDF format, and will be assigned the student's last name as its file name when stored on the server. Because homework is due daily, the professor wants both a means for automatically organizing the assignment submissions by date, and also a means for ensuring that the class slackers can't sneak homework in after the deadline, which is 11:59:59 p.m. daily.

The script offered in Listing 13-2 automates all of this, minimizing administrative overhead for the professor. In addition to ensuring that the file is a PDF, and automatically assigning it the student's specified last name, the script will also create new folders daily, each following the naming convention MM-DD-YYYY.

Listing 13-2. Categorizing Uploaded Files by Date

```
<form action="homework.php" enctype="multipart/form-data" method="post">
    Last Name:<br /> <input type="text" name="name" value="" /><br />
    Homework:<br /> <input type="file" name="homework" value="" /><br />
    <p><input type="submit" name="submit" value="Submit Notes" /></p>
</form>

<?php
# Set a constant
define ("FILEREPOSITORY","/home/www/htdocs/class/homework/");
if (isset($_FILES['homework'])) {
    if (is_uploaded_file($_FILES['homework']['tmp_name'])) {
```

```
    if ($_FILES['homework']['type'] != "application/pdf") {
        echo "<p>Homework must be uploaded in PDF format.</p>";
    } else {

        /* Format date and create daily directory, if necessary. */
        $today = date("m-d-Y");
        if (! is_dir(FILEREPOSITORY.$today)) {
            mkdir(FILEREPOSITORY.$today);
        }

        /* Assign name and move uploaded file to final destination. */
        $name = $_POST['name'];
        $result = move_uploaded_file($_FILES['homework']['tmp_name'],
                            FILEREPOSITORY.$today."/"."$name.pdf");
        /* Provide user with feedback. */
        if ($result == 1) echo "<p>File successfully uploaded.</p>";
            else echo "<p>There was a problem uploading the homework.</p>";

    }

}
}
?>
```

Although this code could stand a bit of improvement, it accomplishes what the professor set out to do. Although it does not prevent students from submitting late homework, that homework will be placed in the folder corresponding with the current date as specified by the server clock.

> **NOTE** *Fortunately for the students, PHP will overwrite previously submitted files, allowing them to repeatedly revise and resubmit homework as the deadline nears.*

Handling Multiple File Uploads

The professor, always eager to push his students to the outer limits of insanity, has decided to require the submission of two daily homework assignments. Always striving for a streamlined submission mechanism, the professor would like both assignments to be submitted via a single interface, and named *student-name1* and *student-name2*. The dating procedure used in the previous listing will be reused in this script. Therefore, the only real puzzle here is to figure out how to submit multiple files via a single form interface.

Earlier in this chapter I mentioned that the $_FILES array is unique because it is the only predefined variable array that is two-dimensional. This is not without reason; the first element of that array represents the file input name, therefore if multiple file inputs exist within a single form, each can be handled separately without interfering with the other. This concept is demonstrated in Listing 13-3.

Listing 13-3. Handling Multiple File Uploads

```php
<form action="multiplehomework.php" enctype="multipart/form-data" method="post">
    Last Name:<br /> <input type="text" name="name" value="" /><br />
    Homework #1:<br /> <input type="file" name="homework1" value="" /><br />
    Homework #2:<br /> <input type="file" name="homework2" value="" /><br />
    <p><input type="submit" name="submit" value="Submit Notes" /></p>
</form>

<?php
/* Set a constant */
define ("FILEREPOSITORY","/home/www/htdocs/class/homework/");
if (isset($_FILES['homework'])) {
    if (is_uploaded_file($_FILES['homework1']['tmp_name']) &&
        is_uploaded_file($_FILES['homework2']['tmp_name'])) {

        if (($_FILES['homework1']['type'] != "application/pdf") ||
            ($_FILES['homework2']['type'] != "application/pdf")) {

            echo "<p>All homework must be uploaded in PDF format.</p>";

        } else {
            /* Format date and create daily directory, if necessary. */
            $today = date("m-d-Y");

            if (! is_dir(FILEREPOSITORY.$today))
                mkdir(FILEREPOSITORY.$today);

            /* Name and move homework #1 */
            $filename1 = $_POST['name']."1";

            $result = move_uploaded_file($_FILES['homework1']['tmp_name'],
                        FILEREPOSITORY.$today."/"."$filename1.pdf");

            if ($result == 1) echo "<p>Homework #1 successfully uploaded.</p>";
            else echo "<p>There was a problem uploading homework #1.</p>";

            /* Name and move homework #2 */
            $filename2 = $_POST['name']."2";

            $result = move_uploaded_file($_FILES['homework2']['tmp_name'],
                        FILEREPOSITORY.$today."/"."$filename2.pdf");

            if ($result == 1) echo "<p>Homework #2 successfully uploaded.</p>";
            else echo "<p>There was a problem uploading homework #2.</p>";

        }
    }
}
?>
```

Although this script is a tad longer due to the extra logic required to handle the second homework assignment, it only differs slightly from Listing 13-2. However, there is one very important matter to keep in mind when working with this or any other script that handles multiple file uploads; the combined file size cannot exceed the upload__max_size or post_max_size configuration directives.

Summary

Transferring files via the Web eliminates a great many inconveniences otherwise posed by firewalls and FTP servers and clients. It also enhances an application's ability to easily manipulate and publish non-traditional files. In this chapter you learned just how easy it is to add such capabilities to your PHP applications. In addition to offering a comprehensive overview of PHP's file upload features, several practical examples were discussed.

In the next chapter, one of my favorite topics of Web development is introduced in excruciating detail: tracking users via session-handling.

CHAPTER 14

Networking with PHP

You may have turned to this page wondering just what PHP could possibly have to offer in regards to networking. After all, aren't networking tasks left to the concern of somebody from that geeky networking group located in the basement of the corporate office? While such a stereotype might have once painted a fairly accurate picture, these days, incorporating networking capabilities into a Web application is commonplace. In fact, Web-based applications are regularly used to monitor and even maintain network infrastructures. The PHP developers, always keen to acknowledge growing needs in the realm of Web application development, and remedy that demand by incorporating new features into the language, have put together a rather amazing array of network-specific functionality.

This chapter is divided into several sections, each of which is previewed here:

- **DNS, servers, and services:** PHP offers a variety of functions capable of retrieving information about the internals of networks, DNS, protocols, and Internet addressing schemes. In this section, I'll introduce these functions and offer several usage examples.

- **Sending e-mail with PHP:** Sending e-mail via a Web application is undoubtedly one of the most commonplace features you can find these days, and for good reason. E-mail remains the Internet's killer application, and offers an amazingly efficient means for communicating and maintaining important data and information. In this section, I'll show you how to effectively imitate even the best e-mail client's "send" functionality via a PHP script.

- **IMAP, POP3, and NNTP:** Although formally known as PHP's IMAP extension, this library is capable of communicating with IMAP, POP3, and NNTP servers. In this section, I'll introduce many of the most commonly used functions found in this library, showing you how to effectively manage an IMAP account via the Web.

- **Streams:** New to version 4.3, streams offer a generalized means for interacting with *streamable* resources, or resources that are read from and written to in a linear fashion. In this section, I'll offer an introduction to this feature.

- **Common networking tasks:** In this section, I'll show you how to use PHP to mimic the tasks commonly carried out by command-line tools, including pinging a network address, tracing a network connection, scanning a server's open ports, and more.

DNS, Services, and Servers

These days, investigating or troubleshooting a network issue often involves gathering a variety of information pertinent to affected clients, servers, and network internals such as protocols, domain name resolution, and IP addressing schemes. PHP offers a number of functions for retrieving a bevy of information about each subject, each of which are introduced in this section.

DNS

The Domain Name System (DNS) is what allows us to use domain names (example.com, for instance) in place of the corresponding not-so-user-friendly IP address, such as 192.0.34.166. The domain names and their complementary IP addresses are stored and made available for reference on domain name servers, which are interspersed across the globe. Typically, a domain will have several types of *records* associated to it, one mapping the IP address to the domain, another for directing e-mail, and another for a domain name alias, for example. Often, network administrators and developers require a means for being able to learn more about various DNS records for a given domain. In this section, I'll introduce a number of standard PHP functions capable of digging up a great deal of information regarding DNS records.

checkdnsrr()

```
int checkdnsrr (string host [, string type])
```

The checkdnsrr() function checks for the existence of DNS records based on the supplied *host* value and optional DNS resource record *type*, returning TRUE if any records are located and FALSE otherwise. Possible record types include:

- A: IPv4 Address Record. Responsible for the host-name-to-IPv4-address translation.

- AAAA: IPv6 Address Record. Responsible for the host-name-to-IPv6-address translation.

- ANY: Looks for any type of record.

- CNAME: Canonical Name Record. A CNAME maps an alias to the real domain name.

- MX: Mail Exchange Record. An MX record determines the name and relative preference of a mail server for the host. This is the default setting.

- NS: Name Server Record. An NS determines the name server for the host.

- PTR: Pointer Record. A PTR is used to map an IP address to a host.

- SOA: Start of Authority Record. An SOA record sets global parameters for the host.

Consider an example. Suppose you wanted to verify whether the domain name example.com has been taken:

```php
<?php
    $recordexists = checkdnsrr("example.com", "ANY");
    if ($recordexists) echo "The domain name has been taken. Sorry!";
    else echo "The domain name is available!";
?>
```

This returns the following:

```
The domain name has been taken. Sorry!
```

You can use this function to verify the existence of a domain of a supplied mail address:

```php
<?php
    $email = "ceo@example.com";
    $domain = explode("@",$email);

    $valid = checkdnsrr($domain[1], "ANY");

    if($valid) echo "The domain has an MX record!";
    else echo "Cannot locate MX record for $domain[1]!";
?>
```

This returns:

```
The domain has an MX record!
```

Note that I did not specifically request for verification of existence of an MX record. Sometimes network administrators will employ other configuration methodologies to allow for mail resolution without using MX records (because MX records are not mandatory). Therefore I like to err on the side of caution and just check for existence of the domain, without specifically requesting that an MX record exists.

dns_get_record()

```
array dns_get_record (string hostname [, int type [, array &authns,
array &addtl]])
```

The dns_get_record() function returns an array consisting of various DNS resource records pertinent to the domain specified by *hostname*. Although by default dns_get_record() returns all records it can find specific to the supplied domain, you can streamline the retrieval process by specifying a *type*, the name of which must be prefaced with DNS_. This function supports all of the types introduced along with checkdnsrr(), in addition to some I'll introduce in a moment. Finally, if you're looking for a full-blown description of this hostname's DNS description, you can pass the *authns* and *addtl* parameters in by reference, which specify that information pertinent to the authoritative name servers and additional records should be also returned.

Assuming that the supplied *hostname* is valid and exists, a call to dns_get_record() returns at least four attributes:

- host: This specifies the name of the DNS namespace to which all other attributes correspond.

- class: Because this function only returns records of class "Internet", this attribute will always read IN.

- type: This determines the record type. Depending upon the returned type, other attributes might also be made available.

- ttl: This is the record's time-to-live, calculating the record's original TTL minus the amount of time that has passed since the authoritative name server was queried.

In addition to the types I introduced in the section on checkdnsrr(), the following domain record types are made available to dns_get_record().

- DNS_ALL: This type retrieves all available records, even those that might not be recognized when using the recognition capabilities of your particular operating system. Use this when you want to be absolutely sure that all available records have been retrieved.

- DNS_ANY: This type retrieves all records recognized by your particular operating system.

- DNS_HINFO: A host information record, used to specify the operating system and computer type of the host. Keep in mind that this information is not required.

- DNS_NAPTR: A naming authority pointer, used to allow for non-DNS compliant names, resolving them to new domains using regular expression rewrite rules. For example, an NAPTR might be used to maintain legacy (pre-DNS) services.

- DNS_NS: A name server record that determines whether the name server is the authoritative answer for the given domain, or whether this responsibility is ultimately delegated to another server.

- DNS_SRV: A services record, used to denote the location of various services for the supplied domain.

In order to forego redundancy I did not include the types already introduced along with checkdnsrr(). Keep in mind that those types are also available to dns_get_record(). Just remember that the type names must always be prefaced with DNS_.

Consider an example. Suppose you want to learn more about the example.com domain:

```php
<?php
    $result = dns_get_record("example.com");
    print_r($result);
?>
```

A sampling of the returned information follows:

```
Array (
    [0] => Array (
        [host] => example.com
        [type] => NS
        [target] => a.iana-servers.net
        [class]  =>  IN
        [ttl]  => 110275
        )
    [1] => Array (
        [host] => example.com
        [type] => A
        [ip] => 192.0.34.166
        [class] => IN
        [ttl] => 88674
        )
)
```

If you were only interested in the name server records, you could execute the following:

```php
<?php
    $result = dns_get_record("example.com","DNS_CNAME");
    print_r($result);
?>
```

This returns the following:

```
Array ( [0] => Array ( [host] => example.com [type] => NS
[target] => a.iana-servers.net [class] => IN [ttl] => 21564 )
[1] => Array ( [host] => example.com [type] => NS
[target] => b.iana-servers.net [class] => IN [ttl] => 21564 ) )
```

getmxrr()

```
int getmxrr (string hostname, array mxhosts [, array weight])
```

The getmxrr() function retrieves the MX records for the host specified by *hostname*. The MX records are added to the array specified by *mxhosts*. If the optional input parameter *weight* is supplied, the corresponding weight values will be placed there, which are the hit prevalence assigned to each server identified by record. An example follows:

```
<?php
   getmxrr("wjgilmore.com",$mxhosts);
   print_r($mxhosts);
?>
```

This returns the following:

```
Array ( [0] => mail.wjgilmore.com)
```

> **NOTE** *I wrote an article for Developer.com* (http://www.developer.com/) *regarding validating e-mail addresses using PHP's* eregi() *and* getmxrr() *functions. Check it out at* http://www.developer.com/lang/php/article.php/3290141.

Services

Although we often use the word "Internet" in a generalized sense, making statements pertinent to using the Internet to chat, read, or download the latest version of some game, what we're actually referring to is one or several Internet *services* that collectively make this communications medium what it is. Examples of these services include HTTP, FTP, POP3, IMAP, and SSH. For various reasons out of the scope of this book, each service commonly operates on a particular communications port. For example, HTTP's default port is 80, and FTP's default port is 23. These days, the widespread need for firewalls at all levels of a network makes knowledge of such matters quite important. Two PHP functions are available for learning more about services and their corresponding port numbers, both of which are introduced in this section.

getservbyname()

```
int getservbyname (string service, string protocol)
```

The getservbyname() function returns the port number of the service corresponding to *service* as specified by the /etc/services file. The *protocol* parameter specifies whether you're referring to the tcp or udp component of this service. Consider an example:

```php
<?php
    echo "HTTP's default port number is: ".getservbyname("http", "tcp");
?>
```

This returns the following:

```
HTTP's default port number is: 80
```

getservbyport()

```
string getservbyport (int port, string protocol)
```

The getservbyport() function returns the name of the service corresponding to the supplied *port* number as specified by the /etc/services file. The *protocol* parameter specifies whether you're referring to the tcp or udp component of the service. Consider an example:

```php
<?php
    echo "Port 80's default service is: ".getservbyport(80, "tcp");
?>
```

This returns the following:

```
Port 80's default service is: http
```

Establishing Socket Connections

In today's networked environment, you'll often want to query services, both local and remote. Often this is done by establishing a socket connection with that service. In this section I'll demonstrate how this is accomplished, using the fsockopen() function.

fsockopen()

resource fsockopen (string *target*, int *port* [, int *errno* [, string *errstring*
[, float *timeout*]]])

The fsockopen() function establishes a connection to the resource designated by
target on port *port*, returning error information to the optional parameters *errno* and
errstring. The optional parameter *timeout* sets a time limit, in seconds, on how long
the function will attempt to establish the connection before failing.

The first example will show how to establish a port 80 connection to www.example.com
using fsockopen(), and output the index page:

```php
<?php
    // Establish a port 80 connection with www.example.com
    $http = fsockopen("www.example.com",80);
    // Send a request to the server
    $req = "GET / HTTP/1.1\r\n";
    $req .= "Host: www.example.com\r\n";
    $req .= "Connection: Close\r\n\r\n";

    fputs($http, $req);

    // Output the request results
    while(!feof($http))
    {
        echo fgets($http, 1024);
    }
    // Close the connection
    fclose($http);
?>
```

This returns the following:

```
HTTP/1.1 200 OK Date: Mon, 05 Jan 2004 02:17:54 GMT Server: Apache/1.3.27 (Unix)
(Red-Hat/Linux) Last-Modified: Wed, 08 Jan 2003 23:11:55 GMT ETag:
"3f80f-1b6-3e1cb03b" Accept-Ranges: bytes Content-Length: 438
Connection: close Content-Type: text/html
You have reached this web page by typing "example.com", "example.net", or
"example.org" into your web browser.
These domain names are reserved for use in documentation and are not available
for registration. See RFC 2606, Section 3.
```

The second example, shown in Listing 14-1, demonstrates fsockopen(), using it to
build a rudimentary port scanner.

Listing 14-1. Creating a Port Scanner with fsockopen()

```php
<?php
    // Give the script enough time to complete the task
    ini_set("max_execution_time",120);

    // Define scan range
    $rangeStart = 0;
    $rangeStop = 1024;

    // Which server to scan?
    $target = "www.example.com";

    // Build an array of port values
    $range =range($rangeStart, $rangeStop);

    echo "<p>Scan results for $target</p>";

    // Execute the scan
    foreach ($range as $port) {
        $result = @fsockopen($target, $port,$errno,$errstr,1);
        if ($result) echo "<p>Socket open at port $port</p>";
    }
?>
```

Scanning the www.example.com Web site, the following output is returned:

```
Scan results for www.example.com:
Socket open at port 22
Socket open at port 80
Socket open at port 443
```

A far lazier means for accomplishing the same task involves using a program execution command like system() and the wonderful free software package Nmap (http://www.insecure.org/nmap/). I'll demonstrate this in the concluding section, "Common Networking Tasks."

pfsockopen()

```
int pfsockopen (string host, int port [, int errno [, string errstring
[, int timeout]]])
```

The pfsockopen() function, or "persistent fsockopen()"), is operationally identical to fsockopen(), except that the connection is not closed once the script completes execution.

Mail

This powerful, yet easily-implemented feature of PHP has long been one of my personal favorites, simply because it's so darned useful. In fact, I'd venture that this will be one of the more popular sections of this chapter, if not this book, because of the commonplace need for such a feature within so many Web applications. In this section I'll show you how to send e-mail using PHP's popular mail() function, demonstrating how to mangle headers, include attachments, and other commonly used tasks. Additionally, I'll delve deep into PHP's IMAP extension, demonstrating numerous features made available via this great library.

In this section I'll introduce the relevant configuration directives, PHP's mail() function, and then conclude the section with several examples highlighting this function's many usage variations.

Configuration Directives

There are five configuration directives pertinent to PHP's mail() function. Pay close attention to the descriptions, because each is platform-specific.

SMTP
Scope: PHP_INI_ALL, Default value: localhost
The SMTP directive sets the Mail Transfer Agent (MTA) for PHP's Windows platform version of the mail function. Note that this is only relevant to the Windows platform, because Unix platform implementations of this function are actually just wrappers around that operating system's mail function. Instead, the Windows implementation depends on a socket connection made to either a local or a remote MTA, defined by this directive.

sendmail_from
Scope: PHP_INI_ALL, Default value: Null
The sendmail_from directive sets the "From" field of the message header. This parameter is only useful on the Windows platform. If you're using a Unix platform, you're constrained to setting this field within the mail function's addl_headers parameter.

sendmail_path
Scope: PHP_INI_SYSTEM, Default value: The default sendmail path
The sendmail_path directive sets the path to the sendmail binary if it's not in the system path, or you'd like to pass additional arguments to the binary. By default, this is set to:

```
sendmail -t -i
```

Keep in mind that this directive only applies to the Unix platform. Windows depends upon establishing a socket connection to an SMTP server specified by the SMTP directive on port smtp_port.

smtp_port
Scope: PHP_INI_ALL, Default value: 25
The smtp_port directive sets the port used to connect to the server specified by the SMTP directive.

mail.force_extra_parameters
Scope: PHP_INI_SYSTEM, Default value: Null
You can use the mail.force_extra_parameters directive to pass additional flags to the sendmail binary. Note that any parameters passed here will replace those passed in via the mail() function's addl_parameters parameter.

As of PHP 4.2.3, the addl_params parameter is disabled if you're running in safe mode. However, any flags passed in via this directive will still be passed in even if safe mode is enabled. In addition, this parameter is irrelevant on the Windows platform.

mail()

```
boolean mail(string to, string subject, string message [, string addl_headers
[, string addl_params]])
```

The mail() function can send an e-mail with a subject of *subject* and a message containing *message* to one or several recipients denoted in *to*. You can tailor many of the e-mail properties using the addl_headers parameter, and can even modify your SMTP server's behavior by passing extra flags via the addl_params parameter.

On the Unix platform, PHP's mail() function is dependent upon the sendmail Mail Transfer Agent (MTA). If you're using an alternative MTA (qmail, for example), you'll need to make use of that MTA's sendmail wrappers. PHP's Windows implementation of the function instead depends upon establishing a socket connection to an MTA designated by the SMTP configuration directive, introduced earlier in this chapter.

I'll devote the remainder of this section to numerous examples highlighting the many capabilities of this simple, yet powerful function.

Sending a Plain Text E-mail

Sending the simplest of e-mails is trivial using the mail() function, done using just the three required parameters. Here's an example:

```php
<?php
    mail("test@example.com", "This is a subject", "This is the mail body");
?>
```

Try swapping out the placeholder recipient address with your own and executing this on your server. The mail should arrive in your inbox within a few moments. If you've executed this script on a Windows server, the From field should denote whatever e-mail address you assigned to the sendmail_from configuration directive. However, if you've executed this script on a Unix machine, you might have noticed a rather odd From address, likely specifying the user "nobody" or "www". Because of the way PHP's mail function is implemented on Unix systems, the default sender will appear as the same user under which the server daemon process is operating. You can change this default though, as is demonstrated in the next example.

Sending an E-mail with Additional Headers

The previous example was a proof-of-concept of sorts, offered just to show you that sending e-mail via PHP can indeed be done. However, it's unlikely that such a bare-bones approach would be taken in any practical implementation. Rather, you'll likely want to specify additional headers such as a Reply-To, Content-Type, and From. To do so, you can use the addl_headers parameter of the mail() function like so:

```php
<?php
    $headers = "From:sender@example.com\r\n";
    $headers .= "Reply-To:sender@example.com\r\n";
    $headers .= "Content-Type: text/plain;\r\n charset=iso-8859-1\r\n";

    mail("test@example.com", "This is the subject", "This is the mail body",
        $headers);
?>
```

When you're using additional headers, make sure that the syntax and ordering corresponds exactly with that found in RFCs 822 and 2822, otherwise unexpected behavior may occur. Certain mail servers have been known to not follow the specifications properly, causing additional odd behavior. Check the appropriate documentation if something appears to be awry.

Sending an E-mail to Multiple Recipients

Sending an e-mail to multiple recipients is easily accomplished by placing the comma-separated list of addresses within the to parameter, like so:

```php
<?php
    $headers = "From:sender@example.com\r\n";
    $recipients = "test@example.com,info@example.com";
    mail($recipients, "This is the subject","This is the mail body", $headers);
?>
```

You can also send to CC: and BCC: recipients, by modifying the corresponding headers. An example follows:

```php
<?php
    $headers = "From:secretary@example.com\r\n";
    $headers .= "Bcc:theboss@example.com\n";
    mail("intern@example.com", "You're fired","Go home, your job is over.",
        $headers);
?>
```

Sending an HTML-formatted E-mail

Although many (myself included) consider HTML-formatted e-mail to rank among of the Internet's greatest annoyances, it's nonetheless a question that comes up repeatedly in regards to PHP's mail() function. Therefore I feel compelled to offer an example, and hope that no innocent recipients are harmed as a result.

Despite the widespread confusion surrounding this task, sending an HTML-formatted e-mail is actually quite easy. It's done simply by setting the Content-Type header to text/html;. Consider an example:

```php
<?php
    // Assign a few headers
    $headers = "From:sender@example.com\r\n";
    $headers .= "Reply-To:sender@example.com\r\n";
    $headers .= "Content-Type: text/html;\r\n charset=\"iso-8859-1\"\r\n";
    // Create the message body.
    $body = "
<html>
    <head>
        <title>Your Winter Quarter Schedule</title>
    </head>
    <body>
    <p>Your Winter quarter class schedule follows.<br />
    Please contact your guidance counselor should you have any questions.
    </p>
    <table>
    <tr>
        <th>Class</th><th>Teacher</th><th>Days</th><th>Time</th>
    </tr>
    <tr>
        <td>Math 630</td><td>Kelly, George</td><td>MWF</td><td>10:30am</td>
    </tr>
    <tr>
        <td>Physics 133</td><td>Josey, John</td><td>TR</td><td>1:00pm</td>
    </tr>
    </table>
    </body>
</html>
    ";
    // Send the message
    mail("student@example.com", "Wi/03 Class Schedule", $body, $headers);
?>
```

Executing this script results in an e-mail that looks like that shown in Figure 14-1.

Wi/03 Class Schedule
sender@example.com
To: student@example.com
_____

Your Winter quarter class schedule follows.
Please contact your guidance counselor should you have any questions.

Class	Teacher	Days	Time
Math 630	Kelly, George	MWF	10:30am
Physics 133	Josey, John	TR	1:00pm

Figure 14-1. An HTML-formatted e-mail

Because of the differences in the way HTML-formatted e-mail is handled by the myriad of mail clients out there, I recommend sticking with plain text formatting for such matters.

Sending an Attachment

If I had a dollar for every time this question has been asked in a newsgroup, I'd be sitting on some island sipping iced tea instead of spending my weekends working on this book. Although I could offer a lengthy and somewhat irrelevant explanation, I'd like to take this opportunity to introduce a wonderful class written and maintained by Richard Heyes (http://www.phpguru.org/) called HTML Mime mail. Available for free download and use under the BSD license, it's a fantastic class for sending MIME-based e-mail. In addition to offering the always intuitive OOP syntax for managing e-mail submissions, it's capable of executing all of the e-mail–specific tasks discussed thus far, in addition to sending attachments.

Like most other classes, using HTML Mime mail is as simple as placing it within your INCLUDE path, and including it into your script like so:

```
include("mimemail/htmlMimeMail.php");
```

Next, I'll instantiate the class and send an e-mail that includes a Word document as an attachment:

```
// Set the From and Reply-To headers
$mail->setFrom('Jason <author@example.com>');
$mail->setReturnPath('author@example.com');

// Set the Subject
$mail->setSubject('Test with attached email');

// Set the body
$mail->setText("Please find attached Chapter 14. Thank you!");

// Retrieve a file for attachment
$attachment = $mail->getFile('chapter14.doc');
```

```
// Attach the file, assigning it a name and a corresponding Mime-type.
$mail->addAttachment($attachment, 'chapter14.doc', 'application/vnd.ms-word');

// Send the email to editor@example.com
$result = $mail->send(array('editor@example.com'));
```

Amazingly easy, huh? Keep in mind that this is only a fraction of the features offered by this excellent class. This is definitely one to keep in mind if you plan on incorporating mail-based capabilities into your application.

IMAP, POP3, and NNTP

PHP offers a powerful range of functions for communicating with the IMAP protocol, dubbed its IMAP extension. Because it's primarily used for mail, I thought it fitting to place it in the "Mail" section. However, the foundational library that this extension depends upon is also capable of interacting with the POP3 and NNTP protocols. For the purposes of this introduction, I'll focus largely on IMAP-specific examples, although in many cases they will work transparently with the other protocols.

Before delving into the specifics of the IMAP extension, however, I'll take a moment to review IMAP's purpose and advantages. IMAP, an acronym for the Internet Message Access Protocol, is the product of Stanford University, first appearing way back in 1986. However, it was at the University of Washington that the protocol really started taking hold as a popular means for accessing and manipulating remote message stores. IMAP affords the user the opportunity to manage mail as if it were local, creating and administering folders used for organization, marking mail with various flags (read, deleted, and replied to, for example), and executing search operations on the store, among many other tasks. These features have grown increasingly useful as users require access to e-mail from multiple locations, home, office and while traveling for example. These days, IMAP is used just about everywhere; in fact, your own place of employment or university likely offers IMAP-based e-mail access; if not, they're way behind the technology curve.

PHP's IMAP capabilities are considerable, with almost 70 functions available through the library. In this section I'll introduce several of the key functions, and provide a few examples that, put together, offer the functionality of a very basic Web-based e-mail client. My goal is to demonstrate some of the basic features of this extension, and offer you a foundation from which additional experimentation can begin. However, before starting this discussion, you'll need to complete a few required configuration-related tasks.

> **TIP** *SquirrelMail (*http://www.squirrelmail.org/*) is a comprehensive Web-based e-mail client written using PHP and the IMAP extension. With support for 40 languages, a very active development and user community, and almost 200 plugins, SquirrelMail remains one of the most promising open source Web-mail products available.*

Requirements

Before you can use PHP's IMAP extension, you'll need to complete a few relatively simple tasks. These tasks are outlined in this section. PHP's IMAP extension depends on the c-client library, which was created and maintained by the University of Washington. You can download the software from their FTP site, located at `ftp://ftp.cac.washington.edu/imap/`. Installing the software is trivial, and will point you to the README file located within the c-client package for instructions. However, there have been a few ongoing points of confusion, some of which I'll outline here:

- The makefile contains a list of ports for many operating systems. You should choose the port that best suits your system and specify it when building the package.

- By default, the c-client software expects that you'll be performing SSL connections to the IMAP server. If you choose not to use SSL for making the connections, be sure to pass `SSLTYPE=none` along on the command line when building the package. Otherwise, PHP will fail during the subsequent configuration.

- If you're planning on using the c-client library solely for allowing PHP to communicate with a remote or preexisting local IMAP/POP3/NNTP server, you do not have to install the various daemons discussed in the README document. Just building the package is sufficient.

- There are reports of serious system conflicts occurring when copying the c-client source files to the operating system's `include` directory. To circumvent such problems, create a directory within that directory called `imap-version#` for example, and place the files there.

Once the c-client build is complete, rebuild PHP using the `--with-imap` flag. To save time, review the output of the `phpinfo()` function, and copy the contents of the "Configure Command" section. This contains the last-used configure command, along with all accompanying flags. Copy that to the command line and tack the following onto it:

```
--with-imap=/path/to/c-client/directory
```

Restart Apache, and you should be ready to move on.

In the following section, I'll concentrate on those functions in the library that you're most likely to use. For the sake of practicality, I'll introduce these functions according to their purposes, starting with the very basic tasks such as establishing a server connection, and ending with some of the more complicated actions you might require, such as renaming mailboxes and moving messages. Keep in mind that these are just a sampling of the functions that are made available by the IMAP extension. Consult the PHP manual for a complete listing.

Establishing and Closing a Connection

Before you do anything with one of the protocols, you need to establish a server connection. As always, once you've completed the necessary tasks, you should close the connection. In this section, I introduce the functions capable of handling both tasks.

imap_open()

```
resource imap_open(string mailbox, string username, string pswd [, int options])
```

The imap_open() function establishes a connection to an IMAP mailbox specified by *mailbox*, returning an IMAP stream on success and FALSE otherwise. This connection is dependent upon three components, the *mailbox*, *username*, and *pswd*. While the latter two components are self-explanatory, it might not be so obvious that *mailbox* should consist of both the server address and the mailbox path. In addition, if the port number used isn't standard (143, 110, and 119 for IMAP, POP3 and NNTP, respectively), you'll need to postfix this parameter with a colon, followed by the specific port number.

The optional *options* parameter is a bitmask consisting of one or more of the following values:

- OP_ANONYMOUS: This NNTP-specific option should be used when you don't want to update or use the .newsrc configuration file.

- CL_EXPUNGE: This option causes the opened mailbox to be expunged upon closure. Expunging a mailbox means that all messages marked for deletion will be destroyed.

- OP_HALFOPEN: Specifying this option tells imap_open() to open a connection, but not any specific mailbox. This option only applies to NNTP and IMAP.

- OP_READONLY: This option tells imap_open() to open the mailbox using read-only privileges.

The following example demonstrates how to open connections to IMAP, POP3, and NNTP mailboxes, respectively:

```php
<?php
    // Open an IMAP connection
    $ms = imap_open("{imap.example.com:143/imap/notls}","jason","mypswd");
    // Open a POP3 connection
    $ms = imap_open("{pop3.example.com:110/pop3/notls}","jason","mypswd");
    // Open an NNTP connection
    $ns = imap_open("{nntp.example.com:119/nntp}","jason","mypswd");
?>
```

> **NOTE** *If you're planning to perform a non-SSL connection, you need to postfix mailbox with the string /imap/notls for IMAP, and /pop3/notls for POP3. This is because PHP assumes an SSL connection by default. Neglecting to use the postfix will cause the attempt to fail.*

imap_close()

```
boolean imap_close(resource msg_stream [, int flag])
```

The imap_close() function closes a previously established stream, specified by *msg_stream*. It accepts one optional *flag*, CL_EXPUNGE, which destroys all messages marked for deletion upon execution. An example follows:

```php
<?php
    // Open an IMAP connection
    $ms = imap_open("{imap.example.com:143}","jason","mypswd");
    // Perform some tasks ...
    // Close the connection, expunging the mailbox
    imap_close($ms, CL_EXPUNGE);
?>
```

Learning More About Mailboxes and Mail

Once you've established a connection, you can begin working with it. Some of the most basic tasks involve retrieving more information about the mailboxes and messages made available via that connection. In this section, I'll introduce several of the functions capable of performing such tasks.

imap_getmailboxes()

```
array imap_getmailboxes(resource msg_stream, string ref, string pattern)
```

The imap_getmailboxes() function returns an array of objects consisting of information about each mailbox found via the stream specified by *msg_stream*. Object attributes include *name*, which denotes the mailbox name, *delimiter*, which denotes the separator between folders, and *attributes*, which is a bitmask denoting the following:

- LATT_NOINFERIORS: This mailbox has no children.

- LATT_NOSELECT: This is a container, not a mailbox.

- LATT_MARKED: This mailbox is "marked," a feature specific to the University of Washington IMAP implementation.

- LATT_UNMARKED: This mailbox is "unmarked," a feature specific to the University of Washington IMAP implementation.

The *ref* parameter repeats the value of the *mailbox* parameter used in the imap_open() function. The *pattern* parameter offers a means for designating the location and scope of the attempt. Setting the pattern to * returns all mailboxes, while setting it to % returns only the current level. For example, you could set *pattern* to /work/% to retrieve only the mailboxes found in the work directory.

Consider an example:

```php
<?php
    // Designate the mail server
    $mailserver = "{imap.example.com:143/imap/notls}";

    // Establish a connection
    $ms = imap_open($mailserver,"jason","mypswd");
    // Retrieve a single-level mailbox listing
    $mbxs = imap_getmailboxes($ms, $mailserver, "INBOX/Staff/%");
    while (list($key,$val) = each($mbxs))
    {
        echo $val->name."<br />";
    }

    imap_close($ms);
?>
```

This returns:

```
{imap.example.com:143/imap/notls}INBOX/Staff/CEO
{imap.example.com:143/imap/notls}INBOX/Staff/IT
{imap.example.com:143/imap/notls}INBOX/Staff/Secretary
```

imap_num_msg()

```
int imap_num_msg(resource msg_stream)
```

This function returns the number of messages found in the mailbox specified by *msg_stream*. An example follows:

```php
<?php
    // Open an IMAP connection
    $user = "jason";
    $pswd = "mypswd";
    $ms = imap_open("{imap.example.com:143}INBOX",$user, $pswd);
    $msgnum = imap_num_msg($ms);
    echo "<p>User $user has $msgnum messages in his inbox.</p>";
?>
```

This returns:

```
User jason has 1,386 messages in his inbox.
```

It's apparent that I have a serious problem organizing my messages.

> **TIP** *If you're interested in receiving just the recently arrived messages (messages that have not been included in prior sessions), check out the* imap_num_recent() *function.*

imap_status()

```
object imap_status(resource msg_stream, string mbox, int options)
```

The imap_status() function returns an object consisting of status information pertinent to the mailbox named in *mbox*. Four possible attributes can be set, depending upon how the *options* parameter is defined. The *options* parameter can be set to one of five possible values:

- SA_MESSAGES: Set the *messages* attribute to the number of messages found in the mailbox.

- SA_RECENT: Set the *recent* attribute to the number of messages recently added to the mailbox. A *recent* message is one that has not appeared in prior sessions. Note that this differs from *unseen* (unread) messages in that unread messages can remain unread across sessions, whereas recent messages are only deemed as such during the first session in which they appear.

- SA_UNSEEN: Set the *unseen* attribute to the number of unread messages in the mailbox.

- SA_UIDVALIDITY: Set the *uidvalidity* attribute to a constant that changes if the UIDs for a particular mailbox are no longer valid. UIDs can be invalidated when the mail server experiences a condition that makes it impossible to maintain permanent UIDs, or when a mailbox has been deleted and re-created.

- SA_ALL: Set all of the available flags.

The following is an example:

```php
<?php
    $mailserver = "{mail.example.com:143/imap/notls}";
    $ms = imap_open($mailserver,"jason","mypswd");
    // Retrieve all of the attributes
    $status = imap_status($ms, $mailserver."INBOX",SA_ALL);
    // How many unseen messages?
    echo $status->unseen;
    imap_close($ms);
?>
```

This returns:

64

The majority of which are spam, no doubt!

Retrieving Messages

Obviously the user is most interested in the information found within the messages sent to him. In this section, I'll show you how to parse these messages for both header and body information.

imap_headers()

```
array imap_headers(resource msg_stream)
```

The imap_headers() function retrieves an array consisting of messages located in the mailbox specified by *msg_stream*. Here's an example:

```php
<?php
    // Designate a mailbox and establish a connection
    $mailserver = "{mail.example.com:143/imap/notls}INBOX/Staff/CEO";
    $ms = imap_open($mailserver,"jason","mypswd");
    // Retrieve message headers
    $headers = imap_headers($ms);

    // Display total number of messages in mailbox
    echo "<strong>".count($headers)." messages in the mailbox</strong><br />";
?>
```

This returns:

`3 messages in the mailbox`

By itself, imap_headers() isn't very useful. After all, you can retrieve the total number of messages using the imap_num_msg() function. Instead, you'll typically use this function in conjunction with another function capable of parsing each of the retrieved array entries. I'll demonstrate how this is accomplished next, using the imap_headerinfo() function.

imap_headerinfo()

`object imap_headerinfo(resource msg_stream, int msg_number [, int fromlength [, int subjectlength [, string defaulthost]]])`

The function imap_headerinfo() retrieves a vast amount of information pertinent to the message *msg_number* located in the mailbox specified by *msg_stream*. Three optional parameters can also be supplied: *fromlength*, which denotes the maximum number of characters that should be retrieved for the from attribute, *subjectlength*, which denotes the maximum number of characters that should be retrieved for the subject attribute, and *defaulthost*, which is presently a placeholder that has no purpose.

In total, 29 object attributes for each message are returned:

- Answered: Has the message been answered? The attribute will be assigned A if answered, blank otherwise.

- bccaddress: A string consisting of all information found in the Bcc header, to a maximum of 1,024 characters.

- bcc[]: An array of objects consisting of items pertinent to the message Bcc header. Each object consists of the following attributes:

  - adl: Known as the at-domain or source route, this attribute is deprecated and rarely, if ever, used.

  - host: Specifies the host component of the e-mail address. For example, if the address was gilmore@example.com, host would be set to example.com.

  - mailbox: Specifies the username component of the e-mail address. For example, if the address was ceo@example.com, the mailbox attribute would be set to ceo.

  - personal: Specifies the "friendly name" of the e-mail address. For example, the From header might read "Jason Gilmore <gilmore@example.com>". In this case, the personal attribute would be set to Jason Gilmore.

- ccaddress: A string consisting of all information found in the Cc header, to a maximum of 1,024 characters.

- cc[ ]: An array of objects consisting of items pertinent to the message Cc header. Each object consists of the same attributes introduced in the bcc[ ] summary.

- date: The date found in the headers of the sender's mail client. Note that this can easily be incorrect or altogether forged. You'll probably want to rely on udate for a more accurate timeframe of when the message was received.

- deleted: Has the message been marked for deletion? This attribute is D if deleted, blank otherwise.

- draft: Is this message in draft format? This attribute is X if draft, blank otherwise.

- fetchfrom: The From header, not to exceed *fromlength* characters.

- fetchsubject: The Subject header, not to exceed *subjectlength* characters.

- followup_to: This attribute is used to prevent the sender's message from being sent to the user when the message is intended for a list. Note that this attribute is not standard, and is not supported by all mail agents.

- flagged: Has this message been flagged? This attribute is assigned F if flagged, blank otherwise.

- fromaddress: A string consisting of all information found in the From header, to a maximum of 1,024 characters.

- from[ ]: An array of objects consisting of items pertinent to the message From header. Each object consists of the same attributes introduced in the bcc[ ] summary.

- in_reply_to: If the message identified by *msg_number* is in response to another message, this attribute specifies the message-id identifying that original message.

- message_id: A string used to uniquely identify the message. A sample message identifier is:

```
<1COCCEE45B00E74D8FBBB1AE6A472E85012C696E>@wjgilmore.com
```

- newsgroups: The newsgroups to which the message has been sent.

- recent: Is this message recent? This attribute is R if the message is recent and seen, N if recent and not seen, and blank otherwise.

- reply_toaddress: A string consisting of all information found in the Reply-To header, to a maximum of 1,024 characters.

- reply_to: An array of objects consisting of items pertinent to the Reply-To header. Each object consists of the same attributes introduced in the bcc[] summary.

- return_path: A string consisting of all information found in the Return-path header, to a maximum of 1,024 characters.

- return_path[]: An array of objects consisting of items pertinent to the message Return-path header. Each object consists of the same attributes introduced in the bcc[] summary.

- subject: The message subject.

- senderaddress: A string consisting of all information found in the Sender header, to a maximum of 1,024 characters.

- sender: An array of objects consisting of items pertinent to the message Sender: header. Each object consists of the same attributes introduced in the bcc[] summary.

- toaddress: A string consisting of all information found in the To header, to a maximum of 1,024 characters.

- to[]: An array of objects consisting of items pertinent to the message To header. Each object consists of the same attributes introduced in the bcc[] summary.

- udate: The date the message was received by the server, formatted in Unix time.

- unseen: Denotes whether the message has been read. This attribute is U if the message is unseen and not recent, and blank otherwise.

The following is an example:

```php
<?php
    // Designate a mailbox and establish a connection
    $mailserver = "{mail.example.com:143/imap/notls}INBOX/Staff/CEO";
    $ms = imap_open($mailserver,"jason","mypswd");

    // Retrieve message headers
    $headers = imap_headers($ms);
```

```
   // Display total number of messages in mailbox
   echo "<strong>".count($headers)." messages in the mailbox</strong><br />";

   // Loop through messages and display subject/date of each
   for($x=1;$x<=count($headers);$x++)
   {
      $header = imap_header($ms,$x);
      echo $header->Subject." (".$header->Date.")<br />";
   }

   // Close the connection
   imap_close($ms);
?>
```

This returns the output shown in Figure 14-2.

3 messages in the mailbox
FWD: Weekly Status Report (Sun, 4 Aug 2004 15:08:04 -500)
Get rich quick! (Mon, 5 Aug 2004 04:27:04 -500)
RE: Course Web site (Tues, 6 Aug 2004 11:55:04 -500)

Figure 14-2. Retrieving message headers

Consider another example. What if you wanted to display in bold those messages that are unread? For sake of space, I'll revise the previous example, but just include the relevant components.

```
<?php
...
for($x=1;$x<=count($headers);$x++)
{
   $header = imap_header($ms,$x);
   $unseen = $header->unseen;
   $recent = $header->recent;
   if ($unseen == "U" || $recent == "N") {
         $flagStart = "<strong>";
         $flagStop = "</strong>";
   }
   echo "<tr>";
   echo "<td>".$header->fromaddress."</td>";
   echo "<td>".$flagStart.$header->Subject.$flagStop."</td>";
   echo "<td>".$header->date."</td>";
   echo "</tr>";
}
echo "</table>";
...
?>
```

Note that you had to perform a Boolean test on two attributes: recent and unseen. Because unseen will be set to U if the message is unseen and not recent, and recent will be set to N if the message is recent and not seen, we can cover our bases by examining if either is true. If so, you have found an unread message.

imap_fetchstructure()

```
object imap_fetchstructure(resource msg_stream, int msg_number [, int options])
```

The imap_fetchstructure() function returns an object consisting of a variety of items pertinent to the message identified by *msg_number*. If the optional *options* flag is set to FT_UID, then it is assumed that the *msg_number* is a UID. There are 17 different object properties, but I'll just point out those that you might find particularly interesting:

- bytes: The message size in bytes.

- encoding: The value assigned to the Content-Transfer-Encoding header. This is an integer ranging from 0 to 5, the values corresponding to 7bit, 8bit, binary, base64, quoted-printable, and other, respectively.

- ifid: This is set to TRUE if a Message-ID header exists.

- id: The Message-ID header, if one exists.

- lines: The number of lines found in the message body.

- type: The value assigned to the Content-Type header. This is an integer ranging from 0 to 7, the values corresponding to Text, Multipart, Message, Application, Audio, Image, Video, and Other, respectively.

Consider an example. The following code will retrieve the number of lines and size, in bytes, of a message:

```php
<?php
    // Open an IMAP connection
    $user = "jason";
    $pswd = "mypswd";
    $ms = imap_open("{imap.example.com:143}INBOX", $user, $pswd);
    // Retrieve information about message number 5.
    $message = imap_fetchstructure($ms,5);
    echo "Message lines: ".$message->lines."<br />";
    echo "Message size: ".$message->bytes." bytes<br />";
?>
```

Sample output follows:

```
Message lines: 15
Message size: 854 bytes
```

imap_fetchoverview()

array imap_fetchoverview(resource *msg_stream*, string *sequence* [, int *options*])

The imap_fetchoverview() function retrieves the message headers for a particular sequence of messages, returning an array of objects. If the optional *options* flag is set to FT_UID, then it is assumed that the *msg_number* is a UID. Each object in the array consists of the 14 attributes:

- answered: Determines whether the message is flagged as answered

- date: The date the message was sent

- deleted: Determines whether the message is flagged for deletion

- draft: Determines whether the message is flagged as a draft

- flagged: Determines whether the message is flagged

- from: The sender

- message-id: The Message-ID

- msgno: The message's message sequence number

- recent: Determines whether the message is flagged as recent

- references: This message's referring Message-ID

- seen: Determines whether the message is flagged as seen

- size: The message's size in bytes

- subject: The message's subject

- uid: The message's UID

Among other things, you can use this function to produce a listing of messages that have not yet been read:

```php
<?php
    // Open an IMAP connection
    $user = "jason";
    $pswd = "mypswd";
    $ms = imap_open("{imap.example.com:143}INBOX",$user, $pswd);
    // Retrieve total number of messages
    $nummsgs = imap_num_msg($ms);
    $messages = imap_fetch_overview($ms,"1:$nummsgs");
    // If message not flagged as seen, output info about it
    while(list($key,$value) = each($messages)) {
        if ($value->seen == 0) {
            echo "<p>Subject: ".$value->subject."<br />";
            echo "Date: ".$value->date."<br />";
            echo "From: ".$value->from."</p>";
        }
    }
?>
```

Sample output follows:

```
Subject: Audio Visual Web site
Date: Mon, 26 Aug 2004 18:04:37 -0500
From: Andrew Fieldpen

Subject: The Internet is broken
Date: Mon, 27 Aug 2004 20:04:37 -0500
From: "Roy J. Dugger"

Subject: Re: Standards article for Web browsers
Date: Mon, 28 Aug 2004 21:04:37 -0500
From: Nicholas Kringle
```

Note the use of a colon to separate the starting and ending message numbers. Also, keep in mind that this function will always sort the array in ascending order, even if you place the ending message number first. Finally, it's possible to selectively choose messages by separating each number with a comma. For example, if you wanted to retrieve information about messages 1 through 3, and 5 you can set *sequence* like so: 1:3,5.

imap_fetchbody()

```
string imap_fetchbody(resource msg_stream, int msg_number, string part_number
[, flags options])
```

The `imap_fetchbody()` function retrieves a particular section (*part_number*) of the message body identified by *msg_number*, returning the section as a string. The optional options *flag* is a bitmask containing one or more of the following items:

- FT_UID: Consider the *msg_number* value to be a UID.

- FT_PEEK: Do not set the message's Seen flag if it isn't already set.

- FT_INTERNAL: Do not convert any newline characters. Instead, return the message exactly as it appears internally to the mail server.

If you leave *part_number* blank, by assigning it an empty string, this function returns the entire message text. You can selectively retrieve message parts by assigning *part_number* an integer value denoting the message part's position. In the following example, I'll retrieve the entire message:

```php
<?php
    // Open an IMAP connection
    $user = "jason";
    $pswd = "mypswd";
    $ms = imap_open("{imap.example.com:143}INBOX",$user, $pswd);
    $message = imap_fetchbody($ms,1,"","FT_PEEK");
    echo $message;
?>
```

Sample output follows:

```
Jason,

Can we create a Web administrator account for my new student?

Thanks
Bill Niceguy

From: "Josh Crabgrass" <crabgrass@example.com>
To: "'Bill Niceguy'" <niceguy@example.com>
Subject: RE: Web site access
Date: Mon, 5 August 2004 10:26:01 -0400
X-Mailer: Microsoft Outlook, Build 10.0.4510
Importance: Normal

Bill,

I'll need an admin account in order to maintain the new Web site.
Thanks,
Josh
```

Composing a Message

Creating and sending messages are likely the two e-mail tasks that take up most of your time. The next two functions demonstrate how both are accomplished using PHP's IMAP extension.

imap_mail_compose()

```
string imap_mail_compose(array envelope, array body)
```

This function creates a MIME message based on the provided *envelope* and *body*. The *envelope* comprises all of the header information pertinent to the addressing of the message, including well-known items such as From, Reply-To, CC, BCC, Subject, and others. The *body* consists of the actual message and various attributes pertinent to its format. Once created, you can do any number of things with the message, including mailing it, appending it to an existing mail store, or anything else for which MIME messages are suitable.

A basic composition example follows:

```php
<?php
    $envelope["from"] = "gilmore@example.com";
    $envelope["to"] = "admin@example.com";
    $msgpart["type"] = TYPETEXT;
    $msgpart["subtype"] = "plain";
    $msgpart["contents.data"] = "This is the message text.";
    $msgbody[1] = $msgpart;
    echo nl2br(imap_mail_compose($envelope,$msbody));
?>
```

This example returns:

```
From: gilmore@example.com
To: admin@example.com
MIME-Version: 1.0
Content-Type: TEXT/plain; CHARSET=US-ASCII
This is the message text.
```

Sending a Message

Once you've composed a message, you can send it using the imap_mail() function, introduced next.

imap_mail()

```
boolean imap_mail(string rcpt, string subject, string msg
[, string addl_headers [, string cc [, string bcc [, string rpath]]]])
```

The imap_mail() function works much like the previously introduced mail() function, sending a message to the address specified by *rcpt*, possessing the subject of *subject* and the message consisting of *msg*. You can include additional headers with the parameter *addl_headers*. In addition, you can CC and BCC additional recipients with the parameters, *cc* and *bcc*, respectively. Finally, the *rpath* parameter is used to set the Return-path header.

I'll revise the previous example so that the composed message is also sent:

```php
<?php
    $envelope["from"] = "gilmore@example.com";
    $msgpart["type"] = TYPETEXT;
    $msgpart["subtype"] = "plain";
    $msgpart["contents.data"] = "This is the message text.";
    $msgbody[1] = $msgpart;
    $message = imap_mail_compose($envelope,$msbody);
    // Separate the message header and body. Some
    // mail clients seem unable to do so.
    list($msgheader,$msgbody)=split("\r\n\r\n",$message,2);
    $subject = "Test IMAP message";
    $to = "jason@example.com";
    $result=imap_mail($to,$subject,$msgbody,$msgheader);
?>
```

Mailbox Administration

IMAP offers the ability to organize mail by categorizing it within compartments commonly referred to as *folders* or *mailboxes*. In this section I'll show you how to create, rename, and delete these mailboxes.

imap_createmailbox()

```
boolean imap_createmailbox(resource msg_stream, string mbox)
```

The imap_createmailbox() function creates a mailbox named *mbox*, returning TRUE on success and FALSE otherwise. The following example uses this function to create a mailbox residing at the user's top-level (INBOX):

```php
<?php
    $mailserver = "{imap.example.com:143/imap/notls}INBOX";
    $mbox = "events";
    $ms = imap_open($mailserver,"jason","mypswd");
    imap_createmailbox($ms,$mailserver."/".$mbox);
    imap_close($ms);
?>
```

Take note of the syntax used to specify the mailbox path:

```
{imap.example.com:143/imap/notls}INBOX/events
```

As is the case with many of PHP's IMAP functions, the entire server string must be referenced as if it were part of the mailbox name itself.

imap_deletemailbox()

```
boolean imap_deletemailbox(resource msg_stream, string mbox)
```

The imap_deletemailbox() function deletes an existing mailbox named *mbox*, returning TRUE on success and FALSE otherwise. For example:

```php
<?php
$mbox = "{imap.example.com:143/imap/notls}INBOX";
if (imap_deletemailbox($ms, "$mbox/staff"))
    echo "The mailbox has successfully been deleted.";
else
    echo "There was a problem deleting the mailbox";
?>
```

Keep in mind that deleting a mailbox also deletes all mail found in that mailbox.

imap_renamemailbox()

```
boolean imap_renamemailbox(resource msg_stream, string old_mbox, string new_mbox)
```

The imap_renamemailbox() function renames an existing mailbox named *old_mbox* to *new_mbox*, returning TRUE on success and FALSE otherwise. An example follows:

```php
<?php
$mbox = "{imap.example.com:143/imap/notls}INBOX";
if (imap_renamemailbox($ms, "$mbox/staff", "$mbox/teammates"))
    echo "The mailbox has successfully been renamed";
else
    echo "There was a problem renaming the mailbox";
?>
```

Message Administration

One of the beautiful aspects of IMAP is that you can manage mail from anywhere. This section offers some insight into how this is accomplished using PHP's functions.

imap_expunge()

```
boolean imap_expunge(resource msg_stream)
```

The imap_expunge() function destroys all messages flagged for deletion, returning TRUE on success and FALSE otherwise. Note that you can automate this process by including the CL_EXPUNGE flag on stream creation or closure.

imap_mail_copy()

```
boolean imap_mail_copy(resource msg_stream, string msglist, string mbox
[, int options])
```

The imap_mail_copy() function copies the mail messages located within *msglist* to the mailbox specified by *mbox*. The optional *options* parameter is a bitmask that accounts for one or more of the following flags:

- CP_UID: The *msglist* consists of UIDs instead of message index identifiers.

- CP_MOVE: Including this flag deletes the messages from their original mailbox after the copy is complete.

imap_mail_move()

```
boolean imap_mail_move(resource msg_stream, string msglist, string mbox
[, int options])
```

The imap_mail_move() function moves the mail messages located in *msglist* to the mailbox specified by *mbox*. The optional *options* parameter is a bitmask accepting the following flag:

- CP_UID: The *msglist* consists of UIDs instead of message index identifiers.

Streams

These days, even trivial Web applications often consist of a well-orchestrated blend of programming languages and data sources. In many such instances, interaction between the language and data source involves reading or writing a linear stream of data, known as a *stream*. For example, invoking the command fopen() results in the binding of a filename to a stream. At that point, that stream can be read from and written to, depending upon the invoked mode setting and on permissions.

Although you might immediately think of calling fopen() on a local file, you might find it interesting to know that you can also create stream bindings using a variety of methods, over HTTP, HTTPS, FTP, FTPS, and even compressing the stream using the zlib and bzip2 libraries. This is accomplished using an appropriate *wrapper*, of which PHP supports several. In this section I'll talk a bit about streams, focusing on stream wrappers and another interesting concept known as *stream filters*.

> **NOTE** *PHP 5 introduces an API for creating and registering your own stream wrappers and filters. You could devote an entire book to the topic, but the majority of readers would not be interested. Therefore, there is no coverage of the matter in this book. If you are interested in learning more, please consult the PHP manual.*

Stream Wrappers and Contexts

A *stream wrapper* is a bit of code that wraps around the stream, managing the stream in accordance with a specific protocol, be it HTTP, FTP, or otherwise. Because PHP supports several wrappers by default, you can bind streams over these protocols transparently, like so:

```php
<?php
    echo file_get_contents("http://www.example.com/");
?>
```

Executing this returns the contents of the www.example.com domain's index page:

```
You have reached this web page by typing "example.com", "example.net",
or "example.org" into your web browser.
These domain names are reserved for use in documentation and are not
available for registration. See RFC 2606, Section 3.
```

As you can see, no other code for handling the fact that I performed an HTTP stream binding was involved. PHP transparently supports binding for the following types of streams: HTTP, HTTPS, FTP, FTPS, filesystem, PHP input/output, and compression.

From Chapter 10 you may remember that the fopen() function accepted a parameter titled *zcontext*. Now that you're a bit more familiar with streams and wrappers, this seems like an opportune time to introduce contexts. Simply put, a context is a set of wrapper-specific options that tweak a stream's behavior. Each supported stream wrapper offers its own set of options. I'll leave it to you to reference these options in the PHP manual; however, I will demonstrate just how one such option can modify a stream's behavior so that the point is made. To use any such context, you first need to create it using the stream_context_create() function, introduced next.

stream_context_create()

```
resource stream_context_create(array options)
```

The stream_context_create() function creates a resource context based on the array of options passed to it. Its purpose is best illustrated with an example. By default, FTP streams do not permit the overwriting of existing files on a remote server. Sometimes, though, you may wish to enable this behavior. To do so, you'll first need to create a context resource, passing in the overwrite parameter, and then pass that resource to set fopen()'s *zcontext* parameter. This process will be made apparent in the following code:

```php
<?php
    $params = array("ftp" => array("overwrite" => "1"));
    $context = stream_context_create($params);
    $fh = fopen("ftp://localhost/", "w", 0, $context);
?>
```

Stream Filters

Sometimes you need to manipulate stream data either as it is read in from or written to some data source. For example, you might want to strip all HTML tags from a stream. Using a *stream filter*, this is a trivial matter. At the time of this writing, three types of stream filters are available: string, conversion, and compression. As of PHP version 5.0 RC1, the string and conversion types were available by default. You can enable the compression filters by installing the zlib_filter package, available via PECL (http://pecl.php.net/). Table 14-1 offers a list of default filters and their corresponding descriptions.

Table 14-1. PHP's Default Stream Filters

FILTER	DESCRIPTION
string.rot13	See the standard PHP function rot13()
string.toupper	See the standard PHP function toupper()
string.tolower	See the standard PHP function tolower()
string.strip_tags	See the standard PHP function strip_tags()
convert.base64-encode	See the standard PHP function base64_encode()
convert.base64-decode	See the standard PHP function base64_decode()
convert.quoted-printable-decode	See the standard PHP function quoted_printable_decode()
convert.quoted-printable-encode	No functional equivalent. In addition to the parameters supported by base64_encode(), it also supports the Boolean arguments binary and force-encode-first, in that order. These arguments specify whether the stream should be handled in binary format, and whether it should be first encoded using base64_encode(), respectively.

To view the filters available to your PHP distribution, use the stream_get_filters() function, introduced next.

stream_get_filters()

```
array stream_get_filters()
```

The stream_get_filters() function returns an array of all registered stream filters. Consider an example:

```
<?php
    print_r(stream_get_filters());
?>
```

This example returns:

```
Array (
    [0] => string.rot13
    [1] => string.toupper
    [2] => string.tolower
    [3] => string.strip_tags
    [4] => convert.*
)
```

I'm not entirely sure why this function lists all of the available string-based filters, but masks the names of the two conversion filters by consolidating the group using an asterisk. As of PHP version 5.0 RC1, there are four conversion filters, namely base64-encode, base64-decode, quoted-printable-encode, and quoted-printable-decode.

To use a filter, you need to pass it through one of two functions, stream_filter_append() or stream_filter_prepend(). Which one you choose depends on the order in which you'd like to execute the filter in respect to any other assigned filters. I'll introduce both functions next.

stream_filter_append()

```
boolean stream_filter_append(resource stream, string filtername
[,int read_write [, mixed params]])
```

The stream_filter_append() function appends the filter *filtername* to the end of a list of any filters currently being executed against *stream*. The optional *read_write* parameter specifies the filter chain (read or write) to which the filter should be applied. Typically you won't need this because PHP will take care of it for you, by default. The final optional parameter, *params*, specifies any parameters that are to be passed into the filter function.

Let's consider an example. Suppose you're writing a form-input blog entry to an HTML file. The only allowable HTML tag is the <br />, therefore you'll want to remove all other characters from the stream as it's written to the HTML file:

```php
<?php
$blog = <<< blog
One of my <b>favorite</b> blog tools is Movable Type.<br />
You can learn more about Movable Type at
<a href="http://www.movabletype.org/">http://www.movabletype.org/</a>.
blog;

    $fh = fopen("042004.html", "w");
    stream_filter_append($fh, "string.strip_tags", STREAM_FILTER_WRITE, "<br>");
    fwrite($fh, $blog);
    fclose($fh);
?>
```

If you open up 042004.html, you'll find the following contents:

```
One of my favorite blog tools is Movable Type.<br />
You can learn more about Movable Type at http://www.movabletype.org/.
```

stream_filter_prepend()

```
boolean stream_filter_prepend(resource stream, string filtername
[,int read_write [, mixed params]])
```

The function stream_filter_prepend() prepends the filter *filtername* to the front of a list of any filters currently being executed against *stream*. The optional *read_write* and *params* parameters correspond in purpose to those described in stream_filter_append().

Common Networking Tasks

Although various command-line applications have long been capable of performing the networking tasks demonstrated in this section, offering a means for carrying them out via the Web certainly can be useful. For example, at work we host a variety of such Web-based applications within our intranet for the IT support department to use when they are troubleshooting a networking problem but don't have an SSH client handy. In addition, they can be accessed via Web browsers found on most modern wireless PDAs. Finally, although the command-line counterparts are far more powerful and flexible, viewing such information via the Web is at times simply more convenient. Whatever the reason, I'm sure you could put some of the applications found in this section to good use.

> **NOTE** *Several examples in this section use the* system() *function. This function is introduced in Chapter 10.*

Pinging a Server

Verifying a server's connectivity is a commonplace administration task. In the following example, I'll show you how to do so using PHP:

```php
<?php
    // Which server to ping?
    $server = "www.example.com";

    // Ping the server how many times?
    $count = 3;

    // Perform the task
    echo "<pre>";
    system("/bin/ping -c $count $server");
    echo "</pre>";

    // Kill the task
    system("killall -q ping");

?>
```

This above code should be fairly straightforward, except for perhaps the system call to killall. This is necessary because the command executed by the system call will continue to execute if the user ends the process prematurely. Because ending execution of the script within the browser will not actually stop the process for execution on the server, you need to do it manually.

Sample output follows:

```
PING www.example.com (192.0.34.166) from 123.456.7.8 : 56(84) bytes of data.
64 bytes from www.example.com (192.0.34.166): icmp_seq=0 ttl=255 time=158 usec
64 bytes from www.example.com (192.0.34.166): icmp_seq=1 ttl=255 time=57 usec
64 bytes from www.example.com (192.0.34.166): icmp_seq=2 ttl=255 time=58 usec

--- www.example.com ping statistics ---
5 packets transmitted, 5 packets received, 0% packet loss
round-trip min/avg/max/mdev = 0.048/0.078/0.158/0.041 ms
```

PHP's program execution functions are great because they allow you to take advantage of any program installed on the server. We'll return to these functions several times throughout this section.

A Port Scanner

Earlier in this chapter, I accompanied the introduction of fsockopen() with a demonstration of how to create a port scanner. However, like many of the tasks introduced in this section, this can be accomplished much more easily using one of PHP's program execution functions. The following example makes use of PHP's system() function and the nmap (network mapper) tool.

```php
<?php
    $target = "www.example.com";
    echo "<pre>";
    system("/usr/bin/nmap $target");
    echo "</pre>";
    // Kill the task
    system("killall -q nmap");
?>
```

A snippet of the sample output follows:

```
Starting nmap V. 2.54BETA31 ( www.insecure.org/nmap/ )
Interesting ports on  (209.51.142.155):
(The 1500 ports scanned but not shown below are in state: closed)
Port        State       Service
22/tcp      open        ssh
80/tcp      open        http
110/tcp     open        pop-3
111/tcp     filtered    sunrpc
```

Subnet Converter

You've probably at one time scratched your head trying to figure out some obscure network configuration issue. Most commonly, the culprit for my woes seems to center around a faulty or unplugged network cable. The second most common problem I face is due to mistakes made when calculating the necessary basic network ingredients: IP addressing, subnet mask, broadcast address, network address, and the like. To remedy this, a few PHP functions and bitwise operations can be coaxed into doing the calculations for you. The example shown in Listing 14-2 will calculate several of these components given an IP address and a bitmask.

Listing 14-2. A Subnet Converter

```html
<form action="netaddr.php" method="post">
<p>
IP Address:<br />
<input type="text" name="ip[]" size="3" maxlength="3" value="" />.
<input type="text" name="ip[]" size="3" maxlength="3" value="" />.
<input type="text" name="ip[]" size="3" maxlength="3" value="" />.
<input type="text" name="ip[]" size="3" maxlength="3" value="" />
</p>

<p>
Subnet Mask:<br />
```

```
<input type="text" name="sm[]" size="3" maxlength="3" value="" />.
<input type="text" name="sm[]" size="3" maxlength="3" value="" />.
<input type="text" name="sm[]" size="3" maxlength="3" value="" />.
<input type="text" name="sm[]" size="3" maxlength="3" value="" />
</p>

<input type="submit" name="submit" value="Calculate" />

</form>

<?php
    if (isset($_POST['submit']))
    {
        // Concatenate the IP form components and convert to IPv4 format
        $ip = implode('.',$_POST['ip']);
        $ip = ip2long($ip);

        // Concatenate the netmask form components and convert to IPv4 format
        $netmask = implode('.',$_POST['nm']);
        $netmask = ip2long($netmask);

        // Calculate the network address
        $na = ($ip & $netmask);
        // Calculate the broadcast address
        $ba = $na | (~$netmask);

        // Convert the addresses back to the dot-format representation and display
        echo "Addressing Information: <br />";
            echo "<ul>";
            echo "<li>IP Address: ". long2ip($ip)."</li>";
            echo "<li>Subnet Mask: ". long2ip($netmask)."</li>";
            echo "<li>Network Address: ". long2ip($na)."</li>";
            echo "<li>Broadcast Address: ". long2ip($ba)."</li>";
            echo "<li>Total Available Hosts: ".($ba - $na - 1)."</li>";
            echo "<li>Host Range: ". long2ip($na + 1)." - ".
                    long2ip($ba - 1)."</li>";
            echo "</ul>";
    }
?>
```

Consider an example. If you supply 192.168.1.101 as the IP address and 255.255.255.0 as the subnet mask, you should see the output shown in Figure 14-3.

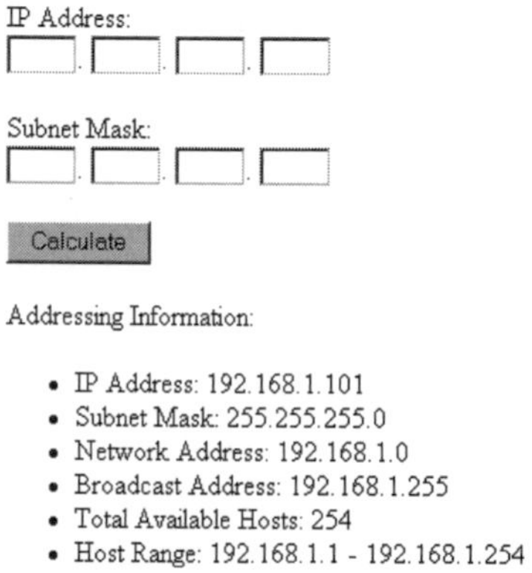

IP Address:

☐.☐.☐.☐

Subnet Mask:

☐.☐.☐.☐

[Calculate]

Addressing Information:

- IP Address: 192.168.1.101
- Subnet Mask: 255.255.255.0
- Network Address: 192.168.1.0
- Broadcast Address: 192.168.1.255
- Total Available Hosts: 254
- Host Range: 192.168.1.1 - 192.168.1.254

Figure 14-3. Calculating network addressing

Testing User Bandwidth

Although various forms of bandwidth-intensive media are commonly used on today's Web sites, keep in mind that not all users have the convenience of a high-speed network connection at their disposal. You can automatically test a user's network speed with PHP by sending the user a relatively large amount of data and then noting the time it takes for transmission to complete.

Create the data file which will be transmitted to the user. This can be anything, really, because the user will never actually see the file. I'd like to suggest creating it by generating a large amount of text and writing it to a file. For example, this script will generate a text file that is roughly 1,500 KB in size:

```php
<?php
    // Create a new file, creatively named "textfile.txt"
    $fh = fopen("textfile.txt","w");
    // Write the word "bandwidth" repeatedly to the file.
    for ($x=0;$x<170400;$x++) fwrite($fh,"bandwidth");
    // Close the file
    fclose($fh);
?>
```

Now I'll write the script that will calculate the network speed. This script is shown in Listing 14-3.

Listing 14-3. Calculating Network Bandwidth

```php
<?php
    // Retrieve the data to send to the user
    $data = file_get_contents("textfile.txt");
    // Determine the data's total size, in Kilobytes
    $fsize = filesize("textfile.txt") / 1024;
    // Define the start time
    $start = time();
    // Send the data to the user
    echo "<!-- $data -->";
    // Define the stop time
    $stop = time();
    // Calculate the time taken to send the data
    $duration = $stop - $start;
    // Divide the file size by the number of seconds taken to transmit it
    $speed = round($fsize / $duration,2);
    // Display the calculated speed in Kilobytes per second
    echo "Your network speed: $speed KB/sec.";
?>
```

Executing this script produces output similar to the following:

```
Your network speed: 249.61 KB/sec.
```

Summary

I wouldn't expect that PHP's networking capabilities to soon replace those tools already offered on the command-line or other well-established clients. Nonetheless, as the Web environment is increasingly targeted for hosting applications of all sorts, I'd venture that you'll quickly find a use for some of the material presented in this chapter.

In the next chapter, I'll introduce what I think is a shining example of how PHP can effectively interact with other enterprise technologies, showing you just how easy it is to interact with your preferred directory server using PHP's LDAP extension.

CHAPTER 15

PHP and LDAP

As CORPORATE HARDWARE and software infrastructures expanded throughout the last
decade, IT staff found themselves overwhelmed with the administrative overhead
required to manage the rapidly growing number of resources being added to the
enterprise. Printers, workstations, servers, switches, and other miscellaneous network
devices all required continuous monitoring and management, as did user resource
access and network privileges.

Quite often the system administrators cobbled together their own internal modus
operandi for maintaining order, systems which were all too often poorly designed,
insecure, and non-scalable. Another alternative, but equally inefficient solution
involved the deployment of numerous disparate systems, each doing its own part to
manage part of the enterprise, yet coming at a cost of considerable overhead because
of the lack of integration. The result was that both users and administrators suffered
from the absence of a comprehensive management solution, at least, until directory
services came along.

Directory services offer system administrators, developers, and end users alike a
consistent, efficient, and secure means for viewing and managing resources such as
people, files, printers, and applications. The structure of these read-optimized data
repositories often closely models the physical corporate structure, an example of
which is depicted in Figure 15-1.

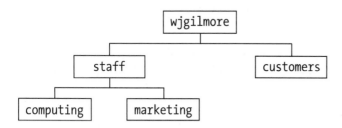

Figure 15-1. A model of the typical corporate structure

As you may imagine, there has long been, and continues to be, a clamoring for powerful directory services products. Numerous leading software vendors have built flagship products, and indeed centered their entire operations around such offerings. The following are just a few of the more widely deployed directory services products:

- Novell Directory Services

- Microsoft Active Directory

- Sun One

- Oracle Collaboration Suite

You might find it interesting to know that all of the above products depend heavily upon an open specification known as the *Lightweight Directory Access Protocol*, or LDAP. In this chapter, you'll be introduced to LDAP, and you will learn how easy it is to talk to LDAP via PHP's LDAP extension. By the end of this chapter, you'll possess the knowledge necessary to begin talking to directory services via your PHP applications. Before delving into this wonderful extension, I'd like to take a few moments to say a few words about LDAP. Although this preliminary information by no means qualifies as an introduction, hopefully it will entice those of you without prior knowledge or experience working with LDAP into taking some time to learn more about this tremendously valuable technology.

An Introduction to LDAP

LDAP is today's de facto means for accessing directory servers, offering a definitive model for storing, retrieving, manipulating and protecting directory data. Perhaps IBM's *LDAP Redbook* best describes LDAP as a protocol that consists of four key models:

- **Information:** Just as a relational database defines the column attributes that data stored in that column must adhere to, LDAP defines the structure of information stored in a directory server.

- **Naming:** LDAP offers a very well-defined structure for determining how LDAP information is navigated, identified, and retrieved. This structure is known as a common directory structure, or *schema*, and closely mimics hierarchical models commonly used to organize information. Examples of such entities include plant and animal taxonomies, corporate organizational hierarchies (similar to the one shown in Figure 15-1), thesauri, and family trees.

- **Function:** LDAP defines what can be done to information stored in a directory server, specifying how data can be retrieved, inserted, updated, and deleted. Furthermore, it defines both the format and the transport method used for communication between an LDAP client and server.

- **Security:** LDAP offers a scheme for determining how and by whom the information stored in an LDAP directory is accessed. Numerous access levels are offered, offering access-privilege levels like read, insert, update, delete, and administrative. Also, the Transport Layer Security (TLS) extension to LDAP v3 offers a secure means for authenticating and transferring data between the client and server through the use of encryption.

You might have inferred from the above summary that LDAP defines both the information store and the communications methodology; and this is indeed the case. The fact that LDAP leaves little to the imagination in regards to implementation is one of the reasons for its widespread use.

Learning More About LDAP

In addition to numerous books written about the topic, the Internet is flush with information about LDAP. I'll offer pointers to some of the more useful online resources in this section:

- **LDAP v3 specification** (http://www.ietf.org/rfc/rfc3377.txt): The official specification of the Lightweight Directory Access Protocol Version 3.

- **The Official OpenLDAP Website** (http://www.openldap.org/): Official Web site of LDAP's widely used open source implementation.

- **Ldapzone.com** (http://www.ldapzone.com/): Another great resource site, with a really cool mascot to boot.

- **IBM LDAP Redbook** (http://www.redbooks.ibm.com/): IBM's free 194-page introduction to LDAP.

Hopefully these resources will prove as useful to you as they long have to me.

PHP and LDAP

I've had the pleasure of writing several LDAP applications using a variety of languages, and yet although I'm a long-time PHP programmer, I never bothered to consider PHP's LDAP capabilities until recently. After doing some initial experimentation, I was quite sorry to have bypassed it for so long, for I believe that PHP's LDAP capabilities are superior to (or at the very least, much more intuitive than) those of many other languages in terms of flexibility and ease of use. This chapter is devoted to a thorough examination of this matter, introducing the bulk of PHP's LDAP functions, and weaving in numerous hints and tips regarding how to make the most of PHP/LDAP integration.

Connecting to the LDAP Server

Working with LDAP is much like working with a database server, in that you must establish a connection to the server before any interaction can begin. PHP's LDAP server connection function is known as ldap_connect().

ldap_connect()

```
resource ldap_connect ([string hostname [, int port]])
```

The ldap_connect() function establishes a connection to the LDAP server specified by *hostname* on port *port*. If the optional port parameter is not specified, and the ldap:// URL scheme prefaces the server or the URL scheme is omitted entirely, then LDAP's standard port 389 is assumed. If the ldaps:// scheme is used, port 636 is assumed. If the connection is successful, a link identifier is returned; on error, FALSE is returned. A simple usage example follows:

```php
<?php
    $ldapHost = "ldap://ad.gilmore.com";
    $ldapPort = "389";
    $ldapLink = ldap_connect($ldapHost, $ldapPort)
                or die("Can't establish LDAP connection");
?>
```

> **NOTE** *Although secure LDAP (LDAPS) is widely deployed, it is not an official specification.*

ldap_start_tls()

```
boolean ldap_start_tls (resource link_id)
```

Although ldap_start_tls() is not a connection-specific function per se, I thought it nonetheless suitable to introduce it in this section because it is typically executed immediately after a call to ldap_connect() if the developer wants to connect to an LDAP server securely using the Transport Layer Security (TLS) protocol. There are a few points worth noting regarding this function:

- TLS connections for LDAP can only take place when using LDAP's version 3 protocol. Because PHP uses LDAP v2 by default, you'll need to specifically declare use of version 3 using ldap_set_option() before making a call to ldap_start_tls(). See the later section, "Configuration Functions" for more information.

- You can call the function ldap_start_tls() before or after binding to the directory, although calling it before makes much more sense if you're interested in protecting bind credentials.

An example follows:

```php
<?php
    $ldapconn = ldap_connect("ldaps://ad.wjgilmore.com");
    ldap_set_option($ldapconn, LDAP_OPT_PROTOCOL_VERSION, 3);
    ldap_start_tls($ldapconn);
?>
```

Binding to the LDAP Server

Once a successful connection has been made to the LDAP server (see ldap_connect()), you'll need to pass a set of credentials under the guise of which all subsequent LDAP queries will be executed. Not surprisingly, these credentials include a username of sorts, better known as an RDN, or Relative Distinguished Name, and password.

ldap_bind()

```
boolean ldap_bind (resource link_id [, string bind_rdn [, string bind_pswd]])
```

Although anybody could feasibly connect to the LDAP server, proper credentials are often required before data can be retrieved or manipulated. This feat is accomplished using ldap_bind(). This function requires at minimum the *link_id* returned from ldap_connect(), and likely a username and password, denoted by *bind_rdn* and *bind_pswd*, respectively. An example follows:

```php
<?php
    $ldapHost = "ldap://ad.gilmore.com";
    $ldapPort = "389";
    $ldapUser = "ldapreadonly";
    $ldapPswd = "iloveldap";

    $ldapLink = ldap_connect($ldapHost, $ldapPort)
                or die("Can't establish LDAP connection");

    ldap_bind($ldapLink, $ldapUser, $ldapPswd)
                or die("Can't bind to the server.");
?>
```

Take note that the credentials supplied to ldap_bind() are created and managed within the LDAP server, and have nothing to do with any accounts residing on the server or workstation from which you are connecting. Therefore, if you are unable to connect anonymously to the LDAP server, you'll need to talk to the system administrator to arrange for an appropriate account.

Closing the LDAP Server Connection

After you have completed all your interaction with the LDAP server, you should clean up after yourself and properly close the connection. One function, ldap_unbind(), is available for doing just this.

ldap_unbind()

```
boolean ldap_unbind (resource link_id)
```

The ldap_unbind() function terminates the LDAP server connection associated with *link_id*. A rather straightforward usage example follows:

```php
<?php
    $ldapUser = "ldapreadonly";
    $ldapPswd = "iloveldap";
    $ldapLink = ldap_connect("ldap://ad.wjgilmore.com", 389)
            or die("Can't establish LDAP connection");
    ldap_bind($ldapLink,"ldapreadonly", "iloveldap")
            or die("Can't bind to LDAP.");
    /* Execute various LDAP-related commands. */
    ldap_unbind($ldapLink)
            or die("Could not unbind from LDAP server.");
?>
```

> **NOTE** *The PHP function* ldap_close() *is operationally identical to* ldap_unbind(), *but because the LDAP API refers to this function using the latter terminology, it is recommended over the former for reasons of readability.*

Retrieving LDAP Data

Because LDAP is a read-optimized protocol, it makes sense that a bevy of useful data search and retrieval functions would be offered within any implementation. Indeed, PHP offers numerous functions for retrieving directory information. I'll examine those functions in this section.

ldap_search()

```
resource ldap_search (resource link_id, string base_dn, string filter
[, array attributes [, int attributes_only [, int size_limit
[, int time_limit [int deref]]]]])
```

The `ldap_search()` function is one you'll almost certainly make use of repeatedly when creating LDAP-enabled PHP applications, because it is the primary means for searching a directory (denoted by *base_dn*) based on a specified filter, denoted by *filter*. A successful search returns a result set, which can then be parsed by other functions that will be introduced later in this section; a failed search returns FALSE. Consider the following example, in which `ldap_search()` is used to retrieve all users with a first name beginning with the letter A:

```
$results = ldap_search($ldapconn, $dn, "givenName=A*");
```

Several optional attributes tweak the search behavior. The first, *attributes*, allows you to specify exactly which attributes should be returned for each entry in the result set. So for example, if you wanted each user's first name, last name, and e-mail addresses, you could include these in the *attributes* list:

```
$results = ldap_search($ldapconn, $dn, "givenName=A*", "givenName,surname,mail");
```

Note that if the *attributes* parameter is not explicitly assigned, all attributes will be returned for each entry, which is quite inefficient if you're not going to make use of all of them. Therefore, making use of this parameter is typically a good idea.

If the optional *attributes_only* parameter is enabled (set to 1), only the attribute types are retrieved. You might use this parameter if you're only interested in knowing whether or not a particular attribute is available in a given entry, and you're not interested in the actual values. If this parameter is disabled (set to 0) or omitted, both the attribute types and their corresponding values are retrieved.

The next optional parameter, *size_limit*, can limit the number of entries retrieved. If this parameter is disabled (set to 0) or omitted, no limit is set on the retrieval count. The following example retrieves both the attribute types and corresponding values of the first five users with first names beginning with A:

```
$results = ldap_search($ldapconn, $dn, "givenName=A*", 0, 5);
```

Enabling the next optional parameter *time_limit* places a limit on the time in seconds devoted to a search. Omitting or disabling this parameter (setting it to 0) results in no set time limit, although such a limit can be (and often is) set within the LDAP server configuration. The next example performs the same search as the previous example, but limits the search to thirty seconds:

```
$results = ldap_search($ldapconn, $dn, "givenName=A*", 0, 5, 30);
```

The eighth and final optional parameter, *deref*, determines how aliases are handled. Because this parameter is used in several functions, I'll save the discussion of its possible values for the later section, "Configuration Options." See the introduction of the LDAP_DEREF_ALWAYS configuration option for more information.

ldap_read()

```
resource ldap_read (resource link_id, string base_dn, string filter
[, array attributes [, int attributes_only [, int size_limit
[, int time_limit [int deref]]]]])
```

You should use the ldap_read() function when you're searching for a specific entry, and can identify that entry by a particular DN, specified by the *base_dn* input parameter. So for example, if I wanted to retrieve just the details of my specific user entry, I might execute:

```php
<?php
    /* Connect and bind to the LDAP server.... */
    $dn = "CN=Jason Gilmore, OU=People, OU=staff, DC=ad, DC=wjgilmore, DC=com";
    $results = ldap_read($ldapconn, $dn,
                        '(objectclass=person)', array("givenName", "sn"));
    $entry = ldap_get_entries($ldapconn, $sr);
    echo "First name: ".$entry[0]["givenname"][0]."<br />";
    echo "Last name: ".$entry[0]["sn"][0]."<br />";
    ldap_unbind($ldapconn);
?>
```

This returns the following:

```
First Name: Jason
Last Name: Gilmore
```

ldap_list()

```
resource ldap_list (resource link_id, string base_dn, string filter
[, array attributes [, int attributes_only [, int size_limit
[, int time_limit [int deref]]]]])
```

The ldap_list() function is identical to ldap_search(), except that the search is only performed on the level immediately below the supplied DN, specified by *base_dn*. See ldap_search() for an explanation of the input parameters.

Working with Entry Values

Chances are that you'll spend the majority of your time gnawing on result entries in an effort to get at their chewy center: the values. Several functions make this very easy, and I'll examine each in this section.

ldap_get_values()

array ldap_get_values (resource *link_id*, resource *result_entry_id*,
string *attribute*)

You'll often want to examine each row of a result set returned by ldap_search(). One way to do this is via the ldap_get_values() function, which retrieves an array of values for an *attribute* found in the entry *result_entry_id*.

```php
<?php
    /* Connect and bind to the LDAP server.... */
    $dn = "CN=Jason Gilmore, OU=People, OU=staff, DC=ad, DC=wjgilmore, DC=com";
    $results = ldap_read($ldapconn, $dn, '(objectclass=person)',
                        array("givenName", "sn", "mail"));
    $firstname = ldap_get_values($ldapconn, $results, "givenname");
    $lastname = ldap_get_values($ldapconn, $results, "sn");
    $mail = ldap_get_values($ldapconn, $results, "mail");

    echo "First name: ".$firstname[0]."<br />";
    echo "Last name: ".$lastname[0]."<br />";
    echo "Email addresses: ";

    $x=0;
    while ($x < $mail["count"]) {
        echo $mail[$x]. " ";
        $x++;
    }
?>
```

This returns:

```
First name: Jason
Last name: Gilmore
Email addresses: gilmore@cob.osu.edu wj@wjgilmore.com wjgilmore@hotmail.com
```

Note that the values must be referenced as an array element, regardless of whether the corresponding attribute is single-valued or multivalued.

ldap_get_values_len()

array ldap_get_values_len (resource *link_id*, resource *result_entry_id*,
string *attribute*)

It's sometimes convenient to store binary data in an LDAP directory, for example a JPEG image of a staff member, or a graduate student's PDF resume. Because binary data must be handled differently from its non-binary counterpart, you must use a special function, ldap_get_values_len()when retrieving it from the data store.

Counting Retrieved Entries

It's often useful to know how many entries were retrieved from a search. PHP offers one explicit function for accomplishing this, ldap_count_entries(). In addition, you'll learn of numerous other methodologies for doing this implicitly through other function introductions in this chapter.

ldap_count_entries()

```
int ldap_count_entries (resource link_id, resource result_id)
```

The ldap_count_entries() function returns the number of entries found in the search result specified by *result_id*. For example:

```
$results = ldap_search($ldapconn, $dn, "sn=G*");
$count = ldap_count_entries($ldapconn, $results);
echo "<p>Total entries retrieved: $count</p>";
```

This returns:

```
Total entries retrieved: 45
```

Retrieving Attributes

You'll often need to learn about the attributes returned from a search. Several functions are available for doing so, each of which is introduced in this section.

ldap_first_attribute()

```
string ldap_first_attribute (resource link_id, resource result_entry_id,
int pointer_id)
```

The ldap_first_attribute() function operates much like ldap_first_entry(), except that it is intended to retrieve the first attribute of the result entry denoted by *result_entry_id*. One point of confusion regarding this function is the *pointer_id* parameter. Although it's an input parameter, ldap_first_attribute() actually uses this parameter to set a pointer that is later used by ldap_next_attribute() if you wish to retrieve the entry's other attributes and their corresponding values. An example follows:

```
$results = ldap_search($ldapconn, $dn, "sn=G*", array(telephoneNumber, mail));
$entry = ldap_first_entry($ldapconn, $results);
$fAttr = ldap_first_attribute($ldapconn, $entry, $pointer);
echo $fAttr;
```

This returns:

```
mail
```

---

ldap_next_attribute()

string ldap_first_attribute (resource *link_id*, resource *result_entry_id*,
int *pointer_id*)

The ldap_next_attribute() function retrieves attributes of the entry specified by
result_entry_id. Using the pointer *pointer_id*, created by a prior call to
ldap_first_attribute(), repeated calls to this function will retrieve each attribute in
the entry. Consider an example:

```
$results = ldap_search($ldapconn, $dn, "sn=G*",
                              array(telephoneNumber, userPrincipalName, mail));
$entry = ldap_first_entry($ldapconn, $results);
$attr = ldap_first_attribute($ldapconn, $entry, $ber);
while ($attr = ldap_next_attribute($ldapconn, $entry, $ber)) echo $attr."<br />";
```

This returns:

```
telephoneNumber
userPrincipalName
mail
```

---

ldap_get_attributes()

array ldap_get_attributes (resource *link_id*, resource *result_entry_id*)

The ldap_get_attributes() function returns a multi-dimensional array of attributes
and their respective values for an entry specified by *result_entry_id*. This function is
quite useful because it allows you the convenience of being able to retrieve a particular
value by referring to its corresponding attribute, in addition to a variety of other useful
information:

- return_value["count"]: The total number of attributes for the entry.

- return_value[0]: The first attribute in the retrieved entry.

- return_value[*n*]: The *n*th attribute in the retrieved entry.

- return_value["*attribute*"]["count"]: The number of values assigned to the
  retrieved entry's *attribute* attribute.

- return_value["*attribute*"][0]: The first value assigned to the retrieved entry's *attribute* attribute.

- return_value["*attribute*"][*n*]: The *n*th + 1 value assigned to the retrieved entry's *attribute* attribute.

Consider an example. Suppose you execute the following search:

```
$results = ldap_search($ldapconn, $dn, "sn=G*", array(telephoneNumber, mail));
```

You then call ldap_first_entry() to designate an initial pointer to the result set:

```
$entry = ldap_first_entry($ldapconn, $results);
```

Finally, you can call ldap_get_attributes(), passing in $entry, to retrieve the array of attributes and corresponding values:

```
$attrs = ldap_get_attributes($ldapconn, $entry);
```

You can then reference that first entry's mail value like so:

```
$emailAddress = $attrs["mail"][0]
```

You could also cycle through all of the attributes like this:

```
while ($x < $attrs["count"]) {
    echo $attrs[$x].": ".$attrs[$x][0]."<br />";
    $x++;
}
```

This returns:

```
(614) 555-4567: jason@wjgilmore.com
```

Of course, it's unlikely that you'll only want the attributes and values from the first entry. You can easily cycle through all retrieved entries with an additional looping block and the ldap_next_entry() function. To demonstrate this, I'll expand upon the previous example:

```
$dn = "OU=People,OU=facstf,DC=ad,DC=cob,DC=ohio-state,DC=edu";

$attributes = array("sn","telephonenumber");

$filter = "memberof=CN=staff,OU=Groups, DC=ad,DC=wjgilmore,DC=com";
$result = ldap_search($ad, $dn, $filter, $attributes);
```

```
$entry = ldap_first_entry($ad, $result);

while($entry) {

    $attrs = ldap_get_attributes($ad, $entry);
    for ($i=0; $i<$attrs["count"]; $i++)
    {
        $attrName = $attrs[$i];
        $values = ldap_get_values($ad,$entry,$attrName);
        for ($j=0; $j < $values["count"]; $j++)
        {
            echo "$attrName: ".$values[$j]."<br />";
        }
    }
    $entry = ldap_next_entry($ad,$entry);
}
```

This returns the following:

```
sn: Gilmore
telephonenumber: 415-555-9999
telephonenumber: 415-555-9876
sn: Reyes
telephonenumber: 212-555-1234
sn: Heston
telephonenumber: 412-555-3434
telephonenumber: 210-555-9855
```

ldap_get_dn()

string ldap_get_dn (resource *link_id*, resource *result_entry_id*)

The ldap_get_dn() function returns the DN of a result entry identified by
result_entry_id, for example:

```
<?php
/* ... Connect to LDAP server and bind to a directory. */
$dn = "OU=People,OU=staff,DC=ad,DC=wjgilmore,DC=com";

/* Search the directory */
$results = ldap_search($ldapconn, $dn, "sn=G*");

/* Grab the first entry of the result set. */
$fe = ldap_first_entry($ldapconn,$results);

/* Output the DN of the first entry. */
echo "DN: ".ldap_get_dn($ldapconn,$fe);
?>
```

This returns:

```
DN: CN=Jason Gilmore,OU=People,OU=staff,DC=ad,DC=wjgilmore,DC=com
```

Sorting and Comparing LDAP entries

Ordering and comparing retrieved entries are often required features when you're working with LDAP data. Two of PHP's LDAP functions accomplish both quite nicely, and each is introduced in this section.

ldap_sort()

boolean ldap_sort (resource *link_id*, resource *result*, string *sort_filter*)

The immensely useful ldap_sort() function can sort a result set based on any of the returned *result* attributes. Sorting is carried out by simply comparing the string values of each entry, rearranging them in ascending order. An example follows:

```php
<?php
    /* Connect and bind */
    $results = ldap_search($ldapconn, $dn, "sn=G*", array("givenname", "sn"));

    ldap_sort($ldapconn, $results, "givenName");

    $entries = ldap_get_entries($ldapconn,$results);

    $count = $entries["count"];

    for($i=0;$i<$count;$i++) {
        echo $entries[$i]["givenname"][0]." ".$entries[$i]["sn"][0]."<br />";
    }

    ldap_unbind($ldapconn);
?>
```

This returns:

```
Jason Gilmore
John Gilmore
Robert Gilmore
```

> **NOTE** *This function is known to produce unpredictable results when you attempt to sort on multivalued attributes.*

ldap_compare()

boolean ldap_compare (resource *link_id*, string *dn*, string *attribute*, string *value*)

The ldap_compare() function offers an easy means for comparing a particular value with a *value* of an *attribute* stored within a given DN, specified by *dn*. This function returns TRUE on a successful comparison, and FALSE otherwise.

For example, if you wanted to compare an entered primary home phone number with that stored in the directory server for a given user, you could execute the following:

```php
<?php
    /* Connect and bind */
    $dn = "CN=Jason Gilmore, OU=People, OU=staff, DC=ad, DC=wjgilmore, DC=com";
    $phone = "614 555-1234";
    if (ldap_compare($ldapconn, $dn, "homePhone", $phone)) {
        echo "<p>Your phone number is up-to-date</p>";
    } else {
        echo "<p>The entered phone number does not match our records.
                    Perhaps you've recently moved?</p>" ;
?>
```

Working with Entries

An LDAP *entry* can be thought of much in the same way as can a database *row*, consisting of both attributes and corresponding values. Several functions are available for peeling such entries of a result set, all of which are introduced in this section.

ldap_first_entry()

resource ldap_first_entry (resource *link_id*, resource *result_id*)

The ldap_first_entry() function retrieves the first entry found in the result set specified by *result_id*. Once retrieved, you can pass it to one of the functions capable of parsing an entry, like ldap_get_values() or ldap_get_attributes().The following example displays the given name and surname of the first user.

```php
<?php
    /* ... Connect to LDAP server and bind to a directory. */
    $dn = "OU=People,OU=staff,DC=ad,DC=wjgilmore,DC=com";

    /* Search the directory  */
    $results = ldap_search($ldapconn, $dn, "sn=G*");

    /* Retrieve the first entry. */
    $firstEntry = ldap_first_entry($ldapconn, $results);

/* Retrieve the given name and surname.*/
    $gn = ldap_get_values($ldapconn, $firstEntry, "givenname");
    $sn = ldap_get_values($ldapconn, $firstEntry, "sn");
    echo "The user's name is $gn $sn.";
?>
```

This returns:

```
The user's name is Jason Gilmore.
```

Note that ldap_get_values() returns an array, and not a single value, even if there is only one item found in the array.

The ldap_first_entry() also serves another important function; it seeds ldap_next_entry() with the initial result set pointer. This matter is discussed in the next section.

ldap_next_entry()

```
resource ldap_next_entry (resource link_id, resource result_entry_id)
```

The ldap_next_entry() function is useful for cycling through a result set, because each successive call will return the next entry until all entries have been retrieved. It's important to note that the first call to ldap_next_entry() in a script must be preceded with a call to ldap_first_entry(), because the *result_entry_id* originates there. In the following example, I'll revise the previous example, this time returning the first and last name of every entry in the result set:

```php
<?php
    /* ... Connect to LDAP server and bind to a directory. */
    $dn = "OU=People,OU=staff,DC=ad,DC=wjgilmore,DC=com";

    /* Search the directory  */
    $results = ldap_search($ldapconn, $dn, "sn=G*");

    /* Retrieve the first entry. */
    $entry = ldap_first_entry($ldapconn, $results);
```

```
    while ($entry) {
        /* Retrieve the given name and surname.*/
        $gn = ldap_get_values($ldapconn, $entry, "givenname");
        $sn = ldap_get_values($ldapconn, $entry, "sn");
        echo "The user's name is $gn[0] $sn[0]<br />";
        $entry = ldap_next_entry($ldapconn, $entry);
    }
?>
```

This returns the following:

```
The user's name is Jason Gilmore
The user's name is Davie Grimes
The user's name is Johnny Groovin
```

ldap_get_entries()

```
array ldap_get_entries (resource link_id, resource result_id)
```

The ldap_get_entries() function offers an easy way to place all members of the result set into a multi-dimensional array. The following list offers the numerous items of information which can be derived from this array:

- return_value["*count*"]: The total number of retrieved entries.

- return_value[*n*]["dn"]: The DN of the *n*th entry in the result set.

- return_value[*n*]["*count*"]: The total number of attributes available in the *n*th entry of the result set.

- return_value[*n*]["*attribute*"]["*count*"]: The number of items associated with the *n*th entry of *attribute*.

- return_value[*n*]["attribute"][*m*]: The *m*th value of the *n*th entry *attribute*.

- return_value[*n*][*m*]: The attribute located in the *n*th entry's *m*th position.

Consider an example:

```
<?php
    /* ... Connect to LDAP server and bind to a directory. */

    /* Search the directory */
    $results = ldap_search($ldapconn, $dn, "sn=G*");
```

```
    /* Create array of attributes and corresponding entries. */
    $entries = ldap_get_entries($ldapconn,$results);

    /* How many entries found? */
    $count = $entries["count"];

    /* Output the surname of each located user. */
    for($i=0;$i<$count;$i++) echo $entries[$i]["sn"][0]."<br />";

    /* Close the connection. */
    ldap_unbind($ldapconn);
?>
```

This returns:

Gilmore
Gosney
Grinch

I'd like to call your attention to the way in which the multi-dimensional array is referenced in the above example:

```
$entries[$i]["sn"][0]
```

This means that the first item (PHP's array indexes always start with zero) of the *i*th element's *sn* attribute is requested. If you were dealing with a multivalued attribute, url for example, you would need to cycle through each element in the url array. This is easily done with the following modification to the above script:

```
    for($i=0;$i<$count;$i++) {
        $entry = $entries[$i];
        $attrCount = $entries[$i]["sn"]["count"];
        for($j=0;$j<$attrCount;$j++) {
            echo $entries[$i]["sn"][j]."<br />";
        }
    }
```

Deallocating Memory

Although PHP automatically deallocates any memory consumed at the conclusion of each script, it does sometimes need to explicitly manage memory before completion. As applied to LDAP, such management could be necessary if numerous large result sets are created within a single script invocation.

ldap_free_result()

```
boolean ldap_free_result (resource result_id)
```

To free up the memory consumed by a result set, use ldap_free_result(), like so:

```php
<?php
    /* connect and bind to ldap server... */
    $results = ldap_search($ldapconn, $dn, "sn=G*");
    /* do something with the result set.
    ldap_free_result($results);
    /* Perhaps perform additional searches... */
    ldap_unbind($ldapconn);
?>
```

Inserting LDAP Data

Inserting data into the directory is as easy as retrieving it. In this section, two of PHP's LDAP insertion functions are introduced.

ldap_add()

```
boolean ldap_add (resource link_id, string dn, array entry)
```

You can add new entries to the LDAP directory with the ldap_add() function. The *dn* parameter specifies the directory DN, and the *entry* parameter is an array specifying the entry to be added to the directory. An example follows:

```php
<?php
    /* Connect and bind to the LDAP server...*/

    $dn = "OU=People,OU=staff,DC=ad,DC=wjgilmore,DC=com";
    $entry["displayName"] = "Julius Caesar";
    $entry["company"] = "Roman Empire";
    $entry["mail"] = "imperatore@wjgilmore.com";
    ldap_add($ldapconn, $dn, $entry) or die("Could not add new entry!");
    ldap_unbind($ldapconn);
?>
```

Pretty simple, huh? But how would you add an attribute with multiple values? Logically, you would use an indexed array:

```php
$entry["displayName"] = "Julius Caesar";
$entry["company"] = "Roman Empire";
$entry["mail"][0] = "imperatore@wjgilmore.com";
$entry["mail"][1] = "caesar@wjgilmore.com";
ldap_add($ldapconn, $dn, $entry) or die("Could not add new entry!");
```

NOTE *Don't forget that the binding user must have the privilege to add users to the directory.*

ldap_mod_add()

```
boolean ldap_mod_add (resource link_id, string dn, array entry)
```

The ldap_mod_add() function is used to add additional values to existing entries, returning TRUE on success and FALSE on failure. Revisiting the previous example, suppose that the user Julius Caesar requested that another e-mail address be added. Because the mail attribute is multivalued, you can just extend the value array using PHP's built-in array expansion capability:

```
$dn = "CN=Julius Caesar, OU=People,OU=staff,DC=ad,DC=wjgilmore,DC=com";
$entry["mail"][] = "ides@wjgilmore.com";
ldap_mod_add($ldapconn, $dn, $entry)
   or die("Can't add entry attribute value!");
```

Note that the $dn has changed here, because you need to make specific reference to Julius Caesar's directory entry.

Suppose that Julius now wants to add his title to the directory. Because the title attribute is single-valued, it can be added like so:

```
$dn = "CN=Julius Caesar,OU=People,OU=staff,DC=ad,DC=wjgilmore,DC=com";
$entry["title"] = "Pontifex Maximus";
ldap_mod_add($ldapconn, $dn, $entry) or die("Can't add entry attribute value!");
```

Updating LDAP Data

Although LDAP data is intended to be largely static, changes are sometimes necessary. PHP offers two functions for carrying out such modifications, one for making changes on the attribute level, and another on the object level. These are ldap_modify() and ldap_rename(), respectively. I'll examine both in this section.

ldap_modify()

```
boolean ldap_modify (resource link_id, string dn, array entry)
```

The ldap_modify() function is used to modify existing directory entry attributes, returning TRUE on success and FALSE on failure. With it, you can modify one or several attributes simultaneously. Consider an example:

```
$dn = "CN=Julius Caesar, OU=People,OU=staff,DC=ad,DC=wjgilmore,DC=com";
$attrs = array("Company" => "Roman Empire", "Title" => "Pontifex Maximus");
ldap_modify($ldapconn, $dn, $attrs);
```

> **NOTE** *The* ldap_mod_replace() *function is an alias to* ldap_modify().

ldap_rename()

```
boolean ldap_rename (resource link_id, string dn, string new_rdn,
string new_parent, boolean delete_old_rdn)
```

The ldap_rename() function is used to rename an existing entry, *dn*, to *new_rdn*. The *new_parent* parameter specifies the newly renamed entry's parent object. If the parameter *delete_old_rdn* is set to TRUE, then the old entry is deleted, otherwise it will remain in the directory as non-distinguished values of the renamed entry.

Deleting LDAP Data

Although it is rare, data is occasionally removed from the directory. Deletion can take place on two levels—removal of an entire object, or removal of attributes associated with an object. Two functions are available for performing these tasks, ldap_delete() and ldap_mod_del(), respectively. Both are introduced in this section.

ldap_delete()

```
boolean ldap_delete (resource link_id, string dn)
```

The ldap_delete() function removes an entire entry (specified by *dn*) from the LDAP directory, returning TRUE on success and FALSE on failure. An example follows:

```
$dn = "CN=Julius Caesar, OU=People,OU=staff,DC=ad,DC=wjgilmore,DC=com";
ldap_delete($ldapconn, $dn) or die("Could not delete entry!");
```

Completely removing a directory object is rare; you'll probably want to remove object attributes rather than an entire object. This feat is accomplished with the function ldap_mod_del(), introduced next.

ldap_mod_del()

```
boolean ldap_mod_del (resource link_id, string dn, array entry)
```

The ldap_mod_del() function removes the value of an entity instead of an entire object. This limitation means it is used more often than ldap_delete(), because it is much more likely that attributes will require removal rather than entire objects. In the following example, user Julius Caesar's "company" attribute is deleted:

```
$dn = "CN=Julius Caesar, OU=People,OU=staff,DC=ad,DC=wjgilmore,DC=com";
ldap_mod_delete($ldapconn, $dn, array("company"));
```

In the following example, all entries of the multivalued attribute "mail" are removed:

```
$dn = "CN=Julius Caesar, OU=People,OU=staff,DC=ad,DC=wjgilmore,DC=com";
$attrs["mail"] = array();
ldap_mod_delete($ldapconn, $dn, $attrs);
```

To remove just a single value from a multivalued attribute, you must specifically designate that value, like so:

```
$dn = "CN=Julius Caesar, OU=People,OU=staff,DC=ad,DC=wjgilmore,DC=com";
$attrs["mail"] = "imperatore@wjgilmore.com";
ldap_mod_delete($ldapconn, $dn, $attrs);
```

Configuration Functions

Two functions are available for interacting with PHP's LDAP configuration options, one for setting the options, and another for retrieving them. These functions are ldap_set_option() and ldap_get_option(), respectively. Each is introduced in this section. However, before introducing these functions, let's take a moment to review the configuration options available to you.

Configuration Options

A number of configuration options are available for tweaking the LDAP's behavior. I'll introduce those options in this section.

> **NOTE** *LDAP uses the concept of aliases to help maintain a directory's namespace as the structure changes over time. An alias looks like any other entry, except that the entry is actually a pointer to another DN, rather than to an entry itself. However, because in certain cases searching directories aliases can result in performance degradation, you may want to control whether or not these aliases are searched, or "dereferenced." You can do so with the option LDAP_OPT_DEREF.*

- LDAP_OPT_DEREF: Determines how aliases are handled during a search. This setting may be overridden by the optional *deref* parameter, available to the ldap_search(), ldap_read(), and ldap_list() parameters. Four settings are available:

  - LDAP_DEREF_ALWAYS: Aliases should always be dereferenced.

  - LDAP_DEREF_FINDING: Aliases should be dereferenced when determining the base object, but not during the search procedure.

  - LDAP_DEREF_NEVER: Aliases should never be dereferenced.

- LDAP_DEREF_SEARCHING: Aliases should be dereferenced during the search procedure but not when determining the base object.

- LDAP_OPT_ERROR: Set to the LDAP error occurring most recently in the present session.

- LDAP_OPT_ERROR_STRING: Set to the last LDAP error message.

- LDAP_OPT_HOST_NAME: Determines the host name for the LDAP server.

- LDAP_OPT_MATCHED_DN: Set to the DN value where the most recent LDAP error occurred from.

- LDAP_OPT_PROTOCOL_VERSION: Determines which version of the LDAP protocol should be used when communicating with the LDAP server.

- LDAP_OPT_REFERRALS: Determines whether returned referrals are automatically followed.

- LDAP_OPT_RESTART: Determines whether LDAP I/O operations are automatically restarted in the case of an error before the operation is complete.

- LDAP_OPT_SIZELIMIT: Constrains the number of entries returned from a search.

- LDAP_OPT_TIMELIMIT: Constrains the number of seconds allocated to a search.

- LDAP_OPT_CLIENT_CONTROLS: Specifies a list of client controls affecting the behavior of the LDAP API.

- LDAP_OPT_SERVER_CONTROLS: Tells the LDAP server to return a specific list of controls with each request.

ldap_get_option()

```
boolean ldap_get_option (resource link_id, int option, mixed return_value)
```

The ldap_get_option() function offers a simple means for returning one of PHP's LDAP configuration options. The parameter *option* specifies the name of the parameter, while *return_value* determines the variable name where the *option* value will be placed. TRUE is returned on success, and FALSE on error. As an example, here's how you retrieve the LDAP protocol version:

```
ldap_get_option($ldapconn, LDAP_OPT_PROTOCOL_VERSION, $value);
echo $value;
```

This returns:

3

Which represents LDAPv3.

ldap_set_option()

```
boolean ldap_set_option (resource link_id, int option, mixed new_value)
```

The ldap_set_option() function is used to configure PHP's LDAP configuration options. The following example sets the LDAP protocol version to version 3:

```
ldap_set_option($ldapconn, LDAP_OPT_PROTOCOL_VERSION, 3);
```

Character Encoding

When transferring data between older to newer LDAP implementations, you need to "upgrade" the data's character set from the older T.61 set, used in LDAPv2 servers, to the newer ISO 8859, used in LDAPv3 servers, and vice versa. Two functions are available for accomplishing this.

ldap_8859_to_t61()

```
string ldap_8859_to_t61 (string value)
```

The ldap_8859_to_t61() function is used for converting from the 8859 to the T.61 character set. This is useful for transferring data between different LDAP server implementations, as differing default character sets are often employed.

ldap_t61_to_8859 ()

```
string ldap_t61_to_8859 (string value)
```

The ldap_t61_to_8859() function is used for converting from the T.61 to the 8859 character set. This is useful for transferring data between different LDAP server implementations, as differing default character sets are often employed.

Working with the Distinguished Name

It's sometimes useful to learn more about the DN of the object you're working with. Several functions are available for doing just this, each of which is introduced in this section.

ldap_dn2ufn()

```
string ldap_dn2ufn (string dn)
```

The ldap_dn2ufn() function converts a Distinguished Name (DN), specified by *dn*, to a somewhat more user-friendly format. This is best illustrated with an example:

```php
<?php
/* Designate the dn */
$dn = "OU=People,OU=staff,DC=ad,DC=wjgilmore,DC=com";

/* Convert the DN to a user-friendly format */
echo ldap_dn2ufn($dn);
?>
```

This returns:

```
People, staff, ad, wjgilmore, com
```

ldap_explode_dn()

```
array ldap_explode_dn (string dn, int only_values)
```

The ldap_explode_dn() function operates much like ldap_dn2ufn(), except that each component of the dn, specified by the input parameter *dn*, is returned in an array rather than in a string. If the include_attributes parameter is set to 0, both the attributes and corresponding values are included in the array elements; if it is set to 1, just the values are returned. Consider this example:

```php
<?php
$dn = "OU=People,OU=staff,DC=ad,DC=wjgilmore,DC=com";
$dnComponents = ldap_explode_dn($dn, 0);
foreach($dnComponents as $component) {
    echo $component."<br />";
}
?>
```

This returns the following:

```
5
OU=People
OU=staff
DC=ad
DC=wjgilmore
DC=com
```

The first line of output is the array size, denoted by the count key.

Error Handling

Although we'd all like to think of our programming logic and code as foolproof, it rarely turns out that way. That said, you should make use of the functions introduced in this section, because they will not only aid you in determining causes of error, but will also provide your end user with the pertinent information he or she needs in the case of an error due not to programming faults, but because of inappropriate or incorrect user actions.

ldap_err2str()

```
string ldap_err2str (int errno)
```

The ldap_err2str() function translates one of LDAP's standard error numbers to its corresponding string representation. For example, error integer 3 represents the time limit exceeded error. Therefore, executing the following function yields an appropriate message:

```
echo ldap_err2str (3);
```

This returns:

```
Time limit exceeded
```

Keep in mind that these error strings might vary slightly, so if you're interested in offering somewhat more user-friendly messages, always base your conversions on the error number rather than an error string.

ldap_errno()

```
int ldap_errno (resource link_id)
```

The LDAP specification offers a standardized list of error codes that might be generated during interaction with a directory server. If you want to customize the otherwise terse messages offered by ldap_error() and ldap_err2str(), or you would like to log the codes, say within a database, you can use ldap_errno() to retrieve this code.

ldap_error()

```
string ldap_error (resource link_id)
```

The ldap_error() function retrieves the last error message generated during the LDAP connection specified by *link_id*. Although the list of all possible error codes is far too long to include in this chapter, I'll offer a few just so you can get an idea of what is available:

- LDAP_TIMELIMIT_EXCEEDED: The predefined LDAP execution time limit was exceeded.

- LDAP_INVALID_CREDENTIALS: The supplied binding credentials were invalid.

- LDAP_INSUFFICIENT_ACCESS: The user has insufficient access to perform the requested operation.

Not exactly user-friendly, are they? If you'd like to offer a somewhat more detailed response to the user, you'll need to set up the appropriate translation logic. However, because the string-based error messages are likely to be modified or localized, it's always best to base such translations on the error number rather than the error string for portability. See ldap_errno() for more information about retrieving these error numbers.

Summary

The ability to interface with powerful third-party technologies such as LDAP through PHP is one of the main reasons I love working with the language. PHP's LDAP support makes it so easy to create Web-based applications that work in conjunction with directory servers, and has the potential to offer a number of great value-added benefits to your user community.

In the next chapter, I'll examine what is probably my favorite PHP feature: session handling. You'll learn how to play "Big Brother," tracking users' preferences, actions, and thoughts as they navigate through your application. Okay, maybe not that last one, but maybe we can request that feature for PHP 6.

CHAPTER 16

Session Handlers

WHILE I WAS OUTLINING this chapter, I took a moment to reflect upon the various occasions I've spoken and written about the process of using HTTP sessions to track user and application data. I recall the need to change my topic introduction several times over the past few years, as standard Web development practices have evolved considerably over the period that I've discussed this subject. Early on, the matter was treated as one of those "gee whiz" tricks that excited only the hardcore developers and dot-coms. However, as application complexity became more prevalent, what once was novelty soon became necessity. These days, foregoing the use of HTTP sessions is more the exception than the norm for most enterprise applications. Therefore, no matter if you're completely new to the realm of Web development, or if you've simply not yet gotten around to integrating this key feature into your development agenda, this chapter is for you.

This chapter introduces what remains one of my favorite features of PHP: session handling. Around since the release of version 4.0, it remains one of the coolest and most talked-about features of the language, yet it is surprisingly easy to use, as you're about to learn. In this chapter I'll cover the entire spectrum of topics surrounding session handling, including its very definition, PHP configuration requirements, and implementation concepts. In addition, I'll not only demonstrate the feature's default session-management features, but I will also show you how to create and define your own customized management plug-in. As always, all of the material will be accompanied with numerous applicable examples. I'll begin, however, at the beginning, and take a moment to define exactly what session handling is all about, and why its such an important part of any Web application.

What Is Session Handling?

The Hypertext Transfer Protocol, better known as HTTP, defines the rules used to transfer text, graphics, video, and all other data via the World Wide Web. It is a *stateless* protocol, meaning that each request is processed without any knowledge of any prior or subsequent requests. Although such a simplistic implementation is a significant contributor to HTTP's ubiquity, this particular shortcoming has long remained a dagger in the heart of developers who wish to create complex Web-based applications that must be able to adjust to user-specific behavior and preferences. To remedy this problem, the practice of storing bits of information on the client's machine, in what are commonly called *cookies* quickly gained acceptance, and offered some relief to this conundrum. However limitations on cookie size, the number of allowed cookies, and various inconveniences surrounding their implementation prompted developers to devise another solution. That solution is known as *session handling*.

Session handling is essentially a clever workaround to this problem of stateless-ness. This is accomplished by tagging each site visitor with a unique identifying attrib-ute, known as the session ID (commonly referred to as a SID) and then correlating that SID with any number of other pieces of data, be it number of monthly visitations, favorite background color, or middle name—you name it. In relational database terms, you can think of the SID as the primary key that ties all the other user attributes together. But how is the SID continually correlated with the user, given the stateless behavior of HTTP? It can be done in two different ways, both of which are introduced in the following sections. The choice of which to implement is entirely up to you.

Cookies

One ingenious means for managing user information actually builds upon the original methodology of using a cookie. As the user executes a request for another page, this data can then later be retrieved as necessary. However, rather than storing the user preferences in the cookie, the SID is stored instead. As the client navigates throughout the site, the SID is retrieved when necessary and the various items of data correlated with that SID are furnished for use within the page. In addition, because the cookie can remain on the client even after a session ends, it can be read in during a subsequent session, meaning that persistence is maintained even across long periods of time and inactivity. Keep in mind, however, that because cookie acceptance is a matter ulti-mately controlled by the client, you must be prepared for the possibility that the user has disabled cookie support within the browser, or that the user takes it upon himself to purge the cookies from his machine.

URL Rewriting

The second method used for SID propagation simply involves appending the SID to every local URL found within the requested page. This results in automatic SID propa-gation whenever the user clicks one of those local links. This method, known as *URL rewriting*, removes the possibility that your site's session-handling feature could be negated if the client disables cookies. However, it is not without its drawbacks. First, URL rewriting does not allow for persistence between sessions, as the process of auto-matically appending an SID to the URL does not continue once the user leaves your site. Second, nothing stops a user from copying that URL into an e-mail and sending it to another user; as long as the session has not expired, the session will continue on the recipient's workstation. Consider the potential havoc that could occur if both users were to simultaneously navigate using the same session, or if the link recipient was not meant to see the data unveiled by that session. For these reasons, I recommend going with the cookie-based methodology. It is up to you to weigh the various factors and arrive at such a decision yourself.

The Session-Handling Process

Because PHP can be configured to autonomously control the entire session-handling process with little programmer interaction, some may choose to consider the gory details somewhat irrelevant. However, there are so many potential variations to the default procedure that taking a few moments to better understand this process would be well worth your time.

The very first task executed by a session-enabled page is to verify whether a valid session already exists, or whether a new one should be initiated. If a valid session doesn't exist, one is generated and correlated with that user, using one of the SID propagation methodologies described earlier. An existing session is located by finding the SID either within the requested URL, or within a cookie. Therefore, if the session name is "sessionid," and it's appended to the URL, you could retrieve the value with the following variable:

```
$_GET['sessionid']
```

If it's stored within a cookie, you can retrieve it like this:

```
$_COOKIE['sessionid']
```

With each page request, this SID is retrieved. Once retrieved, you can either begin correlating information to that SID, or you can retrieve previously correlated SID data. For example, suppose that the user is browsing various news articles on the site. Article identifiers could be mapped to the user's SID, allowing you to compile a list of articles that the user has read, and display it as the user continues to navigate. In the coming sections, you'll learn how to store and retrieve this session information.

> **TIP** *You can also retrieve cookie information via the* $_REQUEST *superglobal. For instance,* $_REQUEST['sessionid'] *will retrieve the SID just as* $_GET['sessionid'] *or* $_COOKIE['sessionid'] *would in the respective scenarios. However, for purposes of clarity, I always suggest using the superglobal that best matches the variable's place-of-origination.*

This process continues until the user ends the session, by closing the browser or navigating to an external site. If you use cookies, and the cookie's expiration date has been set to some date in the future, if the user were to return to the site before that expiration date, the session could be continued as if the user never left. If you use URL rewriting, the session is definitively ended, and a new one must begin the next time the user visits the site.

In the coming sections, you'll learn about the configuration directives and functions responsible for carrying out this process. We'll begin with a review of the former.

Configuration Directives

Twenty-two session configuration directives are responsible for determining the behavior of PHP's session handling functionality. Because these directives play such an important role in determining this behavior, I suggest that you take some time to become familiar with the directives and their possible settings. Each is introduced in this section.

session.save_handler (files, mm, user)
Scope: PHP_INI_ALL, default: `files`
The `session.save_handler` directive determines how the session information will be stored. This data can be stored in three ways: within flat files (`files`), within shared memory (`mm`), or through user-defined functions (`user`). Although the default setting, files, will suffice for many sites, keep in mind that the number of session-storage files could potentially run into the thousands, and even the hundreds of thousands over a given period of time. The shared memory option is the fastest of the three, but also the most volatile because the data is stored in RAM. The third option, although the most complicated to configure, is also the most flexible and powerful, because custom handlers can be created to store the information in any media the developer desires. Later in this chapter you'll learn how to store session data within a MySQL database.

session.save_path (string)
Scope: PHP_INI_ALL, default: `/tmp`
If `session.save_handler` is set to the `files` storage option, then the `session.save_path` directive must point to the storage directory. Keep in mind that this should not be set to a directory located within the server document root, because the information could easily be compromised via the browser. In addition, this directory must be writable by the server daemon.

session.use_cookies (0|1)
Scope: PHP_INI_ALL, default: 1
If you'd like to maintain a user's session over multiple visits to the site, a cookie should be used so that the handlers can recall the SID, and continue with the saved session. If user data is to be used only over the course of a single site visit, then URL rewriting will suffice. Setting this directive to 1 results in the use of cookies for SID propagation; setting it to 0 causes URL rewriting to be used.

Keep in mind that when `session.use_cookies` is enabled, there is no need to explicitly call a cookie-setting function (via PHP's set_cookie(), for example), because this will be automatically handled by the session library. If you choose cookies as the method for tracking the user's session ID, then there are several other directives that one must consider, each of which is introduced in the following entries.

session.use_only_cookies (0|1)
Scope: PHP_INI_ALL, default: 0
This directive ensures that only cookies will be used to maintain the session id, ignoring any attempts to initiate an attack by passing a session ID via the URL. Setting this directive to 1 causes PHP to use only cookies, and setting it to 0 opens up the possibility for both cookies and URL rewriting to be considered.

session.name (string)
Scope: PHP_INI_ALL, default: PHPSESSID
The directive session.name determines the cookie name. The default value can be changed to a name more suitable to your application, or can be modified as needed through the session_name() function, introduced later in this chapter.

session.auto_start (0|1)
Scope: PHP_INI_ALL, default: 0
A session can be initiated explicitly through a call to the function session_start(), or automatically by setting this directive to 1. I prefer disabling this directive and calling the session_start() function as necessary, although this choice is ultimately your call.

session.cookie_lifetime (integer)
Scope: PHP_INI_ALL, default: 0
The session.cookie_lifetime directive determines the session cookie's period of validity. This number is specified in seconds, so if the cookie should live 1 hour, then this directive should be set to 3600. If this directive is set to 0, then the cookie will live until the browser is restarted.

session.cookie_path (string)
Scope: PHP_INI_ALL, default: /
The directive session.cookie_path determines the path in which the cookie is considered valid. The cookie is also valid for all child directories falling under this path. For example, if it is set to /, then the cookie will be valid for the entire Web site. Setting it to /books causes the cookie to only be valid when called from within the http://www.example.com/books/ path.

session.cookie_domain (string)
Scope: PHP_INI_ALL, default: empty
The directive session.cookie_domain determines the domain for which the cookie is valid. This directive is a necessity because it prevents other domains from reading your cookies. The following example illustrates its use:

```
session.cookie_domain = www.example.com
```

If you'd like a session to be made available for site subdomains, say customers.example.com, intranet.example.com and www2.example.com, you could set this directive like this:

```
session.cookie_domain = .example.com
```

session.serialize_handler (string)
Scope: PHP_INI_ALL, default: php
This directive defines the callback handler used to serialize and unserialize data. By default this is handled by an internal handler called php. PHP also supports a second serialization handler, Web Development Data Exchange (WDDX), available by compiling PHP with WDDX support. Staying with the default handler will work just fine for the vast majority of cases.

session.gc_probability (integer)
Scope: PHP_INI_ALL, default: 1
This directive defines the numerator component of the probability ratio used to calculate the frequency in which the garbage collection routine is invoked. The denominator component is assigned to the directive session.gc_divisor, introduced next.

session.gc_divisor (integer)
Scope: PHP_INI_ALL, default: 100
This directive defines the denominator component of the probability ratio used to calculate the frequency in which the garbage collection routine is invoked. The numerator component is assigned to the directive session.gc_probability, introduced previously.

session.gc_maxlifetime (integer)
Scope: PHP_INI_ALL, default: 1440
This directive determines the maximum age (in seconds) of data before it is considered garbage and destroyed. Once destroyed, this data is irretrievable.

session.referer_check (string)
Scope: PHP_INI_ALL, default: empty
Using URL rewriting as the means for propagating session IDs opens up the possibility that a particular session state could be viewed by numerous individuals simply by copying and disseminating a URL. This directive lessens this possibility by specifying a substring that each referrer is checked against. If the referrer does not contain this substring, the session id will be invalidated.

session.entropy_file (string)
Scope: PHP_INI_ALL, default: empty
Those involved in the field of computer science are well aware that what is seemingly random is often anything but. For those skeptical of PHP's built-in session id generation procedure, this directive can be used to point to an additional entropy source that will be incorporated into the generation process. On Unix systems, this source is often /dev/random or /dev/urandom. On Windows systems, installing Cygwin (http://www.cygwin.com/) will offer functionality similar to random or urandom.

session.entropy_length (integer)
Scope: PHP_INI_ALL, default: 0
This directive determines the number of bytes read from the file specified by session.entropy_file. If session.entropy_file is empty, this directive is ignored, and the standard SID-generation scheme is used.

session.cache_limiter (string)
Scope: PHP_INI_ALL, default: nocache
This directive determines whether session pages are cached, and if so, how. Five values are available:

- none: This setting disables the transmission of any cache control headers along with the session-enabled pages.

- nocache: This is the default setting. This setting ensures that every request is first sent to the originating server before offering a potentially cached version.

- private: Designating a cached document as private means that the document will only be made available to the originating user. It will not be shared with other users.

- private_no_expire: This is a variation of the private designation, resulting in no document expiration date being sent to the browser. This was added as a workaround for various browsers that became confused by the Expire header sent along when this directive is set to private.

- public: This setting deems all documents as cacheable, even if the original document request requires authentication.

session.cache_expire (integer)
Scope: PHP_INI_ALL, default: 180
This directive determines the number of seconds that cached session pages are made available before new pages are created. If session.cache_limiter is set to nocache, this directive is ignored.

session.use_trans_sid (0|1)
Scope: PHP_INI_SYSTEM | PHP_INI_PERDIR, default: 0
If session.use_cookies is disabled, the user's unique session ID must be attached to the URL in order to ensure ID propagation. This can be handled explicitly by manually appending the variable $SID to the end of each URL, or automatically by enabling this directive. Not surprisingly, if you commit to using URL rewrites, you should enable this directive to take the possibility of human error out of the rewrite process.

session.hash_function (0|1)
Scope: PHP_INI_ALL, default: 0
The SID can be created using one of two well-known algorithms: MD5 and SHA1. These result in SIDs consisting of 128 and 160 bits, respectively. Setting this directive to 0 results in the use of MD5, while setting it to 1 results in the use of SHA1.

session.hash_bits_per_character (integer)
Scope: PHP_INI_ALL, default: 4
Once generated, the SID is converted from its native binary format to some readable string format. The converter must know whether each character comprises of four, five, or six bits, and looks to session.hash_bits_per_character for the answer. For example, setting this directive to 4 will result in a 32-character string consisting of a combination of the characters 0 through 9 and a through f. Setting it to 5 results in a 26-character string consisting of the characters 0 through 9, and a through v. Finally, setting it to 6 results in a 22-character string consisting of the characters 0 through 9, a through z, A through Z, - and ,. Example SIDs using four, five, and six bits follow, respectively:

```
d9b24a2a1863780e996e5d750ea9e9d2
fine57lneqkvvqmele7h0h05m1
rb68n-8b7Log62RrP4SKx1
```

Note that as the complexity increases, the length decreases.

session.gc_maxlifetime (integer)
Scope: PHP_INI_ALL, default: 1440
This directive determines the duration, in seconds, for which a session is valid. Once this limit is reached, the session information will be destroyed, allowing for the recuperation of system resources. By default, this is set to the unusual value of 1440, or 24 minutes.

url_rewriter.tags (string)
Scope: PHP_INI_ALL, default: a=href,area=href,frame=src,input=src,form=fakeentry
When session.use_trans_sid is enabled, the session id will automatically append the SID to HTML tags located in the requested document before sending the document to the client. However, many of these tags play no role in initiating a server request (unlike a hyperlink or form tag); you can use url_rewriter.tags to tell the server exactly to which tags the SID should be appended. For example:

```
url_rewriter.tags a=href, frame=src, form=, fieldset=
```

Key Concepts

In this section I'll introduce many of the key session-handling tasks, presenting the relevant session functions along the way. Some of these tasks include the creation and destruction of a session, designation and retrieval of the SID, and storage and retrieval of session variables. This introduction sets the stage for the next section, in which I'll offer several practical session-handling examples.

Starting a Session

Remember that HTTP is oblivious to both the user's past and future conditions. Therefore you need to explicitly initiate and subsequently resume the session with each request. Both tasks are done using the session_start() function, introduced below.

session_start()

```
boolean session_start()
```

The function session_start() creates a new session or continues a current session based upon whether it can locate an SID. A session is started simply by calling session_start() like this:

```
session_start();
```

Note that the session_start() function reports a successful outcome regardless of the result. Therefore, using any sort of exception handling in this case will prove fruitless.

NOTE *You can eliminate execution of this function altogether by enabling the configuration directive* session.auto_start. *Keep in mind that this will start or resume a session for every PHP-enabled page however.*

Destroying a Session

Although you can configure PHP's session-handling directives to automatically destroy a session based on an expiration time or probability, sometimes it's useful to manually cancel out the session yourself. For example, you might want to provide the user with the ability to manually log out of your site. When the user clicks the appropriate link, you can erase the session variables from memory, and even completely wipe the session from storage, done through the session_unset() and session_destroy() functions, respectively. Both functions are introduced in this section.

session_unset()

void session_unset()

The session_unset() function will erase all session variables stored in the current session, effectively resetting the session to the state in which it was found upon creation (no session variables registered). Note that this will not completely remove the session from the storage mechanism. If you want to completely destroy the session, see the function session_destroy().

session_destroy()

boolean session_destroy()

The function session_destroy() invalidates the current session by completely removing the session from the storage mechanism. Keep in mind that this will *not* destroy any cookies on the user's browser. However, if you are not interested in using the cookie beyond the end of the session, just set session.cookie_lifetime to 0 (its default value) in the php.ini file.

Retrieving and Setting the Session ID

Remember that the session ID (SID) ties all session data to a particular user. Although PHP will both create and propagate the SID autonomously, there are times when you may wish to both retrieve and set this SID manually. The function session_id() is capable of carrying out both tasks, and is introduced here.

session_id()

```
string session_id([string sid])
```

The function session_id() can both set and get the SID. If it is passed no parameter, the function session_id() returns the current SID. If the optional sid parameter is included, the current SID will be replaced with that value. An example follows:

```
<?php
session_start ();
print "Your session identification number is ".session_id();
?>
```

This results in output similar to the following:

```
Your session identification number is 967d992a949114ee9832f1c11cafc640
```

Creating and Deleting Session Variables

It was once common practice to create and delete session variables via the functions session_register() and session_unregister(), respectively. These days, however, the preferred methodology involves simply setting and deleting these variable just like any other, except that you need to refer to it in the context of the $_SESSION superglobal. For example, suppose you wanted to set a session variable named username:

```
<?php
    session_start();
    $_SESSION['username'] = "jason";
    echo "Your username is ".$_SESSION['username'].".";
?>
```

This would return the following:

```
Your username is jason.
```

To delete the variable, you can use the unset() function:

```
<?php
    session_start();
    $_SESSION['username'] = "jason";
    echo "Your username is: ".$_SESSION['username'].".<br />";
    unset($_SESSION['username']);
    echo "Username now set to: ".$_SESSION['username'].".";
?>
```

This returns:

```
Your username is: jason.
Username now set to: .
```

Encoding and Decoding Session Data

Regardless of the storage media, PHP stores session data in a standardized format consisting of a single string. For example, the contents of a session consisting of two variables, namely username and loggedon, is displayed here:

```
username|s:5:"jason";loggedon|s:20:"Feb 16 2004 22:32:29";
```

Each session variable reference is separated by a semicolon, and consists of three components: the name, length, and value. The general syntax follows:

```
name|s:length:"value";
```

Thankfully, PHP handles the session encoding and decoding autonomously. However, sometimes you might wish to execute these tasks manually. Two functions are available for doing so, session_encode() and session_decode(), respectively.

session_encode()

```
boolean session_encode()
```

The function session_encode() offers a particularly convenient method for manually encoding all session variables into a single string. You might then insert this string into a database and later retrieve it, finally decoding it with session_decode(), for example.

Listing 16-1 offers a usage example. Assume that the user has a cookie containing that user's unique ID stored on a computer. When the user requests the page containing Listing 16-1, the user ID is retrieved from the cookie. This value is then assigned to be the session ID. Certain session variables are created and assigned values, and then all of this information is encoded using session_encode() and inserted into a MySQL database.

Listing 16-1. Using session_encode() to Store Data in a MySQL Database

```php
<?php
    // Initiate session and create a few session variables
    session_start();

    // Set the variables. These could be set via an HTML form, for example.
    $_SESSION['username'] = "jason";
    $_SESSION['loggedon'] = date("M d Y H:i:s");
```

```
    // Encode all session data into a single string and return the result
    $sessionVars = session_encode();
    echo $sessionVars;
?>
```

This returns the following:

```
username|s:5:"jason";loggedon|s:20:"Feb 16 2004 22:32:29";
```

Keep in mind that session_encode() will encode all session variables available to that user, not just those that were registered within the particular script in which session_encode() executes.

session_decode()

```
boolean session_decode(string session_data)
```

Encoded session data can be decoded with session_decode(). The input parameter session_data represents the encoded string of session variables. The function will decode the variables, returning them to their original format, and subsequently return TRUE on success and FALSE otherwise. As an example, suppose that some session data was stored in a MySQL database, namely each SID and the variables $_SESSION['username'], and $_SESSION['loggedon']. In the following script, that data is retrieved from the table and decoded:

```php
<?php
    session_start();
    $sid = session_id();
    mysql_connect("localhost","user","secret");
    mysql_select_db("chapter16");
    $query = "SELECT data FROM usersession WHERE sid='$sid'";
    $result = mysql_query($query);
    $sessionVars = mysql_result($result,0,"data");
    session_decode($sessionVars);
    echo "User ".$_SESSION['username']." logged on at ".$_SESSION['loggedon'].".";
?>
```

This returns:

```
User jason logged on at Feb 16 2004 22:55:22.
```

Keep in mind that this is not the preferred methodology for storing data in a non-standard media! Rather, you can define custom session handlers, and tie those handlers directly into PHP's API. I'll demonstrate how this is accomplished later in this chapter.

Practical Session-Handling Examples

Now that you're familiar with the basic functions that make all of this work, you can consider a couple of real-world examples. In the first example, I'll show you how to create a mechanism that automatically authenticates returning registered site users. In the second example, I'll demonstrate how session variables can be used to provide the user with an index of recently viewed documents. Both examples are fairly commonplace, which should not come as a surprise given their obvious utility. What may come as a surprise is the ease with which you can create them.

> **NOTE** *If you're unfamiliar with the MySQL server and you're confused by the syntax found in the following example, consider reviewing the material found in Chapters 21, 23, and 26.*

Auto-Login

Once a user has logged in, typically by supplying a username and password that uniquely identifies him, it's often convenient to allow the user to later return to the site without having to repeat the process. You can do this easily using sessions, a few session variables, and a MySQL table. Although there are many ways to implement this feature, I'll opt to just check for an existing session variable (namely $username). If that variable exists, the user can pass transparently into the site. If not, a login form is presented.

> **NOTE** *By default the* session.cookie_lifetime *configuration directive is set to 0, which means that the cookie will not persist if the browser is restarted. Therefore, you should change this value to an appropriate number of seconds in order to make the session persist over a period of time.*

Listing 16-2 offers the MySQL table, which I'll call users. This table contains just a few items of information pertinent to a user profile; In a real-world scenario, you would probably need to expand upon this table to best fit your application requirements.

Listing 16-2. The users Table

```
CREATE table users (
->userid mediumint UNSIGNED NOT NULL AUTO_INCREMENT,
->name varchar(25) NOT NULL,
->username varchar(15) NOT NULL,
->pswd varchar(15) NOT NULL,
->PRIMARY KEY(userid));
```

Listing 16-3 contains the snippet used to present the login form to the user if a valid session is not found.

Listing 16-3. The Login Form (login.html)

```
<p>
    <form method="post" action="<?php echo $_SERVER['PHP_SELF']; ?>">
        Username:<br /><input type="text" name="username" size="10" /><br />
        Password:<br /><input type="password" name="pswd" SIZE="10" /><br />
        <input type="submit" value="Login">
    </form>
</p>
```

Finally, Listing 16-4 contains the login employed to execute the auto-login process.

Listing 16-4. Verifying Login Information Using Sessions

```php
<?php
    session_start();
    // Has a session been initiated previously?
    if (! isset($_SESSION['name'])) {
        // If no previous session, has the user submitted the form?
        if (isset($_POST['username']))
        {
            $username = $_POST['username'];
            $pswd = $_POST['pswd'];
            // Connect to the MySQL server and select the database
            mysql_connect("localhost","webuser","secret");
            mysql_select_db("chapter16");
            // Look for the user in the users table.
            $query = "SELECT name FROM users
                        WHERE username='$username' AND pswd='$pswd'";
            $result = mysql_query($query);
            // If the user was found, assign some session variables.
            if (mysql_numrows($result) == 1)
            {
                $_SESSION['name'] = mysql_result($result,0,"name");
                $_SESSION['username'] = mysql_result($result,0,"username");
                echo "You're logged in. Feel free to return at a later time.";
            }
        // If the user has not previously logged in, show the login form
        } else {
            include "login.html";
        }
    // The user has returned. Offer a welcoming note.
    } else {
        $name = $_SESSION['name'];
        echo "Welcome back, $name!";
    }
?>
```

At a time when users are inundated with the need to remember usernames and passwords for every imaginable type of online service, from checking e-mail to library book renewal to reviewing a bank account, providing an automatic login feature when the circumstances permit will be surely welcomed.

Recently Viewed Document Index

How many times have you returned to a Web site, wondering where exactly to find that great PHP tutorial that you nevertheless forgot to bookmark? Wouldn't it be nice if the Web site were able to remember which articles you read, and present you with a list whenever requested? This example demonstrates such a feature.

The solution is surprisingly easy, yet effective. To remember which documents have been read by a given user, you can require that both the user and each document be identified by a unique identifier. For the user, the SID satisfies this requirement. The documents can be identified really in any way you wish, although for the purposes of this example I'll just use the article's title and URL, and assume that this information is derived from data stored in a database table named articles, which is created in Listing 16-5. The only thing to do is to store the article identifiers in session variables, which is done in Listing 16-6.

Listing 16-5. The articles Table

```
mysql>create table articles (
    ->articleid smallint unsigned not null auto_increment,
    ->title varchar(50),
    ->content mediumtext not null,
    ->primary key(articleid));
```

Listing 16-6. The Article Aggregator

```php
<?php
    // Start session
    session_start();
    // Retrieve requested article id
    $articleid = $_GET['articleid'];
    // Connect to server and select database
    mysql_connect("localhost","webuser","secret");
    mysql_select_db("chapter16");
    // Create and execute query
    $query = "SELECT title, content FROM articles WHERE articleid='$articleid'";
    $result = mysql_query($query);
    // Retrieve query results
    list($title,$content) = mysql_fetch_row($result);
    // Add article title and link to list
    $articlelink = "<a href='article.php?articleid=$articleid'>$title</a>";
    if (! in_array($articlelink, $_SESSION['articles']))
        $_SESSION['articles'][] = "$articlelink";
    // Output list of requested articles
```

```
        echo "<p>$title</p><p>$content</p>";
        echo "<p>Recently Viewed Articles</p>";
        echo "<ul>";
        foreach($_SESSION['articles'] as $doc) echo "<li>$doc</li>";
            echo "</ul>";
    ?>
```

The sample output is shown in Figure 16-1.

"PHP 5 and MySQL: Novice to Pro" hits the book stores today!

Jason Gilmore's new book, "PHP 5 and MySQL: Novice to Pro", covers a wide-range of topics pertinent to both the latest releases of PHP and MySQL.

Recently Viewed Articles

- Man sets record for consecutive hours sleep.
- The Ohio State Buckeyes repeat as national champions!
- "PHP 5 and MySQL: Novice to Pro" hits the book stores today!

Figure 16-1. Tracking a user's viewed documents

Creating Custom Session Handlers

User-defined session-handlers offer the greatest degree of flexibility of the three storage methodologies. But to properly implement custom handlers, you must follow a few implementation rules, regardless of the chosen handling methodology. For starters, six functions must be defined, each of which satisfies one required component of PHP's session-handling functionality. Additionally, parameter definitions for each function must be followed, again regardless of whether your particular implementation makes use of the parameter. In this section, I'll outline the purpose and structure of these six functions. In addition, I'll introduce session_set_save_handler(), the function used to magically transform PHP's session-handler behavior into that defined by your custom handler functions. Finally, I'll conclude the section with a demonstration of this great feature, offering a MySQL-based implementation of these handlers. You can immediately incorporate this library into your own application, rendering a MySQL table as the primary storage location for your session information.

- session_open(*$session_save_path*, *$session_name*): This function initializes any elements that may be used throughout the session process. The two input parameters *$session_save_path* and *$session_name* refer to the configuration directives found in the php.ini. I'll use PHP's get_cfg_var() function to retrieve these configuration values in later examples.

- session_close(): This function operates much like a typical handler function does, closing any open resources initialized by session_open(). As you can see, there are no input parameters for this function. Keep in mind that this does not destroy the session. That is the job of session_destroy(), introduced later in this section.

- session_read(*$sessionID*): This function reads the session data from the storage media. The input parameter *$sessionID* refers to the session ID that will be used to identify the data stored for this particular client.

- session_write(*$sessionID*, *$value*): This function writes the session data to the storage media. The input parameter *$sessionID* is the variable name, and the input parameter *$value* is the session data.

- session_destroy(*$SID*): This function is likely the last function you'll call in your script. It destroys the session and all relevant session variables. The input parameter *$SID* refers to the session ID in the currently open session.

- session_garbage_collect(*$lifetime*): This function effectively deletes all sessions that have expired. The input parameter *$lifetime* refers to the session configuration directive session.gc_maxlifetime, found in the php.ini file.

Tying Custom Session Functions into PHP's Logic

Once the six custom handler functions are defined, they must be tied into PHP's session-handling logic. This is accomplished by passing their names into the function session_set_save_handler(). Keep in mind that these names could be anything the developer chooses, but they must accept the proper number and type of parameters as specified in the previous section, and must be passed into the session_set_save_handler() function in this order: open, close, read, write, destroy, and garbage collect. An example depicting how this function is called follows:

```
session_set_save_handler("session_open", "session_close", "session_read",
                         "session_write", "session_destroy",
                         "session_garbage_collect");
```

In the next section, I'll show you how to create handlers that manage session information within a MySQL database. Once defined, I'll tie the custom functions into PHP's session logic using session_set_save_handler().

Custom MySQL-Based Session Handlers

Two tasks must be completed before the MySQL-based handlers can be deployed. The first is to create a database and table that will be used to store the session data, and the second is to create the six custom handler functions. Listing 16-7 offers the MySQL table sessioninfo. For the purposes of this example, I'll assume that this table is found in the database sessions, although you could place this table where you wish.

Listing 16-7. The MySQL Session Storage Table

```
CREATE TABLE sessionInfo (
    ->SID char(32) NOT NULL,
    ->expiration INT UNSIGNED NOT NULL,
    ->value TEXT NOT NULL,
    ->PRIMARY KEY(SID) );
```

Listing 16-8 provides the custom MySQL session functions. Note that I define each of the requisite handlers, making sure that the appropriate number of parameters is passed into each, regardless of whether those parameters are actually used in the function.

Listing 16-8. The MySQL Session Storage Handler

```php
<?php
  /*
  * mysql_session_open()
  * Opens a persistent server connection and selects the database.
  */

  function mysql_session_open($session_path, $session_name) {
      mysql_pconnect("localhost", "username", "secret")
          or die("Can't connect to MySQL server! ");
      mysql_select_db("sessions")
          or die("Can't select MySQL sessions database");
  } // end mysql_session_open()

  /*
  * mysql_session_close()
  * Doesn't actually do anything since the server connection is
  * persistent. Keep in mind that although this function
  * doesn't do anything in my particular implementation, it
  * must nonetheless be defined.
  */

  function mysql_session_close() {
      return 1;
  } // end mysql_session_close()

  /*
  * mysql_session_select()
  * Reads the session data from the database
  */

  function mysql_session_select($SID) {
      $query = "SELECT value FROM sessioninfo
                  WHERE SID = '$SID' AND
                  expiration > ". time();
      $result = mysql_query($query);
      if (mysql_num_rows($result)) {
```

```
            $row=mysql_fetch_assoc($result);
            $value = $row['value'];
            return $value;
        } else {
            return "";
        }
    } // end mysql_session_select()

    /*
     * mysql_session_write()
     * This function writes the session data to the database.
     * If that SID already exists, then the existing data will be updated.
     */

    function mysql_session_write($SID, $value) {
        $lifetime = get_cfg_var("session.gc_maxlifetime");
        $expiration = time() + $lifetime;
        $query = "INSERT INTO sessioninfo
                    VALUES('$SID', '$expiration', '$value')";
        $result = mysql_query($query);
        if (! $result) {
            $query = "UPDATE sessioninfo SET
                        expiration = '$expiration',
                        value = '$value' WHERE
                        SID = '$SID' AND expiration >". time();
            $result = mysql_query($query);
        }
    } // end mysql_session_write()

    /*
     * mysql_session_destroy()
     * Deletes all session information having input SID (only one row)
     */

    function mysql_session_destroy($SID) {
        $query = "DELETE FROM sessioninfo
                    WHERE SID = '$SID'";
        $result = mysql_query($query);
    } // end mysql_session_destroy()

    /*
     * mysql_session_garbage_collect()
     * Deletes all sessions that have expired.
     */

    function mysql_session_garbage_collect($lifetime) {
        $query = "DELETE FROM sessioninfo
                    WHERE sess_expiration < ".time() - $lifetime;
        $result = mysql_query($query);
        return mysql_affected_rows($result);
    } // end mysql_session_garbage_collect()

?>
```

Once these functions are defined, I can then tie them into PHP's handler logic with a call to `session_set_save_handler()`:

```
session_set_save_handler("mysql_session_open", "mysql_session_close",
                         "mysql_session_select",
                         "mysql_session_write",
                         "mysql_session_destroy",
                         "mysql_session_garbage_collect");
```

To test the custom handler implementation, I'll start a session and register a session variable. I'll use the following script:

```
<?php
    INCLUDE "mysqlsessionhandlers.php";
    session_start();
    $_SESSION['name'] = "Jason";
?>
```

After executing this script, let's take a look at the "sessioninfo" table's contents:

```
mysql> select * from sessioninfo;
+------------------------------------------+--------------------+--------------------+
| SID                                      | expiration         | value              |
+------------------------------------------+--------------------+--------------------+
| f3c57873f2f0654fe7d09e15a0554f08         | 1068488659         | name|s:5:"Jason";  |
+------------------------------------------+--------------------+--------------------+
1 row in set (0.00 sec)
```

As expected, a row has been inserted, mapping the SID to the session variable `"Jason"`. This information is set to expire 1,440 seconds after it was created; This value is calculated by determining the current number of seconds after the Unix epoch, and adding 1,440 to it. Note that although 1,440 is the default expiration setting as defined in the `php.ini` file, you are free to change this value to whatever you deem appropriate.

Note that this is not the only way to implement these procedures as they apply to MySQL. You are free to modify this library as you see fit.

Summary

This chapter covered the gamut of PHP's session-handling capabilities. You learned about many of the configuration directives used to define this behavior, in addition to the most commonly used functions that are used to incorporate this functionality into your applications. I closed the chapter with a real-world example of PHP's user-defined session handlers, showing you how to turn a MySQL table into the session-storage media.

In the next chapter, I'll address another advanced, but highly useful topic: templating. Separating logic from presentation is a topic of constant discussion, as well it should be; intermingling the two practically guarantees you a lifetime of application maintenance anguish. Yet actually achieving such separation seems to be a rare feat when it comes to Web applications. It doesn't have to be this way! In the next chapter, I'll show you several commonly used templating methods.

CHAPTER 17

Templating with Smarty

NO MATTER WHAT prior degree of programming experience we had at the time, the over-whelming majority of us started our Web development careers from the very same place; with the posting of a simple Web page. And boy was it easy. Just add some text to a file, save it with an .html extension, and post it to a Web server. Soon enough, you were incorporating animated gifs, JavaScript, and later a powerful scripting language like PHP into your pages. Your site began to swell, first to five pages, then 15, then 50. It seemed to grow exponentially. Then came that fateful decision, the one you always knew was coming, but always managed to cast aside: it was time to redesign the site.

Unfortunately, perhaps because of the euphoric emotions induced by the need to make your Web site the coolest and largest out there, you forgot one of programming's basic tenets: Never mix presentation and logic. Doing so not only introduces the possi-bility that you'll introduce application errors simply by changing the interface, but also essentially nullifies the possibility that you could trust a designer to autonomously maintain the application's "look and feel" without him first becoming a programmer.

Sound familiar?

Although I'd venture that practically all of us have found ourselves in a similar position, it's also worth noting that many who have actually attempted to implement this key programming principle often experience little success. For no matter the application's intended platform, devising a methodology for managing a uniform pre-sentational interface while simultaneously dealing with the often highly complex code surrounding the application's feature set has long been a very difficult affair. So should you simply resign yourself to a tangled mess of logic and presentation? Certainly not!

Although none are perfect, it turns out that there are actually numerous solutions readily available for managing a Web site's presentational aspects almost entirely sepa-rately from its logic. These solutions are known as *templating engines*, and they go a long way towards eliminating the enormous difficulties otherwise imposed by lack of layer separation. In this chapter, I introduce this topic as it applies to PHP, and in par-ticular concentrate upon what is perhaps the most popular PHP-specific templating solution out there: *Smarty*.

What's a Templating Engine?

As the opening remarks imply, regardless of whether you've actually implemented a templating engine solution, it's likely that you're at least somewhat familiar with the advantages of separating application and presentational logic in this fashion. Nonethe-less, it would probably be useful to formally define exactly what one has to gain through using a templating engine.

Simply put, a templating engine aims to separate an application's business logic from its presentational logic. Doing so is beneficial for several reasons, two of which include:

- You can use a single code-base to generate data for numerous outlets: print, the Web, spreadsheets, e-mail-based reports, and others. The alternative solution would involve copying and modifying the code for each outlet, resulting in considerable code redundancy and greatly reducing manageability.

- The application designer (the individual charged with creating and maintaining the interface) can work almost independently of the application developer, because the presentational and logical aspects of the application are not inextricably intertwined. Furthermore, because the presentational logic used by most templating engines is typically more simplistic than the syntax of whatever programming language is being used for the application, the designer is not required to undergo a crash course in that language in order to perform their job.

But how exactly does a templating engine accomplish this separation? Interestingly, most implementations are practically like programming languages unto themselves, offering a well-defined syntax and command set for carrying out various tasks pertinent to the interface. This *presentational language* is embedded in a series of *templates*, each of which contains the presentational aspects of the application, and would be used to format and output the data provided by the application's logical component. A well-defined *delimiter* signals the location in which the provided data and presentational logic is to be placed within the template. A generalized example of such a template is offered in Listing 17-1. This example is based on the syntax of the Smarty templating engine, which is the ultimate focus of this chapter. All popular templating engines follow a very similar structure, however.

Listing 17-1. A Typical Template (index.tpl)

```
<html>
   <head>
      <title>{$pagetitle}</title>
   </head>
   <body>
   {if $name eq "Kirk"}
      <p>Welcome back Captain!</p>
   {else}
      <p>Swab the decks, mate!</p>
   {/if}
   </body>
</html>
```

There are some important items of note regarding this example. First, the delimiters used are curly brackets ({ }). They serve as a signal to the template engine that the data found between the delimiters should be examined and some action potentially taken. Most commonly, this action is simply the placement of a particular variable value. For example, the $pagetitle variable found within the HTML title tags denotes the location where this value, passed in from the logical component, should be placed. Farther down the page, the delimiters are again used to denote the start and conclusion of an if-conditional to be parsed by the engine. If the passed-in $name variable is set to "Kirk," a special message will appear; otherwise, a default message will be rendered.

Because most templating engine solutions, Smarty included, offer capabilities that go far beyond the simple insertion of variable values, its framework must be able to perform a number of tasks that are otherwise ultimately hidden from both the designer and the developer. Not surprisingly, this is best accomplished via object-oriented programming, in which such tasks can be encapsulated. (See Chapters 6 and 7 for an introduction to PHP's object-oriented capabilities.) In Listing 17-2, I'll provide an example of how Smarty is used in conjunction with the logical layer to prepare and render the index.tpl template shown in Listing 17-1. For the moment, don't worry about where this Smarty class resides; I'll get to that soon. Instead, pay particular attention to the fact that the layers are completely separated, and try to understand how this is done in the example.

Listing 17-2. Invoking a Typical Smarty Template

```php
<?php
    // Reference the Smarty class library.
    require("smarty/Smarty.class.php");
    // Create a new instance of the Smarty class.
    $smarty = new Smarty;
    // Assign a few page variables.
    $smarty->assign("pagetitle","Welcome to the Starship.");
    $smarty->assign("name","Kirk");
    // Render and display the template.
    $smarty->display("index.tpl");
?>
```

As you can see, all of the gory implementation details are completely hidden from both the developer and the designer. Now that I've certainly piqued your interest, let's move on to a more formal introduction of Smarty.

Introducing Smarty

Smarty (http://smarty.php.net/) is PHP's "unofficial-official" templating engine, as you might infer from its homepage location. Smarty was authored by Andrei Zmievski and Monte Orte, and is perhaps the most popular PHP templating engine, and undoubtedly the most powerful. Because it was released under the GNU Lesser General Public License (LGPL, http://www.gnu.org/copyleft/lesser.html), Smarty's users are granted a great degree of flexibility in modifying and redistributing the software, not to mention free use.

In addition to a liberal licensing scheme, Smarty offers a powerful array of features, many of which I'll discuss in this chapter. I'll highlight these features here:

- **Powerful presentational logic:** Smarty offers constructs capable of both conditionally evaluating and iteratively processing data. Although it is indeed a language unto itself, its syntax is such that a designer can quickly pick up on it without prior programming knowledge.

- **Template compilation:** To eliminate costly rendering overhead, Smarty converts its templates into comparable PHP scripts by default, resulting in a much faster rendering upon subsequent calls. Smarty is also intelligent enough to recompile a template if its contents have changed.

- **Caching:** Smarty also offers an optional feature for caching templates. Caching differs from compilation in that enabling caching will also prevent the respective logic from even executing, instead just rendering the cached contents. For example, you can designate a time-to-live for cached documents of say, five minutes, and during that time you can forego database queries pertinent to that template.

- **Highly configurable and extensible:** Smarty's object-oriented architecture allows you to modify and expand upon its default behavior. In addition, configurability has been a design goal from the start, offering users great flexibility in customizing Smarty's behavior through built-in methods and attributes.

- **Secure**: Smarty offers a number of features intended to shield the server and the application data from potential compromise by the designer, intended or otherwise.

Keep in mind that all popular templating solutions follow the same core set of implementation principles. Like programming languages, once you've learned one, you'll generally have an easier time becoming proficient with another. Therefore, even if you've decided that Smarty isn't for you, I still invite you to follow along. The concepts you learn in this chapter will almost certainly apply to any other similar solution. Furthermore, it isn't my intention to parrot the contents of Smarty's extensive manual. Instead, I'd like to highlight Smarty's key features, providing you with a jump-start of sorts regarding the solution, all the while keying on general templating concepts.

Installing Smarty

Installing Smarty is a rather simple affair. To start, go to http://smarty.php.net/ and download the latest stable release. Then follow these instructions to get started using Smarty:

1. Untar and unarchive Smarty to some location outside of your Web document root. Ideally, this location would be the same place where you've placed other PHP libraries for subsequent inclusion into a particular application. For example, on Unix this location might be:

    ```
    /usr/local/lib/php5/includes/smarty/
    ```

    On Windows, this location might be:

    ```
    C:\php5\includes\smarty\
    ```

2. Because you'll need to include the Smarty class library into your application, make sure that this location is available to PHP via the include_path configuration directive. Assuming the above locations, on Unix you should set this directive like so:

    ```
    include_path = ".;/usr/local/lib/php5/includes"
    ```

    On Windows, it would be set as:

    ```
    include_path = ".;c:\php5\includes"
    ```

    Remember that you'll need to restart the Web server after making any changes to PHP's configuration file. Also, note that there are other ways to accomplish the ultimate goal of making sure that your application can reference Smarty's library. For example, you could simply provide the complete absolute path to the class library. Another solution involves setting a predefined constant named SMARTY_DIR that points to the Smarty class library directory, and then prefacing the class library name with this constant. Therefore, if your particular configuration renders it impossible for you to modify the php.ini file, keep in mind that this doesn't necessarily prevent you from using Smarty.

3. Complete the process by creating four directories where Smarty's templates and configuration files will be stored.

    *   templates: This directory will host all site templates. You'll learn more about the structure of these templates in the next section.

    *   configs: This directory hosts any special Smarty configuration files you may use for this particular Web site. I'll introduce the specific purpose of these files in a later section.

- templates_c: This directory hosts any templates compiled by Smarty. In addition to creating this directory, you'll need to change its permissions so that the Web server user (typically "nobody") can write to it.

- cache: This directory hosts any templates cached by Smarty, if this feature is enabled.

Although Smarty will by default assume that these directories reside in your Web application's root directory, it's recommended that you place these directories somewhere outside of your Web server's document root. You can change the default behavior using Smarty's $template_dir, $compile_dir, $config_dir, and $cache_dir class members, respectively. So for example, I could modify their locations like so:

```php
<?php
    // Reference the Smarty class library.
    require("smarty/Smarty.class.php");

    // Create a new instance of the Smarty class.
    $smarty = new Smarty;
    $smarty->template_dir="/usr/local/lib/php5/smarty/template_dir/";
    $smarty->compile_dir="/usr/local/lib/php5/smarty/compile_dir/";
    $smarty->config_dir="/usr/local/lib/php5/smarty/config_dir/";
    $smarty->cache_dir="/usr/local/lib/php5/smarty/cache_dir/";
?>
```

With these three steps complete, you're ready to begin using Smarty. To whet your appetite regarding this great templating engine, I'll begin with a simple usage example, and then delve into some of the more interesting and useful features. Of course, the ensuing discussion will be punctuated throughout with applicable examples.

Using Smarty

Using Smarty is like using any other class library. For starters, you just need to make it available to the executing script. This is accomplished easily enough with the require() statement:

```
require("smarty/Smarty.class.php");
```

With that complete, you can then instantiate the Smarty class:

```
$smarty = new Smarty;
```

That's all you need to do to begin taking advantage of its features. Let's pull this all together in a simple example. Listing 17-3 offers a simple design template. Note that there are two "variables" found in the template: $title and $name. Both are enclosed within curly brackets, which are Smarty's default delimiters. These curly bracket delimiters are a sign to Smarty that it should do something with the delimited contents. In the case of this example, the only action would be to replace the variables with the appropriate values passed in via the application logic (presented in Listing 17-4). However, as you'll soon learn, Smarty is also capable of doing a multitude of other tasks, such as executing presentational logic and modifying the text format.

Listing 17-3. A Simple Smarty Design Template (templates/index.tpl)

```
<!doctype html public "-//w3c//dtd html 3.2//en">
<html>
    <head>
        <title>{$title}</title>
    </head>
    <body bgcolor="#ffffff" text="#000000" link="#0000ff"
          vlink="#800080" alink="#ff0000">
    <p>
    Hi, {$name}. Welcome to the wonderful world of Smarty.
    </p>
    </body>
</html>
```

Also note that Smarty expects this template to reside in the templates directory, unless otherwise noted by a change to the $template_dir member.

Listing 17-4 offers the corresponding application logic, which will pass the appropriate variable values into the Smarty template.

Listing 17-4. The index.tpl Template's Application Logic (index.php)

```
<?php
    require("smarty/Smarty.class.php");
    $smarty = new Smarty;
    // Assign two Smarty variables
    $smarty->assign("name", "Jason Gilmore");
    $smarty->assign("title", "Smarty Rocks!");
    // Retrieve and output the template
    $smarty->display("index.tpl");
?>
```

The resulting output is offered in Figure 17-1.

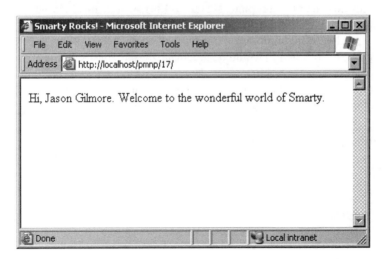

Figure 17-1. The output of Listing 17-4

This elementary example demonstrates Smarty's ability to completely separate the logical and presentational layers of a Web application. However, this is just a smattering of Smarty's total feature set. Before moving on to other topics, I'd like to formally introduce the method used in the previous example to retrieve and render the Smarty template, namely display().

display()

```
void display (string template [, string cache_id [, string compile_id]])
```

This method is ubiquitous within Smarty-based scripts, because it is responsible for the retrieval and display of the template referenced by *template*. The optional parameter *cache_id* specifies the name of the caching identifier. I'll discuss caching in a later section. The other optional parameter, *compile_id*, is used when you want to maintain multiple caches of the same page. This is also discussed in a later section. Because you'll see this method used repeatedly throughout the chapter, I'll forego an example.

Smarty's Presentational Logic

Critics of template engines such as Smarty often complain about the incorporation of some level of logic into the engine's feature set. After all, the idea is to completely separate the presentational and logical layers, right? Although that is indeed the idea, it's not always the most practical solution. For example, without allowing for some sort of iterative logic, how would you output a MySQL result set in a particular format? You couldn't really, at least not without coming up with some rather unwieldy solution. Recognizing this dilemma, the Smarty developers incorporated some rather simplistic, yet very effective application logic into the engine. This is an ideal balance, because Web site designers are often not programmers (and vice versa!).

In this section, you'll learn all about Smarty's impressive presentational features. For organizational reasons, I've separated this discussion into three distinct sections: variable modifiers, control structures, and statements.

Comments

I'll use comments as necessary throughout the remainder of this chapter. Therefore it seems only practical to start by introducing Smarty's comment syntax. Comments are enclosed within the delimiter tags {* and *}, and can consist of a single or multiple lines. A valid Smarty comment follows:

```
{* Some programming note *}
```

Variable Modifiers

As you saw in Chapter 9, PHP offers an extraordinary number of functions capable of manipulating text in just about every which way imaginable. However, you really want to use many of these features from within the presentational layer, for example ensuring that an article author's first and last names are capitalized within the article description. The developer should not always be expected to account for such formatting-specific requirements. As a result, the Smarty developers have incorporated many such presentation-specific capabilities into the library. In this section, I'll introduce many of the more interesting features.

Before starting the overview, I'd like to take a moment to first introduce Smarty's somewhat non-traditional variable modifier syntax. While of course the delimiters are used to signal the requested output of a variable, any variable value requiring modification prior to output followed by a vertical bar, followed by the modifier command, like so:

```
{$var|modifier}
```

You'll see this syntax used repeatedly throughout this section as the modifiers are introduced.

capitalize()

The capitalize function capitalizes the first letter of all words found in a variable. An example follows:

```
$smarty = new Smarty;
$smarty->assign("title", "snow expected in northeast");
$smarty->display("article.tpl");
```

The article.tpl template contains:

```
{$title|capitalize}
```

This returns the following:

```
Snow Expected In Northeast
```

count_words()

The count_words function totals up the number of words found in a variable. An example follows:

```
$smarty = new Smarty;
$smarty->assign("title", "Snow Expected in Northeast.");
$smarty->assign("body", "More than 12 inches of snow is expected to
accumulate overnight in New York.");
$smarty->display("article.tpl");
```

The article.tpl template contains:

```
<strong>{$title}</strong> ({$body|count_words} words)<br />
<p>{$body}</p>
```

This returns:

```
<strong>Snow Expected in Northeast</strong> (10 words)<br />
<p>More than 12 inches of snow is expected to accumulate overnight in New York.</p>
```

date_format()

The date_format function is a wrapper to PHP's strftime() function, and is capable of converting any date/time-formatted string capable of being parsed by strftime() into some special format. Because the formatting flags are documented in the manual, I won't go through the trouble (and paper) to reproduce them. Instead, I'll just provide a usage example:

```
$smarty = new Smarty;
$smarty->assign("title","Snow Expected in Northeast");
$smarty->assign("filed","1072125525");
$smarty->display("article.tpl");
```

The article.tpl template contains:

```
<strong>{$title}</strong><br />
Submitted on: {$filed,"%B %e, %Y"}
```

This returns:

```
<strong>Snow Expected in Northeast</strong><br />
Submitted on: December 22, 2003
```

default()

The default function offers an easy means for designating a default value for a particular variable if the application layer does not return one. For example:

```
$smarty = new Smarty;
$smarty->assign("title","Snow Expected in Northeast");
$smarty->display("article.tpl");
```

The article.tpl template contains:

```
<strong>{$title}</strong><br />
Author: {$author|default:"Anonymous" }
```

This returns:

```
<strong>Snow Expected in Northeast</strong><br />
Author: Anonymous
```

strip_tags()

The strip_tags function removes any markup tags from a variable string. For example:

```
$smarty = new Smarty;
$smarty->assign("title","Snow <strong>Expected</strong> in Northeast");
$smarty->display("article.tpl");
```

The article.tpl template contains:

```
<strong>{$title|strip_tags}</strong>
```

This returns:

```
<strong>Snow Expected in Northeast</strong>
```

---

truncate()

The truncate function truncates a variable string to a designated number of characters. Although the default is 80 characters, you can change it by supplying an input
parameter (demonstrated in the example). You can optionally specify a string that will
be appended to the end of the newly truncated string, for example an ellipsis ("..."). In
addition, you can specify whether the truncation should occur immediately at the designated character limit, or whether a word boundary should be taken into account
(TRUE to truncate at the exact limit, FALSE to truncate at the closest following word
boundary). For example:

```
$summaries = array(
    "Snow expected in the Northeast over the weekend.",
    "Sunny and warm weather expected in Hawaii.",
    "Softball-sized hail reported in Wisconsin."
    );

$smarty = new Smarty;
$smarty->assign("summaries", $summaries);
$smarty->display("article.tpl");
```

The article.tpl template contains:

```
{foreach from=$summaries item=$summary}
    {$summary|truncate:20:"..."|false}<br />
{/foreach}
```

This returns:

```
Snow expected in the...<br />
Sunny and warm weather...<br />
Softball-sized hail...<br />
```

Control Structures

Smarty offers several control structures capable of conditionally and iteratively evaluating passed-in data. I'll review these structures in this section.

if-elseif-else

Smarty's if statement operates much like the identical statement in the PHP language. Like PHP, a number of conditional qualifiers are available, all of which are displayed here:

eq	gt	gte	ge
lt	lte	le	ne
neq	is even	is not even	is odd
is not odd	div by	even by	not
mod	odd by	==	!=
>	<	<=	>=

A simple example follows:

```
{* Assume $dayofweek = 6. *}
{if $dayofweek > 5}
    <p>Gotta love the weekend!</p>
{/if}
```

Consider another example. Suppose you wanted to insert a certain message based on the month. The following example makes use of both conditional qualifiers and the if, elseif, and else statements to carry out this task:

```
{if $month < 4}
   Summer is coming!
{elseif $month ge 4 && $month <= 9}
   It's hot out today!
{else}
   Brrr... It's cold!
{/if}
```

There are a few idiosyncrasies regarding the if, else, and elseif statements. First, the conditional qualifier must always be separated by one space from the operands. Second, you have the choice of enclosing the conditional statement within parentheses, as is required in PHP.

foreach

The foreach tag operates much like the command in the PHP language. As you'll soon see, the syntax is quite different, however. Four parameters are available, two of which are required, and two optional:

- from: This required parameter specifies the name of the target array.

- item: This required parameter determines the name of the current element.

- key: This optional parameter determines the name of the current key.

- name: This optional parameter determines the name of the section. The name is arbitrary and should be set to whatever you deem descriptive of the section's purpose.

Consider an example. Suppose you wanted to loop through the days of the week:

```
require("smarty/Smarty.class.php");
$smarty = new Smarty;
$daysofweek = array("Mon.","Tues.","Weds.","Thurs.","Fri.","Sat.","Sun.");
$smarty->assign("daysofweek", $daysofweek);
$smarty->display("daysofweek.tpl");
```

The daysofweek.tpl file contains:

```
{foreach from=$daysofweek item=day}
    {$day}<br />
{/foreach}
```

This returns the following:

```
Mon.
Tues.
Weds.
Thurs.
Fri.
Sat.
Sun.
```

You can use the key attribute to iterate through an associative array. Consider this example:

```
require("smarty/Smarty.class.php");
$smarty = new Smarty;
$states = array("OH" => "Ohio", "CA" => "California", "NY" => "New York");
$smarty->assign("states",$states);
$smarty->display("states.tpl");
```

The states.tpl template contains:

```
{foreach key=key item=item from=$states }
    {$key}: {$item}<br />
{/foreach}
```

This returns:

```
OH: Ohio
CA: California
NY: New York
```

Although the foreach statement is indeed useful, you should definitely take a moment to learn about the functionally similar, yet considerably more powerful, section statement, introduced later.

foreachelse

The foreachelse tag is used in conjunction with foreach, and operates much like the default tag does for strings, producing some alternative output if the array is empty. An example of a template using foreachelse follows:

```
{foreach key=key item=item from=$titles}
    {$key}: $item}<br />
{foreachelse}
    <p>No states matching your query were found.</p>
{/foreach}
```

Note that foreachelse does not make use of a closing bracket; rather, it is embedded within foreach, much like an elseif is embedded within an if statement.

section

The section function operates in a fashion much like an enhanced for/foreach statement, iterating over and outputting a data array, although the syntax differs significantly. By "enhanced," I mean that it offers the same looping feature as the for/foreach constructs, but with numerous additional options that allow you to exert greater control over the loop's execution. These options are enabled via function parameters. I'll introduce each available option (parameter) here, and then conclude with a few examples:

Two parameters are required:

- name: Determines the name of the section. This is arbitrary and should be set to whatever you deem descriptive of the section's purpose.

- loop: Sets the number of times the loop will iterate. This should be set to the same name as the array variable.

Several optional parameters are also available:

- start: Determines the index position from which the iteration will begin. For example, if the array contains five values, and start is set to 3, then the iteration will begin at index offset 3 of the array. If a negative number is supplied, then the starting position will be determined by subtracting that number from the end of the array.

- step: Determines the stepping value used to traverse the array. By default, this value is 1. For example, setting step to 3 will result in iteration taking place on array indices 0, 3, 6, 9, and so on. Setting step to a negative value will cause the iteration to begin at the end of the array and work backwards.

- max: Determines the maximum number of times loop iteration will occur.

- show: Determines whether or not this section will actually display. You might use this parameter for debugging purposes, and then set it to FALSE upon deployment.

Consider two examples. The first involves iteration over a simple indexed array.

```
require("smarty/Smarty.class.php");
$smarty = new Smarty;
$titles = array(
    "A Programmer's Introduction to PHP 4.0",
    "Practical Python",
    "MySQL"
    );

$smarty->assign("titles",$titles);
$smarty->display("titles.tpl");
```

The titles.tpl template contains:

```
{section name=book loop=$titles}
    {$titles[book]}<br />
{/section}
```

This returns:

```
A Programmer's Introduction to PHP 4.0<br />
Practical Python<br />
MySQL<br />
```

Note the somewhat odd syntax in that the section name must be referenced like an index value would within an array. Also, note that the $titles variable name does double duty, both serving as the reference for the looping indicator and for the actual variable reference.

Now consider an example using an associative array:

```php
require("smarty/Smarty.class.php");
$smarty = new Smarty;
// Create the array
$titles[] = array(
    "title" => "A Programmer's Introduction to PHP 4.0",
    "author" => "Jason Gilmore",
    "published" => "2001"
    );
$titles[] = array(
    "title" => "Practical Python",
    "author" => "Magnus Lie Hetland",
    "published" => "2002"
    );
$smarty->assign("titles", $titles);
$smarty->display("section2.tpl");
```

The section2.tpl template contains:

```
{section name=book loop=$titles}
   <p>Title: {$titles[book].title}<br />
   Author: {$titles[book].author}<br />
   Published: {$titles[book].published}</p>
{/section}
```

This returns:

```
<p>
Title: A Programmer's Introduction to PHP 4.0<br />
Author: Jason Gilmore<br />
Published: 2001
</p>
<p>
Title: Practical Python<br />
Author: Magnus Lie Hetland<br />
Published: 2002
</p>
```

sectionelse

The sectionelse function is used in conjunction with section, and operates much like the default function does for strings, producing some alternative output if the array is empty. An example of a template using sectionelse follows:

```
{section name=book loop=$titles}
    {$titles[book]}<br />
{sectionelse}
    <p>No entries matching your query were found.</p>
{/section}
```

Note that sectionelse does not make use of a closing bracket; rather, it is embedded within section, much like an elseif is embedded within an if statement.

Statements

Smarty offers several statements used to perform special tasks. I'll introduce some of these statements in this section.

include

The include statement operates much like the statement of the same name found in the PHP distribution, except that it is to be used solely for including other templates into the current template. For example, suppose you want to include two files, header.tpl and footer.tpl, into the Smarty template:

```
{include file="/usr/local/lib/pmnp/17/header.tpl"}
{* Execute some other Smarty statements here. *}
{include file="/usr/local/lib/pmnp/17/footer.tpl"}
```

This statement also offers two other features. First, you can pass in the optional assign attribute, which will result in the contents of the included file being assigned to a variable possessing the name provided to assign. For example:

```
{include file="/usr/local/lib/pmnp/17/header.tpl" assign="header"}
```

Rather than outputting the contents of header.tpl, they will be assigned to the variable $header.

A second feature allows you to pass various attributes to the included file. For example, suppose you wanted to pass the attribute title="My home page" to the header.tpl file:

```
{include file="/usr/local/lib/pmnp/17/header.tpl" title="My home page"}
```

Keep in mind that any attributes passed in this fashion are only available within the scope of the included file, and are not available anywhere else within the template.

> **NOTE** *The* fetch *statement accomplishes the same task as* include, *embedding a file into a template, with two differences. First, in addition to retrieving local files,* fetch *can retrieve files using the HTTP and FTP protocols. Second,* fetch *does not have the option of assigning attributes at file retrieval time.*

insert

The insert tag operates in the same capacity as the include tag, except that it's intended to include data that's not meant to be cached. For example, you might use this function for inserting constantly updated data, such as stock quotes, weather reports, or anything else that is likely to change over a short period of time. It also accepts several parameters, one of which is required, and three of which are optional:

- name: Determines the name of the insert function. I'll talk more about this special required parameter shortly.

- assign: This optional parameter can be used when you'd like the output to be assigned to a variable rather than sent directly to output.

- script: This optional parameter can point to a PHP script that will execute immediately before the file is included. You might do this if the output file's contents depends specifically on a particular action performed by the script. For example, you might execute a PHP script that would return certain default stock quotes to be placed into the non-cacheable output.

- var: This optional parameter is used to pass in various other parameters of use to the inserted template. You can pass along numerous parameters in this fashion.

As I alluded to earlier, the name parameter is special. It's used for designating a namespace of sorts specific to the contents intended to be inserted by the insertion statement. When the insert tag is encountered, Smarty will seek to invoke a user-defined PHP function named insert_*name*(), and will pass any variables included with the insert tag via the var parameters to that function. Whatever output is returned from this function will then be output in the place of the insert tag.

Consider an example. Suppose you wanted to insert one of a series of banner advertisements of a specific size within a given location of your template. You might start by creating the function responsible for retrieving the banner id number from the database:

```
function insert_banner($height,$width) {
    $query = "SELECT id FROM banner WHERE height='$height' AND width='$width'
                    ORDER BY RAND() LIMIT 0,1";
    $result = mysql_query($query);
    return mysql_result($result,0,id);
}
```

This banner could then be inserted into the template like so:

```
<img src="/www/htdocs/ads/images/{insert name="banner" height=468 width=60}.gif"/>
```

Once encountered, Smarty will reference any available user-defined PHP function named insert_banner(), and pass it two parameters, namely height and width.

literal

The literal tag signals to Smarty that any data embedded within its tags should be output as-is, without interpretation. It's most commonly used to embed JavaScript and CSS into the template without worrying about clashing with Smarty's assigned delimiter (curly brackets by default). Consider the following example in which some CSS markup is embedded into the template:

```
<html>
<head>
    <title>Welcome, {$user}</title>
    {literal}
        <style type="text/css">
            p {
                margin: 5px;
            }
        </style>
    {/literal}
</head>
...
```

Neglecting to enclose the CSS information within the literal brackets would result in a Smarty-generated parsing error, because it would attempt to make sense of the curly brackets found within the CSS markup (assuming that the default curly-bracket delimiters hasn't been modified).

php

You can use the php function to embed PHP code into the template. Any code found within the {php}{/php} tags will be handled by the PHP engine. An example of a template using this function follows:

```
Welcome to my Web site.<br />
{php}echo date("F j, Y"){/php}
```

The result is:

```
Welcome to my Web site.<br />
December 23, 2003
```

> **NOTE** *A similar, yet more powerful Smarty function also exists, named* include_php.
> *You can use this function to include a separate script containing PHP code into the*
> *template, allowing for cleaner separation. Several other options are available to*
> *this function; consult the Smarty manual for additional details.*

Creating Configuration Files

Developers have long used configuration files as a means for storing data that determines the behavior and operation of an application. For example, the php.ini file is
responsible for determining a great deal of PHP's behavior. With Smarty, template
designers can also take advantage of the power of configuration files. For example,
the designer might use a configuration file for storing page titles, user messages, and
just about any other item you deem worthy of storing in a centralized location.

A sample configuration file (I'll call it app.config) follows:

```
# Global Variables
appName = "PMNP News Service"
copyright = "Copyright 2004 PMNP News Service, Inc."

[Aggregation]
title = "Recent News"
warning = """Copyright warning. Use of this information is for
             personal use only."""

[Detail]
title = "A Closer Look..."
```

The items surrounded by brackets are called *sections*. Any items lying outside of
a section are considered *global*. These items should be defined prior to defining any
sections. In the next section, I'll show you how to use the config_load function to load
in a configuration file, and will also explain how configuration variables are referenced
within templates. Finally, note that the warning variable data is enclosed in triple-
quotes. This syntax must be used in case the string requires multiple lines of the file.

> **NOTE** *Of course, Smarty's configuration files aren't intended to take the place of cas-*
> *cading style sheets (CSS). I recommend using CSS for all matters specific to the site*
> *design (background colors, fonts, and the like), and Smarty configuration files for*
> *matters that CSS is not intended to support, such as page title designations.*

config_load

Configuration files are stored within the `configs` directory, and loaded using the Smarty function `config_load`. Here's how you would load in the example configuration file, `app.config`:

```
{config_load file="app.config"}
```

However, keep in mind that this call will load just the configuration file's global variables. If you'd like to load a specific section, you'll need to designate it using the `section` attribute. So for example, you would use this syntax to load app.config's "Aggregation" section:

```
{config_load file="app.config" section="Aggregation"}
```

Two other optional attributes are also available, both of which are introduced here:

- `scope`: This optional attribute determines the scope of the loaded configuration variables. By default this is set to `local`, meaning that the variables are only available to the local template. Other possible settings include `parent` and `global`. Setting the scope to `parent` makes the variables available to both the local and the calling template. Setting the scope to `global` makes the variables available to all templates.

- `section`: This optional attribute specifies a particular section of the configuration file to load. Therefore, if you're solely interested in a particular section, consider loading just that section rather than the entire file.

Referencing Configuration Variables

Variables derived from a configuration file are referenced a bit differently than other variables. Actually, they can be referenced using several different syntax variations, all of which are introduced in the following sections.

Hash mark

You can reference a configuration variable within a Smarty template by prefacing it with a hash mark (#). For example:

```
{#title}
```

Smarty's `$smarty.config` Variable

If you'd like a somewhat more formal syntax for referencing configuration variables, you can use Smarty's `$smarty.config` variable. For example:

```
{$smarty.config.title}
```

The `get_config_vars()` Method

```
array get_config_vars([string variablename])
```

The get_config_vars() method returns an array consisting of all loaded configuration variable values. If you're interested in just a single variable value, you can pass that variable in as *variablename*. For example, if you were only interested in the $title variable found in the Aggregation section of the above app.config configuration file, you would first load that section using the config_load() function:

```
{config_load file="app.config" section="Aggregation"}
```

You would then call get_config_vars() from within a PHP-enabled section of the template, like so:

```
$title = $smarty->get_config_vars("title");
```

Of course, regardless of the chosen configuration parameter retrieval syntax, don't forget to first load the configuration file using the config_load function.

Using CSS in Conjunction with Smarty

During my initial experimentation with Smarty, it quickly became apparent that there was a clash of syntax between Smarty and CSS, because both depend on the use of curly brackets ({}). Simply embedding CSS tags into the head of an HTML document will result in an "unrecognized tag" error:

```
<html>
<head>
<title>{$title}</title>
<style type="text/css">
    p {
        margin: 2px;
    }
</style>
</head>
...
```

Not to worry, as there are three alternative solutions, and likely there are others as well.

- Use the link tag to pull the style information in from another file:

```
<html>
<head>
    <title>{$title}</title>
    <link rel="stylesheet" type="text/css" href="default.css" />
    </head>
    ...
```

- Use Smarty's literal tag to surround the style sheet information. These tags tell Smarty to not attempt to parse anything within the tag enclosure:

```
<literal>
<style type="text/css">
    p {
        margin: 2px;
    }
</literal>
```

- Change Smarty's default delimiters to something else. You can easily do this by setting the left_delimiter and right_delimiter attributes.

```
<?php
    require("Smarty.class.php");
    $smarty = new Smarty;
    $smarty->left_delimiter = '{{{';
    $smarty->right_delimiter = '{{{';
    ...
?>
```

Although all three solutions resolve the issue, I'd suggest opting for the first, as placing the CSS in a separate file is common practice anyway. In addition, this solution does not require you to modify one of Smarty's key defaults (the delimiter).

Caching

Powerful applications typically require a considerable amount of overhead, often incurred through both costly data retrieval and processing operations. For Web applications, this problem is compounded by the fact that the HTTP protocol is stateless. Thus for every page request, the same operations will be performed repeatedly, regardless of whether the data remains unchanged. This problem is further exacerbated by making the application available on the world's largest network. In an environment, it might not come as a surprise that much ado has been made regarding how to make

Web applications run more efficiently. One particularly powerful solution is also one of the most logical: Convert the dynamic pages into a static version, rebuilding only when the page content has changed or on a regularly recurring schedule. Smarty offers just such a feature, commonly referred to as *page caching*. In this section I'll introduce this feature, and offer a few usage examples.

> **NOTE** *Caching differs from compilation in two ways. First, although compilation reduces overhead by converting the templates into PHP scripts, the actions required for retrieving the data on the logical layer are always executed. Caching reduces overhead on both levels, both eliminating the need to repeatedly execute commands on the logi-cal layer and converting the template contents to a static version. Second, compilation is enabled by default, while caching must be explicitly turned on by the developer.*

If you want to use caching, you'll need to first enable it by setting Smarty's caching attribute like this:

```php
<?php
    require("Smarty.class.php");
    $smarty = new Smarty;
    $smarty->caching = 1;
    $smarty->display("news.tpl");
?>
```

Once enabled, calls to the display() and fetch()methods save the target template's contents in the template specified by the $cache_dir attribute.

Working with the Cache Lifetime

Cached pages remain valid for a lifetime (in seconds) specified by the $cache_lifetime attribute, which has a default setting of 3,600 seconds, or 1 hour. Therefore, if you wanted to modify this setting, you could set it like so:

```php
<?php
    require("Smarty.class.php");
    $smarty = new Smarty;
    $smarty->caching = 1;
    // Set the cache lifetime to 30 minutes.
    $smarty->cache_lifetime = 1800;
    $smarty->display("news.tpl");
?>
```

Any templates subsequently called and cached during the lifetime of this object would assume that lifetime.

It's also useful to override previously set cache lifetimes, allowing you to control cache lifetimes on a per-template basis. You can do so by setting the $caching attribute to 2, like so:

```php
<?php
    require("Smarty.class.php");
    $smarty = new Smarty;
    $smarty->caching = 2;
    // Set the cache lifetime to 20 minutes.
    $smarty->cache_lifetime = 1200;
    $smarty->display("news.tpl");
?>
```

In this case, the news.tpl template's age will be set to 20 minutes, overriding whatever global lifetime value was previously set.

Eliminating Processing Overhead with is_cached()

Earlier in this chapter, I mentioned that caching a template also eliminates processing overhead that is otherwise always incurred when caching is disabled (leaving only compilation enabled). However, this isn't enabled by default. To do so, you need to enclose the processing instructions with an if conditional, and evaluate the is_cached() method, like this:

```php
<?php
    require("Smarty.class.php");
    $smarty = new Smarty;
    $smarty->caching = 1;
    if (!$smarty->is_cached("news.tpl")) {
        $conn = mysql_connect("localhost","news","secret");
        $db = mysql_select_db("news");
        $query = "SELECT rowID, title, author, summary FROM news";
        ...
    }
    $smarty->display("news.tpl");
?>
```

In this example, the news.tpl template's will first be verified as valid. If it is, the costly database access will be skipped. Otherwise, it will be executed.

Creating Multiple Caches per Template

Any given Smarty template might be used to provide a common interface for an entire series of tutorials, news items, blog entries, and the like. Because the same template is used to render any number of distinct items, how can you go about caching multiple instances of a template? The answer is actually easier than you might think. Smarty's developers have actually resolved the problem for you by allowing you to assign a unique identifier to each instance of a cached template via the `display()` method. For example, suppose that you wanted to cache each instance of the template used to render professional boxer's biographies:

```php
<?php
    require("smarty/Smarty.class.php");
    require("boxer.class.php");

    $smarty = new Smarty;

    $smarty->caching = 1;

    try {
        // If the template not already cached, retrieve the appropriate information.
        if (!is_cached("boxerbio.tpl", $_GET['boxerid'])) {
            $bx = new boxer();
            if (! $bx->retrieveBoxer($_GET['boxerid']) )
                throw new Exception("Boxer not found.");
            // Create the appropriate Smarty variables
            $smarty->assign("name", $bx->getName());
            $smarty->assign("bio", $bx->getBio());
        }
        /* Render the template, caching it and assigning it the name
         * represented by $_GET['boxerid']. If already cached, then
         * retrieve that cached template
         */
        $smarty->display("boxerbio.tpl", $_GET['boxerid']);
    } catch (Exception $e) {
        echo $e->getMessage();
    }
?>
```

In particular, take note of this line:

```php
$smarty->display("boxerbio.tpl", $_GET['boxerid']);
```

This line serves double duty for the script, both retrieving the cached version of `boxerbio.tpl` named `$_GET["boxerid"]`, as well as caching that particular template rendering under that name, if it doesn't already exist. Working in this fashion, you can easily cache any number of versions of a given template.

Some Final Words About Caching

Template caching will indeed greatly improve your application's performance, and should seriously be considered if you've decided to incorporate Smarty into your project. However, because most powerful Web applications derive their power from their dynamic nature, you'll need to balance these performance gains with consideration taken for the cached page's relevance as time progresses. In this section I showed you how to manage cache lifetimes on a per-page basis, and execute parts of the logical layer based on a particular cache's validity. Be sure to take these features under consideration for each template.

Summary

Smarty is a powerful solution to a nagging problem that developers face on a regular basis. Even if you don't choose it as your templating engine, I hope that the concepts set forth in this chapter at least convinced you that some templating solution is necessary.

In the next chapter, the fun continues, as we'll turn our attention towards PHP's abilities as applied to one of the newer forces to hit the IT industry in recent years: Web Services. In this chapter, I'll elaborate on a number of interesting new Web Services features both built in to PHP 5 and made available via third-party extensions.

CHAPTER 18

Web Services

THESE DAYS, IT SEEMS as if every few months bring the announcement of some new technology destined to propel each and every one of us into our own personal utopia. You know, the place where all forms of labor are carried out by highly intelligent machines, where software writes itself, and I'm left to do nothing but lie on the beach and have grapes fed to me by well-endowed androids? Most recently, the set of technologies collectively referred to as "Web Services" has been crowned as the keeper of this long-awaited promise. And although the verdict is still out as to whether Web Services will live up to the enormous hype that has surrounded them, there are some very interesting advancements being made in this arena that have drastically changed the way that we think about both software and data within our newly networked world. In this chapter, I'm going to talk about some of the more applicable implementations of Web Services' technologies, and show you how to use PHP to start incorporating them into your Web application development strategy *right now*.

In order to accomplish this goal without actually turning this chapter into a book unto itself, let me start by saying that I do not intend to offer an in-depth introduction to the general concept of Web Services. Devoting a section of this chapter to the matter simply does the topic little justice, and in fact would likely do more harm than good. For a comprehensive introduction, please consult any of the many quality printed and online resources that are devoted to the topic. If you're new to the topic, and are looking for a place to start, I've included a list of my favorite online references at the conclusion of this chapter.

Nonetheless, even if you have no prior experience or knowledge of Web Services, I think that you'll find the discussion in this chapter to be quite easy to comprehend. My intention here is to demonstrate the utility of Web Services through numerous practical demonstrations, employing the use of two great third-party PHP class libraries: Magpie and NuSOAP. I'll also introduce the SOAP and SimpleXML extensions, both of which are new to PHP 5. Specifically I'll discuss the following topics:

- **Why Web Services?** For the uninitiated, I very briefly touch upon the reasons for all of the work behind Web Services, and how they will change the landscape of application development.

- **Real Simple Syndication (RSS):** The forefathers of the World Wide Web had little idea that their accomplishments in this area would lead to what is certainly one of the greatest technological leaps in the history of mankind. However, the extraordinary popularity of the medium caused the capabilities of the original mechanisms to be stretched in ways never intended by their creators. As a result, new methods for publishing information over the Web have emerged, and are starting to have as great an impact on the way we retrieve and review data as did their predecessors. One such technology is known as Real Simple Syndication, or RSS. In this section, I'll introduce RSS, and demonstrate how you can incorporate RSS feeds into your development acumen using a great tool called Magpie.

- **SimpleXML:** New to version 5, the SimpleXML extension offers a new and highly practical methodology for parsing XML. In this section I'll introduce this new feature, and offer several practical examples demonstrating its powerful and intuitive capabilities.

- **SOAP:** The SOAP protocol plays an enormously important role in the implementation of Web Services. I'll touch upon its advantages, and offer an in-depth look into one of the coolest PHP add-ons that I've seen in a while: NuSOAP. In this section you'll learn how to create PHP-based Web Services clients and servers, as well as integrate a PHP Web Service with a C# client. In this section, I'll also introduce PHP's SOAP extension, new to version 5.

> **NOTE** *In several of the examples found throughout this chapter, I reference the URL* `http://www.example.com/`. *When testing these examples, you'll need to change this URL to the appropriate location of the Web Service files on your server.*

Why Web Services?

I've often raised the point that only an academician could have come up with the term *Computer Science*. And indeed it was, because the term is attributed to the visionary George Forsythe, founding head of the Stanford University Computer Science Department. I make this statement only partly in jest, because for those of us in the trenches, there is little doubt that our daily travails often sway more towards the path of artisan than of scientist. This is evident in the way that software has historically been designed. Although the typical developer generally adheres to a loosely defined set of practices and tools, much as an artist generally works with a particular medium and style, he tends to do his own thing and create software in the way he sees most fit. As such, it doesn't come as a surprise that although many programs resemble one another, they rarely follow the same set of rigorous principles such as those scientists might employ when carrying out similar experiments. Numerous deficiencies arise as a result of this refusal to follow generally accepted programming principles, with software being developed at a cost of maintainability, scalability, extensibility, and perhaps most notably, interoperability.

This problem of interoperability has become even more pronounced over the past few years, given the incredible opportunities for cooperation that the Internet has opened up to businesses around the world. However, fully exploiting an online business partnership often, if not always, involves some level of system integration. Therein lies the problem; if the system designers never consider the possibility that they might one day need to tightly integrate their application with another, how will they ever really be able to exploit the Internet to its fullest advantage? Indeed this has been a subject of considerable discussion almost from the onset of this new electronic age.

The proposed solution, collectively referred to as Web Services, is promising. Rather than offer up my own formalized definition of the term, I'll instead defer to the excellent interpretation provided in the W3C's Web Services Architecture document, currently a working draft (http://www.w3.org/TR/ws-arch/):

> *A Web Service is a software system designed to support interoperable machine-to-machine interaction over a network. It has an interface described in a machine-processable format (specifically WSDL). Other systems interact with the Web Service in a manner prescribed by its description using SOAP-messages, typically conveyed using HTTP with an XML serialization in conjunction with other Web-related standards.*

I realize that some of these terms may be alien to the newcomer; not to worry, I'll touch upon them further in a bit. What is important is to keep in mind is that Web Services open up endless possibilities to the enterprise, a sampling of which follow:

- **Software as a service.** Imagine building an e-commerce application that required a means for converting currency among various exchange rates. However, rather than take it upon yourself to devise some means for automatically scraping the Federal Reserve Bank's Web page (http://www.federalreserve.gov/releases/) for the daily released rate, you instead plug in to their (hypothetical) Web Service for retrieving these values. The result is far more readable code, with much less chance for error from presentational changes on the Web page.

- **Say goodbye to Enterprise Application Integration (EAI) as we know it.** Developers currently are forced to devote enormous amounts of time to hacking together one-off solutions to integrate disparate applications. Contrast this with connecting two Web Service–enabled applications, in which the process is highly standardized and based on tried-and-true practices.

- **Write once, reuse everywhere.** Because Web Services offer platform-agnostic interfaces to exposed application methods, they can be simultaneously used by applications running on disparate operating systems. For example, a Web Service running on an e-commerce server might be used to both keep the CEO abreast of inventory numbers via a Windows-based application as well as by a Perl script running on a Linux server that generates daily e-mails to the suppliers.

- **Ubiquitous access.** Because Web Services typically travel over the HTTP protocol, firewalls can by bypassed because port 80 (and 443 for HTTPS) traffic is almost always allowed. Although debate is currently underway as to whether this is really prudent, for the moment it is indeed an appealing solution to the often difficult affair of firewall penetration.

Such capabilities are tantalizing to the developer. Believe it or not, as I'll demonstrate throughout this chapter, you can actually begin taking advantage of Web Services right now.

Ultimately, only one metric will determine the success of Web Services: acceptance. Interestingly, two global companies have already made quite a stir by offering Web Services application programming interfaces (APIs) to their treasured data stores. These companies, the online superstore Amazon.com (`http://www.amazon.com/`) and the famed Google search engine (`http://www.google.com/`), have stirred the imagination of the programming industry with their freely available standards-based Web Services. Since their release, both implementations have sparked the imaginations of programmers worldwide, who have gained valuable experience working with a well-designed Web Services architecture plugged into an enormous amount of data. Given such high-profile deployments, it isn't hard to imagine that other companies will soon follow.

Because these APIs are already widely used within other books and online tutorials, I've opted to instead make use of other examples for the sake of variety. Don't let that stop you from taking the time to experiment with them, however. You can learn more about the Amazon.com and Google APIs via the following links:

```
http://www.amazon.com/webservices/
http://www.google.com/apis/
```

RSS

Given that the entire concept of Web Services largely sprung out of the notion that XML- and HTTP-driven applications would be harnessed to power the next generation of business-to-business applications, it's rather ironic that the first widespread implementation of the Web Services technologies happened on the end-user level. *Real Simple Syndication* (RSS), solves a number of problems that both Web developers and Web users have faced for years.

On the end-user level, all of us can relate to the considerable amount of time consumed by our daily surfing ritual. Most people have a stable of Web sites that they visit on a regular basis, and in some cases, several times daily. For each site, the process is almost identical: visit the URL, weave around a sea of advertisements, navigate to the section of interest, and finally, actually read the news story. Repeat this process numerous times, and the next thing you know, a fair amount of time has passed. Furthermore, given the highly tedious process, it's easy to neglect a particular information resource for days, potentially missing something of interest. In short, leave the process to a human, and something is bound to get screwed up.

Developers face an entirely different set of problems. Once upon a time, attracting users to your Web site involved spending enormous amounts of money on prime-time commercials, magazine layouts, and throwing lavish holiday galas. Then the novelty wore out (and the cash disappeared), and those in charge of the Web sites were forced to actually produce something substantial for their site visitors. Furthermore, they had to do so while working within the constraints of bandwidth limitations, the myriad of Web-enabled devices that sprung up, and an increasingly finicky (and time-pressed) user. Enter RSS.

Who's Publishing in RSS?

Believe it or not, RSS has actually officially been around since early 1999, and in previous incarnations since 1996. However, like many emerging technologies, it remained a niche tool of the "techie" community, at least until recently. The emergence and growing popularity of news aggregation sites and tools has prompted an explosion in terms of the creation and publication of RSS feeds around the Web. These days, you can find RSS feeds just about everywhere, including within these prominent organizations:

- **Yahoo! News:** `http://news.yahoo.com/rss/`

- **Christian Science Monitor:** `http://www.csmonitor.com/rss/`

- **News.com:** `http://www.news.com/`

- **The BBC:** `http://www.bbc.co.uk/syndication/`

- **Wired.com:** `http://www.wired.com/news/rss/`

Given the adoption of RSS in such circles, it isn't really a surprise that we're hearing so much about this great technology these days.

RSS offers a formalized means for encapsulating a Web site's content within an XML-based structure, known as a *feed*. It's based on the premise that most site information shares a similar format, regardless of topic. For example, although sports, weather, and theater are all vastly dissimilar topics, the news items published under each would share a very similar structure, including a title, author, publish date, URL, and description. A typical RSS feed embodies all such attributes and often much more, forcing an adherence to a presentation-agnostic format that can in turn be retrieved, parsed, and formatted in any means acceptable to the end-user, without actually having to visit the syndicating Web site. With just the feed's URL, the user can store it, along with others if he likes, into a tool capable of retrieving and parsing the feed allowing the user to do as he pleases with the information. Working in this fashion, you can use RSS feeds to:

- Browse the rendered feeds using a standalone RSS aggregator application. Examples of popular aggregators include: NewsGator (`http://www.newsgator.com/`), AmphetaDesk (`http://www.disobey.com/amphetadesk/`) and SharpReader (`http://www.sharpreader.net/`). A screenshot of the SharpReader application is shown in Figure 18-1.

- Subscribe to any of the numerous Web-based RSS aggregators, and view the feeds via a Web browser. Examples of popular online aggregators include: NewsIsFree (`http://www.newsisfree.com/`), Bloglines (`http://www.bloglines.com/`), and Feedster (`http://www.feedster.com/`)

- Retrieve and republish the syndicated feed as part of a third-party Web application or service. Moreover Technologies (http://www.moreover.com/) is an excellent example of such a service. Another popular use involves simply incorporating a rendered feed into your own Web site, taking the opportunity to provide additional third-party content to your readers. Later in this section, I'll demonstrate how this is accomplished using the Magpie RSS class library.

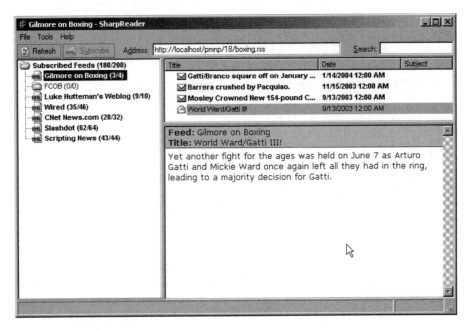

Figure 18-1. The SharpReader interface, created by Luke Hutteman

Sample RSS Syntax

If you're not familiar with the general syntax of an RSS feed, Listing 18-1 offers an example. I'll use this example as a basis for the demonstrations that follow. Although a discussion of RSS syntax specifics is out of the scope of this book, I think that you'll find the structure and tags to be quite intuitive (after all, that's why they call it "Real Simple Syndication").

Listing 18-1. A Sample RSS Feed (boxing.xml)

```
<?xml version="1.0" ?>
<rss version="2.0">
<channel>
    <title>Gilmore on Boxing</title>
    <description>Keen insight into the world of professional
    boxing.</description>
    <link>http://www.gilmoreonboxing.com/</link>
    <item>
```

```
    <title>Mosley Crowned New 154-pound Champion.</title>
    <link>http://www.gilmoreonboxing.com/cs/134</link>
    <description>Shane Mosley came out on top of a bitterly
    contested decision against Oscar De La Hoya for the
    154-pound championship.</description>
    <pubDate>Sat, September 13, 2003 11:56:34 EST</pubDate>
  </item>
  <item>
    <title>World Ward/Gatti III!</title>
    <link>http://www.gilmoreonboxing.com/cs/112</link>
    <description>Yet another fight for the ages was held
    on June 7 as Arturo Gatti and Mickie Ward once again
    left all they had in the ring, leading to a majority
    decision for Gatti.</description>
    <pubDate>Sat, September 6, 2003 23:57:34 EST</pubDate>
  </item>
</channel>
</rss>
```

Now that you're a bit more familiar with the purpose and advantages of RSS, I'll show you how to use PHP to incorporate it into your own development strategy. Although there are numerous RSS tools written for the PHP language, I'm partial to one in particular, and have incorporated it into numerous applications. It's known as Magpie, I'll introduce it next.

MagpieRSS

MagpieRSS is a powerful RSS parser written in PHP by Kellan Elliott-McCrea. It's freely available for download via http://magpierss.sourceforge.net/, and distributed under the GPL license. Magpie offers developers an amazingly practical and easy means for retrieving and rendering RSS feeds, as you'll soon see. In addition, Magpie offers a number of cool features, including:

- **Simple:** Magpie gets the job done with a minimum of effort by the developer. For example, a few lines of code is all it takes to begin retrieving, parsing, and converting RSS feeds into an easily readable format.

- **Non-validating:** If the feed is well formed, Magpie will successfully parse it. This means that it supports all tag sets found within the various RSS versions, as well as your own custom tags.

- **Bandwidth-friendly:** By default, Magpie caches feed contents for 60 minutes, cutting down on use of unnecessary bandwidth. You're free to modify the default to fit caching preferences on a per-feed basis (which I'll demonstrate later). If retrieval is requested after the cache has expired, Magpie will only retrieve the feed if it has been changed (by checking the Last-modified and ETag headers provided by the Web server). In addition, Magpie recognizes HTTP's GZIP content negotiation ability when supported.

Installing Magpie

Like most PHP classes, installing Magpie is as simple as placing the relevant files within a directory that can later be referenced from a PHP script. The instructions for doing so follow:

1. Download Magpie from `http://magpierss.sourceforge.net/`.

2. Extract the package contents to a location convenient for inclusion from a PHP script. I typically like to place third-party classes within an aptly named directory located within the `PHP_INSTALL_DIR/includes/` directory.

3. Include the Magpie class (`rss_fetch.inc`) within your script:

    ```
    require('magpie/rssfetch.php');
    ```

That's it! You're ready to begin using Magpie.

How Magpie Parses a Feed

Magpie parses a feed by placing it into a single object consisting of four fields: `channel`, `image`, `items`, and `textinput`. In turn, `channel` is an array of associative arrays, while the remaining three are associative arrays. I'll now retrieve the `boxing.xml` feed, and output it using the `print_r()` statement:

```php
<?php
    require("magpie/rss_fetch.inc");
    $url = "http://localhost/pmnp/18/boxing.xml";
    $rss = fetch_rss($url);
    print_r($rss);
?>
```

This returns the following (containing only one item for readability):

```
magpierss Object (
    [parser] => Resource id #6
    [current_item] => Array ( )
    [items] => Array (
        [0] => Array (
        [title] => Gatti/Branco square off on January 24th.
        [link] => http://www.gilmoreonboxing.com/cs/125/
        [description] => Brawler Arturo Gatti (36-6) and
        undefeated Gianluca Branco (32-0-1)
        will battle it out on January 24th for the vacant WBC 140-pound title.
        [pubdate] => Wed, January 14, 2004 14:18:50 EST )
    )
    [channel] => Array (
        [title] => Gilmore on Boxing
```

```
     [description] => Keen insight into the world of professional boxing.
     [link] => http://www.gilmoreonboxing.com/
 )
 [textinput] => Array ( )
 [image] => Array ( )
 [parent_field] =>
 Array ( [0] => RDF )
     [current_field] =>
     [current_namespace] =>
     [ERROR] =>
     [last_modified] => Fri, 16 Jan 2004 20:27:31 GMT [etag] =>
                        "2686-27e-6efcae61"
 )
```

Note the presence of the four object attributes. Two of them contain data (items and channel), while the other two are empty. Also note that items is an array of associative arrays, even if only one item is present. In the following examples, I'll demonstrate how the data is peeled from this object and presented in various fashions.

Retrieving an RSS Feed

Based on your knowledge of Magpie's parsing behavior, rendering the feed components should be trivial. Listing 18-2 demonstrates how easy it is to render a retrieved feed within a standard browser.

Listing 18-2. Rendering an RSS Feed with Magpie

```php
<?php
require("magpie/rss_fetch.inc");

// RSS feed location?
$url = "http://localhost/pmnp/18/boxing.xml";
// Retrieve the feed
$rss = fetch_rss($url);

// Format the feed for the browser
$feedTitle = $rss->channel['title'];
echo "Latest News from <strong>$feedTitle</strong>";
foreach ($rss->items as $item) {
    $link = $item['link'];
    $title = $item['title'];
    // Not all items necessarily have a description, so test for one.
    $description = isset($item['description']) ? $item['description'] : "";
    echo "<p><a href=\"$link\">$title</a><br />$description</p>";
}

?>
```

Note that Magpie does all of the hard work of parsing the RSS document, placing the data into easily referenced arrays. Figure 18-2 shows the fruits of this script.

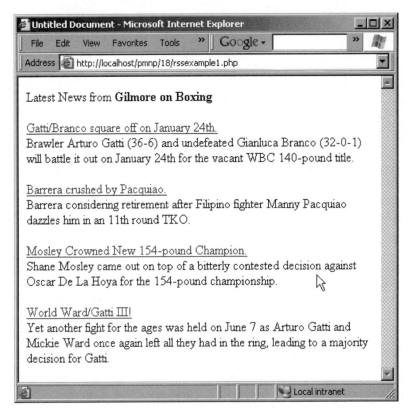

Figure 18-2. Rendering an RSS feed within the browser

Aggregating Feeds

Of course, chances are you're going to want to aggregate multiple feeds and devise some means for viewing them simultaneously. To do so, you can simply modify the Listing 18-2, passing in an array of feeds. I've also added a bit of CSS in order to shrink the space required for output. Listing 18-3 shows the rendered version.

Listing 18-3. Aggregating Multiple Feeds with Magpie

```
<style><!--
p { font: 11px arial,sans-serif; margin-top: 2px;}
//-->
</style>

<?php
require("magpie/rss_fetch.inc");

// Compile array of feeds
$feeds = array(
"http://localhost/pmnp/18/round1/boxing.xml",
"http://news.com.com/2547-1_3-0-5.xml",
"http://slashdot.org/slashdot.rdf");

// Iterate through each feed
foreach ($feeds as $feed) {

    // Retrieve the feed
    $rss = fetch_rss($feed);

    // Format the feed for the browser
    $feedTitle = $rss->channel['title'];
    echo "<p><strong>$feedTitle</strong><br />";

    foreach ($rss->items as $item) {
        $link = $item['link'];
        $title = $item['title'];
        $description = isset($item['description']) ? $item['description'].
                    "<br />" : "";
        echo "<a href=\"$link\">$title</a><br />$description";
    }
    echo "</p>";

}

?>
```

Figure 18-3 depicts the output based on these three feeds.

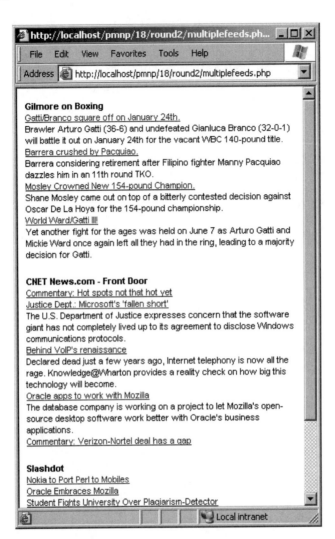

Figure 18-3. Aggregating feeds

Although the use of a static array for containing feeds certainly works, it might be more practical to maintain them within a database table, or at the very least a text file. It really all depends upon the number of feeds you'll be using, and how often you intend on managing the feeds themselves.

Limiting the Number of Displayed Headlines

Some Web site developers are so keen on RSS that they wind up dumping quite a bit of information into their published feeds. However, you might only be interested in viewing only the most recent items, and ignoring the rest. Because Magpie relies heavily on standard PHP language features such as arrays and objects for managing RSS data, limiting the number of headlines is trivial because you can call upon one of PHP's default array functions for the task. The function array_slice() should do the job quite nicely. For example, suppose you want to limit total headlines displayed for a given feed to three. You can use array_slice() to truncate it prior to iteration like so:

```
$rss->items = array_slice($rss->items, 0, 3);
```

Revising the previous script to include this call results in output similar to that shown in Figure 18-4.

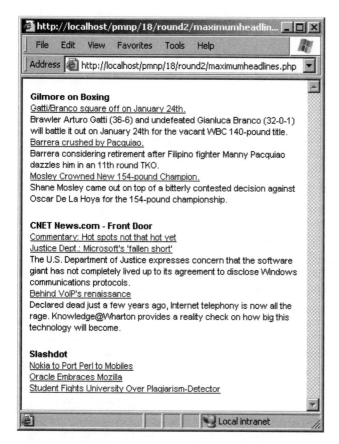

Figure 18-4. Limiting the number of headlines for each feed

Caching Feeds

One final topic I'd like to discuss regarding Magpie is its caching feature. By default, Magpie will cache feeds for sixty minutes, on the premise that the typical feed will likely not be updated more than once per hour. However, some feeds are published more than once an hour, or the feed might be used to publish somewhat more pressing information. (RSS feeds don't necessarily have to be used for browsing news headlines; you could use them to publish information about system health, logs, or any other data that could be adapted to its structure.) In such cases, you may want to consider modifying the default behavior.

To completely disable caching, disable the constant MAGPIE_CACHE_ON, like so:

```
define('MAGPIE_CACHE_ON', 0);
```

To change the default cache time (measured in seconds), you can modify the constant MAGPIE_CACHE_AGE, like so:

```
define('MAGPIE_CACHE_AGE',1800);
```

Finally, you can opt to display an error instead of a cached feed in the case that the fetch fails by enabling the constant MAGPIE_CACHE_FRESH_ONLY:

```
define('MAGPIE_CACHE_FRESH_ONLY', 1)
```

You can also change the default cache location (by default the same location as the executing script), done by modifying the MAGPIE_CACHE_DIR constant:

```
define('MAGPIE_CACHE_DIR', '/tmp/magpiecache/');
```

SimpleXML

Everyone agrees that XML signifies an enormous leap forward in data management and application interoperability. Yet how come it's so darned hard to parse? Although powerful parsing solutions are readily available, DOM, SAX, and XSLT to name a few, each presents a learning curve that is just steep enough to cause considerable gnashing of the teeth among those users interested in taking advantage of XML's practicalities without an impractical time investment. Leave it to an enterprising PHP user to come up with a solution. SimpleXML offers users a very practical and intuitive methodology for processing XML structures, and is enabled by default as of PHP 5. Parsing even complex structures becomes a trivial task, accomplished by loading the document into an object, and then accessing the nodes using field references as you would in typical object-oriented fashion.

I'll use the XML document displayed in Listing 18-4 to illustrate the examples offered in this section.

Listing 18-4. A Simple XML Document

```
<?xml version="1.0" standalone="yes"?>
<library>
    <book>
        <title>Pride and Prejudice</title>
        <author gender="female">Jane Austen</author>
        <description>Jane Austen's most popular work.</description>
    </book>
    <book>
        <title>The Conformist</title>
        <author gender="male">Alberto Moravia</author>
        <description>Alberto Moravia's classic psychological novel.</description>
    </book>
    <book>
        <title>The Sun Also Rises</title>
        <author gender="male">Ernest Hemingway</author>
        <description>The masterpiece that launched Hemingway's
        career.</description>
    </book>
</library>
```

SimpleXML Functions

A number of SimpleXML functions are available for loading and parsing the XML document. I'll introduce those functions in this section, presenting them in a logical order, and several accompanying examples. Once you're acquainted with these functions, I'll offer some real-world examples illustrating SimpleXML's practical implementation.

simplexml_load_file()

```
object simplexml_load_file (string filename)
```

This function loads an XML file specified by *filename* into an object. If a problem is encountered loading the file, FALSE is returned. Consider an example:

```
<?php
    $xml = simplexml_load_file("books.xml");
    var_dump($xml);
?>
```

This code returns:

```
object(simplexml_element)#1 (1) {
["book"]=> array(3) {
   [0]=> object(simplexml_element)#2 (3) {
      ["title"]=> string(19) "Pride and Prejudice"
      ["author"]=> string(11) "Jane Austen"
      ["description"]=> string(32) "Jane Austen's most popular work."
   }
   [1]=> object(simplexml_element)#3 (3) {
      ["title"]=> string(14) "The Conformist"
      ["author"]=> string(15) "Alberto Moravia"
      ["description"]=> string(46) "Alberto Moravia's classic
                                 psychological novel."
   }
   [2]=> object(simplexml_element)#4 (3) {
      ["title"]=> string(18) "The Sun Also Rises"
      ["author"]=> string(16) "Ernest Hemingway"
      ["description"]=> string(56) "The masterpiece that launched
                                 Hemingway's career."
   }
  }
 }
}
```

Note that dumping the XML will not cause the attributes to show. To view attributes, you'll need to use the `attributes()` method, introduced later in this section.

simplexml_load_string()

`object simplexml_load_string (string *data*)`

If the XML document is stored in a variable, you can use the `simplexml_load_string()` function to read it into the object. This function is identical in purpose to `simplexml_load_file()`, except that the lone input parameter is expected in the form of a string rather than a file name.

simplexml_import_dom()

`object simplexml_import_dom(domNode *node*)`

The Document Object Model (DOM) is a W3C specification offering a standardized API for creating an XML document, and subsequently navigating, adding, modifying, and deleting its elements. PHP provides an extension capable of managing XML documents using this standard, titled the DOM XML extension. You can use this function to convert a node of a DOM document into a SimpleXML node, subsequently exploiting use of the SimpleXML functions to manipulate that node.

SimpleXML Methods

Once an XML document has been loaded into an object, several methods are at your disposal. Presently four methods are available, each of which is introduced here.

attributes()

```
object simplexml_element->attributes()
```

XML attributes provide additional information about an XML element. In the sample XML document in Listing 18-4, only the author node possesses an attribute, namely gender, used to offer information about the author's gender. You can use the attributes() method to retrieve these attributes. For example, suppose you wanted to retrieve the gender of each author:

```php
<?php
    $xml = simplexml_load_file("books.xml");
    foreach($xml->book as $book) {
        echo $book->author." is ".$book->author->attributes().".<br />";
    }
?>
```

This example returns:

```
Jane Austen is female.
Alberto Moravia is male.
Ernest Hemingway is male.
```

You can also directly reference a particular book author's gender. For example, suppose you want to determine the gender of the author of the second book in the XML document:

```
echo $xml->book[2]->author->attributes();
```

This example returns:

```
male
```

Often a node will possess more than one attribute. For example, suppose the author node looked like this:

```
<author gender="female" age="20">Jane Austen</author>
```

It's easy to output the attributes with a for loop:

```
foreach($xml->book[0]->author->attributes() AS $a => $b) {
    echo "$a = $b <br />";
}
```

This example returns:

```
gender = female
age = 20
```

asXML()

```
string simplexml_element->asXML()
```

This method returns a well-formed XML 1.0 string based on the SimpleXML object. An example follows:

```
<?php
    $xml = simplexml_load_file("books.xml");
    echo htmlspecialchars($xml->asXML());
?>
```

This example returns the original XML document, except that the newline characters have been removed, and the characters have been converted to their corresponding HTML entities.

children()

```
object simplexml_element->children()
```

Often you might only be interested in a particular node's children. Using the children() method, retrieving them becomes a trivial affair. Suppose for example that the books.xml document was modified so that each book included a cast of characters. The Hemingway book might look like the following:

```
<book>
    <title>The Sun Also Rises</title>
    <author gender="male">Ernest Hemingway</author>
    <description>The masterpiece that launched Hemingway's
    career.</description>
    <cast>
        <character>Jake Barnes</character>
        <character>Lady Brett Ashley</character>
        <character>Robert Cohn</character>
        <character>Mike Campbell</character>
    </cast>
</book>
```

Using the `children()` method, you can easily retrieve the characters:

```php
<?php
   $xml = simplexml_load_file("books.xml");
   foreach($xml->book[2]->cast->children() AS $character) {
      echo "$character<br />";
   }
?>
```

This example returns:

```
Jake Barnes
Lady Brett Ashley
Robert Cohn
Mike Campbell
```

---

xpath()

`array simplexml_element->xpath(string path)`

XPath is a W3C standard that offers an intuitive path-based syntax for identifying XML nodes. For example, referring to the `books.xml` document, you could retrieve all author nodes using the expression: `/library/book/author`. It also offers a set of functions for selectively retrieving nodes based on value.

Suppose you want to retrieve all authors found in the `books.xml` document:

```php
<?php
   $xml = simplexml_load_file("books.xml");
   $authors = $xml->xpath("/library/book/author");
   foreach($authors AS $author) {
      echo "$author<br />";
   }
?>
```

This example returns:

```
Jane Austen
Alberto Moravia
Ernest Hemingway
```

You can also use XPath functions to selectively retrieve a node and its children based on a particular value. For example, suppose you want to retrieve all book titles where the author is named "Ernest Hemingway":

```php
<?php
   $xml = simplexml_load_file("books.xml");
   $book = $xml->xpath("/library/book[author='Ernest Hemingway']");
   echo $book[0]->title;
?>
```

449

This example returns:

```
The Sun Also Rises
```

SOAP

The postal service is amazingly effective at transferring a package from party A to party B, but its only concern is ensuring the safe and timely transmission. They are oblivious to the nature of the transaction, provided that it is in accordance with the postal service's terms of service. As a result, I could send a letter written in English to a fisherman in China, and that letter will indeed arrive without issue, but the recipient would probably not understand a word of it. The same holds true if the fisherman sent me a letter written in his native language; I wouldn't even know where to begin.

This isn't unlike what might occur if two applications attempt to talk to each other across a network. Although they could employ messaging protocols like HTTP and SMTP in much the same way that we make use of the postal service, it's quite unlikely one will be able to say anything of discernible interest to the other. However, if the parties agreed to send data using the same messaging language, and both were capable of understanding messages sent to them, then the dilemma is resolved. Granted, both parties might go about their own way of interpreting that language (more about that in a bit), but nonetheless the commonality is all that's needed to ensure comprehension. Web Services often employ the use of something called SOAP as that common language. Here's the formalized definition of SOAP, as stated within the SOAP 1.2 specification (`http://www.w3.org/TR/SOAP/`):

> *SOAP is a lightweight protocol intended for exchanging structured information in a decentralized, distributed environment. SOAP uses XML technologies to define an extensible messaging framework, which provides a message construct that can be exchanged over a variety of underlying protocols. The framework has been designed to be independent of any particular programming model and other implementation specific semantics.*

Keep in mind that SOAP is only responsible for defining the construct used for the exchange of messages; it does not define the protocol used to transport that message, nor does it describe the features or purpose of the Web Service used to send or receive that message. This means that you could conceivably use SOAP over any protocol, and in fact could route a SOAP message over numerous protocols during the course of transmission. A sample SOAP message is offered in Listing 18-5 (formatted for readability):

Listing 18-5. A Sample SOAP Message

```
<?xml version="1.0" encoding="ISO-8859-1" ?>
    <SOAP-ENV:Envelope SOAP
            ENV:encodingStyle="http://schemas.xmlsoap.org/soap/encoding/"
            xmlns:SOAP-ENV="http://schemas.xmlsoap.org/soap/envelope/"
```

```
            xmlns:xsd="http://www.w3.org/2001/XMLSchema"
            xmlns:xsi="http://www.w3.org/2001/XMLSchema-instance"
            xmlns:SOAP-ENC="http://schemas.xmlsoap.org/soap/encoding/"
          xmlns:si="http://soapinterop.org/xsd">
   <SOAP-ENV:Body>
      <getRandQuoteResponse>
         <return xsi:type="xsd:string">
         "My main objective is to be professional but to kill him.",
            Mike Tyson (2002)
         </return>
      </getRandQuoteResponse>
   </SOAP-ENV:Body>
</SOAP-ENV:Envelope>
```

If you're new to SOAP, it would certainly behoove you to take some time to become familiar with the protocol. I've taken the liberty of citing a few starting points at the conclusion of this chapter. Otherwise, a simple search will turn up a considerable amount of information pertinent to this pillar of Web Services. Regardless, you should be able to follow along with the ensuing discussion quite easily, as the project I introduce, NuSOAP, does a fantastic job of taking care of most of the dirty work pertinent to the assembly, parsing, submission, and retrieval of SOAP messages. Following the NuSOAP discussion, I'll introduce PHP 5's new SOAP extension, showing you how you can create both SOAP clients and servers using native language functionality.

NuSOAP

NuSOAP is a powerful group of PHP classes that make the process of consuming and creating SOAP messages trivial. Written by Dietrich Ayala, NuSOAP works seamlessly with many of the most popular SOAP server implementations, and is released under the LGPL. NuSOAP offers a bevy of impressive features, including:

- **Simplicity:** NuSOAP's object-oriented approach hides many of the details pertinent to the SOAP message assembling, parsing, submission, and reception, allowing the user to concentrate on the application itself.

- **WSDL generation and importing:** NuSOAP will generate a WSDL document corresponding to a published Web Service and can import a WSDL reference for use within a NuSOAP client

- **A proxy class:** NuSOAP can generate a proxy class that allows for the remote methods to be called as if they were local.

- **HTTP-proxying:** For varying reasons (security and auditing are two), some clients are forced to delegate a request to an HTTP proxy, which will in turn perform the request on the client's behalf. That said, any SOAP request would need to pass through this proxy rather than directly querying the service server. NuSOAP offers basic support for specifying this proxy server.

- **SSL:** NuSOAP supports secure communication via SSL if the CURL extension is made available via PHP.

All of these features are discussed in further detail throughout this section. For starters however, you'll need to install NuSOAP. This simple process is introduced next.

> **NOTE** *NuSOAP was originally known as SOAPx4, and in fact is a rewrite of the original project. The name was changed in accordance with an agreement by the project author (Dietrich Ayala) and the company NuSphere, which had at one point sponsored development.*

Installing NuSOAP

Installing NuSOAP is really a trivial affair, done in three steps.

1. Download the latest stable distribution from: `http://dietrich.ganx4.com/nusoap/`.

2. Extract the package contents to a location convenient for inclusion from a PHP script. I typically like to place third-party classes within an aptly named directory located within the `PHP_INSTALL_DIR/includes/` directory.

3. Include the NuSOAP class (`nusoap.php`) within your script:

   ```
   require('nusoap/nusoap.php');
   ```

That's it! You're ready to begin using NuSOAP.

Consuming a Web Service

Rather than go through the motions of creating a useless "Hello World" type example, I'll instead create a client that actually consumes a live, practical Web Service. XMethods, Inc. offers a number of such services via their Website, `http://www.xmethods.net/`. Because I have a particular fascination with the weather, I'll use the "Weather - Temperature" service to retrieve the current temperature based on a given ZIP code. Listing 18-6 offers the PHP client used to consume this service.

> **NOTE** *The services provided via the XMethods, Inc. Web site are intended for demonstrative purposes only. You must abide by their Usage Guidelines, available here:* `http://www.xmethods.net/v2/demoguidelines.html`.

Listing 18-6. Consuming the XMethod's Temperature Web Service

```php
<?php
    // Reference the nusoap class
    require_once('nusoap/nusoap.php');

    // Define the Web service's WSDL
    $serviceWSDL = "http://www.xmethods.net/sd/TemperatureService.wsdl";

    // Define the zip code
    $zipcode = "43210";

    // All parameters must be passed as an array
    $parameters = array('zipcode'=>$zipcode);

    // Create a new soapclient object which references the Web Service.
    $soapclient = new soapclient($serviceWSDL, 'wsdl');

    // Invoke the Web service's getTemp() method, returning
    // the requested temperature/
    $temperature = $soapclient->call('getTemp', $parameters);
    echo "It's $temperature degrees at zip code $zipcode.";
?>
```

Given that it's early January in Ohio as I write this, I wouldn't exactly expect balmy conditions. Indeed this is the case, as I receive the following output:

```
It's 31 degrees at zip code 43210.
```

That was easy! I'm particularly fond of this particular example, because it not only illustrates NuSOAP's powerfully simple API, but also demonstrates first-hand one of the alluring characteristics of Web Services: interoperability. Although the client is PHP-based, the Web Service is actually developed using the Enhydra Application Server, a Java-based product.

> **NOTE** *Enhydra is an Open Source Java/XML application server. Learn more about it at:* http://enhydra.enhydra.org/.

Note that you're not limited to passing a single parameter to a remote method. You can pass in as many as you like, provided that each is added to the parameter array in the order in which the remote method should accept them.

Creating a Method Proxy

You can also access the Web Service's methods directly, as if the service were a local class library. This is done by creating a proxy via the getProxy() method. I'll revise Listing 18-6 to do exactly this. Listing 18-7 offers the revised script.

Listing 18-7. Using NuSOAP's Proxy Class

```php
<?php
    require_once('nusoap/nusoap.php');
    $serviceWSDL = "http://www.xmethods.net/sd/2001/TemperatureService.wsdl";
    $zipcode = "43210";

    $soapclient = new soapclient($serviceWSDL, 'wsdl');

    $proxy = $soapclient->getProxy();
    $temperature = $proxy->getTemp($zipcode);

    echo "It's $temperature degrees at zip code $zipcode.";
?>
```

Returning:

```
It's 31 degrees at zip code 43210.
```

Making the remote method calls in this fashion is quite convenient!

Publishing a Web Service

Of course, you might not only want to consume Web Services, but also publish them. After all, how better to offer your vast compilation of boxing quotes to the world? In this section, I'll show you how to use NuSOAP to create a Web Service that does just this.

For starters, you need to create a MySQL table that hosts the quotes. Although a real-world implementation would involve multiple tables, I'll keep things simple and encapsulate everything in a single table named quotation:

```
CREATE TABLE quotation (
    id SMALLINT UNSIGNED NOT NULL AUTO_INCREMENT,
    boxer varchar(30) NOT NULL,
    quote MEDIUMTEXT NOT NULL,
    year YEAR NOT NULL,
    PRIMARY KEY(id)
    );
```

Assume that this table has been packed with profound statements from the world's greatest fighters. Next, you need to create the Web Service. The commented script is offered in Listing 18-8.

Listing 18-8. The Boxing Quote Web Service (boxing.php)

```php
<?php
   require('nusoap/nusoap.php');

   // Function: getRandQuote()
   // Inputs: None
   // Outputs: A string containing information about a quote,
   //   its attribution, and date.
   function getRandQuote() {
     // Connect to the MySQL DB server and select the database
     mysql_connect("localhost","webserviceuser","secret");
     mysql_select_db("chapter18");

     // Create and execute the query
     $query = "SELECT boxer, quote, year FROM quotation
                     ORDER BY RAND() LIMIT 1";
     $result = mysql_query($query);
     $row = mysql_fetch_array($result);

     // Retrieve, assemble, and return the quote data
     $boxer = $row["boxer"];
     $quote = $row["quote"];
     $year = $row["year"];
     return "\"$quote\", $boxer ($year)";
   }

   // Instantiate a new soap server object
   $server = new soap_server;

   // Register the getRandQuote() method
   $server->register("getRandQuote");

   // Automatically execute any incoming request
   $server->service($HTTP_RAW_POST_DATA);
?>
```

All that's left is to create a client capable of consuming our service. This client is offered in Listing 18-9.

Listing 18-9. A Boxing Web Service Client

```php
<?php
    require_once('nusoap/nusoap.php');
    $serviceURL = "http://localhost/pmnp/18/boxingserver.php";
    $soapclient = new soapclient($serviceURL);
    $quote = $soapclient->call('getRandQuote');
    echo "<p>Your random boxing quotation of the moment:<br />$quote</p>";
?>
```

Contacting the Web Service using this client results in a random quote being retrieved from the `quotation` database table. Sample output follows:

```
"It's easy to do anything in victory. It's in defeat that a man reveals himself.",
Floyd Patterson (1935)
```

Returning an Array

You'll often want to retrieve various items of information from a Web Service, for example a profile of a given fighter. One of the easiest ways to do is by returning an array back to the client. This is accomplished using PHP's default functionality, returning the array just like any other variable. This is demonstrated in Listing 18-10.

Listing 18-10. Returning an Array to the Client

```php
<?php
    require_once('nusoap/nusoap.php');
    // Create a new server
    $server = new soap_server;

    // Register the retrieveBio function
    $server->register("retrieveBio");

    // Define the retrieveBio() function
    function retrieveBio() {
        // Assume that this information was retrieved from a database
        $boxer["name"] = "Muhammed Ali";
        $boxer["age"] = 61;
        $boxer["bio"] = "Ali held the World heavyweight title three times throughout
                         his career.";
        return $boxer;
    }

    $HTTP_RAW_POST_DATA = isset($HTTP_RAW_POST_DATA) ?
    $HTTP_RAW_POST_DATA : '';

    $server->service($HTTP_RAW_POST_DATA);
?>
```

The client can contact the `retrieveBio()` function, and parse the array information using the `list()` statement, like so:

```php
<?php
    require_once('nusoap/nusoap.php');

    // Always create a parameter array
    $params = array();

    // Create a new SOAP client
    $client = new soapclient("http://localhost/pmnp/18/boxing.php");

    // Execute the remote method retrieveBio()
    $boxer = $client->call('retrieveBio', $params);

    // Parse the returned associative array
    $name = $boxer["name"];
    $age = $boxer["age"];
    $bio = $boxer["bio"];

    // Output the information
    echo "<strong>$name</strong> ($age years)<br />$bio";
?>
```

Executing the client results in the following output:

```
<strong>Muhammed Ali</strong> (61 years)<br />
Ali held the World heavyweight title three times throughout his career.
```

Generating a WSDL Document

You'll need to generate a Web Services Definition Language (WSDL) document in order to offer client the opportunity to call methods via a proxy as was demonstrated in Listing 18-7. Doing so via NuSOAP is surprisingly easy, accomplished with few modifications to the servers I've demonstrated thus far. Two additional methods must be called to initiate WSDL configuration and specify the WSDL namespace. These methods are `configureWSDL()` and `schemaTargetNamespace()`, respectively. In addition, because PHP is a loosely typed language, both the input and returned values must be defined using XML Schema, which hints at the data type requirements. Listing 18-11 is a modified version of Listing 18-7, offering WSDL generation support.

Listing 18-11. Generating WSDL

```php
<?php
    require('nusoap/nusoap.php');

    $server = new soap_server();
```

```
// Initiate WSDL configuration
$server->configureWSDL('boxing', 'urn:boxing');

// Designate the WSDL namespace
$server->wsdl->schemaTargetNamespace = 'urn:boxing';

// Register the getRandQuote() function.
$server->register("getRandQuote",
                array('format' => 'xsd:string'),
                array('return' => 'xsd:string'),
                'urn:boxing',
                'urn:boxing#getRandQuote');

function getRandQuote() {
    mysql_connect("localhost","webservicesuser","secret");
    mysql_select_db("wjgilmore");
    $query = "SELECT boxer, quote, year FROM quotation ORDER BY RAND() LIMIT 1";
    $result = mysql_query($query);
    $row = mysql_fetch_array($result);
    $boxer = $row["boxer"];
    $quote = $row["quote"];
    $year = $row["year"];
    return "\"$quote\", $boxer ($year)";
}

$HTTP_RAW_POST_DATA = isset($HTTP_RAW_POST_DATA) ? $HTTP_RAW_POST_DATA : '';
$server->service($HTTP_RAW_POST_DATA);
?>
```

Fault Handling

NuSOAP offers a class for handling errors that may occur during execution. This class, named soap_fault, has four attributes:

- faultactor: This optional attribute indicates which service caused the error.

- faultcode: This required attribute indicates the type of error. There are four possible values: Client, MustUnderstand, Server, and VersionMismatch. A Client error is returned when an error message is found within the message returned by the client. A MustUnderstand error occurs when a mandatory header has been found that is not understood. A Server error occurs when a processing error has occurred on the server. Finally, a VersionMismatch error occurs when incompatible namespaces have been used.

- faultdetail: This optional attribute contains additional information about the error.

- faultstring: This required attribute contains an error description.

These attributes are initialized via the class constructor, like so:

```php
<?php
   if ($bid < 10)
      return new soap_fault("Client", "",
                        "Dollar value must be greater than 10!", "");
   else
      return "Bid accepted";
?>
```

The soap_fault class also offers one method, serialize(). This function returns a complete SOAP message consisting of the fault information. Consider an example:

```php
$fault = new soap_fault("Client", "",
                        "Dollar value must be greater than 10!", "");
$fault->serialize();
```

This returns the following:

```xml
<?xml version="1.0"?>
<SOAP-ENV:Envelope
  SOAP-ENV:encodingStyle="http://schemas.xmlsoap.org/soap/encoding/"

  xmlns:SOAP-ENV="http://schemas.xmlsoap.org/soap/envelope/"
  xmlns:xsd="http://www.w3.org/2001/XMLSchema"
  xmlns:xsi="http://www.w3.org/2001/XMLSchema-instance"
  xmlns:SOAP-ENC="http://schemas.xmlsoap.org/soap/encoding/"
  xmlns:si="http://soapinterop.org/xsd">
<SOAP-ENV:Body>
   <SOAP-ENV:Fault>
      <faultcode>Client</faultcode>
      <faultactor></faultactor>
      <faultstring>Dollar value must be greater than 10!</faultstring>
      <detail><soapVal xsi:type="xsd:string"></soapVal></detail>
   </SOAP-ENV:Fault>
</SOAP-ENV:Body>
</SOAP-ENV:Envelope>
```

Designating an HTTP Proxy

If the client requires use of an HTTP proxy server, it can be set using the setHTTP-Proxy() method. This method takes two arguments: the proxy address and its port:

```php
$client = new soapclient("http://www.example.com/boxing/server.php", 80);
$client->setHTTPproxy("proxy.examplecompany.com", 8080);
```

All subsequent communication with the SOAP server initiated by this client will be routed through the designated proxy.

Debugging Tools

NuSOAP offers a debugging feature, which can be enabled on both the client and server sides. The method for enabling on each is identical, done by setting the debug_flag property to TRUE. For example:

```
$client = new soapclient($endpoint);
$client->debug_flag = true;
```

When debugging via the client, you can then begin accessing debugging information via the property debug_data, like so:

```
echo $client->debug_data;
```

When debugging via the server, the debugging information will automatically be appended to any response. Interestingly, you can also enable server debugging from the client-side by appending ?debug=1 to the Web Service endpoint URL. This causes the server to automatically append the debugging information to the response, as if debugging was enabled on the server side.

Client-side Debugging

Three additional debugging attributes are available to the client:

- request: The request attribute retrieves the request header and accompanying SOAP message. It's called like so:

  ```
  echo $soapclient->request;
  ```

- response: The response attribute retrieves the request response header and its accompanying SOAP message. It's called like so:

  ```
  echo '<xmp>'.$soapclient->response.'</xmp>';
  ```

- debug_str: The debug_str attribute offers detailed information pertinent to the entire request and response process, presented in chronological order and specifying the actor carrying out the particular action.

  ```
  echo $soapclient->debug_str;
  ```

  Because the returned string is quite lengthy, it will be difficult to read if you output it to the browser. You can improve its readability by replacing all newline characters with the br tag via the nl2br() function:

  ```
  echo nl2br($soapclient->debug_str);
  ```

Secure Connections

Security should always be a subject of considerable concern when developing Internet-based applications. One of the de facto security safeguards in widespread use today is the Secure Sockets Layer (SSL) protocol, used to encrypt traffic sent over the Internet. NuSOAP supports SSL connections if the cURL extension is configured for PHP. Due to this extension's popularity, it's been bundled with PHP 5, and is enabled by configuring PHP with the `--with-curl` option.

Secure connections are initiated as is done via the Web browser, prefacing the domain address using https in lieu of http.

PHP 5's SOAP Extension

In response to the community clamor for Web Services' enabled applications, and the popularity of third-party SOAP extensions, a native SOAP extension was incorporated into PHP 5. In this section, I'll talk about this new object-oriented extension, offering several examples demonstrating how easy it is to create SOAP clients and servers. Along the way, you'll learn more about many of the functions and methods available through this extension. Before you can follow along with the accompanying examples, you'll need to take care of a few prerequisites. I'll discuss these prerequisites next.

Prerequisites

PHP's SOAP extension requires the GNOME xml library. You can download the latest stable libxml2 package from http://www.xmlsoft.org/. Binaries are also available for the Windows platform. Version 2.5.4 or greater is required. You'll also need to configure PHP with the `--enable-soap` extension.

Creating a SOAP Client

Creating a SOAP client with the new native SOAP extension is easier than you think. Although several client-specific methods are provided with the SOAP extension, only SoapClient() is required to create a complete WSDL-enabled client object. Once created, it's just a matter of calling the SOAP server's exposed functions. I'll introduce SoapClient() and several other key methods next, guiding you through the process of creating a functional SOAP client as the section progresses. In the later section, "SOAP Client and Server Interaction," I'll offer a complete working example of interaction between a client and server created using this extension.

SoapClient()

```
object SoapClient->SoapClient(mixed wsdl [, array options])
```

The SoapClient() constructor instantiates a new instance of the SoapClient class. The *wsdl* parameter determines whether the class will be invoked in WSDL or non-WSDL mode. If the former, then the parameter will point to the WSDL file, otherwise it will be set to null. The discretionary *options* parameter is an array that accepts the following parameters:

- actor: This parameter specifies the name, in URI format, of the role that a SOAP node must play in order to process the header.

- compression: This parameter specifies whether data compression is enabled. Presently gzip and x-gzip is supported. According to the TODO document, support is planned for HTTP compression.

- exceptions: Enabling this parameter turns on the exception handling mechanism. It is enabled by default.

- login: If HTTP authentication is used to access the SOAP server, this parameter specifies the username.

- password: If HTTP authentication is used to access the SOAP server, this parameter specifies the password.

- proxy_host: This parameter specifies the name of the proxy host when connecting through a proxy server.

- proxy_login: This parameter specifies the proxy server username if one is required.

- proxy_password: This parameter specifies the proxy server password if one is required.

- proxy_port: This parameter specifies the proxy server port when connecting through a proxy server.

- soap_version: This parameter specifies whether SOAP version 1.1 or 1.2 should be used. This defaults to version 1.1.

- trace: If you would like to examine SOAP request and response envelopes, you'll need to enable this by setting it to 1.

Establishing a connection to a Web Service is trivial. Here's an example, in which I'll create a SoapClient object that references the XMethods.net Weather Web Service, first introduced in the NuSOAP discussion earlier in this chapter:

```php
<?php
    $ws = "http://www.xmethods.net/sd/2001/TemperatureService.wsdl";
    $client = new SoapClient($ws);
?>
```

However, just referencing the Web Service really doesn't do you much good. You'll want to learn more about the methods exposed by this Web service. Of course, you can open up the WSDL document in the browser or a WSDL viewer. However, you can also retrieve the methods programmatically using the __getFunctions() method, introduced next.

__getFunctions()

```
array SoapClient->__getFunctions()
```

The __getFunctions() method returns an array consisting of all methods exposed by the service referenced by the SoapClient object. The following example establishes a connection to the XMethods.net Weather Web Service and retrieves a list of available methods:

```php
<?php
    $ws = "http://www.xmethods.net/sd/2001/TemperatureService.wsdl";
    $client = new SoapClient($ws);
    var_dump($client->__getFunctions());
?>
```

This example returns:

```
array(1) {
    [0]=> string(30) "float getTemp(string $zipcode)"
};
```

A single exposed method has been returned, getTemp(), and it accepts a zipcode as its lone parameter. I'll now use this method in an example:

```php
<?php
    $ws = "http://www.xmethods.net/sd/2001/TemperatureService.wsdl";
    $zipcode = "20171";
    $client = new SoapClient($ws);
    echo "It's ".$client->getTemp($zipcode)." degrees at zipcode $zipcode.";
?>
```

This example returns:

```
It's 74 degrees at zipcode 20171.
```

__getLastRequest()

```
string SoapClient->__getLastRequest()
```

When you're debugging, it's useful to view the SOAP request in its entirety, headers and all. You can do so by turning tracing on when creating the SoapClient object, and invoking the __getLastRequest() method after a SOAP request has been executed. This is best explained with an example:

```php
<?php
    $ws = "http://www.xmethods.net/sd/2001/TemperatureService.wsdl";
    $zipcode = "20171";
    $client = new SoapClient($ws,array('trace' => 1));
    $temperature = $client->getTemp($zipcode);
    echo htmlspecialchars($client->__getLastRequest());
?>
```

This example returns (formatted for readability):

```xml
<?xml version="1.0" encoding="UTF-8"?>
<SOAP-ENV:Envelope
    xmlns:SOAP-ENV="http://schemas.xmlsoap.org/soap/envelope/"
    xmlns:ns1="urn:xmethods-Temperature"
    xmlns:xsd="http://www.w3.org/2001/XMLSchema"
    xmlns:xsi="http://www.w3.org/2001/XMLSchema-instance"
    xmlns:SOAP-ENC="http://schemas.xmlsoap.org/soap/encoding/"
    SOAP-ENV:encodingStyle="http://schemas.xmlsoap.org/soap/encoding/">
    <SOAP-ENV:Body><ns1:getTemp>
        <zipcode xsi:type="xsd:string">20171</zipcode>
        </ns1:getTemp>
    </SOAP-ENV:Body>
</SOAP-ENV:Envelope>
```

__getLastResponse()

```
object SoapClient->__getLastResponse()
```

The __getLastRequest() method is useful for reviewing the SOAP request in its entirety, envelope and all. When debugging, it's equally useful to review the response, accomplished using the __getLastResponse() method. As is the case with __getLastRequest(), tracing must be turned on. Consider an example:

```php
<?php
    $ws = "http://www.xmethods.net/sd/2001/TemperatureService.wsdl";
    $zipcode = "20171";
    $client = new SoapClient($ws,array('trace' => 1));
    $temperature = $client->getTemp($zipcode);
    echo htmlspecialchars($client->__getLastResponse());
?>
```

This example returns (formatted for readability):

```
<?xml version='1.0' encoding='UTF-8'?>
<SOAP-ENV:Envelope
    xmlns:SOAP-ENV="http://schemas.xmlsoap.org/soap/envelope/"
    xmlns:xsi="http://www.w3.org/2001/XMLSchema-instance"
    xmlns:xsd="http://www.w3.org/2001/XMLSchema">
    <SOAP-ENV:Body>
        <ns1:getTempResponse xmlns:ns1="urn:xmethods-Temperature"
        SOAP-ENV:encodingStyle="http://schemas.xmlsoap.org/soap/encoding/">
        <return xsi:type="xsd:float">76.0</return>
        </ns1:getTempResponse>
    </SOAP-ENV:Body>
</SOAP-ENV:Envelope>
```

SOAP Server Methods

Creating a SOAP server with the new native SOAP extension is easier than you think.
Although several server-specific methods are provided with the SOAP extension, only
three methods are required to create a complete WSDL-enabled server. I'll introduce
these and other methods, guiding you through the process of creating a functional
SOAP server as the section progresses. In the next section, "SOAP Client and Server
Interaction," I'll offer a complete working example of interaction between a WSDL-
enabled client and server created using this extension. To illustrate this and the next
section, the examples refer to Listing 18-12, which offers a sample WSDL file. Directly
following the listing I'll introduce a few important SOAP configuration directives that
you'll need to keep in mind when building SOAP services using this extension.

Listing 18-12. A Sample WSDL File (boxing.wsdl)

```
<?xml version="1.0" ?>
  <definitions name="boxing"
                targetNamespace="http://www.example.com/boxing"
    xmlns:tns="http://www.example.com/boxing"
    xmlns:xsd="http://www.w3.org/2001/XMLSchema"
    xmlns:soap="http://schemas.xmlsoap.org/wsdl/soap/"
    xmlns="http://schemas.xmlsoap.org/wsdl/">

    <message name="getQuoteRequest">
      <part name="boxer" type="xsd:string" />
    </message>

    <message name="getQuoteResponse">
      <part name="return" type="xsd:string" />
    </message>

    <portType name="QuotePortType">
      <operation name="getQuote">
```

```
        <input message="tns:getQuoteRequest" />
        <output message="tns:getQuoteResponse" />
      </operation>
    </portType>

    <binding name="QuoteBinding" type="tns:QuotePortType">
      <soap:binding
          style="rpc" transport="http://schemas.xmlsoap.org/soap/http" />
      <operation name="getQuote">
        <soap:operation soapAction="" />
          <input>
            <soap:body use="encoded"
              encodingStyle="http://schemas.xmlsoap.org/soap/encoding/" />
          </input>
          <output>
            <soap:body use="encoded"
              encodingStyle="http://schemas.xmlsoap.org/soap/encoding/" />
          </output>
      </operation>
    </binding>

  <service name="boxing">
    <documentation>Returns quote from famous pugilists</documentation>
    <port name="QuotePort" binding="tns:QuoteBinding">
      <soap:address
        location="http://localhost/book/18/boxing/boxingserver.php" />
    </port>
  </service>
</definitions>
```

Important Configuration Directives

There are three important configuration directives that you need to keep in mind when building SOAP services using this extension. I'll introduce those directives in this section.

soap.wsdl_cache_enabled
Scope: PHP_INI_ALL, Default value: 1
This directive determines whether the WSDL caching feature is enabled.

soap.wsdl_cache_dir
Scope: PHP_INI_ALL, Default value: /tmp
This directive determines the location where WSDL documents are cached.

soap.wsdl_cache_ttl
Scope: PHP_INI_ALL, Default value: 86400
This directive determines the time, in seconds, that a WSDL document is cached.

SoapServer()

```
object SoapServer->SoapServer(mixed wsdl [, array options])
```

The SoapServer() constructor instantiates a new instance of the SoapServer class in WSDL or non-WSDL mode. If you require WSDL mode, you need to assign the *wsdl* parameter the WSDL file's location, or else set it to NULL. The discretionary options parameter is an array used to set one or both of the following options:

- actor: This identifies the SOAP server as an actor, defining its URI.

- soap_version: This determines the supported SOAP version, and must be set with the syntax SOAP_x_y, where x is an integer specifying the major version number, and y is an integer specifying the corresponding minor version number. For example, SOAP version 1.2 would be assigned as SOAP_1_2.

The following example creates a SoapServer object referencing the boxing.wsdl file:

```
$soapserver = new SoapServer("boxing.wsdl");
```

Of course, if the WSDL file resides on another server, you can reference it using a valid URI. For example:

```
$soapserver = new SoapServer("http://www.example.com/boxing.wsdl");
```

However, creating a SoapServer object is only one task of several required to create a basic SOAP server. Next, you'll need to export at least one function, a task accomplished using the addFunction() method, introduced next.

> **NOTE** *If you're interested in exposing all methods in a class through the SOAP server, use the method* setClass()*, introduced later in this section.*

addFunction()

```
void SoapServer->addFunction(mixed functions)
```

You can make a function to clients by exporting it using the addFunction() method. In the WSDL file, there is only one function to implement, getQuote(). It takes $boxer as a lone parameter, and returns a string. Let's create this function and expose it to connecting clients:

```php
<?php
    function getQuote($boxer) {
        if ($boxer == "Tyson") {
```

```
            $quote = "My main objective is to be professional
                        but to kill him. (2002)";
    } elseif ($boxer == "Ali") {
        $quote = "I am the greatest. (1962)";
    } elseif ($boxer == "Foreman") {
        $quote = "Generally when there's a lot of smoke,
                    there's just a whole lot more smoke. (1995)";
    } else {
        $quote = "Sorry, $boxer was not found.";
    }
    return $quote;
}

$soapserver = new SoapServer("boxing.wsdl");

$soapserver->addFunction("getQuote");
?>
```

When two or more functions are defined in the WSDL file, you can choose which ones are to be exported by passing them in as an array, like so:

```
$soapserver->addFunction(array("getQuote","someOtherFunction"));
```

Alternatively, if you would like to export all functions defined in the scope of the SOAP server, you can pass in the constant, SOAP_FUNCTIONS_ALL, like so:

```
$soapserver->addFunction(array(SOAP_FUNCTIONS_ALL));
```

It's important to understand that exporting the functions is not all that you need to produce a valid SOAP server. You'll also need to properly process incoming SOAP requests, a task handled for you via the method handle(). This method is introduced next.

handle()

```
void SoapServer->handle([string soap_request])
```

Incoming SOAP requests are received either by way of the input parameter soap_request or the PHP global $HTTP_RAW_POST_DATA. Either way, the method handle() will automatically direct the request to the SOAP server for you. It's the last method executed in the server code. You call it like this:

```
$soapserver->handle();
```

setClass()

```
void SoapServer->setClass(string class_name [, mixed args])
```

Although the addfunction() method works fine for adding functions, what if you want to add class methods? This task is accomplished with the setClass() method, the class_name parameter specifying the name of the class, and the optional args parameter specifying any arguments that will be passed to a class constructor. I'll create a class for the boxing quote service, and export its methods using setClass():

```php
<?php
  class boxingQuotes {
    function getQuote($boxer) {
      if ($boxer == "Tyson") {
        $quote = "My main objective is to be professional
                  but to kill him. (2002)";
      } elseif ($boxer == "Ali") {
        $quote = "I am the greatest. (1962)";
      } elseif ($boxer == "Foreman") {
        $quote = "Generally when there's a lot of smoke,
                    there's just a whole lot more smoke. (1995)";
      } else {
        $quote = "Sorry, $boxer was not found.";
      }
      return $quote;
    }
  }

  $soapserver = new SoapServer("boxing.wsdl");

  $soapserver->setClass("boxingQuotes");
  $soapserver->handle();
?>
```

The decision to use setClass() instead of addFunction() is irrelevant to any requesting clients.

setPersistence()

```
void SoapServer->setPersistence(int mode)
```

One really cool feature of this extension is the ability to persist objects across a session. This is accomplished with the setPersistence() method. This method only works in conjunction with setClass(). Two modes are accepted:

- SOAP_PERSISTENCE_REQUEST: This mode specifies that PHP's session-handling feature should be used to persist the object.

- SOAP_PERSISTENCE_SESSION: This mode specifies that the object is destroyed at the end of the request.

SOAP Client and Server Interaction

Now that you're familiar with the basic premises of using this extension to create both SOAP clients and servers using this new extension, I'll present an example that simultaneously demonstrates both concepts. This SOAP service retrieves a famous quote from a particular boxer, and that boxer's last name is requested using the exposed getQuote() method. It's based on the boxing.wsdl file shown in Listing 18-12. Let's start with the server.

Boxing Server

The boxing server is simple but practical. Extending this to connect to a database server would be a trivial affair. Let's consider the code:

```php
<?php
  class boxingQuotes {
    function getQuote($boxer) {
      if ($boxer == "Tyson") {
        $quote = "My main objective is to be professional
                  but to kill him. (2002)";
      } elseif ($boxer == "Ali") {
        $quote = "I am the greatest. (1962)";
      } elseif ($boxer == "Foreman") {
        $quote = "Generally when there's a lot of smoke,
                  there's just a whole lot more smoke. (1995)";
      } else {
        $quote = "Sorry, $boxer was not found.";
      }
      return $quote;
    }
  }

  $soapserver = new SoapServer("boxing.wsdl");

  $soapserver->setClass("boxingQuotes");
  $soapserver->handle();
?>
```

The client, introduced next, will consume this service.

Boxing Client

The boxing client consists of just two lines, the first instantiating the WSDL-enabled SoapClient() class, and the second executing the exposed method getQuote(), passing in the parameter "Ali":

```php
<?php
  $client = new SoapClient("boxing.wsdl");
  echo $client->getQuote("Ali");
?>
```

Executing the client produces the following output:

```
I am the greatest. (1962)
```

Using a C# Client with a PHP Web Service

Although Linux is in widespread use as a server platform, there is little doubt that the Microsoft Windows operating system continues to dominate the desktop. That said, quite a bit of interest has been generated regarding using Web Services as the tool of choice for affording Windows-based desktop applications to seamlessly integrate with Linux-based server applications. Although I've seen numerous questions posed regarding how this is accomplished, little information has been offered. That said, I'd like to provide a brief yet effective example that demonstrates just how easy it is. To do so, I'll take advantage of Microsoft's .NET platform, which offers fantastic Web Services integration capabilities. I'll use .NET to create a simple console-based application that talks to the PHP-based boxing Web Service built using the NuSOAP extension (Listing 18-8). Although it's simplistic, this example should provide you with enough information to get the ball rolling on more complex applications.

In this final example, I'll try coaxing a C# application and our PHP Web Service into playing nice with each other. I'm particularly fond of this example, because it demonstrates just how easy it is to integrate a Windows desktop application and an open-source server. Because not everybody has a copy of Visual Studio .NET at their disposal, I'll make use of the freely downloadable .NET Framework SDK, which contains all of the tools you need to successfully carry out this experiment. If you're running Visual Studio .NET, the general process is the same, although considerably more streamlined.

For demonstration purposes I'll make use of the PHP-based boxing Web service discussed throughout this chapter. The finished C# client will simply invoke the getRandQuote() function, outputting a random quotation to a console window. Example output is provided in Figure 18-5.

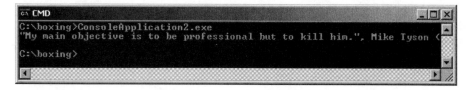

Figure 18-5. Retrieving a random quote via a C# client

If you don't already have it installed, you'll need to download and install the .NET Framework SDK in order to follow along with the example. Because the URL is quite long, I'll save you the trouble of typing it in and instead suggest that you execute a search on the Microsoft site for the package. In addition, you'll need to download the

.NET Framework Redistributable Package, which is also readily available from the Microsoft Web site. If you're unfortunate enough to be using a dial-up connection, consider ordering it on CD, because the package is quite large, topping out at over 100MB.

Once the packages are installed, it's time to begin. For starters, you'll need to generate a C# proxy for the Web Service. You can do this using the Web Services Description Language tool (wsdl.exe), included within the SDK. Reference the WSDL-enabled boxing server script shown in Listing 18-8.

```
wsdl /l:CS /protocol:SOAP http://localhost/pmnp/18/boxing.php?wsdl
```

The result is a file named boxing.cs. Feel free to open it up and examine the file's contents; just be sure not to change anything. Next, you'll compile this proxy as a DLL library. This is necessary because the DLL will be referenced by the C# application so that the Web Service's methods can be called. You compile a DLL like you would any other C# program, using the C# compiler tool (csc.exe):

```
csc /t:library /r:System.Web.Services.dll /r:System.Xml.dll boxing.cs
```

The /r flags tell the compiler to reference these libraries during the compilation process. The result is a file named boxing.dll. In turn, you'll reference this DLL when you compile the C# SOAP client, discussed next.

NOTE *Generating and compiling the proxy via the command line is indeed a tedious process. Bear in mind that the process is automated within Visual Studio .NET, greatly reducing development overhead.*

Finally, create the C# application. Although you could conceivably create a Windows application using a text editor, for health reasons I'd suggest against it. Instead, create a simple console application, shown in Listing 18-13.

Listing 18-13. The C# SOAP Client

```
using System;
using System.Web.Services;
using System.Web.Services.Protocols;
using System.Xml.Serialization;

namespace ConsoleApplication
{
    class boxing
    {
        [STAThread]
        static void Main(string[] args)
        {
            BoxingService bx = new BoxingService();
```

```
        Console.WriteLine(bx.getRandQuote());
      }
   }
}
```

Compile this client, like so:

```
csc boxing.cs /r:boxing.dll
```

What results is a file named boxing.exe. This is the executable C# client. Finally test your program by executing it, like so:

```
C:\vs\proj\pmnp\18\boxing.exe
```

Pending no unforeseen issues, you should see output similar to that shown in Figure 18-5.

Summary

The promise of Web Services and other XML-based technologies has generated an incredible amount of work in this area, with progress regarding specifications, and the announcement of new products and projects happening all of the time. No doubt such efforts will continue, given the incredible potential that this concentration of technologies has to offer.

In the next chapter, you'll turn your attention to the security-minded strategies that developers should always keep at the forefront of their development processes.

CHAPTER 19

Secure PHP Programming

ANY WEB SERVER can be thought of as a castle under constant attack by a sea of barbarians. As history shows, often the attackers' victory isn't entirely dependent upon their degree of skill or cunning, but rather on an oversight by the defenders. The weakest link in the chain of defenses is the one that will likely be the subject of the most intense scrutiny, and ultimately assault. Unfortunately, Web applications are often quite susceptible to numerous weak links, including:

- **User input:** Left unchecked, user input is perhaps the easiest way to wreak serious havoc on an otherwise secure application infrastructure, an assertion backed up by the numerous reports of attacks launched on high-profile Web sites in this fashion. Mangling parameters emanating from Web forms, URL parameters, cookies, and other readily accessible routes all provide attackers with a multitude of routes for striking into the very heart of your application logic.

- **Software vulnerabilities:** Web applications are often constructed from numerous technologies, typically a database server, a Web server, and one or more programming languages, all of which run on one or more operating systems. As a result, you need to constantly keep abreast of exposed vulnerabilities and take the steps necessary to patch the problem before someone takes advantage of it.

- **Elemental exposure:** Web servers and applications are often made available for public use, and so are exposed to all of the abusive elements of the Internet, including worms, viruses, port scanners, script kiddies, and perhaps most frighteningly, determined attackers.

- **The inside job:** Multi-user servers such as those often found in ISPs and educational hosting environments are always susceptible to damage, intentional or otherwise, by a fellow user's actions.

Because each scenario poses significant risk to the integrity of your application, all must be thoroughly investigated and handled accordingly. In this chapter, we'll review many of the steps you can take to hedge against and even eliminate these dangers. Specifically, you'll learn about:

- Securely configuring PHP via its configuration parameters

- The "safe mode" security option

- The importance of validating user data

- Protecting sensitive data through common sense and proper server configuration

- PHP's encryption capabilities

Perhaps the best place to start is with a review of PHP's configuration parameters, as you have the opportunity to take advantage of them right from the very start, prior to doing anything else with the language.

Configuring PHP Securely

PHP offers a number of configuration parameters that are intended to greatly increase PHP's level of security awareness. In this section, I'll touch upon many of the most useful options.

> **NOTE** *Disabling the register_globals directive aids tremendously in the prevention of user-initiated attempts to trick the application into accepting otherwise dangerous data. However, because I already covered this matter in detail in Chapter 3, I'll opt to not repeat the same information in this chapter.*

Safe Mode

Safe mode is of particular interest to those running PHP in a shared-server environment. When enabled, PHP will always verify that the executing script's owner matches the owner of the file the script is attempting to open. This prevents the unintended execution, review, and modification of files not under the ownership of the executing user, provided that the file privileges are also properly configured to prevent modification. Enabling safe mode also poses other significant effects on PHP's behavior. I'll discuss these effects and the numerous safe mode-related parameters that comprise this feature.

safe_mode (boolean)
Scope: PHP_INI_SYSTEM, Default value: 0
Enabling *safe_mode* places restrictions on several potentially dangerous PHP options. You can enable it by setting safe_mode to the boolean value of *on*, or disable it by setting it to *off*. Its restriction scheme is based on comparing the UID (user ID) of the executing script and the UID of the file that that script is attempting to access. If the UIDs are the same, the script can execute; otherwise, the script fails.

Specifically, when safe mode is enabled, several restrictions come into effect:

- Use of all input/output functions (fopen(), file(), and require(), for example) is restricted to only files that have the same owner as the script that is calling these functions. For example, assuming that safe mode is enabled, if a script owned by Mary calls fopen() and attempts to open a file owned by John, it will fail. However, if Mary owns both the script calling fopen() and the file called by fopen(), the function will be successful.

- Attempts by a user to create a new file will be restricted to creating the file in a directory owned by the user.

- Attempts to execute external scripts via functions like popen(), system(), or exec() are only possible when the external script resides in the directory specified by the safe_mode_exec_dir configuration directive. This directive is discussed later in this section.

- HTTP authentication is further strengthened because the UID of the owner of the authentication script is prepended to the authentication realm. User authentication is discussed in further detail in the later section "User Authentication."

- The username used to connect to a MySQL server must be the same as the username of the owner of the file calling mysql_connect().

The following is a complete list of functions, variables, and configuration directives that are affected when safe_mode is enabled:

apache_request_headers()	backticks	chdir()
chgrp()	chmod()	chown()
copy()	dbase_open()	dbmopen()
dl()	exec()	filepro()
filepro_retrieve()	filepro_rowcount()	fopen()
header()	highlight_file()	link()
mail()	max_execution_time	mkdir()
move_uploaded_file()	parse_ini_file()	passthru()
pg_lo_import()	PHP_AUTH variables	popen()
posix_mkfifo()	putenv()	rename()
rmdir()	set_time_limit()	shell_exec()
show_source()	symlink()	system()
touch()	unlink()	

safe_mode_gid (boolean)
Scope: PHP_INI_SYSTEM, Default value: 0
This directive changes safe mode's behavior from verifying user id's before execution to verifying group id's. For example, if Mary and John are in the same user group, Mary's scripts can call fopen() on John's files.

safe_mode_include_dir (string)
Scope: PHP_INI_SYSTEM, Default value: Null
You can use safe_mode_include_dir to designate various paths in which safe mode will be ignored if it's enabled. You might use this function to specify a directory containing various templates that might be incorporated into several user Web sites. You can specify multiple directories by separating each with a semicolon.

safe_mode_exec_dir (string)
Scope: PHP_INI_SYSTEM, Default value: Null
This directive specifies the directory in which any system programs reside that can be executed by functions such as system(), exec(), or passthru(). The safe_mode directive must be enabled for this to work.

safe_mode_allowed_env_vars (string)
Scope: PHP_INI_SYSTEM, Default value: "PHP_"
When safe mode is enabled, you can use this directive to allow certain environment variables to be modified by the executing user's script. You can allow multiple variables to be modified by separating each with a comma.

safe_mode_protected_env_vars (string)
Scope: PHP_INI_SYSTEM, Default value: LD_LIBRARY_PATH
This directive protects certain environment variables from being changed with the putenv() function. By default, the variable LD_LIBRARY_PATH is protected, because of the unintended consequences which may arise if this is changed at runtime. Consult your search engine or Linux manual for more information about this environment variable. Note that any variables declared in this section will override any set by the safe_mode_allowed_env_vars directive.

Other Security-Related Configuration Parameters

In this section I'll review several other configuration parameters that play an important role in better securing your PHP installation.

disable_functions (string)
Scope: PHP_INI_SYSTEM, Default value: Null
For some, enabling safe mode might seem a tad overbearing. Instead, you might want to just disable a few functions. You can set disable_functions equal to a comma-delimited list of function names that you want to disable. Suppose that you wanted to disable the fopen(), popen(), and file() functions. Just set this directive like so:

```
disable_functions = fopen,popen,file
```

Note that this directive does not depend on whether safe mode is enabled.

disable_classes (string)

Scope: PHP_INI_SYSTEM, Default value: Null

Given the new functionality offered by PHP's embrace of the object-oriented paradigm, it likely won't be too long before you're using large sets of class libraries. However, there may be certain classes found within these libraries that you'd rather not make available. You can prevent the use of these classes with the disable_classes directive. For example, suppose you wanted to completely disable the use of two classes, named *administrator* and *janitor*:

```
disable_classes = "administrator, janitor"
```

Note that the influence exercised by this directive does not depend on the safe_mode directive.

doc_root (string)

Scope: PHP_INI_SYSTEM, Default value: Null

This directive can be set to a path that specifies the root directory from which PHP files will be served. If the doc_root directive is set to nothing (empty), it will be ignored, and the PHP scripts are executed exactly as the URL specifies. If safe mode is enabled and doc_root is not empty, no PHP scripts outside of this directory will be executed.

max_execution_time (integer)

Scope: PHP_INI_ALL, Default value: 30

This directive specifies how many seconds a script can execute before being terminated. This can be useful to prevent users' scripts from eating up CPU time. By default, this is set to 30 seconds. If you set it to zero, no time limit will be set.

memory_limit (integer)

Scope: PHP_INI_ALL, Default value: 8M

This directive specifies, in megabytes, how much memory a script can use. By default, this is set to 8M. Note that you cannot specify this value in terms other than megabytes, and that you must always follow the number with an M. This directive is only applicable if --enable-memory-limit was enabled when you configured PHP.

open_basedir (string)

Scope: PHP_INI_SYSTEM, Default value: Null

PHP's open_basedir directive can establish a base directory to which all file operations will be restricted, much like Apache's DocumentRoot directive. This prevents users from entering otherwise restricted areas of the server. For example, suppose all Web material is located within the directory /home/www. To prevent users from viewing and potentially manipulating files like /etc/passwd via a few simple PHP commands, consider setting open_basedir like so:

```
open_basedir = "/home/www/"
```

Note that the influence exercised by this directive does not depend on the safe_mode directive.

sql.safe_mode (integer)
Scope: PHP_INI_SYSTEM, Default value: 0
When enabled, sql.safe_mode ignores all information passed to mysql_connect() and mysql_pconnect(), instead using localhost as the target host. The user under which PHP is running is used as the username (quite likely the Apache daemon user), and no password is used.

user_dir (string)
Scope: PHP_INI_SYSTEM, Default Value: Null
This directive specifies the name of the directory in a user's home directory where PHP scripts must be placed in order to be executed. For example, if user_dir is set to scripts and user "Johnny" wants to execute somescript.php, then Johnny must create a directory named scripts in his home directory and place somescript.php in it. This script can then be accessed via the URL http://www.example.com/~johnny/scripts/somescript.php. This directive is typically used in conjunction with Apache's UserDir configuration directive.

Hiding the Configuration Details

Many programmers prefer to wear their decision to deploy Open Source software as a badge for the world to see. However, it's important to realize that every tidbit of information you release about your project may provide an attacker with vital clues that can ultimately be used to penetrate your server. That said, I'd like to suggest an alternative approach of letting your application stand on its own merits while keeping quiet about the technical details whenever possible. Although obfuscation is only a part of the total security picture, it's nonetheless a strategy that should always be kept in mind. In this section I'll introduce several very easy, but effective strategies you can undertake in this regard.

Eliminate Server and Software Signatures

Some software offers a signature of sorts, intended primarily for administrative purposes, which displays several valuable details regarding its version and capabilities. Apache and PHP both offer such a feature, which I suggest disabling. In this section, I'll show you how this feature is controlled.

Hiding Apache

Apache outputs a server signature included within all document requests, and within server-generated documents (a 500 Internal Server Error document, for example). Two configuration directives are responsible for controlling this signature: ServerSignature and ServerTokens.

ServerSignature

The ServerSignature directive is responsible for the insertion of that single line of output pertaining to Apache's server version, server name (set via the ServerName directive), port, and compiled-in modules. When enabled and working in conjunction with the ServerTokens directive (introduced next), it's capable of displaying output like this:

```
Apache/2.0.44 (Unix) DAV/2 PHP/5.0.0b3-dev Server at www.example.com Port 80
```

Obviously, the Apache version, operating system, and compiled-in modules are items you'd rather keep to yourself. Therefore consider disabling this directive by setting it to Off.

ServerTokens

The ServerTokens directive determines which degree of server details are provided if the ServerSignature directive is enabled. Six options are available, including: Full, Major, Minimal, Minor, OS, and Prod. An example of each is given in Table 19-1.

Table 19-1. Options for the ServerTokens *Directive*

OPTION	EXAMPLE
Full	Apache/2.0.44 (Unix) DAV/2 PHP/5.0.0b3-dev
Major	Apache/2
Minimal	Apache/2.0.44
Minor	Apache/2.0
OS	Apache/2.0.44 (Unix)
Prod	Apache

Although this directive is moot if ServerSignature is disabled, if for some reason ServerSignature must be enabled, I suggest setting this directive to Prod.

Hiding PHP

PHP offers a directive similar to Apache's ServerSignature. It's called expose_php, and is introduced here.

expose_php (boolean)
Scope: PHP_INI_SYSTEM, Default value: 1
When enabled, the directive expose_php appends its details to the server signature. For example, if ServerSignature is enabled and ServerTokens is set to Full, and this directive is enabled, the relevant component of the server signature would look like:

```
Apache/2.0.44 (Unix) DAV/2 PHP/5.0.0b3-dev Server at www.example.com Port 80
```

When disabled, it will look like this:

```
Apache/2.0.44 (Unix) DAV/2 Server at www.example.com Port 80
```

Remove all Instances of phpinfo() Calls

The phpinfo() function offers a great tool for viewing a summary of PHP's configuration on a given server. However, left unprotected on the server, these files are a veritable gold mine for attackers. For example, this function yields information pertinent to the operating system, PHP and Web server versions, configuration flags, and a detailed report regarding all available extensions and their versions. Leaving this information accessible to an attacker will greatly increase the likelihood that a potential attack vector will be revealed and subsequently exploited.

Unfortunately, it appears that many developers are either unaware or unconcerned with such disclosure, because typing phpinfo.php into my favorite search engine yields roughly 21,600 results, many of which reside within the root directory of the server Web site. A quick refinement of my search to include other key terms resulted in a subset of the initial results (old, vulnerable PHP versions) which would serve as prime candidates for attack due to the use of known insecure versions of PHP, Apache, IIS, and various supported extensions.

Allowing others to view the results from phpinfo() is essentially equivalent to providing the general public with a roadmap to many of your server's technical characteristics and shortcomings. Don't fall victim to an attack simply because of laziness or a lackadaisical concern regarding the availability of this data.

Change the Document Extension

PHP-enabled documents are often easily recognized by their unique extension, of which the most common include .php, .php3, and .phtml. Did you know that this can easily be changed to any other extension you wish, even .html, .asp, or .jsp? Just change the line in your httpd.conf file that reads:

```
AddType application/x-httpd-php .php
```

Adding whatever extension you please, for example:

```
AddType application/x-httpd-php .asp
```

Of course, you'll need to be sure that this does not cause a conflict with other technologies installed on the server.

Hiding Sensitive Data

Although the discussion regarding the sheer number of phpinfo() enabled files made available on the Internet might have persuaded you otherwise, you might find it a surprise to know that many developers tend to believe that if a document isn't linked to a page on a Web site, it isn't accessible. Obviously, this is hardly the case. Any document located in a Web server's document tree, and possessing adequate privilege, is fair game for retrieval by any mechanism capable of executing the GET command. As an exercise, create a file, and inside this file type "my secret stuff." Save this file into your public HTML directory under the name of secrets with some really strange extension like .zkgjg. Obviously, the server isn't going to recognize this extension, but it's going to attempt to serve up the data anyway. Now, go to your browser and request that file, using the URL pointing to that file. Scary, isn't it?

Of course, the user would need to know the name of the file he's interested in retrieving. However, just like the presumption that a file containing the phpinfo() function will be named phpinfo.php, a bit of cunning and the ability to exploit deficiencies in the Web server configuration are all one really needs to have some luck in finding otherwise restricted files. Fortunately, there are two simple ways to definitively correct this problem, both of which are described in this section.

Take Heed of the Document Root

In Apache's httpd.conf file you'll find a configuration directive named DocumentRoot. This is set to the path that you would like the server to consider to be the public HTML directory. If no other safeguards have been undertaken, any file in this path is considered fair game in terms of being served to a user's browser, even if the file does not have a recognized extension. It is not possible for a user to view a file that resides outside of this path. Therefore, it is a very good idea to always place your configuration files outside of the DocumentRoot path.

To retrieve these files, you can use include() to include those files into any PHP files. For example, assume that you set your document root to:

```
DocumentRoot C:/apache2/htdocs      # Windows
DocumentRoot /www/apache/home       # Unix
```

Suppose you have a configuration file containing the access variables (hostname, username, and password) for your MySQL database. You certainly wouldn't want anyone to view that file, so it would be a good idea to place it outside of the document root. Therefore, you could save that file to:

```
C:/Apache/restricted/      # Windows
/usr/local/restricted/     # Unix
```

When you need to use this access information, just include these files using the full pathname where needed. For example:

```
REQUIRE("C:/apache2/restricted/mysqlaccess.inc");      # Windows
```

```
REQUIRE("/usr/local/restricted/mysqlaccess.inc");      # Unix
```

Of course, if safe mode is disabled, other users with the capability to execute PHP scripts on the machine may still be able to include that file into their own scripts. Therefore, in a multi-user environment, it would be a good idea to couple this safeguard with directives such as safe_mode and open_basedir.

Denying Access to Certain File Extensions

A second way to prevent users from viewing certain files is to deny access to certain extensions by configuring the httpd.conf file Files directive. Assume that you don't want anyone to access files having the extension .inc. Simply place the following in your httpd.conf file:

```
<Files *.inc>
    Order allow,deny
    Deny from all
</Files>
```

After making this addition, restart the Apache server, and you will find that access is denied to any user making a request to view a file with the extension .inc via the browser. However, you can still include these files in your scripts. Incidentally, if you search through the httpd.conf file, you will see that this is the same premise used to protect access to .htaccess.

Sanitizing User Data

Neglecting to properly review and sanitize user-input data at *every* opportunity could afford attackers the opportunity to do massive internal damage to your information store and operating system, deface or delete Web files, and even gain unrestricted access to your server. I'll illustrate this important matter with a real-world example. Suppose that you offered an on-line service that generated PDFs from an input URL. A great tool for accomplishing just this is HTMLDOC, a program that converts HTML documents to indexed HTML, Adobe PostScript, and PDF files. HTMLDOC can be invoked from the command line, like so:

```
%>htmldoc --webpage -f webpage.pdf http://www.wjgilmore.com/
```

> **NOTE** *HTMLDOC is a product of Easy Software Products, and is released under the GNU General Public License. Learn more about it at* http://www.easysw.com.

This results in the creation of a PDF named webpage.pdf, which would contain a snapshot of my Web site's index page. Of course, most users will not have command-line access to your server, so you'd need to create a much more controlled interface to the service, perhaps the most obvious of which is via a Web page. Using PHP's passthru() function (introduced later in this chapter), you can call HTMLDOC and return the desired PDF, like so:

```
$document = $_POST['userurl'];
passthru("htmldoc --webpage -f webpage.pdf $document);
```

However, what if an enterprising attacker took the liberty of passing through additional input, unrelated to the desired HTML page, entering something like this:

```
http://www.wjgilmore.com/ ; cd /usr/local/apache/htdocs/; rm –rf *
```

Most Unix shells would interpret passthru() request as three separate commands! The first command is this:

```
htmldoc --webpage -f webpage.pdf http://www.wjgilmore.com/
```

The second command is this:

```
cd /usr/local/apache/htdocs/
```

And the final one is this:

```
rm -rf *
```

This would remove your entire Web document tree! One way to safeguard such attempts is to sanitize user input before it is passed to any of PHP's program execution functions. Three standard functions are conveniently available for doing so: escapeshellarg(), escapeshellcmd(), and strip_tags().

escapeshellarg()

string escapeshellarg (string *arguments*)

The escapeshellarg() function delimits *arguments* with single quotes and prefixes (escapes) quotes found within *arguments*. The effect is that when *arguments* is passed to a shell command, it will be considered a single argument. This is significant because it lessens the possibility that an attacker could masquerade additional commands as shell command arguments. Therefore, in the nightmare scenario I outlined earlier, the entire user input would be enclosed in single quotes, like so:

```
'http://www.wjgilmore.com/ ; cd /usr/local/apache/htdoc/; rm –rf *'
```

HTMLDOC would simply return an error because it could not resolve a URL possessing this syntax, instead of deleting an entire directory tree.

escapeshellcmd()

```
string escapeshellcmd (string command)
```

The escapeshellcmd() function operates under the same premise as escapeshellarg(), sanitizing potentially dangerous input through the escaping of shell metacharacters. These characters include: # & ; ` , | * ? , ~ < > ^ ( ) [ ] { } $ \\.

To illustrate just how ugly things could get if you were to neglect validation of user input, suppose that you offered users the ability to execute system commands, such as ls -l. However, if the user entered something like `rm -rf * ` (note the backticks), and you were to then either echo this input or insert it into exec() or system(), it could potentially recursively delete files and directories from your server. You can eliminate these problems by first cleaning up the command with escapeshellcmd().If you pass this offending input through escapeshellcmd(), the string would be converted to \ `rm -rf \ *\ `.

strip_tags()

```
string strip_tags(string str [, str allowed_tags])
```

Another problem that arises from user input is the introduction of HTML content. This can be particularly problematic when the information is displayed back to the browser, as is the case with a message board. The introduction of HTML tags into a message board could alter the display of the page, causing it to be displayed incorrectly, or not at all. This problem can be eliminated by passing the user input through strip_tags().

The function strip_tags()removes all HTML tags from a string. The input parameter *str* is the string that will be examined for tags, while the optional input parameter *allowed_tags* specifies any tags that you would like to be allowed in the string. For example, italic tags (<i></i>) might be allowable, but table tags such as <td></td> could potentially wreak havoc on a page. An example follows:

```php
<?php
    $input = "I <td>really</td> love <i>PHP</i>!";
    $input = strip_tags($input,"<i></i>");
    // $input now equals "I really love <i>PHP</i>!"
?>
```

Data Encryption

Encryption can be defined as the translation of data into a format that is intended to be unreadable by anyone except the intended party. The intended party can then decode, or decrypt, the encrypted data through the use of some secret, typically a secret key or password. PHP offers support for several encryption algorithms. Several of the more prominent ones are described here.

> **TIP** *For more information about encryption, I recommend the book,* Applied Cryptography: Protocols, Algorithms, and Source Code in C *by Bruce Schneier (John Wiley & Sons, 1995).*

PHP's Encryption Functions

Encryption over the Web is largely useless unless the scripts running the encryption schemes are operating on a secured server. Why? Because PHP is a server-side scripting language, information must first be sent to the server in plain text format *before* it can be encrypted. There are many ways that an unwanted third party can watch this information as it is transmitted from the user to the server if the user is not operating via a secured connection. For more information about setting up a secure Apache server, check out http://www.apache-ssl.org. If you're using a different Web server, refer to your documentation. Chances are that there is at least one, if not several, security solutions for your particular server.

md5()

```
string md5(string str)
```

MD5 is a third-party hash algorithm often used for creating digital signatures (among other things), which can be used to uniquely identify the sending party. It is considered to be a "one-way" hashing algorithm, which means there is no way to dehash data that has been hashed using md5().

The MD5 algorithm can also be used as a password verification system. Because it is (in theory) extremely difficult to retrieve the original string that has been hashed using the MD5 algorithm, you could hash a given password using MD5, and then compare that encrypted password against those that a user enters in order to gain access to restricted information.

For example, assume that your secret password "toystore" has an MD5 hash of 745e2abd7c52ee1dd7c14ae0d71b9d76. You can store this hashed value on the server and compare it to the MD5 hash equivalent of the password the user attempts to enter. Even if an intruder got hold of the encrypted password, it wouldn't make much difference, because that intruder couldn't return the string to its original format through conventional means. An example of hashing a string using md5() follows:

```php
<?php
    $val = "secret";
    $hash_val = md5 ($val);
    // $hash_val = "c1ab6fb9182f16eed935ba19aa830788";
?>
```

Often hash data pertaining to a user will be stored in a database. In fact, such practice is so widespread that many databases, MySQL included, offer a hashing function. For example, suppose you want to hash a password before storing it in a table. You could form the query like so:

```
$query = "INSERT INTO users VALUES('Jason Gilmore', md5('secretpswd')";
```

Remember that in order to store a complete hash, you'll need to set the field length to 32 characters.

The md5() function will satisfy most hashing needs. There is another much more powerful hashing alternative, made available via the Mhash extension. I'll introduce this extension in the next section.

mhash

mhash is an open-source library that offers an interface to a wide number of hash algorithms. Authored by Nikos Mavroyanopoulos and Sascha Schumann, mhash can significantly extend PHP's hashing capabilities. Integrating the mhash module into your PHP distribution is rather simple:

1. Go to http://mhash.sourceforge.net and download the package source.

2. Extract the contents of the compressed distribution and follow the installation instructions as specified in the INSTALL document.

3. Compile PHP with the --with-mhash option.

On completion of the installation process, you have the functionality offered by mhash at your disposal. In this section, I'll introduce the most prominent of the five functions made available to PHP when the mhash extension is included.

mhash()

```
string mhash(int hash, string data [, string key])
```

The function mhash() offers support for a number of hashing algorithms, allowing developers to incorporate checksums, message digests, and various other digital signatures into their PHP application. Hashes are also used for storing passwords. mhash currently supports the hashing algorithms listed here:

CRC32	CRC32B	GOST
HAVAL	MD5	RIPEMD128
RIPEMD160	SHA1	SNEFRU
TIGER		

Consider an example. Suppose you wanted to immediately encrypt a user's chosen password at the time of registration (which is typically a good idea). You could use mhash() to do so, setting the *hash* parameter to your chosen hashing algorithm, and *data* to the password you want to hash:

```php
<?php
    $userpswd = "mysecretpswd";
    $pswdhash = mhash(MHASH_SHA1, $userpswd);
    echo "The hashed password is: ".bin2hex($pswdhash);
?>
```

This returns the following:

```
The hashed password is: 07c45f62d68d6e63a9cc18a5e1871438ba8485c2
```

Note that you must use the bin2hex() function to convert the hash from binary mode to hexadecimal so that it can be formatted in a fashion easily viewable within a browser.

Via the optional parameter *key*, mhash() is also capable of determining message integrity and authenticity. If you pass in the message's secret key, mhash() will validate whether the message has been tampered with by returning the message's Hashed Message Authentication Code (HMAC). You can think of the HMAC as a checksum for encrypted data. If the HMAC matches the one that would be published along with the message, then the message has arrived undisturbed.

mcrypt

mcrypt is a popular data-encryption package available for use with PHP, providing support for two-way encryption (that is, encryption and decryption). Before you can use it, you'll need to follow these installation instructions:

1. Go to http://mcrypt.sourceforge.net/ and download the package source.

2. Extract the contents of the compressed distribution and follow the installation instructions as specified in the INSTALL document.

3. Compile PHP with the --with-mcrypt option.

mcrypt supports a number of encryption algorithms, all of which are listed here:

ARCFOUR	BLOWFISH	CAST
DES	ENIGMA	GOST
IDEA	LOKI	MARS
PANAMA	RC (2, 4, and 6)	RIJNDAEL
SAFER (64, 128, and PLUS)	SERPENT (128, 192, and 256)	SKIPJACK
TEAN	THREEWAY	3DES
TWOFISH (128, 192, and 256)	WAKE	XTEA

In this section, I'll introduce just a sample of the more than 35 functions made available via this PHP extension. For a complete introduction, please visit the PHP manual.

mcrypt_encrypt()

```
string mcrypt_encrypt(string cipher, string key, string data, string mode
[, string iv])
```

The mcrypt_encrypt() function encrypts *data*, returning the encrypted result. The parameter *cipher* names the particular encryption algorithm, and the parameter *key* determines the key used to encrypt the data. The *mode* parameter specifies one of the six available encryption modes: electronic codebook, cipher block chaining, cipher feedback, 8-bit output feedback, N-bit output feedback, and a special stream mode. Each is referenced by an abbreviation: ecb, cbc, cfb, ofb, nofb, and stream, respectively. Finally, the *iv* parameter initializes the cbc, cfb, ofb, and certain algorithms used in stream mode. Consider an example:

```
<?php
    $ivs = mcrypt_get_iv_size(MCRYPT_DES, MCRYPT_MODE_CBC);
    $iv = mcrypt_create_iv($ivs, MCRYPT_RAND);
    $key = "F925T";
    $message = "This is the message I want to encrypt.";
    $enc = mcrypt_encrypt(MCRYPT_DES, $key, $message, MCRYPT_MODE_CBC, $iv);
    echo bin2hex($enc);
?>
```

This returns:

```
f5d8b337f27e251c25f6a17c74f93c5e9a8a21b91f2b1b0151e649232b486c93b36af467914bc7d8
```

You can then decrypt the text with the mcrypt_decrypt() function, introduced next.

mcrypt_decrypt()

```
string mcrypt_decrypt(string cipher, string key, string data, string mode
[, string iv])
```

The mcrypt_decrypt() function decrypts a previously encrypted *cipher*, provided that the *cipher*, *key*, and *mode* are the same as those used to encrypt the data. Go ahead and insert the following line into the previous example, directly after the last statement:

```
echo mcrypt_decrypt(MCRYPT_DES, $key, $enc, MCRYPT_MODE_CBC, $iv);
```

This returns:

```
This is the message I want to encrypt.
```

The methods in this section are only those that are in some way incorporated into the PHP extension set. However, you are not limited to these encryption/hashing solutions. Keep in mind that you can use functions like popen() or exec()with any of your favorite third-party encryption technologies, PGP (http://www.pgpi.org/) or GPG (http://www.gnupg.org/), for example.

Summary

Hopefully the material presented in this chapter provided you with a few important tips, and more importantly, got you thinking about the many attack vectors that your application and server face. However, it's important to understand that the topics described in this section are but a tiny sliver of the total security pie. If you're new to the subject, take some time to learn more about some of the more prominent security-related Web sites. Regardless of your prior experience, you need to devise a strategy for staying abreast of breaking security news. I've found that subscribing to the newsletters from both the more prevalent security-focused Web sites and from the product developers to be the best way to do so. However, your strategic preference is somewhat irrelevant; what is important is that you have one and stick to it, lest your castle be conquered.

CHAPTER 20

SQLite

As of PHP 5.0, support for the open-source database server SQLite (http://www.sqlite.org/) is enabled by default. This was done in response to both the decision to unbundle MySQL from version 5 due to licensing discrepancies, and a realization that users might benefit from the availability of another powerful database server which none-theless requires measurably less configuration and maintenance as compared to similar products. In this chapter, I'll introduce both SQLite and PHP's ability to interface with this surprisingly capable database server.

SQLite

SQLite is a very compact, multi-platform SQL database engine written in C. Practically SQL92-compliant, SQLite offers many of the core database management features made available by competing products such as MySQL, PostgreSQL, and Oracle, yet at considerable savings in terms of cost, learning curve, and administration investment. Some of SQLite's more compelling characteristics include:

- SQLite stores an entire database in a single file, allowing for easy backup and transfer.

- SQLite's entire database security strategy is based entirely on the executing user's file permissions. So for example, user "web" might own the Web server daemon process, and through a script executed on that server, an attempt is made to open and write to a SQLite database named pmnp.db. Whether this user is capable of doing so depends entirely on the permissions set on the pmnp.db file.

- SQLite offers default transactional support, automatically integrating commit and rollback support.

- SQLite is available under a public domain license (it's free) for both the Microsoft Windows and Unix platforms.

Although I won't discuss SQLite's installation and configuration procedures (a precompiled binary is available for Windows, and it's the usual "configure-make-make install" procedure for Linux), I will offer a brief guide to the SQLite command-line interface. The reason for doing so is two-fold. First, it will provide you with at least an introductory look at this useful client. In additional, the steps demonstrated will create the data that will serve as the basis for all subsequent examples in this chapter.

Using the SQLite Command-line Interface

The SQLite command-line interface operates much the same as the MySQL client (mysql) in that it offers a simple means for interacting with the SQLite database server. With this tool, you can create and maintain databases, execute administrative processes such as backups and scripts, and tweak the client's behavior. To start the client, open up a terminal window and start SQLite with the help option:

```
%>sqlite -help
```

Before exiting back to the command-line, you'll be greeted with the command's usage syntax and a menu consisting of numerous options. Note that the usage syntax specifies that a filename is required to enter the SQLite interface. This filename is actually the name of the database. When supplied, a connection to this database will be opened, if the executing user possesses adequate permissions to do so. If the supplied database does not exist, it will be created, again if the executing user possesses the necessary privileges.

As an example, create a test database named pmnp.db. This database consists of a single table, employee. In this section, I'll use SQLite's command-line program to create the database, table, and sample data. Although no replacement for the documentation, the intention is that it will also serve as a brief primer for familiarizing yourself with the very basic aspects of SQLite and its command-line interface.

1. Open a new SQLite database.

   ```
   %>sqlite pmnp.db
   ```

2. Create a table.

   ```
   sqlite>create table employee (
   ...> empid integer primary key,
   ...>name varchar(25),
   ...>title varchar(25));
   ```

3. Check the table structure for accuracy:

   ```
   sqlite>.schema employee
   ```

4. Insert a few data rows.

   ```
   sqlite> insert into employee values(NULL,"Jason Gilmore","Chief Slacker");
   sqlite> insert into employee values(NULL,"Sam Spade","Technologist");
   sqlite> insert into employee values(NULL,"Ray Fox","Comedian");
   ```

5. Query the table just to ensure that all is correct.

   ```
   sqlite>select * from employee;
   ```

You should see:

```
1|Jason Gilmore|Chief Slacker
2|Sam Spade|Technologist
3|Ray Fox|Comedian
```

6. Quit the interface with the following command:

    ```
    sqlite>.quit
    ```

Note that a period (.) prefaces the quit command. This syntax requirement holds true for all commands available under the help menu.

PHP's SQLite Library

If you're familiar with PHP's MySQL library, the SQLite functions introduced in this section will be very familiar. In fact, for many of the functions the name is the only real differentiating factor. If you have a background in MySQL, picking up SQLite should be a snap. Even if you're entirely new to the concept, don't worry; I think you'll find these functions are extremely easy to use.

SQLite Directives

One PHP configuration directive is pertinent to SQLite. It's introduced in this section.

sqlite.assoc_case (0,1,2)
Scope: PHP_INI_ALL, Default value: 0
The sqlite.assoc_case directive determines the case used for referring to column names. By default, this directive is set to 0, which retains the case used in the table definitions. If it's set to 1, the names will be converted to uppercase. If it's set to 2, the names will be converted to lowercase.

Opening a Connection

Before you can retrieve or manipulate any data located in an SQLite database, you must first establish a connection. Two functions are available for doing so, sqlite_open() and sqlite_popen().

sqlite_open()

```
resource sqlite_open(string filename [,int mode [,string &error_message]])
```

The sqlite_open() function opens an SQLite database, first creating the database if it doesn't already exist. The *filename* parameter specifies the database name, and the optional *mode* parameter determines the access privilege level under which the database will be opened, and is specified as an octal value (the default is 0666) as might be used to specify modes in Unix. Currently, this parameter is unsupported by the API. The optional *error_message* parameter is actually automatically assigned a value specifying an error if the database could not be opened. If the database is successfully opened, the function will return a resource handle pointing to that database.

> **NOTE** *Unlike many other database servers, SQLite does not differentiate between establishing a connection with the database server and opening a database. For example, a typical execution sequence involving MySQL requires that* mysql_connect() *is used to establish a connection to the server, and then* mysql_select_db() *opens a particular database. This is not the case with SQLite, where both tasks are consolidated under the* sqlite_open() *(or* sqlite_popen()*) command.*

Consider an example:

```php
<?php
    $sqldb = sqlite_open("/home/book/20/pmnp.db") or die("Could not connect!");
?>
```

This will either open an existing database named pmnp.db, create a database named pmnp.db within the directory /home/book/20/, or result in an error, likely because of privilege problems. If you experience problems creating or opening the database, be sure that the user owning the Web server process possesses adequate permissions for writing to this directory.

sqlite_popen()

```
resource sqlite_popen(string filename [,int mode [,string &error_message]])
```

The function sqlite_popen() operates identically to sqlite_open(), except that it uses PHP's persistent connection feature in an effort to conserve resources. The function first verifies whether a connection already exists; if it does, it will reuse this connection, otherwise a new one will be created. Because of the performance improvements offered by this function, you should use sqlite_popen() instead of sqlite_open().

Closing a Connection

Good programming practice dictates that you close pointers to resources once you're finished with them. This maxim holds true for SQLite; once you've completed working with a database, you should close the open handle. One function, sqlite_close(), accomplishes just this.

sqlite_close()

```
void sqlite_close(resource dbh)
```

The function `sqlite_close()` closes the connection to the database resource specified by *dbh*. You should call it after all necessary tasks involving the database have been completed. An example follows:

```php
<?php
    $sqldb = sqlite_open("pmnp.db");
    // Perform necessary tasks
    sqlite_close($sqldb);
?>
```

Note that if a pending transaction has not been completed at the time of closure, the transaction will automatically be rolled back.

Querying a Database

The majority of your time spent interacting with a database server takes the form of SQL queries. The functions `sqlite_query()` and `sqlite_unbuffered_query()` offer the main vehicles for submitting these queries to SQLite and returning the subsequent result sets. You should pay particular attention to the specific advantages of each, however, because applying them inappropriately can negatively impact performance and capabilities.

sqlite_query()

```
resource sqlite_query(resource dbh, string query)
```

The `sqlite_query()` function executes an SQL query, *query*, against the database specified by *dbh*. If the query is intended to return a result set, FALSE is returned if the query fails. All other queries return TRUE if the query was successful, and FALSE otherwise.

In order to provide a practical example, other functions are used in this example that have not yet been introduced. Not to worry; just understand that the `sqlite_query()` function is responsible for sending and executing an SQL query. Soon enough, you'll learn the specifics regarding the other functions used in the example.

```php
<?php
    $sqldb = sqlite_open("pmnp.db");
    $results = sqlite_query($sqldb, "SELECT * FROM employee");
    while (list($empid, $name) = sqlite_fetch_array($results)) {
        echo "Name: $name (Employee ID: $empid) <br />";
    }
    sqlite_close($sqldb);
?>
```

This yields the following results:

```
Name: Jason Gilmore (Employee ID: 1)
Name: Sam Spade (Employee ID: 2)
Name: Ray Fox (Employee ID: 3)
```

Keep in mind that sqlite_query() will only execute the query and return a result set; it will not output or offer any additional information regarding the returned data. To do so, you'll need to pass the result set into one or several other functions, all of which are introduced in the following sections.

sqlite_unbuffered_query()

resource sqlite_unbuffered_query(resource *dbh*, string *query*)

The sqlite_unbuffered_query() can be thought of an optimized version of sqlite_query(), identical in every way except that the result set is returned in a format intended to be used in the order in which it is returned, without any need to search or navigate it in any other way. This function is particularly useful if you're solely interested in dumping a result set to output, an HTML table or a text file, for example.

Because this function is optimized for returning result sets intended to be output in a straightforward fashion, you cannot pass its output to functions like sqlite_num_rows(), sqlite_seek(), or any other function with the purpose of examining or modifying the output or output pointers. If you require the use of such functions, use sqlite_query() to retrieve the result set instead.

Parsing Result Sets

Once a result set has been returned, you'll likely want to do something with the data. The functions in this section demonstrate the many ways that you can parse the result set.

sqlite_fetch_array()

array sqlite_fetch_array(resource *result* [, int *result_type* [, bool *decode_binary*]])

The sqlite_fetch_array() function returns an associative array consisting of the items found in the *result* set's next available row, or returns FALSE if no more rows are available. The optional *result_type* parameter can be used to specify whether the columns found in the result set row should be referenced by their integer-based position in the row or by their actual name. Specifying SQLITE_NUM enables the former, while SQLITE_ASSOC enables the latter. You can return both referential indexes by specifying SQLITE_BOTH. Finally, the optional *decode_binary* parameter determines whether PHP will decode the binary-encoded target data that had been previously encoded using the function sqlite_escape_string(). This function is introduced in the later section, "Working With Binary Data."

Consider an example:

```php
<?php
    $sqldb = sqlite_open("pmnp.db");
    $results = sqlite_query($sqldb, "SELECT * FROM employee");
    while ($row = sqlite_fetch_array($results,SQLITE_BOTH)) {
        echo "Name: $row[1] (Employee ID: ".$row['empid'].")<br />";
    }
    sqlite_close($sqldb);
?>
```

This returns:

```
Name: Jason Gilmore (Employee ID: 1)
Name: Sam Spade (Employee ID: 2)
Name: Ray Fox (Employee ID: 3)
```

Note that I chose to use the SQLITE_BOTH option so that the returned columns could be referenced both by their numerically indexed position as well as by their name. Although it's not entirely practical, this example serves as an ideal means for demonstrating the function's flexibility.

One great way to render your code a tad more readable is to use PHP's list() function in conjunction with sql_fetch_array(). With it, you can both return and parse the array into the required components all on the same line. I'll revise the previous example to take this idea into account:

```php
<?php
    $sqldb = sqlite_open("pmnp.db");
    $results = sqlite_query($sqldb, "SELECT * FROM employee");
    while (list($empid, $name) = sqlite_fetch_array($results)) {
        echo "Name: $name (Employee ID: $empid)<br />";
    }
    sqlite_close($sqldb);
?>
```

sqlite_array_query ()

array sqlite_array_query (resource *dbh*, string *query* [, int *res_type*
[, bool *decode_binary*]])

The sqlite_array_query() function consolidates the capabilities of sqlite_query() and sqlite_fetch_array() into a single function call, both executing the query and returning the result set as an array. The input parameters work exactly like those introduced in the component functions sqlite_query() and sqlite_fetch_array(). According to the PHP manual, this function should only be used for retrieving result sets of fewer than 45 rows; however in this case it will provide both a considerable improvement in performance, and in certain cases a slight reduction in total lines of code. Consider an example:

```php
<?php
    $sqldb = sqlite_open("pmnp.db");
    $rows = sqlite_array_query($sqldb, "SELECT empid, name FROM employee");
    foreach ($rows AS $row) {
        echo $row["name"]." (Employee ID: ".$row["empid"].")<br />";
    }
    sqlite_close($sqldb);
?>
```

This returns:

```
Jason Gilmore (Employee ID: 1)
Sam Spade (Employee ID: 2)
Ray Fox (Employee ID: 3)
```

sqlite_column()

```
mixed sqlite_column(resource result, mixed index_or_name [, bool decode_binary])
```

The sqlite_column() function is useful if you're interested in just a single column from a given *result* row or set. You can retrieve the column either by *name* or by *index* offset. Finally, the optional *decode_binary* parameter determines whether PHP will decode the binary-encoded target data that had been previously encoded using the function sqlite_escape_string(). This function is introduced in the later section, "Working With Binary Data."

For example, suppose you retrieved all rows from the employee table. Using this function, you could selectively poll columns, like so:

```php
<?php
    $sqldb = sqlite_open("pmnp.db");
    $results = sqlite_query($sqldb,"SELECT * FROM employee WHERE empid = '1'");
    $name = sqlite_column($results,"name");
    $empid = sqlite_column($results,"empid");
    echo "Name: $name (Employee ID: $empid) <br />";
    sqlite_close($sqldb);
?>
```

This returns:

```
Name: Jason Gilmore (Employee ID: 1)
```

Ideally, you'll want to use this function when you're working with result sets consisting of numerous columns, or with particularly large columns.

sqlite_fetch_single()

```
string sqlite_fetch_single(resource row_set [, int result_type
[, bool decode_binary]])
```

The sqlite_fetch_single() function operates identically to sql_fetch_array() except that it returns just the value located in the first column of the *row_set*.

> **TIP** *This function has an alias:* sqlite_fetch_string(). *Except for the name, it's identical in every way.*

Consider an example. Suppose you're interested in querying the database for a single column. To reduce otherwise unnecessary overhead, you should opt to use sqlite_fetch_single() over sqlite_fetch_array(), like so:

```php
<?php
    $sqldb = sqlite_open("pmnp.db");
    $results = sqlite_query($sqldb,"SELECT name FROM employee WHERE empid < 3");
    while ($name = sqlite_fetch_single($results)) {
        echo "Employee: $name <br />";
    }
    sqlite_close($sqldb);
?>
```

This returns:

```
Employee: Jason Gilmore
Employee: Sam Spade
```

Retrieving Result Set Details

You'll often want to learn more about a result set than just its contents. Several SQLite-specific functions are available for determining information such as the returned field names, and the number of fields and rows returned. These functions are introduced in this section.

sqlite_field_name()

```
string sqlite_field_name(resource result, int field_index)
```

The sqlite_field_name() function returns the name of the field located at the index offset *field_index* found in the *result* set. For example:

```php
<?php
    $sqldb = sqlite_open("pmnp.db");
    $results = sqlite_query($sqldb,"SELECT * FROM employee");
    echo "Field name found at offset #0: ".sqlite_field_name($results,0)."<br />";
    echo "Field name found at offset #1: ".sqlite_field_name($results,1)."<br />";
    echo "Field name found at offset #2: ".sqlite_field_name($results,2)."<br />";
    sqlite_close($sqldb);
?>
```

This returns:

```
Field name found at offset #0: empid
Field name found at offset #1: name
Field name found at offset #2: title
```

As is the case with all numerically indexed arrays, remember that the offset starts at zero, and not one.

sqlite_num_fields()

```
int sqlite_num_fields(resource result_set)
```

The sqlite_num_fields() function returns the number of columns located in the *result_set*. For example:

```php
<?php
    $sqldb = sqlite_open("pmnp.db");
    $results = sqlite_query($sqldb, "SELECT * FROM employee");
    echo "Total fields returned: ".sqlite_num_fields($results)."<br />";
    sqlite_close($sqldb);
?>
```

This returns:

Total fields returned: 3

---

sqlite_num_rows()

int sqlite_num_rows(resource *result_set*)

The sqlite_num_rows() function returns the number of rows located in the *result_set*. An example follows:

```php
<?php
    $sqldb = sqlite_open("pmnp.db");
    $results = sqlite_query($sqldb, "SELECT * FROM employee");
    echo "Total rows returned: ".sqlite_num_rows($results)."<br />";
    sqlite_close($sqldb);
?>
```

This returns:

Total rows returned: 3

Manipulating the Result Set Pointer

Although SQLite is indeed a database server, in many ways it behaves much like what you experience when working with file I/O. One such way involves the ability to move the row "pointer" around the result set. Several functions are offered for doing just this, all of which are introduced in this section.

sqlite_current()

array sqlite_current(resource *result* [, int *result_type* [, bool *decode_binary*]])

The sqlite_current() function is identical to sqlite_fetch_array() in every way except that it does not advance the pointer to the next row of the *result* set. Instead, it only returns the row residing at the current pointer position. If the pointer already resides at the end of the result set, FALSE is returned.

sqlite_has_more()

```
boolean sqlite_has_more(resource result_set)
```

The sqlite_has_more() function determines whether the end of the *result_set* has been reached, returning TRUE if additional rows are still available, and FALSE otherwise. An example follows:

```php
<?php
    $sqldb = sqlite_open("pmnp.db");
    $results = sqlite_query($sqldb, "SELECT * FROM employee");
    while ($row = sqlite_fetch_array($results,SQLITE_BOTH)) {
        echo "Name: $row[1] (Employee ID: ".$row['empid'].")<br />";
        if (sqlite_has_more($results)) echo "Still more rows to go!<br />";
            else echo "No more rows!<br />";
    }
    sqlite_close($sqldb);
?>
```

This returns:

```
Name: Jason Gilmore (Employee ID: 1)
Still more rows to go!
Name: Sam Spade (Employee ID: 2)
Still more rows to go!
Name: Ray Fox (Employee ID: 3)
No more rows!
```

sqlite_next()

```
boolean sqlite_next(resource result)
```

The sqlite_next() function moves the result set pointer to the next position, returning TRUE on success and FALSE if the pointer already resides at the end of the result set.

sqlite_rewind()

```
boolean sqlite_rewind(resource result)
```

The sqlite_rewind() function moves the *result* set pointer back to the first row, returning FALSE if no rows exist in the result set, and TRUE otherwise.

sqlite_seek()

```
boolean sqlite_seek(resource result, int row_number)
```

The sqlite_seek() function moves the pointer to the row specified by *row_number*, returning TRUE if the row exists, and FALSE otherwise. Consider an example in which an employee of the month will be randomly selected from a result set consisting of the entire staff:

```php
<?php
    $sqldb = sqlite_open("pmnp.db");
    $results = sqlite_query($sqldb, "SELECT empid, name FROM employee");

    // Choose a random number found within the range of total returned rows
    $random = rand(0,sqlite_num_rows($results)-1);

    // Move the pointer to the row specified by the random number
    sqlite_seek($results, $random);

    // Retrieve the employee ID and name found at this row
    list($empid, $name) = sqlite_current($results);
    echo "Randomly chosen employee of the month: $name (Employee ID: $empid)";
    sqlite_close($sqldb);
?>
```

This returns the following (this only shows one of three possible outcomes):

```
Randomly chosen employee of the month: Ray Fox (Employee ID: 3)
```

One point of common confusion that arises in this example regards the starting index offset of result sets. The offset always begins with zero, and not one, which is why you need to subtract 1 from the total rows returned in this example. As a result, the randomly generated row offset integer must fall within a range of zero and one less than the total number of returned rows.

Working with Binary Data

SQLite is capable of storing binary information in a table, such as a GIF or JPEG image, a PDF, or a Microsoft Word document. However, unless you treat this data carefully, errors in both storage and communication could arise. Several functions are available for carrying out the tasks necessary for managing this data, one of which is introduced in this section. The other two relevant functions are introduced in the next section.

sqlite_escape_string()

```
string sqlite_escape_string(string item)
```

Certain data intended for storage in a database must be taken into special consideration, either for reasons pertinent to the database's particular implementation, to the
ability of some other technology's capability to work with that data which may be later
retrieved from the database, or both. As a result, many databases, including MySQL,
PostgreSQL, and SQLite, employ special features capable of handling this data as necessary. For example, SQLite expects that single quotes signal the delimitation of a
string. However, because this character is often used within data which you might want
to include in a table column, a means is required for tricking the database server into
ignoring them on these occasions. This is commonly referred to as "escaping" these
special characters, often done by prefacing the special character with some other character, a single-quote (') for example. Although you can do this manually, a function is
available that will do the job for you. The sqlite_escape_string() function escapes
any single quotes and other binary-unsafe characters intended for insertion in an
SQLite table found in *item*.

I'll use this function to escape an otherwise invalid query string:

```php
<?php
    $str = "As they always say, this is 'an' example.";
    echo sqlite_escape_string($str);
?>
```

This returns:

```
As they always say, this is ''an'' example.
```

If the string contains a NULL character, or begins with 0x01, circumstances that
have special meaning when working with binary data, sqlite_escape_string() will
take the steps necessary to properly encode the information so that it can be safely
stored and later retrieved.

> **NOTE** *The NULL character typically signals the end of a binary string. 0x01 is the
> escape character used within binary data. Therefore, to ensure that it was properly
> interpreted by the binary data parser, it would need to be decoded.*

When you're using user-defined functions, a topic discussed in the next section,
you should never use this function. Instead, use the sqlite_udf_encode_binary() and
sqlite_udf_decode_binary() functions. Both are introduced in the next section.

Creating and Overriding SQLite Functions

An intelligent programmer will take every opportunity to reuse code. Because many database-driven applications often require the use of a core task set, there are ample opportunities to make use of this virtue. Such tasks often seek to manipulate database data, producing some sort of outcome based on the retrieved data. As a result, it would be quite convenient if the task results could be directly returned via the SQL query, like so:

```
sqlite>SELECT convert_salary_to_gold(salary)
   ...> FROM employee WHERE empID=1";
```

PHP's SQLite library offers a means for registering and maintaining customized functions such as this. In this section, I'll show you how this is accomplished.

sqlite_create_function()

```
boolean sqlite_create_function(resource dbh, string func, mixed callback
[, int num_args])
```

The sqlite_create_function() function enables you to register custom PHP functions as an SQLite user-defined function (UDF). For example, this function would be used to register the convert_salary_to_gold() function discussed in the opening paragraphs of this section, like so:

```php
<?php
    /* Define gold's current price-per-ounce. */
    define("PPO",400);

    /* Calculate how much gold an employee can purchase with salary. */
    function convert_salary_to_gold($salary)
    {
        return $salary / PPO;
    }

    /* Connect to the SQLite database. */
    $sqldb = sqlite_open("pmnp.db");

    /* Create the user-defined function. */
    sqlite_create_function($sqldb,"salarytogold", "convert_salary_to_gold", 1);

    /* Query the database using the UDF. */
    $query = "select salarytogold(salary) FROM employee WHERE empid=1";
    $result = sqlite_query($sqldb, $query);
    list($salaryToGold) = sqlite_fetch_array($result);

    /* Display the results. */
    echo "The employee can purchase: ".$salaryToGold." ounces.";
```

```
    /* End the database connection. */
    sqlite_close($sqldb);
?>
```

Assuming user Jason makes $10,000 per year, you can expect the following output:

```
The employee can purchase 25 ounces.
```

---

sqlite_udf_encode_binary()

```
string sqlite_udf_encode_binary(string data)
```

The sqlite_udf_encode_binary() function encodes any binary data intended for storage within a SQLite table. Use this function instead of sqlite_escape_string() when you're working with data sent to a user-defined function.

sqlite_udf_decode_binary()

```
string sqlite_udf_decode_binary(string data)
```

The sqlite_udf_decode_binary() function decodes any binary data previously encoded with the sqlite_udf_encode_binary() function. Use this function when you're returning possibly binary unsafe data from a user-defined function.

Creating Aggregate Functions

When you work with database-driven applications, it's often useful to derive some value based on some collective calculation of all values found within a particular column or set of columns. Several such functions are commonly made available within an SQL server's core functionality set. A few such commonly implemented functions, known as *aggregate functions*, include sum(), max() and min(). However, you might require a custom aggregate function not otherwise available within the server's default capabilities. SQLite compensates for this by offering the ability to create your own. The function used to register your custom aggregate functions, sqlite_create_aggregate(), is introduced in this section.

sqlite_create_aggregate()

```
boolean sqlite_create_aggregate(resource dbh, string func, mixed step_func,
mixed final_func [, int num_args])
```

The sqlite_create_aggregate() is used to register a user-defined aggregate function, *step_func*. Actually it registers two functions: *step_func*, which is called on every row of the query target, and *final_func*, used to return the aggregate value back to the caller. Once registered, you can call *final_func* within the caller by the alias *func*. The optional *num_args* parameter specifies the number of parameters the aggregate function should take. Although the SQLite parser attempts to discern the number if this parameter is omitted, you should always include it for clarity's sake.

Consider an example. Building on the salary conversion example from the previous section, suppose you wanted to calculate the total amount of gold employees could collectively purchase:

```php
<?php
    /* Define gold's current price-per-ounce. */
    define("PPO",400);

    /* Create the aggregate function. */
    function total_salary(&$total,$salary)
    {
        $total += $salary;
    }

    /* Create the aggregate finalization function. */
    function convert_to_gold(&$total)
    {
        return $total / PPO;
    }

    /* Connect to the SQLite database. */
    $sqldb = sqlite_open("pmnp.db");

    /* Register the aggregate function. */
    sqlite_create_aggregate($sqldb, "computetotalgold", "total_salary",
            "convert_to_gold",1);

    /* Query the database using the UDF. */
    $query = "select computetotalgold(salary) FROM employee";
    $result = sqlite_query($sqldb, $query);
    list($salaryToGold) = sqlite_fetch_array($result);

    /* Display the results. */
    echo "The employees can purchase: ".$salaryToGold." ounces.";

    /* End the database connection. */
    sqlite_close($sqldb);
?>
```

If your employees' salaries total $16,000, you could expect the following output:

```
The employees can purchase 40 ounces.
```

Summary

The administrative overhead required of many database servers often outweighs the advantages of added power they offer to many projects. SQLite offers an ideal remedy to this dilemma, providing a fast and capable back end at a cost of minimum maintenance. Given SQLite's commitment to standards, ideal licensing arrangements, and quality, consider saving yourself time, resources, and money by using SQLite for your future projects.

The next chapter signals the start of the second major book topic, another popular database server named MySQL. In this chapter, you'll learn all about the software, its history and community, and gain valuable insight into why it's the world's most popular Open Source database server.

CHAPTER 21

MySQL:
The Disruptive Database

THE MYSQL RELATIONAL DATABASE server was born out of an internal company project spearheaded by employees Michael "Monty" Widenius and David Axmark. First released to the general public in 1995 by way of their Uppsala, Sweden–based software company TCX DataKonsult AB, the software soon proved so popular that its creators quickly realized its potential and founded MySQL AB, a company based entirely around MySQL-specific service and product offerings. Profitable since its inception, MySQL AB has since grown by leaps and bounds, establishing offices in several countries, attracting considerable venture capital funding in 2001, and announcing numerous high-profile partnerships with several IT heavyweights, including Silicon Graphics, Veritas, Novell, and Rackspace.

From its first public release in 1995, MySQL's developers placed particular emphasis on software performance and scalability. The result is a highly optimized product that was lacking in many features considered standard for enterprise database products: stored procedures, triggers, and transactions for example. Yet the product caught the attention of a vast number of users more interested in speed and scalability than in capabilities that would in many cases often go unused anyway. With the release of subsequent versions came the addition of additional features, and with it, users. Today, there are more than four million active MySQL installations worldwide, with over 35,000 copies of the software downloaded daily (http://www.mysql.com/company/factsheet.html). These users include some of the most widely known companies and organizations in the world, such as Yahoo!, NASA, the United States Census Bureau, Google, the New York Stock Exchange, Sun Microsystems, Nortel Networks, and Cisco (http://www.mysql.com/press/MySQL_userlist.pdf). Later in this chapter, I'll take a closer look at how a few of these users are putting MySQL to work, and in some cases, saving millions of dollars in the process.

What is it about MySQL that makes it so popular? I'll take a moment to highlight just a few key features MySQL has to offer. Afterwards, I'll offer some specific information pertinent to two major milestone releases of the product, namely versions 4 and 5.

Performance

As I mentioned, the MySQL developers have taken great pains to optimize every imaginable aspect of the code base. Although much of this is the result of intelligent application-development strategies, there are several very specific optimization features worth mentioning:

Multiple Table Handlers

Anybody who has taken a computer science class or worked on any substantial application knows that algorithms are particularly adept at certain tasks and particularly maladapted for others. Therefore, it's crucial to choose the right algorithm for the job for your application to perform efficiently under duress. MySQL takes a similar tack, offering three different types of generalized mechanisms, or *table handlers*, for managing data. Each of the three table handlers, HEAP, InnoDB, and MyISAM, bears its own strengths and weaknesses and should be applied selectively to best fit the intended use of your data. Because a single database could consist of several tables, each with its own specific purpose, MySQL affords you the opportunity of simultaneously using different table handlers in a single database. I'll further introduce these handlers in Chapter 24.

Query Caching

Query caching is one of MySQL's greatest speed enhancements. Simple and highly effective when enabled, MySQL will store SELECT queries, along with their corresponding results, in memory. As subsequent queries are executed, MySQL will compare them against the cached queries; if they match, MySQL will forego the costly database retrieval and instead simply dump the cached query result. To eliminate outdated results, mechanisms are also built in for automatically removing the cached results and recaching them upon the next request.

Full-Text Indexing and Searching

The release of MySQL version 3.23.23 was accompanied with the addition of full-text indexing and searching capabilities, a feature that greatly enhances the performance of mining data from text-based columns (namely CHAR, VARCHAR, TINYTEXT, TEXT, MEDIUMTEXT, and LONGTEXT). This feature also enables you to produce results in order of relevance in accordance with how closely the query matches the row.

Replication

Version 3.23.15 saw the addition of MySQL's replication feature. Replication allows for a database located within one MySQL server to be duplicated on another, which provides a great number of advantages. For instance, just having a single slave database in place can greatly increase availability, because it could be immediately brought online if the master experiences a problem. If you have multiple machines at your disposal, client queries can be spread across the master and multiple slaves, considerably reducing the load that would otherwise be incurred on a single machine. Another advantage involves backups; rather than take your application offline while a backup is completed, you could instead execute the backup on a slave, allowing your application to incur zero downtime.

Platform Flexibility

At the time of this writing, optimized MySQL binaries were available for twelve platforms, including Dec OSF, FreeBSD, IBM AIX, HP-UX, Linux, Mac OS X, Novell Netware, OpenBSD, QNX, SGI Irix, Solaris, and Microsoft Windows. Furthermore, MySQL also makes the source code available for download if binaries are not available for your platform, or if you want to perform the compilation yourself.

Advanced Security and Configuration Options

MySQL sports a vast array of security and configuration options, enabling you to wield total control over just about every imaginable aspect of its operation. For example, with MySQL's configuration options you can control things like:

- The location of MySQL's data store, the daemon owner, default language, default port, and other key global characteristics.

- The amount of memory allocated to threads, the query cache, temporary tables, table joins, and index key buffers.

- Various aspects of MySQL's networking capabilities, including how long it will attempt to perform a connection before aborting, whether it will attempt to resolve DNS names, the maximum allowable packet size, and more.

MySQL's security options are equally impressive, allowing you to manage things like:

- The total number of queries, updates, and connections allowed on an hourly basis.

- Whether a user must present a valid SSL certificate in order to connect to the database.

- Which actions are available to a user for a given database, table, and even column. For example, you might allow a user update privileges for the email column of a corporate employee table, but deny deletion privileges.

In addition, MySQL tracks numerous metrics regarding all aspects of database interaction, among other things the total incoming and outgoing bytes transferred, counts of every query type executed (insert, select, update, delete), total threads open, running, cached, and connected. It also tracks the number of queries that have surpassed a certain execution threshold, total queries stored in the cache, if it's enabled, uptime, and much more. Such numbers prove invaluable for continuously tuning and optimizing your server throughout its lifetime.

Because of the importance of these options, I'll return to them repeatedly throughout the forthcoming chapters. Specifically, I devote part of Chapter 22 to MySQL configuration, and the whole of Chapter 25 to the matter of MySQL security.

Internationalization and Localization

Although MySQL uses English-compatible settings by default, users can make use of over 30 character sets used in conjunction with over 20 languages. With these settings, you can control the language used for error and status messages, how MySQL sorts data, and which character set is used to store data in the tables.

Flexible Licensing Options

MySQL is available under two licensing options: the GNU General Public License (GPO), and the commercial license. The open-source license allows you to use MySQL free of charge to develop open-source applications, provided that you also adhere to the terms of the GPL. The commercial license is available if you would rather not release or redistribute your project code, or otherwise build non-GPL compliant applications. If you go with the non-GPL option, pricing is quite agreeable, with the MySQL Classic (nontransactional) version of the database server running $249 per license, and the MySQL Pro version (transactional-capable) running $495, according to the latest information on the MySQL.com Web site. Special pricing arrangements are available for both versions if you want to purchase multiple copies. See the MySQL Web site for more details.

A (Hyper)Active User Community

Although many open-source projects enjoy an active user community, I tend to define MySQL's as hyperactive. For starters, the company strives to release an updated version every four to six weeks, resulting in a constant stream of bug fixes and feature enhancements. In addition, there are thousands of open-source projects underway that depend upon MySQL as the back end for managing a broad array of information, including server log files, e-mail, images, Web content, help desk tickets, and gaming statistics. If you require advice or support, you can use your favorite search engine to consult one of the hundreds of tutorials written regarding every imaginable aspect of the software, browse MySQL's gargantuan manual, or pose a question in any of the high-traffic MySQL-specific newsgroups. In fact, I've often found that when researching MySQL, the problem isn't so much one of whether I'll find what I'm looking for, but where to begin!

MySQL 4

The March 25, 2003, production release of MySQL 4.0 marked a major milestone in the software's history. After 18 months of development releases and several years of labor, the completed product was made available to the general public, bringing several new features to the table that many have long been considered standard among any viable enterprise database product. I'll enumerate some of the feature highlights here:

- **Addition of InnoDB to the standard distribution:** The InnoDB table handler, which has been available to users since version 3.23.34a, was made part of the standard distribution as of version 4.0. The InnoDB tables bring a host of new features to MySQL users, including transactions, foreign key integrity, and row-level locking. I'll introduce the InnoDB table handler in Chapter 24 and discuss transactions in Chapter 29.

- **Query caching:** Query caching, which was made available in version 4.0.1, greatly improves the performance of selection queries by storing query results in memory and retrieving those results directly, rather than repeatedly querying the database for the same result set.

- **An embedded MySQL server:** An embedded MySQL server makes it possible to integrate a full-featured MySQL server into embedded applications. Embedded applications power things like kiosks, CD-ROMs, Internet appliances, cell phones, and PDAs.

- **Subqueries:** Subqueries can greatly reduce the complexity otherwise required of certain queries, offering the ability to embed select statements inside other select statements. As of version 4.1, MySQL users can now enjoy the use of standards-based subquery operations.

- **Secure connections via the Secure Sockets Layer (SSL):** Using solely unencrypted client-server connections raises the possibility that the data and the authentication credentials could be intercepted and even modified by some uninvited third-party. As of version 4.0, encrypted connections can be established between MySQL and any client supporting Secure Sockets Layer (SSL) technology. I'll introduce this feature in Chapter 25.

MySQL 5

An alpha release of MySQL 5 was made available for download on January 21, 2004. This release really signifies a major advancement of the product; I predict that this version will ultimately signal MySQL AB's arrival in the enterprise database server arena, substantially cutting into the market share of its entrenched competitors. Certainly a bold statement! However, given the ambitious array of features already available or presently under development for this version, perhaps the prediction isn't so far fetched after all. I'll enumerate some of the feature highlights here:

- **Complete foreign key support:** A *foreign key* is a key found in a given table that references a primary key found in another table. Such keys are used to identify a relationship among rows in different tables. Already available for the InnoDB table handler, foreign key support is scheduled to be made available for all handlers as of version 5.1.

- **Stored procedures:** A stored procedure is a set of SQL statements that is stored in the database and made available in the same manner as SQL functions such as min() or rand(). Based on the requirements as set forth by the latest pending SQL standard, SQL:2003, the addition of stored procedures fulfills one of the last major feature deficiencies of MySQL.

- **Triggers:** Scheduled for release with version 5.1, triggers are essentially a stored procedure that is invoked based on the occurrence of a defined event. Triggers are often used to preserve data integrity by reviewing and manipulating data when a particular event occurs, such as deleting keyed data in a particular table.

Prominent MySQL Users

As you learned in the opening paragraphs of this chapter, MySQL boasts quite a list of prominent users. In this section, I'll offer some additional insight into a few of my favorite implementations.

Yahoo! Finance

When you think of one of the true Internet heavyweights, the online portal Yahoo! almost assuredly pops into the mind. Although most would think that this corporate juggernaut is devoted to commercial IT solutions, http://www.yahoo.com/ actually operates on the FreeBSD platform, an open-source Unix variant. However, Yahoo's preference for experimenting with and even deploying open-source solutions might not be more pronounced than its move to power companion Web site http://finance.yahoo.com/ using FreeBSD and a MySQL back end. No small feat, considering that the Web site processes billions (with a *b*) of page views monthly, on average.

Jeremy Zawodny, one of the Yahoo! Finance database developers, is so proud of MySQL's efficiency that he actually embeds the Yahoo! MySQL server statistics in his e-mail signature. To provide an idea of just how much traffic their MySQL installation processes on a regular basis, the following is his signature from a February 6, 2004, newsgroup posting:

```
MySQL 4.0.15-Yahoo-SMP: up 145 days, processed 1,515,422,676 queries
(120/sec. avg)
```

For more information about the Yahoo! Finance MySQL deployment, check out this article: http://www.mysql.com/articles/us/yahoo_finance.html.

NASA

The National Aeronautics and Space Administration (NASA) has long been heralded as one of the most ingenious United States governmental institutions, not only for its famed space walks and lunar landings, but also for its ability to continually succeed despite shoestring funding. This ongoing budget dilemma recently worked its way into the NASA department responsible for maintaining the NAIS (NASA Acquisition Internet Service, `http://nais.nasa.gov/`), the service responsible for maintaining and providing access to NASA's competitive solicitations for outside contract opportunities. Faced with a pending restructuring of Oracle licensing agreements, the NAIS staff was forced to search for an alternative database solution.

According to NAIS developer Jim Sudderth, NAIS chose MySQL, basing this decision on three motives: cost, support, and compatibility (`http://www.mysql.com/articles/us/nasa.html`). He clarifies their reasoning with a reference to the savings in cost for technical support alone, which worked out to roughly one percent of the technical support expenditure required of Oracle (`http://www.gcn.com/vol19_no33/enterprise/3275-1.html`). Perhaps even more important, NAIS's team leader stated that they actually noticed a performance increase as a result of the switch (`http://www.fcw.com/fcw/articles/2000/1204/pol-nasa-12-04-00.asp`).

U.S. Census Bureau

Although it owns a site license for Oracle, the U.S. Census Bureau relies on MySQL to power three of its most successful and highest-traffic Web sites (`http://www.mysql.com/press/user_stories/us_census.html`). The first of these sites, FedStats (`http://www.fedstats.gov/`), is the primary online resource for retrieving statistical information produced by the U.S. government. This site offers access to a document repository of more than 200,000 documents interspersed among over 70 federal agencies.

The second Web site, MapStats (`http://www.fedstats.gov/qf/`), offers statistical information regarding states, counties, and various other geographical regions found around the United States. MapStats aggregates data dispersed across numerous resources, offering 70,000 records of information regarding these subjects.

The third Web site, QuickFacts (`http://quickfacts.census.gov/`), provides Census information as applied to the various states and counties around the U.S. According to a previously referenced case study posted to the MySQL Web site, the site serves an average of 120,000 pages daily.

Summary

From internal project to global competitor, MySQL has indeed come a very long way in just a few short years. In this chapter, I offered a brief overview of this climb to stardom, detailing MySQL's history, progress, and future. I also touched upon just a few of the thousands of successful user stories, highlighting the use of MySQL at Yahoo!, NASA, and the U.S. Census Bureau.

In the following chapters, I'll further acquaint you with many of MySQL's basic topics, covering the installation and configuration process, the many MySQL clients, table structures, and its security features. If you're new to MySQL, this material will prove invaluable for getting up to speed regarding the basic features and behavior of this powerful database server. If you're already quite familiar with MySQL, I still suggest browsing through the material; at the very least, it should serve as a valuable reference.

CHAPTER 22

Installing and Configuring MySQL

THIS CHAPTER OFFERS a general introduction to the MySQL database server installation and configuration process. I don't intend this as a replacement for MySQL's excellent (and mammoth) user's manual; I'll instead opt to highlight the key procedures of immediate interest to anybody interested in quickly and efficiently readying the database server for use. In total, the following topics are covered:

- An important note about the PHP 5 distribution

- Downloading instructions

- Distribution variations

- Installation procedures (source, binary, RPMs)

- Setting the MySQL administrator password

- Starting and stopping MySQL

- Installing MySQL as a system service

- MySQL configuration

By the chapter's conclusion, you'll have learned how to install and configure an operational MySQL server. Before delving into this discussion however, I'd like to point out a recent change that is sure to confuse many long-time PHP/MySQL developers.

An Important Note about the PHP 5 Distribution

The PHP and MySQL developers have long enjoyed a close relationship. The respective technologies are like two peas in a pod, bread and butter, wine and cheese; you get the picture. This popularity prompted the PHP developers early on to bundle the MySQL client libraries with the distribution, and enable the extension by default in version 4. However, as a result of licensing issues that transpired due to MySQL AB's decision to release their product under the GPL, the PHP developers decided to unbundle the libraries and disable the extension in PHP 5. Likely because of the subsequent community turmoil over this decision, MySQL AB released an optional GPL license extension for PHP, which permits the distribution of "derivative works that are formed with GPL-licensed MySQL software and with software licensed under version 3.0 of the PHP license" (`http://www.mysql.com/products/licensing/opensource-license.html`). That said, if your software doesn't satisfy this constraint, you're free to use MySQL's GPL version. Alternatively, you should purchase the appropriate commercial license. I'll talk a bit more about licensing issues in a later section.

Regardless of the exception, it's unlikely that the MySQL client libraries will be rebundled with PHP anytime soon. Therefore, you'll need to include the `--with-mysql[=DIR]` configuration option when you're building PHP, specifying the path to the MySQL installation directory.

On Windows, you'll need to do two things to enable MySQL support with PHP 5. After successfully installing MySQL, open up the `php.ini` file and uncomment the following line:

```
extension=php_mysql.dll
```

Next, copy the `libmysql.dll` file, located in the PHP 5 home directory, to your Windows system directory. On Windows 95, 98, or ME, this is typically `C:\Windows\system`; on WindowsNT or 2000 this is typically `C:\winnt\system32\` or `C:\winnt40\system32\`; on Windows XP this is typically `C:\windows\system32\`. Restart Apache and you should be all set.

Downloading MySQL

Given that MySQL is Open Source software, you might presume that obtaining it is as simple as navigating to the MySQL site and downloading a copy, and indeed, it is that easy. However, there are a few issues that one should keep in mind when proceeding to download the latest distribution. I'll discuss these matters in this section.

The official MySQL Web site receives a large amount of traffic. To speed your download and aid in the offloading of traffic from the official site, you should use the closest mirror. A list of mirrors hosting the latest MySQL version is available at `http://www.mysql.com/downloads/mirrors.html`.

Three versions of MySQL 4 are available for download. You should choose the version that best fits your specific needs.

- **Standard:** The standard version should suit the needs of most users. It offers all of MySQL's common features, including InnoDB transactional support. Note that you can pick and choose from features not offered by default with this version (RAID, for example); you'll simply need to compile from source and include the necessary flags rather than use the standard binary distribution.

- **Max:** The Max version contains every MySQL feature under the sun, including everything offered by the Standard version, in addition to SSL and RAID support. Note that at the time of this writing, not all of these features have been thoroughly tested; therefore you should only choose this version if you're interested in experimenting with the latest features, or if your particular application makes one or more of these features a necessity.

NOTE *The Windows distribution consists of both the Standard and Max binaries.*

- **Debug:** The Debug version is identical to the Max distribution; the only difference is that it's compiled with the --with-debug=full option. Don't use this version for production purposes, because the additional debugging mechanisms will greatly reduce performance. You should only use this version if in the course of developing your application, you require extensive debugging information, or if you're attempting to decipher a potential bug in the MySQL code itself.

Licensing Issues

It is unfortunate that many scoff at the idea of compensating Open Source developers, despite the fact that many a career has been made (mine included) using the software developed by the tireless efforts of countless developers from around the globe. The MySQL developers are no different, and have made the database server freely available for download since the first public release in 1996. Their convictions regarding the value of Open Source software were made even more evident with the June, 2000 decision to release MySQL under the GPL (General Public License). But what made this move particularly dramatic was that it was announced after the formation of MySQL AB, a for-profit company founded by the core members of the MySQL development team. In addition to offering their product line for free under the GPL, MySQL AB also offers low-cost commercial and support licenses. I touch upon reasons why you might choose one licensing option or the other in Chapter 21.

Although by all accounts the company is doing tremendously well, you should consider purchasing a license to ensure that development will continue into the future. A single "MySQL Classic" license (which does not include transactional capabilities) costs $249.00, while a single "MySQL Pro" license (which includes the InnoDB transactional storage engine) costs $495.00. Certainly a small price to pay when compared to the alternatives, wouldn't you say?

Installing MySQL

After suffering through the deployment of a wide variety of database servers, I'm happy to announce that the MySQL installation process is quite painless. In fact, after a few iterations I'm confident that your future installation or upgrade sessions will take just a few minutes to complete.

In this section, you'll learn how to install MySQL on both the Linux and Windows platforms. In addition to offering comprehensive step-by-step installation instructions, I discuss topics that often confuse both newcomers and regular users alike, including distribution format vagaries, system-specific problems, and more.

> **NOTE** *Throughout the remainder of this chapter, the constant* INSTALL-DIR *is used as a placeholder for MySQL's base installation directory. Consider modifying your system path to include this directory.*

Linux

Although MySQL has been ported to at least ten platforms, its Linux distribution remains the most popular. This isn't surprising, because both products are commonly used in conjunction with running Web-based services. In this section I'll cover the installation procedures for all three of MySQL's available Linux distribution formats: RPM, source, and binary.

RPM, Source, or Binary?

Software intended for the Linux operating system often offers several distribution formats. MySQL is no different, offering source, binary, and RPM versions of each released version. Because I'm always an advocate of flexibility and choice, I'll offer instructions for all three. Because you just guess which best suits your particular situation, you should read all three sections carefully before settling upon a format, and perform additional research if necessary.

> **NOTE** *You'll need to be logged in as root to execute the installation procedure. In addition, I'll assume that you've placed the downloaded MySQL distribution in* /usr/src, *although you could conceivably initiate the installation process from any directory.*

The RPM Installation Process

The Red Hat Package Manager (RPM) provides an amazingly simply means for installing and maintaining software. RPM offers a common command interface for installing, upgrading, uninstalling, and querying software, largely eliminating the learning curve historically required of general Linux software maintenance. Given these advantages, it might not come as a surprise that RPM is the officially recommended way for installing MySQL on Linux.

> **TIP** *Although you'll learn a few of the Red Hat Package Manager's more useful and common commands in this section, it hardly scratches the surface of its capabilities. That said, if you're unfamiliar with the RPM, take some time to learn more about it at* http://www.rpm.org/.

MySQL offers RPMs for the x86, IA64, and AMD64 processors. A number of RPMs are available for each. To carry out the examples found throughout the remainder of this book, you'll need to download at least two:

- The MySQL server (MySQL-VERSION.i386.rpm)

- The MySQL client (MySQL-client-VERSION.rpm)

Download these packages, saving them to your preferred distribution repository directory. I prefer to store my packages in the /usr/src directory, but the location has no bearing on the final outcome of the installation process.

Learning More about the Package

Before commencing with the installation, you should learn more about each package. Executing the following command offers a succinct description of the package architecture and its contents:

```
%>rpm -qp --info MySQL-VERSION.i386.rpm
```

Executing the following command displays all packaged files and their installation destination:

```
%>rpm -qpl MySQL-VERSION.i386.rpm
```

Installing the MySQL RPMs

You can install the MySQL RPM with a single command:

```
%>rpm -i MySQL-VERSION.i386.rpm
```

Upon execution, the installation process will begin. Assuming all goes well, you will be informed that the initial tables have been installed, and that the mysqld daemon has been started.

Keep in mind that this will only install MySQL's server component. If you want to connect to the server from the same machine, you'll need to install the client RPM:

```
%>rpm -i MySQL-client-VERSION.i386.rpm
```

If the installation procedure is successful, no output will result. Believe it or not, the initial databases have also been created, and the MySQL server daemon is running. Continue on to the section, "Set the MySQL Administrator Password."

Uninstalling the MySQL RPMs

Uninstalling MySQL is as easy as installing it, involving only a single command:

```
%>rpm -e MySQL-VERSION
```

To be sure, the MySQL RPMs offer a painless and effective means to an end. However, this convenience comes at the cost of flexibility. For example, the installation directory is not relocatable; that is, you are bound to the predefined installation path as determined by the packager. This is not necessarily a bad thing, but the flexibility is often nice, and sometimes necessary. If your personal situation requires that added flexibility, read on.

The Binary Installation Process

A binary distribution is simply precompiled source code, typically created by developers or contributors with the intention of offering users a platform-specific optimized distribution. At the time of this writing, MySQL binaries were available for the Dec OSF, FreeBSD, IBM AIX, HP-UX, Linux, Mac OS X, Novell Netware, OpenBSD, QNX, SGI Irix, Solaris, and Windows platforms. Although I'll focus solely on the Linux installation process, keep in mind that the procedure is largely identical for all platforms except for Windows, which I'll devote special attention to in the next section.

To install the MySQL binary on Linux, you need to have tools capable of unzipping and untarring the binary package. Most Linux distributions come with the GNU `gunzip` and `tar` tools, which are capable of carrying out these tasks.

> **NOTE** *According to the MySQL Web site, the binary created for a Pentium x686 machine running Linux kernel 2.2.x is compiled with the following flags:*
>
> ```
> CFLAGS="-O3 -mpentiumpro" CXX=gcc CXXFLAGS="-O3 -mpentiumpro
> -felide-constructors -fno-exceptions -fno-rtti" ./configure
> --prefix=/usr/local/mysql --enable-assembler
> --with-mysqld-ldflags=-all-static --disable-shared
> --with-extra-charsets=complex
> ```

You can download the MySQL binary for your platform by navigating to the MySQL Web site downloads section. Unlike the RPMs, the binaries come with both the server and client packaged together, so you'll only need to download a single package. Download this package, saving them to your preferred distribution repository directory. I prefer to store my packages in the /usr/src directory, but the location has no bearing on the final outcome of the installation process.

Although the binary installation process is a tad more involved than an RPM in terms of keystrokes, it is only slightly more complicated in terms of required Linux knowledge. This process can be divided into four steps:

1. Create the necessary group and owner.

   ```
   %>groupadd mysql
   %>useradd -g mysql mysql
   ```

2. Decompress the software to the intended directory. The GNU `gunzip` and `tar` programs are recommended.

   ```
   %>cd /usr/local
   %>gunzip < /usr/local/mysql-VERSION-OS.tar.gz | tar xvf -
   ```

3. Link the installation directory to a common denominator:

    ```
    %>ln -s FULL-PATH-TO-MYSQL-VERSION-OS mysql
    ```

4. Install the MySQL database. `mysql_install_db` is a shell script that logs in to
    the MySQL database server, creates all of the necessary tables, and populates
    them with initial values.

    ```
    %>cd mysql
    %>scripts/mysql_install_db
    %>chown -R root .
    %>chown -R mysql data
    %>chgrp -R mysql .
    ```

    That's it! Proceed to the section, "Set the MySQL Administrator Password!".

The Source Installation Process

The MySQL developers have gone to great lengths to produce optimized RPMs and
binaries for a wide array of operating systems, and you should use them whenever
possible. However, if you are working with a platform for which no binary exists, you
require a particularly exotic configuration, or you happen to be a control freak (which
I realize many of you are), then you also have the option to install from source. The
process is actually only slightly longer than the binary installation procedure.

The source installation process is indeed somewhat more complicated than
installing binaries or RPMs. For starters, you should possess at least rudimentary
knowledge using build tools like GNU gcc and make, and have them installed on your
operating system. I'll assume that if you've chosen to not heed my advice regarding
using the binaries, you know all of this already. Therefore, I'll simply forge ahead with
the installation instructions, provided in six easy steps:

1. Create the necessary group and owner.

    ```
    %>groupadd mysql
    %>useradd -g mysql mysql
    ```

2. Decompress the software to the intended directory. The GNU gunzip and tar
    programs are recommended.

    ```
    %>cd /usr/local
    %>gunzip < /usr/local/mysql-VERSION.tar.gz | tar xvf -
    %>cd mysql-VERSION
    ```

3. Configure, make, and install MySQL. A C++ compiler and make program is
    required. Recent versions of the GNU gcc and make programs are strongly rec-
    ommended. Keep in mind that COMPILER-FLAGS is merely a placeholder for any
    precompilation variables that should be set, and --CONFIGURATION-FLAGS a
    placeholder for any configuration settings that determine several important

characteristics of the MySQL server, such as installation location. I'll leave it to you to decide which flags best suit your special needs.

```
%>COMPILER-FLAGS ./configure --CONFIGURATION-FLAGS
%>make
%>make install
```

> **NOTE** *According to the MySQL website, it is crucial to include* -fno-exceptions *within the compiler flags. Omitting this flag could result in an unstable binary. Including* -felide-constructors *and* -fno-rtti *is also suggested. In total, the following compiler flags are suggested:*
>
> ```
> CFLAGS="-03" CXX=gcc CXXFLAGS="-03 -felide-constructors \
> -fno-exceptions -fno-rtti" ./configure --prefix=/usr/local/mysql \
> --enable-assembler --with-mysqld-ldflags=-all-static
> ```

4. Install the MySQL database. mysql_install_db is a shell script that logs in to the MySQL database server, creates all of the necessary tables and populates them with initial values.

   ```
   %>scripts/mysql_install_db
   ```

5. Update the installation permissions.

   ```
   %>chown -R root  /usr/local/mysql
   %>chown -R mysql /usr/local/mysql/var
   %>chgrp -R mysql /usr/local/mysql
   ```

6. Copy the MySQL configuration file into its typical location. I'll talk more about the role of this configuration in a later section.

   ```
   %>cp support-files/my-medium.cnf /etc/my.cnf
   ```

That's it! Proceed to the section, "Set the MySQL Administrator Password!".

Windows 2000 Advanced Server

Open-source products continue to make headway on the Microsoft Windows server platform, with historically predominant Unix-based technologies like the Apache Web server, PHP, the Perl and Python programming languages, and more recently, MySQL, continuing to gain popularity on what was once considered taboo ground for free software. In addition, for many users, myself included, the Windows environment offers an ideal testing ground for Web/database applications that will ultimately be moved to a production Linux environment.

This section highlights the MySQL binary installation process targeted for the Windows platform. Although you could compile the software from source, I suspect that the most users will opt to use the binary instead (a choice recommended by both MySQL AB and myself). Therefore, I'll concentrate solely on that procedure.

> **TIP** *The MySQL installation process for Windows Server 2003 is identical to that discussed in this section.*

You can download the MySQL binary for your platform by navigating to the MySQL Web site downloads section. Unlike the RPMs, the binaries come with both the server and client packaged together, so you only need to download a single package. Download this package, saving it to your preferred distribution repository directory. I prefer to store my packages in the C:\packages directory, but the location has no bearing on the final outcome of the installation process.

Like many Windows programs, a convenient GUI installer is available for installing the binary. The process follows:

1. Decompress the zip file to a convenient installation location, such as C:\TEMP\mysql. Any Windows-based decompression program capable of working with zip files should work just fine; Winzip (http://www.winzip.com/) is a particularly popular compression package.

2. Double-click the Setup.exe icon to start the installation process.

3. Read and click through the welcome and informational prompts.

4. Either accept or change the installation destination directory. The default is C:\mysql. You're free to change this default, but I do suggest placing the installation directory within the logical drive root directory (for example D:\mysql, E:\mysql).

5. You'll next be prompted to choose between the "Typical", "Compact", and "Custom" setup variations. At the time of this writing, the "Custom" installation process seems to be a placeholder, because you cannot actually modify the installation contents, I assume that in the near future you'll be able to choose this method if you'd like to forego installation of certain components, including documentation and examples, or are interested in installing only the client or server. For the moment, choosing "Typical" is the recommended option.

6. The installation process will begin. Hang tight until the process ends, and the Setup Complete window appears. Click the Finish button.

That's it! Proceed to the next section and set the MySQL administrator password.

Set the MySQL Administrator Password

By default, the root (administrator) account password is left blank. Although I find this practice questionable, it has long been the standard procedure and I suspect it will be this way for some time into the future. You must take care to add a password immediately! You can do so with the SET PASSWORD command, like so:

```
%>mysql -u root mysql
%>SET PASSWORD FOR root@localhost=PASSWORD('secret');
```

Of course, choose a password that is a tad more complicated than *secret*. MySQL will let you dig your own grave in the sense that passwords such as "123", "abc", and your mother's name are all perfectly acceptable. I suggest choosing a password that is at least eight characters long, and consists of a combination of numeric and alphabetical characters of varying case.

Failing to heed this advice means that anybody with access to the operating system can shut down the daemon, not to mention completely destroy your database server and its data. Although there is nothing wrong with doing a little experimentation immediately after the installation process, you should consider setting the MySQL administrator password immediately.

Starting and Stopping MySQL

The MySQL server daemon is controlled via a single program, located in the INSTALL-DIR/bin directory. Instructions for controlling this daemon for both the Linux and Windows platforms is offered in this section.

Controlling the Daemon Manually

Although you'll ultimately want the MySQL daemon to automatically start and stop in conjunction with the operating system, you'll often need to manually execute this process during the configuration and later application testing stages. In this section, I'll show you how to do so on both the Linux and Windows platforms.

Starting MySQL on Linux

The script responsible for starting the MySQL daemon is called mysqld_safe, and is located in the INSTALL-DIR/bin directory. Keep in mind that this script can only be started by a user possessing sufficient execution privileges; typically either root or a member of the group *mysql*.

```
%>cd INSTALL-DIR
%>./bin/mysqld_safe --user=mysql &
```

Keep in mind that mysqld_safe will not execute unless you first change to the INSTALL-DIR directory. In addition, the trailing ampersand is required, because you'll want the daemon to run in the background.

> **TIP** *Before version 4.0,* mysqld_safe *was known as* safe_mysqld. *Frankly, I don't know why this change was made; nonetheless, all of the options available to* safe_mysqld *are also available under the new naming convention. Although at the time of this writing a symbolic link was included in the distribution, pointing* safe_mysqld *to* mysqld_safe, *don't count on this link being there for future releases.*

The `mysqld_safe` script is actually a wrapper around the mysqld server daemon, offering features not available by calling mysqld directly, such as run-time logging and automatic restart in case of error. You'll learn more about `mysqld_safe` in the later section, "Configuring MySQL."

Stopping MySQL on Linux

Although the MySQL server daemon can only be started by a user possessing the file system privileges necessary to execute the `mysqld_safe` script, it can be stopped by a user possessing the proper privileges as specified within the MySQL privilege database. Keep in mind that this privilege is typically left solely to the MySQL root user, not to be confused with the operating system root user! Don't worry too much about this right now; just understand that MySQL users are not the same as operating system users, and that the MySQL user attempting to shut down the server must possess adequate permissions for doing so. I'll offer a proper introduction to `mysqladmin` along with the other MySQL clients in Chapter 23, and delve into issues pertinent to MySQL users and the MySQL privilege system in Chapter 26.

```
shell>cd INSTALL-DIR/bin
shell>mysqladmin -u root -p shutdown
Enter password: *******
```

Assuming that the proper credentials have been supplied, you will be returned to the command prompt without notification of the successful shutdown of the MySQL server. In the case of an unsuccessful shutdown attempt, an appropriate error message is offered.

Starting MySQL on Windows

Because the standard MySQL distribution for Windows offers both the standard and the MySQL-Max server binaries, take heed as to which one you use, because each offers a different set of features. In fact, there are a total of five different binaries, listed in Table 22-1.

Table 22-1. Windows Binaries

BINARY	DESCRIPTION
mysqld	Compiled with complete debugging capabilities, and support for InnoDB and BDB tables, and symbolic links. Use this binary only if you are attempting to validate a potential bug in the MySQL distribution.
mysqld-max	Optimized binary with support for InnoDB and BDB tables, and symbolic links.
mysqld-max-nt	Optimized binary with support for InnoDB and BDB tables, symbolic links, and named pipes.
mysqld-nt	Optimized binary for Windows NT/2000/XP.
mysqld-opt	Optimized binary also offering support for transactional tables as of version 4.0.

Once you've chosen the binary that best fits your situation, navigate to the `INSTALL-DIR/bin` folder and double-click the relevant icon. MySQL will begin running as a background process.

Stopping MySQL on Windows

Because the MySQL server daemon is stopped using a command hailing from the mysqladmin client, the process for stopping this daemon is platform-agnostic. Thus the process is exactly the same as was discussed in the preceding Linux section:

```
%>cd INSTALL-DIR/bin
%>mysqladmin -u root -p shutdown
Enter password: *******
```

See this section's Linux counterpart for further information regarding the use of `mysqladmin`.

Starting and Stopping MySQL Automatically

When the occasion arises that a server needs to be rebooted, or unexpectedly shuts down, it is imperative that all such mission-critical services are properly exited, and automatically reactivated on system boot. Thankfully, such matters are trivially accomplished on both the Linux and Windows platforms.

Linux

Linux is capable of operating in several different system states, each of which is defined by the set of services made available to the user when that state is in control of the system. Eight such runlevels are available, although typically only seven are of interest to the user. Red Hat's relevant runlevels are listed in Table 22-2.

Table 22-2. Red Hat's System Runlevels

RUNLEVEL	DESCRIPTION
0	Halt
1	Single-user mode
2	Empty (user-definable)
3	Full multi-user mode (no windowing)
4	Empty (user-definable)
5	Full multi-user mode (with windowing)
6	Reboot

Although a thorough introduction of the Linux runlevels is out of the scope of this book, the following points should give you a fair idea of how this operates:

- The system's default runlevel is configured in the file /etc/inittab.

- Red Hat's default runlevel is 3.

- Runlevels 2 and 4 are typically used for custom configurations involving services not otherwise required in the standard runlevels 3 and 5.

- Red Hat's runlevel designations are stored in /etc/rc.d/. Each runlevel possesses it's own folder, and is numbered accordingly. For example, the runlevel 3 folder is rc3.d.

- Whether and in what order services are started or terminated within each runlevel is determined by examining the first three characters of each symbolic link found in the respective runlevel folder. If the symbolic link begins with an S, that service will be initiated in that runlevel. If it begins with a K, it will be terminated. The two-digit integer following this first character determines the order in which that service will be initiated or terminated. The higher the number, the later its fate will be addressed.

Starting MySQL on Boot

To ensure that the MySQL daemon automatically starts on system boot, an addition to runlevel three is required.

```
%>ln -s INSTALL-DIR/support-files/mysql.server /etc/rc.d/init.d/mysql
%>ln -s /etc/rc.d/init.d/mysql /etc/rc.d/rc3.d/S99mysql
```

Stopping MySQL on Shutdown or Reboot

To ensure that the MySQL daemon properly exits upon system shutdown or reboot, additions to the appropriate runlevels (zero and six, respectively) are required. Note that the following steps assume that you have first executed the steps required to ensure that MySQL starts on boot.

```
%>ln -s /etc/rc.d/init.d/mysql /etc/rc.d/rc0.d/K01mysql
%>ln -s /etc/rc.d/init.d/mysql /etc/rc.d/rc6.d/K01mysql
```

Once you've made these changes, you should take a few moments to ensure that the MySQL shutdown and bootup process is properly working. This involves simply shutting down, starting, and finally rebooting the server, each time reviewing the server process list to ensure that MySQL is running.

Windows

On the Windows platform, any application installed as a service can be configured to start automatically and properly upon system boot, and stop upon system shutdown or reboot. This practice is no different with MySQL.

Installing MySQL as a Service

To install MySQL as a service, open a command-line prompt and execute:

```
C:\>INSTALL-DIR/bin/mysqld-max-nt --install
```

If you've chosen another binary, replace `mysqld-max-nt` accordingly. Note that this presupposes that you have added the path to the MySQL `bin` directory to the system path. If not, you must first `cd` to the proper directory before executing the service installation command. If you installed MySQL in accordance with the installation path suggested by the installer, this directory is `C:\mysql`.

> **TIP** *You should add the MySQL bin directory to your system path. This is accomplished by navigating to: Start ➤ Settings ➤ Control Panel ➤ System ➤ Advanced, and clicking on Environment Variables. Edit the Path Environment Variable, concatenating* `C:\mysql\bin;` *to the end of the string.*

Once the binary is installed, navigate to the Services Administration Panel via Start ➤ Settings ➤ Control Panel ➤ Administrative Tools ➤ Services. This panel is depicted in Figure 22-1. Ensure that the mysql service's Startup Type is set to Automatic. If not, right click the mysql service and select Properties. Change the Startup Type setting to Automatic and press OK.

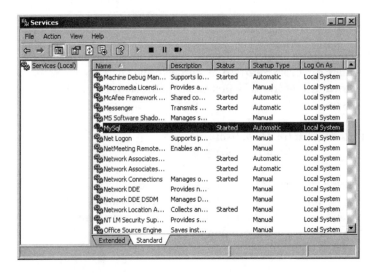

Figure 22-1. The Windows Services administrator

Uninstalling the MySQL Service

Uninstalling the MySQL service is as simple as starting it. To uninstall the MySQL service, execute:

```
C:\>INSTALL-DIR/bin/mysqld-max-nt remove
```

Keep in mind that if you uninstall the MySQL service, it will not automatically restart should the system require rebooting.

Configuring and Optimizing MySQL

Unless otherwise specified, MySQL assumes a default set of configuration settings upon each start of the MySQL server daemon. Although this default likely suits a number of users in need of nothing more than a standard deployment, it's quite likely that you'll want to make at least a few rudimentary changes to the default configuration. Such changes will not only better adapt your deployment to your specific hosting environment, but could also greatly enhance the performance of your application based on its behavioral characteristics. For example, some applications might be update-intensive, prompting you to adjust the resources MySQL requires for handling write/modification queries. Other applications might need to handle a large number of user connections, prompting a change to the number of threads allocated to new connections. Thankfully, MySQL is highly configurable; as you'll learn in this and later chapters, administrators have the opportunity to manage just about every aspect of its operation.

In this section, I'll offer an introduction to many of the configuration parameters that affect the general operation of the MySQL server. Because configuration and optimization is such an important aspect of maintaining a healthy server (not to mention a sane administrator), I'll return to this topic repeatedly throughout the remainder of the book.

mysqld_safe

You may have noticed that previous sections we referred to the MySQL server daemon as `mysqld`. Although this is indeed the daemon, you actually rarely directly interact with it; rather, you interface to the daemon through a wrapper called `mysqld_safe`. The `mysqld_safe` wrapper adds a few extra safety-related logging and system-integrity features to the picture when the daemon is started. Given these useful features, `mysqld_safe` is the preferred way to start the server, although you should keep in mind that it's only a wrapper, and should not be confused with the server itself.

More than 190 MySQL server configuration parameters are at your disposal, capable of fine-tuning practically every conceivable aspect of the daemon's operation, including MySQL's memory usage, logging sensitivity, and boundary settings, such as maximum number of simultaneous connections, temporary tables, and connection errors, among others. If you'd like to view a summary of all options available to the command, execute:

```
%>INSTALL-DIR/bin/mysqld --help
```

Note that in this context you should call `mysqld` and not `mysqld_safe`. Because `mysqld_safe` is a wrapper around `mysqld`, all options available to the latter are available to the former. In this section I'll highlight several of the more commonly used parameters.

Configuration and Optimization Parameters

In this section I'll introduce several configuration and optimization parameters that play key roles in MySQL's general operation.

back_log

A well-tuned MySQL server is capable of working with many connections simultaneously. Each connection must be received and delegated to a new thread by the main MySQL thread, a task that, although trivial, isn't instantaneous. The `back_log` parameter determines the number of connections that are allowed to queue up while this main thread deals with a particularly heavy new connection load. By default this is set to 50.

datadir

It's common practice to place the MySQL data directory in a non-standard location, on another disk partition, for example. Using the `datadir` option, you can redefine this path. For example, I commonly mount a second drive to `/data`, and store my databases in a directory called `mysql`:

```
%>./bin/mysqld_safe --datadir=/data/mysql --user=mysql &
```

Keep in mind that you'll need to copy or move the MySQL permission tables to this new location. Because MySQL's databases are stored in files, you can do so using operating system commands typical for performing such actions, such as `mv` and `cp`. If you're using a GUI, you can drag and drop these files to the new location.

default-table-type

As you'll learn in Chapter 24, MySQL supports several table types, each of which has its own advantages and disadvantages. If you regularly make use of a particular table type (MyISAM is the default), you might want to set it as the default using this parameter. For example, you could set the default to HEAP like so:

```
%>./bin/mysqld_safe --default-table-type=heap
```

init_file

You can execute a series of SQL commands at daemon startup by placing them in a text file and assigning that filename to init_file. For example, suppose you want to clear a table used for storing session information with each start of the MySQL server. Place the following query in a file named mysqlinitcmds.sql and assign it to init_file like so:

```
%>./bin/mysqld_safe --init_file=/usr/local/mysql/scripts/mysqlinitcmds.sql &
```

key_buffer_size

The key_buffer_size parameter determines the amount of memory allocated to storing index blocks. Larger key buffers allow for the storage of more index blocks, resulting in faster key lookup because the decreased chance that a disk-read is required.

log_long_format

This parameter defines a file to which all queries that aren't using indexes are logged. Viewing such a log file could be useful for studying possible improvements to your queries and table structures.

log_slow_queries

This parameter defines a file to which all queries taking longer than long_query_time seconds to execute are logged. Each time that query execution time surpasses this limit, the slow_queries counter is incremented. Studying such a log file using the mysqldumpslow utility could be useful for determining bottlenecks in your database server.

max_allowed_packet

In the world of MySQL, a packet is equivalent to both a single SQL statement and a single row returned to the requesting client. As of MySQL 4.01, the max_allowed_packet parameter can be as large as the total amount of server RAM. This parameter is really only of any concern if you are storing particularly large values in one or more columns, such as BLOBs.

max_connections

This parameter determines the maximum number of simultaneous database connections. By default this is set to 100. You can check the maximum number of connections simultaneously opened by your database by reviewing the max_used_connections parameter, available by executing SHOW STATUS. If you see this number approaching the century mark, consider bumping the maximum upward. Keep in mind that as the number of connections increase, so will memory consumption, because MySQL allocates additional memory to every connection it opens.

mysqld-version

Given that some distributions offer numerous binary variations, it's useful to be able to switch amongst them at startup. This option offers a convenient means for doing so. If you don't include this flag or its variant (--mysqld=), mysqld-max will be started, if it exists. If mysqld-max doesn't exist, then it will start mysqld.

net_buffer_length

The net_buffer_length parameter determines the initial buffer allocation for each client-server connection. This buffer may grow as large as max_allowed_packet bytes in size.

port

By default, MySQL communicates on port 3306; however, you can reconfigure this to listen on any other port using this parameter.

read_buffer_size

The read_buffer_size parameter determines the memory provided to any thread executing a sequential table scan.

skip-name-resolve

Enabling this parameter prevents MySQL from resolving hostnames. This means that all Host column values in the grant tables consist either of an IP address or localhost. If you're planning on using solely IP addresses or localhost, enable this parameter.

skip-networking

Enabling this parameter prevents MySQL from listening for TCP/IP connections, a wise idea if your MySQL installation resides on the same server from which you'll be initiating connections.

table_cache

This parameter determines the number of tables that can be opened simultaneously. The larger the number, the more memory that could be potentially consumed, because MySQL needs to allocate memory to every table opened. By default, this is set to 64 MB. If, after running MySQL for some time, the parameter opened_tables is set to a high number, you should increase the this setting.

thread_cache_size

For performance reasons, MySQL can store a set number of threads in a cache, the number of which is determined by this parameter. For every new connection, MySQL will first consult this cache, reusing one of the cached threads if available. If the cache is empty, MySQL will create a new thread. Therefore, if your deployment requires large numbers of new connections, consider raising this value from its default of 0.

user=[username]

The MySQL daemon should run as a non-root user, minimizing the damage if an attacker were to ever successfully enter the server via a MySQL security hole. Although the common practice is to run the server as user mysql, you can run it as any existing user, provided that the user is the owner of the data directories. For example, suppose you want to run the daemon using the user mysql:

```
%>./bin/mysqld_safe --user=mysql &
```

The my.cnf File

You've already learned that such changes can be made on the command line when starting the MySQL daemon via its wrapper, mysqld_safe. However, there exists a much more convenient methodology for tweaking the start-up parameters, as well as the behaviors of many MySQL clients, including mysqladmin, myisamchk, myisampck, mysql, mysqlcheck, mysqld, mysqldump, mysqld_safe, mysql.server, mysqlhotcopy, mysqlimport, and mysqlshow. You can maintain these tweaks within MySQL's configuration file, my.cnf.

At startup, MySQL looks in several directories for this file, with each directory determining the scope of the parameters declared within. The location and relative scope of each directory is highlighted here:

- /etc/my.cnf (C:\my.cnf or windows-sys-directory\my.ini on Windows): Global configuration file. All MySQL server daemons located on the server refer first to this file. Note the extension of .ini if you choose to place the configuration file in the Windows system directory. Also note that MySQL's Windows distribution supports only global configuration files.

- DATADIR/my.cnf: Server-specific configuration. This file is placed in the directory of the directory referenced by the server installation. A somewhat odd, yet crucial characteristic of this configuration file is that it references only the data directory specified at configuration time, even if a new data directory is specified at run-time. Note that MySQL's Windows distribution does not support this feature.

- --defaults-extra-file=*name*: The file specified by the supplied filename, complete with absolute path. Note that MySQL's Windows distribution does not support this feature.

- ~/.my.cnf: User-specific configuration. This file is expected to be located in the user's home directory. Note that MySQL's Windows distribution does not support this feature.

You should understand that MySQL attempts to read from each of these locations at startup. If multiple configuration files exist, parameters read in later take precedence over earlier parameters. Although you could create your own configuration file, you should base your file off of one of four preconfigured my.cnf files, each of which are supplied with the MySQL distribution. These templates are housed in INSTALL-DIR/support-files. The purpose of each is defined in Table 22-3.

Table 22-3. MySQL Configuration Templates

NAME	DESCRIPTION
my-huge.cnf	Intended for high-end production servers tasked with primarily running MySQL, and containing of 1GB to 2GB of RAM.
my-large.cnf	Intended for medium-sized production servers tasked with primarily running MySQL, and containing around 512MB of RAM.
my-medium.cnf	Intended for low-end production servers containing little memory (less than 128MB).
my-small.cnf	Intended for minimally equipped servers, possessing nominal RAM (less than 64MB).

So what does this file look like? Here's a partial listing of the my-large.cnf configuration template:

```
# Example mysql config file for large systems.
#
# This is for large system with memory = 512M where the system runs mainly
# MySQL.

# The following options will be passed to all MySQL clients
[client]
#password       = your_password
port            = 3306
socket          = /tmp/mysql.sock

# Here follows entries for some specific programs

# The MySQL server
[mysqld]
port            = 3306
socket          = /tmp/mysql.sock
```

```
skip-locking
key_buffer=256M
max_allowed_packet=1M
table_cache=256
sort_buffer=1M
record_buffer=1M
myisam_sort_buffer_size=64M

[mysqldump]
quick
max_allowed_packet=16M

[mysql]
no-auto-rehash
# Remove the next comment character if you are not familiar with SQL
#safe-updates

...
```

> **NOTE** *If your* my-large.cnf *file looks similar to this, but the variables are prefaced with* set-variable, *not to worry. This was the standard way of setting variables within MySQL's configuration files prior to version 4.0.2. Although this still works in later versions, it has been deprecated.*

Looks fairly straightforward, right? And indeed it is. Configuration files can really be summarized in three succinct points:

- Comments are prefaced with a hash mark.

- Variables are assigned exactly like they would be when assigned along with the call to mysqld_safe, except that they are not prefaced with the double-hyphen.

- The context of these variables are set by prefacing the section with the intended beneficiary, enclosed in square brackets. For example, if you wanted to tweak the default behavior of mysqldump, you would begin with:

  ```
  [mysqldump]
  ```

  You would then follow it with the relevant variable settings, like so:

  ```
  quick
  max_allowed_packet = 16M
  ```

  This context is assumed until the next square-bracket setting is encountered.

Summary

This chapter set the stage for starting experimentation with the MySQL server. You not only learned how to install and configure MySQL, but also learned a bit regarding how to optimize the installation to best fit your administrative and application preferences. I'll revisit configuration and optimization issues throughout the remainder of this book as necessary.

In the next chapter, I'll introduce MySQL's many clients, which offer a convenient means for interacting with many facets of the server.

CHAPTER 23

The Many MySQL Clients

MySQL COMES WITH quite a few utilities, or *clients*, each of which provide interfaces for carrying out various tasks pertinent to server administration. In this chapter, I'll offer a general overview of the most commonly used clients, and provide an in-depth introduction to the most prominent two of the bunch, namely *mysql* and *mysqladmin*. Because the MySQL manual already does a fantastic job at providing a general overview of each, I've instead opted to focus upon those features that you're most likely to regularly use in your daily administration activities. I'll then conclude the chapter with a brief survey of three third-party GUI-based administration applications.

> **NOTE** *A common cause of confusion surrounds the unfortunate clash of names when referring to the* mysql *client, MySQL database server, and* mysql *database. When referring to the client or database,* mysql *is always formatted in all lowercase, whereas any references to the database server will appear as MySQL. Confusion between the* mysql *client and database should be eliminated due to the context in which the term appears.*

Each MySQL client offers a bevy of options capable of tweaking its default behavior. Because many of these options and their resulting effects are shared by several, and in some cases, all clients, let's take a moment to review these standard options and their corresponding behaviors.

Standard Client Options

In this section I'll highlight several of the options shared by many, if not all, of the mysql clients introduced in this chapter. I've divided the options into two categories: connection options and standard options. Although all indeed fall under the general theme of "standard options," the particularly important nature of the connection options warrants special reference. To start however, I'd like to make note of a few simple rules that you should keep in mind when using options:

- Options can be passed to clients in three ways: via the command-line, environment variables, or configuration files. If you plan on using a particular option repeatedly, the preferred way to set it is through a configuration file. MySQL's configuration files were first introduced in Chapter 22.

- Any options assigned via the command-line override assignments located in configuration files or environment variables.

- Options are case-sensitive. For example, `-p` denotes password, but `-P` denotes port number.

- When you pass options via the command line, they are prefaced with either one hyphen or two, depending upon whether you're using short or long form. When they are passed in a configuration file, they are not prefaced with hyphens at all.

- Some options require you to assign a value, and others provoke a certain behavior simply by being referenced. If an option requires a value, I'll say as much when I introduce it.

- If an option requires a value, and the option's long form is used, you assign this value by following the option with an equals sign and then the value. For example, if you're referencing the hostname option's long form, you could assign it `www.example.com` like so:

```
--host=www.example.com
```

When you use the short form, you assign a value by simply noting the value directly after the option. You can include a space for readability, although you're not constrained to do so. For example:

```
-h www.example.com
```

The only option that does not follow this format is the password option. I'll explain why this is so in the next section.

Connection Options

There are six connection options which could come into play when starting a `mysql` client. Each of these options is introduced below.

- `--host=name`, `-h`: The target database host. If you're connecting to the localhost, you can omit this option.

- `--user=name`, `-u`: The connecting user's username.

- `--password[=name]`, `-p`: The connecting user's password. Although you can include the password on the command line, it is unadvisable because it could be logged to a command history file, causing a considerable security risk. Instead, upon execution you'll be prompted for the password, which will not be echoed back to the screen when you enter it. Regardless of which route you choose, keep in mind that neither protects against password sniffing through network monitoring when you connect to a remote host, because the password, along with all other connection information, is be transmitted unencrypted unless MySQL's SSL capabilities are used. See Chapter 25 for more information about MySQL's SSL feature.

- `--pipe, -W`: Specifies that named pipes will be used to connect to the server.

- `--port=port_num, -P`: Specifies the port to use when connecting to the MySQL server. Note that you can't just specify a non-standard port (3306 is the default) without configuring the MySQL server daemon to listen on that port. You can do so simply by passing this same option to `mysqld` at startup time.

- `--socket=/path/to/socket, -s`: For localhost connections, a socket file is required. By default this file is created in `/tmp/` on Unix machines. On Windows machines, this option determines the name of the pipe (by default this name is MySQL) used for local connections when named pipes are used.

General Options

The following list highlights many of the options available to all or most clients. You can verify whether a particular client supports a given option by outputting the client's help page with the option `--help`.

- `--compress, -C`: Enable compression for the protocol used for client/server communication.

- `--defaults-file=/path/to/configuration/file`: At startup, each client typically searches in several locations for configuration files, and applies the settings accordingly. You can override this behavior by specifying the location of a configuration file with this option.

- `--defaults-extra-file=/path/to/configuration/file`: Read this file after all other configuration files have been read. You might use such a file during application testing, for example.

- `--help, -?`: Output help information before exiting. You can pipe the results through a pager to facilitate reading. For example:

```
%>mysql --help | more
```

- `--no-defaults`: Ignore all configuration files.

- `--print-defaults`: Output the options that will be used by the client as defined within configuration files and environment variables.

- `--silent, -s`: Decrease client chatter, or output. Note that this option does not necessarily suppress all output.

- `--variable-name=value`: Set a variable's value. Note that the option isn't actually called "variable-name." Rather, this is intended as a placeholder for the name of whatever variable you're trying to modify.

- `--verbose, -v`: Output more output than would occur by default.

- `--version, -V`: Exit after outputting client version information.

mysql

The mysql client is an extremely useful SQL shell, capable of managing almost every conceivable aspect of a MySQL server, including creating, modifying, and deleting tables and databases, setting user access privileges, viewing and modifying the server configuration, and querying table data. Although the majority of the time you'll likely be working with MySQL via a GUI or an API, I suspect that you'll nonetheless find mysql invaluable for carrying out various administration tasks. Its general usage syntax follows:

```
mysql [options] [database_name] [non-interactive_arguments]
```

mysql can be used in interactive and non-interactive mode, both of which I'll examine in this section. Regardless of which you use, you'll typically need to provide connection options. Although exactly which credentials you'll need to provide depends upon your specific server configuration (a matter discussed in detail in Chapter 25), you typically need a hostname (`--host=, -h`), username (`--user=, -u`), and password (`--password=, -p`). Often you'll want to include the target database name (`--database=, -D`) to save the extra step of executing the USE command once you've entered the client. Although order is irrelevant, the connection options are generally entered like so:

```
%>mysql -h yourhostname -u yourusername -p -D databasename
```

Note that the password is not included on the command line. For example, consider an attempt to connect to a MySQL server residing at www.example.com using the username jason, the password secret, and the database company:

```
%>mysql -h www.example.com -u jason -p -D company
```

At this point you might include other options, many of which are introduced in the following section, or press Enter to be prompted for the password. If your credentials are valid, you'll be granted access to the client interface, or you will be permitted to executive whatever non-interactive arguments are included on the command line.

Key mysql Options

Like all clients introduced in this chapter, mysql offers a number of useful options. I'll introduce many of the most important options here.

- --auto-rehash: By default, mysql creates hashes of database, table, and column names to facilitate auto-completion (you can auto-complete database, table, and column names with the Tab key). You can disable this behavior with the option --no-auto-rehash. If you'd like to re-enable it, use this option.

- --column-names: By default, mysql includes the column names at the top of each result set. You can disable them with the option --no-column-names. If you'd like to re-enable this behavior, use this option.

- --database=*name*, -D: This option determines which database will be used. If you're using mysql interactively, you can also switch between databases as necessary with the USE command.

- --default-character-set=character_set: Set the character set.

- --disable-tee: If you've enabled logging of all queries and the results with the option --tee or with the command tee, you can disable it will this option.

- --execute=*query*, -e *query*: This option executes a query without having to actually enter the client interface. You can execute multiple queries with this option by separating each with a semicolon. Be sure to enclose the query in quotes so that the shell does not misinterpret it as multiple arguments.

- --force, -f: When used in non-interactive mode, MySQL can read and execute queries found in a text file. By default, execution of these queries stops if an error occurs. This option causes execution to continue regardless of errors.

- --html, -H: This option outputs all results in HTML format. See the corresponding tip in the section "Useful mysql Tips" for more information about this option.

- --no-auto-rehash, -A: By default, mysql creates hashes of database, table, and column names in order to facilitate auto-completion. Although this is convenient, it does slow startup. If you don't require this feature, including this option will suppress hash creation, thereby speeding startup time.

- --pager[*=pagername*]: Many queries will produce more information than can fit on a single screen. You can tell mysql to present results one page at a time by assigning a pager. Examples of valid pagers include more and less. Presently this command is only valid on Unix platform. You can also set a pager while inside the mysql client using the \P command.

- `--safe-updates`, `-U`: This option causes `mysql` to ignore all `DELETE` and `UPDATE` queries in which the `WHERE` clause is omitted. This is a particularly useful safeguard for preventing against accidental mass deletions or modifications. See the corresponding tip in the section "Useful `mysql` Tips" for more information about this option.

- `--skip-column-names`: By default, `mysql` includes headers containing column names at the top of each result set. You can disable inclusion of these headers with this option.

- `--tee=`*name*: This option causes `mysql` to log all commands and the resulting output to the file specified by *name*. This is particularly useful for debugging purposes. You can disable logging at any time while inside `mysql` by issuing the command notee, and can later re-enable it with the command tee. See the corresponding tip in the section "Useful `mysql` Tips" for more information about this option.

- `--vertical`, `-E`: This option causes `mysql` to display all query results in a vertical format. This format is often preferable when you're working with tables that contain several columns. See the corresponding tip in the section "Useful `mysql` Tips" for more information about this option.

- `--xml`, `-X`: Including this option causes all results to be output in XML format. See the corresponding tip in the section "Useful `mysql` Tips" for more information about this option.

Using mysql in Interactive Mode

To use `mysql` in interactive mode, you'll need to first enter the interface. As already explained, you do so by passing along appropriate credentials. Building on the previous example, suppose you wanted to interact with the `company` database located on the `www.example.com` server:

```
%>mysql -h www.example.com -u jason -p -D company
Enter password:
Welcome to the MySQL monitor.  Commands end with ; or \g.
Your MySQL connection id is 95 to server version: 4.1.0-alpha-max-log

Type 'help;' or '\h' for help. Type '\c' to clear the buffer.

mysql>
```

Once you're connected via the mysql client, you can begin executing SQL commands. For example, to view a list of all existing databases, you'd use this command:

```
mysql>SHOW databases;
```

To switch to (or use) another database, the mysql database for example, use this command:

```
mysql>USE mysql;
```

> **NOTE** *To switch to the* mysql *database, you'll almost certainly require root access. If you don't have root access, and have no other databases at your disposal, you can switch to the* test *database, created by MySQL at installation time, or use the* mysqladmin *client to create a new database.*

Once you've switched to the mysql database context, you can view all tables with this command:

```
mysql>SHOW TABLES;
```

This returns the following:

```
+-----------------+
| Tables_in_mysql |
+-----------------+
| columns_priv    |
| db              |
| func            |
| host            |
| tables_priv     |
| user            |
| user_info       |
+-----------------+
7 rows in set (0.01 sec)
```

To view the structure of one of those tables, use this command:

```
mysql>DESCRIBE host;
```

This returns:

```
+-----------------------+------------------+------+-----+---------+-------+
| Field                 | Type             | Null | Key | Default | Extra |
+-----------------------+------------------+------+-----+---------+-------+
| Host                  | char(60) binary  |      | PRI |         |       |
| Db                    | char(64) binary  |      | PRI |         |       |
| Select_priv           | enum('N','Y')    |      |     | N       |       |
| Insert_priv           | enum('N','Y')    |      |     | N       |       |
| Update_priv           | enum('N','Y')    |      |     | N       |       |
| Delete_priv           | enum('N','Y')    |      |     | N       |       |
| Create_priv           | enum('N','Y')    |      |     | N       |       |
| Drop_priv             | enum('N','Y')    |      |     | N       |       |
| Grant_priv            | enum('N','Y')    |      |     | N       |       |
| References_priv       | enum('N','Y')    |      |     | N       |       |
| Index_priv            | enum('N','Y')    |      |     | N       |       |
| Alter_priv            | enum('N','Y')    |      |     | N       |       |
| Create_tmp_table_priv | enum('N','Y')    |      |     | N       |       |
| Lock_tables_priv      | enum('N','Y')    |      |     | N       |       |
+-----------------------+------------------+------+-----+---------+-------+
14 rows in set (0.00 sec)
```

You can also execute SQL queries such as INSERT, SELECT, UPDATE, and DELETE. For example, suppose you want to select all values residing in the Host, User, and password columns of the user table, found in the mysql database, and order it by the Host:

```
mysql>SELECT Host, User, password FROM user ORDER BY Host;
```

In summary, you can execute any query via the mysql client that MySQL is capable of understanding.

Viewing Configuration Variables and System Status

You can view a comprehensive listing of all server configuration variables via the SHOW VARIABLES command:

```
mysql>SHOW VARIABLES;
```

As of version 4.1.0 alpha, this command returns 131 different system variables. If you'd like to just view just a particular variable, say the default table type, you can use this command in conjunction with LIKE:

```
mysql>SHOW VARIABLES LIKE "table_type";
```

This returns:

```
+---------------+--------+
| Variable_name | Value  |
+---------------+--------+
| table_type    | MYISAM |
+---------------+--------+
1 row in set (0.00 sec)
```

Viewing system status information is equally as trivial:

mysql>**SHOW STATUS;**

This returns:

```
+-------------------------+--------+
| Variable_name           | Value  |
+-------------------------+--------+
| Aborted_clients         | 0      |
| Aborted_connects        | 0      |
| Bytes_received          | 334    |
| Bytes_sent              | 11192  |
...
| Threads_running         | 1      |
| Uptime                  | 231243 |
+-------------------------+--------+
143 rows in set (0.00 sec)
```

As of version 4.1.0 alpha, this returns 143 different status variables. To view just a single item from the status report, say the total amount of bytes sent:

mysql>**SHOW STATUS LIKE "bytes_sent";**

This returns:

```
+---------------+-------+
| Variable_name | Value |
+---------------+-------+
| Bytes_sent    | 11088 |
+---------------+-------+
1 row in set (0.00 sec)
```

Using mysql in Batch Mode

The mysql client also offers batch mode capabilities, used for both importing data into a database and for piping output to another destination. For example, you can execute SQL commands residing in a text file simply by piping the file into the mysql client, like so:

```
%>mysql [options] < /path/to/file
```

I regularly use this feature to retrieve statistics that I then send over e-mail to myself each night. For example, suppose that I want to monitor the number of slow executing queries that have taken place on the server. I'll start by creating a user with no password named mysqlmonitor, granting the user only usage privileges on the mysql database. I'll then create a file named mysqlmon.sql and add the following line to it:

```
show status like "slow_queries";
```

Next I can place the following in my crontab:

```
0 3 * * * mysql -u monitor < mysqlmon.sql | mail -s "Slow queries" jason@example.com
```

This will cause an e-mail titled "Slow queries" to be sent to jason@example.com at 3 a.m. each morning. The e-mail body will contain a number consisting of the value of the status variable slow_query.

You can also execute a file while already logged into the mysql client using the source command:

```
mysql>source textfilename;
```

Paging Output

You can page through output using your operating system's paging commands. For example:

```
%>mysql < queries.sql | more
```

Quitting mysql

You can exit the mysql client in a variety of ways: quit, exit, \q, and Ctrl-D all do the job.

Useful mysql Tips

In this section I'll enumerate a few mysql-specific tips that I find quite useful, yet perhaps aren't immediately recognized as available to the beginner.

Displaying Results Vertically

Use the \G option to display query results in a vertical output format. This renders the returned data in a significantly easier-to-read fashion. Consider this example in which all rows are selected from the mysql.db table using this option:

```
mysql>use mysql;
mysql> select * from db\G;
*************************** 1. row ***************************
    Host: %
    Db: test%
    User:
    Select_priv: Y
    Insert_priv: Y
    Update_priv: Y

    ...
*************************** 2. row ***************************

    ...
```

Logging Queries

Log all queries and their results to a log file. This is particularly useful for debugging purposes. You can initiate logging with the tee or \T option, followed by a filename. For example, suppose you want to log the session to a file named session.sql:

```
mysql>\T session.sql
Logging to file 'session.sql'
mysql>show databases;
+------------+
| Database   |
+------------+
| mysql      |
| test       |
+------------+
```

Once logging begins, the output exactly as you see it here will be logged to session.sql. If you want to disable logging at anytime during the session, execute notee, or \t.

Getting Server Statistics

Executing the status, or \s command will retrieve a number of useful statistics regarding the current server status, including uptime, version, TCP port, connection type, total queries executed, average queries per second, and more.

Preventing Accidents

Suppose that you managed a table consisting of 10,000 newsletter members, and one day decided to use the mysql client to delete a test account that you had used during the development phase. It's been a long day, and without thinking you execute:

```
mysql>DELETE FROM subscribers;
```

Rather than:

```
mysql>DELETE FROM subscribers WHERE email="test@example.com";
```

Whoops, you just blew away your entire subscriber base. Hope you performed a recent backup. The --safe-updates option prevents such inadvertent mistakes by refusing to execute any DELETE or UPDATE query that is not accompanied with a WHERE clause.

Modifying the mysql Prompt

I regularly work with several MySQL databases, each of which resides on its own server. To make sure that I always know where I am, I modify the default prompt to include the hostname. You can do this in several ways:

First, you can modify the prompt on the command-line when logging into mysql:

```
%>mysql -u jason --prompt="(\u@\h) [\d]> " -p company
```

Once you're logged into the console, the prompt will appear like so:

```
(jason@localhost) [company]>
```

You can also make the change in the my.cnf file under the [mysql] section:

```
[mysql]
...
prompt=(\u@\h) [\d]>
```

Finally, you can do it via the MYSQL_PS1 environment variable:

```
%>export MYSQL_PS1="(\u@\h) [\d]> "
```

> **NOTE** *A complete list of flags available to the prompt are available in the MySQL manual.*

Output Table Data in HTML and XML

This cool but largely unknown feature of the mysql client allows you to output query results in XML and HTML formats, using the --xml (-X), and the --html (-H) options, respectively. For example, suppose you want to create an XML file consisting of the databases found on a given server. You could place the command SHOW DATABASES in a text file and then invoke the mysql client in batch mode like so:

```
%>mysql -X < showdb.sql > serverdatabases.xml
```

The result is that a file named serverdatabases.xml will be created and consist of output similar to the following:

```
<?xml version="1.0"?>
<resultset statement="show databases">
  <row>
        <Database>bookmarkdb</Database>
  </row>
  <row>
        <Database>bookmarks</Database>
  </row>
</resultset>
```

Although not without a few flaws (for example, the HTML code is not XHTML-compliant), this feature can be quite useful for certain applications.

mysqladmin

The mysqladmin utility is used to carry out a wide array of administrative tasks, perhaps most notably creating and destroying databases, monitoring server status, and shutting down the MySQL server daemon. Like mysql, you need to pass in the necessary access credentials to make use of the mysqladmin functionality.

For example, you can examine all server variables and their values, by executing:

```
%>mysqladmin -u root -p variables
Enter password:
```

If you've supplied valid credentials, a long list of parameters and corresponding values will scroll by. If you want to page through the results, you can pipe this output to more or less if you're using Linux, or more if you're using Windows.

mysqladmin Commands

Although mysql is essentially a free-form SQL shell, allowing any SQL query recognized by MySQL, mysqladmin's scope is much more limited, recognizing a predefined set of commands. I'll introduce those commands in this section.

- create *databasename*: Create a new database, the name of which is specified by *databasename*. Note that each database must possess a unique name. Attempts to create a database using a name of an already existing database will result in an error.

- drop *databasename*: Delete an existing database, the name of which is specified by *databasename*. Once a request to delete the database is submitted, you will be prompted to confirm the request in order to prevent accidental deletions.

- extended-status: Provide extended information regarding the server status. This is the same as executing show status from within the mysql client.

- flush-hosts: Flush the host cache tables. You'll need to use this command if a host's IP address changes. Also, you'll need to use this command if the MySQL daemon receives a number of failed connection requests from a specific host (the exact number is determined by the max_connect_errors variable), because that host will be blocked from attempting additional requests. Executing this command removes the block.

- flush-logs: Close and reopen all logging files.

- flush-status: Reset status variables, setting them to zero.

- flush-tables: Close all open tables and terminate all running table queries.

- flush-threads: Purge the thread cache.

- flush-privileges: Reload the privilege tables. If you're using the GRANT and REVOKE commands rather than directly modifying the privilege tables using SQL queries, you do not need to use this command.

- kill id[,id2[,idN]]: Terminate the process(es) specified by id, id2, through idN. You can view the process numbers with the processlist command.

- password *new-password*: Change the password of the user specified by -u to *new-password*.

- ping: Verify that the MySQL server is running by pinging it, much like a Web or mail server might be pinged.

- `processlist`: Output a list of all running MySQL server daemon processes.

- `reload`: Alias of the command `flush-privileges`.

- `refresh`: Combines the tasks carried out by the commands `flush-tables` and `flush-logs`.

- `shutdown`: Shut down the MySQL server daemon. Note that you cannot restart the daemon using `mysqladmin`. Instead, it must be restarted using the mechanisms as introduced in Chapter 22.

- `status`: Output various server statistics, such as uptime, total queries executed, open tables, average queries per second, and running threads.

- `start-slave`: Start a slave. This is used in conjunction with MySQL's replication feature.

- `stop-slave`: Stop a slave. This is used in conjunction with MySQL's replication feature.

- `variables`: Output all server variables and their corresponding values.

- `version`: Output version information and server statistics.

The Other Utilities

Like the `mysql` and `mysqladmin` clients, all utilities introduced in this section can be invoked with the `--help` option.

mysqldump

The `mysqldump` client is used to export existing table data, table structures, or both from the MySQL server. If requested, the exported data can include all necessary SQL statements required to re-create the dumped information. Furthermore, you can specify whether to dump one, some, or all databases found on the server, or even just specific tables in a given database.

You can invoke `mysqldump` using any of the following three syntax variations:

```
%>mysqldump [options] database [tables]
%>mysqldump [options] --databases [options] database1 [database2...]
%>mysqldump [options] --all-databases [options]
```

Let's consider a few examples. The first example dumps just the table structures of all databases found on a local server to a file named output.sql:

```
%>mysqldump -u root -p --all-databases --no-data > mysql-data-structures.sql
```

Note that the output is being directed to a file; otherwise, the output would be sent to standard output, the screen. Also, keep in mind that the .sql extension is not required. I use this extension merely for reasons of convenience; you can use any extension you wish.

The next example dumps just the data of a single database, company.

```
%>mysqldump -u root -p --no-create-info company > mysql-data-structures.sql
```

The final example dumps both the structure and the data of two tables located in the company database, including drop table queries before each create statement. This is particularly useful when you need to repeatedly re-create an existing database, because attempting to create already existing tables results in an error, thus the need for the drop queries.

```
%>mysqldump -u root -p --add-drop-table company product staff > output.sql
```

For a thorough introduction of this immensely useful utility, see Chapter 30.

mysqlshow

The mysqlshow utility offers a convenient means for determining which databases, tables, and columns exist on a given database server. Its usage syntax follows:

```
mysqlshow [options] [database [table [column]]]
```

For example, suppose you want to view a list of all available databases:

```
%>mysqlshow -u root -p
```

To view all tables in a particular database, such as mysql:

```
%>mysqlshow -u root -p mysql
```

To view all columns in a particular table, such as the mysql database's db table:

```
%>mysqlshow -u root -p mysql db
```

Note that what is displayed depends entirely upon the furnished credentials. In these examples, I used the root user, which implies that I'll have all information at my disposal. However, other users will likely not have as wide-ranging access. Therefore, if you're interested in surveying all available data structures, use the root user.

mysqlhotcopy

You can think of the mysqlhotcopy utility as an optimized mysqldump, using Perl, the MySQL DBI module, and various optimization techniques to back up one or several databases, writing the data to a file (or files) of the same name as the database is being backed up. Although optimized, this utility comes at somewhat of a disadvantage in the sense that it can only be run on the same machine on which the target MySQL server is running. If you require remote backup capabilities, take a look at mysqldump or MySQL's replication features. Although I'll review mysqlhotcopy in considerable detail in Chapter 30, it seems appropriate to offer at least a condensed introduction in this chapter.

Three syntax variations are available:

```
%>mysqlhotcopy [options]  database1 [/path/to/target/directory]
%>mysqlhotcopy [options] database1...databaseN /path/to/target/directory
%>mysqlhotcopy [options] database./regular-expression/
```

As is the norm, numerous options are available for this utility, a few of which I'll demonstrate in the usage examples. In the first example, the company and mysql databases are copied to a backup directory.

```
%>mysqlhotcopy -u root -p company mysql /usr/local/mysql/backups
```

The following variation of the first example adds a default file extension to all copied database files:

```
%>mysqlhotcopy -u root -p --suffix=.sql company mysql /usr/local/mysql/backups
```

For the last example, a backup of all tables in the company database that begin with the word sales is created:

```
%>mysqlhotcopy -u root -p company./^sales/ /usr/local/mysql/backups
```

Like all other MySQL utilities, you must supply proper credentials to use mysqlhotcopy's functionality. In particular, the invoking user needs to have select privileges for those tables being copied. In addition, you need write access to the target directory. Finally, the Perl DBI::mysql module must be installed.

> **TIP** *Although, like all other utilities, you can learn more about* mysqlhotcopy *by invoking it with the* --help *option, more thorough documentation can be had via perldoc. Execute* perldoc mysqlhotcopy *for a comprehensive guide.*

mysqlimport

The mysqlimport utility offers a convenient means for importing data from a delimited text file into a database. It is invoked using the following syntax:

```
%>mysqlimport [options] database textfile1 [textfile2...]
```

This utility is particularly useful when migrating to MySQL from another database product or legacy system. This is because the vast majority of storage solutions (MySQL included) are capable of both creating and parsing delimited data. An example of a delimited data file follows:

```
Hemingway, Ernest\tThe Sun Also Rises\t1926\n
Steinbeck, John\tOf Mice and Men\t1937\n
Golding, William\tLord of the Flies\t1954
```

In this example, each item (field) of data is delimited by a tab (\t), and each row by a newline (\n). Keep in mind that the delimiting characters are a matter of choice, because most modern storage solutions offer a means for specifying both the column and the row delimiters when creating and reading delimited files. Suppose these rows were placed in a file called books.sql, and that you wanted to read this data and write it to a database aptly called books:

```
%>mysqlimport -u root -p --fields-terminated-by=\t \
>--lines-terminated-by=\n books books.sql
```

The executing user requires INSERT permissions for writing the data to the given table, in addition to FILE privileges in order to make use of mysqlimport.

myisamchk

Although it is widely acknowledged that MySQL is quite stable, certain conditions out of its control can result in corrupt tables. Such corruption can wreak all sorts of havoc, including preventing further insertions or updates, and even resulting in the temporary (and in extreme cases, permanent) loss of data. If you experience any table errors or oddities, you can use the myisamchk utility to check MyISAM table indices for corruption, and repair them if necessary. It's invoked using the following syntax:

```
%>myisamchk [options] /path/to/table_name.MYI
```

In the absence of any options, myisamchk just checks the designated table for corruption. For example, suppose you want to check the table named staff that resides in the company database:

```
%>myisamchk /usr/local/mysql/data/company/staff.MYI
```

Varying degrees of checks are also available, each of which requires additional time, but more thoroughly reviews the table for errors. Although the default is simply check (--check), there also exists a medium check (--medium-check) and an extended check (--extend-check). Only use the extended check for the most severe of cases, because medium check will catch the overwhelming majority of errors, and consume considerably less time. You can also review extended information for each of these checks by supplying the --information (-i) option, which offers various table-specific statistics.

If problems are identified with the table, you'll be notified accordingly. If an error is found, you can ask myisamchk to attempt to repair it by supplying the --recover (-r) option:

```
%>myisamchk -r /usr/local/mysql/data/company/staff.MYI
```

Note that what is presented here is just a smattering of the options available to this utility. Definitely consult the manual before using it to check or repair tables. Also, you should only run myisamchk when the MySQL daemon is not running. If you don't have the luxury of taking your database server offline, take a look at the next utility, mysqlcheck.

mysqlcheck

As of version 3.23.38, the mysqlcheck utility offers users the means for checking and, if necessary, repairing corrupted tables while the MySQL server daemon is running. It can be invoked in any of the three following ways:

```
%>mysqlcheck [options] database [tables]
%>mysqlcheck [options] --databases database1 [database2...]
%>mysqlcheck [options] --all-databases
```

In addition to the typical user credentials and concerned databases and tables, you can specify whether you want to analyze (-a), repair (-r), or optimize (-o) by passing in the appropriate parameter. So for example, suppose the staff table, located in the table company, became corrupted due to sudden hard-drive failure. You could repair it by executing:

```
%>mysqlcheck -r company staff
```

Like myisamchk, mysqlcheck is capable of finding and repairing the overwhelming majority of errors. In addition, it offers a wide-ranging array of features. Therefore, before you use it to resolve any mission-critical problems, take some time to consult the MySQL manual to ensure that you're using the most effective set of options.

Third-Party Client Programs

Although the MySQL command-line clients offer an efficient, powerful means for working with the server, many users prefer the convenience of point-and-click interaction offered by GUI-based clients. Many such clients are available, several of which are available under open-source licensing arrangements. In this section, I'll introduce three of the more prominent products, offering information pertinent to features, screenshots, pricing schedules (if applicable), and download instructions.

MySQL Administrator

MySQL Administrator, a product of MySQL AB, was released to the public on January 21, 2004. Although at the time of publication the product was still deemed an alpha release, and is indeed not without its quirks, the sheer number of capabilities presented by the software make it already apparent that MySQL Administrator will soon be a critical component of every administrator's toolset.

Features

MySQL Administrator offers a number of compelling features:

- Interfaces for managing every conceivable aspect of the server, including the daemon service, users and privileges, configuration variables, logging, and more. A screenshot of the user management interface is offered in Figure 23-1.

- Real-time graphical monitoring of connection and memory usage, traffic, SQL queries, replication status, and user connections. This monitor is depicted in Figure 23-2.

- Although disabled at press time, a GUI-based means for managing and even automating backups has been built into the application. A backup restoration mechanism is also integrated into the application, although that, too, was disabled at press time.

- Comprehensive user administration that allows the administrator to manage each user's username, password, privileges, and resource usage. Additionally, administrators can maintain contact information for each user, including their name, e-mail address, description, additional contact information, and even a picture.

Availability

As is the case with all MySQL products, MySQL Administrator is released under both a GPL and a commercial license. At press time, no pricing information was available for the commercial version. MySQL Administrator is available for download on the MySQL AB Web site, `http://www.mysql.com/`. Binaries for both Linux and Windows are available, as is the source code.

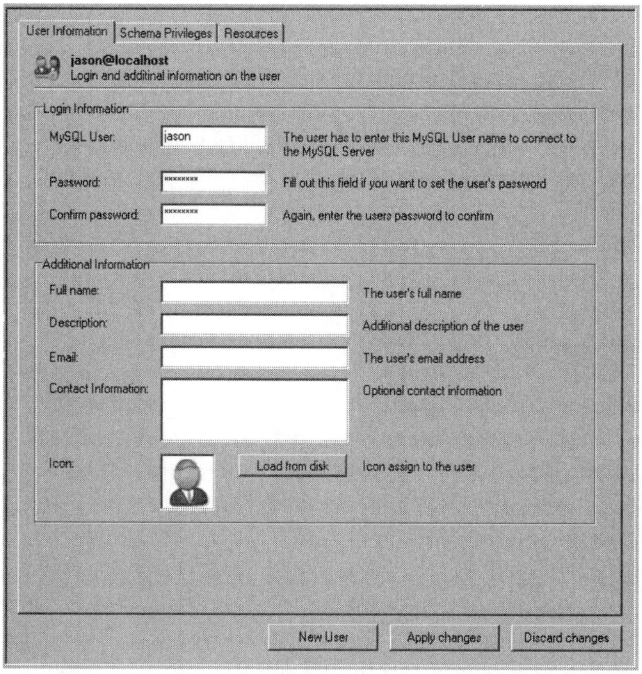

Figure 23-1. The user administration interface

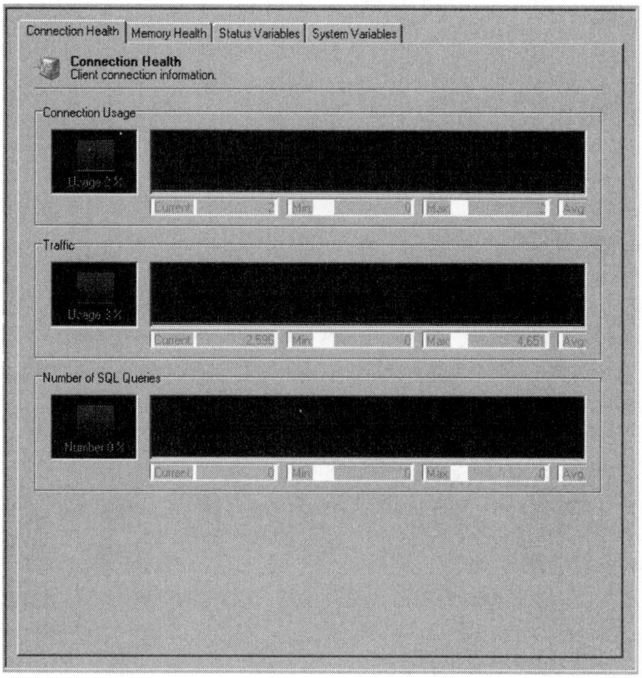

Figure 23-2. Monitoring key server metrics

phpMyAdmin

phpMyAdmin is a Web-based MySQL administration application written in PHP. It's not only very stable (it has been in development since 1998), but it's also feature-rich thanks to an enthusiastic development team and user community. I can personally vouch for the quality of this product, having used it on a daily basis for several years; I wouldn't know what to do without it.

Features

phpMyAdmin offers a number of compelling features:

- phpMyAdmin is browser-based, allowing you to easily manage remote MySQL databases from anywhere you have access to the Web. SSL is also transparently supported, allowing for encrypted administration if your server offers this feature. A screenshot of the interface used to manage tables in the mysql database is offered in Figure 23-3.

- Administrators can exercise complete control over user privileges, passwords, and resource usage, as well as create, delete, and even copy user accounts.

- Real-time interfaces are available for viewing uptime information, query and server traffic statistics, server variables, and running processes.

- Developers from around the world have translated phpMyAdmin's interface into 47 languages, including English, Chinese (traditional and simplified), Arabic, French, Spanish, Hebrew, German, and Japanese.

- phpMyAdmin offers a highly optimized point-and-click interface that greatly reduces the possibility of user-initiated errors.

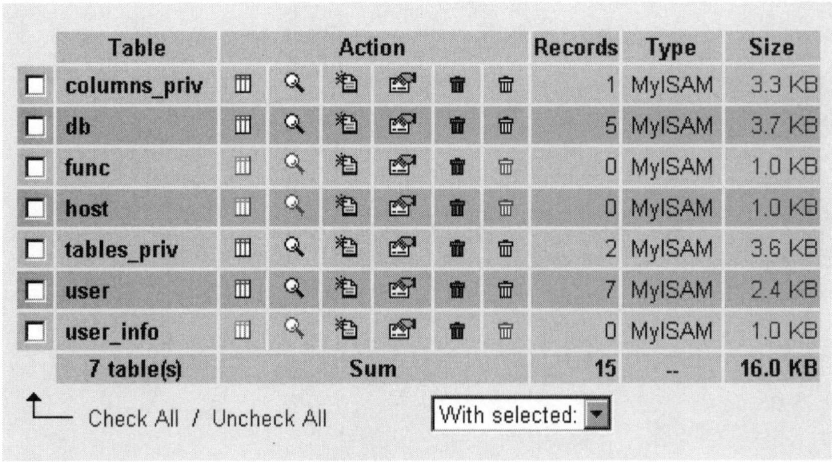

Table	Action						Records	Type	Size
☐ columns_priv	⊞	🔍	📄	🖼	🗑	🗑	1	MyISAM	3.3 KB
☐ db	⊞	🔍	📄	🖼	🗑	🗑	5	MyISAM	3.7 KB
☐ func	⊞	🔍	📄	🖼	🗑	🗑	0	MyISAM	1.0 KB
☐ host	⊞	🔍	📄	🖼	🗑	🗑	0	MyISAM	1.0 KB
☐ tables_priv	⊞	🔍	📄	🖼	🗑	🗑	2	MyISAM	3.6 KB
☐ user	⊞	🔍	📄	🖼	🗑	🗑	7	MyISAM	2.4 KB
☐ user_info	⊞	🔍	📄	🖼	🗑	🗑	0	MyISAM	1.0 KB
7 table(s)	Sum						15	--	16.0 KB

Check All / Uncheck All   With selected: ▼

Figure 23-3. Overview of the MySQL database

Availability

phpMyAdmin is released under the GNU General Public License. The official php-MyAdmin Web site, http://www.phpmyadmin.net/, offers source downloads, news, mailing lists, a live demo, and more.

Navicat

Navicat is a standalone MySQL database administration application that presents a host of user-friendly tools through a rather slick interface. Navicat has been under development for almost three years and is very stable. It also boasts an impressive list of clientele from around the globe.

Features

Navicat offers a number of compelling features:

- A slick interface closely resembling features found in Microsoft Access, providing backup, filter, and import wizards, and convenient sorting and search interfaces.

- Comprehensive user management features, including a unique tree-based privilege administration interface that allows you to quickly add and delete database, table, and column rights.

- Integrated with the Windows Task Manager to schedule database backups.

- Impressive data import and export features, capable of importing from nine standard formats, and exporting to 19 industry standard formats. Navicat's data export utility is shown in Figure 23-4.

- Supports MySQL's SSL feature.

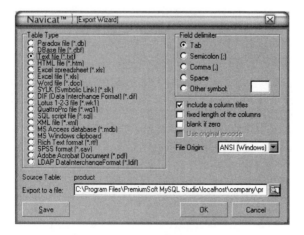

Figure 23-4. Navicat's data export utility

Availability

Navicat is a product of PremiumSoft CyberTech LTD and is available for download at
http://www.navicat.com/. Unlike the other two solutions, Navicat is not free, and at the
time of writing cost $95.00 for commercial use, and $75.00 for educational use. You can
download a fully functional 30-day evaluation version. Binary downloads are available
for Microsoft Windows, Mac OS X, and Linux platforms.

Summary

In this chapter, I introduced MySQL's many clients, and provided special attention to
two of the most important of the bunch: `mysql` and `mysqladmin`. I also offered some
insight into the most prevalent third-party management applications. Because administration is such a key aspect of maintaining a healthy database server, I'd like to recommend experimenting with all of them so as to determine which route best fits your
specific database management situation.

In the next chapter, I'll address another key aspect of MySQL: table structures.
You'll learn about the various table types and the supported data types and attributes.
Also, I'll run through numerous examples regarding how to create, modify, and use
databases, tables, and columns.

CHAPTER 24

MySQL Table Structures

TAKING TIME TO properly design your project's table structures is key to its success. Neglecting to do so can have dire consequences on not only storage requirements, but also on application performance, maintainability, and data integrity. In this chapter, you'll become better acquainted with the many facets of MySQL table design. By its conclusion, you will be familiar with the following topics:

- The purpose, advantages, disadvantages, and relevant configuration parameters of MySQL's table types, namely BDB, HEAP, InnoDB, ISAM, MERGE, and MyISAM.

- The purpose and range of MySQL's supported data types. To facilitate later reference, I've broken these data types into three categories: date and time, numeric, and textual.

- MySQL's table attributes, which serve to further modify the behavior of a data column.

- The MySQL commands used to create, modify, navigate, review, and alter both databases and tables.

Table Types

A relational database *table* is a data structure used to store and organize information. You can picture a table as a grid consisting of both *rows* and *columns*, much like a spreadsheet. For example, you might design a table intended to store employee contact information, and that table might consist of five columns: employee ID, first name, last name, e-mail address, and phone number. Because my organization consists of four employees, this table would consist of four rows, or *records*.

Although this example is simplistic, it clearly depicts the purpose of a table: as a vehicle for general data storage. However, database tables are also used in a number of other ways, some of which are rather complex. For example, databases are also commonly used to store *transactional* information. Simply defined, a *transaction* is a group of tasks that is collectively considered to be a single unit of work. If all of the unit tasks succeed, then the table changes will be executed, or *committed*. If any fail, then all of the results of the preceding and proceeding tasks must be annulled, or *rolled back*. You might use transactions for procedures such as user registration, inventory management, or e-commerce, in which it's imperative that all steps are correctly carried out in order to ensure data consistency. As you might imagine, such abilities require some overhead due to the additional features that must be incorporated into the table.

> **NOTE** *MySQL's transactional features are introduced in Chapter 29.*

Still other tables aren't intended to store any long-term information, and in fact are actually created and maintained entirely in a server's RAM or in a special temporary file to ensure a high degree of performance, at the risk of high volatility. Others exist solely to ease maintenance and review of a collection of identical tables, offering a single interface for simultaneously interacting with all of them. I could continue, but I think the point has been made. There are many types of tables, each with their specific purpose, advantages, and disadvantages. Accordingly, you should always take care to choose the table type that best fits the requirements of your application. In this section, I'll introduce MySQL's six available table types, outlining the purpose, advantages, and disadvantages of each.

ISAM

The ISAM table handler was MySQL's first, and has since been deprecated in deference to its successor, MyISAM (introduced in the next section). ISAM tables are slower and less reliable than their younger counterpart, and they are not operating system independent. Although this handler is still available, it's likely that support will entirely disappear from the distribution in a future version. As a result, you should stay away from this table type. If you've inherited an older MySQL deployment, you should definitely consider converting ISAM tables to a more capable type. Later in this section I demonstrate how that's accomplished.

MyISAM

MyISAM is MySQL's default table handler as of version 3.23. It resolves a number of deficiencies suffered by its predecessor. For starters, MyISAM tables are operating system independent, meaning that you can easily port them from a Windows server to a Linux server. In addition, MyISAM tables are typically capable of storing more data at a cost of less storage space than their older counterpart. MyISAM tables also have the convenience of a number of data integrity and compression tools at their disposal, all of which are bundled with MySQL.

MyISAM tables cannot handle transactions, meaning that you should use this type for all of your non-transactional needs, so as not to incur the extra overhead required of transactional table types such as InnoDB and BDB (both of which are introduced later in this section). The MyISAM table handler is particularly adept when applied to the following scenarios:

- **Select-intensive tables:** The MyISAM handler is quite fast at sifting through large amounts of data, even in a high-traffic environment.

- **Insert-intensive tables:** MyISAM's concurrent insert feature allows for data to be selected and inserted simultaneously. For example, the MyISAM handler would be a great candidate for managing mail or Web server log data.

The MyISAM table handler is such an important component of MySQL that considerable effort has been invested in its optimization. One key way in which this has been done is through the creation of three MyISAM subtypes: *static, dynamic,* and *compressed.* MySQL will automatically apply the best type in accordance with the specifics of the table structure. I'll introduce each of these subtypes next.

MyISAM Static

MySQL automatically uses the static MyISAM variant if the size of all table columns are static (that is, the xBLOB, xTEXT, or VARCHAR data types are not used). Performance is particularly high with this type of table because of the low overhead required to both maintain and access data stored in a predefined format. However, this advantage comes at a tradeoff for space, because each column requires the maximum amount of space allocated for each column, regardless of whether that space is actually used. Take for example two otherwise identical tables used to store user information. One table, user_static, uses the static CHAR data type to store the user's username and password:

```
create table user_static (
rowID smallint unsigned not null auto_increment,
username char(15) not null,
pswd char(15) not null,
primary key(rowID));
```

The other table, dubbed user_dynamic, uses the dynamic VARCHAR data type:

```
create table user_dynamic (
rowID smallint unsigned not null auto_increment,
username varchar(15) not null,
pswd varchar(15) not null,
primary key(rowID));
```

Because user_static uses solely static fields, it automatically assumes the MyISAM-static form, while the other assumes the MyISAM-dynamic form (introduced in the next section). Now insert a single row into each:

```
insert into user_static set rowID=NULL, username="jason", pswd="secret";
insert into user_dynamic set rowID=NULL, username="jason", pswd="secret";
```

Inserting just this single row into each will result in user_static being a little over 60 percent larger than user_dynamic (33 bytes versus 20 bytes). This is because the static table always consumes the space specified within the table definition, while the dynamic table only consumes the space required of the inserted data. However, don't take this trivial example as an endorsement for using only MyISAM-dynamic. Instead, take a moment to read more about this table type's characteristics, including its disadvantages, introduced next.

MyISAM Dynamic

MySQL automatically uses the dynamic variant if even one table column has been defined as dynamic (use of xBLOB, xTEXT, or VARCHAR). Although a MyISAM-dynamic table consumes significantly less space than its static counterpart, the savings in space comes at a disadvantage of performance. If a field's contents change, that the location will likely need to be moved, causing fragmentation. As the data set becomes increasingly fragmented, data access performance will suffer accordingly. Two remedies are available for this problem:

- Use static data types whenever possible.

- Use OPTIMIZE TABLE on a regular basis, which defragments the database. This feature of MySQL is introduced in Chapter 30.

MyISAM Compressed

Sometimes you'll create tables that are intended as read-only throughout the lifetime of your application. If this is the case, you can significantly reduce their size by converting them into MyISAM-compressed tables by using the myisamchk utility. Given certain hardware configurations (a fast processor and slow hard drive, for example), performance savings could be significant.

MERGE Tables

MyISAM also offers an additional variant that isn't as prominently used as the others, but is nonetheless quite useful in certain situations. This variant, known as a MERGE table, is actually an aggregation of identical MyISAM tables. Why is this useful? Consider that databases are often used for storing time-specific data: sales information, server logs, and flight timetables all immediately come to mind as prime candidates in this regard. As you might imagine, though, such data stores can easily become excessively large and quite unwieldy. As a result, a common storage strategy is to break the data up into numerous tables, with each name pertinent to a particular time-block. For example, I might create twelve identical tables for storing server log data, assign each a name corresponding with each month of the year, and use each according to the current month. However, I'd also like to produce reports based on data spread across all twelve tables. Rather than write error-prone queries that take all the tables into account, I can MERGE them together and enjoy the convenience of writing single-table queries. Once complete, the table can simply be dropped without affecting the original data.

Converting ISAM Tables to MyISAM

If you've been using MySQL since before version 3.23, chances are that any preexisting tables are of the ISAM handler-type. If this is the case, you should convert all such tables to the MyISAM type. Surprisingly, doing so is quite trivial, accomplished with a single ALTER command for each table:

```
ALTER TABLE table_name TYPE=MYISAM;
```

Alternatively, you can use the mysql_convert_table_format utility, which is bundled with the MySQL server. This client works much like mysql or mysqladmin, requiring authorization before any commands are executed. As an example, suppose you wanted to convert all ISAM tables located in a legacy database named clients to MyISAM:

```
%>mysql_convert_table_format -u root -p --type='MYISAM' clients
```

You can also specifically enumerate the tables that you'd like to convert. For example, suppose that there only two tables that require conversion (namely, companies and staff) in the clients database:

```
%>mysql_convert_table_format -u root -p --type='MYISAM' clients companies staff
```

Note that this script is capable of converting between BDB, ISAM, and MyISAM tables.

InnoDB

InnoDB is a robust transactional table handler that has been under active development for over a decade and released under the GNU GPL License. InnoDB has been embraced by such Internet heavyweights as Yahoo!, Slashdot, and Google, and offers users a powerful solution for working with very large data stores. It has been available to MySQL users since version 3.23.34a and has proved such a popular and effective solution for transactional applications that support has been enabled by default since version 4.0.

> **NOTE** *InnoDB is developed and maintained by Innobase Oy, Inc., based out of Helsinki, Finland. You can learn more about the company and the great InnoDB project at* http://www.innodb.com/.

Although InnoDB is commonly grouped with other table types, as I've done here, it's actually a complete database back end unto itself. InnoDB table resources are managed using dedicated buffers, which can be controlled like any other MySQL configuration parameters. InnoDB also brings other great advances to MySQL by way of row-level locking and foreign key constraints.

InnoDB tables are ideal for the following scenarios, among others:

- **Update-intensive tables:** The InnoDB handler is particularly adept at handling multiple simultaneous update requests.

- **Transactions:** The InnoDB handler is the only standard MySQL handler that supports transactions, a requisite feature for managing sensitive data such as financial or user registration information.

- **Automated crash recovery:** Unlike other handlers, InnoDB tables are capable of automatically recovering from a crash. Although MyISAM tables can also be repaired after a crash, the process can take significantly longer.

HEAP

MySQL's HEAP table handler was created with one goal in mind: speed. To attain the fastest response time possible, the logical storage media is system memory. Although storing table data in memory does indeed offer impressive performance, keep in mind that if the mysqld daemon crashes, all HEAP data will be lost.

This gain in speed comes at a cost of several drawbacks. For example, HEAP tables do not support the VARCHAR, BLOB, or TEXT data types, because all HEAP tables are stored in fixed-record-length format. In addition, automatically incrementing columns (via the AUTO_INCREMENT attribute) are not supported. Various searching deficiencies should also be considered; for example, HEAP requires use of the entire key for row searching, whereas MyISAM tables can execute a search using a key prefix. Of course, you should keep in mind that HEAP tables are intended for a specific scope, and aren't intended for long-term storage of data. Among others, you might consider using a HEAP table when your data is:

- **Negligible:** The target data is relatively small in size and accessed very frequently. Remember that storing data in memory will prevent that memory from being used for other purposes. Note that you can control the size of HEAP tables with the parameter max_heap_table_size. This parameter acts as a resource safeguard, placing a maximum limit on the size of a HEAP table.

- **Transient:** The target data is only temporarily required, and during its lifetime must be made immediately available.

- **Relatively inconsequential:** The sudden loss of data stored in HEAP tables would not have any substantial negative effect on application services, and certainly should not have a long-term impact on data integrity.

BDB

The BerkeleyDB (BDB) table handler, created and maintained by Sleepycat Software, Inc. (http://www.sleepycat.com/), was the first to bring transactional capabilities to MySQL. The prominence of this table type has been diminished considerably since the introduction of the more tightly integrated InnoDB table type, prompting the removal of the BDB table drivers from the standard MySQL distribution. You can, however, continue to use the BDB table type, if you so choose, by installing the MySQL-Max version of the database server.

....

Table Handler FAQ

There is often a bit of confusion surrounding various issues pertinent to table handlers. That said, I thought I'd devote a sidebar to frequently asked questions that I often encounter via e-mail and within newsgroups.

Is it wrong to use multiple table handlers within the same database?

Not at all. In fact, unless you're working with a particularly simple database, it's quite likely that your application would benefit from using multiple table types. It's always a good idea to carefully consider the purpose and behavior of each table in your database and choose an appropriate table handler accordingly. Don't take the lazy way out and just go with the default handler; it could detrimentally affect your application's performance in the long term.

How can I specify a handler at creation time, or change it later?

You can selectively assign table types at creation time by passing along the attribute TYPE=TABLE_TYPE, and you can convert a table later with the ALTER command or by using the mysql_convert_table_format script, which comes with your MySQL distribution.

I need speed! What's the fastest table handler?

Because HEAP tables are stored in memory, they offer extremely fast response time. However, keep in mind that anything stored in memory is highly volatile and is going to disappear if MySQL crashes or is shut down. Although HEAP tables certainly serve an important purpose, you might want to consider other optimization routes if speed is your goal. You can start by taking time to properly design your tables, always choosing the best possible data type and handler. Also, be diligent in optimizing your queries and MySQL server configuration, and of course never skimp on the server hardware. In addition, you can take advantage of other MySQL features, such as query caching.

....

Data Types and Attributes

It makes sense that you would want to wield some level of control over the data placed into each column of a MySQL table. For example, you might want to make sure that the value doesn't surpass a maximum limit, fall out of the bounds of a specific format, or even constrain the allowable values to a predefined set. To help in this task, MySQL offers an array of data types that can be assigned to each column in a table. Each forces the data to conform to a predetermined set of rules inherent to that data type, for example size, type (string, integer, or decimal, for instance), and format (ensuring that it conforms to a valid date or time representation, for example).

The behavior of these data types can be further tuned through the inclusion of *attributes*. In this section, I'll introduce both MySQL's supported data types, as well as many of the commonly used attributes. Because many data types support the same attributes, I'll forego repetition of the attribute definition, instead grouping the definitions under the heading "Data Type Attributes." I will make note of any special behavior as necessary, however.

Data Types

In this section, I'll introduce MySQL's supported types, offering information about the name, purpose, format, and range of each. To facilitate later reference, I've taken the liberty of breaking them down into three categories: *date and time, numeric,* and *string*.

Date and Time Data Types

Numerous types are available for representing time- and date-based data. I'll introduce those types in this section.

DATE

The DATE data type is responsible for storing date information. Although MySQL displays DATE values in a standard YYYY-MM-DD format, the values can be inserted using either numbers or strings. For example, both 20040810 and 2004-08-10 would be accepted as valid input. The range is 1000-01-01 to 9999-12-31, and the storage requirement is three bytes.

> **NOTE** *For all date/time data types, MySQL will accept any type of non-alphanumeric delimiter to separate the various date and time values. For example,* 20040810, 2004*08*10, 2004, 08, 10, *and* 2004!08!10 *are all the same as far as MySQL is concerned.*

DATETIME

The DATETIME data type is responsible for storing a combination of date and time information. Like DATE, DATETIME values are stored in a standard format YYYY-MM-DD HH:MM:SS; the values can be inserted using either numbers or strings. For example, both 20040810153510 and 2004-08-10 15:35:10 would be accepted as valid input. Its range is 1000-01-01 00:00:00 to 9999-12-31 23:59:59. The storage requirement is eight bytes.

TIME

The TIME data type is responsible for storing time information and supports a range not only large enough to represent both standard and military-style time formats, but also to represent extended time intervals. This range is -838:59:59 to 838:59:59, and the storage requirement is three bytes.

TIMESTAMP[(M)]

The TIMESTAMP data types differs from DATETIME in that MySQL automatically updates it to the current date and time whenever an insert or update operation affecting it is executed. TIMESTAMP values are displayed in HH:MM:SS format, and like the DATE and DATETIME data types, you can assign values using either numbers or strings. Timestamp values can be displayed in the following formats: YYYYMMDDHHMMSS (M=14), YYMMDDHHMMSS (M=12), YYYYMMDD (M=8), and YYMMDD (M=6) format. The range of TIMESTAMP is 1970-01-01 to "sometime in the year 2037," according to the MySQL manual. Its storage requirement is four bytes.

Note that as of version 4.1, you cannot specify the size. Starting with version 4.1, you are constrained to a TIMESTAMP column format that corresponds exactly to that of DATETIME.

YEAR[(2|4)]

The YEAR data type is responsible for storing year-specific information, supporting numerous ranges according to context:

- **Two-digit number:** 1 to 99

- **Four-digit number:** 1901 to 2155

- **Two-digit string:** "00" to "99"

- **Four-digit string:** "1901" to "2155"

Its storage requirement is one byte.

Numeric Data Types

Numerous types are available for representing numerical data. I'll introduce these types in this section.

> **NOTE** *Many of the numeric data types allow you to constrain the maximum display size, denoted by the M parameter following the type name in the following definitions. Many of the floating-point types allow you to specify the number of digits that should follow the decimal point, denoted by the D parameter. These parameters, along with related attributes, are optional and are indicated as such by their enclosure in square brackets.*

BIGINT [(M)]

The BIGINT data type offers MySQL largest integer range, supporting a signed range of –9,223,372,036,854,775,808 to 9,223,372,036,854,775,807, and an unsigned range of 0 to 18,446,744,073,709,551,615. The storage requirement is eight bytes.

INT [(M)] [UNSIGNED] [ZEROFILL]

The INT data type offers MySQL's second-largest integer range, supporting a signed range of –2,147,483,648 to 2,147,483,647, and an unsigned range of 0 to 4,294,967,295. The storage requirement is four bytes.

MEDIUMINT [(M)] [UNSIGNED] [ZEROFILL]

The MEDIUMINT data type offers MySQL's third-largest integer range, supporting a signed range of –8,388,608 to 8,388,607, and an unsigned range of 0 to 16,777,215. The storage requirement is three bytes.

SMALLINT [(M)] [UNSIGNED] [ZEROFILL]

The SMALLINT data type offers MySQL's fourth-largest integer range, supporting a signed range of –32,768 to 32,767, and an unsigned range of 0 to 65,535. The storage requirement is two bytes.

TINYINT [(M)] [UNSIGNED] [ZEROFILL]

The TINYINT data type is MySQL's smallest integer range, supporting a signed range of –128 to 127, and an unsigned range of 0 to 255. The storage requirement is one byte.

DECIMAL([M[,D]]) [UNSIGNED] [ZEROFILL]

The DECIMAL data type is a floating-point number stored as a string, supporting a signed range of –1.7976931348623157E+308 to –2.2250738585072014E-308, and an unsigned range of 2.2250738585072014E–308 to 1.7976931348623157E+308. The decimal point and minus sign are ignored when determining the number's total size. The storage requirement is M+2 bytes if D is greater than 0, M+1 bytes if D is equal to 0, and D+2 if M is less than D.

DOUBLE([M,D]) [UNSIGNED] [ZEROFILL]

The DOUBLE data type is a double-precision floating-point number, supporting a signed range of –1.7976931348623157E+308 to –2.2250738585072014E–308, and an unsigned range of 2.2250738585072014E–308 to 1.7976931348623157E+308. The storage requirement is eight bytes.

FLOAT([M,D]) [UNSIGNED] [ZEROFILL]

This FLOAT data type variation is MySQL's single precision floating-point number representation, supporting a signed range of –3.402823466E+38 to –1.175494351E–38, and an unsigned range of 1.175494351E–38 to 3.402823466E+38. The storage requirement is four bytes.

FLOAT (precision) [UNSIGNED] [ZEROFILL]

This FLOAT data type variant is provided for ODBC compatibility. The degree of precision can range between 1 to 24 for single precision, and 25 to 53 for double precision. The range is the same as that defined in the preceding FLOAT definition. The storage requirement is four bytes if precision is less than 24, and eight bytes if precision is between 25 and 53.

MySQL's String Data Types

Numerous types are available for representing string data. I'll introduce these types in this section.

[NATIONAL] CHAR(Length) [BINARY | ASCII | UNICODE]

The CHAR data type offers MySQL's fixed-length string representation, supporting a maximum length of 255 characters. If an inserted string does not occupy Length spaces, the remaining space will be padded by blank spaces. When retrieved, these blank spaces will be omitted. If Length is one character, the user can omit the length reference, simply using CHAR. You can also specify a zero-length CHAR in conjunction with the NOT NULL attribute, which will allow only NULL or "". The NATIONAL attribute is available for compatibility reasons, because this is how SQL-99 specifies that the default character set should be used for the column, which MySQL already does by default. Supplying the BINARY attribute causes the values in this column to be sorted in case-sensitive fashion; omitting it causes them to be sorted in case-insensitive fashion.

Starting with version 4.1.0, if Length is greater than 255, the column will automatically be converted to the TEXT type. Also starting with this version, including the ASCII attribute will result in the application of the Latin1 character set to the column. Finally, beginning with version 4.1.1, including the UNICODE attribute will result in the application of the ucs2 character set to the column.

The storage requirement is Length bytes, where Length is between 1 and 255.

[NATIONAL] VARCHAR(Length) [BINARY]

The VARCHAR data type is MySQL's variable-length string representation, supporting a maximum length of 255 characters. The NATIONAL attribute is available for compatibility reasons, because this is how SQL-99 specifies that the default character set should be used for the column, which MySQL already does by default. Supplying the BINARY attribute causes the values in this column to be sorted in case-sensitive fashion; omitting it causes them to be sorted in case-insensitive fashion. The storage requirement is Length + 1 byte, where Length is between 1 and 255.

LONGBLOB

The LONGBLOB is MySQL's largest binary string representation, supporting a maximum length of 4,294,967,295 characters. The storage requirement is the total number of characters + 4 bytes.

LONGTEXT

The LONGTEXT data type is MySQL's largest non-binary string representation, supporting a maximum length of 4,294,967,295 characters. The storage requirement is the total number of characters + 4 bytes.

MEDIUMBLOB

The MEDIUMBLOB data type is MySQL's second-largest binary string representation, supporting a maximum of 16,777,215 characters. The storage requirement is the total number of characters + 3 bytes.

MEDIUMTEXT

The MEDIUMTEXT data type is MySQL's second-largest non-binary text string, capable of storing a maximum length of 16,777,215 characters. The storage requirement is the total number of characters + 3 bytes.

BLOB

The BLOB data type is MySQL's third-largest binary string representation, supporting a maximum length of 65,535 characters. The storage requirement is the total number of characters + 2 bytes.

TEXT

The TEXT data type is MySQL's third-largest non-binary string representation, supporting a maximum length of 65,535 characters. The storage requirement is the total number of characters + 2 bytes.

TINYBLOB

The TINYBLOB data type is MySQL's smallest binary string representation, supporting a maximum length of 255 characters. The storage requirement is the total number of characters + 1 bytes.

TINYTEXT

The TINYTEXT data type is MySQL's smallest non-binary string representation, supporting a maximum length of 255 characters. The storage requirement is the total number of characters + 1 bytes.

ENUM("member1","member2",... "member65,535")

The ENUM data type provides a means for storing a maximum of one member chosen from a predefined group consisting of a maximum of 65,535 distinct members. The choice of members is restricted to those declared in the column definition. If the column declaration includes the NULL attribute, then NULL will be considered a valid value and will be the default. If NOT NULL is declared, the first member of the list will be the default. The storage requirement is 1 byte for enumerations not surpassing 255 values, and 2 bytes for those consisting of greater than 255 values.

SET("member1", "member2",... "member64")

The SET data type provides a means for specifying zero or more values chosen from a predefined group consisting of a maximum of 64 members. The choice of values is restricted to those declared in the column definition. The storage requirement is 1, 2, 3, 4, or 8 values, depending on the number of members. You can determine the exact requirement with this formula: $(N+7)/8$, where N is the set size.

Data Type Attributes

Although this list is not exhaustive, I'll cover those attributes you'll most commonly use, as well as those that will be used throughout the remainder of this book.

AUTO_INCREMENT

The AUTO_INCREMENT attribute takes away a level of logic that would otherwise be necessary in many database-driven applications: the ability to assign unique integer identifiers to newly inserted rows. Assigning this attribute to a column will result in the assignment of the last insertion id +1 to each newly inserted row.

MySQL requires that the AUTO_INCREMENT attribute be used in conjunction with a column designated as the primary key. Furthermore, only one AUTO_INCREMENT column per table is allowed. An example of a AUTO_INCREMENT column assignment follows:

```
rowID SMALLINT NOT NULL AUTO_INCREMENT PRIMARY KEY
```

BINARY

The BINARY attribute is only used in conjunction with CHAR and VARCHAR values. When columns are assigned this attribute, they will be sorted in case-sensitive fashion (in accordance with their ASCII machine values). This is in contrast to the case-insensitive sorting when the BINARY attribute is omitted. An example of a BINARY column assignment follows:

```
hostname CHAR(25) BINARY NOT NULL
```

DEFAULT

The DEFAULT attribute ensures that some constant value will be assigned when no other value is available. This value must be a constant, because MySQL does not allow functional or expressional values to be inserted. Furthermore, this attribute cannot be used in conjunction with BLOB or TEXT fields. If the NULL attribute has been assigned to this field, the default value will be null if no default is specified. Otherwise (specifically, if NOT NULL is an accompanying attribute), the default value will depend on the field data type.

An example of a DEFAULT attribute assignment follows:

```
subscribed ENUM('0','1') NOT NULL DEFAULT '0'
```

INDEX

If all other factors are equal, the use of indexing is often the single most important step you can take towards speeding your database queries. Indexing a column creates a sorted array of keys for that column, each of which points to its corresponding table row. Subsequently searching this ordered key array for the input criteria results in vast increases in performance over searching the entire unindexed table, because MySQL will already have the sorted array at its disposal. The following example demonstrates how a column used to store employee's last names can be indexed:

```
CREATE TABLE employee (
    empid VARCHAR(9) NOT NULL,
    firstName VARCHAR(15) NOT NULL,
    lastName VARCHAR(25) NOT NULL,
    email VARCHAR(45) NOT NULL,
    phone VARCHAR(10) NOT NULL,
    INDEX lastName (lastName),
    PRIMARY KEY(ssn));
```

Alternatively, an index could be added after a table has been created by making use of MySQL's CREATE INDEX command:

```
CREATE INDEX lastName ON employee (firstName(7));
```

In this example, I took the opportunity to offer a slight variation on the previous one. This time I indexed only the first seven characters of the first name, because more letters probably won't be necessary to differentiate among first names. Because performance is better when smaller indexes are used, you should strive to use them whenever practical.

NATIONAL

The NATIONAL attribute is used only in conjunction with the CHAR and VARCHAR data types. When specified, it ensures that the column uses the default character set, which MySQL already does by default. In short, this attribute is offered as an aid in database compatibility.

NOT NULL

Defining a column as NOT NULL will disallow any attempt to insert a NULL value into the column. Using the NOT NULL attribute where relevant is always suggested, because it results in at least baseline verification that all necessary values have been passed to the query. An example of a NOT NULL column assignment follows:

```
zipcode VARCHAR(10) NOT NULL
```

NULL

Simply stated, the NULL attribute means that no value can exist for the given field. Keep in mind that NULL is a mathematical term specifying "nothingness," rather than an empty string or zero. When a column is assigned the NULL attribute, it is possible for the field to remain empty regardless of whether the other row fields have been populated.

The NULL attribute is assigned to a field by default. Typically, you will want to avoid this default, ensuring that empty values will not be accepted into the table. This is accomplished through NULL's antithesis, NOT NULL, introduced above.

PRIMARY KEY

The PRIMARY KEY attribute is used to guarantee uniqueness for a given row. No values residing in a column designated as a PRIMARY KEY are repeatable nor nullable within that column. It's quite common to assign the AUTO_INCREMENT attribute to a column designated as a primary key, because this column doesn't necessarily have to bear any relation to the row data, other than acting as its unique identifier. However, there are two other ways for ensuring a record's uniqueness:

- **Single-field primary keys:** Single-field primary keys are typically used when there is a pre-existing, non-modifiable unique identifier for each row entered into the database, such as a part number or Social Security number. Note that this key should never change once set.

- **Multiple-field primary keys:** Multiple-field primary keys can be useful when it is not possible to guarantee uniqueness from any single field within a record. Thus, multiple fields are conjoined to ensure uniqueness. When such a situation arises, it is often a good idea to simply designate an AUTO_INCREMENT integer as the primary key, to alleviate the need to somehow generate unique identifiers with every insertion.

The following three examples demonstrate creation of the auto-increment, single-field, and multiple-field primary key fields, respectively.

Creating an automatically incrementing primary key:

```
CREATE TABLE staff (
    staffID SMALLINT NOT NULL AUTO_INCREMENT,
    fName VARCHAR(15) NOT NULL,
    lName VARCHAR(25) NOT NULL,
    email VARCHAR(55) NOT NULL,
    PRIMARY KEY(staffID));
```

Creating a single-field primary key:

```
CREATE TABLE citizen (
    ssID VARCHAR(9) NOT NULL,
    fName VARCHAR(15) NOT NULL,
    lName VARCHAR(25) NOT NULL,
    zipcode VARCHAR(9) NOT NULL,
    PRIMARY KEY(ssID));
```

Creating a multiple-field primary key:

```
CREATE TABLE friend (
    fName VARCHAR(15) NOT NULL,
    lName VARCHAR(25) NOT NULL,
    nickname varchar(15) NOT NULL,
    PRIMARY KEY(lName, nickName));
```

UNIQUE

A column assigned the *UNIQUE* attribute will ensure that all values possess distinct values, except that NULL values are repeatable. You typically designate a column as UNIQUE in order to ensure that all fields within that column are distinct, for example to prevent the same e-mail address from being inserted into a newsletter subscriber table multiple times, while at the same time acknowledging that the field could potentially be empty (NULL). An example of a column designated as UNIQUE follows:

```
email VARCHAR(55) UNIQUE
```

ZEROFILL

The *ZEROFILL* attribute is available to any of the numeric types and will result in the replacement of all remaining field space with zeroes. For example, the default width of an unsigned INT is 10, therefore a zero-filled INT value of 4 would be represented as 0000000004. An example of a ZEROFILL attribute assignment follows:

```
odometer MEDIUMINT UNSIGNED ZEROFILL NOT NULL
```

Given this definition, the value 35,678 would be returned as 0035678.

Working with Databases and Tables

Learning how to manage and navigate MySQL databases and tables will be one of the first tasks you'll want to master. In this section, I'll highlight several key tasks.

Working with Databases

In this section, I'll demonstrate how to create, select, and delete MySQL databases.

Creating a Database

There are two common ways to create a database. Perhaps the easiest is to create it using the CREATE DATABASE command from within the mysql client:

```
mysql>CREATE DATABASE company;
Query OK, 1 row affected (0.00 sec)
```

You can also create a database via the mysqladmin client:

```
%>mysqladmin -u root -p create company
Enter password:
%>
```

Common problems for failed database creation include insufficient or incorrect permissions, or an attempt to create a database that already exists.

Using a Database

Once the database has been created, you can designate it as the default working database by "using" it, done with the USE command:

```
mysql>USE company;
Database changed
```

Alternatively, you can switch directly into that database when logging in via the mysql client by passing its name on the command line, like so:

```
%>mysql -u root -p company
```

In both cases, you'll immediately have the database tables and data at your disposal upon executing each command.

Deleting a Database

You delete a database in much the same fashion as you create one. You can delete it from within the mysql client with the DROP command, like so:

```
mysql>DROP DATABASE company;
Query OK, 1 row affected (0.00 sec)
```

Alternatively, you can delete it from the mysqladmin client. The advantage of doing it in this fashion is that you're prompted prior to deletion:

```
%>mysqladmin -u root -p drop company

Enter password:
Dropping the database is potentially a very bad thing to do.
Any data stored in the database will be destroyed.

Do you really want to drop the 'company' database [y/N] y
Database "company" dropped
%>
```

Working with Tables

In this section, I'll demonstrate how to create, list, review, delete, and alter MySQL database tables.

Creating a Table

A table is created using the CREATE TABLE statement. Although there are a vast number of options and clauses specific to this statement, it seems a bit impractical to introduce them all in what is an otherwise informal introduction, that said I'll instead opt to introduce various features of this statement as they become relevant in future sections. Nonetheless, general usage will be demonstrated here. As an example, let's create the employee table first discussed at the start of this chapter:

```
CREATE TABLE employee (
    empID TINYINT UNSIGNED NOT NULL AUTO_INCREMENT,
    firstname VARCHAR(25) NOT NULL,
    lastname VARCHAR(25) NOT NULL,
    email VARCHAR(45) NOT NULL,
    phone VARCHAR(10) NOT NULL,
    PRIMARY KEY(empID));
```

Keep in mind that a table must consist of at least one column. Also, you can always go back and alter a table structure after it has been created. Later in this section I'll demonstrate how this is accomplished via the ALTER TABLE statement.

> **TIP** *As a rule, I like to always declare my MySQL tables in lowercase format and in the singular form. Of course, the choice is up to you; what is important is that you choose a format and stick with it. Take it from experience, constantly having to look up the exact format of table names because a set format was never agreed upon can be quite annoying.*

You can also create a table regardless of whether you're currently using the target database. Simply prepend the table name with the target database name like so: database_name.table_name.

Conditionally Creating a Table

By default, MySQL generates an error if you attempt to create a table that already exists. To avoid this error, the CREATE TABLE statement offers a clause that can be included if you want to simply abort the table creation attempt if the target table already exists. For example, suppose you distributed an application that relied on a MySQL database for storing data. Because some users would download the latest version as a matter of course for upgrading, while others would download it for the first time, your installation script requires an easy means for creating the new user's tables while not causing undue display of errors during the upgrade process. This is done via the IF NOT EXISTS clause. For example, suppose you wanted to create the employee table only if it doesn't already exist:

```
CREATE TABLE IF NOT EXISTS employee (
    empID TINYINT UNSIGNED NOT NULL AUTO_INCREMENT,
    firstname VARCHAR(25) NOT NULL,
    lastname VARCHAR(25) NOT NULL,
    email VARCHAR(45) NOT NULL,
    phone VARCHAR(10) NOT NULL,
    PRIMARY KEY(empID));
```

Note that one oddity of this action is that the output does not specify whether the table was created. Both variations display the "Query OK" message before returning to the mysql command prompt.

Copying a Table

It's trivial to create a new table based on an existing one. The following query produces an exact copy of the employee table, naming it employee2:

```
CREATE TABLE employee2 SELECT * FROM employee;
```

An identical table, `employee2`, will be added to the database.

Sometimes you might be interested in creating a table based on just a few columns found in a preexisting table. You can do so by simply specifying the columns within the `CREATE SELECT` statement:

```
CREATE TABLE employee3 SELECT firstname,lastname FROM employee;
```

Creating a Temporary Table

Sometimes it's useful to create tables that will have a lifetime only as long as the current session. For example, you might need to perform several queries on a subset of a particularly large table. Rather than repeatedly run those queries against the entire table, you can create a temporary table for that subset and then run the queries against it instead. This is accomplished by using the `TEMPORARY` keyword in conjunction with the `CREATE TABLE` statement:

```
CREATE TEMPORARY TABLE emp_temp SELECT firstname,lastname FROM employee;
```

Temporary tables are created as any other table would be, except that they're stored in the operating system's designated temporary directory, typically `/tmp` or `/usr/tmp` on Linux. You can override this default by setting MySQL's `TMPDIR` environment variable.

> **NOTE** *As of MySQL 4.0.2, ownership of the* `CREATE TEMPORARY TABLE` *privilege is required in order to create temporary tables. See Chapter 25 for more details about MySQL's privilege system.*

Viewing a Database's Available Tables

You can view a list of the tables made available to a database with the `SHOW TABLES` statement:

```
mysql>USE company;
Database changed
mysql>SHOW TABLES;
+--------------------+
| Tables_in_company2 |
+--------------------+
| employee           |
+--------------------+
1 row in set (0.00 sec)
```

Viewing Table Structure

You can view a table structure using the DESCRIBE TABLE statement:

```
mysql>DESCRIBE employee;
```

```
+-----------+---------------------+------+-----+---------+----------------+
| Field     | Type                | Null | Key | Default | Extra          |
+-----------+---------------------+------+-----+---------+----------------+
| empID     | tinyint(3) unsigned |      | PRI | NULL    | auto_increment |
| firstname | varchar(25)         |      |     |         |                |
| lastname  | varchar(25)         |      |     |         |                |
| email     | varchar(45)         |      |     |         |                |
| phone     | varchar(10)         |      |     |         |                |
+-----------+---------------------+------+-----+---------+----------------+
```

Deleting a Table

Deleting a table, or *dropping* it, is accomplished via the DROP TABLE statement. Its syntax follows:

```
DROP [TEMPORARY] TABLE [IF EXISTS] tbl_name [, tbl_name,...]
```

For example, you could delete your employee table as follows:

```
DROP TABLE employee;
```

You could also simultaneously drop the employee2 and employee3 tables created in previous examples like so:

```
DROP TABLE employee2 employee3;
```

Altering a Table Structure

You'll find yourself often revising and improving your table structures, particularly in the early stages of development. However, you don't have to go through the hassle of deleting and re-creating the table every time you'd like to make a change. Rather, you can alter the table's structure with the ALTER statement. With this statement, you can delete, modify, and add columns as you deem necessary. Like CREATE TABLE, the ALTER TABLE statement offers a vast number of clauses, keywords, and options. I'll leave it to you to look up the gory details in the MySQL manual, and instead I'll offer several examples intended to get you started quickly. Let's begin with adding a column. Suppose you want to track each employee's birth date with the employee table:

```
ALTER TABLE employee ADD COLUMN birthdate DATE;
```

The new column is placed at the last position of the table. However, you can also control the positioning of a new column using an appropriate keyword, including FIRST, AFTER, and LAST. For example, I could place the birthdate column directly after the lastname column, like so:

```
ALTER TABLE employee ADD COLUMN birthdate DATE AFTER lastname;
```

Whoops, you forgot the NOT NULL clause! You can modify the new column:

```
ALTER TABLE employee CHANGE birthdate birthdate DATE NOT NULL;
```

Finally, after all that, you decide that it isn't necessary to track the employee's birth dates. Go ahead and delete the column:

```
ALTER TABLE employee DROP birthdate;
```

Summary

In this chapter, you learned about the many ingredients that go into MySQL table design. I kicked off the discussion with a survey of MySQL's table handlers, discussing the purpose and advantages of each. This discussion was followed by an introduction to MySQL's supported data types, offering information about the name, purpose, and range of each. I then examined many of the most commonly used attributes, which serve to further tweak column behavior. I concluded the chapter with a short tutorial on basic MySQL administration commands, demonstrating how databases and tables are created, deleted, perused, and altered.

In the next chapter, we'll dive into another key MySQL feature: security. You'll learn all about MySQL's powerful privilege tables, as well as learn more about how to secure the MySQL server daemon and create secure MySQL connections using SSL.

CHAPTER 25

Securing MySQL

I'M SURE THAT when you exit your automobile, you take a moment to lock the doors and set the car alarm, if you have one. It's almost an automatic reaction, because you know that the possibility of the car or its contents being stolen will dramatically increase if you don't take such rudimentary, yet effective precautions. Ironically, the IT industry at-large seems to take the opposite approach when creating the vehicles used to maintain enterprise data. Both IT systems and applications are rife with open doors leading to intellectual property theft, damage, and even destruction as a result of electronic attacks. Often, such occurrences take place not because the technology did not offer deterrent features, but simply because the implementer never bothered to put these deterrents into effect.

In this chapter, I'll introduce numerous aspects of MySQL's highly effective security model. In particular, I'll describe MySQL's user privilege system in lurid detail, showing you how to create users, manage privileges, and change passwords. Additionally, I'll demonstrate MySQL's secure (SSL) connection feature, and will show you how to place limitations on user resource consumption. While no amount of discussion will force all of you to implement these features, I hope that the examples and anecdotes interspersed throughout this chapter will be enough to sway the majority of readers into taking the time to do so. After completing this chapter, you should be familiar with the following topics:

- What steps you should take immediately after starting the mysqld daemon for the first time

- How to secure the mysqld daemon

- MySQL's access privilege system

- The GRANT and REVOKE functions

- User account management

- Creating secure MySQL connections with SSL

Let's start at the beginning: what you should do *before doing anything else* with your MySQL database server.

What You Should Do First

This section outlines several rudimentary, yet very important tasks you should undertake immediately after completing the installation and configuration process outlined in Chapter 22.

- **Patch the operating system and any installed software.** Software security alerts seem to be issued on a weekly basis these days, and although they are annoying, it's absolutely necessary that you take the steps to ensure that your system is fully patched. With exploit instructions and tools readily available on the Internet, a malicious user with even little experience in such matters will have little trouble taking advantage of an unpatched server. Don't take solace in the fact that you're running a Unix-based environment; patches come out almost as often, if not more so, than the supposedly bug-ridden Windows platform. The bottom line is that you should develop an official patching strategy and stick with it, regardless of your chosen operating system.

- **Disable all unused system services.** Always take care to eliminate all unnecessary potential server attack routes before you place it on the network. These attack vectors are almost exclusively the result of insecure system services, often ones running on the system unbeknownst to the system administrator. The rule of thumb these days is that if you're not going to use the service, turn it off.

- **Tighten the database server firewall.** Although shutting off unused system services is a great way to lessen the probability of a successful attack, it doesn't hurt to add a second layer of security by closing all unused ports. For a dedicated database server, I typically close off all ports below 1024 except for 22 (SSH), 3306 (MySQL), and a handful of "utility" ports like 123 (NTP). In short, if you don't intend for traffic to travel on a given port, close it off altogether. In addition to making such adjustments on a dedicated firewall appliance or router, also consider taking advantage of the operating system's firewall. Both Microsoft Windows Server 2000/2003 and Unix-based systems have built-in firewalls at your disposal.

- **Audit the database server's user accounts.** Particularly if a pre-existing server's purpose has been reassigned to hosting the organization's database, make sure that all non-privileged users are disabled, or better, deleted. Although MySQL users and operating system users are completely unrelated, the mere fact that they have access to the server environment raises the possibility that damage could be done, inadvertently or otherwise, to the database server and its contents. To completely ensure that nothing is overlooked during such an audit, I suggest reformatting all attached drives and reinstalling the operating system.

- **Set the MySQL root user password.** By default, the root (administrator) account password is left blank. Although I find this practice questionable, this has long been the standard procedure, and I suspect it will be this way for some time. You must take care to add a password immediately! You can do so with the SET PASSWORD command, like so:

```
%>mysql -u root mysql
%>SET PASSWORD FOR root@localhost=PASSWORD('secret');
%>FLUSH PRIVILEGES;
```

Of course, choose a password that is a tad more complicated than *secret*. MySQL will let you dig your own grave in the sense that passwords such as *123*, *abc*, and your dog's name are perfectly acceptable. I suggest choosing a password that is at least eight characters in length, and consists of a mixture of numeric and alphabetical characters of varying case.

Securing the mysqld Daemon

There are several security options you can use when you start the mysqld daemon. These options are introduced in this section.

- --skip-networking: Enabling this option prevents the use of TCP/IP sockets when connecting to MySQL. If your application and database reside on the same server, you should definitely consider including this option.

- --skip-name-resolve: Enabling this option prevents the use of hostnames when connecting to the MySQL database, instead allowing only IP addresses or localhost.

- --safe-show-database: Enabling this option causes the SHOW DATABASES command to return only those databases for which the user possesses some sort of privilege. If you're running version 4.02 or higher, this option is enabled by default.

- --skip-show-database: This option prevents any user that does not possess the SHOW DATABASES privilege from using the command entirely. As of version 4.02, the Show_db_priv column located the user table mimics this feature. (See the next section for more information about the user table.)

- --local-infile: Disabling this option by setting it to 0 disables use of the command LOAD DATA LOCAL INFILE. See Chapter 30 for more information about this command.

- --safe-user-create: Enabling this option prevents any user from creating new users via the GRANT command if they do not also possess the INSERT privilege for the user table.

The MySQL Access Privilege System

Protecting your data from unwarranted review, modification, or deletion, accidental or otherwise, should always be your primary concern. Yet balancing a secure database with an expected level of user convenience and flexibility is often a difficult affair. The delicacy of this balance becomes obvious when you consider the wide array of access scenarios that might exist in any given environment. For example, what if a user requires modification, but not insertion privileges? How do you authenticate a user who might need to access the database from a number of different IP addresses? What if you wanted to provide a user read access to only certain table columns, while restricting the rest? You can imagine the nightmarish code that might result from incorporating such features into the application logic. Thankfully, the MySQL developers have relieved you of these tasks, integrating fully-featured authentication and authorization capabilities into the server. This is commonly referred to as the MySQL access privilege system.

How the Privilege System Works

MySQL's privilege system revolves around two general concepts: *authentication* and *authorization*. The first, *authentication*, determines whether a user is even allowed to connect to the server. The second, *authorization*, determines whether the user possesses adequate privileges to execute query requests. Because authorization cannot take place without successful authentication, you can think of this process as taking place in stages.

The Two Stages of Access Control

The general privilege control process takes place in two distinct steps: *connection authentication* and *request verification*. Together, these steps are carried out in five distinct phases:

1. The user table determines whether the incoming connection should be accepted or rejected. This is done by matching the specified host and the user to a row contained within the table. The execution of Step 1 completes the authentication phase of the privilege control process.

2. Step 2 initiates the request verification phase of the privilege control process. If the connection is accepted, the corresponding privileges as granted within the user table are examined. If any of these privileges are enabled (set to y), then the user will have *global* privileges, for any database, to act in the capacity granted by that privilege. Of course, in most cases, all of these privileges will be disabled, which causes Step 3 to occur.

3. The db table is examined, verifying which databases this user is allowed to interact with. Any corresponding privileges enabled in this table correspond to all tables within those databases that the user is allowed to interact with.

4. If a row in the db table is found to have a matching user but an empty host value, the host table is then examined. If a matching host value is found, the user will have those privileges for that database as indicated in the host table,

and not the db table. This is done to allow for host-specific access on a given database.

5. Finally, if a user attempts to execute a command that has not been granted in the user, db, or host tables, the tables_priv and columns_priv tables are examined, to determine whether the user is able to execute that command on the table(s) or column(s) in question.

As you may have gathered from the process breakdown, the system examines privileges started with the very broad and ending with the very specific. Let's consider a concrete example.

Tracing Through a Real-World Connection Request

The example takes the following variables into account:

- **Database:** company

- **Table:** widgets

- **User:** jason

- **Connecting from:** www.example.com

- **Password:** secret

- **Scenario:** User jason would like to insert a new row into the widgets table.

Upon submission of the insertion request, MySQL follows this procedure:

1. Does this user jason@www.example.com require a secure connection? If yes, and user jason@www.example.com has connected without the required security certificate, deny the request and end the control procedure. If no, proceed to Step 2.

2. Has user jason@www.example.com exceeded any resource usage limitations? If yes, deny the request and end the control procedure. If no, proceed to Step 3.

3. Does user jason@www.example.com possess the necessary privileges to connect to the database server? If yes, proceed to Step 4. If no, deny access and end the control procedure. This step ends the authentication component of the privilege control mechanism.

4. Does user jason@www.example.com possess global insertion privileges? If yes, accept and execute the insertion request. If no, proceed to Step 5.

5. Does user jason@www.example.com possess insertion privileges for the company database? If yes, accept and execute the insertion request. If no, proceed to Step 6.

6. Does the user possess insertion privileges for the widget table columns specified in the insertion request? If yes, accept and execute the insertion request. If no, deny the request and end the control procedure.

By now you should be beginning to understand the generalities surrounding MySQL's access control mechanism. However, the picture isn't complete until you're familiar with the technical underpinnings of this process. I'll introduce this matter next.

Where Is Access Information Stored?

MySQL's privilege verification information is stored in the mysql database, which is installed by default along with the database server. Specifically, five tables found in this database play an important role in the authentication and privilege verification process. These tables are:

- user: This table determines which users can log in to the database server from which host.

- db: This table determines which user can access which database.

- host: This table is an extension of the db table, offering additional host names from which a user can connect to the database server.

- tables_priv: This table determines which users can access specific tables of a particular database.

- columns_priv: This table determines which users can access specific columns of a particular table.

In this section, I'll delve into the details pertinent to the purpose and structure of each privilege table.

The user Table

The user table is unique in the sense that it is the only privilege table to play a role in both stages of the privileged request procedure. During the authentication stage, it's responsible for granting user access to the MySQL server. In the request authorization stage, it determines whether those users granted access to the server have been assigned *global* privileges for working with the MySQL server. That is, any privilege enabled in this table will allow a user to work in some capacity (dependent upon exactly which privileges have been enabled) with all databases located on that MySQL server.

The user table possesses another defining characteristic: it is the only one to store privileges pertinent to the administration of the MySQL server. For example, this table is responsible for determining which users are allowed to execute commands relevant to the general functioning of the server, such as shutting down the server, reloading user privileges, and viewing and even killing existing client processes. Needless to say, this table plays quite an important role in the access privilege procedure.

Because of its wide-ranging responsibilities, user is the largest of the privilege tables, containing a total of thirty fields: three scope, and the rest privilege. Table 25-1 offers information regarding the columns found in the user table, including their names, data types, attributes, and default values. Following the table, I'll offer a more thorough introduction of each column's purpose.

Table 25-1. Overview of the user *Table*

COLUMN	DATA TYPE	NULL	DEFAULT
Host	varchar(60) binary	No	No default
User	varchar(16) binary	No	No default
Password	varchar(16) binary	No	No default
Select_priv	enum('N','Y')	No	N
Insert_priv	enum('N','Y')	No	N
Update_priv	enum('N','Y')	No	N
Delete_priv	enum('N','Y')	No	N
Create_priv	enum('N','Y')	No	N
Drop_priv	enum('N','Y')	No	N
Reload_priv	enum('N','Y')	No	N
Shutdown_priv	enum('N','Y')	No	N
Process_priv	enum('N','Y')	No	N
File_priv	enum('N','Y')	No	N
Grant_priv	enum('N','Y')	No	N
References_priv	enum('N','Y')	No	N
Index_priv	enum('N','Y')	No	N
Alter_priv	enum('N','Y')	No	N
Show_db_priv	enum('N','Y')	No	N
Super_priv	enum('N','Y')	No	N
Create_tmp_table_priv	enum('N','Y')	No	N
Lock_tables_priv	enum('N','Y')	No	N
Execute_priv	enum('N','Y')	No	N
Repl_slave_priv	enum('N','Y')	No	N
ssl_type	enum('','ANY','X509','SPECIFIED')	No	0
ssl_cipher	blob	No	0
x509_issuer	blob	No	0
x509_subject	blob	No	0
max_questions	int(11) unsigned	No	0
max_updates	int(11) unsigned	No	0
max_connections	int(11) unsigned	No	0

Host

The Host column specifies the hostname that determines the host address from which a user can connect. Addresses can be stored as either hostnames, IP addresses, or wildcards. Wildcards can consist of either the % or _ character. In additionally, netmasks may be used to represent IP subnets. Several example entries follow:

- www.example.com
- 192.168.1.2
- %
- %.example.com
- 192.168.1.0/255.255.255.0
- localhost

User

The User column specifies the case-sensitive user name capable of connecting to the database server. Although wildcards are not permitted, blank values are. If the entry is empty, any user arriving from the corresponding Host entry will be allowed to log in to the database server. Example entries follow:

- jason
- Jason_Gilmore
- secretary5

Password

The Password column stores the encrypted password supplied by the connecting user. Although wildcards are not allowed, blank passwords are. Therefore, make sure that all users are provided with a corresponding password to alleviate potential security issues.

Passwords are stored in a one-way hashed format, meaning that they cannot be retrieved. As of version 4.1, the number of bytes required to store a password increased from 16 bytes to 41 bytes. Therefore, if you're importing data from a pre-4.1 version, and you want to take advantage of the added security offered by the longer hashes, you'll need to increase the size of the Password column to fit the new space requirement. You can do so by either manually altering the table with the ALTER command, or by running the utility mysql_fix_privilege_tables. If you choose not to, or cannot, then MySQL will still allow you to fix and maintain passwords; it will simply continue to use the old methodology for doing so.

User Identification

MySQL identifies a user not just by the supplied username, but by the combination of supplied user and originating host. For example, jason@localhost is entirely different from jason@www.wjgilmore.com. Furthermore, keep in mind that MySQL will always apply the most specific set of permissions that match the supplied user@host combination. Although this may seem obvious, sometimes unforeseen consequences can happen. For example, it's often the case that multiple rows match the requesting user/host identity; Even if a wildcard entry that satisfies the supplied user@host combination is seen before a later entry that perfectly matches the identity, the privileges corresponding to that perfect match will be used instead of the wildcard match. Therefore, always take care to ensure that the expected privileges are indeed supplied for each user. Later in this chapter I'll show you how to view privileges on a per-user basis.

The user Privileges

The remainder of the rows comprise the user privilege columns. I'll introduce each in this section.

- Select_priv: Determines whether the user can select data via the SELECT command.

- Insert_priv: Determines whether the user can insert data via the INSERT command.

- Update_priv: Determines whether the user can modify existing data via the UPDATE command.

- Delete_priv: Determines whether the user can delete existing data via the DELETE command.

- Create_priv: Determines whether the user can create new databases and tables.

- Drop_priv: Determines whether the user can delete existing databases and tables.

- Reload_priv: Determines whether the user can execute various commands specific to flushing and reloading of various internal caches used by MySQL, including logs, privileges, hosts, queries, and tables.

- Shutdown_priv: Determines whether the user can shut down the MySQL server. You should be very wary of providing this privilege to anybody except the root account.

- Process_priv: Determines whether the user can view the processes of other users via the SHOW PROCESSLIST command.

- File_priv: Determines whether the user can execute the SELECT INTO OUTFILE and LOAD DATA INFILE commands.

- Grant_priv: Determines whether the user can grant privileges already granted to that user to other users. For example, if the user can insert, select, and delete information located in the foo database, and has been granted the Grant privilege, that user can grant any or all of these privileges to any other user located in the system.

- References_priv: Currently just a placeholder for some future function; it currently serves no purpose at this time.

- Index_priv: Determines whether the user can create and delete table indexes.

- Alter_priv: Determines whether the user can rename and alter table structures.

- Show_db_priv: Determines whether the user can view the names of all databases residing on the server, including those for which he possesses adequate access privileges. As a rule of thumb, I suggest disabling this for all users unless there is a particularly compelling reason otherwise.

- Super_priv: Determines whether the user can execute certain powerful administrative functions, such as the deletion of user processes via the KILL command, the changing of global MySQL variables using SET GLOBAL, and the execution of various commands pertinent to replication and logging.

- Create_tmp_table: Determines whether the user can create temporary tables.

- Lock_tables_priv: Determines whether the user can block table access/modification using the LOCK TABLES command.

- Execute_priv: Determines whether the user can execute stored procedures. Note that stored procedures are not yet implemented (they will be available in MySQL 5.0). Therefore this column is currently just a placeholder for that future function.

- Repl_slave: Determines whether the user can read the binary logging files used to maintain a replicated database environment. This user resides on the master system, and facilitates the communication between the master and the client machines.

- Repl_client: Determines whether the user can determine the location of any replication slaves and masters.

The Remaining Columns

The remaining columns are so interesting that I've devoted entire sections to them later in this chapter. You can learn more about the max_questions, max_updates, and max_connections columns in the section "Limiting User Resources." You can learn more about the ssl_type, ssl_cipher, x509_issuer, and x509_subject columns in the section "Secure MySQL Connections."

The db Table

The db table is used to assign privileges to a user on a per-database basis. It is examined if the requesting user does not possess global privileges for the task he's attempting to execute. If a matching user/host/database triplet is located in the db table, and the requested task has been granted for that row, then the request is executed. If the user/host/database/task match is not satisfied, one of two events will occur:

- If a user/db match is located, but the host is blank, then MySQL will look to the host table for help. The purpose and structure of the host table is introduced in the next section.

- If a user/host/database triplet is located, but the privilege is disabled, MySQL will next look to the tables_priv table for help. The purpose and structure of the tables_priv table is introduced in a later section.

Wildcards, represented by the % and _ characters, may be used in both the Host and Db columns, but not in the User column. Like the user table, the rows are sorted so that the most specific match takes precedence over less-specific matches. An overview of the db table's structure is presented in Table 25-2.

Table 25-2. Overview of the db *Table*

COLUMN	DATA TYPE	NULL	DEFAULT
Host	char(60)	No	No default
Db	char(64)	No	No default
User	char(16)	No	No default
Select_priv	enum('N','Y')	No	N
Insert_priv	enum('N','Y')	No	N
Update_priv	enum('N','Y')	No	N
Delete_priv	enum('N','Y')	No	N
Create_priv	enum('N','Y')	No	N
Drop_priv	enum('N','Y')	No	N
Grant_priv	enum('N','Y')	No	N
References_priv	enum('N','Y')	No	N
Index_priv	enum('N','Y')	No	N
Alter_priv	enum('N','Y')	No	N
Create_tmp_table_priv	enum('N','Y')	No	N
Lock_tables_priv	enum('N','Y')	No	N

The host Table

The host table only comes into play if the db table's host field is left blank. You might leave the db table's host field blank if a particular user needs access from various hosts. Rather than reproducing and maintaining several user/host/db instances for that user, only one is added (with a blank Host field), and the corresponding hosts addresses are stored in the host table's host field.

Wildcards, represented by the % and _ characters, may be used in both the Host and Db columns, but not in the User column. Like the user table, the rows are sorted so that the most specific match takes precedence over less-specific matches.

Table 25-3. Overview of the host Table

COLUMN	DATA TYPE	NULL	DEFAULT
Host	char(60) binary	No	No default
Db	char(64) binary	No	No default
Select_priv	enum('N','Y')	No	N
Insert_priv	enum('N','Y')	No	N
Update_priv	enum('N','Y')	No	N
Delete_priv	enum('N','Y')	No	N
Create_priv	enum('N','Y')	No	N
Drop_priv	enum('N','Y')	No	N
Grant_priv	enum('N','Y')	No	N
References_priv	enum('N','Y')	No	N
Index_priv	enum('N','Y')	No	N
Alter_priv	enum('N','Y')	No	N
Create_tmp_table_priv	enum('N','Y')	No	N
Lock_tables_priv	enum('N','Y')	No	N

The tables_priv Table

The tables_priv table is intended to store table-specific user privileges. It comes into play only if the user, db and host tables do not satisfy the user's task request. To best illustrate its use, consider an example. Suppose that user jason from host www.wjgilmore.com wants to execute an update query on the table staff located in the database company. Once the request is initiated, MySQL will begin by reviewing the user table to see if jason@www.wjgilmore.com possesses global insertion privileges. If this is not the case, the db and host tables will next be reviewed for database-specific insertion privileges. If these tables to not satisfy the request, MySQL will then look to the tables_priv table to verify whether user jason@www.wjgilmore.com possesses the insertion privilege for the table staff found in the company database.

An overview of the tables_priv table can be found in Table 25-4.

Table 25-4. Overview of the tables_priv *Table*

COLUMN	DATA TYPE	NULL	DEFAULT
Host	char(60) binary	No	No default
Db	char(64) binary	No	No default
User	char(16) binary	No	No default
Table_name	char(60) binary	No	No default
Grantor	char(77)	No	No default
Timestamp	timestamp	Yes	Null
Table_priv	tableset	No	No default
Column_priv	columnset	No	No default

Because of space limitations, I've used the term *tableset* as a placeholder for set(Select, Insert, Update, Delete, Create, Drop, Grant, References, Index, Alter). The term *columnset* is a placeholder for set(Select, Insert, Update , References).

All of the columns found in the tables_priv table should be familiar, except for the following:

Table_name

The Table_name column determines the table to which the table-specific permissions set within the tables_priv table will be applied.

Grantor

The Grantor column specifies the username of the user granting the privileges to the user.

Timestamp

The Timestamp column specifies the exact date and time when the privilege was granted to the user.

Table_priv

The Table_priv column determines which table-wide permissions are available to the user. The following privileges can be applied in this capacity: Select, Insert, Update, Delete, Create, Drop, Grant, References, Index, and Alter.

Column_priv

The Column_priv column stores the names of any column-level privileges assigned to that user for the table referenced by the Table_name column. The purpose for doing so is undocumented, although I suspect that it is done in an effort to improve general performance.

The columns_priv Table

The columns_priv table is responsible for setting column-specific privileges. It comes into play only if the user, db/host, and tables_priv tables are unable to determine whether the requesting user has adequate permissions to execute the requested task.

An overview of the columns_priv table can be found in Table 25-5.

Table 25-5. Overview of the columns_priv *Table*

COLUMN	DATA TYPE	NULL	DEFAULT
Host	char(60) binary	No	No default
Db	char(64) binary	No	No default
User	char(16) binary	No	No default
Table_name	char(60) binary	No	No default
Column_name	char(64) binary	No	No default
Timestamp	timestamp	Yes	Null
Column_priv	columnset	No	No default

All columns found in this table should be familiar, except for Column_name. The Column_name column specifies the name of the table column affected by the GRANT command.

User and Privilege Management

The tables located in the mysql database are no different from any other relational tables in the sense that their structure and data can be modified using typical SQL commands. In fact, up until version 3.22.11, this was exactly how the user information found in this database was managed. However, with this release came a new, arguably much more intuitive methodology for managing this crucial data. With it, users can be both created and disabled, and their access privileges can be both granted and revoked on the fly. Their exacting syntax eliminates potentially horrendous mistakes that could otherwise be introduced due to a malformed SQL query (for example, forgetting to include the WHERE clause in an UPDATE query).

The GRANT and REVOKE Commands

This improved administration feature centers around two commands, namely GRANT and REVOKE, responsible for adding and deleting of users and access privileges. These commands offer a great deal of granular control over who controls practically every conceivable aspect of the server and its contents, from who can shut down the server, to who can modify information residing within a particular table column. Table 25-6 offers a list of all possible privileges that can be granted or revoked using these commands.

> **TIP** *Although modifying the mysql tables using standard SQL syntax is deprecated, you are not prevented from doing so. Just keep in mind that any changes made to these tables must be followed up with the* flush privileges *command. Because this is an outmoded method for managing user privileges, I won't go into further details regarding this matter. See the MySQL documentation for further information.*

Table 25-6. Privileges Managed by GRANT *and* REVOKE

NAME	DESCRIPTION
All Privileges	Affects all privileges except for WITH GRANT OPTION
Alter	Affects the use of the ALTER TABLE command
Create	Affects the use of the CREATE TABLE command
Create Temporary Tables	Affects the use of the CREATE TEMPORARY TABLE command
Delete	Affects the use of the DELETE command
Drop	Affects the use of the DROP TABLE command
Execute	Affects the user's ability to run stored procedures (MySQL version 5.0)
File	Affects the use of SELECT INTO OUTFILE and LOAD DATA INFILE
Grant Option	Affects the user's ability to delegate privileges
Index	Affects the use of the CREATE INDEX and DROP INDEX commands
Insert	Affects the use of the INSERT command
Lock Tables	Affects the use of the LOCK TABLES command
Process	Affects the use of the SHOW PROCESSLIST command
References	Placeholder for a future MySQL feature
Reload	Affects the use of the FLUSH command-set.
Replication Client	Affects the user's ability to query for the location of slaves and masters
Replication Slave	Required privilege for replication slaves
Select	Affects the use of the SELECT command
Show Databases	Affects the use of the SHOW DATABASES command
Shutdown	Affects the use of the SHUTDOWN command
Super	Affects the use of administrator-level commands such as CHANGE MASTER, KILL thread, mysqladmin debug, PURGE MASTER LOGS, and SET GLOBAL
Update	Affects the use of the UPDATE command

In this section, the GRANT and REVOKE commands are introduced in some detail, followed by numerous examples demonstrating their usage.

GRANT

You use the GRANT command when you need to assign new privileges to a user or group of users. This privilege assignment could be as trivial as granting a user only the ability to connect to the database server, or as drastic as providing a few colleagues root MySQL access (not recommended of course, but possible). The command syntax follows:

```
GRANT privilege_type [(column_list)] [, privilege_type [(column_list)] ...]
    ON {table_name | * | *.* | database_name.*}
    TO user_name [IDENTIFIED BY 'password']
        [, user_name [IDENTIFIED BY 'password'] ...]
    [REQUIRE {SSL|X509} [ISSUER issuer] [SUBJECT subject]]
    [WITH GRANT OPTION]
```

At first glance, the GRANT syntax can look intimidating, however it really is quite simple to use. I'll present some examples in the following sections so you can become better acquainted with this command.

> **NOTE** *As soon as a* GRANT *command is executed, any privileges granted in that command take effect immediately.*

Creating a New User

In the first example, I'll create a new user and assign that user a few database-specific privileges. User michele would like to connect to the database server from IP address 192.168.1.103 with the password secret. The following provides her access, select, and insert privileges for all tables found in the books database:

```
mysql>GRANT select, insert ON books.* TO michele@192.168.1.103
        ->IDENTIFIED BY 'secret';
```

Upon execution, two privilege tables will be modified, namely the user and db. Because the user table is responsible for both access verification and global privileges, a new row must be inserted, identifying this user. However, all privileges found in this row will be disabled. Why? Because the GRANT command is specific to just the books database. The db table will contain the user information relevant to map user michele to the books table, in addition to enabling the Select_priv and Insert_priv columns.

Adding Privileges to an Existing User

Now suppose that user michele needs the update privilege for all tables residing in the books database. This is again accomplished with GRANT:

```
mysql>GRANT update ON books.* TO michele@192.168.1.103;
```

Once executed, the row identifying the user michele@192.168.1.103 in the db table is modified so that the Update_priv column is enabled. Note that there is no need to restate the password when adding privileges to an existing user.

Granting Table-Level Privileges

Now suppose that in addition to the previously defined privileges, user michele@192.168.1.103 requires delete privileges for two tables located within the books database, namely the authors and editors tables. Rather than provide this user with carte blanche to delete data from any table in this database, you can limit privileges so that she only has the power to delete from those two specific tables. Because two tables are involved, two GRANT commands are required:

```
mysql>GRANT delete ON books.authors TO michele@192.168.1.103;
Query OK, 0 rows affected (0.07 sec)
mysql>GRANT delete ON books.editors TO michele@192.168.1.103;
Query OK, 0 rows affected (0.01 sec)
```

Because this is a table-specific privilege setting, only the tables_priv table will be touched. Once executed, two new rows will be added to the tables_priv table. This assumes that there are not already pre-existing rows mapping the authors and editors tables to michele@192.168.1.103. If this is the case, those pre-existing rows will be modified accordingly to reflect the new table-specific privileges.

Granting Multiple Table-Level Privileges

A variation on the previous example is to provide a user with multiple permissions that are restricted to a given table. Suppose that a new user, rita, connecting from multiple addresses located within the wjgilmore.com domain, was tasked with updating author information, and thus was only in need of select, insert, and update privileges for the authors table:

```
mysql>GRANT select,insert,delete ON books.authors TO rita@'%.wjgilmore.com'
    ->identified by 'secret';
```

Executing of this GRANT statement results in two new entries to the mysql database: a new row entry within the user table (again, just to provide rita@%.wjgilmore.com with access permissions), and a new entry within the tables_priv table, specifying the new access privileges to be applied to the authors table. Keep in mind that because the privileges only apply to a single table, there will be just one row added the tables_priv table, with the Table_priv columns set to Select, Insert, Delete.

Granting Column-Level Privileges

Finally, consider an example that affects just the column-level privileges of a table. Suppose you want to grant update privileges on books.authors.name for user nino@192.168.1.105:

```
mysql>GRANT update (name) ON books.authors TO nino@192.168.1.105;
```

REVOKE

The REVOKE command is responsible for deleting previously granted privileges from a user or group of users. The syntax follows:

```
REVOKE privilege_type [(column_list)] [, privilege_type [(column_list)] ...]
    ON {table_name | * | *.* | database_name.*}
    FROM user_name [, user_name ...]
```

As with GRANT, the best way to understand use of this command is through some examples. The following examples demonstrate how to revoke permissions from and even delete existing users.

> **NOTE** *If the* GRANT *and* REVOKE *syntax is not to your liking, and you'd like a some-what more wizard-like means for managing permissions, check out the Perl script* mysql_setpermission. *Keep in mind that although it offers a very easy-to-use inter-face, it does not offer all of the features that* GRANT *and* REVOKE *have to offer. This script is located in the* MYSQL-INSTALL-DIR/bin *directory, and assumes that Perl and the DBI and DBD::MySQL modules have been installed.*

Revoking Previously Assigned Permissions

Sometimes you need to remove one or more previously assigned privileges from a particular user. For example, suppose you want to remove the UPDATE privilege from user rita@192.168.1.102 for the database books:

```
mysql>REVOKE insert ON books.* FROM rita@192.168.1.102;
```

Revoking Table-Level Permissions

Now suppose you want to remove both the previously assigned UPDATE and INSERT privileges from user rita@192.168.1.102 for the table authors located in the database books:

```
mysql>REVOKE insert, update ON books.authors FROM rita@192.168.1.102;
```

Note that this example assumes that you've granted table-level permissions to user rita@192.168.1.102. The REVOKE command will not downgrade a database-level GRANT (one located in the db table), removing the entry and inserting an entry in the tables_priv table. Instead, in this case it will simply remove reference to those privileges from the tables_priv table. If only those two privileges are referenced in the tables_priv table, then the entire row is removed.

Revoking Columnar-Level Permissions

Finally, suppose that you had previously granted a column-level delete permission to user rita@192.168.1.102 for the column name located in books.authors, and now you would like to remove that privilege:

```
mysql>REVOKE insert (name) ON books.authors FROM rita@192.168.1.102;
```

In all of these examples, it's possible that user rita could still be able to exercise some privileges within a given database if the privileges were not explicitly referenced in the REVOKE command. If you want to be sure that the user forfeits all permissions, you can revoke all privileges like so:

```
mysql>REVOKE all privileges on books.* from rita@192.168.1.102;
```

However, if your intent is to definitively remove the user from the mysql database, be sure to read the next section.

Deleting a User

A common question regarding REVOKE is pertinent to how it goes about deleting a user. The simple answer to this is that it doesn't at all. For example, suppose that you revoke all privileges from a particular user, say with the command:

```
mysql>REVOKE all privileges on books.* from rita@192.168.1.102;
```

Although this command does indeed remove the row residing in the db table pertinent to rita@192.168.1.102's relationship with the books database, it does *not* remove that user's entry from the user table. This is done presumably so that you could later reinstate this user without having to reset the password. If you're sure that this user will not be required in the future, you'll need to manually remove the row using the DELETE command.

GRANT and REVOKE Tips

The following list offers various tips to keep in mind when you're working with GRANT and REVOKE.

- You can grant privileges for a database that doesn't yet exist.

- If the user identified by the GRANT command does not exist, it will be created.

- If you create a user without including the IDENTIFIED BY clause, no password will be required for login.

- If an existing user is granted new privileges, and the GRANT is accompanied by an IDEN-TIFIED BY clause, the user's old password will be replaced with the new one.

- Table-level GRANTs only support the following privilege types: alter, create, delete, drop, grant option, index, insert, select, and update.

- Column-level GRANTs only support the following privilege types: insert, select, and update.

- The _ and % wildcards are supported when referencing both database and host names in GRANT commands. Because the _ character is also valid in a MySQL database name, you'll need to escape it with a backslash if it's required in the GRANT.

- You can't reference *.* in an effort to remove a user's privileges for all databases. Rather, each must be explicitly referenced by a separate REVOKE command.

Reviewing Privileges

Although you can review a user's privileges simply by selecting the appropriate data from the privilege tables, this strategy can become increasingly unwieldy as the tables grow in size. Thankfully, MySQL offers a much more convenient means (two, actually) for reviewing user-specific privileges. I'll examine both in this section.

SHOW GRANTS FOR

The SHOW GRANTS FOR user command displays the privileges granted for a particular user. For example:

```
mysql>SHOW GRANTS FOR rita@192.168.1.102;
```

This yields the table shown in Figure 25-1.

```
+-----------------------------------------------------------------------------------------------+
| Grants for rita@192.168.1.102                                                                 |
+-----------------------------------------------------------------------------------------------+
| GRANT USAGE ON *.* TO 'rita'@'192.168.1.102' IDENTIFIED BY PASSWORD '428567f408994404'        |
| GRANT INSERT (name) ON `books`.`authors` TO 'rita'@'192.168.1.102'                             |
+-----------------------------------------------------------------------------------------------+
2 rows in set (0.00 sec)
```

Figure 25-1. Typical results of the SHOW GRANTS FOR *command*

As with the GRANT and REVOKE commands, you must make reference to both the username and the originating host in order to uniquely identify the target user.

mysqlaccess

The mysqlaccess command is a Perl script used to view access privilege summaries of MySQL users. It also reports possible security loopholes introduced through improper user-privilege configuration. Consider an example. Suppose you wanted to review user rita@192.168.1.103's access to the database books:

```
%>./mysqlaccess 192.168.1.103 rita book -u root -p
```

This produces the output show in Figure 25-2.

```
Access-rights
for USER 'rita', from HOST '192.168.1.102', to DB 'book'
       +-----------------+---+ +-------------------+---+
       | Select_priv     | N | | Show_db_priv      | N |
       | Insert_priv     | N | | Super_priv        | N |
       | Update_priv     | N | | Create_tmp_table_priv | N |
       | Delete_priv     | N | | Lock_tables_priv  | N |
       | Create_priv     | N | | Execute_priv      | N |
       | Drop_priv       | N | | Repl_slave_priv   | N |
       | Reload_priv     | N | | Repl_client_priv  | N |
       | Shutdown_priv   | N | | Ssl_type          | ? |
       | Process_priv    | N | | Ssl_cipher        | ? |
       | File_priv       | N | | X509_issuer       | ? |
       | Grant_priv      | N | | X509_subject      | ? |
       | References_priv | N | | Max_questions     | 0 |
       | Index_priv      | N | | Max_updates       | 0 |
       | Alter_priv      | N | | Max_connections   | 0 |
       +-----------------+---+ +-------------------+---+
BEWARE:  Everybody can access your DB as user `rita' from host `192.168.1.102'
      :  WITHOUT supplying a password.
      :  Be very careful about it!!

The following rules are used:
  db    : 'No matching rule'
  host  : 'Not processed: host-field is not empty in db-table.'
  user  : '192.168.1.102','rita','','N','N','N','N','N','N','N','N','N','N','N','N',
N','N','N','N','N','N','N','N','N','N','','','','','0','0','0'
```

Figure 25-2. Typical mysqlaccess *output*

To learn more about mysqlaccess, execute one or both of the following commands:

```
%>mysqlaccess --help
%>mysqlaccess --howto
```

Limiting User Resources

Monitoring resource usage is always a good idea, but it is particularly important when you're offering MySQL in a hosted environment, such as an ISP. If you're concerned with such a matter, you will be happy to learn that as of version 4.0.2 it's possible to limit the consumption of MySQL resources on a per-user basis. These limitations are managed like any other privilege, via the privilege tables. In total, three privileges concerning the use of resources exist, and all three are located in the user table. Each is introduced in this section, followed by a few examples.

- max_connections: Determines the maximum number of times the user can connect to the database per hour.

- max_questions: Determines the maximum number of queries (using the SELECT command) that the user can execute per hour.

- max_updates: Determines the maximum number of updates (using the INSERT and UPDATE commands) that the user can execute per hour.

Consider a couple examples. In the first, I'll limit user dario@%.wjgilmore.com's number of connections per hour to 3600, or an average of one per second:

```
mysql>GRANT insert, select, update ON books.* TO dario@'%.wjgilmore.com'
    >identified by 'secret' WITH max_connections_per_hour 3600;
```

In the next example, I'll limit the total number of updates user dario@'%'.wjgilmore.com can execute per hour to 10,000:

```
mysql>GRANT insert, select, update ON books.* TO dario@'%.wjgilmore.com'
    >identified by 'secret' WITH max_updates_per_hour 10000;
```

Secure MySQL Connections

Data flowing between a client and MySQL server is not unlike any other typical network traffic; it could potentially be intercepted and even modified by a malicious third-party. Sometimes this isn't really an issue, because the database server and clients often reside on the same internal network, and for many, on the same machine. However, if your project requirements result in the transfer of data over insecure channels, you now have the option to use MySQL's built-in security features to encrypt that connection. As of version 4.0.0, it became possible to encrypt all traffic between the mysqld server daemon and any client using SSL (Secure Sockets Layer) and the X509 encryption standard.

To implement this feature, you need to complete these prerequisite tasks first:

- The OpenSSL library must be installed. This is available for download at `http://www.openssl.org/`.

- MySQL must be configured with the `--with-vio` and `--with-openssl` flags.

You can verify whether MySQL is ready to handle secure connections by logging into the MySQL server and executing:

```
mysql>SHOW VARIABLES LIKE 'have_openssl'
```

Once these prerequisites are complete, you'll either need to create or purchase both a server certificate and a client certificate. The processes for accomplishing either task are out of the scope of this book. You can get information about this process on the Internet, so take a few moments to perform a search and you'll turn up numerous resources.

Grant Options

There are a number of grant options that determine the user's SSL requirements. I'll introduce those options here.

require ssl

This grant option forces the user to connect over SSL. Any attempts to connect in an insecure fashion will result in an "Access denied" error. An example follows:

```
mysql>grant insert, select, update on company.* to jason@client.wjgilmore.com
    >identified by 'secret' require ssl;
```

require x509

This grant option forces the user to provide a valid Certificate Authority (CA) certificate. This would be required if you want to verify the certificate signature with the CA certificate. Note that this option does not cause MySQL to be concerned about the origin, subject, or issuer. An example follows:

```
mysql>grant insert, select, update on company.* to jason@client.wjgilmore.com
    >identified by 'secret' require SSL require X509;
```

Note that this option doesn't specify which CAs are valid and which are not. Any CA that verified the certificate would be considered valid. If you'd like to place a restriction on which CAs are considered valid, see the next grant option.

require issuer

This grant option forces the user to provide a valid certificate, issued by a valid CA issuer. Several additional pieces of information must be included with this, including the country of origin, state of origin, city of origin, name of certificate owner, and certificate contact. An example follows:

```
mysql>grant insert, select, update on company.* to jason@client.wjgilmore.com
    >identified by 'secret' require SSL require issuer 'C=US, ST=Ohio, L=Columbus,
    >O=WJGILMORE, OU=ADMIN, CN=db.wjgilmore.com/Email=admin@wjgilmore.com'
```

require subject

This grant option forces the user to provide a valid certificate including a valid certificate "subject". An example follows:

```
mysql>grant insert, select, update on company.* to jason@client.wjgilmore.com
    >identified by 'secret' require SSL require subject 'C=US, ST=Ohio, L=Columbus,
    >O=WJGILMORE, OU=ADMIN, CN=db.wjgilmore.com/Email=admin@wjgilmore.com'
```

require cipher

This grant option enforces the use of recent encryption algorithms by forcing the user to connect using a particular cipher. The options currently available include: EDH, RSA, DES, CBC3, and SHA. An example follows:

```
mysql>grant insert, select, update on company.* to jason@client.wjgilmore.com
        >identified by 'secret' require SSL require cipher 'DES-RSA';
```

SSL Options

The options introduced in this section are used by both the server and the connecting client to determine whether SSL should be used, and if so, the location of the certificate and key files.

--ssl

This option simply acts as a signal that SSL should be used. More specifically, when used in conjunction with the mysqld daemon, it tells the server that SSL connections should be allowed. Used in conjunction with the client, it signals that a SSL connection will be used. Note that including this option does not ensure, nor require, that an SSL connection is used. In fact, my own tests have shown that the option itself is not even required to initiate an SSL connection. Rather, the accompanying flags, introduced here, determine whether a SSL connection is successfully initiated.

--ssl-ca

This option specifies the location and name of a file containing a list of trusted SSL certificate authorities. For example:

```
--ssl-ca=/home/jason/openssl/cacert.pem
```

--ssl-capath

This option specifies the directory path where trusted SSL certificates in privacy-enhanced mail (PEM) format are stored.

--ssl-cert

This option specifies the location and name of the SSL certificate used to establish the secure connection. For example:

```
--ssl-cert=/home/jason/openssl/mysql-cert.pem
```

--ssl-cipher

This option specifies which encryption algorithms are allowable. The cipher-list syntax is the same as that used by the command:

```
%>openssl ciphers
```

For example, to allow just the Triple-DES and Blowfish encryption algorithms, this option would be set as so:

```
--ssl-cipher=des3:bf
```

`--ssl-key`

This option specifies the location and name of the SSL key used to establish the secure connection. For example:

```
--ssl-key=/home/jason/openssl/mysql-key.pem
```

In the next sections you'll learn how to use these options on both the command line and within the my.cnf file.

Starting the SSL-enabled MySQL Server

Once you have both the server and client certificates in hand, you can start the SSL-enabled MySQL server like so:

```
%>./bin/mysqld_safe --user=mysql --ssl-ca=$OPENSSL/cacert.pem \
 >--ssl-cert=$OPENSSL/server-cert.pem --ssl-key=$OPENSSL/server-key.pem &
```

Where $OPENSSL refers to the path pointing to the SSL certificate storage location.

Connecting Using an SSL-enabled Client

You can then connect to the SSL-enabled MySQL server using the following command:

```
%>mysql --ssl-ca=$OPENSSL/cacert.pem --ssl-cert=$OPENSSL/client-cert.pem \
 >--ssl-key=$OPENSSL/client-key.pem -u jason -h www.wjgilmore.com -p
```

Again, $OPENSSL refers to the path pointing to the SSL certificate storage location.

Storing SSL Options in the my.cnf File

Of course, you don't have to pass the SSL options via the command-line. Instead, you can place them within a my.cnf file. An example my.cnf file follows:

```
[client]
ssl-ca    = /home/jason/openssl/cacert.pem
ssl-cert  = /home/jason/openssl/client-cert.pem
ssl-key   = /home/jason/openssl/client-key.pem

[mysqld]
ssl-ca    = /usr/local/mysql/openssl/ca.pem
ssl-cert  = /usr/local/mysql/openssl/cert.pem
ssl-key   = /usr/local/mysql/openssl/key.pem
```

Frequently Asked Questions

Because the SSL feature is so new, there is still some confusion surrounding its usage. In this section, I'll attempt to offer some relief by answering some of the most commonly asked questions regarding this topic.

I'm using MySQL solely as a backend to my Web application, and I am using HTTPS to encrypt traffic to and from the site. Do I also need to encrypt the connection to the MySQL server?

This depends on whether the database server is located on the same machine as the Web server. If this is the case, then encryption will likely only be beneficial if you consider your machine itself to be insecure. If the database server resides on a separate server, then the data could potentially be traveling unsecured from the Web server to the database server, and therefore it would warrant encryption. There is no steadfast rule regarding the use of encryption. You can only reach a conclusion after a careful weighing of security and performance factors.

I understand that encrypting Web pages using SSL will degrade performance. Does the same hold true for the encryption of MySQL traffic?

Yes, your application will take a performance hit, because every data packet must be encrypted while traveling to and from the MySQL server.

How do I know that the traffic is indeed encrypted?

The easiest way to ensure that the MySQL traffic is encrypted is to create a user account that requires SSL, and then try to connect to the SSL-enabled MySQL server by supplying that user's credentials and a valid SSL certificate. If something is awry, you'll receive an "Access denied" error.

On what port does encrypted MySQL traffic flow?

The port number remains the same (3306) regardless of whether you're communicating in encrypted or unencrypted fashion.

Summary

An uninvited database intrusion can wipe away months of work and erase inestimable value. Therefore, although the topics covered in this chapter generally lack the glamour of other feats such as creating a database connection and altering a table structure, the importance of taking the time to thoroughly understand them cannot be understated. I strongly recommend that you take adequate time to understand MySQL's security features, because they should be making a regular appearance in all of your MySQL-driven applications.

In the next chapter, I'll introduce PHP's MySQL library, showing you how to manipulate MySQL database data through your PHP scripts.

CHAPTER 26

PHP's MySQL Functionality

THE PHP SCRIPTING LANGUAGE and MySQL database server are two distinct technologies, each with its own purpose, history, development team, and technological impact. Yet, both seem to be inextricably linked in that each owes the other an enormous amount of gratitude for the role played in the popularity each has enjoyed over the past few years. As you might imagine, the integration possibilities surrounding the two technologies are quite powerful. This chapter introduces MySQL's PHP API, presenting many of its functions and offering numerous usage examples. By the conclusion, you will be quite familiar with how to retrieve, insert, update, and delete MySQL data, as well as perform a wide variety of administrative actions important to any database-driven application.

NOTE *At the time of writing, an experimental extension called* mysqli, *or* Improved MySQL *had just been released. This extension is intended for use with MySQL 4.1 and greater, as it provides additional features not available to the original MySQL extension. Consult the PHP manual for more information about this new extension.*

Prerequisites

Before getting into the meat of this chapter, there are a few preliminary items worth mentioning. The first, "User Privileges," touches upon an essential topic involving how PHP (and any other MySQL API, for that matter) handles user privileges when connecting to a MySQL database server. The second, "Sample Data," introduces the dummy table I'll use in examples throughout this chapter.

User Privileges

Keep in mind that as far as MySQL is concerned, PHP is just another API; the rules of interaction are no different than those followed when interacting with MySQL in any other way. A PHP script intent on communicating with MySQL must still make a connection to the MySQL server, and in typical usage, must select a database to interact with. All such actions, in addition to the queries that would follow such a sequence, require that they are carried out by a user who has adequate privileges to do so.

These privileges are communicated and verified whenever a user connects to the MySQL server, as well as every time a command requiring privilege verification is submitted. However, you'll only need to identify the executing user at the time of connection; unless another connection is made later within the script, that user's identity is assumed for the remainder of the script's execution. In the coming sections, you'll learn how to use two functions, namely mysql_connect() and mysql_pconnect(), to connect to the MySQL server and pass in these credentials.

Sample Data

By now you know that I'm fond of using a cohesive set of sample data throughout a given chapter. This chapter is no different. The following table, product, located within a database named company, is used for all relevant examples in the following pages.

```
CREATE TABLE product (
rowID INT NOT NULL AUTO_INCREMENT,
productid varchar(8) NOT NULL,
name varchar(25) NOT NULL,
price DECIMAL(5,2) NOT NULL,
description MEDIUMTEXT NOT NULL,
PRIMARY KEY(rowID)
)
```

PHP's MySQL Commands

PHP's MySQL API offers more than 45 functions capable of performing a wide array of tasks. The remainder of this chapter is devoted to an introduction to these functions. Rather than introduce these functions in alphabetical order, I'll opt to introduce them in a "need to know" fashion; that is, in an order that will most quickly help you to begin building useful database-driven applications. Those functions that are absolutely necessary to begin working with a MySQL database via PHP are introduced first, followed by those that, although not absolute necessities, are nonetheless quite useful.

Establishing and Closing a Connection

Several functions are responsible for establishing and closing a connection to the MySQL database server. To initiate a connection to a MySQL database, mysql_connect() and mysql_pconnect() are available. Although both accomplish the same goal, establishing a connection that will subsequently be used to execute database transactions, their respective means are quite different. To close a connection, the function mysql_close() is used. All of these functions are introduced in this section.

mysql_connect()

```
resource mysql_connect([string hostname [:port] [:/path/to/socket]
[, string username] [, string password]])
```

The function mysql_connect() is used to establish an initial connection with the MySQL server. Once a successful connection is established, you can go about selecting databases for subsequent interaction.

Note that all parameters are optional, because MySQL's privilege tables can be configured to accept a non-authenticated connection. You probably won't ever use mysql_connect() in this fashion, however. Typically, you'll invoke this function by passing in three parameters: *hostname*, *username*, and *password*. The *hostname* specifies the server name or IP address of the MySQL server, while the *username* and *password* input parameters should correspond to a username and password specified in the MySQL server privilege tables. MySQL autonomously retrieves the client host address so that the *hostname/username/password* identity can be determined. See Chapter 25 if this doesn't make sense. An optional port number can be included along with the host, in addition to an optional socket path when a local host is specified. If the *hostname* parameter is empty, mysql_connect() attempts to connect to the local host. For the sake of completeness, I'd like to note that there are other parameters available to this function, but they're used so infrequently that I didn't think them worth discussing. See the manual for additional information.

An example connection call follows:

```
@mysql_connect("localhost", "webuser", "secret")
or die("Could not connect to MySQL server!");
```

In this case, localhost is the server host, webuser is the username, and secret is the password. The @ preceding the mysql_connect() function will suppress any error message that results from a failed attempt (a feature available to all functions). Instead the user will see the custom message specified in the die() call.

Note I did not have to explicitly return a value from the mysql_connect() call, although a resource reference is created. This is fine when only a single MySQL server connection comes into play within your application. However, when you make connections to multiple MySQL servers on multiple hosts, a link ID must be explicitly generated so that subsequent commands can be directed to the intended MySQL server. For example:

```
<?php
    $link1 = @mysql_connect("www.somehost.com", "webuser", "abcde")
                or die("Could not connect to MySQL server!");
    $link2 = @mysql_connect("www.someotherhost.com", "webuser", "secret")
                or die("Could not connect to MySQL server!");
?>
```

Now $link1 and $link2 can be referenced as needed in subsequent queries. Later in this chapter, you'll learn how these link IDs are used in queries to specify the intended server.

mysql_pconnect()

```
resource mysql_pconnect([string hostname [:port] [:/path/to/socket]
[, string username] [, string password])
```

The function mysql_pconnect() is identical in purpose to mysql_connect(): establishing a connection to a MySQL server. However, it is functionally more efficient than its sibling because it first checks for an already open connection before establishing another.

If a link already exists, the existing link will be used instead of opening another. If a link does not already exist, mysql_pconnect() will establish a new one.

I'll forego an example, because mysql_pconnect()'s execution is identical to mysql_connect(). Just keep in mind that like mysql_connect(), it must be called within each script in which you intend on interacting with the MySQL database server. In addition, remember that you don't need to explicitly close the connection (using the function mysql_close(), introduced later in this chapter) at the conclusion of a script that has invoked mysql_pconnect(), because connections are pooled.

mysql_close()

```
boolean mysql_close ([resource link_id])
```

Once you have finished querying the MySQL server, you should close the connection. Closing a connection isn't required, however, because PHP's garbage collection feature will take care of the matter for you. The function mysql_close() closes the connection corresponding to the optional input parameter link_id. If the link_id input parameter is not specified, the most recently opened link is assumed.

A usage example follows:

```php
<?php
    @mysql_connect("localhost", "webuser", "secret")
    or die("Could not connect to MySQL server!");
    @mysql_select_db("company")
    or die("Could not select database!");
    echo "You're connected to a MySQL database!";
    mysql_close();
?>
```

In this example, there is no need to specify a link identifier, because only one open server connection exists when mysql_close() is called.

Storing Connection Information in a Separate File

In the spirit of secure programming practice, it's often a good idea to change passwords on a regular basis. Yet because a connection to a MySQL server must be made within every script requiring access to a given database, it's possible that functions such as mysql_connect() and mysql_pconnect() are strewn throughout a large number of files, making such changes difficult. The easy solution to such a dilemma should not come as a surprise; store this information in a separate file and then include that file into your script as necessary. For example, I might store my mysql_connect() function in a header file named mysql.connect.php, like so:

```php
<?php
@mysql_connect("localhost","intranetmanager","secret")
or die("Could not connect to MySQL server!");
?>
```

I can then include this file as necessary, like so:

```php
<?php
    include "mysql.connect.php";
    // begin database selection and queries.
?>
```

Securing Your Connection Information

If you're new to web scripting, it might be rather disconcerting to learn that information as important as MySQL connection parameters, including the password, is stored in plain text within a file. Indeed this is the case, although there are a few steps you can take to ensure that unwanted guests are not able to obtain this important data:

- Use system-based user permissions to ensure that only the user owning the Web server daemon process is capable of reading the file. On Unix-based systems, this means changing the file ownership privileges to that of the user running the Web process and setting the connection file permissions to -r--------.

- If you're connecting to a remote MySQL server, keep in mind that this information will be passed in plain text unless appropriate steps are taken to encrypt that data during transit. Your best bet is to use Secure Socket Layer (SSL) encryption.

- Several script encoding products are available that will render your code unreadable to all but those possessing the necessary decoding privileges, while at the same time leaving the code's executability unaffected. The Zend encoder (http://www.zend.com/) is probably the best known of this product line, although several other solutions exist. Keep in mind that unless you have other specific reasons for encoding your source, you should consider other protection alternatives (such as the one mentioned in the first bullet point) to alleviate the additional maintenance overhead incurred by this procedure.

Choosing a Database

Once you've established a successful connection with the MySQL server, you can select a database residing on that server. This is accomplished with mysql_select_db().

mysql_select_db()

```
boolean mysql_select_db (string db_name [, resource link_id])
```

The mysql_select_db() function selects a database for subsequent use within a script, returning TRUE on success and FALSE otherwise. A link to the intended database is created by passing its name, indicated by the input parameter *db_name*, into the function. If multiple connections are open, *link_id* must be specified. An example of how a database is selected using mysql_select_db() follows:

```php
<?php
   @mysql_connect("localhost", "webuser", "secret")
   or die("Could not connect to MySQL server!");
   @mysql_select_db("company")
   or die("Could not select database!");
?>
```

Querying MySQL

Regardless of how you intend to interact with a MySQL database via a PHP script, the process remains the same. A SQL statement is created and passed to a function tasked with executing the query. In this section, the two functions capable of this task are introduced, namely mysql_query() and mysql_db_query().

mysql_query()

```
resource mysql_query(string query, [resource link_id])
```

The mysql_query() function is responsible for executing the *query*. If the optional input parameter *link_id* is included, the query will be sent to the connection associated by that value; otherwise the most recently opened link is used.

If select, show, describe, or explain queries are passed into the function, the return value will be either a resource identifier on success or FALSE on failure. All other queries return of TRUE on success and FALSE on failure. Like all other PHP functions, the query can be passed in directly, by enclosing it within quote marks, or by first assigning it to a variable and then passing in the variable. I prefer the latter, because it tends to result in somewhat tidier code, not to mention code that's easier to debug by way of echo statements. Consider an example:

```php
<?php
   /* Connect to MySQL server and select database. */
   $linkID = @mysql_connect("localhost","user","secret")
                  or die("Could not connect to MySQL server");
   @mysql_select_db("company") or die("Could not select database");

   /* Create and execute query. */
   $query = "INSERT INTO product set productid='abcd123', name='pants',
            price='45.20'";
   $result = mysql_query($query);

   /* Close connection to database server. */
   mysql_close();
?>
```

Because an insert statement was used, either TRUE or FALSE will be returned, allowing you to easily determine whether or not the query was successfully executed. Pretty simple, right? Indeed, for queries intended to insert, update, and delete data from the server, it is this easy. However, retrieving data is a tad more involved. As I stated earlier in this section, a successful query involving a describe, explain, select, or show statement will return a resource identifier. Alone, this identifier is pretty useless. However, it can be passed into a number of functions that can provide much more interesting information regarding the query. I'll examine these functions in the next section.

mysql_db_query()

resource mysql_db_query(string *database*, string *query* [, resource *link_id*])

The function mysql_db_query() is equivalent to mysql_query(), except for that it also selects a database before executing the query, saving the user the added step of calling mysql_select_db(). For example:

```php
<?php
    /* Connect to MySQL server and select database. */
    $linkID = @mysql_connect("localhost","user","secret")
                    or die("Could not connect to MySQL server");
    /* Create and execute query. */
    $query = "INSERT INTO product set productid='abcd123', name='pants',
            price='45.20'";
    $result = mysql_db_query("company", $query);

    /* Close connection to database server. */
    mysql_close();
?>
```

Note that in this example I eliminated the call to mysql_select_db(). Although it does consolidate code, for clarity's sake I prefer to include this call, and I'll base all subsequent examples on this premise.

Retrieving and Displaying Data

This section introduces many of the functions that you will (or at least, should) become most familiar with when using MySQL's PHP API, because these functions play an important role in retrieving the data returned from a select query.

mysql_result()

```
mixed mysql_result(resource result_set, int row [, mixed field])
```

This is the simplest, although the most inefficient, of the array of data retrieval functions. It retrieves data from one *field* of the specified *row* found in the *result_set*. While the *field* must be called by name, the *row* must be called by integer offset. For example:

```php
<?php
    ...
    $query = "SELECT productid, name FROM product ORDER BY name";
    $result = mysql_query($query);
    $productid = mysql_result($result, 0, "productid");
    $name = mysql_result($result, 0, "name");
    ...
?>
```

This returns the values of the product and name fields located in the very first row of the result set specified by $result. What if you want to output the values of these fields for all returned rows? You'll need to use a looping conditional, like so:

```php
<?php
    ...
    $query = "SELECT productid, name FROM product ORDER BY name";
    $result = mysql_query($query);
    for ($count=0; $count <= mysql_numrows($result); $count++)
    {
        $productid = mysql_result($result, $count, "productid");
        $name = mysql_result($result, $count, "name");
        echo "$name ($productid) <br />";
    }
    ...
?>
```

Although this is not terrible, mysql_result() requires quite a bit of verbosity on the part of the coder; after all, what if there are ten, fifteen, or fifty table fields? That's right, one mysql_result() call is required for each. Thankfully, four other functions offer a much easier way to retrieve this row information: mysql_fetch_row(), mysql_fetch_array(), mysql_fetch_assoc(), and mysql_fetch_object(). Each is introduced in the following sections.

> **TIP** *If a field name is aliased within the query, use the alias rather than the actual field name within* mysql_result().

mysql_fetch_row()

```
array mysql_fetch_row(resource result_set)
```

This function retrieves an entire row of data from result_set, placing the values in an indexed array. This might not seem like it offers a particularly significant advantage over mysql_result(); after all you still have to cycle through the array, pulling out each value and assigning it an appropriate variable name, right? Although you could do this, you might find using this function in conjunction with list() to be particularly interesting. (The list() function was introduced in Chapter 5.) Consider this example:

```php
<?php
   ...
   $query = "SELECT productid, name FROM product ORDER BY name";
   $result = mysql_query($query);
   while (list($productid, $name) = mysql_fetch_row($result))
   {
      echo "$name ($productid) <br />";
   }
   ...
?>
```

Using the list() function and a while loop, you can assign the field values to a variable as each row is encountered.

mysql_fetch_array()

```
array mysql_fetch_array(resource result_set [,int result_type])
```

The mysql_fetch_array() function is really just an enhanced version of mysql_fetch_row(), offering you the opportunity to retrieve each row of the result_set as an associative array, a numerically indexed array, or both. By default, it retrieves both arrays; you can modify this default behavior by passing one of the following values in as the result_type:

- MYSQL_ASSOC: Returns the row as an associative array, with the key represented by the field name and the value by the field contents.

- MYSQL_NUM: Returns the row as a numerically indexed array, with the ordering determined by the ordering of the field names as specified within the array. If an asterisk is used (signaling the query to retrieve all fields), the ordering will correspond to the field ordering in the table definition. Designating this option results in mysql_fetch_array() operating in the same fashion as mysql_fetch_row().

- MYSQL_BOTH: Returns the row as both an associative and a numerically indexed array. Therefore, each field could be referred to in terms of its index offset, as well as its field name. This is the default.

For example, suppose you only want to retrieve a result set using associative indices:

```
$query = "SELECT productid, name FROM product ORDER BY name";
$result = mysql_query($query);
while ($row = mysql_fetch_array($result,MYSQL_ASSOC))
{
    $name = $row['name'];
    $productid = $row['productid'];
    echo "Product:  $name ($productid) <br />";
}
```

If you wanted to retrieve a result set solely by numerical indices, you would make the following modifications to the example:

```
$query = "SELECT productid, name FROM product ORDER BY name";
$result = mysql_query($query);
while ($row = mysql_fetch_array($result,MYSQL_NUM))
{
    $name = $row[1];
    $productid = $row[0];
    echo "Product:  $name ($productid) <br />";
}
```

mysql_fetch_assoc()

array mysql_fetch_assoc(resource *result_set*)

This function operates identically to mysql_fetch_array() when MYSQL_ASSOC is passed in as the *result_type* parameter.

mysql_fetch_object()

object mysql_fetch_object(resource *result*)

This function operates identically to mysql_fetch_array(), except that an object is returned rather than an array. Rehashing the first example used in the introduction to mysql_fetch_array():

```
$query = "SELECT productid, name FROM product ORDER BY name";
$result = mysql_query($query);
while ($row = mysql_fetch_object($result))
{
    $name = $row->name;
    $productid = $row->productid;
    echo "Product:  $name ($productid) <br />";
}
```

Inserting Data

Inserting data into the database is carried out very much in the same fashion as retrieving information, except that the query will often contain variable data. Following an example is the best way to learn this process. Suppose that your company's inventory specialist requires a means for inserting new product information from anywhere. Not surprisingly, the most efficient way to do so is to provide him with a Web interface. Figure 26-1 depicts this Web form and is followed up with Listing 26-1, which shows the form source code, called insert.php.

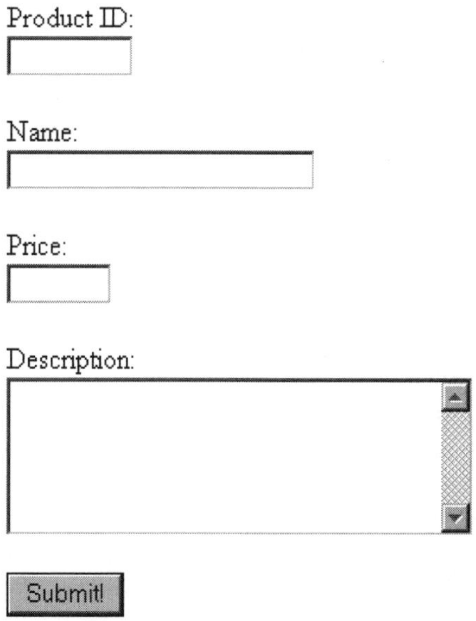

Product ID:

Name:

Price:

Description:

Submit!

Figure 26-1. Product insertion form

Listing 26-1. Product Insertion Form Code (insert.php)

```
<form action="<?php echo $_SERVER['PHP_SELF'];?>" method="post">
    <p>
        Product ID:<br />
        <input type="text" name="productid" size="8" maxlength="8" value="" />
    </p>
    <p>
        Name:<br />
        <input type="text" name="name" size="25" maxlength="25" value="" />
    </p>
    <p>
        Price:<br />
        <input type="text" name="price" size="6" maxlength="6" value="" />
```

```
        </p>
        <p>
            Description:<br />
            <textarea name="description" rows="5" cols="30"></textarea>
        </p>
        <p>
            <input type="submit" name="submit" value="Submit!" />
        </p>
    </form>
```

Listing 26-2 contains the source code for the database insertion logic.

Listing 26-2. Inserting Form Data into a MySQL Table

```php
<?php
    // If the submit button has been pressed
    if (isset($_POST['submit']))
    {
        // Connect to the server and select the database
        $linkID = @mysql_connect("localhost","webuser","secret")
                or die("Could not connect to MySQL server");
        @mysql_select_db("company") or die("Could not select database");
        // Retrieve the posted product information.
        $productid = $_POST['productid'];
        $name = $_POST['name'];
        $price = $_POST['price'];
        $description = $_POST['description'];

        // Insert the product information into the product table
        $query = "INSERT INTO product SET productid='$productid', name='$name',
                price='$price', description='$description'";

        $result = mysql_query($query);

        // Display an appropriate message
        if ($result) echo "<p>Product successfully inserted!</p>";
        else echo "<p>There was a problem inserting the product!</p>";

        mysql_close();
    }
    // Include the insertion form
    include "insert.php";
?>
```

Modifying Data

Data modification is ultimately the product of three queries: one that provides the user with the means for selecting target data for modification, a second that provides the user with an interface for modifying the data, and a third that carries out the modification request. Target selection can take place via a variety of interfaces: radio buttons, checkboxes, selectable lists, you name it. Listing 26-3 offers a selectable list created from a list of products found in the product table. Although I'll just show the form, you could easily create the form contents using the create_dropdown() function first introduced in Chapter 11.

Listing 26-3. A Populated Selectable List

```
<form action="modify.php" method="post">
<select name="rowID">
<option name="">Choose a product:</option>
<option name="2">Apples</option>
<option name="1">Bananas</option>
<option name="3">Oranges</option>
</select>
<input type="submit" name="submit" value="Submit" />
</form>
```

Listing 26-4 contains the conditional invoked once the product has been selected for modification.

Listing 26-4. Modifying Form Data (modify.php)

```
if (isset($_POST['submit']))
{
    $rowID = $_POST['rowID'];

    $query = "SELECT name, productid, price, description FROM product
                    WHERE rowID='$rowID'";

    $result = mysql_query($query);
    list($name,$productid,$price,$description) = mysql_fetch_row($result);
    include "modifyform.php";
}
```

The modifyform.php file, shown here, populates a form very similar to that used in the insertion process.

```
<form action="<?php echo $_SERVER['PHP_SELF'];?>" method="post">
<input type="hidden" name="rowID" value="<?php echo $rowID;?>">
    <p>
        Product ID:<br />
        <input type="text" name="productid" size="8" maxlength="8"
```

```
                        value="<?php echo $productid;?>" />
    </p>
    <p>
       Name:<br />
       <input type="text" name="name" size="25" maxlength="25"
                        value="<?php echo $name;?>" />
    </p>
    <p>
       Price:<br />
       <input type="text" name="price" size="6" maxlength="6"
                        value="<?php echo $price;?>" />
    </p>
    <p>
       Description:<br />
       <textarea name="description" rows="5" cols="30">
        <?php echo $description;?></textarea>
    </p>
    <p>
         <input type="submit" name="submit" value="Submit!" />
    </p>
</form>
```

The final step of the modification process involves actually executing the update query.

```
<?php
if (isset($_POST['submit']))
{
    $rowID = $_POST['rowID'];
    $productid = $_POST['productid'];
    $name = $_POST['name'];
    $price = $_POST['price'];
    $description = $_POST['description'];

    $query = "UPDATE product SET productid='$productid', name='$name',
                    price='$price', description='$description'
                    WHERE rowID='$rowID'";

    $result = mysql_query($query);

    if ($result) echo "<p>The product has been successfully updated.</p>";
    else echo "<p>There was a problem updating the product.</p>";

}
?>
```

Keep in mind that this is just one of a vast number of ways you can go about modifying data within a PHP script. Also, for sake of illustrating the crux of the topic, I omitted all code required for sanity checking information entered by the user. Such controls are central to ensuring proper functionality of this, as well as any other mechanism used for updating database information.

Deleting Data

Like data modification, data deletion is a three-step process, involving target data selection, the deletion request, then request execution. As with data modification, explaining data deletion is probably best served with an example. The following example demonstrates selecting multiple data rows for deletion via checkboxes. I'll forego the code used to create the checkbox-oriented listing, as the procedure is quite similar to that described in Chapter 11 in the section "Working with Multi-Valued Form Components." The important point to bear in mind is that each checkbox possesses the rowID value for the respective row. Figure 26-2 shows what such a generated listing might look like.

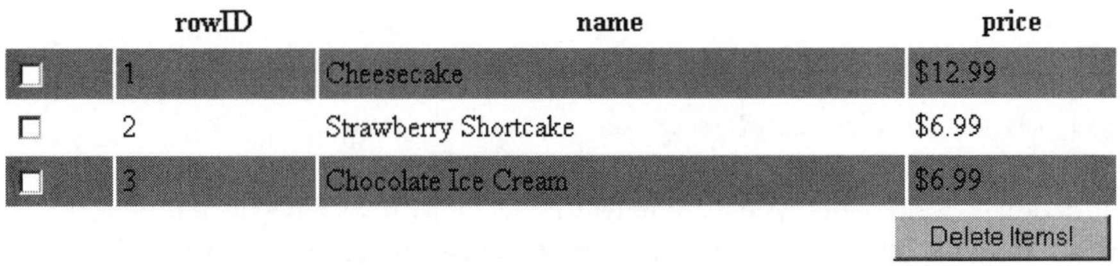

	rowID	name	price
☐	1	Cheesecake	$12.99
☐	2	Strawberry Shortcake	$6.99
☐	3	Chocolate Ice Cream	$6.99

Delete Items!

Figure 26-2. Deleting multiple items using checkboxes

Deleting the chosen rows is trivial. Pointing the form action to the following code snippet will take care of the matter quite nicely:

```php
<?php
    mysql_connect("localhost","webuser","secret");
    mysql_select_db("company");

    if (isset($_POST['submit']))
    {
        foreach($count=0; $count < count($_POST['rowID']); $count++)
        {
            $rowID = $_POST['rowID'][$count];
            $query = "DELETE FROM product WHERE rowID='$rowID'";

            $result = mysql_query($query);

            if ((mysql_affected_rows() == 0) || mysql_affected_rows() == -1) {
                echo "<p>There was a problem deleting some of the selected
                    items.</p>";
                exit;
            }
        }
        echo "<p>The selected items were successfully deleted.</p>";
    }
?>
```

As you can see, the deletion process is like all of the other processes described thus far. One important point worth noting, however, is the use of mysql_affected_rows() to ensure that the row in question was properly deleted. If this function returns 0, no rows were found; if it returns -1, a query error occurred. Otherwise, it returns the total number of rows affected by the deletion query, which in this situation should always be one. You'll learn more about this function in the next section.

Rows Selected and Rows Affected

You'll often want to be able to determine the number of rows returned by a select query, or the number of rows affected by an insert, update, or delete query. Two functions, introduced in this section, are available for doing just this.

mysql_num_rows()

```
int mysql_num_rows(resource result_set)
```

This function is useful when you want to learn how many rows have been returned from a select query statement. It takes as input one parameter: the query result, result_set. For example:

```php
<?php
    $query = "SELECT name FROM product WHERE price > 15.99";
    $result = mysql_query($query);
    echo "There are ".mysql_num_rows($result)." product(s) priced above \$15.99.";
?>
```

Sample output follows:

```
There are 5 product(s) priced above $15.99.
```

Keep in mind that mysql_num_rows() is only useful for determining the number of rows retrieved by a select query. If you'd like to retrieve the number of rows affected by an insert, update, or delete query, see mysql_affected_rows(), introduced next.

mysql_affected_rows()

```
int mysql_affected_rows([resource link_id])
```

This function retrieves the total number of rows affected by an insert, update, or delete query. No input parameters are required; it assumes the last result of the most recently established database link by default. An optional link id, link_id, can be input if the affected rows of another link identifier is desired. An example follows:

```php
<?php
    $query = "UPDATE product SET price = '39.99' WHERE price='34.99'";
    $result = mysql_query($query);
    echo "There were ".mysql_affected_rows()." product(s) affected. ";
?>
```

Sample output follows:

There were 2 products affected.

Retrieving Database and Table Information

Several functions are available for retrieving information about the databases and
tables that reside on a MySQL server. These functions are introduced in this section.

mysql_list_dbs()

resource mysql_list_dbs([resource *link_id*])

The mysql_list_dbs() function retrieves the names of all databases found on the
server. If the optional *link_id* parameter is included, then the names of the databases
located on the server specified by that *link_id* will be retrieved; otherwise the names
of those databases found on the most recently opened database server connection will
be used. An example follows:

```php
<?php
    mysql_connect("localhost","webuser","secret");
    $dbs = mysql_list_dbs();
    echo "Databases: <br />";
    while (list($db) = mysql_fetch_row($dbs))
    {
        echo "$db <br />";
    }
?>
```

Sample output follows:

Databases:
company
mysql
test

mysql_db_name()

```
string mysql_db_name(resource result_set, integer index)
```

The mysql_db_name() function retrieves the name of the database located at position *index* of the *result_set* returned by mysql_list_dbs().

mysql_list_tables()

```
resource mysql_list_tables(string database [, resource link_id])
```

The mysql_list_tables() function retrieves the names of all tables located within the *database*. If the optional *link_id* parameter is included, it assumes that the *database* resides on the server specified by that identifier. Otherwise, the most recently opened *link_id* is assumed.

```php
<?php
    mysql_connect("localhost","webuser","secret");
    $tables = mysql_list_tables("company");
    while (list($table) = mysql_fetch_row($tables))
    {
        echo "$table <br />";
    }
?>
```

This returns:

```
product
staff
news
```

mysql_tablename()

```
string mysql_tablename(resource result_set, integer index)
```

The mysql_tablename() function retrieves the name of the table located at position *index* of the *result_set* returned by mysql_list_tables(). Modifying the previous example:

```php
<?php
    mysql_connect("localhost","webuser","secret");
    $tables = mysql_list_tables("company");
    $count = 0;
    while ($count < mysql_numrows($tables))
    {
        echo mysql_tablename($tables,$count)."<br />";
        $count++;
    }
?>
```

This returns:

```
product
staff
news
```

Retrieving Field Information

Several functions are available for retrieving information about the fields in a given table. Each of these functions are introduced in this section, with a concluding comprehensive example offered at the section's conclusion.

mysql_fetch_field()

```
object mysql_fetch_field(resource result [, int field_offset])
```

The mysql_fetch_field() function retrieves an object containing information pertinent to the field specified by field_offset. In all, twelve object properties are available, including:

- name: The field name

- table: The field table

- max_length: The field's maximum length

- not_null: Set to 1 if the field cannot be set to null, 0 if it can

- primary_key: Set to 1 if the field is a primary key, 0 otherwise

- unique_key: Set to 1 if the field is a unique key, 0 otherwise

- multiple_key: Set to 1 if the field is a non-unique key, 0 otherwise

- numeric: Set to 1 if the field is numeric, 0 otherwise

- blob: Set to 1 if the field is a blob, 0 otherwise

- type: The field data type

- unsigned: Set to 1 if the field is unsigned, 0 otherwise

- zerofill: Set to 1 if the column is zero-filled, 0 otherwise

Consider an example:

```php
<?php
    mysql_connect("localhost","webuser","secret");
    mysql_select_db("company");
    $query = "SELECT * FROM product LIMIT 1";
    $result = mysql_query($query);
    $fields = mysql_num_fields($result);
    for($count=0;$count<$fields;$count++)
    {
        $field = mysql_fetch_field($result,$count);
        echo "<p>$field->name $field->type ($field->max_length)</p>";
    }
?>
```

This returns the following:

```
rowID int (1)
productid string (4)
name string (10)
price real (5)
description blob (33)
```

mysql_num_fields()

```
integer mysql_num_fields(resource result_set)
```

The mysql_num_fields() function returns the number of fields located in the result_set. For example:

```php
<?php
    ...
    $query = "SELECT productid, name FROM product ORDER BY name";
    $result = mysql_query($query);
    echo "Total number of fields returned: ".mysql_num_fields($result).".<br />";
    ...
?>
```

This returns:

```
Total number of fields returned: 2.<br />
```

mysql_list_fields()

```
resource mysql_list_fields(string database_name, string table_name
[, resource link_id])
```

The mysql_list_fields() function retrieves the names of all fields located in *table_name*. This table resides on the database indicated by database_name. If the optional link_id parameter is included, it assumes that the *database* resides on the server specified by that identifier. Otherwise, the most recently opened *link_id* is assumed.

You can use mysql_list_fields() instead of a query to return the total number of fields found in a table:

```php
<?php
    $fields = mysql_list_fields("company","product");
    echo "Total number of fields returned: ".mysql_num_fields($fields).".<br />";
    ...
?>
```

mysql_field_flags()

string mysql_field_flags(resource *result_set*, integer *field_offset*)

The mysql_field_flags() function retrieves all options assigned to the field located in position *field_offset* of the *result_set*.

```php
$query = "SELECT productid as Product_ID, name FROM product ORDER BY name";
$result = mysql_query($query);
$row = mysql_fetch_row($result);

echo mysql_field_flags($result, 0);
```

This returns:

```
not-null
```

mysql_field_len()

integer mysql_field_len(resource *result_set*, integer *field_offset*)

The mysql_field_len() function retrieves the length of the field residing in the *field_offset* position of *result_set*.

```php
$query = "SELECT description FROM product WHERE productid='tsbxxl'";
$result = mysql_query($query);
$row = mysql_fetch_row($result);

echo mysql_field_len($result, 0);
```

This returns:

```
16777215
```

This particular number is returned because a mediumtext column's maximum length is 16,777,215 characters. Incidentally, if you wanted to insert the appropriate commas in the integer, you could pass it through PHP's number_format() function, like this:

```
echo number_format(mysql_field_len($result, 0));
```

This produces:

```
16,777,215
```

mysql_field_name()

```
string mysql_field_name(resource result_set, int field_offset)
```

This function returns the name of the field specified by the *field_offset* position of *result_set*.

```
$query = "SELECT productid as Product_ID, name FROM product ORDER BY name";
$result = mysql_query($query);
$row = mysql_fetch_row($result);

echo mysql_field_name($result, 0);
```

This returns:

```
Product_ID
```

mysql_field_type()

```
string mysql_field_type(resource result_set, int field_offset)
```

This function returns the type of the field specified by the *field_offset* position of *result_set*.

```
$query = "SELECT productid as Product_ID, name FROM product ORDER BY name";
$result = mysql_query($query);
$row = mysql_fetch_row($result);

echo mysql_field_type($result, 0);
```

This returns:

---
string

---

mysql_field_table()

```
string mysql_field_table(resource result_set, int field_offset)
```

This function returns the name of the table that contains the field specified by the *field_offset* position of *result_set*.

```
$query = "SELECT productid as Product_ID, name FROM product ORDER BY name";
$result = mysql_query($query);
$row = mysql_fetch_row($result);

echo mysql_field_table($result, 0);
```

This returns:

---
product

Viewing Table Properties

The script shown in Listing 26-5 pulls together many of the functions introduced in this section, demonstrating how you can easily view table information for a given database with the browser. Two functions are defined for this purpose: view_db_properties() and view_table_properties(). The view_db_properties() function takes as input a database name, calling mysql_list_tables() to enumerate a list of tables located within that database. Each table name is then passed to view_table_properties(), where several other pre-defined functions are invoked, namely mysql_num_fields(), mysql_field_name(), mysql_field_type(), mysql_field_len(), and mysql_field_flags(), each doing its part to paint a complete picture of the table in question.

Listing 26-5. Viewing Table Properties

```php
<?php
mysql_connect("localhost","webuser","secret");

// The view_db_properties() function retrieves table information for
// the database defined by the input parameter $db, and invokes
// view_table_properties() for each table instance located within
// that database.
```

```php
function view_db_properties($db)
{

   mysql_select_db($db);

   $tables = mysql_list_tables($db);

   while (list($tableName) = mysql_fetch_row($tables))
   {
      echo "<p>Table: <b>$tableName</b></p>";
      echo "<table border='1'>";
      echo "<tr><th>Field</th><th>Type</th><th>Length</th><th>Flags</th>";
      echo view_table_properties($tableName);
      echo "</table>";
   }


}

// The view_table_properties() function retrieves
// field properties for the table defined by the input parameter $table. */

function view_table_properties($table)
{

   $tableRows = "";

   // Retrieve a single row from the table,
   // giving us enough field information to determine field properties.

   $result = mysql_query("SELECT * FROM $table LIMIT 1");
   $fields = mysql_num_fields($result);
   for($count=0; $count < $fields; $count++)
   {
      // Retrieve field properties
      $name = mysql_field_name($result,$count);
      $type = mysql_field_type($result,$count);
      $length = mysql_field_len($result,$count);
      $flags = mysql_field_flags($result,$count);

      $tableRows .= "<tr><td>$name</td>
                        <td>$type</td>
                        <td>$length</td>
                        <td>$flags</td></tr>";
   }

   return $tableRows;

}

view_db_properties("company");

?>
```

Executing this script against the company database, you can expect to view output similar to that shown in Figure 26-3.

Table: **product**

Field	Type	Length	Flags
rowID	int	10	not_null primary_key unsigned auto_increment
productid	string	8	not_null
name	string	25	not_null
price	real	7	not_null
description	blob	16777215	not_null blob

Figure 26-3. Viewing detailed table structure data

Retrieving Error Information

Developers always strive towards that nirvana known as bug-free code. In all but the most trivial of projects, however, such yearnings are almost always left unsatisfied. Therefore, properly detecting errors and returning useful information to the user is a vital component of efficient software development. In this section, I'll introduce two functions that are useful for deciphering and communicating MySQL errors.

mysql_error()

```
string mysql_error([resource link_id])
```

This function returns the error message generated by the last MySQL function, or an empty string if no error occurred. If the optional *link_id* parameter is included, the most recently occurring error emanating from that identifier will be used; otherwise the most recently opened server link is assumed. The message language is dependent upon the MySQL database server, because the target language is passed in as a flag at server startup. A sampling of the English-language messages follow:

```
Sort aborted
Too many connections
Couldn't uncompress communication packet
```

As you can see, the messages aren't exactly user-friendly, at least to the non-geeks using your application. Therefore, you might consider simply foregoing use of this function, and instead suppressing error output altogether and offering a warm-and-fuzzy message in the case of error:

```
@mysql_connect("localhost","user","pswd")
or die("I couldn't connect to the MySQL database server! Sorry about your luck!");
```

> **TIP** *MySQL's error messages are available in twenty languages and are stored in*
> `MYSQL-INSTALL-DIR/share/mysql/LANGUAGE/`.

mysql_errno()

```
integer mysql_errno([resource link_id])
```

Error numbers are often used in lieu of a natural language message to ease software internationalization efforts and allow for customization of error messages. This function returns the error code generated from the execution of the last MySQL function, or zero if no error occurred. If the optional `link_id` parameter is included, then the most recently occurring error emanating from that identifier will be used; otherwise the most recently opened server link is assumed. An example follows:

```php
<?php
    @mysql_connect("localhost","blah","blah");
    echo "Mysql error number generated: ".mysql_errno();
?>
```

This returns:

```
Mysql error number generated: 1045
```

Helper Functions

Numerous system-related functions are also available and capable of providing valuable information about MySQL server threads, status, connection types, and client and server versions. Each of these functions is introduced in this section.

mysql_client_encoding()

```
int mysql_client_encoding([resource link_id])
```

This function returns the default character set used for the most recently established connection. If an optional link identifier `link_id` is passed into the function, the character set used for that connection will be returned instead.

mysql_real_escape_string()

string mysql_real_escape_string(string *unescaped_string* [, resource *link_id*])

This highly useful function escapes all special characters intended to be included in an SQL statement. An example follows:

```
$description = "It's a savory reproduction of Grandma Mimi's favorite recipe!";
$description = mysql_real_escape_string($description);
// $description = "It\'s a savory reproduction of Grandma Mimi\'s favorite recipe!";
```

> **NOTE** *Neglecting to escape these special characters will result in query failure, so be sure to take the necessary steps to ensure that this matter is resolved.*

mysql_stat()

string mysql_stat([resource *link_identifier*])

This function returns a string containing several statistics pertinent to the MySQL server's status, including uptime, threads, executed queries, slow queries, opened tables, flushed tables, currently open tables, and average queries per second.

```
<?php
    $status = explode(' ', mysql_stat());
    foreach($status as $value) echo $value."<br />";
?>
```

This returns:

```
Uptime: 15641173
Threads: 1
Questions: 25118
Slow queries: 0
Opens: 139
Flush tables: 1
Open tables: 30
Queries per second avg: 0.002
```

Note that the uptime is listed in seconds. You'll need to run the value through a conversion function to obtain a more meaningful measurement.

mysql_thread_id()

```
int mysql_thread_id([resource link_id])
```

The mysql_thread_id() function retrieves the process id of the currently executing thread. If the optional *link_id* parameter is included, the thread pertinent to that server specified by that identifier will be examined. Otherwise, the most recently opened connection is assumed.

mysql_list_processes()

```
resource mysql_list_processes([resource link_id])
```

The mysql_list_processes() function retrieves a result set containing a list of all current MySQL server threads. If the optional *link_id* parameter is included, the processes pertinent to that server specified by that identifier will be examined. Otherwise, the most recently opened connection is assumed. Once the result set is parsed using mysql_fetch_assoc() or another similar function, eight properties are available: process id (id), user, host, database (db), running command (command), time-of-execution (time), execution state (state), and additional information (info). An example follows:

```php
<?php
mysql_connect("localhost","intranetmanager","secret");

$processes = mysql_list_processes();

echo "<table>";
echo "<tr><th>ID</th><th>User</th><th>Host</th><th>DB</th>
         <th>Command</th><th>Time</th><th>State</th><th>Info</th>
         </tr>";

while ($row = mysql_fetch_row($processes))
{
    list($id,$user,$host,$db,$command,$time,$state,$info) = $row;
    echo "<tr><td>$id</td><td>$user</td>
             <td>$host</td><td>$db</td><td>$command</td>
             <td>$time</td><td>$state</td><td>$info</td>
             </tr>";
}

echo "</table>";
?>
```

mysql_get_server_info()

string mysql_get_server_info([resource *link_id*])

The mysql_get_server_info() function retrieves the version signature of the MySQL server. If the optional *link_id* parameter is included, the version of the MySQL server specified by that identifier will be retrieved. Otherwise, the most recently opened connection is assumed. For example:

```php
<?php
    mysql_connect("localhost","webuser","secret");
    echo mysql_get_server_info();
?>
```

This returns:

```
4.0.5-beta-max-nt
```

mysql_get_host_info()

string mysql_get_host_info([resource *link_id*])

The mysql_get_host_info() function returns information pertinent to the type of connection used to connect to the MySQL server. If the optional *link_id* parameter is included, connection information for that MySQL server will be retrieved. Otherwise, the most recently opened connection is assumed. For example:

```php
<?php
    mysql_connect("localhost","webuser","secret");
    echo mysql_get_host_info();
?>
```

This returns:

```
localhost via TCP/IP
```

mysql_get_client_info()

```
string mysql_get_client_info()
```

The `mysql_get_client_info()` function returns information pertinent to the client library version. For example:

```php
<?php
    mysql_connect("localhost","webuser","secret");
    echo mysql_get_client_info();
?>
```

This returns:

```
3.23.49
```

Summary

If you're new to combining PHP and MySQL, I hope that I've answered many of your initial questions regarding what PHP's MySQL library can do. If you're already well versed in the matter, hopefully this chapter will serve as a valuable reference for moving forward. Regardless of your level of expertise, this chapter sets the stage for some of the more advanced topics found in the remaining four chapters.

In these remaining chapters, I'll touch upon a variety of topics bound to come up when you're developing PHP/MySQL applications. I'll start with a broad overview of the basic, yet crucial features pertinent to practically every such application, discussing the nuances of working with query data. The following chapters will focus on three advanced topics, namely working with indexes and fulltext searches, transactions, and finally data import and export. I'll devote the initial sections of each chapter to a MySQL-specific overview and then delve into the topic as it applies to PHP.

## CHAPTER 27

Practical
Database Queries

IN THE PREVIOUS CHAPTER I introduced you to PHP's MySQL extension, and demonstrated basic queries involving data selection. I also showed you how to use Web forms and MySQL queries to insert, modify, and delete database data. In this chapter, I'd like to expand on this foundational knowledge, demonstrating numerous concepts that you're bound to return to repeatedly while creating database-driven Web applications using the PHP language. In particular, I'll show you how to implement the following concepts:

- **A MySQL database class:** Managing your database queries using a class not only results in cleaner application code, but also affords you the ability to quickly and easily extend and modify query capabilities as necessary. In this section, I'll offer a MySQL database class implementation, and provide several introductory examples to get you familiar with its behavior.

- **Tabular output:** Listing query results in an easily readable format is one of the most commonplace tasks you'll implement when building database-driven applications. In this section, I'll show you how to create these listings using XHTML tables. I'll also demonstrate how to link each result row to a corresponding detailed view.

- **Sorting tabular output:** Often query results are ordered in a default fashion, by product name, for example. But what if the user would like to reorder the results using some other criteria, such as price? In this section, I'll show you how to provide table sorting mechanisms that let the user search on any column.

- **Paged results:** Database tables often consist of hundreds, even thousands, of results. When large result sets are retrieved, it often makes sense to separate these results across several pages, and provide the user with a mechanism to navigate back and forth between these pages. In this section, I'll show you an easy way to do so.

Note that the intent of this chapter isn't to provide a single, solitary means for carrying out these tasks, but to provide you with some general insight regarding how one might go about their implementation. If your mind is racing regarding how you can build upon these ideas after you've finished this chapter, I'll consider my goal successfully met.

Sample Data

For the examples found in this chapter, I'll continue using the product table created in the last chapter. For your convenience I'll reprint the table here:

```
CREATE TABLE product (
    rowID int not null auto_increment,
    productid varchar(8) not null,
    name varchar(25) not null,
    price decimal(5,2) not null,
    description mediumtext not null,
    primary key(rowID)
)
```

Creating a MySQL Database Class

Although I introduced PHP's MySQL library in Chapter 26, you probably won't want to reference these functions directly within your scripts. Rather, you should encapsulate them within a class, and then use the class to interact with the database. Listing 27-1 offers the base functionality that one would expect to find in such a class.

Listing 27-1. A MySQL Data Layer Class (mysql.class.php)

```php
<?php
class mysql {
    private $linkid;     // MySQL link identifier
    private $host;       // MySQL server host
    private $user;       // MySQL user
    private $pswd;       // MySQL password
    private $db;         // MySQL database
    private $result;     // Query result
    private $querycount; // Total queries executed

    /* Class constructor. Initializes the $host, $user, $pswd
       and $db fields. */
    function __construct($host, $user, $pswd, $db) {
        $this->host = $host;
        $this->user = $user;
        $this->pswd = $pswd;
        $this->db = $db;
    }

    /* Connects to the MySQL database server. */
    function connect() {
        try {
            $this->linkid = @mysql_connect($this->host,$this->user,$this->pswd);
            if (! $this->linkid)
                throw new Exception("Could not connect to the MySQL server.");
```

```
   }
   catch (Exception $e) {
      die($e->getMessage());
   }
}

/* Selects the MySQL database. */
function select() {
   try {
      if (! @mysql_select_db($this->db, $this->linkid))
         throw new Exception("Could not connect to the MySQL database.");
   }
   catch (Exception $e) {
      die($e->getMessage());
   }
}

/* Execute database query. */
function query($query) {
   try {
      $this->result = @mysql_query($query,$this->linkid);
      if (! $this->result)
         throw new Exception("The database query failed.");
   }
   catch (Exception $e) {
      echo($e->getMessage());
   }
   $this->querycount++;
   return $this->result;
}
/* Determine total rows affected by query. */
function affectedRows() {
   $count = @mysql_affected_rows($this->linkid);
   return $count;
}

/* Determine total rows returned by query. */
function numRows() {
   $count = @mysql_num_rows($this->result);
   return $count;
}

/* Return query result row as an object. */
function fetchObject() {
   $row = @mysql_fetch_object($this->result);
   return $row;
}

/* Return query result row as an indexed array. */
function fetchRow() {
   $row = @mysql_fetch_row($this->result);
```

```
        return $row;
    }

    /* Return query result row as an associative array. */
    function fetchArray() {
        $row = @mysql_fetch_array($this->result);
        return $row;
    }

    /* Return total number queries executed during
       lifetime of this object. Not required,
       but interesting nonethless. */
    function numQueries() {
        return $this->querycount;
    }


}
?>
```

The code found in Listing 27-1 should be quite easy to comprehend at this point in the book; therefore I've taken the liberty of going light on the comments. There is one point that I'd like to raise, however, pertinent to the output of exceptions. In order to keep matters simple, I've chosen to use die() statements for outputting exceptions specific to both connecting to the database server and selecting a database, while instead a failed query will not be fatally returned. Depending upon your particular needs, this implementation might not exactly suit your needs, but it should work just fine for the purposes of this book.

I'll devote the remainder of this section to several examples, each aimed to better familiarize you with use of the MySQL class.

Why Use the MySQL Database Class?

If you're new to object-oriented programming, you may still be unconvinced of the class-oriented approach, and you may be thinking about directly embedding the MySQL functions in the application code. In hopes of remedying such reservations, I'd like to illustrate the advantages of the class-based strategy with two examples. Both examples implement the simple task of querying the company database for a particular product name and price. However, the first example does so by calling the MySQL functions directly from the application code, while the second uses the MySQL class library shown in Listing 27-1.

```
<?php
    // Connect to the database server and select a database
    $linkid = @mysql_pconnect("localhost","jason","secret")
        or die("Could not connect to the MySQL server.");
    $db = @mysql_select_db("company", $linkid)
        or die("Could not connect to the MySQL database.");
```

```
    // Execute the query
    $result = @mysql_query("SELECT name, price FROM product ORDER by rowID")
        or die("The database query failed.");
    // Output the results
    while($row = mysql_fetch_object($result))
        echo "$row->name (\$$row->price)<br />";
?>
```

The next example uses the MySQL class.

```
<?php
    include "mysql.class.php";
    // Create a new mysql object
    $mysqldb = new mysql("localhost","jason","secret","company");
    // Connect to the database server and select a database
    $mysqldb->connect();
    $mysqldb->select();
    // Execute the query
    $mysqldb->query("SELECT name, price FROM product ORDER by rowID");
    // Output the results
    while ($row = $mysqldb->fetchObject())
        echo "$row->name (\$$row->price)<br />";
?>
```

Both examples return output similar to the following:

```
PHP T-Shirt ($12.99)
MySQL T-Shirt ($10.99)
```

The latter example offers numerous advantages:

- The code is cleaner. Intertwining logic, data queries, and error messages results in jumbled code.

- Because the database access code is encapsulated in the class, changing database types is trivial.

- Encapsulating the error messages in the class allows for easy modification and internationalization.

- Any changes to the PHP's MySQL API can easily be implemented through the class. Imagine having to manually modify MySQL function calls spread throughout fifty application scripts! If you're considering a later move to MySQL 4.1, you'll need to migrate to PHP 5's mysqli library. Encapsulating your MySQL functions in a class will render this migration trivial. Incidentally, because at the time of this writing the official release of MySQL 4.1 is not expected for some time, I've decided to omit discussion of this new extension.

Executing a Simple Query

Before delving into somewhat more complex topics involving this class, I'd like to take a moment to offer a few introductory examples. For starters, I'll show you how to connect to the database server, choose a database, and retrieve some data using a simple query:

```php
<?php
    include "mysql.class.php";

    // Create new mysql object
    $mysqldb = new mysql("localhost","jason","secret","company");

    // Connect to database server and select database
    $mysqldb->connect();
    $mysqldb->select();

    // Query the database
    $mysqldb->query("SELECT name, price FROM product
                        WHERE productid='tshirt01'");

    // Retrieve query result as an object
    $row = $mysqldb->fetchObject();

    // Output the data
    echo "$row->name (\$$row->price)";
?>
```

This example returns:

```
PHP T-Shirt ($12.99)
```

Retrieving Multiple Rows

Now consider a slightly more involved example. The following script retrieves all rows from the product table, ordering the results by name.

```php
<?php
    include "mysql.class.php";

    // Create new mysql object
    $mysqldb = new mysql("localhost","jason","secret","company");

    // Connect to database server and select database
    $mysqldb->connect();
    $mysqldb->select();
```

```
    // Query the database
    $mysqldb->query("SELECT name, price FROM product ORDER BY name");
    // Output the data
    while ($row = $mysqldb->fetchObject())
        echo "$row->name (\$$row->price)<br />";
?>
```

This returns:

```
MySQL Coffee Cup ($4.99)
Perl Hat ($16.99)
PHP T-Shirt ($12.99)
```

Counting Queries

I thought that it might be interesting to illustrate how easy it is to extend the capabilities of a data class, just one of the advantages of embedding the MySQL functionality in this fashion (see the sidebar for other advantages). I've created a method called numQueries() that retrieves the value of the private field $querycount. This field is incremented every time a query is executed, allowing me to keep track of the total number of queries executed throughout the lifetime of an object. The following example executes two queries and then outputs the number of queries executed:

```
<?php
    include "mysql.class.php";

    // Create new mysql object
    $mysqldb = new mysql("localhost","jason","secret","company");

    // Connect to database server and select database
    $mysqldb->connect();
    $mysqldb->select();

    // Execute a few queries
    $query = "SELECT name, price FROM product ORDER BY name";
    $mysqldb->query($query);
    $query2 = "SELECT name, price FROM product WHERE productid='tshirt01'";
    $mysqldb->query($query2);

    // Output the total number of queries executed.
    echo "Total number of queries executed: ".$mysqldb->numQueries()." <br />";
?>
```

This example returns the following:

```
Total number of queries executed: 2
```

Tabular Output

Viewing retrieved database data in a coherent, user-friendly fashion is key to the success of a Web application. HTML tables have been used for years to satisfy this need for uniformity, for better or for worse. Because this feature is so commonplace, it makes sense to encapsulate this functionality in a function, and call that function whenever database results should be formatted in this fashion. In this section, I'll demonstrate one way to accomplish this; I've used this function for quite some time now and don't know what I would do without it.

For reasons of convenience, I'll create this function in the format of a method and add it to the MySQL data class. To facilitate this method, I'll also need to add two more helper methods, one for determining the number of fields in a result set, and another for determining each field name:

```
/* Return the number of fields in a result set. */
function numberFields() {
   return @mysql_num_fields($this->result);
}

/* Return a field name given an integer offset. */
function fieldName($offset) {
   return @mysql_field_name($this->result, $offset);
}
```

I'll use these methods along with other methods in the MySQL data class to create an easy and convenient method named getResultAsTable(), used to output table-encapsulated results. I find this method highly useful for two reasons in particular. First, it automatically converts the field names into table headers, and second, it automatically adjusts to number of fields found in the query. It's a one-size-fits-all solution for formatting needs of this sort. The method is presented in Listing 27-2.

Listing 27-2. The getResultAsTable() *Method*

```
function getResultAsTable() {

   if ($this->numrows() > 0) {

      // Start the table
      $resultHTML = "<table border='1'>\n<tr>\n";
```

```
        // Output the table header
        $fieldCount = $this->numberFields();
        for ($i=0; $i < $fieldCount; $i++) {
            $rowName = $this->fieldName($i);
            $resultHTML .= "<th>$rowName</th>";
        } # end for

        // Close the row
        $resultHTML .= "</tr>\n";

        // Output the table data
        while ($row = $this->fetchRow()) {
            $resultHTML .= "<tr>\n";
            for ($i = 0; $i < $fieldCount; $i++)
                $resultHTML .= "<td>".htmlentities($row[$i])."</td>";
            $resultHTML .= "</tr>\n";
        } # end while

        // Close the table
        $resultHTML .= "</table>";
    } else {
        $resultHTML = "No results found";
    }
    return $resultHTML;
}
```

Using getResultAsTable() is easy, as is demonstrated in the following code snippet:

```
<?php
    include "mysql.class.php";

    $mysqldb = new mysql("localhost","jason","secret","company");

    $mysqldb->connect();

    $mysqldb->select();

    // Execute the query
    $mysqldb->query("SELECT name as Product,
                     price as Price,
                     description as Description FROM product");

    // Return the result as a table
    echo $mysqldb->getResultAsTable();
?>
```

Example output is displayed in Figure 27-1.

Product	Price	Description
Linux Hat	8.99	A hat that says 'I Love Linux'.
MySQL Coffee Cup	4.99	Display your database allegiance to the breakfast crew with this 10 oz. coffee cup
Perl Coffee Cup	5.99	Shine like a pearl in the morning with this Perl coffee cup.
Perl Hat	16.99	Spread the good vibe by wearing this Perl baseball cap with pride. The text states, "Perl is for lovers".
PHP Coffee Cup	3.99	Relax, you're having a PHP-powered breakfast with this 10 oz coffee cup.
PHP T-Shirt	12.99	Wear this PHP T-shirt with pride.

Figure 27-1. Creating table-formatted results

Linking to a Detailed View

Often a user will want to do more with the results than just view them. For example, the user might want to learn more about a particular product found in the result, or he might want to add the product to his shopping cart. An interface that offers such capabilities is presented in Figure 27-2.

Product	Price	actions
Linux Hat	8.99	View Detailed	Add to Cart
MySQL Coffee Cup	4.99	View Detailed	Add to Cart
Perl Coffee Cup	5.99	View Detailed	Add to Cart
Perl Hat	16.99	View Detailed	Add to Cart
PHP Coffee Cup	3.99	View Detailed	Add to Cart
PHP T-Shirt	12.99	View Detailed	Add to Cart

Figure 27-2. Offering actionable options in the table output

As it currently stands, the getResultsAsTable() method doesn't offer the ability to accompany each row with actionable options. In this section, I'll show you how to modify the code to provide this functionality. Before delving into the code, however, I'd like to raise a few points.

For starters, I want to be able to pass in actions of varying purpose and number. That said, I'll pass the actions in as a string to the function. However, because the actions will be included at the end of each line, I won't know what primary key to tack on to each action until the row is rendered. This is essential, because the destination script needs to know which item is targeted. Therefore, run-time replacement on a pre-defined string must occur when the rows are being formatted and output. I'll use the string VALUE for this purpose. An example action string follows:

```php
$actions = '<a href="viewdetail.php?rowid=VALUE">View Detailed</a> |
           <a href="addtocart.php?rowid=VALUE">Add to Cart</a>';
```

Of course, this also implies that an identifying key must be included in the query. The product table's primary key is rowID. In addition, this key should be placed first in the query, because the script needs to know which field value is to serve as the replacement for VALUE. Finally, because you probably don't want the rowID to appear in the formatted table, the counters used to output the table header and data will need to be incremented by one.

The updated getResultAsTable() method follows. For your convenience, I've bolded those lines that have either changed or are new.

```
function getResultAsTable($actions) {

  if ($this->numrows() > 0) {

    // Start the table
    $resultHTML = "<table border='1'>\n<tr>\n";

    // Output the table header
    $fieldCount = $this->numberFields();
    for ($i=1; $i < $fieldCount; $i++) {
      $rowName = $this->fieldName($i);
      $resultHTML .= "<th>$rowName</th>\n";
    } # end for

    $resultHTML .= "<th>actions</th></tr>\n";

    // Output the table data

    while ($row = $this->fetchRow()) {
      $resultHTML .= "<tr>\n";
      for ($i = 1; $i < $fieldCount; $i++)
        $resultHTML .= "<td>".htmlentities($row[$i])."</td>\n";

      // Replace VALUE with the correct primary key
      $action = str_replace("VALUE", $row[0], $actions);
      // Add the action cell to end of the row
      $resultHTML .= "<td nowrap> $action</td>\n</tr>\n";

    } # end while

    // Close the table
    $resultHTML .= "</table>\n";
  } else {
    $resultHTML = "No results found";
  }
  return $resultHTML;
}
```

The process for executing this method is almost identical to the original. The key difference is that this time you have the option of including actions:

```php
<?php
    include "mysql.class.php";
    $mysqldb = new mysql("localhost","jason","secret","company");
    $mysqldb->connect();
    $mysqldb->select();

    $mysqldb->query("SELECT rowID, name as Product,
                        price as Price
                        FROM product ORDER BY name");

    $actions = '<a href="viewdetail.php?rowid=VALUE">View Detailed</a> |
                <a href="addtocart.php?rowid=VALUE">Add to Cart</a>';

    echo $mysqldb->getResultAsTable($actions);
?>
```

Executing this code will produce output similar to that found in Figure 27-2.

Sorting Output

When I display query results, I often order the information using criteria that I think would be most convenient for the user. For example, if the user wanted to view a list of all products in the product table, I would output the results in ascending alphabetical order according to product name. However, some users may want to order the information using some other criteria, by price for example. Often, such mechanisms are implemented by linking listing headers, for example the table headers used in the previous examples. Clicking any of these links will cause the table data to be sorted using that header as the criterion. In this section, I'll demonstrate this concept, again modifying the most recent version of the getResultAsTable() method. However, only one line requires modification, specifically:

```php
$resultHTML .= "<th>$rowName</th>";
```

I'll change this line to read:

```php
$resultHTML .= "<th>
                <a href=\"".$_SERVER['PHP_SELF']."?sort=$rowName\">$rowName</a>
                </th>";
```

The executing code looks quite similar to that used in previous examples, except that now a dynamic SORT clause must be inserted into the query. A ternary operator, introduced in Chapter 3, is used to determine whether the user has clicked on one of the header links:

```php
$sort = (isset($_GET['sort'])) ? $_GET['sort'] : "name";
```

If a sort parameter has been passed via the URL, that value will be the sorting criteria. Otherwise, a default of name is used.

```
$mysqldb->query("SELECT rowID, name as Product,
                 price as Price FROM product ORDER BY $sort ASC");
```

The complete executing code follows:

```php
<?php
    include "mysql.class.php";
    $mysqldb = new mysql("localhost","jason","secret","company");
    $mysqldb->connect();
    $mysqldb->select();

    // Determine what kind of sort request has been submitted.
    // By default this is set to sort by name
    $sort = (isset($_GET['sort'])) ? $_GET['sort'] : "name";

    // Query the database
    $mysqldb->query("SELECT rowID, name as Product,
                     price as Price FROM product ORDER BY $sort ASC");

    $actions = '<a href="viewdetail.php?rowid=VALUE">View Detailed</a> |
                <a href="addtocart.php?rowid=VALUE">Add to Cart</a>';

    echo $mysqldb->getResultAsTable($actions);
?>
```

Loading the script for the first time results in the output being sorted by name. Example output is shown in Figure 27-3.

Product	Price	actions
Linux Hat	8.99	View Detailed	Add to Cart
MySQL Coffee Cup	4.99	View Detailed	Add to Cart
Perl Coffee Cup	5.99	View Detailed	Add to Cart
Perl Hat	16.99	View Detailed	Add to Cart
PHP Coffee Cup	3.99	View Detailed	Add to Cart
PHP T-Shirt	12.99	View Detailed	Add to Cart

Figure 27-3. The product table output sorted by the default name

Clicking the Price header re-sorts the output. This sorted output is shown in Figure 27-4.

Product	Price	actions
PHP Coffee Cup	3.99	View Detailed | Add to Cart
MySQL Coffee Cup	4.99	View Detailed | Add to Cart
Perl Coffee Cup	5.99	View Detailed | Add to Cart
Linux Hat	8.99	View Detailed | Add to Cart
PHP T-Shirt	12.99	View Detailed | Add to Cart
Perl Hat	16.99	View Detailed | Add to Cart

Figure 27-4. The product table output sorted by price

Creating Paged Output

If you've perused any e-commerce sites or search engines, you're familiar with the practice of separating query results into several pages. This feature is convenient not only to enhance readability, but also to further optimize page loading. You might be surprised to learn that adding this feature to your Web site is a trivial affair. In this section, I'll demonstrate how it's accomplished.

This feature depends in part on SQL's LIMIT clause. The LIMIT clause is used to specify both the starting point and the number of rows returned from a SELECT query. Its general, its syntax looks like this:

```
LIMIT [offset,] number_rows
```

For example, if I wanted to limit returned query results to just the first five rows, I could construct the following query:

```
SELECT name, price FROM product ORDER BY name ASC LIMIT 5
```

Because I intend to start from the very first row, this is the same as:

```
SELECT name, price FROM product ORDER BY name ASC LIMIT 0,5
```

However, if I wanted to start from the fifth row of the result set, I would construct the following query:

```
SELECT name, price FROM product ORDER BY name ASC LIMIT 5,5
```

Because this syntax is so convenient, you only need to determine three variables to create mechanisms for paging throughout the results:

- **The number of entries per page:** This is entirely up to you. Alternatively, you could easily offer the user the ability to customize this variable. This value is passed into the number_rows component of the LIMIT clause.

- **The row offset:** This value depends on what page is presently loaded. This value is passed by way of the URL so that it can be passed to the offset component of the LIMIT clause. I'll show you how to calculate this value in the following code.

- **The total number of rows in the result set:** This is required knowledge because the value is used to determine whether the page needs to contain a next link.

Interestingly, no modifications to the MySQL database class are required. Because this concept seems to cause quite a bit of confusion, I'll guide you through the code first, and then offer the example in its entirety in Listing 27-3. The first section is typical of any script using the MySQL data class:

```php
<?php
    include "mysql.class.php";
    $mysqldb = new mysql("localhost","jason","secret","company");
    $mysqldb->connect();
    $mysqldb->select();
```

Next I'll specify the maximum number of entries that should appear on each paged result:

```php
    $pagesize = 2;
```

Next, I'll use a ternary operator to determine whether the $_GET['recordstart'] parameter has been passed by way of the URL. This parameter determines the offset from which the result set should begin. If it has, I'll assign it to $recordstart; otherwise $recordstart is set to 0:

```php
    $recordstart = (isset($_GET['recordstart'])) ? $_GET['recordstart'] : 0;
```

Next, the database query is executed and the data output. Note that the record offset is set to $recordstart, and the number of entries to retrieve is set to $pagesize:

```php
    $mysqldb->query("SELECT name, price FROM product
                    ORDER BY name LIMIT $recordstart,$pagesize");
    // Output the result set
    $actions = '<a href="viewdetail.php?rowid=VALUE">View Detailed</a> |
                    <a href="addtocart.php?rowid=VALUE">Add to Cart</a>';
    echo $mysqldb->getResultAsTable($actions);
```

Next, I need to determine the total number of rows available, accomplished by removing the LIMIT clause from the original query. However, to optimize the query, I'll use the count() function rather than retrieving a complete result set:

```php
    $mysqldb->query("select count(rowID) as count FROM product");
    $row = $mysqldb->fetchObject();
    $totalrows = $row->count;
```

Finally, the previous and next links are created. The previous link is created only if the record offset, $recordstart, is greater than zero. The next link is created only if some records remain to be retrieved, meaning that $recordstart + $pagesize must be less than the $totalrows:

```php
// Create the 'previous' link
if ($recordstart > 0) {
    $prev = $recordstart - $pagesize;
    $url = $_SERVER['PHP_SELF']."?recordstart=$prev";
    echo "<a href=\"$url\">Previous Page</a> ";
}

// Create the 'next' link
if ($totalrows > ($recordstart + $pagesize)) {
    $next = $recordstart + $pagesize;
    $url = $_SERVER['PHP_SELF']."?recordstart=$next";
    echo "<a href=\"$url\">Next Page</a>";
}
```

Sample output is shown in Figure 27-5. The complete code listing is presented in Listing 27-3.

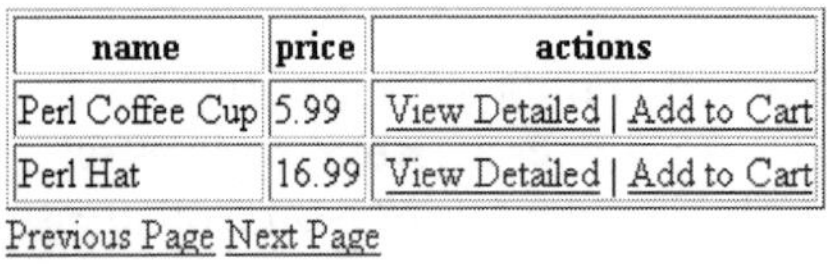

name	price	actions
Perl Coffee Cup	5.99	View Detailed | Add to Cart
Perl Hat	16.99	View Detailed | Add to Cart

Previous Page Next Page

Figure 27-5. Creating paged results (two results per page)

Listing 27-3. Paging Database Results

```php
<?php

include "mysql.class.php";
$mysqldb = new mysql("localhost","jason","secret","company");
$mysqldb->connect();
$mysqldb->select();

// Set number entries per page
$pagesize = 2;

// What is our record offset?
$recordstart = (isset($_GET['recordstart'])) ? $_GET['recordstart'] : 0;
```

```
// Execute the SELECT query, including a LIMIT clause
$mysqldb->query("SELECT name, price FROM product
                  ORDER BY name LIMIT $recordstart, $pagesize");

// Output the result set
$actions = '<a href="viewdetail.php?rowid=VALUE">View Detailed</a> |
           <a href="addtocart.php?rowid=VALUE">Add to Cart</a>';
echo $mysqldb->getResultAsTable($actions);

// Determine whether additional rows are available
$mysqldb->query("select count(rowID) as count FROM product");
$row = $mysqldb->fetchObject();
$totalrows = $row->count;

// Create the 'previous' link
if ($recordstart > 0) {
    $prev = $recordstart - $pagesize;
    $url = $_SERVER['PHP_SELF']."?recordstart=$prev";
    echo "<a href=\"$url\">Previous Page</a> ";
}

// Create the 'next' link
if ($totalrows > ($recordstart + $pagesize)) {
    $next = $recordstart + $pagesize;
    $url = $_SERVER['PHP_SELF']."?recordstart=$next";
    echo "<a href=\"$url\">Next Page</a>";
}
?>
```

Listing Page Numbers

If you have several pages of results, the user might wish to traverse them in a non-linear order. For example, the user might choose to jump from page one to page three, then page six, then back to page one again. Thankfully, providing users with a linked list of page numbers is surprisingly easy. Building on Listing 27-3, you start by determining the total number of pages, and assigning that value to $totalpages. You determine the total number of pages by dividing the total result rows by the chosen page size, and round upwards using the ceil() function:

```
$totalpages= ceil($totalrows / $pagesize);
```

Next, you determine the current page number, and assign it to $currentpage. You determine the current page by dividing the present record offset ($recordstart) by the chosen page size ($pagesize), and adding one to account for the fact that LIMIT offsets start with 0:

```
$currentpage = ($recordstart / $pagesize ) + 1;
```

Next, create a function titled pageLinks(), and pass it four parameters:

- $totalpages: This total result pages is stored in the aforementioned $totalpages variable.

- $currentpage: The current page, stored in the aforementioned $currentpage variable.

- $pagesize: The chosen page size, stored in the aforementioned $pagesize variable.

- $parameter: The name of the parameter used to pass the record offset by way of the URL. Thus far I've used recordstart, so I'll stick with that in the following example.

The pageLinks() function follows:

```php
function pageLinks($totalpages, $currentpage, $pagesize,$parameter) {

    // Start at page one
    $page = 1;

    // Start at record zero
    $recordstart = 0;

    // Initialize $pageLinks
    $pageLinks = "";

    while ($page <= $totalpages) {
        // Link the page if it isn't the current one
        if ($page != $currentpage) {
            $pageLinks .= "<a href=\"".$_SERVER['PHP_SELF']."
                        ?$parameter=$recordstart\">$page</a> ";
        // If the current page, just list the number
        } else {
            $pageLinks .= "$page ";
        }
            // Move to the next record delimiter
            $recordstart += $pagesize;
            $page++;
    }
    return $pageLinks;
}
```

Finally, you call the function like so:

```
echo "<p>Pages: ".
    pageLinks($totalpages,$currentpage,$pagesize,"recordstart").
    "</p>";
```

Sample output of the page listing, combined with other components introduced throughout this chapter, is shown in Figure 27-6.

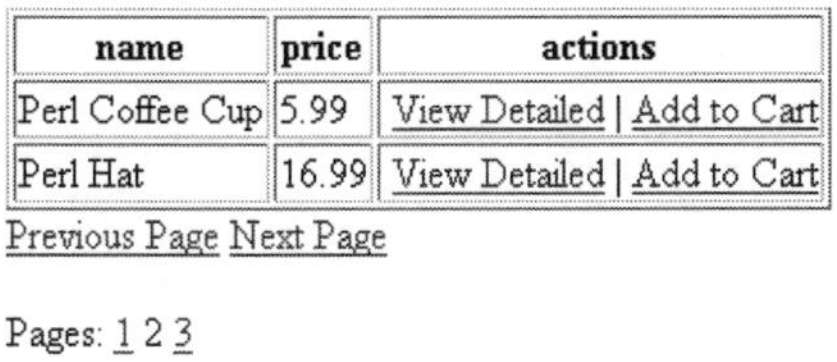

name	price	actions
Perl Coffee Cup	5.99	View Detailed | Add to Cart
Perl Hat	16.99	View Detailed | Add to Cart

Previous Page Next Page

Pages: 1 2 3

Figure 27-6. Generating a numbered list of page results

Summary

In this chapter, I offered insight into some of the most common general tasks you'll encounter when developing data driven applications. I started by providing a MySQL data class, and offered some basic usage examples involving this class. Next I showed you a convenient and easy methodology for outputting data results in tabular format, then showed you how to add actionable options for each output data row. I continued to build upon this material, showing you how to sort output based on a given table field. Finally, I showed you how to spread query results across several pages, and demonstrated how to create linked page listings, enabling the user to navigate the results in a non-linear fashion.

In the next chapter I'll introduce MySQL's data indexing and full-text search capabilities, and show you how to execute Web-based database searches using PHP.

CHAPTER 28

Indexes and Searching

In Chapter 24, I briefly introduced the concept of PRIMARY and UNIQUE keys, defining the role of each and showing you how to recognize and incorporate them into your table structures. However, indexes play such an important role in database development that I think it worth devoting some additional time to these features. In this chapter, I'll further introduce you to these important concepts. I'll also show you how to create Web interfaces used to search MySQL databases. In particular, I'll discuss the following topics:

- **Database indexing:** In this section I'll introduce you to general database indexing terminology and concepts, and show you how to create primary, unique, normal, and full-text MySQL indexes.

- **Forms-based searches:** In the second-half of this chapter, I'll show you how to create PHP-enabled search interfaces for querying your presumably newly indexed MySQL tables.

Database Indexing

Generally speaking, there are three advantages you have to gain by introducing indexing into your MySQL database development strategy:

- **Query optimization:** An index is essentially an ordered (or indexed) subset of table columns, with each row entry pointing to its corresponding table row. Working within the indexed subset allows for much faster processing of query requests, because it eliminates the need to search the entire table, instead opting to concentrate on just a relatively small slice.

- **Data uniqueness:** Often a means is required for identifying a data row based on some value, or values that are known to be unique to that row. For example, consider a table that stores information about company staff members. This table might include information about the staff member's first and last name, telephone number, and social security number. Although it's possible that two or more staff members could share the same name (John Smith for example), and that sharing an office could necessitate use of the same phone number, you know that no two should possess the same social security number.

- **Text searching:** With the introduction of full-text indexes in MySQL version 3.23.23, users now have the opportunity to optimize searching against even large amounts of text located in any field indexed as such.

There are four general categories of indexes: primary, unique, normal, and full-text. Each type is introduced in this section.

> **NOTE** *In the context of the material covered in this chapter, the terms* key *and* index *are synonyms and can be used interchangeably.*

Primary Key Indexes

The primary key index is the most common type of index found in relational databases. It's generally accepted practice that a row's primary index value is determined by an automatically incrementing integer value, specific to the key's column. This guarantees that, regardless of whether pre-existing rows are subsequently deleted, every row will have a unique primary index. For example, suppose you want to create a database of useful Web sites for your company's IT team. This table might look like the following:

```
CREATE TABLE webresource (
    rowID tinyint unsigned not null auto_increment,
    name varchar(75) not null,
    url varchar(200) not null,
    description mediumtext not null,
    primary key(rowID));
```

> **NOTE** *You can only have one automatically incrementing column per table, and that column must be designated as the primary key.*

It is typically ill advised to create a primary index that allows the developer to divine some information about the row it represents. I'll demonstrate why with an illustration. Rather than use an integer value as the webresource table's primary index, suppose you decide to make the most of this column by combining information about the url domain and first three letters of the description. The repercussions involved in making such a decision should be obvious; first, what happens when the description changes? Although updating the index to reflect the new description would be trivial, what happens if another site just so happens to already possess a row ID value of exaphp? Should you call it exaphp1, or perhaps devise some other means for handling such exceptions? Save yourself the hassle and always use a primary index that offers no insight into the data it represents; rather, it is an autonomous vehicle with the sole purpose of ensuring the ability to uniquely identify a data record.

Unique Indexes

Like a primary index, a unique index prevents duplicate values from being created. However, the difference is that only one primary index is allowed per table, whereas multiple unique indexes are supported. With this possibility in mind, it might be worth revisiting the webresource table from the previous section. Although it's conceivable that two Web sites could share the same name, for example "Great PHP resource," it wouldn't make sense to repeat URLs. This sounds like an ideal unique index:

```
CREATE TABLE webresource (
    rowID mediumint unsigned not null auto_increment,
    name varchar(75) not null,
    url varchar(200) not null unique,
    description mediumtext not null,
    primary key(rowID));
```

As I mentioned, it's possible to designate multiple fields as unique in a given table. Consider an example. Suppose you wanted to prevent contributors to the link repository from repeatedly designating non-descriptive names ("cool site," for example) when inserting a new Web site. Revisiting the original webresource table, I will define the name column as unique:

```
CREATE TABLE webresource (
    rowID mediumint unsigned not null auto_increment,
    name varchar(75) not null unique,
    url varchar(200) not null unique,
    description mediumtext not null,
    primary key(rowID));
```

You can also specify a multiple-column unique index. For example, suppose you wanted to allow your contributors to insert duplicate url values, and even duplicate name values, but you did not want duplicate name and url combinations to appear. You can enforce such restrictions by creating a multiple-column unique index. Revisiting the original webresource table:

```
CREATE TABLE webresource (
    rowID mediumint unsigned not null auto_increment,
    name varchar(75) not null,
    url varchar(200) not null,
    unique(name,url),
    description mediumtext not null,
    primary key(rowID));
```

Given this configuration, the following name and value pairs could all simultaneously reside in the same table:

```
Apress site, http://www.apress.com/
Apress site, http://blogs.apress.com/
Blogs, http://www.apress.com/
Apress blogs, http://blogs.apress.com/
```

However, attempting to insert any of the preceding combinations again will result in an error, because duplicate combinations of name and url are illegal.

Normal Indexes

Quite often you'll want to optimize searches on fields other than those designated as primary or even unique. Because this is a commonplace occurrence, it only makes sense that it should be possible to optimize such searches by indexing these fields. Such indexes are typically called *normal*, or *ordinary*.

Single-Column Normal Indexes

A single-column normal index should be used if a particular column in your table will be the focus of a considerable number of your selection queries. For example, suppose an employee profile table consists of four columns: a unique row ID, first name, last name, and e-mail address. You know that the majority of the searches will be specific to either the employee's last name, or the e-mail address. You should create one normal index for the last name and a unique index for the e-mail address, like so:

```
CREATE TABLE employee (
    rowID smallint unsigned not null auto_increment,
    firstname varchar(35) not null,
    lastname varchar(35) not null,
    email varchar(55) not null unique,
    index (lastname),
    primary key(rowID));
```

Building on this idea, MySQL offers the feature of creating partial-column indexes, based on the idea that the first *N* characters of a given column will often be enough to ensure uniqueness, where *N* is specified within the index creation parameters. Doing so both requires less disk space and is considerably faster than indexing the entire column. Revisiting the previous example, you can imagine that the first five characters of the last name suffices to ensure accurate retrieval:

```
create table employee (
    rowID smallint unsigned not null auto_increment,
    firstname varchar(35) not null,
    lastname varchar(35) not null,
    email varchar(55) not null unique,
    index (lastname(5)),
    primary key(rowID));
```

Often however, selection queries are a function of including multiple columns. After all, more complex tables might require a query consisting of several columns before the desired data can be retrieved. Run time on such queries can be decreased greatly through the institution of multiple-column normal indexes, discussed next.

Multiple-Column Normal Indexes

Multiple-column indexing is recommended when you know that a number of specified columns will often be used together in retrieval queries. MySQL's multi-column indexing approach is based upon a strategy known as *left-most prefixing*. Left-most prefixing states that any multiple-column index, including columns A, B, and C will improve performance on queries involving the following column combinations:

- A, B, C

- A, B

- A

Here's how you create a multiple-column MySQL index:

```
create table employee (
    rowID smallint unsigned not null auto_increment,
    lastname varchar(35) not null,
    firstname varchar(35) not null,
    email varchar(55) not null unique,
    city varchar(100) not null,
    index name (lastname, firstname),
    primary key(rowID));
```

Broadly speaking, two indexes have been created (in addition to the primary key index). The first is the unique index for the e-mail address. The second is a multiple-column index, consisting of two columns, `lastname` and `firstname`. This is quite useful, because it increases the search speed when queries involve any of the following column combinations:

- `lastname, firstname`

- `lastname`

Driving this point home, the following queries would benefit from the multiple-column index:

```
SELECT email FROM employee WHERE lastname="Geronimo" AND firstname="Ed";
SELECT lastname FROM employee WHERE lastname="Geronimo";
```

While the following queries would not:

```
SELECT lastname FROM employee WHERE firstname="Ed";
SELECT email FROM employee WHERE city="Columbus";
```

In order to gain performance on these two queries, you'd need to create separate indexes for both `firstname` and `city`.

Full-Text Indexes

The latest of MySQL's index types to be introduced is the full-text index, available as of version 3.23.23. Full-text indexes offer an efficient means for searching text stored in `CHAR`, `VARCHAR`, or `TEXT` data types. Before delving into examples, a bit of background regarding MySQL's special handling of this index is in order.

Because MySQL assumes that full-text searches will be implemented for sifting through large amounts of natural language text, so a mechanism must be in place for retrieving data that produces results that best fit the user's desired result. More specifically, if a user were to search using a string like "Apache is the world's most popular web server," the words *is* and *the* should probably play little or no role in determining result relevance. In fact, MySQL will split searchable text into words, by default eliminating any word of less than four characters. I'll discuss how you can modify this behavior later in this section.

Creating a full-text index is much like creating indexes of other types. As an example, I'll revisit the `webresource` table created earlier in this chapter, indexing its `description` column using the `fulltext` variant:

```
CREATE TABLE webresource (
    rowID tinyint unsigned not null auto_increment,
    name varchar(75) not null,
    url varchar(200) not null,
    description mediumtext not null,
    fulltext(description),
    primary key(rowID));
```

In addition to the typical primary index, a full-text index consisting of the `description` column has been created. For demonstration purposes, I'll fill in the table with the data found here:

ROWID	NAME	URL	DESCRIPTION
1	Python.org	`http://www.python.org/`	The official Python Website
2	MySQL manual	`http://dev.mysql.com/doc/`	The MySQL reference manual
3	Apache site	`http://httpd.apache.org/`	Great Apache site! Includes Apache 2 manual
4	PHP: Hypertext Preprocessor	`http://www.php.net/`	The official PHP Web site
5	Apache Week	`http://www.apacheweek.com/`	Offers a dedicated Apache 2 section

Although creating of this index variant is like its brethren, retrieval queries based on the full-text index are different. SELECT queries make use of two special MySQL functions, MATCH() and AGAINST(). With these functions, natural language searches can be executed against the full-text index, like so:

```
SELECT name,url FROM webresource WHERE MATCH(description)
    AGAINST('Apache 2');
```

The results returned look like this:

```
+-------------+-------------------------+
| name        | url                     |
+-------------+-------------------------+
| Apache site | http://httpd.apache.org |
| Apache Week | http://www.apacheweek.com |
+-------------+-------------------------+
```

This lists the rows in which "Apache" is found in the description column, in order of highest relevance. Remember that the 2 is ignored because of its length. When MATCH() is used in a WHERE clause, relevance is defined in terms of how well the returned row matches with the search string. Alternatively, the functions can be incorporated into the query body, returning a list of weighted scores for matching rows; the higher the score, the greater the relevance. An example follows:

```
SELECT MATCH(articleSummary, description) AGAINST('Apache 2')
    FROM webresource;
```

Upon execution, MySQL will search every row in the article table, calculating relevance values for each, like so:

```
+-----------------------------------------+
| match(description) against('Apache 2') |
+-----------------------------------------+
|                                      0 |
|                                      0 |
|                       0.57014514171969 |
|                                      0 |
|                       0.38763393589171 |
+-----------------------------------------+
```

Starting with version 4.01, Boolean-oriented full-text searches were introduced. I'll introduce this search variation later in this section.

Stopwords

As I mentioned earlier, MySQL will by default ignore any keywords of less than four characters. These words, along with those found in a predefined list built into the MySQL server, are known as *stopwords*, or words that should be ignored. You can exercise a good deal of control over stopword behavior by modifying the following MySQL variables:

- ft_min_word_len: You can qualify words that don't meet a particular length as stopwords. You can specify the minimum required length using this parameter. If you change this parameter, you'll need to restart the MySQL server daemon and rebuild the indexes.

- ft_max_word_len: You can also qualify words that exceed a particular length as stopwords. You can specify this length using this parameter. If you change this parameter, you'll need to restart the MySQL server daemon and rebuild the indexes.

- ft_max_word_len_for_sort: This parameter is presently not used.

- ft_stopword_file: This file contains a list of 544 English words that will automatically be filtered out of any search keywords. You can change this to point to another list by setting this parameter to the path and name of the requested list. Alternatively, if you have the option of recompiling the MySQL source, you can modify this list by opening up myisam/ft_static.c and editing the predefined list. In the first case, you'll need to restart MySQL and rebuild the indexes, while in the second case you'll need to recompile MySQL according to your specifications and rebuild the indexes.

> **NOTE** *Rebuilding MySQL's indexes is accomplished with the command* REPAIR TABLE *table_name* USE_FRM, *where* table_name *represents the name of the table that you would like to rebuild.*

Note that stopwords are ignored by default because it is presumed that they occur too frequently in common language to be pertinent. This can have unintended effects, because MySQL will also automatically filter out any keyword that is found to exist in over 50 percent of the records. Take heed of what happens, for example, if all contributors add a URL pertinent to the Apache Web server, and accordingly all include the word *Apache* in the description. Therefore, executing a full-text search looking for the term *Apache* will produce what are surely unexpected results: no records found. If you can recompile the MySQL source, you can disable this behavior by opening up myisam/ftdefs.h and locating the line:

```
#define GWS_IN_USE GWS_PROB
```

Change this line to:

```
#define GWS_IN_USE GWS_FREQ
```

Recompile the MySQL source to your specifications, and this feature will be disabled. Note, however, that although this behavior might be more suitable to a user's expectations, it will effectively negate MySQL's ability to order results by relevancy when the MATCH() function is used in the WHERE clause.

Boolean FULLTEXT Searches

Boolean full-text searches offer more granular control over search queries, allowing you to explicitly identify which words should and should *not* be present in candidate results. For example, Boolean full-text searches can retrieve rows that possess the word *Apache*, but not *Navajo*, *Woodland*, or *Shawnee*. Similarly, you can ensure that results include at least one keyword, all keywords, or no keywords; you are free to exercise considerable filtering control over returned results. Such control is maintained via a number of recognized Boolean operators. Several of these operators are presented in Table 28-1.

Table 28-1. Full-Text Search Boolean Operators

OPERATOR	DESCRIPTION
+	A leading plus-sign ensures that the ensuing word is present in every result row.
-	A leading minus-sign ensures that the ensuing word is not present in any row returned.
*	A tailing asterisk allows for keyword variations, provided that the variation begins with the string specified by the preceding word.
" "	Surrounding double-quotes ensure that result rows contain that enclosed string, exactly as it was entered.
< >	Preceding greater-than and less-than symbols are used to decrease and increase an ensuing word's relevance to the search rankings, respectively.
( )	Parentheses are used to group words into subexpressions

Consider a few brief examples. The first example returns rows containing *Apache*, but not *manual*:

```
select name,url from webresource where match(description)
    against('+Apache -manual' in boolean mode);
```

The next example returns rows containing the word *Apache*, but not *Shawnee*, or *Navajo*:

```
select name, url from webresource where match(description)
    against('+Apache -Shawnee -Navajo' in boolean mode);
```

The final example returns rows containing *web* and *scripting,* or *php* and *scripting,* but ranks "web scripting" lower than "php scripting":

```
SELECT name, url FROM webresource WHERE MATCH(description)
   AGAINST(+(<web >php) +scripting);
```

Note that this last example will only work if you lower the ft_min_word_len parameter to 3.

Indexing Best Practices

The following list offers a few tips that you should always keep in mind when incorporating indexes into your database development strategy:

- Only index those columns that are required in WHERE and ORDER BY clauses. Indexing columns in abundance will only result in unnecessary consumption of hard drive space, and will actually slow performance when altering table information. Performance degradation will occur on indexed tables because every time a record is changed, the indexes must be updated.

- If you create an index such as INDEX(firstname, lastname), don't create INDEX(firstname), because MySQL is capable of searching an index prefix. However, keep in mind that only the prefix is relevant; this multiple-column index will not apply for searches that only target lastname.

- Use the attribute not null for those columns in which you plan on indexing, so that null values will never be stored.

- Use the --log-long-format option to log queries that aren't using indexes. You can then examine this log file and adjust your queries accordingly.

- The EXPLAIN statement helps you determine how MySQL will execute a query, showing you how and in what order tables are joined. This can be tremendously useful for determining how to write optimized queries, and whether indexes should be added. Please consult the MySQL manual for more information about the EXPLAIN statement.

Forms-Based Searches

The ability to easily drill down into a Web site using hyperlinks is one of the behaviors that made the Web such a popular media. However, as both Web sites and the Web grew exponentially in size, the ability to execute searches based on user-supplied keywords evolved from convenience to necessity. In this section, I'll offer several examples demonstrating how easy it is to build Web-based search interfaces for searching a MySQL database. To implement these examples, I'll continue many of the methods found in the MySQL data class first introduced in Chapter 27.

Performing a Simple Search

Many effective search interfaces involve a single text field. For example, suppose you want to provide the human resources department with the ability to look up employee contact information by last name. To implement this task, the query will examine the lastname column found in the employee table. A sample interface for doing so is shown in Figure 28-1.

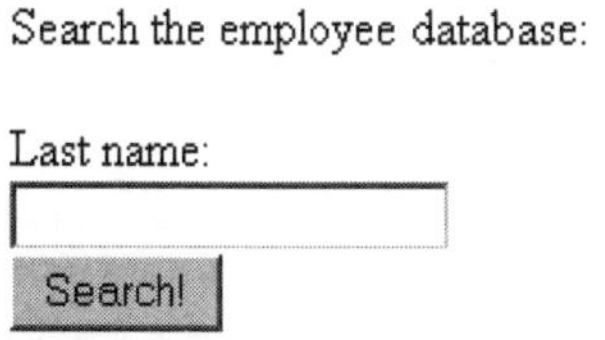

Search the employee database:

Last name:

Search!

Figure 28-1. A simple search interface

Listing 28-1 implements this interface, passing the requested last name into the search query. If the number of returned rows is greater than zero, each is output; otherwise, an appropriate message is offered.

Listing 28-1. Searching the Employee Table (simplesearch.php)

```
<p>
Search the employee database:<br />
<form action="simplesearch.php" method="post">
   Last name:<br />
   <input type="text" name="lastname" size="20" maxlength="40" value="" /><br />
   <input type="submit" value="Search!" />
</form>
</p>

<?php
   // If the form has been submitted with a supplied last name
   if (isset($_POST['lastname'])) {

      include "mysql.class.php";
      // Connect to server and select database
      $mysqldb = new mysql("localhost","jason","secret","company");
      $mysqldb->connect();
      $mysqldb->select();

      // Set the posted variable to a convenient name
      $lastname = $_POST['lastname'];

      // Query the employee table
      $mysqldb->query("SELECT firstname, lastname, email FROM employee
                  WHERE lastname='$lastname'");
```

```
        // If records found, output firstname, lastname, and email field of each
        if ($mysqldb->numrows() > 0) {
            while ($row = $mysqldb->fetchobject())
                echo "$row->lastname, $row->firstname ($row->email)<br />";
        } else {
            echo "No results found.";
        }
    }
?>
```

Therefore, entering *Gilmore* into the search interface would return results similar to the following:

Gilmore, Jason (gilmore@example.com)

Extending Search Capabilities

Although this simple search interface is effective, what happens if the user doesn't know the employee's last name? What if the user knows another piece of information, such as the e-mail address? I'll modify the original example so that it can handle input originating from the form depicted in Figure 28-2.

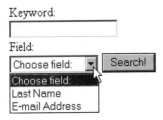

Figure 28-2. The search form revised

Listing 28-2 offers the code involved to implement these extended capabilities.

Listing 28-2. Extending the Search Capabilities (searchextended.php)

```
<p>
Search the employee database:<br />
<form action="searchextended.php" method="post">
    Keyword:<br />
    <input type="text" name="keyword" size="20" maxlength="40" value="" /><br />
    Field:<br />
```

```
    <select name="field">
        <option value="">Choose field:</option>
        <option value="lastname">Last Name</option>
        <option value="email">Email Address</option>
        </select>
    <input type="submit" value="Search!" />
</form>
</p>

<?php
    // If the form has been submitted with a supplied keyword
    if (isset($_POST['field'])) {

        include "mysql.class.php";
        // Connect to server and select database
        $mysqldb = new mysql("localhost","jason","secret","company");
        $mysqldb->connect();
        $mysqldb->select();

        // Set the posted variables to a convenient names
        $keyword = $_POST['keyword'];
        $field = $_POST['field'];

        // Create the query
        if ($field == "lastname" ) {
            $mysqldb->query("SELECT firstname, lastname, email
                        FROM employee WHERE lastname='$keyword'");
        } elseif ($field == "email") {
            $mysqldb->query("SELECT firstname, lastname, email
                        FROM employee WHERE email='$keyword'");
        }

        // If records found, output firstname, lastname, and email field of each
        if ($mysqldb->numrows() > 0) {
            while ($row = $mysqldb->fetchobject())
                echo "$row->lastname, $row->firstname ($row->email)<br />";
        } else {
            echo "No results found.";
        }
    }
?>
```

Therefore, setting the field to *Email Address* and inputting *gilmore@example.com* as the keyword would return results similar to the following:

```
Gilmore, Jason (gilmore@example.com)
```

Of course, in both examples, you'd need to put additional controls in place to sanitize data and ensure that the user receives detailed responses if he supplies invalid input. Nonetheless, the basic search process should be apparent.

Performing a Full-Text Search

Performing a full-text search is really no different from executing any other selection query; only the query looks different, a detail that remains hidden from the user. I'll implement the search interface depicted in Figure 28-3, demonstrating how to search the webresource table's description field.

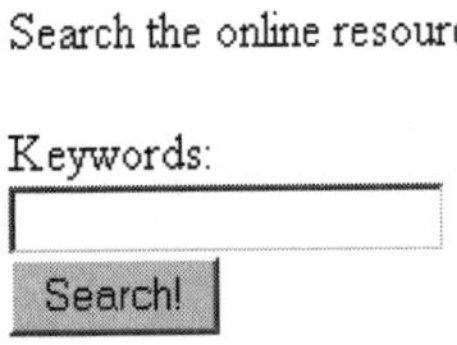

Search the online resources database:

Keywords:

[   ]

[Search!]

Figure 28-3. A full-text search interface

Listing 28-3 shows the code required to implement these full-text search capabilities.

Listing 28-3. Implementing Full-Text Search

```
<p>
Search the online resources database:<br />
<form action="fulltextsearch.php" method="post">
    Keywords:<br />
    <input type="text" name="keywords" size="20" maxlength="40" value="" /><br />
    <input type="submit" value="Search!" />
</form>
</p>

<?php
    // If the form has been submitted with supplied keywords
    if (isset($_POST['keywords'])) {
        include "mysql.class.php";
        // Connect to server and select database
        $mysqldb = new mysql("localhost","root","","company");
        $mysqldb->connect();
        $mysqldb->select();


        $keywords = $_POST['keywords'];
        // Create the query
        $mysqldb->query("SELECT name, url FROM webresource
                        WHERE MATCH(description) AGAINST('$keywords')");

        // Output retrieved rows or display appropriate message
        if ($mysqldb->numrows() > 0) {
            while ($row = $mysqldb->fetchobject())
```

```
            echo "<a href=\"$row->url\">$row->name</a><br />";
      } else {
         echo "No results found.";
      }
   }
}
?>
```

To extend the user's full-text search capabilities, consider offering a help page demonstrating MySQL's Boolean search features.

Summary

Table indexing is a sure-fire way to optimize queries. In this chapter, I introduced this topic, and showed you how to create primary, unique, normal, and full-text indexes. I then demonstrated how easy it is to create PHP-enabled search interfaces for querying your MySQL tables.

In the next chapter, I'll introduce MySQL's transactional feature, and show you how to incorporate transactions into your Web applications by extending the MySQL data class first introduced in Chapter 27.

## CHAPTER 29

Transactions

IN THIS CHAPTER, I'll introduce MySQL's transactional capabilities and demonstrate how transactions are executed both via a MySQL client and from within a PHP script. By its conclusion, you'll possess a general understanding of transactions, how they're implemented by MySQL, and how transactions can be used in your PHP applications. For starters, however, I'll formally define the transaction.

What's a Transaction?

A *transaction* is an ordered group of database operations that are perceived as a single unit. A transaction is deemed successful if all operations in the group succeed, and unsuccessful if even a single operation fails. If all operations complete successfully, that transaction will be *committed*, and its changes made available to all other database processes. If an operation fails, the transaction will be *rolled back*, and the effects of all operations comprising that transaction will be annulled. Any changes effected during a transaction will be made solely available to the thread owning that transaction, and will remain so until those changes are indeed committed. This prevents other threads from potentially making use of data that may soon be negated due to a rollback, which would result in a corruption of data integrity.

Transactional capabilities are a crucial part of enterprise databases, as many business processes consist of multiple steps. Take for example a customer's attempt to make an online purchase. At checkout time, his shopping cart will be compared against existing inventories to ensure availability. Next the customer must supply his billing and shipping information, at which point his credit card will be checked for the necessary available funds and then debited. Next, the product inventories will be deducted accordingly, and the shipping department will be notified of the pending order. If any of these steps fail, then none of them should occur. Imagine the customer's dismay to learn that his credit card had been debited, even though the product never arrives because of inadequate inventory. Likewise, you wouldn't want to deduct inventory or even ship the product if the credit card is invalid, or if insufficient shipping information was provided.

On more technical terms, a transaction is defined by its ability to follow four tenets, embodied in the acronym ACID. These four pillars of the transactional process are introduced here:

- **Atomicity:** All steps of the transaction must be successfully completed, otherwise none of the steps will be committed.

- **Consistency:** All steps the transaction must be successfully completed, or all data will revert to the state it was in before the transaction began.

- **Isolation:** The steps carried out by any as-of-yet incomplete transaction must remain isolated from the system until the transaction has been deemed complete.

- **Durability:** All committed data must be saved by the system in such a way that in the event of a system failure, the data can be successfully returned to a valid state.

As you learn more about MySQL's transactional support throughout this chapter, it will become apparent just how important it is that these tenets are followed in order to ensure database integrity.

MySQL's Transactional Capabilities

MySQL support for transactions started with version 3.23.34a and is enabled by default in all versions of MySQL 4.0 and greater. Transactions are supported by two of MySQL's table handlers: InnoDB and BDB, both of which were first introduced in Chapter 24. In this section, I'll explain transactions as applied to InnoDB, discussing the system requirements and configuration parameters available to the InnoDB handler. Next I'll offer a brief explanation regarding how exactly InnoDB goes about ensuring ACID-compliance. I'll conclude the section with a detailed usage example and a list of tips to keep in mind when working with InnoDB transactions. All of this sets the stage for the concluding part of this chapter, where I'll demonstrate how you can incorporate transactional capabilities into your PHP applications.

System Requirements

In this chapter, I'll focus on the transactions as applied to the InnoDB table handler, because its capabilities are enabled by default as of MySQL 4.0. You can verify whether InnoDB tables are made available to you by executing this command:

```
mysql>SHOW VARIABLES LIKE 'have_innodb';
```

You should see the following:

```
+---------------+-------+
| Variable_name | Value |
+---------------+-------+
| have_innodb   | YES   |
+---------------+-------+
1 row in set (0.00 sec)
```

If not, you'll need to upgrade your MySQL distribution to a version offering support for InnoDB. If you're still using a pre–4.0 version greater than 3.23.34, you can enable support by recompiling MySQL with the `--with-innodb` option.

Table Creation

Creating a table of type InnoDB is really no different from the process required to create a table of any other type. You simply make use of the CREATE TABLE statement, and create the table as you see fit. Note that unless the MySQL daemon is started with the --default-table-type=InnoDB flag, you're going to need to explicitly specify that you'd like the table to be created as an InnoDB type at the time of creation. For example:

```
CREATE TABLE customer (
->rowID SMALLINT UNSIGNED NOT NULL AUTO_INCREMENT,
->name VARCHAR(45) NOT NULL,
->PRIMARY KEY(rowID)
->) TYPE=InnoDB;
```

Once created, a *.frm file (in this example, a customer.frm file) is stored in the respective database directory, the location of which is denoted by MySQL's datadir parameter and defined at daemon startup. This file contains data dictionary information required by MySQL. Unlike MyISAM tables, however the InnoDB engine requires that all InnoDB data and index information is stored in a *tablespace*. This tablespace can actually consist of numerous disparate files (or even raw disk partitions), which are located by default in MySQL's datadir directory. This is a pretty powerful feature, because it means that you can create databases that far exceed that maximum allowable file size imposed by many operating systems by simply concatenating new files to the tablespace as necessary. How all of this behaves is dependent upon how you define the pertinent InnoDB configuration parameters, introduced next.

InnoDB Configuration Parameters

A number of configuration parameters are made available for tweaking InnoDB's behavior. I'll introduce these parameters in this section. Note that you should review and set many of these variables from the very start, as doing so will positively affect performance.

innodb_additional_mem_pool_size

In addition to caching table data and indexes, you can improve InnoDB performance by allocating cache memory to other internal items required for its operation. This memory can be allocated through this parameter. It's recommended that you set this to at least 2MB, although it should be increased accordingly in proportion to the number of InnoDB tables used in your project.

innodb_buffer_pool_size

This parameter is similar to MySQL's key_buffer parameter, but specific to InnoDB tables. It determines how much memory will be set aside to cache table data and indexes. Like key_buffer, higher settings improve performance, and should be increased accordingly as system RAM is added.

innodb_data_file_path

This parameter name is somewhat misleading, because it not only specifies paths to all InnoDB data files, but also the initial size allocation, maximum allocation, and whether the file size should be increased once it surpasses the starting allocation delimiter. The parameter's general format follows:

```
path-to-datafile:size-allocation[:autoextend[:max-size-allocation]]
```

For example, suppose you wanted to create a single datafile named myibdata1 with an initial size of 100MB and have it auto-extend an additional 8MB each time the current size limit is reached (8MB is the default extension value when autoextend is specified). However, you don't want this file to surpass 1GB:

```
innodb_data_home_dir =
innodb_data_file_path = /data/myibdata1:100M:autoextend:max:1GB
```

Later, you note that this file is indeed approaching the predesignated 1GB limit. You can then add another data file, like so:

```
innodb_data_home_dir =
innodb_data_file_path = /data2/myibdata1:100M:autoextend:max:1GB;
/data2/myibdata2:100M:autoextend:max:2GB;
```

Note that in these examples I first set innodb_data_home_dir to blank, because ultimately the data files resided in separate locations (/data/ and /data2/). If you'd like all InnoDB data files to reside in the same location, you can specify that common location using innodb_data_home_dir and then just provide the file names when designating them with innodb_data_file_path. Not defining these values at all will result in a file named ibdata1 being created in datadir.

innodb_data_home_dir

This parameter specifies the common part of the path in which the InnoDB table-spaces are to be created. By default, this is MySQL's default data directory, denoted by the MySQL parameter datadir.

innodb_file_io_threads

This parameter determines the number of file I/O threads available to InnoDB tables. The MySQL developers suggest a value of 4 for non-Windows platforms.

innodb_flush_log_at_trx_commit

Setting this parameter to 1 will result in the writing of the log to disk each time a transaction is committed. To improve performance, you could set this to either 0 or 2, at the risk of losing some data in the case of a crash. Setting it to 0 means that the transaction log is written to the log file and the log file is flushed to disk once per second. Setting it to 2 means that the transaction log is written to the log with each commit, but the log file is flushed to disk once per second.

innodb_log_archive

Because MySQL currently recovers InnoDB tables using its own log files, this parameter should be set to 0.

innodb_log_arch_dir

MySQL currently ignores this parameter, although it may be used in subsequent releases. Presently, it should be set to the same value as set for innodb_log_group_home_dir.

innodb_log_buffer_size

This parameter determines the size in megabytes of RAM used for writing log files. Larger buffer sizes improve performance, although an unexpected crash could result in lost table data. The MySQL developers suggest values ranging between 1MB and 8MB.

innodb_log_file_size

This parameter determines the size of database log files in megabytes. Larger settings improve general performance but also increase the time required to restore a crashed database.

innodb_log_files_in_group

To improve performance, MySQL can write log information to several files in a circular fashion. The developers recommend setting this parameter to 3.

innodb_log_group_home_dir

This parameter determines the location of the files specific to a log group, the number of which is determined by innodb_log_files_in_group. By default, this location is set to MySQL's datadir.

innodb_lock_wait_timeout

InnoDB has its own built-in deadlock detection mechanisms, which result in a rollback of the pending transaction. However, if you use MySQL's LOCK TABLES statement or some third-party transactional engine in conjunction with InnoDB, InnoDB will be unable to recognize the deadlock. To eliminate this possibility, you can set innodb_lock_wait_timeout to an integer value signifying the number of seconds MySQL will wait before allowing other transactions to modify data that could ultimately be affected by a transaction rollback.

skip-innodb

Enabling this parameter prevents the InnoDB table driver from being loaded, a recommended step when you're not using InnoDB tables.

Sample Project

I'll illustrate the topics discussed throughout this chapter by basing the examples on a few relevant components of an online swap meet. I'll prepare for these examples by creating two InnoDB tables: participant and trunk in a database named company. The purpose of each table, along with the structure, is presented here. Once you've created the tables, take a moment to add some sample data, also provided in the following section.

The participant Table

This table stores information about each of the swap meet participants, including their names, e-mail addresses, and available cash.

```
CREATE TABLE participant (
->rowID SMALLINT UNSIGNED NOT NULL AUTO_INCREMENT,
->name VARCHAR(35) NOT NULL,
->email VARCHAR(45) NOT NULL,
->cash DECIMAL(5,2) NOT NULL,
->PRIMARY KEY(rowID)
->) TYPE=InnoDB;
```

The trunk Table

This table stores information about each item owned by the participants, including the owner, name, description, and price.

```
CREATE TABLE trunk (
->rowID SMALLINT UNSIGNED NOT NULL  AUTO_INCREMENT,
->owner SMALLINT UNSIGNED NOT NULL REFERENCES participant(rowID),
->name VARCHAR(25) NOT NULL,
->price DECIMAL(5,2) NOT NULL,
->description MEDIUMTEXT NOT NULL,
->PRIMARY KEY(rowID)
->) TYPE=InnoDB;
```

Adding Some Sample Data

Next, add a few rows of data to all three tables. To keep things simple, add two participants, Jason and Jon, and a few items for their respective trunks.

```
mysql>INSERT INTO participant SET name="Jason",
       ->email="jason@example.com", cash="100.00";
mysql>INSERT INTO participant SET name="Jon",
       ->email="jon@example.com", cash="150.00";
mysql>INSERT INTO trunk SET owner=2, name="Abacus", price="12.99",
       ->description="Low on computing power? Use an abacus!";
mysql>INSERT INTO trunk SET owner=2, name="Magazines", price="6.00",
       ->description="Stack of computer magazines.";
mysql>INSERT INTO trunk SET owner=1, name="Lottery ticket", price="1.00",
       ->description="Great gift for the eternal optimist.";
```

A Simple Example

To get better acquainted with exactly how InnoDB tables behave, I'll run through a simple transactional example from the command line. This example will demonstrate how two swap meet participants would go about exchanging an item for cash. Before examining the code, take a moment to review the pseudocode:

1. Participant Jason requests an item, say the abacus located in participant Jon's virtual trunk.

2. Participant Jason transfers a cash amount of $12.99 to participant Jon's account. The effect of this is the debiting of the amount from Jason's account, and the crediting of an equivalent amount to Jon's account.

3. Ownership of the abacus is transferred to participant Jason.

As you can see, each step of the process is crucial to the overall success of the procedure. Therefore, we'll turn the process into a transaction to ensure that our data cannot become corrupted due to the failure of a single step. Although in a real-life scenario there are other steps, such as ensuring that the purchasing participant possesses adequate funds, I'll keep the process simple so as not to detract from the main topic.

You start the transaction process by issuing the START TRANSACTION command:

```
mysql>START TRANSACTION;
Query OK, 0 rows affected (0.00 sec)
```

NOTE *The command BEGIN is an alias of* START TRANSACTION. *Although both accomplish the same task, it's recommended that you use the latter, because it conforms to SQL-99 syntax.*

Next, deduct an amount of $12.99 from Jason's account:

```
mysql>UPDATE participant SET cash=cash-12.99 WHERE rowID=1;
Query OK, 1 row affected (0.00 sec)
```

Next, credit an amount of $12.99 to Jon's account:

```
mysql>UPDATE participant SET cash=cash+12.99 WHERE rowID=2;
Query OK, 1 row affected (0.00 sec)
```

Next, transfer ownership of the abacus to Jason:

```
mysql>UPDATE trunk SET owner=1 WHERE name="Abacus" AND owner=2;
Query OK, 1 row affected (0.00 sec)
```

Take a moment to check the participant table to ensure that the cash amount has been debited and credited correctly.

```
mysql>SELECT * FROM participant;
```

This returns:

```
+-------+-------+-------------------+--------+
| rowID | name  | email             | cash   |
+-------+-------+-------------------+--------+
|     1 | Jason | jason@example.com |  87.01 |
|     2 | Jon   | jon@example.com   | 162.99 |
+-------+-------+-------------------+--------+
2 rows in set (0.01 sec)
```

Also take a moment to check the trunk table; you'll see that ownership of the abacus has indeed changed. Keep in mind, however, that because InnoDB tables must follow the ACID tenets, this change is currently only available to the thread executing the transaction. To illustrate this point, start up a second mysql client, again logging in and changing to the company database. Check out the participant table. You'll see that the participant's respective cash values remain unchanged. Checking the trunk table will also show that ownership of the abacus has not changed. This is because of the isolation component of the ACID test. Until you COMMIT the change, any changes made during the transaction process will not be made available to other threads.

Although the updates indeed worked correctly, suppose that one or several had not. Return to the first client window and negate the changes by issuing the command ROLLBACK:

```
mysql>ROLLBACK;
```

Now again execute the SELECT command:

```
mysql>SELECT * FROM participant;
```

This returns:

```
+-------+-------+-------------------+--------+
| rowID | name  | email             | cash   |
+-------+-------+-------------------+--------+
|     1 | Jason | jason@example.com | 100.00 |
|     2 | Jon   | jon@example.com   | 150.00 |
+-------+-------+-------------------+--------+
2 rows in set (0.00 sec)
```

Note that the participant's cash holdings have been reset to their original values. Checking the trunk table will also show that ownership of the abacus has not changed. Try repeating the above process anew, this time committing the changes using the COMMIT command rather than rolling them back. Once the transaction is committed, return again to the second client and review the tables; you'll see that the committed changes are made immediately available.

> **NOTE** *You should realize that until the COMMIT or ROLLBACK commands are issued, any data changes taking place during a transactional sequence will not take effect. This means that if the MySQL server crashes before committing the changes, the changes will not take place, and you'll need to start the transactional series for those changes to occur.*

In a later section, we'll re-create this process using a PHP script.

Backing Up and Restoring InnoDB Tables

You can back up your InnoDB tables in three ways:

- Perform a binary backup of your database by shutting down MySQL and copying all of your InnoDB data files, log files, and .frm files to a safe place.

- Take a snapshot of just the tables with the mysqldump command. Although InnoDB data is collectively stored in a tablespace, you can use mysqldump to take a current snapshot of an InnoDB table just like you would with an MyISAM table.

- Use MySQL's replication features, with which InnoDB tables integrate seamlessly.

Data restoration is also accomplished in a variety of ways. Three commonly practiced methods follow:

- If the MySQL daemon crashes, InnoDB will execute its own restore process when the daemon restarts.

- If you'd like to recover a MySQL database to the location as specified by the most recent binary backup, you can use the mysqlbinlog client.

- If you used mysqldump to create a snapshot of the table(s), you could simply drop the table and re-create it by feeding the dump file back into MySQL like so:

```
%>mysql -u root -p databasename < dumpfile.sql
```

Usage Tips

In this section, I'll offer some tips to keep in mind when using MySQL transactions.

- Issuing the START TRANSACTION command is the same as setting the AUTOCOMMIT variable to 0. The default is AUTOCOMMIT=1, which means that each statement is committed as soon as it's successfully executed. This is the reasoning for beginning your transaction with the START TRANSACTION command, because you don't want each component of a transaction to be committed upon execution.

- Only use transactions when it's critical that the entire process executes successfully. For example, the process for adding a product to a shopping cart is critical; browsing all available products is not. Take such matters into account when designing your tables, because it will affect performance.

- You cannot roll back data-definition language statements; that is, any statement used to create or drop a database, or create, drop, or alter tables.

- Transactions cannot be nested. Issuing multiple START TRANSACTION commands before a COMMIT or ROLLBACK will have no effect.

- If you update a non-transactional table during the process of a transaction and then conclude that transaction by issuing ROLLBACK, an error will be returned, notifying you that the non-transactional table will not be rolled back.

- Take regular snapshots of your InnoDB data and logs by backing up the binary log files, as well as using mysqldump to take a snapshot of the data found in each table.

Building Transactional Applications with PHP

Integrating MySQL's transactional capabilities into your PHP applications really isn't any major affair; you just need to remember to start the transaction at the appropriate time and then either commit or roll back the transaction once the relevant operations have completed. In this section, I'll demonstrate the general methodology for conducting transactions with PHP. By its completion, you should be quite familiar with the general process involved for incorporating this important feature into your applications.

Of course, you should continue using our MySQL class first created in Chapter 27. Therefore, begin by adding three additional methods to your mysql class: begintransaction(), commit(), and rollback(), the purposes of each should be quite self-explanatory by now.

```
function begintransaction() {
    $this->query("START TRANSACTION");
}
function commit() {
    $this->query("COMMIT");
}

function rollback() {
    $this->query("ROLLBACK");
}
```

Because these commands typically don't result in errors, I'll forego incorporating exception handling.

Beware of mysql_query()

The mysql_query() function behaves in a fashion that perhaps isn't as intuitive as you might think. Not completely understanding its behavior can play major havoc in your transactional logic. The confusion arises from the manner in which it determines success and failure. For DESCRIBE, EXPLAIN, SELECT, and SHOW queries, mysql_query() returns a resource identifier on success and FALSE on error. Makes sense, right? However, for all other types of queries (INSERT, UPDATE, DELETE, etc.), mysql_query()

returns TRUE on success and FALSE on error. This also makes sense, except that TRUE simply means that the query was legal. It does not necessarily mean that anything occurred. For example, I might execute the following:

```
$query = "UPDATE participant SET name = 'Gilmore' WHERE name='Don'";
echo mysql_query($query);
```

Based on the test information you inserted at the beginning of this chapter, this query will not update any rows, because there is no participant listed by the name of "Don." However, mysql_query() nonetheless returns TRUE, because the query was valid. This could be a major problem when it comes to transactions, because you need to know for sure whether the intended outcome has occurred. To handle the transaction properly, you need to both check for proper query execution and determine whether any rows were affected. You can do this with the function mysql_affected_rows(), first introduced in Chapter 26. For example, you could rewrite this code to determine whether or not the query was valid and whether any row was affected, like so:

```
$query = "UPDATE participant SET name = 'Gilmore' WHERE name='Don'";
$result = mysql_query($query);
if ($result AND mysql_affected_rows($result) == 1) echo "TRUE";
else echo "FALSE";
```

This would return FALSE.

This concept is key to using MySQL database transactions in conjunction with PHP, so it will be incorporated into the following example.

The Swap Meet Revisited

In this example, you'll recreate the previously demonstrated swap meet scenario, this time using PHP. Keeping the non-relevant details to a minimum, the page would display a product and offer the user the means for adding that item to their shopping cart; it might look like this:

```
<p>
    <strong>Abacus</strong><br />
    Owner: Jon<br />
    Price: $12.99<br />
    Low on computing power? Use an abacus!<br />
    <form action="purchase.php" method="post">
        <input type="hidden" name="itemid" value="1" />
        <br />
        <input type="submit" value="Purchase!" />
    </form>
</p>
```

As you would imagine, the data displayed in this page could easily be extracted from the participant and trunk tables in the database. Rendered in the browser, this page would look like Figure 29-1.

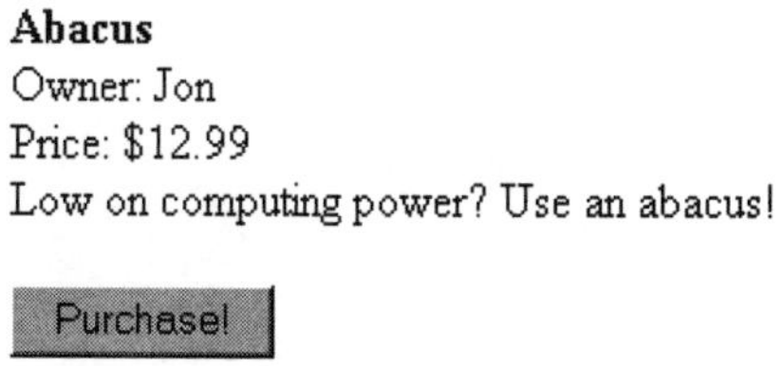

Abacus
Owner: Jon
Price: $12.99
Low on computing power? Use an abacus!

[Purchase!]

Figure 29-1. A typical product display

Clicking the Purchase! button would take the user to the purchase.php script. One variable is passed along, namely $_POST['itemid']. Using this variable in conjunction with some hypothetical class methods for retrieving the participant and trunk item primary keys, you can use MySQL transactions to add the product to the database and deduct and credit the participants' accounts accordingly.

Listing 29-1. Swapping Items with purchase.php

```php
<?php
    session_start();
    include "mysql.class.php";
    /* Retrieve the participant's primary key using some fictitious
       class that refers to some sort of user session table,
       mapping a session ID back to a specific user.
    */
    $participant = new participant();
    $buyerid = $participant->getparticipantkey();

    /* Give the POSTed item id a friendly variable name */
    $itemid = $_POST['itemid'];

    /* Retrieve the item seller and price using some fictitious item class. */
    $item = new item();
    $sellerid = $item->getitemowner ($itemid);
    $price = $item->getprice($itemid);

    // Instantiate the mysql class
    $mysqldb = new mysql("localhost","webuser","secret","company");

    // Connect to the MySQL server and select the database
    $mysqldb->connect();
    $mysqldb->select();
```

```
// Start by assuming the transaction operations will all succeed
$transactionsuccess = TRUE;

// Start the transaction
$mysqldb->begintransaction();

/* Debit buyer's account. */

$query = "UPDATE participant SET cash=cash-$price WHERE rowID='$buyerid'";
$result = $mysqldb->query($query) ;
if (!$result OR $result->affectedrows() != 1 )
   $transactionsuccess = FALSE;

/* Credit seller's account. */
$query = "UPDATE participant SET cash=cash+$price WHERE rowID='$sellerid'";
$result = $mysqldb->query($query) ;
if (!$result OR $result->affectedrows() != 1 )
   $transactionsuccess = FALSE;

/* Update trunk item ownership. If it fails, set
   $transactionsuccess to FALSE. */
$query = "UPDATE trunk SET owner='$buyerid'
        WHERE rowid='$itemid'";
$result = $mysqldb->query($query) ;
if (!$result OR $result->affectedrows() != 1 )
   $transactionsuccess = FALSE;

/* If $transactionsuccess is TRUE, commit the transaction, otherwise
   roll back the changes.
*/
if ($transactionsuccess) {
   $mysqldb->commit();
   echo "The swap took place! Congratulations!";
} else {
   $mysqldb->rollback();
   echo "There was a problem with the swap!";
}
?>
```

As you can see, both the status of the query and the affected rows were checked after the execution of each step of the transaction. If either failed at any time, $transactionsuccess was set to FALSE and all steps were rolled back at the conclusion of the script. Of course, you could optimize this script to start each query in lockstep, taking place only after it was determined that the prior had in fact correctly executed, but I'll leave that exercise to you.

Summary

Database transactions are of immense use when modeling your business processes, because they help to ensure the integrity of your organization's most valuable asset: its information. If you use them prudently, they are a great asset to keep in mind when building database-driven applications.

In the next and final chapter, not only will I demonstrate just how easy it is to use MySQL's default utilities to both import and export large amounts of data, but I'll also show you how to use simple PHP scripts to do cool things such as format forms-based information for viewing via a spreadsheet application, such as Microsoft Excel.

CHAPTER 30

Importing and Exporting Data

BACK IN THE STONE AGE, cavemen never really had any issues with data incompatibility, as stones and one's own memory were the only storage medium. Copying data involved pulling out the old chisel and getting busy on a new slab of granite. Now, of course, the situation is much different. Hundreds of data storage strategies exist, the most commonplace of which include spreadsheets and various types of databases. Working in a complex, often convoluted fashion, you often need to convert data from one storage type to another, say between a spreadsheet and a relational database, or between an Oracle database and MySQL. If this is done poorly, you could spend hours, and even days and weeks massaging the converted data into a useable format. This chapter seeks to eliminate that conundrum, introducing MySQL's data import and export utilities, as well as various techniques and concepts central to lessening the pain involved in performing such tasks.

By the conclusion of this chapter, you should be familiar with the following topics:

- Common data formatting standards recognized by most mainstream storage products

- The `select into outfile` SQL statement

- The `load data infile` SQL statement

- The `mysqlimport` utility

- How to use PHP to mimic MySQL's built-in import utilities

Before delving into the core topics, I'll take a moment to review the sample data used as the basis for examples used in this chapter. Afterwards, I'll review the basic concepts surrounding MySQL's import and export strategies.

Sample Table

If you would like to execute the examples as you proceed through the chapter, the following table will be the focus of each demonstration:

```
CREATE TABLE sales (
    orderNumber INT UNSIGNED NOT NULL AUTO_INCREMENT,
    purchaseTimeStamp TIMESTAMP NOT NULL,
    productID VARCHAR(10) NOT NULL,
    quantity SMALLINT NOT NULL,
    PRIMARY KEY(orderNumber));
```

This table is used to track basic sales information for some hypothetical company. Although it lacks some of the columns you might find in a real-world implementation, I'll forego a somewhat more practical representation in an attempt to keep the focus on the concepts introduced in this chapter.

Attaining a Happy Medium

Even if you're a burgeoning programmer, you're probably already quite familiar with software's exacting demands when it comes to data. All i's must be dotted and t's crossed; a single out-of-place character is enough to produce unexpected results. Therefore, you can imagine the issues that might arise when attempting to convert data from one format to another. Thankfully, a particular formatting strategy has become commonplace: delimitation.

Information structures like database tables and spreadsheets share a similar conceptual organization. Each is broken down into rows and columns, each of which is further broken down into cells. Therefore, you can convert between formats as long as you institute a set of rules for determining how the columns, rows, and cells are recognized. An application utility will read in this data, and make the conversions necessary for adapting the data to its own formatting standards. Typically, two characters or character sequences are used as delimiters, separating each cell within a row, and each row from the following. For example, a table with fields delimited by commas and rows delimited by the newline character might look like this:

```
345,2003-06-19 01:13:42,3005xl,4
346,2003-06-19 01:35:04,1223m,1
347,2003-06-19 04:20:38,3005m,2
```

Many data import and export utilities revolve around the concept of data delimitation, MySQL's included.

Exporting Data

As your computing environments grow increasingly complex, you'll probably need to share your data among various disparate systems and applications. Sometimes you won't be able to cull this information from a central source; rather, it must be constantly retrieved from the database, prepped for conversion, and finally converted into a format recognized by target. In this section, I'll show you how to easily export MySQL data using the SQL statement select into outfile.

> **NOTE** *Another commonly used data export tool, mysqldump, is introduced in Chapter 23. Although officially it's intended for data backup, it serves a secondary purpose as a great tool for creating data export files.*

select into outfile

The select into outfile SQL statement is actually a variant of the SELECT query. It's used when you want to direct query output to a text file. This file can then be opened by a spreadsheet application, or imported into another database like Microsoft Access, Oracle, or any other software supporting delimitation. Its general syntax format follows:

```
SELECT [select options go here] INTO {OUTFILE  | DUMPFILE} filename
    export_options
    FROM table_references [additional select options go here]
```

I'll introduce the key command options here:

- OUTFILE: Selecting this option results in the query result being output to the text file. The formatting of the query result is dependent upon how the EXPORT OPTIONS are set. These options are introduced below.

- DUMPFILE: Selecting this option over OUTFILE results in the query results being written as a single line, omitting column or line terminations. This is useful when exporting binary data such as a graphic or a Word file. Keep in mind that you cannot choose OUTFILE when exporting a binary file, or the file will be corrupted. Also, note that a DUMPFILE query must target a single row; combining output from two binary files doesn't make any sense, and an error will be returned if you attempt it. Specifically, the error returned is, "Result consisted of more than one row."

- EXPORT OPTIONS: The export options determine how the table fields and lines will be delimited in the outfile. Their syntax and rules match exactly those used in load data infile, introduced later in this chapter. Rather than repeat this information, please see that section for a complete dissertation.

Usage Tips

There are a few items worth noting regarding use of select into outfile:

- If a target file path is not specified, MySQL's data directory will be used.

- The executing user must possess the selection privilege (SELECT_PRIV) for the target table(s).

- If a target file path is specified, the MySQL daemon owner must possess adequate privileges to write to the target directory.

- One particularly odd side effect of this process leaves the target file world-writeable. This is because the MySQL server daemon user can't create a file owned by anyone else other than itself. Therefore the file must be made world-writeable so that its contents can be manipulated.

- The query will fail if the target text file already exists.

- Export options cannot be included if the target text file is a DUMPFILE.

A Simple Example

I'll start with a simple example, and then conclude this section on a somewhat more practical note. Suppose you wanted to export January, 2003 sales data to a tab-delimited text file, consisting of lines delimited by newline characters:

```
SELECT * INTO OUTFILE /intranet/www/sales/0103.txt
      FIELDS TERMINATED BY '\t' LINES TERMINATED BY '\n'
      FROM company.sales
      WHERE MONTH(saleDate) = '1' AND YEAR(saleDate) = '2003';
```

Assuming that the executing user has select privileges for the sales table found in the company database, and the mysql daemon process owner can write to the /intranet/www/sales/ directory, the 0103.txt file will be created, with the following data written to it:

```
3454    2003-01-01 00:43:15    4421y   4
3455    2003-01-15 01:15:24    5433zb  3
3456    2003-01-27 01:15:24    9873m   12
```

Exporting MySQL Data to Microsoft Excel

Now I'll provide a highly practical example, one that I use on a regular basis. Suppose the marketing department would like to draw a parallel between a recent sidewalk graffiti campaign and a recent rise in sales. To do so, they require the sales data for the month of July. Of course, a marketing meeting would be nothing without pie charts; therefore, they'd like the data provided in Excel format. Because Excel can convert delimited text files, you execute the following query:

```
SELECT * INTO OUTFILE "/www/intranet/spreadsheets/july-sales.xls"
    FIELDS TERMINATED BY '\t', LINES TERMINATED BY '\n' FROM sales
    WHERE MONTH(purchaseTimeStamp) = '7';
```

This file is then retrieved via a predefined folder located on the corporate intranet, and opened in Microsoft Excel. A window similar to Figure 30-1 will appear.

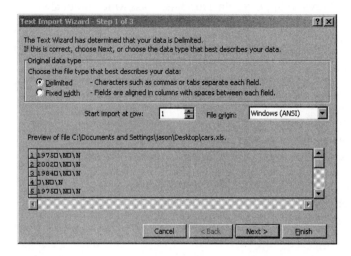

Figure 30-1. Microsoft Excel's Text Import Wizard

If it isn't already selected, choose the Delimited radio button, and proceed to the next window, the second step of the Text Import Wizard. That window is shown in Figure 30-2.

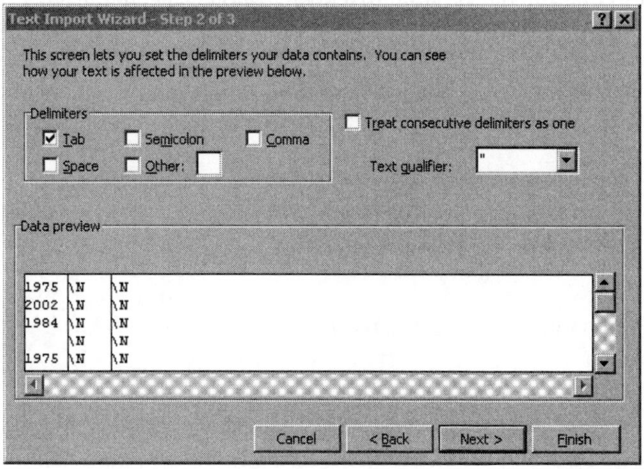

Figure 30-2. Choosing the delimiter in Excel

Figure 30-2 displays the second step of the Text Import Wizard. In this step, you'll choose the cell delimiter specified in the select into outfile statement. Clicking Next takes you to the final screen, where you'll have the opportunity to convert any of the imported columns to one of Excel's supported data formats; a task which is not always necessary, so I'll forego including this screen shot. Click Finish, and the data will open up in normal Excel fashion.

In the next section, I'll switch directions a bit; you'll learn how to migrate delimited data from third-party sources into MySQL.

Importing Data

If you've invested the time to read this book, I can imagine that you're planning on making MySQL a significant part of your application infrastructure. Therefore, you're probably already thinking about how you're going to migrate existing data, possibly from several sources, into your new database environment. In this section, you'll learn about the two built-in tools MySQL offers for importing delimited datasets into a table: load data infile and mysqlimport.

> **TIP** *You might use the* mysqlimport *client in lieu of* load data infile *when you need to create batch imports executed from a* cron *job.*

load data infile

The load data infile statement, a command executed much like a query is within the mysql client, is used to import delimited text files into a MySQL table. Its generalized syntax follows:

```
LOAD DATA [LOW_PRIORITY | CONCURRENT] [LOCAL] INFILE 'FILE_NAME.TXT'
[REPLACE | IGNORE]
INTO TABLE TABLE_NAME
[FIELDS
    [TERMINATED BY 'CHARACTER'] [[OPTIONALLY] ENCLOSED BY 'CHARACTER']
    [ESCAPED BY 'CHARACTER']
]
[LINES
    [STARTING BY 'CHARACTER'] [TERMINATED BY 'CHARACTER']
]
[IGNORE NUMBER LINES]
[(COLUMN_NAME, ...)]
```

Certainly one of MySQL's longer query commands you've seen thus far, isn't it? Yet it's this wide array of options that make this feature so powerful. I'll break each component down:

- `LOW PRIORITY`: This option forces execution of the command to be delayed until no other clients are reading from the table.

- `CONCURRENT`: Used in conjunction with a MyISAM table, this option allows other threads to retrieve data from the target table while the command is executing.

- `LOCAL`: This option declares that the target infile must reside on the same server as the client executing the command. If omitted, the target infile must reside on the same server hosting the MySQL database.

- `REPLACE`: This option results in the replacement of existing rows with new rows possessing identical primary or unique keys.

- `IGNORE`: Including this option has the opposite effect of `REPLACE`. Read-in rows with primary or unique keys matching an existing table row will be ignored.

- `FIELDS TERMINATED BY 'character'`: This option signals how fields will be terminated. Therefore, `TERMINATED BY ','` means that each field will end with a comma, like so:

```
24,2003-09-27 14:45:05,4746xxl,9
```

  Note that the last field does not end in the comma character. This is because it isn't necessary, as typically this option is used in conjunction with the `LINES TERMINATED BY 'character'` option. Encountering the character specified by this other option by default also delimits the last field in the file, as well as signals to the command that a new line (row) is about to begin.

- `[OPTIONALLY] ENCLOSED BY 'character'`: This option signals that each field will be enclosed by a particular character. Note that this does not eliminate the need for a terminating character. Revising the previous example, using the option `FIELDS TERMINATED BY ',' ENCLOSED BY '"'` implies that each field is enclosed by a pair of double quotes, and delimited by a comma, like so:

```
"24","2003-09-27 14:45:05","4746xxl","9"
```

  The optional `OPTIONALLY` flag denotes that character strings only require enclosure by the specified character pattern. Fields containing only integers, floats, and so on need not be enclosed.

- ESCAPED BY `'character'`: In the case that the character denoted by the ENCLOSED BY option appears within any of the fields, it must be escaped to ensure that the field is not incorrectly read in. However, this escape character must be defined by ESCAPED BY so that it can be recognized by the command. For example, FIELDS TERMINATED BY `','` ENCLOSED BY `''` ESCAPED BY `'\\'` would allow the following fields to be properly parsed:

```
'jason@wjgilmore.com', 'I\'ll return to your Website everyday!',
'Five stars'
```

- LINES: The following two options are pertinent to how lines are started and terminated, respectively:

  - STARTING BY `'character'`: This option defines the character intended to signal the beginning of a line, and thus a new table row. My experience has been that use of this option is skipped in preference to the next option.

  - TERMINATED BY `'character'`: This option defines the character intended to signal the conclusion of a line, and thus the end of a table row. Although it could conceivably be anything, this character is most often the newline (\n) character. In many Windows-based files, the newline character is often represented as \r\n.

- IGNORE *x* LINES: This option tells the command to ignore the first *x* lines. This is useful when the target file contains header information.

- [(column_name,...)]: If the number of fields located in the target file does not match the fields in the target table, you'll need to specify exactly which columns are to be filled in by the file data. For example, if the target file containing sales information only consisted of two fields, purchaseTimeStamp and quantity, rather than the four fields used in prior examples (orderNumber, purchaseTimeStamp, productID, quantity), yet in the target table all four fields remained, the command would have to be written like so:

```
load data local infile 'sales.txt'
into table cars (purchaseTimeStamp, quantity);
```

> **TIP** *If you would like the order of the fields located in the target file to be rearranged as they are read in for insertion into the table, you can do so by rearranging the order via this option.*

A Simple Example

I'll present a basic example, revolving around the sales theme. Suppose you want to import a file titled productreviews.txt, which contains the following information:

```
'43','wj@wjgilmore.com','I love the new Website!'
'44','areader@example.com','Why don\'t you sell shoes?'
'45','anotherreader@example.com','The search engine works great!'
```

The target table, aptly titled productreviews, has three fields, and they are in the same order (commentID, email, comment) as the information found in cars.txt.

```
load local data infile 'productreviews.txt' INTO TABLE productreviews FIELDS
TERMINATED BY ',' ENCLOSED BY '\'' ESCAPED BY '\\' LINES TERMINATED BY '\n';
```

Choosing the Target Database

In the example shown above, you might have noticed that although I referred to the target table, the target database was not clearly defined. This is because load data infile will assume that target table resides in the currently selected database. Alternatively, you can specify the target database by prefixing it with the database name, like so:

```
load local data infile 'cars.txt' into table inventory.cars;
```

If you execute load data infile before choosing a database, or without explicitly specifying the database in the query syntax, an error will occur.

Security and load data infile

There are a few security issues that you should keep in mind regarding load data infile:

- The executing user must possess the FILE privilege.

- If you want to read files residing on a connecting client, (load data local infile) you can disable it altogether by starting the mysqld daemon with --local-infile=0.

- The infile must reside either within MySQL's data directory, or be world-readable.

mysqlimport

The mysqlimport client is really just a command-line version of the load data infile SQL query. Its general syntax follows:

```
%>mysqlimport [options] database textfile1 [textfile2 ... textfileN]
```

Useful Options

Before reviewing any examples, I'll take a moment to explain the many options offered by mysqlimport:

- --columns, -c: This option should be used when the number or ordering of the fields in the target file do not match those found in the table. For example, suppose you were inserting the following target file:

```
3005x1,2003-06-19 01:13:42,4,789
1223m,2003-06-19 01:35:04,1,790
3005m,2003-06-19 04:20:38,2,791
```

Yet the table listed the fields in the orderID, purchaseTimeStamp, productID, and quantity. Therefore, you can rearrange the input fields during the parsing process so that the data is inserted in the proper location by including this option:

```
--columns=productID,purchaseTimeStamp,quantity,orderID
```

- --compress, -C: Including this option compresses the data flowing between the client and the server, assuming that both support compression. This option is most effective if you're loading a target file that does not reside on the same server as the database.

- --debug, -#: This option is used to create trace files when debugging.

- --delete, -d: This option deletes the target table's contents before importing the target file's data.

- --fields-terminated-by=, --fields-enclosed-by=, --fields-optionally-enclosed-by=, --lines-terminated-by=: These four options determine mysqlimport's behavior in terms of how both fields and lines are recognized during the parsing procedure. See the command load data infile, introduced earlier in this chapter, for a complete introduction.

- --force, -f: Including this option causes mysqlimport to continue execution even if errors occur during execution.

- --help: Including this option generates a short help file, and a comprehensive list of the options discussed in this section.

- --host, -h: This option specifies the server location of the target database. The default is localhost.

- --ignore, -i: This option causes mysqlimport to ignore any rows located in the target file that share the same primary or unique key as a row already located in the table.

- --ignore-lines=*n*: This option tells mysqlimport to ignore the first *n* lines of the target file. It's useful when the target file contains header information that should be disregarded.

- --lock-tables, -l: This option write-locks all tables located in the target database for the duration of mysqlimport's execution.

- --local, -L: This option specifies that the target file is located on the client. By default, it is assumed that this file is located on the database server; therefore, you'll need to include this option if you're executing this command remotely, and have not uploaded the file to the server.

- --*password=your_password*, *-pyour_password:* This option is used to specify the password component of your authentication credentials. If the *your_password* part of this option is omitted, you will be prompted for the password.

- --port, -P: If the target MySQL server is running on a nonstandard port (MySQL's standard port is 3306), you need to specify that port value with this option.

- --replace, -r: This option causes mysqlimport to overwrite any rows located in the target file that share the same primary or unique key as a row already located in the table.

- --silent, -s: This option tells mysqlimport to output only error information.

- --socket, -S: This option should be included if a nondefault socket file had been declared when the MySQL server was started.

- --user, -u: By default, mysqlimport compares the name/host combination of the executing system user to the mysql privilege tables, ensuring that the executing user possesses adequate permissions to carry out the requested operation. Because it's often useful to perform such procedures under the guise of another user, you can specify the "user" component of credentials with this option.

- `--verbose`, `-v`: This option causes `mysqlimport` to output a host of potentially useful information pertinent to its behavior.

- `--version`, `-V`: This option causes `mysqlimport` to output version information and exit.

A Simple Example

A simple demonstration of `mysqlimport` involves the update of inventory audit information from the workstation of an accountant located in the fictitious company's fiscal department to the MySQL intranet database:

```
%>mysqlimport -h intranet.example.com  -u fiscal -p --replace --compress --local \
 ->company C:\audit\inventory.txt
```

This command, executed at will by the accountant, results in the compression and transmission of the data found in the local text file (`C:\audit\inventory.txt`) to the table inventory located in the company database. Note that `mysqlimport` will strip the extension from each text file, and use the resulting name as the table into which to import the text file's contents.

A Practical Example

Some time ago, I was asked to build a corporate Web site for a pharmaceutical corporation that, among other things, allowed buyers to browse descriptions and pricing information for roughly 10,000 products. This information was maintained on a mainframe, and the data was synchronized on a regular basis to the MySQL database residing on the Web server. To accomplish this, I set up a one-way trust between the machines, and created two shell scripts: the first, located on the mainframe, was responsible for dumping the data (in delimited format) from the mainframe, and then pushing this data file via sftp to the Web server. The second script, located on the Web server, was responsible for executing `mysqlimport`, loading this file to the MySQL database. This script was quite trivial to create, and looked like this:

```
#!/bin/sh
/usr/local/mysql/bin/mysqlimport --delete --silent \
--fields-terminated-by='\t' --lines-terminated-by='\n' \
products /ftp/uploads/products.txt
```

To keep the logic involved to a bare minimum, I executed a complete dump of the entire mainframe database each night, and deleted the entire MySQL table before beginning the import. This served to ensure that all new products were added, changes to existing product information was updated, and any products that were deleted were removed. To prevent the credentials from being passed in via the command-line, I created a system user named productupdate, and placed a my.cnf file in the user's home directory, which looked like this:

```
[client]
host=localhost
user=productupdate
password=secret
```

I then changed the permissions and ownership on this file, setting the owner to
mysql and allowing only the mysql user to read the file. The final step involved adding
the necessary information to the productupdate user's crontab, which executed the
script each night at 2 a.m. The system ran flawlessly from the first day.

Loading Table Data with PHP

For security reasons, ISPs often disallow the use of load data infile, as well as many
of MySQL's packaged clients like mysqlimport. However, such limitations do not necessarily mean that you are out of luck when it comes to importing data, because you
can mimic load data infile and mysqlimport functionality using a PHP script. The
following script uses PHP's file-handling functionality and a handy function known as
fgetcsv() to open and parse the delimited automobile data listed at the beginning of
this section:

```php
<?php
/* Connect to the MySQL server and select the cars database. */
$conn = mysql_connect("localhost","someuser","secret");
$db   = mysql_select_db("cars");

/* Open and parse the cars.csv file. */
$fh = fopen("cars.csv", "r");
while ($line = fgetcsv($fh, 1000, ","))
{
    $year = $line[0];
    $make = $line[1];
    $color = $line[2];

    /* Insert the data into the carcollection table. */
    $query = "INSERT INTO carcollection SET year='$year',
             make='$make',color='$color'";
    $result = mysql_query($query);
}
fclose($fh);
mysql_close();
?>
```

Keep in mind that execution of such a script might time out before completing
the insertion of a particularly large dataset. If you think that this might be the case, set
PHP's max_execution_time configuration directive at the beginning of the script. Alternatively, consider using Perl or another MySQL API to do the job at the system level.

Summary

MySQL's import and export utilities are powerful tools for migrating data to and from your MySQL database. Using them effectively can spell the difference between a maintenance nightmare and a triviality.

This concludes the book. I hope you enjoyed reading it as much as I enjoyed writing it. Best of luck!

Index